HERITAGE

Dear Valued Legacy Client,

Please accept this complimentary copy of *The Secret History of the First U.S. Mint* as a token of our appreciation for your continued business.

It's a fun and educational read for anyone interested in the history of our nation's monetary production. The authors, Joel Orosz and Leonard Augsburger, are friends and longtime clients. For their efforts on this wonderful book, they received the Book of the Year Award from the Numismatic Literary Guild. I think you'll agree that they are well-deserving of such recognition.

Although Heritage has expanded into other collecting areas, our primary focus remains on rare coins and currency. As the world's largest numismatic auctioneer, we are dedicated to maintaining our leadership role through professionalism, innovation and customer service. Bottom line: We're grateful for clients like you!

On behalf of my partners and our dedicated staff, we wish you continued success in your collecting endeavors and look forward to being of continued service.

Sincerely,

Greg Rohan

Todd Imhof

THE WORLD'S LARGEST NUMISMATIC AUCTIONEER

HERITAGE HA.com
AUCTIONS

The Secret History of the First U.S. Mint

How Frank H. Stewart Destroyed
—and Then Saved—
a National Treasure

Joel J. Orosz
Leonard D. Augsburger

Foreword by
Eric P. Newman

Whitman
Publishing, LLC
PUBLISHING SINCE 1934

© 2011 Whitman Publishing, LLC
3101 Clairmont Road • Suite G • Atlanta, GA 30329

Correspondence concerning this book may be directed to the publisher, ATTN: *Secret History of the First U.S. Mint*, at the address above.

ISBN: 079483244X
Printed in China

If you enjoy *The Secret History of the First U.S. Mint*, you will also enjoy *History of the United States Mint and Its Coinage*, by David W. Lange; *America's Money, America's Story*, 2nd edition, by Richard Doty; and *Striking Change*, by Michael F. Moran.

For a complete catalog of numismatic reference books, supplies, and storage products, visit Whitman Publishing online at www.whitmanbooks.com.

Whitman®

Contents

About the Authors iv

Dedication iv

Foreword, *by Eric P. Newman* v

Preface vii

Acknowledgments ix

Introduction: The Declaration House: Foreshadowing of the First Mint's Fate xi

Chapter 1: The Man, the Mint, and the Masterpieces. 1

Chapter 2: Frank Huling Stewart: The Man Who Owned the First United States Mint 12

Chapter 3: "A Very *Mean* House": The First United States Mint, 1792–1911. 30

Chapter 4: The Frank H. Stewart Collection: Relics of the First United States Mint. 70

Chapter 5: The Frank H. Stewart Collection: Coins Created at the First United States Mint 94

Chapter 6: Frank H. Stewart's Commissioned Artworks: Edwin Lamasure's *Cradle of Liberty*
and *Ye Olde Mint* 118

Chapter 7: Frank H. Stewart's Commissioned Artworks: John Ward Dunsmore's *Inspection of the
First Dies* and *Washington Inspecting the First Money Coined by the United States* 158

Chapter 8: Artworks Inspired by Frank H. Stewart's Commissions: Frank J. Reilly's *Director of
the First U.S. Mint Inspecting Initial Coinage, Philadelphia, 1792* and Hy Hintermeister's
Washington Examining the First Coins 190

Chapter 9: The Fate of the Stewart Collection: Congress Hall, the National Park Service,
and Rowan University. 204

Chapter 10: The Last Days of Frank H. Stewart 216

Afterword: The Mint as It Was, the Mint as Stewart Fixed It in Memory 244

Appendix A: The Stewartiana Catalog 251

Appendix B: Frank H. Stewart Purchases From Chapman Sales. 276

Appendix C: Early Fire Insurance Surveys of the First Mint Campus 279

Appendix D: Seventh Street Lot Numbering. 282

Appendix E: The Frank H. Stewart Photographs of the First Mint Demolition 283

Notes 293

Selected Bibliography (Focusing on Significant Numismatic References) 315

Index 317

An award-winning numismatic biographer, **Joel J. Orosz** (right) received the ANA Heath Literary Award in 2000. He is the historian and a longtime board member of the Numismatic Bibliomania Society and a frequent contributor to its journals, *The Asylum* and *E-Sylum*. Orosz is distinguished professor emeritus of philanthropic studies at the Dorothy A. Johnson Center for Philanthropy of Grand Valley State University, Grand Rapids, Michigan. Co-author **Leonard D. Augsburger** (left) wrote *Treasure in the Cellar*, published in 2008 by the Maryland Historical Society. Secretary-treasurer of the Liberty Seated Collectors Club and a board member of the Numismatic Bibliomania Society, he has authored many articles for both organizations and received numerous awards from the Numismatic Literary Guild. Augsburger, a software engineer by trade, has been employed in the telecommunications industry since 1987.

DEDICATIONS

For Florence: My muse everlasting
J.J.O.

To Debra: Love's true picture
L.D.A.

ABOUT THE FOREWORD AUTHOR

Eric P. Newman, a devoted collector and researcher of American coins and paper money since the 1930s, has long been recognized as one of our most important numismatic scholars and authors. He is the recipient of nearly every honor within the discipline, both national and international, including more Heath Literary Awards (from the American Numismatic Association) than any other writer. He has earned the prestigious medals of the American Numismatic Society, the Royal Numismatic Society, and the American Numismatic Association. His scholarship includes diverse works on American colonial coins, paper money, banking, Missouriana, Shakespearean drama, and American history. *Early Paper Money of America*—just one of the classic standard references he has authored—was recently published in its fifth edition. In 1986, Newman was inducted into the ANA Numismatic Hall of Fame. The Newman Money Museum is located in his home city of St. Louis, on the campus of Washington University.

Foreword

Thomas Jefferson, on December 15, 1775, seems to have written the earliest comment on the future coinage of a U.S. Mint, this being prior to the Declaration of Independence and while the Continental Congress was struggling to undertake some national control. His words were: "To expedite the striking of monies ordered by the Congress to be struck." The *Journal of the Continental Congress* reported these words to be in Jefferson's own handwriting. A committee had been selected to prepare an agenda for items to be considered during the 1775 Christmas holiday recess of the Continental Congress. Jefferson was placed on the committee and prepared thoughts for a program of action. The holiday recess never occurred because of unfinished work of the Congress, and thus the committee never met. Yet Jefferson had initiated his hope and his specific intent for a national metallic coinage to be created. His early thinking was not in vain.

Jefferson continued to devote his energies for many of the following years to create a sound U.S. coinage. When, in 1789, he became U.S. secretary of state under President George Washington, he was selected to supervise the creation of the first U.S. Mint. He received early and steady cooperation from Alexander Hamilton, who became U.S. secretary of the treasury in 1789 and whose duties would otherwise have included such a mint.

The circulation of money in America under the control of combined British Colonial and American governing bodies during the period just prior to the American Revolution, and continuing through the Revolution until the Treaty of Paris in 1783, was in total turmoil. The paper money issued by the American colonies, by the American states, and by the Continental Congress became the victim of inflation and ended up worthless. The specie in circulation was from many different foreign countries (primarily from colonial Spanish and Portuguese sources), and those Americans using such coinage needed to use visual identification of the insignia, size, and denomination and then determine quality with respect to the weight and fineness of each piece presented. This included the problem of recognizing counterfeits and becoming aware of deliberate metal removal by filing and other means. The copper coins in American circulation were primarily counterfeit, short-weight, and/or debased British and Irish halfpence and farthings that had been imported mostly from Birmingham, England, as a fraud on the American public. A trickle of 1773 Virginia copper halfpence struck at the English Royal (Tower) Mint circu-

lated in the American South, but the bulk of the coinage was melted or hoarded in Virginia after late delivery and value uncertainties.

There also was Imaginary Money used in five separate large American geographical areas, each area having a different ratio for its nominal pounds, shillings, and pence to the Spanish dollar or piece of eight reals. Many transactions in this Imaginary Money were recorded by book entry on merchants' records. The value of Imaginary Money was published in almanacs, newspapers, broadsides, and so forth, to help the common people conduct transactions for necessities.

About July 1776 there appeared several varieties of Continental Currency experimental coins struck primarily in pewter and about the size of a Spanish dollar. Some of these coins contained the initials E G (Elisha Gallaudet, an engraver of New York City). There is nothing known as to any authorization for them, and there is no known written mention of their existence for almost a decade after their 1776 distribution. Their design and legends were copied from the February 17, 1776, fractional paper money authorized and issued by the Continental Congress. Whether any official documents covering this Continental Currency coinage were lost remains a mystery.

The thinking continued as to what to do about coinage for the United States. Robert Morris, as the U.S. superintendent of finance (from 1781 through 1784), recommended in 1782 a proposal using the basics of all of the American Imaginary Money systems as a common denominator for the parts of the Spanish dollar. In 1783 he arranged for coinage of patterns made for that proposal using the legend NOVA CONSTELLATIO, and denominations from five units up to 1,000 units were struck in Philadelphia by Benjamin Dudley with participation by John Jacob Eckfeldt, the German immigrant machinist whose family dominated the future first U.S. Mint and beyond. The Morris thinking was considered so impractical that Jefferson, Hamilton, and others determined to change it almost completely.

Then came a deluge of copper coinage for American use emitted as speculative ventures by a myriad of sources: in 1785 a New York City private firm in which Robert Morris was a silent partner introduced into circulation copper coinage about the size of a British halfpence, minted in England and copying the legend NOVA CONSTELLATIO. Then Vermont, Connecticut, and New

Jersey authorized private contractors to mint similar-size copper pieces that carried their respective state names, and this coinage continued through 1788. A secret mint called Machin's Mills on Orange Lake near Newburgh, New York, was established and minted counterfeit British halfpence of various dates from 1787 through 1788. Unauthorized New York coppers with the legend NOVA EBORAC were minted in New Haven, Connecticut, in 1787. Massachusetts authorized cents and half cents with its commonwealth name on them, and these were coined there from 1787 through 1788. The U.S. Congress, in 1787—induced by bribery and corrupt political influence—authorized a private contractor (James Jarvis) to mint copper coins known as Fugio coppers. These coins weighed only about 3/4 of the federal standard of 157.5 grains for one cent, as previously set by a congressionally appointed "Grand Committee" acting from May 13, 1785, and thereafter. These Fugio coppers were struck in New Haven, Connecticut, in secrecy. There were also other small private mintages of coppers and experimental copper coinage with various American designs and legends. All of the foregoing copper coinages except those of Massachusetts were of less weight than the one cent provided for by federal standard.

The American use of foreign specie coins, Imaginary Money, and the proliferation of unreliable copper coinages resulted in an overwhelming stimulant for a prompt solution by the U.S. government to restore public confidence by stabilizing money circulation. It became clear that it was critically important to establish a reliable U.S. Mint. The economic health of the American people depended on it.

Private contractors continued to seek authorization to strike coins for the United States. English minters in 1791 struck quantities of samples of WASHINGTON PRESIDENT copper one-cent pieces and in 1792 coined an improved design to include 13 stars. Peter Getz of Lancaster, Pennsylvania, submitted 1792 half dollar–size trial coinage with a numeric presidential legend (G. WASHINGTON PRESIDENT I) in accordance with pending congressional legislation. That coinage was immediately deemed unacceptable.

It was obvious that having gold and silver coinage minted in Europe was impractical because of the risk of sea transport to the United States. Copper coinage minted in England for the United States was somewhat practical because much copper was produced and refined there. When the first U.S. Mint was under construction in Philadelphia, quantities of copper were purchased from Swedish and English sources, and the U.S. Mint advertised in a Philadelphia newspaper to buy copper. An English source thereafter furnished many copper planchets for the first U.S. Mint.

In the thinking for the development and operation of a U.S. Mint, many problems had to be solved. Sufficient water power was not available in Philadelphia or New York or in a future possibility of the new federal capital along the Potomac River. The advantage of steam power was known in America from the successful Boulton & Watt private enterprise in Soho, near Birmingham, England, but the Royal Mint in London had not introduced that type of energy. Steam power in the United States was not then sufficiently developed. Therefore, the first U.S. Mint had to rely on the power of horses and the strength and physical coordination of men, which, although very burdensome, had the virtue of reliability. With mechanical skills available there, the location of choice was Philadelphia.

Jefferson's hope and dream came true after about 18 years of the struggle and devotion of many. The coins minted at the first U.S. Mint are evidence of its achievement. The exciting historical detail of that establishment is outstandingly presented by the book which follows.

Eric P. Newman
St. Louis, Missouri

Preface

Authors are notorious for underestimating the work that must be done in order to write a book, but in the long history of publishing, few writers have ever misjudged the magnitude of the task before them quite so spectacularly as those who wrote the volume you now hold in your hands. Recounting how this project expanded—perhaps "metastasized" would be more accurate—from a modest article into a profusely illustrated tome may prove instructive to anyone contemplating a seemingly simple literary project.

In February of 2006, the authors' attention was fixed on topics well-removed from Frank H. Stewart and the first U.S. Mint. Leonard Augsburger was focused on another city (Baltimore) in another century (the 20th), in the homestretch of research for his book, *Treasure in the Cellar*, the first thoroughly documented history of the great gold coin hoard literally unearthed in Depression-era Baltimore. Joel J. Orosz's attention was fixed on America's "small beginning" in coinage, the 1792 half disme. It was this diminutive coin, of course, that served as the (unseen) focal point of John Ward Dunsmore's celebrated painting, *Washington Inspecting the First Money Coined by the United States*. Like most numismatists, the authors knew just enough about Dunsmore's canvas to be dangerous: it was painted around the time of World War I; it was commissioned by the man who wrote the *History of the First United States Mint*; and it represented the triumph of artistic license over historical accuracy.

Orosz, still fixated upon half dismes, began to ask logical questions about the Dunsmore painting, such as whether the artist may have painted more than one version, and if so, where the original and the copies may currently reside. He sought the help of selected numismatic scholars, and Augsburger replied with a citation, discovered during his Baltimore coin hoard research, which suggested that *Washington Inspecting* may once have been in the possession of the U.S. Secret Service. Orosz was intrigued by this surprising information, a correspondence on the subject ensued, and on February 27, 2006, Augsburger e-mailed Orosz the following proposal: "an article on the Dunsmore painting would be the perfect sort of piece for the *Numismatist*. . . . What do you think, should we co-author it?" Orosz enthusiastically accepted the invitation, agreeing that enough data might be available to support a short article in a numismatic journal.

It did not take long for the writing partners to discover that their compact and tidy research project would be, in fact, neither compact nor tidy. Almost immediately, they realized that it was all but impossible to seriously study one painting that Stewart commissioned without studying the other, and therefore Edwin Lamasure's *Ye Olde Mint* was added to the research docket. An understanding of the pictures was impossible unless one understood the artists, but surprisingly, there was not a good biography of either Dunsmore or Lamasure in existence, so the project expanded to include the lives of the painters. As the authors' research progressed, they encountered other artworks that clearly had been inspired by Stewart's two commissions: *Director of the First U.S. Mint Inspecting Initial Coinage, Philadelphia, 1792*, by Frank Reilly; and *Washington Examining the First Coins*, by Henry "Hy" Hintermeister. These artists, too, proved bereft of reliable biographies. Then, evidence of a forged copy of *Washington Inspecting* came to light (artist understandably unknown), and a legitimate copy of *Ye Olde Mint* (by Natalie Hause) surfaced as well. The "modest article" had clearly morphed into a monograph, if not a full-fledged book.

The expanding roster of artworks was daunting enough, but it was matched by the topic's growth in other directions. There was no way to tell the full story of the paintings without discussing their patron, Frank H. Stewart, but his numismatic notoriety notwithstanding, Stewart was devoid of a published biography. And it was hopeless to write Stewart's life story unless one was willing to delve into his life's work, the turn-of-the-20th-century electrical supply business in Philadelphia. Nor was it practical to tell the story of Stewart the businessman without including where he conducted that business, namely the property on which the buildings of the first Mint once stood. True, this history had been told idiosyncratically by Stewart himself, and more thoroughly by Don Taxay in *The United States Mint and Coinage*, but comprehensively by no one. The intricacies of land ownership, building construction, damage, repair, and sale over more than three centuries now became part of what was beginning to appear, like the universe, to be an ever-expanding system. And the enlargement only continued, for the Dunsmore and Lamasure canvases, as it turned out, were only a small part of a large aggregation of coins, medals, and mechanical artifacts from the first Mint that Stewart had collected and then donated to Congress Hall, then a museum located within the Independence Hall complex. The authors now faced the fact that completing the project would require them to conduct extensive research and produce fluent writing on subjects as diverse as art history, biography, Philadelphia heritage, business history, the evolution of the U.S. Mint, the development of coin-making technology, and—oh yes—several aspects of numismatics.

Fortunately, or perhaps frighteningly, there proved to be an almost inexhaustible well of primary resources to draw upon, the sheer number and geographical range of which did little to reduce the authors' carbon footprints. No city can match Philadelphia for the sheer number of Stewart- and first Mint–related materials. Independence National Historical Park holds the bulk of the Stewart collection of numismatic and first Mint artifacts, along with a rich archive of documentary material. So comprehensive is this assemblage that Independence Hall has loaned a superb selection to the fourth U.S. Mint (including *Washington Inspecting* and *Ye Olde Mint*), which are displayed in the mezzanine-level exhibit area. The Historical Society of Pennsylvania, the Library Company of Philadelphia, and the American Philosophical Society, among their encyclopedic collections, contain invaluable information about the first Mint. The Philadelphia City Archives holds a wealth of information about the Mint property's evolution over the years. Time and again, the authors visited this formidable array of repositories, eventually developing a new understanding of W.C. Field's famous gibe, "All things considered, I'd rather be in Philadelphia."

For all its resources, however, Philadelphia does not enjoy a monopoly of Stewartiana. The mother lode actually resides at Rowan University in Glassboro, New Jersey, a trove so rich that it took repeated research visits to completely mine its resources. Major metropolises also offered much of value. New York City provided the New-York Historical Society, the Fraunces Tavern Museum, the American Numismatic Society, and the Salmagundi Club; Washington, D.C., the Archives of American Art and the Copyright Office; Chicago the Newberry and Chicago Public libraries. Smaller towns also had their roles to play, such as Woodbury, New Jersey (Gloucester County Historical Society and probate records), and even

Lithopolis, Ohio (Dunsmore art archives). All told, the authors spent the equivalent of 15 weeks in archives large and small, gathering documentary evidence that had been undisturbed for decades.

This accounting of sources, as exhaustive (and exhausting) as it is, has not yet mentioned the almost limitless resources of the Internet. Endless hours peering at Google search results produced data by the gigabyte-load, ranging from the discovery of entire repositories, such as the collection at Lithopolis, to the uncovering of arcane details, to the identity of descendants of key players in the Mint's history. Among those brought to light were living leaves on the family trees of Adam Eckfeldt, John Ward Dunsmore, Edwin Lamasure, and even Frank H. Stewart himself.

This tsunami of primary and secondary information transformed the anticipated article into a monograph, then into a very substantial book, and made infinite jest of the authors' initial assessment of the time and resources needed to completely tell the story. Rarely, indeed, have two authors been so wrong about a subject, but never have any writers been so happy to have been so mistaken. Frank H. Stewart, who saved so many artifacts and enabled the writing of so much history, has never before received due credit for his accomplishments. To bring just recognition to his memory at long last has rendered every note transcribed and every trip taken worth the time and effort expended. It is no overstatement to say that it has become an honor and a privilege to bring this project to a successful conclusion. In summary, we recall the words of Stewart himself, and count ourselves among those he encouraged:

> It is my hope that this little volume will encourage others to do . . . what I have attempted to do . . . possibly not without errors, because the town and hall clocks have tolled the hour of midnight many times while I worked and thought of men, things and buildings that are gone.[1]

Acknowledgments

Amy Adamo, director of the Fraunces Tavern Museum, made its Dunsmore painting collection accessible, and offered useful introductions; **John W. Adams** made valuable suggestions and reviewed the manuscript; **Greg Allen** provided correspondence from Mint Director Mary Brooks; **James Almoney** shared details of his father's donation of a Dunsmore copy to the U.S. Secret Service; **Christine Armstrong,** of Armstrong Studio Associates, took photographs of Lamasure-related material.

Benjamin Franklin Bailar furnished useful insights about Benjamin Franklin; **Bruce Balderson** shared information about the Ocean City Fishing Club; **David Baugh** gave invaluable advice on navigating the Philadelphia City Archives; **John Baumgart** photographed tokens and medals; **Thomas W. Becker,** author of *The Coin Makers*, shared slides he took of *Ye Olde Mint* in 1967; **Jordan Berman,** of The Illustrated Gallery, handled the Frank Reilly painting and offered research leads; **Betty Birdsong,** program specialist, Historian's Office, U.S. Mint, provided helpful data; **Mark Borckardt** furnished a previously unpublished photograph of the Front Building of the first Mint; **Q. David Bowers** helped in numerous ways, including research suggestions, reviewing the manuscript, and providing an image; **Ray Bracken,** of RJB Photography, photographed the Ocean County Coin Club Dunsmore lithograph as well as artifacts in the Stewart Collection at Rowan University; **Bill Burd** opened his library for research; **Roger W. Burdette** offered constant encouragement to the authors and reviewed the manuscript.

Frank Campbell assisted at the American Numismatic Society library; **Irene Coffey,** curator of the Franklin Institute of Philadelphia, made helpful research suggestions; **Steve Crain** assisted with information on the Dunsmore calendar in his collection.

Charles Davis furnished useful information about Dunsmore lithographs and Frank H. Stewart's publications; **Beth Deisher,** editor of *Coin World*, published letters and articles relating to Frank H. Stewart and the first U.S. Mint; **Karie Diethorn,** chief curator of Independence Hall National Park, went above and beyond the call of duty in facilitating research on the Stewart Old Mint collection, including providing access to artifacts both at Independence Hall and those on loan to the U.S. Mint; **Patricia Drodofsky,** librarian at the Wagnalls Library in Lithopolis, made the Dunsmore art archive available for inspection.

The descendants of **Adam Eckfeldt** generously shared family photos and documents from the family archive; **Michael Ewing** shared his wide-ranging knowledge of Edwin Lamasure's artistic oeuvre and provided images.

Donald Farish, president of Rowan University, provided a tour of the former Frank H. Stewart residence in Woodbury, New Jersey; the late **Harry Forman** shared his reminiscences on a number of Stewart-related topics, particularly the forged "Dunsmore" painting; **Kay Freeman** generously shared her research and her insights on a variety of pertinent topics; **Gordon Frost** furnished helpful suggestions.

Richard T. Gayley provided help on the Main Line Coin Club medal; **Bob Giannini,** curator, Independence Hall National Park, supplied information on coins excavated from the park's grounds; **Robert Goler,** curator at the U.S. Mint, opened doors for research at the Mint; **Mary Ann Gonzales,** curator of the Stewart Room at Rowan University, was extremely helpful in guiding research at this invaluable repository during numerous visits; **Roy Goodman,** curator of the American Philosophical Society, furnished many fruitful research leads; **Tim Grant,** of the Public Affairs Office at the U.S. Mint, was helpful in providing access to the Old Mint collection artifacts on loan to the Mint, as well as portraits of early Mint employees; **Barbara Gregory,** editor-in-chief of *The Numismatist*, published an article about Frank H. Stewart and the first Mint; **Frank Greenberg** provided information about his large-format Dunsmore calendar; **Ellen Gruber,** executive director of the Wagnalls Library, made its Dunsmore collection available for research.

Elizabeth Hahn located items in the American Numismatic Society library; **Dan Hamelberg** opened his incomparable library for research and also furnished one-of-a-kind photographs for illustrations; **Thomas Hansen** took the photographs of the Joseph Reilly painting and the Natalie Hause portrait of David Rittenhouse; **Natalie Hause** provided information about two of her paintings, a copy of *Ye Olde Mint* and a portrait of David Rittenhouse; **Krista Hesselbein,** of *Coin World*, helped by finding reprints of relevant articles; **Hugh Hetzer** shared indispensable data and leads about the Hintermeisters, both father and son; **Robert Hoge,** curator of the American Numismatic Society, arranged for the authors to deliver the Groves Lecture in 2008, and also to speak to a meeting of the New York Numismatic Club; **Wayne Homren,** editor and publisher of *The E-Sylum*, the electronic newsletter of the Numismatic Bibliomania Society, offered invaluable services as a forum for research queries and responses, as well as a "bully pulpit" from which to make announcements of new finds; **Jack Howes** provided photography from the Eric Newman collection; **Gene Hynds** furnished information on George Soley.

Joanne Isaac, of the American Numismatic Society, helped the authors plan and deliver their Groves Forum presentation in 2008. **Katie Jaeger** made valuable suggestions; **Mary Jenkins,** curator at Independence National Historical Park, provided helpful information; **D. Wayne (Dick) Johnson** furnished useful research leads, and was particularly helpful in securing a photograph of the Hintermeister print in his possession; **R.W. Julian** was generous in sharing research findings, and reviewed the manuscript; **Tom Jurkowsky,** director of public affairs at the U.S. Mint's Washington, D.C., headquarters, provided information on artifacts in the Mint's collection.

Ute Wartenberg Kagan provided the resources of the American Numismatic Society; **Alexander Katlan** was helpful in facilitating research at both the Fraunces Tavern Museum and the Salmagundi Club; **Jeremy Katz** photographed both the Dunsmore and the Lamasure paintings at Independence Hall National Park as well as tokens, medals and coins in the Old Mint collection, plus portraits in possession of the Philadelphia Mint; **George Frederick Kolbe** was generous with his expertise on many topics, especially those bearing on Dunsmore lithographs and bibliographical issues; **Bob Korver** located Stewart memorabilia, including gavels made from first Mint timbers; **John Kraljevich** located a number of "impossible" items; **Susan Kriete,** Print Room reference librarian at the New-York Historical Society, helped to secure illustrations; **Kurt Krueger** shared information on his copy of Dunsmore's *Inspecting.* **Bob Lamasure** graciously shared information about his grandfather, Edwin Lamasure Jr.; **David Lange** assisted with research about the Lamasure painting; **Tracy Leach,** Curator, Fraunces Tavern Museum, was instrumental in gaining access to Dunsmore canvases; **Sandra C. LeRoy** typed first drafts of several chapters; **Michael Levin,** of the U.S. Mint in San Francisco, was helpful with regard to *Ye Olde Mint*; **Karen Lightner** assisted with images in the Print and Picture collection of the Free Library of Philadelphia; **Jon Lusk** provided photography from the Noyes/Lusk DVD Project, and the off-center Sheldon 1796 NC-7 large cent, cut down and restruck with Breen-3a half cent dies (p. 100) is © Noyes/Lusk DVD Project.

Jim Majoros assisted in many ways, especially with regard to the Dunsmore lithograph owned by the Ocean County Coin Club; **Rick Martin** provided important information about the Hintermeisters, both father and son; **Sydney Martin,** editor of the C4 Newsletter, published a Stewart-themed article; **Itty Matthew,** New-York Historical Society photographer, took photographs of Dunsmore material; **Chris McCawley** supplied information about his 1993 personal medal featuring *Ye Olde Mint*; **Tim McConnell** provided useful data; **Matt Mille,** detectorist, shared information about his find near the first Mint property; **David H. Mitchell,** of Independence Hall National Park, supplied technical assistance; **Barbara Mitnick** offered good advice; **Karl Moulton** read an early draft and gave constructive suggestions; **Douglas A. Mudd,** curator, American Numismatic Association, used the resources of the ANA Museum to aid the research.

Eric P. Newman threw the resources of the Newman Money Museum's library and coin collection behind the project, wrote the foreword for this book, and read drafts, offering trenchant criticisms and eliminating errors.

Joyce Olsen at the Stewart Room at Rowan University was constantly helpful during research visits; **Peter Ostrander** assisted on the subject of R.P. Bolton. **W. David Perkins** shared information about the Dunsmore lithograph in his possession, early dollar attributions, and offered many other research leads and good suggestions; **Suzanne Prabucki,** curator, Fraunces Tavern Museum, was helpful in researching Dunsmore; **Barbara Price,** curator, Gloucester County Historical Society, supplied much useful information and research suggestions regarding Stewart.

Thomas Serfass, curator, Newman Money Museum, assisted with research on many arcane topics; **Craig Sholley** deconstructed the case for the so-called "First Mint Press" and reviewed the manuscript; **Steve Sitarski,** of Independence Hall National Park, was helpful in research of the Old Mint collection; **David Sklow** was generous in sharing his incomparable collection of first Mint postcards and furnished many other research leads; **Cynthia Smith** generously made key research materials available; **Pete Smith** provided crucial assistance in many ways, particularly around the questions regarding the first Mint's physical plant, and also painted the first illustration to depict all of the first Mint's buildings as they appeared circa 1828; he also reviewed the manuscript and provided images; **David Sundman** helped to publicize the project.

Saul Teichman supplied good advice regarding early patterns; **Amber Thompson,** librarian, American Numismatic Association, assisted in many ways with research; **Coxey Toogood,** curator at Independence Hall National Park, offered research leads.

Sarah J. Weatherwax, curator of Prints and Photographs, Library Company of Philadelphia, was extremely helpful in securing graphics; **Alan Weinberg** provided photographs of 1792 coinage; **Craig Whitford** shared his deep knowledge of the first Mint and provided excellent leads to find obscure resources; **Robert Whitney** and **Steve Whitney** were generous in supplying information about their grandfather, Joseph Massetti; **Scott Wixon,** of the New-York Historical Society, made available numerous Dunsmore items; **Carl Wolf** invited the authors to speak to the Chicago Coin Club about Stewart and the first Mint in December of 2007.

Vicken Yegparian reviewed the manuscript and offered valuable criticism; **David Yoon,** editor of *The Asylum,* the journal of the Numismatic Bibliomania Society, published a Stewart-themed article.

Isabel Ziegler, associate curator, Independence Hall National Park, organized the session at which the Dunsmore and Lamasure paintings were photographed.

Introduction
THE DECLARATION HOUSE: FORESHADOWING OF THE FIRST MINT'S FATE

It may not be the "greatest story ever told" in American numismatics, but it is perhaps the most improbable of tales, and certainly the most contradictory. How did a modest farmer's son named Frank Huling Stewart grow up to buy the first U.S. Mint? How did it come to pass that a hero who made it his mission to preserve "Ye Olde Mint," as he fondly called it, become the villain who demolished it? How did a high school dropout come to write the book that, after the passage of more than eight decades, still remains the definitive history of the nation's first coin factory? How did a man who had no pretensions to being a numismatist assemble an important collection of the first Mint's coinage, and donate it to the public? How did a businessman whose acquaintance with the fine arts was but fleeting come to commission, from first-rate artists such as John Ward Dunsmore and Edwin Lamasure, the paintings that, down to this very day, define our mental image of the first U.S. Mint? And how on earth was it that the proprietor of the Frank H. Stewart Electric Company was not christened "Frank H. Stewart"?

Yes, the story of Frank H. Stewart and the first U.S. Mint contains contradictions by the carload, with plot twists so melodramatic that a Hollywood screen writer would have blushed to devise them. Yet, implausible as it all is, every one of these things actually happened. A poor boy made good, bought the Mint, labored to preserve it, failed, demolished it, but in the process gathered a significant coin collection, wrote an indispensable history, and commissioned enduringly influential art works. Most of what we know about this humble, but highly historic, cluster of brick and frame buildings we know because of Frank H. Stewart's exertions. Above all, the artistic record that he commissioned has indelibly fixed the image of that enterprise into our minds, and, as we shall see, it has inspired many subsequent artists—both nefarious and not—to take brush in hand on numismatic subjects. Here, for the first time, is the full story of the paradoxical man and his self-appointed mission—initially to conserve, eventually to level, finally to commemorate—the first Mint of the United States.

Fittingly enough, the convoluted tale of Frank H. Stewart and the first Mint begins not with him at all, but rather with another man, and in another century. The century was the enlightened 18th, and the man was the Sage of Monticello, Thomas Jefferson. How the author of the Declaration of Independence became the starting point for the saga of Frank H. Stewart and the first Mint makes for a fascinating story all in itself.

THE MYSTERY OF THE MISSING "DECLARATION HOUSE"

In Frank H. Stewart's 1924 book, *History of the First United States Mint*, he revealed that his impetus to save the first U.S. Mint stemmed from an earlier failed attempt at preservation:

> One of the most pathetic ineffectual attempts ever made to save an historic building was that of Thomas Donaldson, a local newspaper man of Philadelphia. He published a book that made me wish to avoid the mistake that was made when the Declaration House was destroyed, but the first United States Mint, like the building in which Jefferson wrote the Declaration of Independence, had to give way to business growth.[1]

The whole affair of the Declaration House stuck in Stewart's craw for a long time, for in 1947 he again commented:

> What happened to the place where Thomas Jefferson lived at 7th and Market Streets, Philadelphia, when he drafted the Declaration of Independence? It was destroyed of course, but a newspaper man wrote a book about it. There was no public interest then.[2]

Donaldson's efforts may have been no more successful than Stewart's, but they certainly were not pathetic. This "newspaper man" was in fact successful in settling a 50-year-old dispute over the precise location of the "Declaration House" (with the aid, interestingly enough, of two pioneering numismatists), and he did manage to salvage some of that building's materials. The book to which Stewart referred is *The House in which Thomas Jefferson Wrote the Declaration of Independence*, which Donaldson wrote and privately printed in 1898. This lively—and at times scathing—account of his search for the true Declaration House is marred by his fondness for quoting Irish- and African-Americans in dialect, a very common practice in the 1890s.[3] That foible aside, the tale Donaldson tells is one of history forgotten, invented, and finally recovered. Most of all, it reads as an uncannily prescient rehearsal for Frank H. Stewart's ultimately unsuccessful preservation campaign that was fated to unfold nearly 20 years afterwards.

Present-day readers may be surprised to learn that Mr. Donaldson had to expend considerable effort in identifying the house in which Jefferson wrote the Declaration, but it was simply the case that Philadelphians of the late

18th and early 19th centuries were so preoccupied with surviving a revolution, creating a new republic, and building a great city, that they had but little time to record these significant events as they transpired. Then, too, the Quaker City was the home of so many history-making personalities, sites, and events during the Revolutionary and early federal years (1774 through 1801) that the few chroniclers then in place simply could not keep up. In any case, the Declaration House was hardly the only landmark to go missing, for the location of the President's House, where George Washington and John Adams lived while Philadelphia was the temporary national capital, was forgotten and subsequently rediscovered,[4] and for a time the location of the first U.S. Mint was in dispute, as well.[5]

Frank H. Stewart, 1873–1948, taken in 1913.

Thomas Donaldson's *The House in which Thomas Jefferson Wrote the Declaration of Independence*, 1898.

The Declaration House, photographed by Frederick De Bourg Richards, 1856.

This confusion about the precise location of the Declaration House should not be misconstrued as a matter of indifference among the good people of Philadelphia. Indeed, those citizens had strongly held, if not always well-informed, notions of just where the celebrated house's exact location might be. Early numismatists, even those outside of the Quaker City, also had more than a passing interest, as evidenced by the New England Numismatic and Archaeological Society's addition to its Cabinet, at its meeting on July 19, 1866, of "a picture of the House where Jefferson wrote the Declaration of Independence."[6] The report does not state, however, which of the various claimant buildings was depicted: for over the years, multiple structures were advanced as the hallowed location.

Thanks largely to Donaldson's research, we can confidently recount where Jefferson wrote the immortal words declaring that all men are created equal. Thomas Jefferson arrived at Philadelphia in mid-May 1776, as one of Virginia's delegates to the Second Continental Congress. He lodged for a short time with Benjamin Randolph on Chestnut Street. On May 23, 1776, in search of quieter quarters, he turned to the outskirts of the thriving city. There, on the southwest corner of High (already popularly known as Market) and South Seventh Streets, the young delegate found the peaceful rooms he prized on the second floor of a new three-story brick house that had been finished only weeks before.[7]

Philadelphia in 1776 was home to about 35,000 inhabitants, the most populous city in Britain's American provinces. Only six years shy of celebrating its centennial, the capital of Quaker William Penn's proprietorship boasted many sophisticated amenities, including Surgeon's Hall, the Library Company of Philadelphia, and the American Philosophical Society, respectively the first medical school, subscription library, and learned society in the colonies, not to mention an array of lovely churches and imposing stately homes.[8] From its humble beginnings clinging to the banks of the Delaware River, Penn's city had expanded westward, and by 1776, the neighborhood that surrounded the intersection of Market and South Seventh was, although still suburban in character, rapidly becoming an urbanized and bustling location. Just a block to the south was the capacious mansion of Joseph Carpenter, built in 1701 as a country seat; a block to the east of that estate, along Walnut Street, stood the impressive State House, which post-Revolutionary Americans would come to know as Independence Hall. And, if one was in the mood for a nip of the hard stuff, Michael Shubert operated a distillery just a half block up the street, at numbers 37 and 39 North Seventh.[9]

On June 1, 1775, Jacob Graff Jr., a well-respected brick layer, purchased the lot at the southwest corner of Market and South Seventh Streets. By the late spring of 1776, he had constructed a three-story "double house" (duplex) that fronted Market Street on its north side, with its long dimension running along South Seventh Street. Graff's new home showcased his masonry talents, alternating dark and light bricks in a striking checkerboard pattern.[10] The entire second floor was composed of two rooms flanking a central staircase, a bedroom on the south, and a parlor on the north. These are the rooms that Jefferson rented, and it was in the parlor that he drafted the Declaration.[11] When he looked up from his writing and glanced out either of the parlor's two north-facing windows, he had a clear view of Mr. Shubert's distillery, the future site of the first U.S. Mint.

The Graff House, at 700 Market Street, did not long remain in the builder's hands after the stirring events of 1776. On July 24 of the following year, Graff sold it to Jacob Hiltzheimer, who eventually built another house adjoining it at 702 Market Street. In or about the year 1798, the brothers Simon and Hyman Gratz purchased both buildings from Mr. Hiltzheimer, thus giving rise to a century's worth of confusion among historians, who would grapple, often unsuccessfully, over the similarity between the names "Graff" and "Gratz." At some point prior to 1852, the Gratz brothers added a fourth floor to the original Graff House.[12]

During the decades following the Revolution, as Hiltzheimer and the brothers Gratz altered the original site, Philadelphians' memories of those glorious days steadily ebbed. Then, as the golden anniversary of the Declaration approached, the "Freedom City" experienced a revival of the Spirit of '76. Almost immediately, controversies erupted as to the exact location where Jefferson had penned the first draft of American liberty. The 50th anniversary of the Declaration—punctuated by the remarkable coincidence of the simultaneous demise of its two chief architects, Thomas Jefferson and John Adams, on July 4, 1826—came and went without settling the controversy. As Thomas Donaldson recorded 72 years later, there were four separate houses that were reputed to be—by their various proponents—the one and only place where the quiet Virginia polymath had written himself into the pages of history.[13] The four candidates were:

- The Indian Queen Inn, three blocks to the east of the Graff House, near the southwest corner of Market and South Fourth Streets,
- A brick house just a few steps south of Graff's home, at numbers 8 and 10 South Seventh Street, (west side) later known as Kelly's Oyster House,
- The brick house next door to Graff's at 702 Market Street, built by Jacob Hiltzheimer,
- The Graff House itself.[14]

It was the preparation for another major anniversary of the Declaration—the United States Centennial Celebration of 1876—that piqued Donaldson's interest in finding the exact location of the Declaration House. Good newspaper man that he was, Donaldson conducted an investigation of the claimants, and quickly eliminated the pretenders. He discovered that Jefferson himself (as will shortly be explained) testified that he did not write the Declaration at the Indian Queen Inn. Neither Kelly's Oyster House nor the home at 702 Market Street were in existence in 1776, having been built from 1796 to 98 and 1796, respectively.[15] Hence, by a process of elimination, only the Graff House remained as a viable candidate.

PIONEER NUMISMATISTS PROVIDE THE ANSWER

Donaldson, however, sought proof positive that the building at 700 Market Street was the authentic location, and in the process of investigating, he discovered that two pioneering numismatists had already, unbeknownst to the rest of the world, established this fact. In 1825, during the run-up to the golden anniversary of the Declaration, Dr. James Mease had stepped into the fray. Mease, by then retired from a distinguished medical career (he had toiled beside Dr. Benjamin Rush during the horrendous 1793 yellow fever epidemic that had closed the U.S. Mint), was Philadelphia's foremost antiquarian. He was the author of

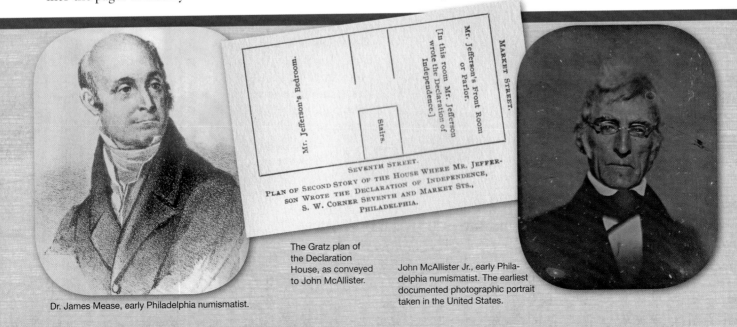

MARKET STREET.

Mr. Jefferson's Front Room or Parlor.

[In this room Mr. Jefferson wrote the Declaration of Independence.]

Mr. Jefferson's Bedroom.

Stairs.

SEVENTH STREET.

PLAN OF SECOND STORY OF THE HOUSE WHERE MR. JEFFERSON WROTE THE DECLARATION OF INDEPENDENCE, S. W. CORNER SEVENTH AND MARKET STS., PHILADELPHIA.

Dr. James Mease, early Philadelphia numismatist.

The Gratz plan of the Declaration House, as conveyed to John McAllister.

John McAllister Jr., early Philadelphia numismatist. The earliest documented photographic portrait taken in the United States.

A Picture of Philadelphia, an 1811 guide book that had just come out in a second edition in 1824, which contained one of the first published descriptions of the U.S. Mint. He had also written, in 1821, the first article published in the United States on a numismatic topic, "Description of Some of the Medals Struck in Relation to Important Events in North America, Before and Since the Declaration of Independence by the United States."[16] With his wide-ranging interests, the good doctor enjoyed an extensive acquaintance among America's leading statesmen, scientists, and men of letters.

Mease decided the most practical way to settle the dispute over the Declaration House location was to simply ask the author. Accordingly, on September 8, 1825, he posed the question in a letter to the Sage of Monticello, who replied as follows, on September 16:

> At the time of writing that instrument [the Declaration] I lodged in the house of a Mr. Gratz, a new brick house, 3 stories high, of which I rented the second floor, consisting of a parlor and bedroom ready furnished. In that parlor I wrote habitually, and in it wrote this paper particularly. . . . The proprietor, Gratz, was a young man, son of a German and then newly married. I think he was a brick layer and that his home was on the south side of Market Street, probably between Seventh and Eighth Streets. . . . I have some idea that it was a corner house, but no other recollections throwing any light on the question.[17]

Jefferson's memory, nearly 50 years after the fact, was remarkably faithful to actual events. Although he fell victim to the Graff/Gratz confusion, all of the other details he provided to Dr. Mease were accurate. Unfortunately, the good doctor did not widely publicize the letter (its only appearance in print for many years appears to have been in Nicholas Biddle's *Eulogium*, a memorial volume published after Jefferson's death in 1826), and this conclusive proof that Graff's was the Declaration House, having never been widely distributed, was very quickly forgotten.

Decades later, another early Philadelphia numismatist, John McAllister Jr., turned his attention to the Declaration House mystery. A genuine prodigy who had enrolled in the University of Pennsylvania at the age of 10 and graduated six years later, McAllister inherited a successful optical company (one of its customers was Thomas Jefferson) and made it bigger and better. John McAllister and Son flourished so admirably that, prior to turning 50, he retired to dedicate his life to his wide-ranging avocational interests. Operating from his home, "Retsilla" ("Allister" spelled backwards), at 194 Chestnut Street, McAllister both made and recorded history. He devised, in 1858, the new numbering system that rationalized the chaotic addresses of Philadelphia's streets (a system still used in street numbering to this day). McAllister has also been credited with coining the word "telegraph," and it is generally agreed that his May 6, 1840, sitting for a daguerreotype resulted in the earliest documented photographic portrait taken in the United States. Like many others in the Mint's home town, he was bitten by the coin bug, and from 1826 through 1858, kept an extraordinary archive of clippings from the Philadelphia newspapers on numismatic subjects.[18]

Truly, McAllister was a man of many interests, but his consuming passion was antiquarianism, and more specifically, that of a recorder of fugitive historical facts. The most celebrated of those transcriptions occurred on April 9, 1844, when he interviewed the retired Chief Coiner of the U.S. Mint, Adam Eckfeldt, who told him that 1792 half dismes—the first coins issued by the U.S. Mint—were struck from $100 worth of silver bullion or specie deposited by President George Washington. For years, the authorship of this memorandum was misattributed to Jonas McClintock, then a refiner at the Mint. We now know, however, that McAllister wrote three copies of this memorandum. The discovery copy was found in the celebrated Leary's book store in downtown Philadelphia, nearly a century after its creation, preserved because it had been glued onto the flyleaf of an old European numismatic book.[19]

McAllister generated another memorandum in 1855, as he sought to pinpoint the location of the Declaration House. In his search for the truth, like any good historian, he looked to primary sources, and sought out Mr. Hyman Gratz, the long-time co-owner of the Graff House. According to the testimony of Miss Agnes McAllister, John, Jr.'s daughter:

> Mr. Hyman Gratz sketched for my father a plan of the house (southwest corner of Seventh and Market Streets) as it was in 1776. This, with some account of the property, which my father had collected and made a note of, he inserted in his copy of Mr. Biddle's "Eulogium" [of Thomas Jefferson].[20]

It appears that the proprietor of Retsilla made a regular practice of conserving important memoranda by gluing them into books on pertinent subjects, and what book could be more pertinent than that which reprinted Jefferson's letter to Dr. Mease? This particular memorandum, with its accompanying map, accurately described the two rooms that comprised the second floor of the Graff House, and correctly stated that the Gratz brothers, during the long period of their ownership, had added a fourth story. Thomas Donaldson noted that, when the Graff House was being demolished, he verified the correctness of both McAllister's map and written description.[21] Like Dr. Mease, however, John McAllister Jr. failed to publicize his discoveries, so the controversy was still simmering 20 years later in 1875, when the forthcoming U.S. Centennial Celebration again brought it to the fore of public attention in the Quaker City.

THE FALL (AND RISE) OF THE DECLARATION HOUSE

Thanks to the researches of these numismatic "M&Ms"—Mease & McAllister—Thomas Donaldson was able to quickly settle a half century's worth of disputes, and conclusively identify the Graff house as the proper location.[22] Donaldson, however, did not have long to savor his accomplishment, for in 1881 or 1882, the Graff House and its next-door neighbor at 702 Market (the house built by Jacob Hiltzheimer) were put up for sale for $80,000. In late 1882, both became the property of the Penn National Bank, a growing concern that—ominously—was casting about for a place to build a brand new headquarters building.[23]

For all of his reverence for Jefferson and ardor to preserve the Graff House, Donaldson proved curiously slow in reacting to this threat. Perhaps he believed that others wealthier and better-connected than a newspaper reporter should and would take the lead, and indeed, he records halfhearted attempts made by a couple of the city's movers and shakers to relocate the home to Philadelphia's bucolic Fairmount Park and also to the University of Pennsylvania.[24] No viable effort materialized, though, and Donaldson, believing that it was now inevitable that the Graff House was going to be razed by the Penn National Bank, decided "to buy the material of the house and rebuild it in some proper place."[25] He turned to his friend, Spencer Fullerton Baird, the second Secretary of the Smithsonian Institution, for help. According to Donaldson, "[Baird] thought that if I would buy the material and put it away for a time, we could prevail upon some patriotic citizen of fortune . . . to rebuild it at Washington in the National Museum grounds."[26] Sad to state, the Graff House never had the chance to migrate by the side of the Smithsonian "Castle" on the National Mall, for Baird soon after passed away, the "patriot of fortune" never stepped forward, and the whole scheme died aborning.

Died, that is, save for one particular. Perhaps to compensate for his slow start, Donaldson now vigorously pursued the first part of the late Secretary Baird's suggestion and cut a deal with Mr. Gillies Dallett, the Penn National Bank's venerable president, to pay $500 for the salvageable building materials from the Graff House. Donaldson did not realize, however, that President Dallett was suffering from a "defective memory" and the bank president utterly forgot their bargain. As Donaldson awaited notification, Dallett ordered the Graff House demolished, a fact which the newspaper man discovered only while riding a horse-drawn streetcar down Market Street the morning on which the demolition commenced, February 28, 1883. In high dudgeon, Donaldson rushed to Dallett's office, where the embarrassed president owned up to having forgotten their previous agreement. Although it was now too late to salvage everything Donaldson wanted, for the reduced consideration of $75, he secured the second floor exterior bricks, the window lintels and sills, and much of the interior woodwork, including doorways and the stairway.[27] This material he temporarily stored nearby in the basement of a building at 710 Market Street.[28] Donaldson personally supervised the removal of the salvaged material over a 12-day period, and attempted to document the demolition process by turning to the photographic firm operated by Frederick F. Gutekunst Jr. (1831–1917) and his brother, Lewis.[29] This partnership is familiar to numismatists for having produced the photographic plate named in the title of Dr. Edward Maris's

REMAINS OF THE DECLARATION HOUSE, JANUARY, 1898.
Material from the Declaration House, No. 700 Market street, Philadelphia, purchased from Thomas Little, contractor for its demolition, under cover on a lot in Philadelphia, in January, 1898. The house to the left was built out of material from the buildings of the Centennial Exposition at Philadelphia, in 1876.

The remains of the Declaration House, 1898.

Plaque placed upon the Penn National Bank, c. 1900, marking the lifetime of the Declaration House, 1775–1883.

great work, *A Historic Sketch of the Coins of New Jersey, with a Plate*, as well as plates of coins for several sales by the Chapman Brothers.[30] There would be no photos of the Graff House's demolition, however, for the firm declared it to be too dark and cloudy to take any exposures. The razing of the Declaration House nearly did in the would-be savior, as well, for he contracted a cold and a severe case of tonsillitis, which confined him to bed for two weeks.[31]

After his recovery, Donaldson moved the salvaged materials from 710 Market Street to a shed on the vacant lot next door to his own home at 132 North 40th Street.[32] He then launched a long campaign to persuade, and if necessary to shame, the city of Philadelphia into building a reconstruction of the Declaration House that would incorporate the materials he had salvaged. Philadelphians, however, proved just as indifferent to the Declaration House in pieces as they were when it was intact, and as the years passed, even Donaldson grew weary of being a voice in the historical wilderness. A melancholy coda to his long quest is found in a photograph taken in January 1898, depicting the salvaged remains of the Declaration House lying under an irregular and porous covering of modern lumber.[33] This photo was featured, as a sort of "exhibit A" of neglect, in Donaldson's last attempt to scold Philadelphia into action, *The House in Which Thomas Jefferson Wrote the Declaration of Independence* (1898). This sometimes caustic call to arms came to nothing, as well, leading Donaldson to the threshold of despair. As the new century rang in, he began to give away to friends, piece by piece, the remains of the Graff House.

As Donaldson lost heart, the Penn National Bank, which had completed its massive stone headquarters building at 700 and 702 Market Street in 1884, seemed certain to endure there long after the lonely preservationist's quixotic vision of reconstruction was forgotten. Indeed, the bank outlived the dreamer, but not, as it turned out, the dream. By the mid-20th century, the fortress-like building was deemed obsolete, and was demolished. In its place, directly on the site that had been occupied by the Graff House, came another boarder named Tom: the Tom Thumb Hamburger Stand. For more than 20 years thereafter, the very spot where had occurred the apotheosis of Enlightenment ideals became the haunt of the poodle skirt and the soda jerk.[34]

Finally, in 1975, almost a century after he first had proposed it, Donaldson's idea of a reconstructed Declaration House became a reality, as the Tom Thumb was razed, and the U.S. National Park Service erected a facsimile of Jacob Graff Jr.'s home in its accustomed place at 700 Market Street. Donaldson would be proud that two of the lintels he rescued back in 1883 today frame the parlor windows on the second floor: the Declaration Room of the Declaration House.[35]

THE DECLARATION HOUSE AND THE FIRST MINT

It is undeniable that the impetus for Thomas Donaldson's preservationist initiative—the shade of "Long Tom" Jefferson—also served to drive Frank H. Stewart down the same path. For just as Jefferson's words imparted historical significance upon the Graff House, so did his works as the Cabinet officer responsible for the first Mint imbue that institution—and its physical site—with an aura of historical consequence. That these two historic plots are within half a block of each other must have only served to strengthen the connection in Stewart's mind. Thomas Donaldson had failed the memory of the Sage of Monticello. Frank H. Stewart, in his turn, hoped to do better.

Thomas Jefferson, the Sage of Monticello, at 33 years, the age at which he authored the *Declaration*.

The modern-day recreation of the Declaration House, facing southwest.

Ironies abound in history, and the ironies connecting 700 Market Street with the first Mint a half block away go far beyond the Jefferson connection. Both were historically significant sites that only Philadelphia could claim, but that literally only one person in Philadelphia cared to save. In both cases, that man tried to rally others to the cause, but failed, and eventually chronicled his experiences in a book that is still the definitive record of its subject. Both sites surrendered numismatic treasures when they were demolished.[36] And finally, there is a direct connection in time. Donaldson was still engaged in his long twilight struggle to reconstruct the Graff House in 1895 when Stewart moved his company into the Seventh Street neighborhood; and Donaldson was donating the last of

his artifacts in 1911, at the very climax of Stewart's campaign to save the first Mint.[37]

For all of their similarities, however, one key difference remains: today, a replica of the Graff House, built on its original site, and incorporating a few of its original components, greets visitors to Philadelphia, while no facsimile of the first Mint is to be found (and even its location has utterly disappeared under a monolithic federal building). This first Mint of the United States, however, lives on in the memories and the consciousness of numismatists because of the labors of just one man: Frank H. Stewart. It is now time to meet the man, to remember the Mint, and to appreciate the masterpieces of the illustrators' art that Stewart commissioned to commemorate it.

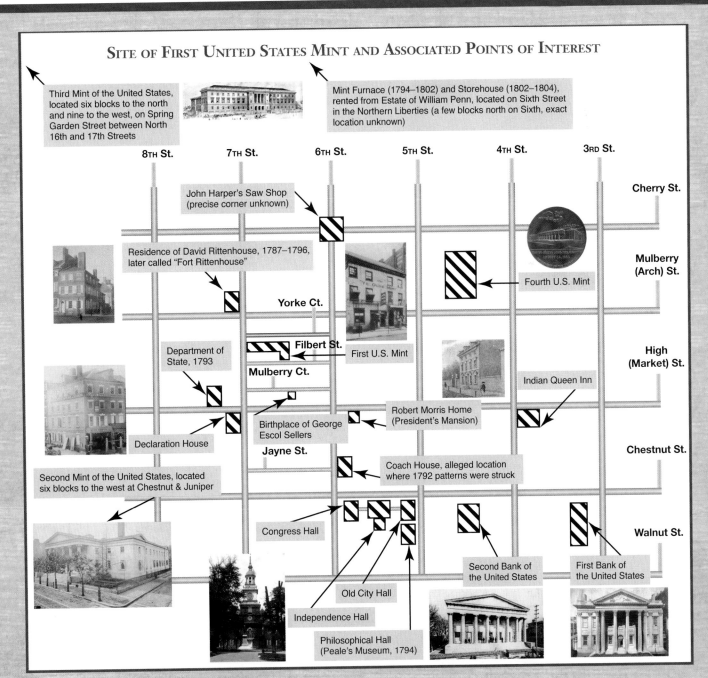

Site of the first U.S. Mint and associated points of interest.

Lit Brothers Department Store,
North Seventh Street, *ca.* 1898.

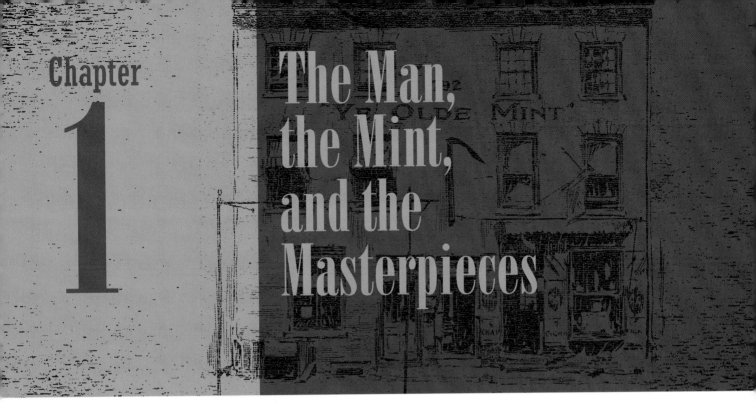

Chapter 1

The Man, the Mint, and the Masterpieces

Like specters from another era, the wooden doorjambs and joists from the Graff House continued to rot on the empty lot next to 132 North 40th Street, unused, unwanted, and unclaimed, throughout the "Gay 90s," and into the new 20th century. Thomas Donaldson may have failed to convince anyone to build a replica of the Declaration House, but it seemed that everyone else in Philadelphia was involved in a building project; the city continued to bustle, more historical landmarks tumbled down, and commerce continued to be king. The old North Seventh Street neighborhood was part of this metamorphosis, with the famous Lit Brothers Department Store, Philadelphia's answer to Macy's and Marshall Field's, going up on Seventh just north of the Penn National Bank headquarters, which occupied the old Graff House site. Progress was on the march.

Still, across Seventh Street and just a few steps north of the bustling Lit Brothers store, tradition abided. For here, at numbers 37 and 39, was located a humble cluster of small brick and frame buildings that, by the end of the 19th century, had stood watch over this neighborhood for more than 100 years. The structures were now owned by the Kates family, landlords of long standing, and were let out to a variety of commercial firms. Long ago, the buildings had resigned their initial purpose, as the first U.S. Mint—the Kates family had owned them now for three generations—and the venerable exteriors were showing their age. Sooner or later, the aged Mint facilities would yield to the pry bar, and another chapter of the early history of the United States would be gone forever.

The old neighborhood, however, had a new resident, a young go-getter named Frank H. Stewart, who owned an eponymous electrical supply company with a rapidly expanding clientele. By sheer chance, in 1895 he occupied the premises at 35 North Seventh—literally next door to the old Mint—and, by even greater serendipity, he was an amateur historian. The needs of his expanding business caused him to cast his eyes upon the dilapidated buildings next door, which appealed to him both for potential business expansion and for their *bona fide* historical association. And always present in his consciousness was the melancholy fate of the Graff House—a fate he wished for the neighboring buildings to be spared. As the 1890s gave way to the new 20th century, the man had met the Mint.

The saga of Frank H. Stewart and the first U.S. Mint is comprised of obscure truths and embellished yarns; of exceptional devotion and callous indifference; of documentary poverty and visual riches. On the face of it, the saga is a bewildering welter of twice-told tales punctuated by maddening gaps in the historical record. On closer examination, however, it resolves itself into three distinct elements: the man, the Mint, and the masterpieces. In order to untwist the tale, each element will be introduced in this chapter and fully explained in the subsequent chapters.

THE MAN

Frank H. Stewart could easily have served as a model protagonist for the novels of his contemporary, Horatio Alger Jr. Like Alger's young heroes, Stewart entered adulthood with very modest prospects but used "luck and pluck" to rise in the world. In common with many other late 19th-century entrepreneurs, young Frank found in the monotonous and exhausting toil of the family farm an enormous incentive to discover a more congenial way to earn a living. The plucky lad felt education could help him escape, and although he never finished high school, he earned a degree from Prickett's Business School in Philadelphia.[1] He tried various occupations, but finally had the good fortune to land in the electrical supply business just as it was taking off. Frank H. Stewart started his self-named company in January 1894,[2] and by the next year his headquarters was at 35 North Seventh Street, immediately south of the first Mint's yard at numbers 37 and 39.[3] Business was booming, and in 1907, the Frank H. Stewart Electric Company purchased numbers 37 and 39, plus the adjoining properties at 629 and 631 Filbert Street (former Mint parcels, all), from the Kates family, who had owned them since the United States government sold them as surplus in 1835.[4] Along with the property came at least six of the original buildings still standing; hence, Stewart became the "master of the Mint."

For most businessmen in the early 20th century, the next step would have been abundantly clear. Most of the Mint buildings were more than 100 years old, and each one looked every minute of it. The sooner these Federal-era fleabags could be razed and replaced by a modern commercial building, the better it would be, not just for the needs of a growing company, but for the sake of the entire neighborhood. These rattletraps had an unfortunate tendency to catch on fire, and on at least one occasion, the Philadelphia Fire Department was suspected of damaging beyond repair the roof of the largest of the old Mint's buildings, in hopes that the structure would be demolished.[5] Frank H. Stewart, however, had an understanding that transcended that of the typical turn-of-the-century businessman; his vision extended beyond the next quarter's results to contemplate posterity's judgment.

It is true that in his early years, Stewart had focused intently upon his Alger-like rise in the business world.

With commercial success, however, came a broadening of his outlook and interests. Fraternal and social organizations, along with civic projects, became a consuming passion.[6] Transcending all other enthusiasms was his intense interest in history, especially local history, expressed most overtly in his presidency, for more than 20 years, of the Gloucester County Historical Society in New Jersey. There is no evidence to suggest that his 1895 decision to move to 35 North Seventh Street was based on anything more than commercial considerations, but living next door to history must have piqued his interest. Now, in 1907, Frank Stewart owned every lot and every surviving building of the first U.S. Mint. Had a Babbit-like businessman acquired these structures, the property would have soon resembled Jericho—with the walls "a-tumblin' down"—but the historian in Stewart felt there had to be another way. He would save the Mint's history—at least the most important parts of it—if he could.

Over the years, a number of misconceptions have grown up around Stewart's preservation efforts from 1907, when he bought the property, to 1911, when he demolished the last of the old Mint buildings and replaced them with a modern six-story tower for his own company. A significant misconception is that he was an ardent historic preservationist. In fact, Stewart never claimed such a title. Few people realize that among his first acts after becoming "master of the Mint" was to demolish what he called the "Smelting Building."[7] In *Ye Olde Mint*, the iconic painting that Stewart commissioned artist Edwin Lamasure to create, there are three brick buildings, ranging from left to right across the canvas. According to Stewart, the single-story structure to the left was the Smelting Building; the two-story building in the middle was the Coinage Building; and the three-story edifice on the right was the Administration Building (the roof of which Philadelphia fire fighters stood accused of deliberately destroying). Stewart believed that the Smelting Building was neither historically significant nor structurally sound, so he leveled it without hesitation or ceremony.

Another misconception is that Stewart commissioned *Ye Olde Mint* and a companion work, *Washington Inspecting the First Money Coined by the United States*, a painting by John Ward Dunsmore, in an effort to rally support for the preservation of the first Mint's buildings. In fact, all of the Mint structures had been occupying space in a landfill for years before he commissioned the paintings, in 1914 and 1915 respectively.[8] The purpose of these artworks, therefore, was to commemorate the structures and activities of the first Mint (a purpose, as we will see, they fulfilled very well).

Perhaps the greatest of these misunderstandings, however, is the belief that Stewart was motivated in his preservationist efforts by the stirring success stories of the field: the invalid Ann Pamela Cunningham rallying women from across the nation to save Mount Vernon, and the Levy family's multigenerational stewardship that preserved Monticello. In fact, Stewart's inspiration came not from glorious success, but rather from the failure of Thomas Donaldson's campaign to save the Graff House. In a February 20, 1925, radio broadcast (made, incidentally, from the Lit Brothers Department Store in-house radio station, the call letters of which were, naturally, WLIT), Stewart made his motivations very clear:

> The destruction of historic buildings in Philadelphia has been going forward without much regard to their historical or sentimental value. The loss of the building in which Jefferson wrote the Declaration of Independence was described in a book by Thomas Donaldson, published in 1898. He tried to buy the building in order that it might be re-erected on some other site, and failed. The only reason I mention this is because it made a tremendous impression on me. I made up my mind that none should ever criticize me for destroying the first United States Mint without an attempt at preservation.[9]

Clearly, Frank H. Stewart was driven more by the fear of failure than by the expectation of success. This motivation, however, did not translate into timely action on Stewart's part. In an uncanny echo of Thomas Donaldson's initial passivity in his attempt to preserve the Graff House, Stewart had owned the first Mint property for

four years before he made a strong effort to have the city of Philadelphia take possession of what he called the Coinage Building (the middle structure in the Lamasure painting). In fact, Stewart did not make his first approach to the city until July 7, 1911, only a month before he planned to demolish all of the buildings on the site in order to clear the way for the new headquarters of the Frank H. Stewart Electric Company.[10] Philadelphia mayor John E. Reyburn and the executive officer of the Permanent Comprehensive Plans Committee, George W.B. Hicks, claimed to be favorably disposed toward Stewart's offer to donate the Coinage Building to the city, but noted that it would require an appropriation to accept it, and that only the City Council, which had adjourned for the summer, could authorize an appropriation.[11] Whether Reyburn and Hicks were truly receptive, or whether they were using the Council's adjournment as a rationalization for inaction, is debatable. What is known is that the clock ran out, and Stewart reluctantly gave the order to clear the old Mint site.

While there is little doubt that Stewart could have done more to save the Mint complex, and might have preserved at least one building if he had acted with more energy, there is also no question that he was markedly successful at commemorating the first Mint. He carefully preserved information in the form of photographs, drawings, and

Deed conveying the Mint property from the U.S. government to the Kates family, 1835. Note the signature of Andrew Jackson in the lower right-hand corner.

A view of the Stewart Electric Company at 35 North Seventh Street, *ca.* 1905, prior to the expansion to 37 and 39 North Seventh. From a Frank H. Stewart Electric Company catalog.

eventually paintings that collectively have fixed the image of the first U.S. Mint in the minds of subsequent generations. Without this work, we would have only a handful of depictions of the Administration Building (the three-story structure on the right-hand side of the Lamasure painting) by which to remember the entire complex. As the buildings were being demolished, Stewart carefully collected planchets and other artifacts of the coinage process, along with structural relics, such as locks and iron security bars, and donated them to public collections. And, like Donaldson before him, Stewart distributed artifacts of the Mint to friends.[12] In short, virtually every image we have of the first U.S. Mint, and nearly every authentic artifact, we have because Frank H. Stewart commissioned it, salvaged it, donated it, or published it. Without this "master of the Mint" the story of our nation's first coinage factory would be all but lost to posterity.

THE MINT

Today's visitors to the fourth U.S. Mint, located at Arch and Fifth Streets in Philadelphia, cannot fail to be impressed by the sheer physical scale of its operations. It is billed as the world's largest coinage facility, and its dimensions confirm this superlative claim. The Mint's single floor sprawls over three city blocks, more than five acres of ground.[13] The ceiling soars several stories above the shop floor, and Croesus himself would envy its output of as many as 14 billion coins per year.[14] For all its hulking size and space-age technology, that the fourth Mint is located in Philadelphia is essentially a relic of the American Revolution. Its roots extend, in an unbroken line, to the humble "starter Mint" that was created in Philadelphia during George Washington's first term as president, in 1792, when the Quaker city was the temporary capital of the fledgling United States of America. By all rights, it should have moved to the new Federal City on the Potomac in 1801, as did the rest of the central government's departments. On six occasions from 1801 until 1823, however, the Pennsylvania Congressional Delegation cobbled together enough votes to keep the Mint in its ancestral home city. Finally, in 1828, the Pennsylvanians achieved the prize they sought: the nation's prime coinage facility was permanently lodged in Philadelphia.[15]

Those who visit the fourth Mint today may be surprised to discover how close it is physically to its very first mailing address. They simply need to saunter two blocks west on Arch Street, then turn left down the east side of North Seventh Street. Less than half a block south of Arch, they will encounter a handsome bronze plaque affixed to a brick wall, marking the location of the first U.S. Mint. Each corner of the rectangular plaque is adorned with a raised medallion depicting the four iterations of that institution that have graced Philadelphia. Focusing on the medallion of the first Mint, the visitor notices three buildings, arranged left to right across the medallion's field, each of brick, and each progressively taller. This medallic depiction was directly copied, of course, from Edwin Lamasure's *Ye Olde Mint*, and more precisely, from the Frank H. Taylor version of Lamasure's masterpiece, of which more will be said later.

The first and fourth (current) U.S. Mints in Philadelphia, featured on a postal cover issued upon the occasion of the 200th anniversary of the Mint and signed by attendees of the Mint Bicentennial program. Included are the signatures of Mint engravers Frank Gasparro and Elizabeth Jones.

It requires more than a little imagination, however, to visualize this site on North Seventh Street as the home of Lamasure's three humble brick structures. Today, the massive ten-story bulk of the William J. Green, Jr. Federal Building, opened in 1974, has erased all evidence, not only of the first Mint, but also of the Frank H. Stewart Electric Company Building that succeeded it. Under the southwest corner of the megalith called the Green Building lie the sites of all four of the Mint's lots and all 10 of its edifices, not to mention the quaintly-named alleyways that bounded and bisected its yard: Sugar, Bone, and Yorke's Court.[16]

This much we know for certain, but little else about the first Mint was as it appeared on the surface. Stewart's decision to ask Lamasure to paint only three buildings makes *Ye Olde Mint* a misleading image. At its height of operations, as previously mentioned, there were no fewer than 10 structures crowding the yard. This fact is in turn misleading; that there were 10 free-standing buildings implies that the yard must have been quite expansive. In fact, the 10 structures ranged in size from modest to tiny, and they were crammed together so tightly because the entire yard occupied much less than half the area of a modern football field. Moreover, edifices on neighboring lots crowded the Mint on three sides.[17]

Adding to the confusion are contemporary descriptions of the first Mint that place it on North Seventh Street, between Mulberry Street on the north and High Street on the south; no map of Philadelphia today depicts thoroughfares named "Mulberry" or "High." This mystery is easily solved, however, for the City of Brotherly Love has also been, throughout its history, the city of changing street names and addresses. Pennsylvania's lord proprietor, William Penn, had named Mulberry Street for the trees that flanked it, and High Street because it was to be the village's main thoroughfare. Philadelphians, however, soon began to refer to Mulberry as "The Arch Street," due to a sizeable bridge that spanned it, and High Street, which hosted Philadelphia's central shopping district, became known as "The Market Street."[18] The street names were not officially changed until the Consolidation Act of 1854, long after the first Mint had been sold, thus leaving a legacy of confusion to befuddle the modern-day reader.

One overriding reality about the first Mint, the one fact that would have been self-evident to anyone viewing it in person, was its Lilliputian proportions. The biggest of its 10 buildings was a mere 36 feet, 10 inches wide: barely enough yardage for a single first down in football. The main service "road" to the yard, the ominously-named Bone Alley, was a scant four feet wide: at points in the yard, a child could stand smack in the middle of it and touch Mint buildings on either side.

From the very beginning, the Mint failed to impress Philadelphians and visitors alike. Moreau de St. Mery, a French expatriate, in 1798, noted that "it is not busy because the chief money is *piastre gourdes* [Spanish silver dollars]. . . . Thus the Mint, as one might say, is merely a curiosity."[19]

As the years passed, the first Mint became something of a civic embarrassment to Philadelphians, who rarely steered tourists in its direction. Consequently, we have very few accounts of visits made there. One tourist who was not

Plaque marking the first Mint site in Philadelphia.

deterred, B.L.C. Wailes of Natchez, Mississippi, wrote in his journal for December 28, 1829, "Visited U.S. Mint. The establishment is carried on in a very mean house." He then added hopefully: "A new building, it is said, is now being prepared for its reception."[20] By 1858, another writer, Caspar Souder, could compare the old and new:

> The beautiful structure at present occupied by the Mint, presents a strong contrast, in respect to size, convenience and general appearance, with the obscure and humble building in Seventh street, in which the establishment was originally located. The old rough-cast house in Seventh street has fallen from its high estate, and it is now used as workshops by different handcraftsmen.[21]

Mr. Wailes thus got it right on both counts. The Mint in 1829 was resident in wretched buildings on a yard so small that George Washington could have literally flung a Spanish silver dollar across it in any direction. By 1829, the government was indeed planning a

splendid Greek revival temple of numisma to replace it, although the changeover would not actually occur until 1833. The federal government also took its sweet time in disposing of its surplus property, finally selling it at auction in 1835 to one Michael Kates, who, along with two generations of descendants, rented out the buildings to tenants for the next 72 years.[22] Finally, his grandnephew, J. Louis Kates, sold it to a businessman who was also his next-door neighbor on North Seventh Street: Frank Huling Stewart.[23]

THE MASTERPIECES

The last of the 10 buildings that the first U.S. Mint had erected on its yard, and that the Kates family had rented out for generations, fell to the pry bars in 1911 at Frank H. Stewart's behest. In their place rose a new "Mint" edifice, although no coins were ever struck there, for when Stewart erected a six-story tower as the headquarters for his company, he called it the "Old Mint Building." Stewart enjoyed the paradox, noting that it was "probably the first new building to be called an old building in the history of architecture."[24] This was not quite true, for several new bank buildings, for example, were called the "Old National Bank." More than mere whimsy dictated the choice of this name; Stewart displayed an intuitive grasp of what later students of business would call "branding." He immediately created an "Old Mint" line of electrical supplies and aggressively marketed the line to his clientele.

From his vantage point in his new Old Mint Building, Stewart fretted that he would share the

The second Mint of the United States, at Chestnut and Juniper Streets in Philadelphia.

fate of Thomas Donaldson, for he had failed to save the first Mint just as Donaldson had failed to save the Graff Home.[25] Stewart, however, was able to assemble all of his peculiar talents—his strong affinity for history, his business acumen, and his distinctive grasp of the branding process—to escape Donaldson's lot. He may not have preserved the first Mint, but he could successfully commemorate it. He capitalized on the Mint's rich history, used business methods to fuel a commemorative campaign, and branded the entire effort as the work of the Frank H. Stewart Electric Company. This three-pronged strategy proved so successful that virtually every knowledgeable numismatist today remembers Frank H. Stewart more as the man who labored mightily to save the first Mint, than as the man who leveled it. How was this thoroughly modern feat of image transformation performed? Ironically, it occurred through the agency of a thoroughly old-fashioned means of communication: commissioning a pair of artists to capture on canvas the first Mint's main buildings, and an epochal (if apocryphal) scene from its storied past.

Stewart turned first to the buildings. He had made a careful record of the structures before he demolished them: measuring their dimensions, photographing their interiors and exteriors, noting any unusual features. After a long search for authentic images of the first Mint proved a complete dry hole, Stewart hired a noted local artist, a magazine illustrator named Frank H. Taylor, to make a drawing of the Mint façade. Taylor's effort was a good beginning, but the master of the Mint decided that the task required talent beyond anything that Philadelphia had to offer. He later wrote that, "It occurred to me that it would be a job worthy of one of America's foremost artists. With that thought in mind, I made an arrangement through the Osborne Company to have Edwin Lamasure paint the picture after I had obtained all of the data available.[26] The Osborne Company employed prominent artists to paint canvases, which were then lithographed and customized for companies to adorn promotional giveaway items. Osborne's stable of artists tended toward rustic and whimsical scenes, and one of the foremost exponents of that genre was Edwin Lamasure (1867–1916). Of French extraction, Lamasure worked exclusively in water colors and favored rural scenes in Maryland and Virginia, near his home in Washington, D.C. Some he liked so much that he painted the same landscape in all four seasons. Besides being reproduced on calendars, Lamasure's work was widely distributed in other advertising media, including magazines, posters, blotters, and flyers. *Ye Olde Mint* was not Lamasure's only foray into numismatics, for he had been employed as an engraver at the Bureau of Engraving and Printing during the 1880s.[27]

Like all illustrators excepting perhaps Norman Rockwell, Lamasure has been slighted by art historians and collectors alike, often dismissed as a mere "draftsman" who did work for hire for commercial concerns such as the Osborne

Early rendering of the first Mint, probably by Frank H. Taylor.

Edwin Lamasure Jr.

A shipment of Stewart Electric Company catalogs promoting the "Old Mint" brand.

Company. This problem was exacerbated, in his case, by the difficulty nearly everyone had in spelling his last name. Even Frank H. Stewart, who commissioned at least three paintings from him, was wont to misspell his surname as "Lamazure,"[28] while later authors have been guilty of even greater atrocities: for example, Robert P. Hilt II, in his book *Die Varieties of Early United States Coins: Volume 1,* mangled it as "Lainazure."[29] Lamasure, however, was a better artist than many think, and the best possible proof of this assertion is the impact of his painting, *Ye Olde Mint,* on the numismatic hobby.

In 1913, as Frank H. Stewart was pondering a campaign to commemorate the first Mint, he purchased Lamasure's painting of the south façade of Independence Hall, entitled *The Cradle of Liberty,* and used this scene on one of two versions of the Frank H. Stewart Electric Company calendar for 1914. He was greatly pleased with the results, and promptly commissioned Lamasure to paint *Ye Olde Mint.* As he had the year before, Stewart purchased the painting and then reproduced it for his calendar for the coming (1915) year.[30] As previously mentioned, Stewart provided Lamasure with his research and Taylor's sketch of the Mint's buildings, yet both he and his artist managed to garble reality. Only three of the 10 buildings were depicted, the close-crowding neighboring structures were omitted, making it appear to be a rural setting, and incongruous details were included, such as a lady who sold taffy on Philadelphia's streets, and Nero, the Mint's watchdog, who was let out only at night, and within the fenced-in yard of the Mint.

Paradoxically, however, while getting it all wrong, Lamasure got it all right. The spacious setting, ironically, echoed William Penn's original conception of the city of Philadelphia—large city lots populated with gentlemen who owned even larger estates on the outskirts of town.[31] Further, Lamasure's composition of the three main buildings of the first Mint flows from left to right across the yard, with each building bigger than its predecessor, creating an impression of movement and progress. Inaccurate though the setting may be, it evokes a sense of nostalgia by its implicit comparison of the modest brick buildings with the Brobdingnagian U.S. Mint of today. Lamasure's work struck a chord with numismatists of its era, and that chord has echoed down for generations since. *Ye Olde Mint* has been reproduced countless times, on everything from dignified Assay Commission Medals to kitschy Christmas ornaments. It is not only featured on the medallion marking the site of the first Mint; the original painting hangs today in the visitor's center of the fourth Philadelphia Mint. It clearly meets the definition of an iconic work, for it quite simply has created the image that we all carry in our minds of the first Mint's buildings and yard.

Having succeeded so admirably in commemorating the physical plant, Stewart turned in 1915 to dramatizing a pivotal moment of the Mint's rich history. The 1916 calendar of the Frank H. Stewart Electric Company featured a scene at which Mint Director David Rittenhouse presented the very first coins struck by the institution, the 1792 half dismes, to President and Mrs. George Washington.

Ye Olde Mint, the original watercolor by Edwin Lamasure Jr.

Painting this scene would require the talents of an artist who had demonstrated the ability to create pleasing portraits of Washington, and Stewart found this man in the person of John Ward Dunsmore (1856–1945), a prolific painter of historical tableaux.

Dunsmore, like Lamasure, has been given short shrift by art historians. Had he been born a century earlier, when historical painting was much in vogue, he would have fared markedly better. Working as he did during the dawn of the age of the "modern" in art, however, his meticulously researched and well-crafted historical canvases seemed somewhat anachronistic. Today, Dunsmore's work clearly belongs to a bygone era.

For Frank H. Stewart, however, Dunsmore had impeccable credentials for the task of imagining the presentation scene, for he had studied in Europe, directed Detroit's art museum, and run his own school of painting.[32] Even more important, Dunsmore was a serious student of the Revolutionary era. A member of the New-York Historical Society, the artist chaired their "Field Committee," which conducted excavations of Revolutionary War encampments, both British and Continental, on northern Manhattan Island. Dunsmore used the relics found in these digs, along with his own collection of historical clothing, to ensure verisimilitude in his period paintings.[33] Among these were a series on the career of George Washington, which made him the perfect painter for Stewart's purposes.

John Ward Dunsmore, *ca.* 1920.

If Lamasure's *Ye Olde Mint* vexes purists with its historical inaccuracies, Dunsmore's *Washington Inspecting* renders purists apoplectic. First of all, the scene is a fabrication; there is no historical evidence which confirms that there ever was a formal presentation of the half dismes. Then there is the "cast of thousands" aspect, evocative of John Trumbull's *Declaration of Independence*, for Dunsmore included just about every luminary of Washington's first administration in the picture. Besides the president, Mrs. Washington, and Mint Director David Rittenhouse, the group includes Thomas Jefferson, Mr. and Mrs. Alexander Hamilton, Washington's personal secretary Tobias Lear, and Mint notables Henry Voigt (chief coiner) and Adam Eckfeldt (later chief coiner, but in 1792 only an occasional contractor for the Mint).[34] The small touches of the painting also annoy sticklers for historical detail. What is a grandfather's clock doing in the coinage room? And why is that oriental rug on the floor of what was essentially a factory?

Lithographic copy of *Washington Inspecting the First Money Coined by the United States*, by John Ward Dunsmore.

Like Lamasure's scene, however, Dunsmore's counterfactual tableau underlines a larger truth. The artist set the scene in the actual first floor of the Coinage Building (the middle structure in the Lamasure painting), as gleaned from photographs taken by Frank H. Stewart before he demolished the edifice. (It was not known until much later that the half dismes were struck elsewhere, before the Mint's buildings were ready for business.)[35] The grandfather's clock was one that had been made by Rittenhouse, and both the furniture and the coinage equipment in the painting were carefully copied from pieces in the possession of the U.S. Mint in 1915.[36] In short, the picture may be historically incorrect, but it was painted with careful and thematic attention to historical detail.

Washington Inspecting is also true in a larger sense. Just as the precise scene depicted in Emanuel Leutze's *Washington Crossing the Delaware* never occurred, but the picture accurately conveys the heroism of the commander in chief during a critical moment of the Revolution, so too does *Washington Inspecting* convey the larger truth that Washington staunchly supported the creation and development of the first U.S. Mint, with considerable assistance from Jefferson, Hamilton, and Rittenhouse. Both paintings invoke an emotional response that transcends their shortcomings as historical documents. Charles Weisgerber's

The Birth of Our Nation's Flag (1892) is in the same vein. The painting portrays a scene devoid of documentary confirmation, yet it powerfully associates Washington with the creation of the American standard. As a result, the story of Betsy Ross and "Old Glory" is ubiquitous in the American elementary school.

The 1976 Assay Commission medal featured a rendering of *Washington Crossing the Delaware*, engraved by Frank Gasparro. Another numismatic connection to the image exists in the person of Benjamin Rush, early treasurer of the U.S. Mint and signer of the Declaration of Independence. Rush spent Christmas morning, 1776, with General Washington, just before Washington's crossing. Rush's biographer tells the story:

> Rush reports him [Washington] much depressed, lamenting "the ragged state of his army in affecting terms." He tried to assure Washington that Congress would come to his support in his present difficulties and distress. While they were talking, the General was playing with his pen and ink and one of the pieces of paper on which he had been scribbling fell to the floor near Rush's feet. On it was written the phrase, "Victory or Death." That same evening, Christmas night, Washington made his famous crossing of the

The Birth of Our Nation's Flag, from a postcard.

Delaware. . . . In the morning came the news of Washington's successful crossing, his silent descent upon Trenton and his capture of a thousand Hessian troops by surprise. . . . Rush learned that at the surprise attack on Trenton the passwords for the troops had been "Victory or Death."[37]

Even more so than *Ye Olde Mint*, *Washington Inspecting* meets the definition of an iconic image. It has inspired artists like Hy Hintermeister and Frank J. Reilly to paint derivative scenes, and even has been forged on at least one occasion. It, too, has been reproduced on calendars, post cards, medals, and tokens. Dunsmore's canvas has given American numismatists a creation myth, peopled with the nation's founding heroes, and it meshes nicely with Lamasure's three humble Federal-era brick buildings to tell a tale of republican simplicity and civic virtue at the dawn of American nationhood. Looking at the two paintings together, it takes no great imagination to visualize George Washington striding the short block and a half from the president's house at Sixth and Market to pay a call on Director Rittenhouse at the Mint, even if there is scant reliable evidence that the president ever did so.[38] Accurate these pictures are not, but influential they certainly have been.

These, then, are the irreducible elements of our story: one man, one Mint, and two masterpieces of popular art. By appointing himself the first Mint's commemorator in chief, Frank H. Stewart made people forget that he was also its destroyer. By serving as Stewart's subject, the little Mint achieved the esteem after it was gone that it had never earned when still standing. And by creating an idealized image of the first Mint in every numismatist's brain, the two masterpieces became Stewart's most potent tools in his quest for commemoration. The man understood his mission well. In his address upon laying the cornerstone of his new Old Mint Building, on January 27, 1912, Stewart said simply, "Every one of us here assembled owes a tribute to the past and a legacy to the future."[39] In his efforts to commemorate the first Mint, he certainly paid tribute to the past, and in commissioning two masterpieces, he definitely created a legacy for the future. The rest of this book will examine Stewart, the Mint he commemorated, and the legacy he created, not only for the living, but for all generations of numismatists to come.

Benjamin Rush, engraving by Christian Gobrecht.

David Rittenhouse, first director of the U.S. Mint; portrait by Natalie Hause.

Frank H. Stewart Electric Company showroom
at 35 North Seventh Street, *ca.* 1898

Chapter 2

Frank Huling Stewart: The Man Who Owned the First United States Mint

The story of the man, Frank H. Stewart, begins with the United States Centennial of American Independence. The year 1876 brought the Centennial Exhibition, the first world's fair in the United States (the 1853 Crystal Palace Exhibition in New York City was a private commercial venture), to the city of Philadelphia. The world's fairs were the Olympics of their time, international events planned years in advance and executed on a gargantuan scale. Indeed, the Main Exhibition Building, a temporary structure erected in Philadelphia's Fairmount Park, had a footprint of over 20 acres. Thousands of exhibitors and millions of the public, including the parents of Frank H. Stewart,[1] flocked to this extravaganza of technology and agriculture to witness for the first time marvels such as Bell's telephone and Remington's typewriter, an example of which incongruously landed in the inventory of one E.B. Mason, a 19th-century Philadelphia coin dealer.[2] Also on the numismatic front, side trips to the Philadelphia Mint were a popular attraction, and a total of 600,000 visitors made the Mint a decidedly crowded venue during the summer and fall of 1876. The *American Journal of Numismatics* commented:

> They came from all of the States and all lands, from 9 to 12 A.M. [sic, 12 P.M. is intended], to see the collection of coins and the minting operations. How they passed through without choking up the workshops, and without helping themselves occasionally, may be a wonder to those who can imagine such an array; but a certain routine, and a proper disposition of guides, prevented any loss, except what occurred in picking pockets.[3]

Among the 600,000 were a number of the numismatically uninitiated, according to one old-time collector who later described his visit to the Mint Cabinet in 1876:

> I had an introduction to the governor of the mint and was asked to wait until the rush of visitors was over when I could be shown over at leisure. While waiting I watched the crowd of country people who had come to see the exhibition looking over the mint collection. One attendant was especially detailed to show the "widow's mite." As he called out "this way to see the widow's mite," many of the

United States
Centennial medal, 1876
(Julian CM-11).

crowd, although they could not tell this particular piece, went and gazed with awe and wonder on what they believed to be the actual coin dropped by the poor widow into the temple treasury.[4]

To satiate the throngs an explosion of Centennial-themed medal and token issues emerged, seemingly as numerous as the Philadelphia Mint visitors themselves, but more accurately on the order of a thousand different varieties.[5] Two years later, coin dealer Édouard Frossard sounded like a 21st-century collector complaining about the ubiquitous issues of the U.S. Mint:

> Mr. John W. Haseltine informs us that his next coin sale will contain many Centennial medals from a private collection, a number of which he had never seen or heard of. Mr. H. adds: "There are now no new Centennial medals being made," a welcome piece of information, for the interest in Centennial medals has of late decreased in a ratio proportionate to the increase of the posthumous article.[6]

THE AGE OF ELECTRICITY

The whole Centennial affair marked the emergence of post-Reconstruction America on the world stage, and along with this power came the debut of another, for a careful observer at the Exhibition would have also seen a number of experimental electric lights on display.[7]

Electric lighting was already well known among the scientific community but remained impractical on a commercial scale. Edison's incandescent innovation was still three years off, and his was one of any number of concerns striving to turn electric lighting into an economically viable enterprise. Besides Edison, the most notable attempt, at least in Philadelphia, was the introduction of the electric arc light, championed by The Brush Electric Light Company of Philadelphia. The Brush Company was rebuffed by the city council in its initial attempts to sell electric service to the city, and so lit upon the idea of giving it away at no cost for the first year, in hopes that luxury would become necessity. On December 3, 1881, to much fanfare, Brush illuminated the length of Chestnut Street between the Delaware and Schuylkill rivers. "Chestnut Street was better lit upon Saturday and Sunday nights than at any time in its history," thought one newspaper.[8] Someone peering south down Seventh Street from the first U.S. Mint site would have been much attracted by the nascent, glowing light two blocks away. Free hookups for residential customers followed next, as Frank H. Stewart wrote many years later:

> The electric light companies did nearly all of their own wiring and in many instances it was done free of cost in order to inveigle the house owner to give electricity a trial.[9]

Brush had marketed their product well, and demand throughout Philadelphia quickly brought a rash of com-petitors, along with multiple standards for electric services and devices. It was much like the evolution of the personal computer a hundred years later, as companies schemed against each other and carefully weighed the costs of cooperation and standardization against the ultimate prize of market hegemony. Philadelphia may have been an eastern city, but the electric business there, and anywhere else for that matter, was just as unsettled as the contemporary wild West. Poles 40 feet high crisscrossed the city carrying power lines, a spider's web in the sky, and competing companies even ran electrical lines on the same streets.[10] As Frank H. Stewart recalled, "At this time needless to say there were no city ordinances prohibiting the running of overhead wires without a permit."[11] Compounding the chaos was the lack of central generating stations, and department stores like Wanamaker's simply used their own isolated plants.

The government was no different from anyone else, and as late as 1897 in Washington, D.C., the Bureau of Engraving and Printing was trying to furnish their own generator space for local electrification. Edwin Lamasure Sr., BEP accountant and father of the painter, commented:

> I knew the Director of the Bureau had the matter in contemplation; that he had spoken of it some time ago and regretted that we did not have the space; but since then we have had an addition to the middle wing there, and it does give now the room for dynamos, so we could do it; and he has it in hand, and is very much interested in getting from Congress some permanent buildings down in the yard.[12]

The BEP was apparently not located close enough to the power grid to "tap in," but even for those who lived near the established electric lines there remained a lack of equipment standards—electric lamps which worked with the service of one company might very well be inoperable if a resident moved to a different section of the city covered by a different firm. As Stewart put it, the different standards "made nearly as many combinations as a Yale lock on a burglar proof safe."[13]

The various electric and gas concerns of Philadelphia consolidated over time, but the process of networking turbogenerators, burying electric lines, and supplying a standard electric service with ever increasing usage and geographical demands consumed much industrial capital over the next 50 years. The consolidated Philadelphia Electrical Company, by 1927, represented the growth from the primitive demonstrations at the 1876 Centennial, to half a million customers and 7,000 employees.[14] Meanwhile, World's Fairs continued to showcase the proliferating technology, and numismatists were not far behind, striking a medal which commemorated the five-acre Electrical Building at the 1893 World's Columbian Exposition in Chicago.[15] A California exposition followed suit the following year, executing several medals dedicated to the electric tower erected in the San Francisco fairgrounds.[16] The Bureau of Engraving and Printing was next, producing what some today consider its finest work—the series of 1896 $5 Silver Certificate Note, featuring a winged Liberty holding aloft an electric light bulb.[17] Ironically, the BEP itself was not electrified at the time. Yet, the Age of Electricity presented great opportunity for ambitious newcomers, and fortuitously, one Frank Steward was born in New Jersey on May 7, 1873.[18]

FRANK STEWARD, THE INFANT ELECTRIC

Stewart, as he came to be known, grew up in and around Sharptown, New Jersey, about 30 miles southwest of Philadelphia. Stewart traced his paternal line to one Joseph Steward, an ancestor emigrating from England to the colonies in 1682. Beyond that, the Steward name was thought to have originated in Scotland, "descended from Banquo, Thane of Lochaber," according to a cousin of Stewart's,[19] referring of course to the character immortalized in Shakespeare's *Macbeth*. Stewart, however, was a thoroughly American figure, unencumbered by any weight of history, even as he came to be fascinated by the study of the past.

Stewart's father, Eli, of Salem County, New Jersey, spent much of his life as a farmer, with the exception of a few years in Illinois, where he was engaged in selling lightning rods. He married at the late age of 47, in 1872, to the widow Mary Emma Oliphant. Frank was born the following year, and his brother Burnett followed six years later. A family genealogist recorded of Eli:

> He was slow in speech and movement, and talked but little. During the years he spent in Sharptown [Salem County, New Jersey] he kept himself well posted on the topics of the day, and was usually very interesting when he could be induced to talk. He was extremely fond of playing checkers, and no small portion of his time when he lived in Sharptown was spent in the shops and stores at the game.... Like his brothers he was a member of the Methodist Church and a man of unimpeachable character.[20]

Thirty miles from Philadelphia was a good way into the country in 1873, and thus Stewart's early life was set in an agricultural tableau. "Children were not pampered then as now," Stewart wrote much later,[21] echoing the identical observation of all elder generations, though to be sure Stewart experienced his fair share of manual labor in the farming community. "Farm life was tiresome work," he recalled in the 1930s:

> We got up at 4:15 in the Summer season; took care of the stock; got our breakfasts and almost faced the rising sun on the way up the road to the fields. A Summer day's field work ended at 6 p.m., which was torture to a frail boy.[22]

Stewart's parents were more or less like everyone in rural America, living off the land and not much else.

> The biggest thing in their overworked lives was the mortgage on [the] . . . farm. We would often ship things by boat from Coursens Landing [sic, Course's Landing, New Jersey, is likely intended] to Philadelphia and the boatmen would come around and say that the wagon loads of produce did not net enough to pay the freight. This happened often on grapes, apples, and watermelons so it was more than disheartening to be a farmer or a farmer's son. . . . We lived off the farm with the exception of sugar, molasses and kerosene.[23]

1896 $5 Silver Certificate, featuring an electrified Liberty (Fr-268).

While Stewart "learned to dislike farm life to the fullest extent,"[24] he seemed to retain some sense of nostalgia for his childhood, or at least for the collected accoutrements thereof:

> A single barrel breech loading shot gun, a Filbert rifle, a pepper box pistol, a lot of muskrat traps, a rabbit hound, a flock pigeons, a fishing pole and other boy like possessions that would be ruled out of order except on a farm where the chance of damage was small. . . . The gun now decorates a deer's head and antlers and reminds the writer of the farm in Mannington [township] and the mill pond of Sharptown.[25]

Stewart's "chance of damage" became a reality more than once. Then as now, farming life was fraught with danger, men and machines and fate not always in harmony. Stewart's biographer explained:

Frank H. Stewart, *ca.* 1885.

Frank H. Stewart, *ca.* 1888.

Mr. Stewart remembers spending many an hour at night, sitting as still as a mouse in a homemade canoe, with a white rag tied over the end of the gun for a sight, trying to shoot muskrats. He carried this gun until one day, through mishandling the gun while reloading, a bullet grazed his eyebrow, and he almost lost an eye. When Frank returned home and his parents questioned him about the wound, the boy told them that he had fallen while hunting. Mr. Stewart said, "I was no George Washington."[26]

On another occasion, Stewart was struck in his left leg by a pitchfork falling from a hay wagon. The resulting wound caused much trouble later in his life.[27] Along with the dangers of rural existence came the blessings of the small village, and Sharptown in this regard was like any other tiny community, a place where everybody knew everybody. Stewart clearly relished the memories of family reunions, a virtual town hall gathering, as his father came from a family of 14:

> The Steward picnics held every year on the knoll in the woods at Course's Landing on August 16 were always in the boyhood of the compiler attended by one hundred or more of the family. The pies, cakes, meats, watermelons, cantaloupes, lemon and apple butters and other good things to eat cannot be forgotten.[28]

Despite the occasional sentimentality, Stewart had little tolerance for the romanticism of rural life:

> All the "hocus pocus" about the gentility and independence of the farmer of my youth was a myth despite what it may be nowadays."[29]

Thus, Stewart purposed early to extract himself from the rural milieu into which he had been born:

> Some time during the Summer of 1887 the compiler [Stewart] saw a cartoon, in a semi-weekly New York newspaper, of a bookkeeper seated on a high stool, facing a tall desk with an oil lamp overhead. The bookkeeper had a pen over one ear and did not seem to have any real work to do except to occasionally move a few figures. . . . The cartoon had done its work and the boy decided by some hook or crook to become a bookkeeper.[30]

Stewart's father evidently thought enough of the idea to bankroll his oldest son, and so Frank, at the age of 17, found himself enrolled at Prickett's College of Commerce, located at Broad and Chestnut streets in downtown Philadelphia. Alone in the big city, Stewart plunged into his studies, even paying extra for "illuminating gas" in his room so as to study by night. The man who eventually turned the First U.S. Mint into an electrical supply house thus started his urban voyage only a few blocks away from the decrepit building on Seventh Street, using the precursor of electricity to power his way through the world of commerce.

PHILADELPHIA FREEDOM

Leaving behind his rural existence, Stewart began to absorb the sights of the city, most notably the Mint Cabinet and Independence Hall, both of which he visited shortly after his arrival in 1890:

> Nov 22. I made a tour through the mint saw their mineral cabinet and collection of coins among them two silver Dollars of 1804 and one 20$ gold piece of 1849 the only one known of, another of the first ever coined by man, 7th century B.C. One side of which represented a man's head as perfect as any coin of modern times. Afternoon went into the old state house which contains relics of 'ye olden time' the old liberty bell & yolk on which is inscribed Proclaim liberty unto all the inhabitants thereof and the sword of 'Mad Anthony' Wayne. Pieces of the charter oak and treaty tree and a link of the iron cable placed across the Hudson by Arnold [reference is made to a chain spanning the Hudson River, erected as a barrier to oppose British ships] the original Declaration of Independence[.] Franklin's air pump[.][31]

Both institutions would come to play a large part in Stewart's life. For now, the ambitious youth completed his bookkeeping course in one academic year and finished at the top of his class, graduating in 1891. Ambition or not, Frank still came across as a yokel, at least in the eyes of the Prickett's administration. Stewart explained:

> The proprietor told him that he was entitled to be salutatorian or valedictorian at the commencement exercise but that he was too young or too green for the task. This was true, because he had never seen a commencement exercise and did not know the meaning of the honor. A preacher's son substituted to the entire satisfaction of all concerned before an audience of three thousand persons in the Academy of Music.[32]

Along with the graduation, Frank Steward became Frank H. Stewart:

> The story is this. The proprietor of a Business College [Prickett's Business School], while making out a list of graduates, whereon the writer [Stewart] was Number One, asked what his middle name was. Being quite unsophisticated at the age of eighteen and feeling that is was necessary for the dignity of the occasion, he manufactured one right then and there and adopted the name Huling, which he has never used since. Frank H. had a somewhat pleasing sound compared with Frank and thus it came about when he gave his name to his first employer in Philadelphia.[33]

Prickett's botched the name even further, using "Hulings" rather than "Huling" in the commencement program.[34] Stewart's employer took care of the rest of the name change:

The writer's employer had some business cards printed Frank H. Stewart, which while somewhat wrong, made no difference to him, but when he, too, went into business a quandary presented itself. He was known by the alias and not by his real name. The line of least, or no resistance, was to let good enough alone. So it was and is.[35]

Others in the Steward family felt likewise, including Stewart's brother William Burnett Stewart (Stewart's parents seem to have graced his brother with a middle name, while Frank went wanting[36]), who also adopted the "Stewart" spelling. Stewart explained it:

> A few of the Stewards who entered the business fields in Philadelphia within the last fifty years have adopted the name Stewart for no sensible reason beyond the fact that it was easy to be known as Stewart and a constant inconvenience to insist on Steward as the correct name.[37]

Later, he expressed some regret at the name change:

> Everyone called him "Stewart," and he says he very foolishly put that name on his letter and bill heads, and then it became too late to rectify a boyish mistake.[38]

In any case, at the age of 18, Frank H. Stewart had literally made a name for himself, completed his formal education, and was now ready to take his place in the business

Prickett's Business School graduation program, 1892.

world of Philadelphia. Stewart always remembered his motivation as a young man:

> The country boy works harder in the city than the city boy because he knows if he does not make good he will have to go back to the manual labor of the country. Fear of hard work left behind always reminds the boy of the farm that punishment awaits him if he fails to win his way in a large city. In other words, fear rather than a greater brain capacity is the motive power behind him.[39] I have never known a single one to go back. They have either gone forward or died in the attempt.[40]

Regardless of fear or brain power, both of which Stewart possessed in ample quantity, there was no getting around the general business conditions in the 1890s. The United States, coming into its own as a world power, in some sense became a victim of its own success. New technology seems to always attract speculation, as promising as the beauty of a Dutch tulip on April Fool's Day, and the late 19th century was no exception. The "Dutch tulips" of the 1870s and 1880s were the railroads, crisscrossing the country and selling the public on the idea that connectedness was always a good thing, and would surely generate fortune for all. Indeed, iron and steel boomed and anyone supplying infrastructure to the expanding rail grid had a reasonable expectation of success. But, like the "information superhighway" many years in the future, the rail industry over-expanded, stretching operators heavily invested in blasting their way across the mountainous American frontier. Many rail interests and their supporting banks went bankrupt or consolidated, resulting in much unemployment and economic malaise, hardly "gay" as the 1890s are romanticized.

Along with reduced transport costs and other technological advances, agriculture was next in line. Commodity prices plummeted, the United States now in a mode of overproduction and underconsumption. Concurrent recession in Europe reduced demand for American foodstuffs, and soon farmers could not meet mortgage payments, further squeezing available credit. The "Great American Dream" was reduced to a faint chimera, to the extent that immigration fell severely in the latter portion of the 1890s. Thus, even the "tired," "poor," and "huddled masses," "yearning to breathe free," thought the chances of finding good air might be better away from the "spacious skies" of America, where the "amber waves" had more sellers than buyers. The American population, reactionary as always, voted heavily against the current administration in the midterm election of 1894, and thus the majority of the country leaned Republican for a good while.

Given the mood of the times, Stewart's father must have been rather surprised, when, in the fall of 1891, Stewart wrote home that he was quitting his first job out of school, working the want ad counter of the Philadel-

phia *Item* newspaper (which was coincidentally located on Seventh Street in Philadelphia, hardly a block south of the First U.S. Mint). Frank H. Taylor, who we shall meet again, described the newspaper:

> The small building at the north-west corner of Lodge alley, (Jayne street), and Seventh street was, for many years, the publishing office of that now defunct but once widely read newspaper, the *Item*. This sheet was started in 1847 by "Colonel" Thomas Fitzgerald, as a weekly. In later times the *Item* became a daily and put forth a Sunday edition, always prone to "play up" topics of local sensation, and never without the traditional "chip on the shoulder," the *Item*, steered ably by its redoubtable founder and his sons, provided the sort of reading matter best relished in the horny-headed purlieus [outskirts] of old Philadelphia.[41]

With no comment on the paper's editorial policy, Stewart was frustrated with his lack of upward mobility,[42] and felt that additional skills in stenography might bring him closer to his dream job of being a bookkeeper. His father supported the young man's decision, though Stewart was forced to move back home to Sharptown as his parents offered to pay tuition but no board. Stewart lived as a student commuter, traveling by horse to nearby Woodstown, then by train to Philadelphia. Stewart re-enrolled at Prickett's, and upon completion of the five-month course entered the electrical business on May 15, 1892,[43] being hired by one O.D. Pierce, a Philadelphia electrical contractor.[44] It was still an era "when most persons were afraid of electricity," Stewart recalled.[45] Stewart, ever the writer, promptly authored the Pierce catalog, the first such emission to offer electrical lighting supplies to the citizens of Philadelphia.[46] Pierce evidently was impressed with the youthful go-getter, enough to quickly promote him from a clerical position into sales, and within a few months Stewart found himself dispatched throughout Pennsylvania and New Jersey as a traveling salesman. Indeed, Pierce went as far as to grant the new employee power of attorney.[47] Stewart forged a number of productive relationships with area contractors, but not enough to save the firm, which was caught up in the Panic of 1893 and closed up shop in January of the following year.[48]

Stewart, now only 20 years old and in the face of an economic depression, made the seemingly idiotic decision to open his own electrical supply wholesale business. Stewart's motivation was not the brash overconfidence of a young man. Instead, "fear rather than a greater brain capacity" was the watchword of the day. As Stewart put it, "the 20-acre fields began to worry him."[49] But fear did not get in the way of careful preparation. Stewart had saved nearly $500 from his salary at Pierce, and there was the Pierce client list as well. Stewart's father kicked in another two hundred, and the nascent business had a capital stake. Stewart's chips were all on the table, but this was not a reckless gambler at work. He had labored intensely ever since his arrival in the Freedom City, and if he believed in anything, it was in Frank H. Stewart. Thus, the young man invested his entire bankroll in the most promising new enterprise in Philadelphia: the Frank H. Stewart Electric Company. The same moment inextricably tied Stewart to the First U.S. Mint, for Stewart made the fateful decision to launch his new enterprise in a humble basement at 20 North Seventh, across the street from the century-old, broken-down coinage factory.[50] The die was cast.

Despite the economic malaise, Stewart's timing was by no means ill-fated. The electrical concerns, especially in large cities, were learning that their resources were better spent investing in the electrical generation infrastructure, rather than on connecting individual customers to the power grid. In their stead rose a host of local contractors to deal with the mundane matter of wiring individual residences and linking to Philadelphia Electric. To again draw upon an analogy with the modern Internet, today we likewise see the Googles of the 21st century concentrate on storing and serving information, leaving the business of distribution to others. Stewart perceived the need to service the local contractors, and so became one of the first wholesale electrical supply distributors in the city.[51] From his basement office at 20 North Seventh Street, Stewart ordered from such giants as General Electric and played middleman to the new profession of electrical tradesman.

Presenting in business as "Frank H. Stewart Manufacturer and Dealer in General Electrical Supplies," the new firm was launched in January, 1894, and first listed in the Philadelphia city directory of 1895.[52] Stewart moved about in 1894, doing business from other locations besides 20 North Seventh, including 1208 Green Street (probably his residence[53]) and 41 North Seventh. On May 16, 1895, Stewart settled in at 35 North Seventh, where he would remain a long time, renting half of the first floor and half of the basement for $50 a month.[54] Stewart seems to have regretted the frequent moving around central Philadelphia, for later he advised new businessman to beware of "removals," as "moving from one place to another is hazardous."[55] Two years later Stewart doubled his space, signing a lease for "all that Store and Basement No. 35 North Seventh Street," at $1,100 per year.[56] Stewart rented 35 North Seventh for many years, eventually purchasing the property in 1919.[57] Both this, and Stewart's previous location at 41 North Seventh, were of course adjacent to the former U.S. Mint.

The Seventh Street area turned into something of an "electrical district," with a number of competitors all within a block of Stewart. The Metropolitan Electric Supply Company set up a few doors to the north, while the Franklin Electric Company was located across the street.[58] Stewart acknowledged the power of location, remarking that "A beginner should start on a good business street even though it be in a basement as mine was."[59]

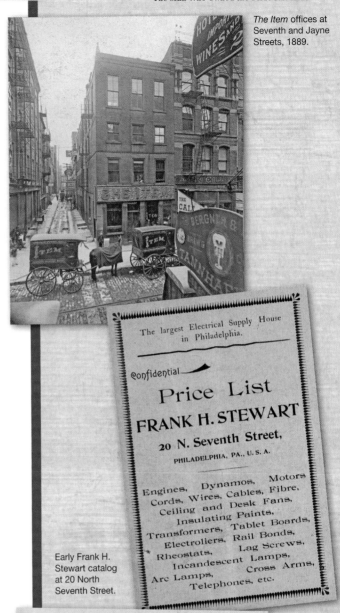

The Item offices at Seventh and Jayne Streets, 1889.

Early Frank H. Stewart catalog at 20 North Seventh Street.

Frank H. Stewart Electric Company exterior at 35 North Seventh Street, *ca.* 1905.

STEWART'S ROSE

Stewart launched his eponymous business in 1894, and on May fifth of that same year met his future bride, Abigail Rose Kirby (who went by Rose). Rose was a prolific diarist, and while her diaries (preserved until at least the 1970s) are today missing, Stewart himself extracted portions which dealt with their courtship, presented forthwith (edited for readability).[60] Rose was 17 in 1894, and writes much to reinforce the idea that matters of the heart are a timeless aspect of human experience.

5/5/1894. Saturday. Festival wore my red dress & pansies. Introduced by Lizzie Cooper to Frank Stewart & C. Oliphant [possibly a half-brother of Frank]. Had cream lemonade cake and candy. All went to our house. Oliphant took Lizzie home. Had a nice talk with Frank Stewart. Made engagement for Sunday night.

Abigail Rose
Kirby, wife of
Frank H. Stewart,
ca. 1900.

Rose in 1909,
with companion,
in Florida.

5/6/1894. Sunday Frank Stewart came at 6:30. Driving through Sharptown. Went to Presbyterian church.

5/12/1894. Saw Frank Stewart on train. He wanted to know if I would go and out with him tomorrow night – said yes.

5/22/1894. Received letter from Frank.

5/26/1894. Saturday. Frank Stewart and I drove to Sharptown in carriage to the festival. Ate strawberry cream cake & candy,

6/16/1894. Saturday. Lizzie Cooper party with Frank Stewart. Had a lovely time. Home at 12:30. Wore new white dress.

7/4/1894. Received letter from Frank.

7/11/1894. Received letter from Frank.

7/13/1894. Received letter from Frank.

7/14/1894. 18 yrs. old today.

7/15/1894. On Crispens[?] portico when Frank drove past—came to see if I would go out driving. Went home 9:30. Lemonade and cake will never give him anymore.

7/24/1894. Received letter from Frank.

7/25/1894. Received letter from Frank.

7/26/1894. Received letter from Frank.

7/27/1894. Received letter from Frank.

8/3/1894. Jolly party of 14. It was the shortest and loveliest and happiest and best day I have spent for years. Home at 10.

8/12/1894. Frank brought me some roses.

9/15/1894. Went to church. Stewart & I started. Would not speak all the way down.

9/23/1894. Stewart came at 6:30. Wore my challis dress. I hate him. Home before 9. Quarreled & spatted. He put out the light as I was bound to read. Told him he would be sorry if he didn't light up. He wouldn't and went and got in big chair. Would not speak to him. He got hat. Said he was going home. Went to the door and stood there about 10 minutes. Came back, shut the door, lit the lamp & sat down. Before he went home we made up. Think he is right nice for all.

10/13/1894. Tomorrow night I find out what ails him. He can go. He doesn't have to come here. I think he is downright mean. He might say what ails him. If he is tired of coming why doesn't he stop. So sorry I wrote that letter but it was not my fault.

10/14/1894. Frank came at 7:30. I noticed quite a change as soon as he came in. I could have him at the North Pole for all that he noticed me. We had three fights with fountain pen. We were completely covered with ink before finishing. It was half a sheet &

sounded as if written on an iceberg. If he can't write better letters he need not waste his ink on me as they are not appreciated.

10/27/1894. Stewart came at 9:10. Momma went to the door. She said I was upstairs. But before I could get to the door he was gone. If he can't get here before that time he had better stay away altogether.

11/5/1894. I really miss Frank. I wish he could come next week. I think I well appreciate him when he comes home again.

11/22/1894. Frank sick for two week's illness. If Frank would only get well I'll be happy though I wonder if I do like him or not. I wish I knew.

11/29/1894. Thanksgiving Day. Received a letter from Frank & threw it in stove.

12/2/1894. Wrote to Frank. I made it as short & as cool as possible. I don't care. I can send as good as I get.

12/6/1894. Well a letter came this morning he said he thought I was not myself when I wrote that letter.

12/10/1894. Received a letter from Frank. He wrote eight pages – but I felt tempted to burn them all. He is a mystery.

12/13/1894. I did not get any letter. Now I think that is mean. As I have written twice. He can keep his letters. It will be a cool time when I write again very soon.

12/15/1894. I am upstairs packing away Stewart's letters and pictures. I am going to forget that there ever was a Frank H. Stewart I think it is a mean underhanded trick he had played. Why couldn't he say he was tired. The Lord knows I was tired six months ago. Let him go.

12/30/1894. Didn't hear from Frank for over a week so I wrote him a note asking if he were mad. Also to say so. Sent my letter on the train. Received one on the 5 P.M. [afternoon train]. He said he was not tired. He had been expecting to hear from me so I expect we'll wander on again.

1/1/1895. Sent Frank flowers. They were lovely about two dozen different colored carnations.

1/5/1895. Saw Frank. Well I thought I would drop. Didn't say one sensible thing.

1/7/1895. At store [likely on North Seventh Street in Philadelphia]. I looked up & saw Stewart. He coolly marched back & sat down – shut up store, etc. He stayed until 9:15. We couldn't find anything to talk about. Wrote a long letter to him tonight.

1/20/1895. About 6:30 some one knocked—went to door & there stood Frank. After 12 weeks. Well we put in a full evening. He surely was full. He didn't leave there until 1:40. He doesn't look so awfully bad.

1/27/1895. When some one knocked went to door & there was Frank sitting on the railing. We had a lovely argument on women as drummers [a contemporary term for salespeople]. He said no lady was a drummer. I said there were lady drummers. Not either would give in. Frank didn't go home until 20 min. of one. He is surely a great child.

2/15/1895. Frank goes to Ohio.

2/20/1895. Well – I guess things have come to a standstill between Frank and me. Oh, dear. I wish I had not been so hateful and queer. If he doesn't write this week or come I shall send his photos back.

2/21/1895. Received letter from Frank. Well, if I wasn't glad – about the nicest letter he ever wrote I am so glad.

2/25/1895. Barton [identity unknown] asked me to go to Washington party. Told him I would let him know. Wrote to Frank asking him about it.

2/26/1895. Received letter from Frank this morning. Well it was cool, sarcastic & almost insulting. But I thought I would hurt myself laughing over it. Told Barton I could not go.

3/5/1895. Wrote to my boy tonight. The night of the party and I don't care a snap about going.

3/10/1895. Sunday. Frank came about quarter of seven. We had a strong argument on if a hen and half lay an egg and a half in a day and a half then how many eggs did one hen lay? I said 1 egg. He said 2/3 of an egg. After Nat & Clarkson left we hardly said a word. I got mad at him twice. We had a scrapping match before he went home. He didn't go home until quarter to two.

3/15/1895. Received quite a long letter from Frank Has invited me to go to Boston—so guess I'll go.

3/27/1895. Did not write to Frank last night. Have found out a few things about that fellow. Who can you trust? I thought he was the soul of honor. Anything but deceit. Never let a fellow be too sure of you. Sorry I did not find it out sooner. Haven't had any fun for some time but think I shall.

4/7/1895. Sunday Frank came at 7:30. We went out & took a walk. Well, if we didn't have one fine time. Such a racket. Frank got up to go. He was mad then cried & he came back we talked it all over & made up. Better friends than ever. He went home at 2 in the morning.

4/27/1895. We quarrel all the time. He surely is contrary and I am too.

No further data are recorded, but it is a safe bet that Frank and Rose continued their on-again, off-again romance for several iterations before putting closure to the matter, when they were married on August 26, 1896.[61]

GROWING PAINS

The $200 stake from Stewart's father did not last long, for two years later, by 1896, Stewart was in hock to the old man for $3,000.[62] Stewart had started the business on a pure commission basis, perhaps good for some profit but not for much growth, as Stewart recalled:

> A beginner can often times make arrangements to represent some manufacturer on a consignment or commission basis. While this is not true merchandising it may help at the start[63]…For the first two months I carried no stock and sold only on a commission for the factories but soon saw that I was not going to get a new position or get ahead on that basis so I . . . bought about two wheelbarrow loads of merchandise which I kept in the basement on the floor.[64]

With stock came the need for capital to purchase and house Stewart's growing inventory of electrical supplies. Stewart took on a partner in March, 1895, one P. Logan Bockius, who thought enough of the young go-getter to invest $2,500 in Stewart's fledgling enterprise.[65] Bockius evidently had great faith in the 21-year-old youth, to invest the 2010 equivalent of over $60,000, but the partnership did not persist. Stewart told the story:

> After a few months I . . . took in a partner. . . . Mr. Bockius was with me close to a year. I would go out on the road and get orders and he would look after the details of the management of the little basement store, and stock. The . . . action on my part soon proved to be a mistake because of the smallness of the business and the partnership was dissolved and my partner very kindly took my note for his share of the business for the very simple reason I could not pay in cash.[66]

Stewart also appealed to old friends back in rural New Jersey for working capital,[67] but in the end his father appears to have served as the chief banker. Stewart made his case for an additional $2,000 in an 1896 letter sent to the coun-

try from which he desperately wanted to escape. The four-page sales pitch to his father does much to illuminate the state of Stewart's electrical business at the time:

> I am carrying at a rough guess at least six thousand dollars worth of stock and have bills outstanding due me about three thousand dollars or in all about nine thousand dollars. . . . I am running a square business in one of the large cities of this country on this capital and have a credit for any amount of stock I see fit to buy because I have paid my bills and treated people honestly. I am considered by my acquaintances the growing part of the electrical supply business. . . . I get down here at eight thirty in the morning and leave at six o'clock at night and work like a slave all day. . . . To day I am doing a business between twenty and twenty five thousand a year on three thousand dollars capital. . . . This business did not succeed any other business but every dollars worth of stuff that goes out because I have been the direct means of selling it. . . . My stock is such that I can fill any orders promptly and I am getting the largest contracting business in the town because I am now carrying a stock.

Stewart was turning his capital eight times a year, an intense pace, and constantly aligning the flow of cash between creditors and customers. He continued:

> I cannot stand the strain much longer and can get $2000 if you see fit to indorse [sic] for me. You can be secured by the 2000$ [sic] worth of assets that I have in case anything should happen to me. . . . I am now making some little money which will show for itself in the course of time but that does not help a raging headache or pay off bills. . . . I do not ask you for the money nor ask you to get it for me but if you think the outlook warrants it I can get the money if you will endorse for me which while it makes you responsible you can be secured with two dollars for every one.

Stewart saved a carrot for the wrap-up:

> I have got to have a book keeper and if I can get the money I can give Burnett [Stewart's younger brother, at this time seventeen years old] a job at five dollars a week but he can never enter this business as a partner unless I am paid fifteen hundred dollars a year for what time I spend in working it up, again I do not want a partner anyway…You can think this matter over carefully and let me have your ultimatum regarding it. I would not ask for it if I did not need it nor would I ask for it if I thought it an unsafe investment.[68]

Whether Eli Stewart responded affirmatively is unknown, but what is known is that W. Burnett Stewart went to work for his brother, eventually holding a small capital stake in the company, and ultimately becoming the treasurer of the company. Burnett evidently joined his brother very early in the game, for in 1910 he was referred to as the oldest employee in the company.[69]

F. H. STEWART.   P. L. BOCKIUS.

Stewart and Bockius, from a July 1895 issue of *Electrical World*.

FRANK H. STEWART INCORPORATED

Stewart's sales, if not profits, were meteoric in the early years of the enterprise. The company turnover in its first year, 1894, was a mere $4,000, but this was increased to $100,000 by 1901, and in 1907 eclipsed the $500,000 mark.[70] There was not a single setback, each year substantially outperforming the previous. Profits were more illusory: Stewart netted but four percent during his first $100,000 year. He fared much better the following year, doubling his margin and delivering a $12,000 profit.[71] The days of begging Dad for a few thousand were over.

Stewart officially incorporated the Frank H. Stewart Electric Company in the state of Pennsylvania in 1904. He held over 90 percent of the total stock issue, while his brother William Burnett Stewart held five percent, and a number of other investors held smaller amounts.[72] The corporate charter summed up the business:

> Philadelphia, June 15, 1904. Capital, $100,000. Buying, selling, assembling, trading or dealing in all kinds of electrical supplies, gas and electric fixtures, lamps, globes, dynamos, electrical machinery, art metal work, and all other articles of commerce of a like character at wholesale and retail.[73]

William Burnett Stewart served as treasurer of the firm, while majority stockholder Frank H. Stewart naturally assumed the presidency of his enterprise. William was also an inventor, or at least enough of one to have a patent issued in 1911.[74] "As it is well known, where electrical . . . cords are used for a connection between a wall . . . and a lamp or other device, it often occurs that the conductor may be too long, in which event it is necessary to provide

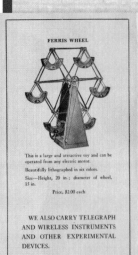

Stewart Electric Company toy circular, undated.

Christmas tree light advertisement, from *Stewart's Current Flashes*, 1921.

Frank H. Stewart Electric Company stock certificate, 1904.

means for taking up the slack," Stewart wrote of his contraption in the patent application. To address the irritation of the housekeeper, Stewart offered up a clamp which could conveniently gather the loose wire into a smaller and presumably safer bunch. Burnett also received a patent for an electrical socket bushing, while Frank, not to be outdone, patented two inventions himself, both related to the aforementioned problem of managing excessively long electrical cords.[75]

The two brothers sold primarily to the electrical trade in the 1890s, as electricity was foreign to the layman and feared by many. The corporate charter indicated retail intentions as well, and by the 1920s Stewart was selling radios, vacuum cleaners, batteries, fans, washing machines—in short every large and small appliance the expanding industry could divine.[76] A 1921 Stewart holiday circular tempted the buying public with the latest fixtures, including Santa Claus-shaped electric Christmas tree ornaments.[77] Electric toys for the children were not far behind.

Industrial concerns were equally sensitive to electric stimulation. Stewart Electric sold, for example, industrial lighting, noting in a catalog, "For the effective and economical production of work, it is important that a sufficient intensity of light be provided. . . . It has been found by careful tests that Productive Intensities have increased production from 6 to 33% over than in poorly lighted rooms and workshops."[78] The whole endeavor was wildly successful—Stewart's $500,000 volume in 1907 would be the equivalent of over $10,000,000 today. And early in 1911, the firm reported a profit for the previous year of $43,000—roughly a million in modern terms.[79] At the age of 34, the local boy in the big city had more than made good, now a principal stockholder in a profit-producing juggernaut.

THE GOOD LIFE

While dedicated to hard work and fair dealing, Stewart was no slave to the office. He would eventually retire in 1928 at the age of 55,[80] and beginning with the purchase of the first Mint in 1907 seems to have dedicated increasing amounts of time to historical and genealogical research, fishing, traveling, and institutional politics. In an autobiographical sketch, Stewart described himself:

> Mr. Stewart is a curious mixture of Business man, Sportsman, Archaeologist, Numismatist and Historian. He is a director or officer in over a dozen varied institutions. . . . He is historian of the New Jersey Society of Pennsylvania and Director of the Genealogical Society of Pennsylvania, as well as President of the Ocean City, N.J. Fishing Club [where Stewart maintained a summer residence], composed of over three hundred of the crack fisherman of the New Jersey Coast; and it is fair to say that Mr. Stewart exercises the prerogatives of a fisherman without

flinching when he tells of the marvelous escapes from death while being towed in small boats by giant fish of the seven seas. He specializes in salt water fish and has fished in many out of way places.[81]

Stewart was married, but like his hero George Washington, never had children, allowing more time for avocational pursuits.[82] His first love was history, especially that of southern New Jersey, which he explained thus:

> One day in June 1886, when I was a boy about thirteen years old, while hoe harrowing corn on my father's farm, I noticed what seemed to be an elongated oval shaped brown dry leaf. I stopped the horse, picked up the supposed leaf and was amazed to find it was a stone knife. The discovery was an important one in my life. . . . During the next two years I found many arrow heads, pieces of pottery and one or two tomahawks, which I saved. . . . From the above my friends may naturally suspect that my trend toward local history has its inception in finding the stone knife on Salem Creek in 1886, which is a fact. . . . it is a worth while subject, especially for boys, because it may lead to other important hobbies or studies as it did in my case.[83]

Like many collectors, Stewart put boyhood fascinations to the side as a young professional. But as time and resources allowed, the old passions were rekindled, and Stewart determined to resume his former pursuits. The fate of his childhood collection, unfortunately, was such as is common to adults who trust parents with their belongings:

> After I had established a business in Philadelphia, I found that all work and no diversion was wearing me down and I looked around for a hobby. I decided that the collection of Indian relics would be beneficial. The next time I went to Sharptown I asked my mother to get out the relics I had found on the farm and was somewhat dismayed to learn that she had given a Methodist preacher his choice of my small collection, including the first stone knife I had ever seen, mentioned above.[84]

Stewart went on to rebuild the collection, and also wrote widely on southern New Jersey history, under the imprimatur of the Gloucester County (New Jersey) Historical Society, of which he was conveniently president and patron in chief. One of the Society trust funds was named after his parents, Eli and Mary Burnett Steward.[85] Stewart was obsessed with original documents, noting that:

> There is nothing I like better than to dig in manuscript records of one, two, or three centuries ago. For the last ten years I have hardly read a book because of my preference for the things that have never been published. In this way I get things unabridged and undiluted.[86]

Stewart, with minimal formal academic training, was not capable of interpreting history and reframing it in compelling and enduring ways; yet, so dogged was his perseverance in hunting and preserving original documents that today his work cannot be ignored. Stewart seemed to know his limits, as many of his writings are little more than formalized presentations of original source materials. His *chef d'oeuvre*, *History of the First United States Mint*, of which much more will be said later, is somewhat in the same vein, relying heavily on recitation of archival material first unearthed by Stewart.

STEWART MEETS THE MINT

The continued growth of the Frank H. Stewart Electric Company in the early 1900s created a need for physical expansion, much like the first U.S. Mint 75 years previous. Stewart complained:

> For a great many years we have been more or less hampered by not having sufficient room to satisfactorily handle our congested stocks located in old buildings and neighboring warehouses. . . .[87]

Stewart, who had operated at 20 North Seventh, 41 North Seventh, and now 35 North Seventh, finally aimed his dart true and struck the bull's-eye upon the site of the former Mint at 37 through 39 North Seventh, directly adjacent to the 35 North Seventh property. Stewart purchased 37 through 39 North Seventh, along with an adjoining property, 631 Filbert, on April 20, 1907, from J. Louis Kates and Frederick Snyder, who were acting as executors for the estate of John L. Kates. The purchase price was $45,000.[88] The deed of transfer, normally a tedious tangle of rods and furlongs, related at least some idea of the romance of moment, referring to 37 through 39 North Seventh as "the 'Old Mint' property." And while the First Mint had been subject to an annual ground rent of "Twenty-one Spanish coined silver pieces of eight," Stewart had no such obligation, for the ground rent had been extinguished in 1890.[89]

Stewart made quick use of the additional space, at least on the Filbert lot:

> He immediately tore down the small building located in the rear of the property and erected a building which was connected with the property 35 North Seventh Street. . . . This helped for a while.[90]

A more nuanced account of that property appeared in *History of the First U.S. Mint*:

> The building 631 Filbert street was a wooden shack that was probably used at one time as the Mint stable; connected to it on the rear was a one and a half story brick building known as the smelting house. These two small buildings which had no basement were demolished in the latter part of 1907. . . .[91]

Stewart built a four-story building in their place, at a cost of $15000.[92] The remaining structures, the Front and Middle Buildings of the first U.S. Mint, awaited their fate. In the meantime, a new consciousness of the Old Mint began to take root in Stewart's busy brain.

STEWART'S OLD MINT BRAND

Branding was a byproduct of the Industrial Revolution, for mass-produced goods, distributed widely, required distinction in order to compete with locally sourced products. Still a relatively young concept in Stewart's time, branding ultimately exploded in the 1950s, sparked by the warm glow of the television set. Creation of a brand aimed to instill familiarity and confidence in a company, and this was a concept that Stewart understood well. "Experience has shown that a business slogan or a trade mark has been helpful," Stewart thought.[93]

Stewart's first attempt at a corporate identity took shape on his 1894 company letterhead, which featured a clenched fist surrounded by a glory of electric rays, staring down a dragon with its head retreating and tailed curled in submission to the almighty power of the new technology. The idea perhaps played to a public with little scientific comprehension of electric force, appealing to mythological imagery in order to equate fantasy with the new reality. Stewart recalled some of the misperceptions of the era:

> The public generally speaking had their own ideas about electricity. They thought that the staples used to tack down the wires would shut off the flow of current and that while it might flow down the wires it certainly would not go up a hill. Because it was called a fluid they thought it was governed by the same laws. Others were surprised that it was possible to touch a dynamo without getting a shock.[94]

Stewart slew the dragon quickly, for by 1896 he held forth simply as "Frank H. Stewart & Co. Electrical Supplies," using an engraving of an electric light bulb to round out his letterhead. (Later, the Zenith Corporation's "thunderbolt" logo evoked Stewart's early electric rays.) Steady business growth for a decade, along with the purchase of the old Mint property in 1907, inspired Stewart to reassert his earlier creativity, so the Old Mint brand was born shortly after the purchase of the property in April, 1907.

Stewart's launch of the Old Mint brand advertising campaign took shape upon the façade of the first Mint Front Building at 37 through 39 North Seventh Street, where he had applied the phrase "1792 YE OLDE MINT." Stewart's application took place soon after he purchased the building. Contemporary newspaper photographs depict a blank façade at the time of the April, 1907, purchase.[95] But, by November, a newspaper clipping depicts "YE OLDE MINT" on the building front.[96]

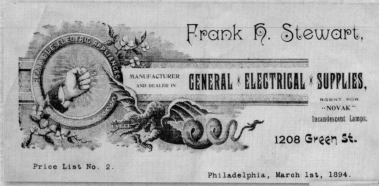

Price List No. 2.

Philadelphia, March 1st, 1894.

1894 Stewart Electric Company letterheads.

1896 Stewart Electric Company letterhead.

OLD UNITED STATES MINT TO BE TORN DOWN

Building situated at 37 and 39 N. 7th st., erected in 1792 by Congress and used as a Mint until 1833. It is now to be torn down and a four-story warehouse erected in its place.

37 through 39 North Seventh Street, from the *Evening Bulletin*, April 24, 1907.

37 through 39 North Seventh Street, from the *North American*, September 8, 1907.

And by August, 1908, Stewart produced a postcard depicting the Mint building with the "Ye Olde Mint" moniker.[97] In December, 1909, Stewart further disseminated the brand in his pamphlet entitled *Ye Olde Mint*, which featured as its frontispiece an image of the now decorated façade. This date is fixed by a letter from S. Hudson Chapman, Philadelphia coin dealer, acknowledging receipt of Stewart's pamphlet.[98] *The Numismatist* of January, 1910, added:

> Since the site, a few years ago, became the property of Mr. Frank H. Stewart, a member of the American Numismatic Association, that part of the first mint structure facing on the street was prominently marked by Stewart: "1792, YE OLDE MINT."[99]

Stewart refined the Old Mint brand concept in 1910, for in that year the following explanation appeared in his pamphlet, *For the Man Who Buys Electrical Supplies:*

> Our trade mark [STEWART'S OLD MINT GOLD STANDARD], illustrated herewith, stands for quality above ordinary expectations. It refers to the fact the gold standard of coins issued by the old mint from 1792 to time of the discontinuance of its operations was above those issued afterwards. The gold then contained in a ten-dollar gold piece would today be worth ten dollars and sixty-five cents, and was therefore about six per cent more valuable than subsequent standards.[100]

37 through 39 North Seventh Street, now with *Ye Olde Mint* on the façade, from a Frank H. Stewart Electric Company postcard, 1908.

Stewart was correct, for the coinage law of January 18, 1837, reduced the fineness of U.S. gold coins from 0.9167 to 0.900, and weight of the $10 eagle from 270 grams to 258. U.S. gold coins had been overvalued (that is, an eagle had contained more than $10 worth of gold), since at least 1799. Speculators exported them to take advantage of this premium, and gold coinage did not circulate for long. Starting in 1834, when the quarter and half eagles were reduced in weight and fineness, and with the act of 1837 reducing the fineness of the eagles, the remaining pre-1834 gold coins were removed from circulation, as they were returned to the Mint for recoinage (although rare examples were saved for the Mint Cabinet of coins by Adam Eckfeldt). The failure of gold to circulate was not necessarily desirable from an economic perspective, but Stewart apparently felt that the fine points of financial theory would not detract from his marketing campaign. In any case, Stewart had neatly tied together his possession of the Old Mint with a bit of historical trivia, and created a vehicle to promote his business interest. The resulting trademark, "Stewart's Old Mint Gold Standard," thus personified the three great endeavors of Stewart's life—the creation of a successful company, the exploration of the first U.S. Mint, and an avid avocation for history. Stewart went even further, tying the Stewart brand to the inevitable march of human progress, a concept less dubious in the pre-World War I era:

> If the electrical supplies you use come from us you are helping to put STEWART'S OLD MINT GOLD STANDARD electrical supplies where they belong, at the head of the powerful marching hosts of an all-conquering science.[101]

While the exact birth date of the Old Mint brand is unknown, it was certainly in full effect at the Stewart Electric Company by May of 1910, for in that month a reception and dinner was held at Kugler's restaurant at 1412 Chestnut, a few blocks' walk from the Old Mint building. The banquet was a celebration of all things Old Mint, for the menu featured a variety of mint-themed delicacies, starting with an appetizer of "MILLED EDGE P'S," featuring what apparently was an entrée, "PIECE OF WATCHDOG a la RITTENHOUSE," and wrapping up with "CRUCIBLES OF MOLTEN METAL" for dessert. (Years later, the coin dealer Thomas Elder followed suit at a New York City numismatic banquet. His menu cataloged sirloin steak as "unattributed," while baked potatoes and green peas were described as "a mixed lot, containing some good specimens."[102]) In 1924, at a Stewart Electric Company picnic, the order of ceremonies began with the "Presentation of Uniforms to the Ball Teams, 1792 Half-Dimes vs. 1828 Half-Cents."[103]

Stewart further drove the "Old Mint" name throughout his line of electrical products. A handbill for Stewart's soldering salts shamelessly plugged the brand:

The Electrician stood on a ladder high
And gazed at the ceiling hard,
Then let out a mighty cry
For "Stewart's Old Mint Gold Standard"

The weak rhyme is unsigned, but likely Stewart himself must be blamed as the unlicensed poet. If only literary talent had matched enthusiasm! Stewart similarly sold "Old Mint Electrical Bells," "Old Mint Push Buttons," and so forth. Stewart embedded the Old Mint logo as a watermark on the company stationary, and used the symbol in his letterhead as well. The letterhead is found in two flavors—one using "STEWART'S OLD MINT GOLD STANDARD," and a second, incorporating Edwin Lamasure's *Ye Olde Mint*, now promoting "OLD MINT ELECTRICAL SUPPLIES." Stewart naturally thought highly of his own brand, writing in 1920:

> In the case of my own concern our trade mark is worth at least a quarter of a million dollars and I personally would not sell it for that. The letters, "G.E." of the General Electric Company, the "W." of the Westinghouse Company, the "Hotpoint" name, are other illustrations.[104]

Although Stewart strived to connect the Old Mint electrical brand with the history of first U.S. Mint, this association no longer resonates with the general public, or even with numismatists. While the Frank H. Stewart Electric Company calendars featuring *Ye Olde Mint* and *Washington Inspecting the First Money Coined by the United States* both included the Old Mint logo, today these images themselves are far better known than the calendars, which are quite scarce. For all of Frank H. Stewart's promotional ability, the Old Mint brand has been greatly exceeded by these two depictions of the first Mint. The irony is that without the Old Mint brand, neither of these artworks would have ever been conceived. And, of course, the Old Mint brand itself would not have been possible without the real old Mint as its inspiration.

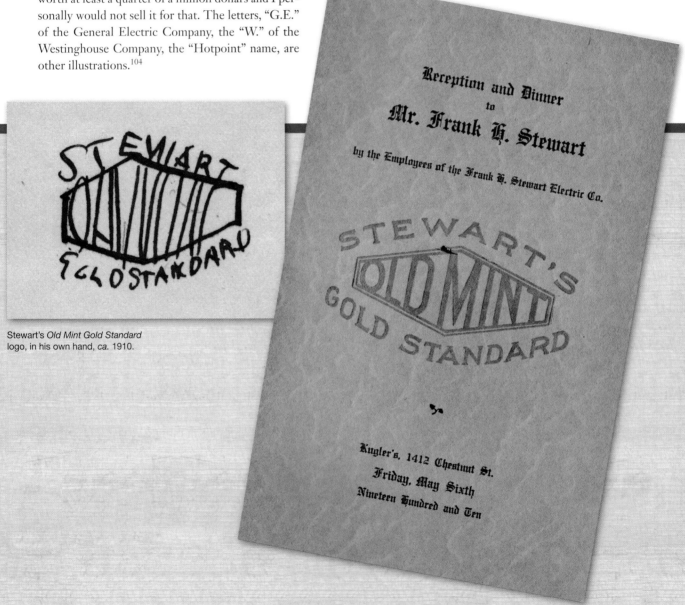

Stewart's *Old Mint Gold Standard* logo, in his own hand, *ca.* 1910.

Frank H. Stewart Electric Company banquet program cover, 1910.

Handbill for Frank H. Stewart Electric Company soldering salts.

THE ELECTRICIAN STOOD ON A LADDER HIGH
AND GAZED AT THE CEILING HARD,
THEN LET OUT A MIGHTY CRY
FOR "STEWART'S OLD MINT GOLD STANDARD"
SOLDERING SALTS

1/2 LB. BOTTLES - 25 CENTS EACH
1 LB. " - 40 " "

FRANK H. STEWART ELECTRIC CO.

35 N. Seventh Street   Philadelphia

OLD MINT ELECTRIC BELLS

044455   044449   044450

No.		Price
044449	2½-inch adjustable Iron Box Bells	$0.32
044450	3-inch adjustable Iron Box Bells	.33
044455	Special tone fancy gong Iron Box Bells	.50

Old Mint branding in the Frank H. Stewart Electric Company product line.

FRANK H. STEWART ELECTRIC COMPANY

OLD MINT PUSH BUTTONS
These are high grade Bronze Push Buttons with German silver contacts.

No. 511   No. 530   No. 531   No. 536   No. 570

No.	Size	Style	Price	Add for postage
511	1⅝ inches	Cast Screw Cap	$0.25 each	$0.05
530	2x4 inches	Wrought Bronze	.40 each	.05
531	2x4 inches	Wrought Bronze	.40 each	.05
536	2x4 inches	Wrought Bronze	.45 each	.05
570	2⅜ inches	Cast Bronze	.30 each	.05

Furnished in polished bronze, brushed brass or oxidized copper finishes.

FRANK H. STEWART ELECTRIC CO.

OLD MINT BUILDING
37 & 39 NORTH SEVENTH STREET
PHILADELPHIA

ELECTRICAL
SUPPLIES

Frank H. Stewart Electric Company letterhead, 1911.

FRANK H. STEWART ELECTRIC CO.

OLD MINT BUILDING
35, 37 & 39 NORTH SEVENTH STREET
PHILADELPHIA

ELECTRICAL
SUPPLIES

Frank H. Stewart Electric Company letterhead, 1918.

FRANK H. STEWART

PRESIDENT
FRANK H. STEWART ELECTRIC CO.

OLD MINT BUILDING
37 & 39 N. SEVENTH STREET
PHILADELPHIA

Frank H. Stewart business card.

The rear of the Front Building, from Stewart's *History of the First United States Mint*, showing the Watch House behind 39 North Seventh (right).

Chapter 3

"A Very *Mean* House": The First United States Mint, 1792–1911

From "The Man," Frank H. Stewart, our attention now shifts to "The Mint," that humble cluster of brick and frame structures that served as the new nation's first coinage factory from 1792 to 1833. In making that transition, we leave behind the cheerful realm of data and fact that documents Stewart's life, and enter the dour domain of fragmentary and fugitive information, of nonexistent illustrations and half-baked speculations, of shopworn wisdom and oft-repeated falsehoods. Much of what we wish to know about the first Mint is all but unknowable, and some of what we think we know about it is in fact untrue. Before tackling the treacherous task of reconstructing what we can about this elusive institution, it would be well to explain why it is so difficult to recount the true tale of its history and evolution:

- As already noted, Philadelphians have long delighted in changing the names—and even, in the mid-19th century, the addresses—of their streets. Thus, High Street became Market Street, and Mulberry became Arch. The address of the Mint's lots facing North Seventh Street were numbers 27 and 29 during the entire time that the first Mint was in operation, but in 1856, the addresses changed to numbers 37 and 39, with all neighboring North Seventh lot numbering changing, as well (appendix D). Sometimes, the changes piled bewilderingly one atop another. For example, the 14-foot-wide alley that defined the first Mint's southern border was known, at various times and among different residents, as Sugar Alley, Farmer's Alley, Elder Street, Zane Street, and Filbert Street. As a result, simply keeping the geography straight presents the historian with a continual challenge.
- Records of the construction and daily operation of the Mint's buildings, if they were ever created in the first place, have survived in only fragmentary and scattered pieces. Thus even basic questions, such as when a building was erected, the materials from which it was constructed, its number of stories, and the purposes it served over time, are usually known only in part, if at all.
- In those rare cases when information is available regarding the construction of a building, the development of the structure over the years

31

as its functions changed, or as it was damaged and rebuilt, was not thoroughly documented. Thus an edifice that began its service as a single-story frame structure might have been reconstructed with a two-story brick exterior after having been damaged by fire.

- The only plan of the first Mint made when it was in service is a hand-drawn map from 1828 that is neither to scale nor at all detailed. The only comprehensive plans of the Mint are insurance descriptions created February 16, 1837, two years after the first Mint was sold to Michael Kates, and years later, in 1860. The only photographs and paintings of the site were created long after the government had abandoned the Mint, and, as we have seen, the paintings were not historically accurate. Nor do any of the illustrations depict all of the buildings in the Mint's yard.

- Due to the foregoing, and to an unfortunate tendency on the part of some chroniclers of the Mint's development toward filling in the gaps with speculation, successive historians have added to the confusion by disagreeing with each other over the sequence in which the Mint erected its structures, the uses to which they were put, and the names by which they were called. As we shall see, some of them made outright errors, further muddying the waters.

As a result, then, of shifting street names, poor to non-existent records, 41 years of undocumented evolution and remodeling, a dearth of reliable visual depictions, and discordant or downright confused chroniclers, the task facing any would-be historian of "Ye Olde Mint" is reminiscent of Churchill's famous assessment of the Soviet Union: "A riddle wrapped in a mystery inside an enigma." Any reconstruction of that history must, of course, rely on facts, but since reliable data are so scarce, it is sometimes necessary to fill in blanks with expert opinion, deductions, and even informed conjectures, properly identified. In so doing, the authors will be guided by the advice of Raymond H. Williamson, an unjustly forgotten pioneer of scholarship in American numismatics. Writing in the cradle age of serious numismatic research, Williamson admonished: "Great care should be exercised in separating the facts from the probabilities, and the probabilities from the conjectures. In any case, verbatim quotations from the source material are desirable, either in the text or in an appendix; only then can the reader judge for himself as to the validity of the writer's assumptions."[1] To begin that sobering task, it will be necessary to start with the man who put the "Penn" into Pennsylvania, the lord proprietor himself.

THE MINT YARD: FROM PENN TO RITTENHOUSE

William Penn, a member of the Society of Friends, received the Royal Charter to establish Pennsylvania in 1681. The next year, he traveled to his new realm and made a Treaty of Friendship with its native inhabitants, the Lenni Lenape (in English, the Delawares), extinguishing their claims for £1,000 (a generous sum by the standards of the day). The proprietor, accompanied by his surveyor, Thomas Holme, had to go 100 miles up the broad Delaware River to find a suitable site for his new capital city, which Penn named Philadelphia, because of his determination to make literal truth of its Greek meaning: "city of brotherly love."

The site Penn and Holme chose lies on a peninsula formed by the Delaware and one of its principal tributaries, the Schuylkill. The land that was destined to become Philadelphia was actually in the hands of three European farmers, so Penn had to make one more purchase to found his new world metropolis. Holme created a rectangular grid for the new city, bordered on the north by present-day Vine Street; on the south by South Street; on the west by the curving banks of the Schuylkill; and on the east by the wide expanse of the Delaware. This 1,280-acre plot was cut into four quadrants by two perpendicular bisecting streets, the east-west High Street (now Market), and the north-south Broad Street. Holme lined his gridiron streets with commodious lots, and purchasers could claim additional free lots in the "Liberty Lands" to the north of the city.[2] A public square was also set aside for what we would today call green space in each of the four quadrants. The proprietor sold off hundreds of the lots to eager purchasers, but retained considerable holdings for later migrants, as well as a significant reserve for himself. Unfortunately many of the buyers subdivided the lots, leaving several as narrow as 17 feet across. They also cut up the blocks with alleys and courts, creating the patchwork quilt of land ownership that the makers of the Mint would encounter in 1792.

The sheer regularity of Holme's plan was a reaction to the medieval cities of Europe that had grown organically around meandering rivers or ancient winding lanes. Holme's rational gridiron was easy to understand and eased the plight of resident and traveler alike, but it did not meet with universal approval. A British traveler named Thomas Hamilton, writing in 1831, just as the first U.S. Mint was nearing the end of its run, left this barbed commentary on the fruit of Holme's efforts:

> Philadelphia is mediocrity personified in brick and mortar. It is a city laid down by square and rule, a sort of habitable problem . . . a mathematical infringement on the rights of individual eccentricity . . . a rigid and prosaic despotism of right angles and parallelograms.[3]

The land destined to become the yard of "Ye Olde Mint" lay in the northeast quadrant. Under Penn's initial plan, most of the east-west streets were named for trees, while most north-south roads were numbered in accordance with the grid system.[4] The first major street to the north of High Street (later, Market) was Mulberry Street (later, Arch). One of the numbered streets intersecting the parallel thoroughfares of Market and Arch was North Seventh. Here, along the eastern side of this roadway, between Market and Arch, William Penn had retained considerable real estate.

On August 12, 1699, the proprietor conveyed what would become the first Mint's yard, and much more acreage besides, to the Pennsylvania Land Company. This entity held it for nearly 60 years, until Boxing Day—December 26, 1758—when it sold the tract to separate owners. The three lots that were destined to become the nucleus of the Mint's holdings were reunited the following year through a purchase by Dr. Richard Farmer. The good doctor, in turn, sold the land, on September 1, 1760, to a local distiller named Michael Shubert, who erected buildings suitable for his trade, and busily produced ardent spirits at this location for nearly three decades. By the early 1790s, however, Shubert's finances, to use the delicate language of the day, had become "embarrassed," and so the property was sold on May 27, 1790, by sheriff James Ash, to Frederick Hailer, who plied the medieval trade of surgeon barber.[5]

The three lots that Dr. Richard Farmer purchased back in 1759 were the birthplace of the first Mint, but their form was fixed long before there was a United States. All of them followed Thomas Holme's 1682 plan, and measured a mere 17 or 18 feet across. The diminutive size of such lots can be seen on portions of Holme's 1682 map of the new city, particularly on prime parcels close to the Delaware and Schuylkill rivers. Another peculiarity was the shape created by the three lots; since one sat to the east of the other two, and extended farther south, the entire Mint yard at first looked like a capital "L." On the map, the long part of the L ran east and west, with the base jutting to the south. The lots themselves were located on the block to the north of Market Street, and just south of Arch Street. The two lots forming the long arm of the L fronted North Seventh Street, at numbers 37 and 39 (although the original street numbers were 27 and 29, the modern system of numbering will be used here). The lot forming the base of the L extended south from the two lots on North Seventh to a small alleyway running parallel to both Market and Arch, the address of which was number 631 Sugar Alley. How and why this peculiar little parcel was chosen as the home of the first U.S. Mint was largely the decision of one man, a remarkable polymath known as "the American Newton."

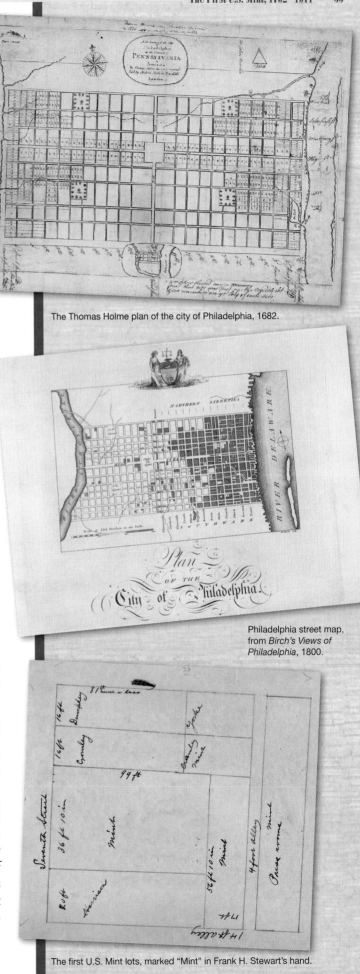

The Thomas Holme plan of the city of Philadelphia, 1682.

Philadelphia street map, from *Birch's Views of Philadelphia*, 1800.

The first U.S. Mint lots, marked "Mint" in Frank H. Stewart's hand.

George Washington, from an
engraving by Asher Durand.

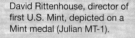

David Rittenhouse, director of
first U.S. Mint, depicted on a
Mint medal (Julian MT-1).

David Rittenhouse, engraving based on a painting from 1792.

In 1732—the same year that George Washington was born in Virginia—David Rittenhouse first saw the light of day in Philadelphia. Like his friend Benjamin Franklin, Rittenhouse pursued interests both prosaic and philosophical (in the 18th-century scientific sense of the latter term). Franklin was a printer; Rittenhouse was a clockmaker. Franklin became a celebrated scientist through his experimentation with electricity; Rittenhouse gained scientific plaudits for constructing an elegant orrery, which modeled the planets' rotation about the sun, and especially for accurately measuring the solar parallax during the transit of Venus across the sun in 1769. His home, on the northwest corner of Arch and North Seventh, boasted a fully equipped astronomical observatory. Such was Rittenhouse's scientific stature that, in 1791, after Franklin's death, he was elected president of the American Philosophical Society, then the highest honor for an American scientist. By 1792, though, the year in which he turned 60, Rittenhouse was unwell, and wanted nothing more than to concentrate on his study of the heavens. Another ailing sexagenarian, however, had more earthbound plans for him.

George Washington was nearing the end of his first presidential term in 1792, and during the early part of that year was contemplating retirement. Much unfinished business intruded upon those plans: near the top of Washington's list was the task of creating a federal Mint. The young United States was still bereft of many of the attributes of a sovereign nation, and among the most glaring of these gaps was the country's inability to coin its own money. This had been inevitable when America was a province of Great Britain, but it had become intolerable more than three years after the ink had dried on the federal Constitution. President Washington recalled that the British nation had, a century before, turned to its foremost scientist, Sir Isaac Newton, to become master of the Royal Mint; the president decided to make history repeat itself by naming the "American Newton," David Rittenhouse, to be the founding director of the U.S. Mint.

The Mint Act passed Congress on April 2, 1792, and on April 13, 1792, the president placed the eminent astronomer's name before the U.S. Senate.[6] Rittenhouse delayed a formal response due to his ill health, for it was not until July 1, 1792, that he signed his oath of office. Although he had not officially accepted his commission, surviving evidence makes it clear that Rittenhouse was performing the Mint director's duties long before July 1. In a letter written to President Washington on June 9, 1792, Secretary of State Thomas Jefferson, the cabinet officer in charge of the infant U.S. Mint, forwarded a letter "on the subject of procuring a house for the mint" from Rittenhouse. "Mr. Rittenhouse thinks the house in 7th Street can be bought for 1600£. . . . Thos. J. concurs in opinion with Mr. Rittenhouse that it will be better to buy this house, and submits the same to the President."[7]

A week later, Rittenhouse informed Jefferson that

> I have bargained with the owner for the House and Lot on Seventh Street, between Arch and Market Streets, of which you saw the Draught for the Use of the Mint. The price £1600 in Cash, Pennsylvania Currency, Subject to a Ground-rent of 21 Dollars An. Payable to the Friends Alms-House.[8]

On July 9, David Rittenhouse, by now formally installed as director of the Mint, wrote Washington with news that his plans for purchasing the North Seventh Street plot had come to fruition. Rittenhouse informed Washington that he had hired Henry Voigt as acting chief coiner, and Voigt had several workmen busy making equipment and dies for half cents, cents, half dismes and dismes. Rittenhouse then revealed to the president that, "I have purchased on account of the United States, a House and Lot which I hope will be found convenient for the Mint."[9] Since no building in the yard was ready, half dismes—the first coins produced under the authority of the United States—were struck from July 11 to 13 at the cellar of saw manufacturer John Harper, which was located at North Sixth and Cherry, only one block east and a block and a half north of the new Mint's site.

Rittenhouse never shared a rationale for his choice of the three lots—numbers 37 and 39 North Seventh and number 631 Sugar Alley—to serve as the Mint's yard, but proximity must have been a compelling factor. The director himself lived only a half block north, on the northwest corner of Arch and North Seventh, at number 245 Arch Street.[10] Henry Voigt, the first chief coiner, was listed (at least during the first years of operation) at the Mint itself: number 39 North Seventh.[11] Indeed, the 1800 and 1810 federal censuses place the Voigt household at 39 North Seventh. The 1810 census lists Voigt and a household of six there. The 1800 census, while not explicitly listing house numbers, places Voigt and a household of 10 next to Jacob Cromley (known to have resided in the adjacent lot north at 41 North Seventh). There was also a tradition among the descendants of the Mint's first assayer, Albion Coxe, that Coxe influenced President Washington in the choice of site for the Mint, but this is not corroborated by any contemporary documents.[12] The Mint would come to pay dearly for all of this convenience, however, for it outgrew the tiny tract almost immediately. Less than three years later, a congressional committee chaired by Elias Boudinot, who would soon become the Mint's third director, stated flatly that "The lots on which the [buildings] are built, from a principle of economy, were so restricted in size, that they are now found to be much too small, and so insufficient as greatly to hinder the several operations, and delay the business."[13]

THE MINT'S YARD

For the purchase price of $4,266.67, then, David Rittenhouse had made the first U.S. Mint heir to a parcel of (relatively) ancient and (mostly) honorable provenance, where booze had been bottled and blood had been let, with a cramped yard occupied by a decrepit distillery, and characterized by its distinctive "L" shape. Over the four decades to follow, the boundaries of that original tract would be expanded, and the buildings upon it erected, enlarged, burned, razed, purchased, and even rented. The tale of the territorial expansion can be told with some assurance, but the true story of the buildings can only be glimpsed through a glass, darkly. Recounting both of these evolutions is essential in order to understand the first Mint's operations and impact.

Elias Boudinot, Mint director 1795–1805.

From the moment he secured these three lots for the United States, David Rittenhouse was faced with two vexing problems: the Mint's yard was too small, and its security was too easily breached. The two lots fronting North Seventh Street collectively measured only 36 feet 10 inches wide, and 99 feet deep. The third lot, at number 631 Sugar Alley, was 17 feet wide by 56 feet, 10 inches deep. Therefore, when combined, the lots were nearly 37

Rittenhouse residence at the northwest corner of Seventh and Arch. Sketch by Frank H. Taylor.

feet wide by 116 feet deep, with a small rectangle 17 feet wide by 20 feet deep running to the south to form the base of the "L."[14] To place this into perspective, the Mint's first yard covered only eight percent of the square footage required by a National Football League playing field today. As Elias Boudinot noted in his report, this Lilliputian space was inadequate to even the immediate needs of the Mint, much less being able to accommodate future growth. The diminutive dimensions of the lots meant that the Mint's buildings would have to crowd the very boundaries of the yard, making them vulnerable to any passerby with a larcenous intent.

Both of the director's problems, fortuitously enough, had a single solution: more land. It was easier to understand the solution, however, than to implement it, for even in 1792, the North Seventh Street neighborhood was a crowded place; any expansion would have to displace neighbors who were literally cheek by jowl (since their lots were so small, Philadelphians were accustomed to building right up to the edges of their property lines). This meant that the Mint was completely surrounded by neighboring private dwellings. To the immediate south on North Seventh, at number 35, was a neighbor named Harrison. To the north were two more lots, at numbers

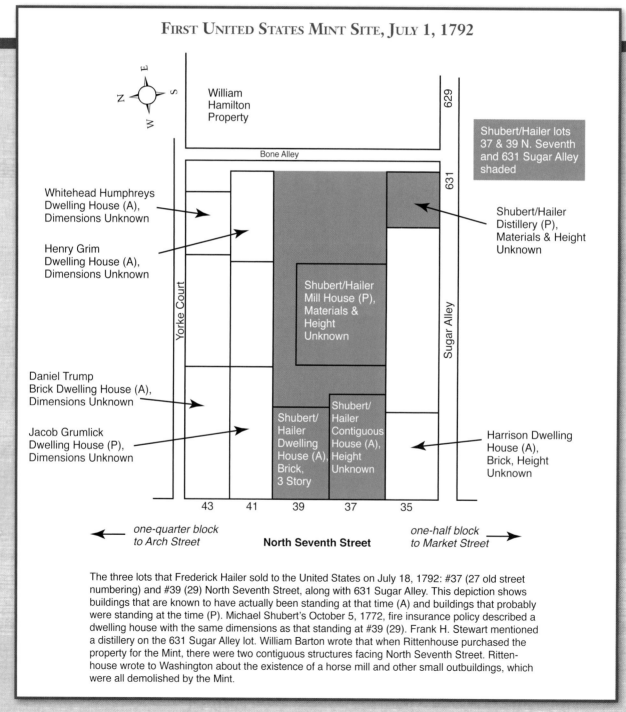

FIRST UNITED STATES MINT SITE, JULY 1, 1792

William Hamilton Property

Bone Alley

629

631

Shubert/Hailer lots 37 & 39 N. Seventh and 631 Sugar Alley shaded

Whitehead Humphreys Dwelling House (A), Dimensions Unknown

Henry Grim Dwelling House (A), Dimensions Unknown

Shubert/Hailer Distillery (P), Materials & Height Unknown

Yorke Court

Shubert/Hailer Mill House (P), Materials & Height Unknown

Sugar Alley

Daniel Trump Brick Dwelling House (A), Dimensions Unknown

Jacob Grumlick Dwelling House (P), Dimensions Unknown

Shubert/Hailer Dwelling House (A), Brick, 3 Story

Shubert/Hailer Contiguous House (A), Height Unknown

Harrison Dwelling House (A), Brick, Height Unknown

43   41   39   37   35

← one-quarter block to Arch Street

North Seventh Street

one-half block → to Market Street

The three lots that Frederick Hailer sold to the United States on July 18, 1792: #37 (27 old street numbering) and #39 (29) North Seventh Street, along with 631 Sugar Alley. This depiction shows buildings that are known to have actually been standing at that time (A) and buildings that probably were standing at the time (P). Michael Shubert's October 5, 1772, fire insurance policy described a dwelling house with the same dimensions as that standing at #39 (29). Frank H. Stewart mentioned a distillery on the 631 Sugar Alley lot. William Barton wrote that when Rittenhouse purchased the property for the Mint, there were two contiguous structures facing North Seventh Street. Rittenhouse wrote to Washington about the existence of a horse mill and other small outbuildings, which were all demolished by the Mint.

First Mint campus, July 1, 1792.

41 and 43, with both lots divided into two parcels, each with a house upon them. The western portion of number 41, bordering on North Seventh Street, held the home of Jacob Grumlick. The eastern portion of number 41, bordering on the rather ominously named Bone Alley (which ran parallel to North Seventh Street and perpendicular to Sugar Alley, thus forming the eastern boundary of these original Mint lots), hosted the dwelling house of Henry Grim.[15] The western section of number 43 was the location of Daniel Trump's house, while the eastern portion of the same lot was home to Whitehead Humphreys. The Humphreys property connects Benjamin Franklin to the Mint, for Humphreys had borrowed £600 from Franklin. In 1797 the Franklin estate sued the Humphreys estate to recover the debt, and as a result this parcel was sold to Robert E. Griffith.[16]

Bone Alley, in fact, became the bane of David Rittenhouse's tenure as Mint director. Its status as the "eastern front" bounding the Mint's lot at 631 Sugar Alley created an ongoing security problem. Despite its extremely narrow width (a mere four feet), Bone Alley was a public right-of-way, providing Henry Grim's sole access to Sugar Alley. Moreover, the buildings on the lot immediately to the east of Bone Alley, at number 629 Sugar Alley, formerly owned by George Montea, now the property of William Hamilton, were right on top of the Mint's yard, making for a very porous border.[17]

Rittenhouse, therefore, was a man on a mission to acquire more land, and his campaign began auspiciously on October 4, 1794, when the Mint paid $1,200 to secure number 629 Sugar Alley from William Hamilton, thus providing an additional parcel 20 feet, six inches wide by 88 feet deep on the east side of Bone Alley.[18] Rittenhouse now controlled Bone Alley on both sides for most of its length, but still could not close it because it continued to provide Henry Grim's access to Sugar Alley. So the director's priority quite naturally became acquiring Grim's property on the eastern section of number 41 North Seventh, along with Whitehead Humphreys's parcel next door on the eastern section of number 43. This objective eluded both Rittenhouse and his successor, Henry William De Saussure. Just how seriously De Saussure took this quest can be gleaned from the report he made to Congress upon resigning his post in December of 1795:

> Amongst the unpleasant circumstances which attend the contracted scale upon which the mint has been erected, there is one of very serious import. The owner of a small lot adjoining the mint, has a right of passage through the interior of the lots of the mint. This exposes the works to improper intrusion, and prevents the complete control over the workmen, which is essential to the well ordering of the business. A small sum of money would have purchased that lot some time ago. I believe it may still be had, reasonably.[19]

The United States Congress, however, had turned churlish about appropriating even small sums of money to the Mint for property purchases. Some congressmen felt that the startup costs had been too high, and many were disappointed by the small output of coinage during the Mint's first couple of years. By December 1794, as previously mentioned, Congressman Elias Boudinot was chairing a committee to investigate the entire situation. The Boudinot report eventually exonerated the Mint's officers, but suspicions lingered.[20] Consequently, Rittenhouse and his successors labored in vain for more than a decade to get funding to buy the Grim and Humphreys parcels. Extracting money from Congress for anything was problematic; Elias Boudinot, the Mint's third director, complained that as late as 1802 the employees of the Mint were still being paid 1792 wages.[21]

THE BUILDINGS: REVISING FRANK H. STEWART'S INTERPRETATIONS

Frank H. Stewart, of course, eventually came to own the historic buildings that sat upon the Mint's yard, and he was the first to attempt a systematic examination of how, when, and why they were constructed. To his credit, Stewart saved much data, made many connections, and got most of the story right. On the other hand, he made a pair of ill-advised decisions and one outright error that, in combination, distort our understanding of the first U.S. Mint down to the present day. First, in commissioning the painting of *Ye Olde Mint* by Edwin Lamasure, Stewart focused on only three of the 10 Mint buildings, and only at one moment in their decades-long history, thus leading

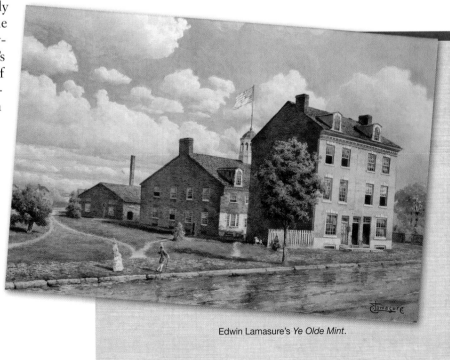

Edwin Lamasure's *Ye Olde Mint.*

viewers to forget that there were other structures, and that the appearance of even the three depicted buildings changed over time. Second, he chose to name the buildings by the functions he presumed them to fill. This practice is problematic for a number of reasons, not the least of which is that, in some cases, there is no way of determining exactly what purpose a particular building served, or when it served it. Smelting surely occurred in what Stewart called the Smelting Building, for example, but there is evidence that it was also used to cut planchets. Stewart's designation of another structure as the Coinage Building implies exclusivity, but proof exists that coins were struck in three other buildings in the Mint complex. Stewart's Administration Building housed administrators, but at various times it was also home to weighers, refiners, coiners, and coin presses. To identify an edifice in the old Mint complex purely by presumed function, therefore, is usually misleading at best and at worst, dead wrong.

To be fair to Frank H. Stewart, he eventually came to understand this fact, for in his 1924 book, *History of the First United States Mint*, he reluctantly concluded that "it is impossible to state with entire accuracy just what use was made of the buildings from time to time."[22] By then, however, he had been calling the three buildings depicted in *Ye Olde Mint* the Administration, Coinage, and Smelting Buildings for so long that the usage became general among numismatists.

To avoid replicating these unhelpful patterns, the authors will focus on the totality of the Mint's yard and structures. The total view will be achieved with aid of a map drawn by Mint director Samuel Moore in 1828, a map and survey created on February 16, 1837, for the Franklin Fire Insurance Company of Philadelphia, a map drawn in 1860 for the Hexamer Insurance Company, and a painting created by numismatic historian Pete Smith in 2009, none of which were available to Frank H. Stewart. Taken in combination with new archival findings, these visual aids will help create a new, more comprehensive picture of the first Mint's physical appearance. A more precise identification of the first Mint's buildings will be accomplished, for the most part, by referring to them by location, rather than by presumed function. Thus, the three structures in the Lamasure painting of *Ye Olde Mint*, which Stewart identified (from right to left) as the Administration, Coinage, and Smelting Buildings, we will call the Front, Middle and Rear buildings. In other cases, such as the structures along Bone Alley, the identification will be more generic: Shop 1, Shop 2, etc. Only when the use of the building is known and was largely unchanged over time—such as the Mill House—will it be labeled by function. What this system lacks in romance will be compensated for by much greater historical accuracy.

Stewart's outright error grew out of enthusiasm for the old Mint buildings he had purchased, and was exacerbated by a rare failure to do his homework. He was very proud that the middle of the three structures in Lama-

sure's *Ye Olde Mint* picture, which Stewart was wont to call the "Coinage Building," was—as he firmly believed—the first structure erected by the United States federal government. Stewart initially made a blanket statement in 1909 claiming this status for all three of the buildings in the Lamasure picture, "because they were the first erected by the authority of the Federal Government for public use."[23] Four years later, he settled on the Middle Building as the very first one: "The old building we tore down was the first United States Mint, and also the first public building erected by the authority of Congress." When Stewart commissioned artist John Ward Dunsmore to capture aspects of the old Mint on canvas, he encouraged Dunsmore to take the Middle Building as his subject, which, as we shall see, Dunsmore did in preliminary sketches. There is strong reason to doubt that the sole function of the Middle Building was to strike coins, and no question, as will be demonstrated subsequently, that it was not the first one erected in the Mint's yard. But one thing is utterly certain: Neither this structure, nor any other once standing on the yard of the first Mint, was the first edifice constructed by the federal government.

James Rankin Young, in his book *The United States Mint at Philadelphia*, published in 1903, said that the Mint "constructed the third building for government use erected by the United States Government. The first government building was erected at the Lazaretto, on Tinicum Island, in the Delaware River, near the lower part of Philadelphia. This was used for quarantine purposes; and the second, built at Chelsea, Massachusetts, as a marine hospital."[24] Young does not give precise construction dates for these structures; but at least two others also predate the Mint edifices. The Portland Head Light in Cape Elizabeth, Maine, was begun by the state of Massachusetts in 1787. Congress appropriated $1,500 in 1790 to complete it, and work on it was finished on January 10, 1791.[25] Less than three months later, on March 31, 1791, the federal government let a contract for the construction of the old Cape Henry Lighthouse at Virginia Beach, Virginia. It was completed in late October of 1792, only shortly after the first of the Mint buildings.[26] It is indisputable, therefore, that the Mint structures were neither the first to be funded, nor the first to be constructed, by the United States government.

Moreover, Stewart was informed of this fact *before* he made his claim. Edgar H. Adams, a numismatic scholar of no mean achievements, sent Stewart a letter on November 29, 1908, in which he shared the information provided by James Rankin Young. Stewart ignored this data, possibly because it contradicted a local tradition in which he very much wanted to believe.[27] Stewart's false claim about the Middle Building, unfortunately, has been repeated in all of the major reference books on the Mint, and has become as ineradicable as kudzu in the annals of American numismatics. The Mint itself is likewise complicit, laying claim to the title of "the first public building authorized by the Congress of the United States," as engraved on the reverse of the 1929 Assay Commission medal.

THE BUILDINGS: 1792–1793

Although we know that the Mint buildings were not the first funded or constructed by the federal government, we know precious little else about them, at least not with certainty. In trying to piece together the history of their construction, we must begin with Thomas Jefferson's previously quoted June 9, 1792, letter to George Washington. David Rittenhouse, whether motivated by a principle of economy, as Elias Boudinot later concluded, or by convenience to himself, or some combination of the two impulses, had personally chosen the three tiny lots on North Seventh Street as the preferred site for the first U.S. Mint:

> Th. Jefferson, with his respects to the President, incloses him a letter from Mr. Rittenhouse on the subject of procuring a house for the Mint. Mr. Rittenhouse thinks the house on Seventh Street can be bought for £1,600. . . . The outhouses will save the necessity of new erections, and there is a horse mill,

which will save the building one for the rolling mill; so that on the whole Thomas J. concurs in opinion with Mr. Rittenhouse that it will be better to buy this house; and submits the same to the President. A plan for the ground and building is inclosed.[28]

Edgar H. Adams, 1908, from the ANA Convention photograph.

Frustratingly, neither the original letter from Rittenhouse to Jefferson, nor the plan for Michael Shubert's grounds and buildings, can be located today. What can be gleaned from Jefferson's letter, however, is that Frederick Hailer's Seventh Street property included a home, a horse mill, and outbuildings, one of which had sheltered Michael Shubert's old distillery. Stewart believed the distillery was located on the lot

240 W. 42d st.,
N. Y. City,
Nov. 29, 1908.

Mr. Frank H Stewart,
Philadelphia, Pa.

Dear Sir: Your letters of the 23d just to promptly came to hand and I am much interested in its contents. In all the references to the old mint with a single exception that I have seen the statement is made that it was the first U.S. building. That exception occurs in the book entitled "The United State Mint," by James Rankin Young, published at Philadelphia in 1903, and sold at the present mint. He states that "the first Government building was erected at the Lazaretto, on Tincum Island, in the Delaware River, near the lower part of Philadelphia. This

was used for quarantine purposes and the second built at Chelsea, Mass, as a marine hospital."

This was my authority and his work being of quite recent issue I thought perhaps the author had found additional information.

Trusting that this is satisfactory, and always glad to hear from you at any time I am,

Sincerely, yours
E. H. Adams

Adams letter to Stewart, 1908.

at 631 Sugar Alley (where the Mint would build its stable), for he spoke of "Michael Shubert's old distillery on Farmer Street [Sugar Alley] in the rear."[29]

In his *History of the First United States Mint*, he added another structure to the mix: "Frederick Hailer, surgeon barber, and wife Christiana, deeded on July 18, 1792, the land and distill-house and frame tenement building built by Shubert to the United States Government and the Mint Buildings were erected thereon."[30] Was Shubert's house the same building as the tenement that Stewart mentions? A 1791 Philadelphia directory lists Michael Shubert as a distiller at 39 North Seventh.[31] A copy of Shubert's October 5, 1772, fire insurance policy identifies his dwelling house as "17 feet 9 inches front by 31 feet deep 3 story high." These are precisely the same dimensions of the structure that would eventually stand on lot number 39 of the U.S. Mint: the northern half of the Front Building. Unfortunately, the only address given for this house by the insurance policy is "Seventh Street between High & Mulberry Streets."[32]

Stewart was quite certain that the Mint inherited a tenement house when it made the purchase from Hailer. Stewart's source for that information was a handwritten transcription of the original deed conveying the two North Seventh Street lots (numbers 37 and 39), along with the Sugar Alley lot to the east, from Frederick and Christiana Hailer to the United States of America. Stewart apparently hired a researcher to transcribe this information, for the transcriptions are not in his hand. The deed, dated July 18, 1792, begins by noting that Congress had authorized the president of the United States to purchase buildings and put them in proper condition to serve as a Mint for the nation. Then comes the following passage:

> and the Pres. hath in pursuance thereof caused to be purchased from the said Frederick Hailer and C[hristiana] husband & wife for the purpose aforesaid a certain messuage or tenement—Distill House and two contiguous lots of ground therewith belonging, one of the lots being situate in the East side of 7th Street from the River Delaware in the said city of Phila.[33]

Stewart understood that this description treated the two lots facing North Seventh Street as a unit with the second lot being the one that fronted Sugar Alley. He may also have known that the now archaic Old French term "messuage" meant, according to Samuel Johnson's 1756 *A Dictionary of the English Language*, "the house and grounds set aside for household uses." What Stewart did not realize, however, was that the phrase "messuage or tenement" was standardized boilerplate language in eighteenth century land deeds. He apparently read it literally, and decided that there was a tenement building on the Shubert/Hailer property. It is possible, of course, that this was literally true, but not likely. If the use of the phrase "messuage or tenement" was proof positive, then nearly every lot in Philadelphia would have hosted a tenement house.

If the tenement house was a figment of Stewart's misreading of the deed, what buildings did stand upon the two lots fronting North Seventh Street when the Mint bought the Shubert/Hailer property? The strongest testimony comes from an eyewitness, William Barton, remembered today as the co-designer of the Great Seal of the United States, who was also David Rittenhouse's nephew and advisor. In his 1813 biography of his uncle, Barton told the story this way:

> As soon as he had determined to accept the Directorship of the Mint, he began to make suitable arrangements for carrying the institution into operation. Towards this end, he suggested to the Secretary of State the expediency of purchasing the two contiguous houses and lots of ground, conveniently situated, for the establishment; in preference to taking buildings upon lease.[34]

This definitive statement was made by a man who played a role in events of 1792. Barton was an unsuccessful candidate for treasurer of the Mint in 1792,[35] but he was a close informal advisor to his uncle. As one contemporary put it, "he was the favored nephew, and confidential friend, of his Uncle Rittenhouse, who usually advised with and consulted him, in the first organization of the Mint establishment . . . besides which, it cannot be questioned that a more exemplary private character than Mr. Barton is not to be found."[36]

Barton's recollection is confirmed by the testimony of an 1826 visitor to the Mint: "I also saw . . . the mint of the United States, which is established here. In the year 1793 [sic; 1792] when Philadelphia was still the seat of government . . . this mint was located in a newly-built private house, ..." Further corroboration comes from an unattributed account published in the *Philadelphia Press* on August 1, 1857. The article states that the Mint was established "in a building which had been originally erected as a dwelling house, but which was enlarged for Mint purposes by various additions, not very sightly or accommodating, at the side and rear."[37] This article obviously treats the number 37 and number 39 halves of the Front Building as a unit, and refers to the Rear Building as the addition to the rear, and the stable, built on the number 629 Sugar Alley lot, as the addition to the side. It is highly likely, as we shall see, that Barton was correct that the Shubert/Hailer house and another home stood side-by-side at numbers 39 and 37 when Rittenhouse purchased the property.

Before any Mint buildings could go up, however, Shubert's decrepit distillery would have to come down. Stewart notes that on July 19, 1792, the day after the deed was signed that conveyed the property from Frederick Hailer, a gang of eight carpenters plus other workmen began demolishing Shubert's distillery; by July 31, the site was cleared, and foundation work was being done for a new building.[38] Jefferson's letter, Stewart's account, and Barton's assertion, however, supply questions as well as answers.

1. Was the Shubert/Hailer House retained and/or renovated for the use of the Mint?
2. Was the existing horse mill building converted for a similar use by the Mint?
3. How many of the outbuildings were retrofitted for the Mint's use, and how many were demolished?

The best source of answers for these questions is an expense accounting that David Rittenhouse sent to Thomas Jefferson on March 25, 1793. The second entry in this accounting reads: "For erecting two New brick buildings, Furnaces, a Frame Mill House & stable & c. $775.44."[39] The answer to the second question is thus decided: the Mint either demolished the existing horse mill building, or renovated it to be a furnace, and they constructed a new Mill House. The frame stable was also constructed before March of 1793. This information, however, leaves the first and third questions unanswered. If one counts the two halves of the Front Building separately, there were three brick structures standing on the three original Mint lots as of March 25, 1793, and according to Rittenhouse's report, two of them were newly constructed by the Mint. But which ones?

It seems highly likely that the Shubert/Hailer dwelling house at number 39 North Seventh was retained. The edifice that ultimately stood at number 39 had precisely the same measurements as the Shubert/Hailer house, and it seems unlikely that the Mint would tear it down only to build an exact replica on the same site. As noted, a 1793 Philadelphia directory and the 1800 and 1810 federal censuses list chief coiner Henry Voigt and family residing at 39 North Seventh. Most convincingly, beginning on September 3, 1792, and running every other day in *Dunlap's American Advertiser* through at least October 23, the Mint inserted a notice offering to buy copper for its operations. Interested parties were directed to inquire at the Mint, the address of which was given as number "29 North Seventh" (number 39 in modern numbering).[40] Since number 39 was open for business by early September, this leaves only about a month to demolish a pre-existing structure and build a new one, which seems an unreasonably short time frame. Number 39, therefore, was not one of the newly constructed brick buildings.

As for the contiguous "twin" of the Shubert/Hailer house at number 37, all evidence points to it being one of the new brick structures mentioned by Rittenhouse. Don Taxay seemed to settle the question when he wrote that Rittenhouse's March 25, 1793, expense account records that an original house was razed and a new brick building was erected in its place; unfortunately, the March 25 expense account contains no such confirmation.[41] One piece of evidence suggests that the house at number 37 was renovated

William S. Barton, nephew of David Rittenhouse, engraving by Christian Gobrecht.

(perhaps the original structure was faced with brick to match the half at number 39), for when Frank H. Stewart demolished the Front Building, he noted that "The floors in 37 and 39 were mostly three boards thick, one floor having been put down over another."[42] Alternatively, a letter written by Mint director Elias Boudinot to Treasury Secretary Albert Gallatin on March 22, 1802, suggests that the Mint constructed the number 37 half of the Front Building after buying the Mint yard. Boudinot lists among the Mint's real estate "Two lots on Seventh Street . . . with a dwelling house on the north lot, and a shell of a house on the south lot."[43] In Samuel Johnson's 1756 *A Dictionary of the English Language*, one of the meanings of "shell" is given as "the outer part of a house." Boudinot seems to be suggesting, therefore, that number 39 was a dwelling house and number 37 was never a dwelling house, although it was constructed to appear like one. Another reason to believe that the Mint built number 37 is the ground floor passageway between it and number 39 that led into the Mint yard. Such a passageway made sense for an institution like the Mint; it would make little sense for a private landowner like Frederick Hailer.[44] In either case, whether number 37 was renovated or constructed by the Mint, there is every reason to believe that it was one of the two brick buildings mentioned in Rittenhouse's March 25, 1793, expense reporting.

What was the second brick building? Rittenhouse's March 25, 1793, expense account is unequivocal in stating that the Mint built a Mill House and a stable, but as we shall see, both of these were frame structures. This means that the second brick edifice had to be the Rear Building. The fact that this structure was built without a basement suggests that it was indeed one of the products of the initial building blitz of 1792–1793. In fact, Don Taxay believed it to be the first constructed in the Mint's yard.[45]

There can be little question that when Rittenhouse stated, in his July 9, 1792, letter to President Washington, that "considerable alterations must be made, and some small new buildings erected"[46] he was displaying a knack for quiet understatement, for from July of 1792 to March of 1793, Rittenhouse unleashed a frenzy of construction and renovation on North Seventh Street. The Shubert/Hailer outbuildings were all razed, for the distillery, horse mill, and stable were replaced by at least five Mint structures: the two houses that comprised the Front Building, the Mill House, the Rear Building, and the stable. Rittenhouse also mentioned "furnaces" in the March 25, 1793, expense report. It seems plausible that these were initially located in the Mill House and Rear Building, for a subsequent insurance survey mentioned a "forge" as located in the latter structure. Later the Mint would have separate buildings to house furnaces, but in its first years, small furnaces were probably adequate to meet the demands of modest coinage runs.

Although no detailed records survive as to when buildings were begun and finished, there are both *ex post facto* descriptions and financial records that offer evidence for rapid construction of five structures in the Mint's yard. On November 20, 1794, Rittenhouse reported to Congress that "The expenses of the Mint have hitherto been chiefly applied only preparatory towards carrying on the business of the establishment; in erecting the necessary buildings, furnaces for melting, refining, assaying, & c."[47] This assertion was confirmed by Elias Boudinot in his February 9, 1795, investigative committee report to Congress. The future Mint director explained that one of the factors that had initially delayed coin production was the need to create the Mint's physical plant: "The buildings were all to be completed before the works could be begun."[48] Clearly, the first two years of the Mint's operation were dominated by the creation of its physical plant; the first year primarily to construct the buildings, and the second year mainly to stock them with adequate equipment.

These observations by the Mint's first and third directors are corroborated by extant financial records. In 1798, a comprehensive accounting of the warrants drawn on the U.S. treasury by the Mint from its inception in July of 1792, through December 31, 1797, was presented to Congress. The first heading, "Incidental and Contingent Expenses and Repairs of the Mint," was defined as "the amount expended for the requisite buildings and repairs, and procuring apparatus, making machines, wages of the workmen, and other expenses, including three lots of ground, with buildings thereon purchased for carrying on the operations of the Mint." Excluding the costs of property purchases (which were listed separately under this heading), and further excluding the costs of bullion purchases and the salaries of the Mint's officers (which also were listed under separate subheadings), the quarterly incidental and contingent expenses, in round numbers, were as follows:[49]

July–September, 1792	$3,245 (average)
October–December, 1792	3,245 (average)
January–March, 1793	3,245 (average)
April–June, 1793	2,122
July–September, 1793	1,172
October–December, 1793	1,536
January–March, 1794	2,658
April–June, 1794	1,828
July–September 1794	3,665
October–December, 1794	3,044
January–March, 1795	7,147
April–June, 1795	5,371
July–September, 1795	5,180
October–December, 1795	6,979

January–March, 1796	3,146
April–June, 1796	2,695
July–September, 1796	2,879
October–December, 1796	1,765 (average)
January–March, 1797	1,765 (average)
April–June, 1797	1,765 (average)
July–September, 1797	1,765 (average)
October–December, 1797	2,077

Although the data are muddied by combining costs for buildings, repairs, apparatus, workmen's wages, and other expenses into a single category, it is still possible to infer that the high average expenditures for the Mint's first three quarters (1792–93) funded a significant amount of construction. Not only were the average amounts expended during the first three quarters dramatically higher than expenditures during the succeeding five quarters, it was also the case that incidental and contingent spending for the Mint's first three quarters would not be exceeded until the first three quarters of 1795: shortly after the October 4, 1794, purchase of the lot at 629 Sugar Alley would make possible building or renovating the four shops later resident on that lot. The total cost of buildings, lots, and machinery for the first Mint was estimated by a congressional committee in 1828 to be about $36,000.[50] Expenditures for the Mint's first three quarters (July 1792–March 1793), and the four quarters of 1795, total $34,412. Adding the cost of the Mint's four lots brings the total to $39,878. Although this number includes an undetermined amount in workmen's salaries and other expenses, the timing and amounts of spending spikes immediately following property purchases make it very likely that the great bulk of the Mint's buildings went up during two periods of concentrated construction in 1792–93 and in 1795.

If the Mint erected and/or renovated at least nine of its buildings (the five already discussed and the four shops on the lot at 629 Sugar Alley) in two bursts of activity in 1792–93 and 1795, then it seems highly likely that several of the Mint's buildings were under construction and/or renovation simultaneously during these two brief periods. All of the structures were clearly necessary in order to strike coins, and all were self-contained; there would be no reason, therefore, to erect them in sequence, making the commencement of one await the completion of another. Moreover, as we have seen, it is highly likely that the number 39 North Seventh half of the Front Building was simply converted from Michael Shubert's dwelling house, and if so, it had been standing since at least 1772.

Despite the likelihood that the Mint built multiple structures simultaneously, nearly every history of this institution asserts that the Middle Building, the one that Frank H. Stewart called the Coinage Building, was the first one erected in the yard. The source of this claim was Stewart himself, for he notes that the "foundation stone" for the Mint's first building was laid by David Rittenhouse at 10:00 a.m. on July 31, 1792; the framework was raised by August

25, and the building completed by September 7. "This account," wrote Stewart, "refers to what I have called the Coinage Building."[51] Why was Stewart so certain that the Middle Building was the first structure the Mint built? It turns out that it was mostly an aesthetic judgment. "Inasmuch as considerable attempt at ornamentation was made on the front of the coinage building, it was quite probable that this was the first building erected."[52]

We now know that this is simply wrong. The Middle Building, as we shall see, was actually the last of the first Mint's edifices to be constructed; it was not erected until 1816. From 1792 until it burned to the ground in early 1816, the Mill House stood where the Middle Building would eventually be constructed. The structure that Stewart mentioned as being completed by September 7 was likely the Rear Building, which Taxay was probably correct in stating was the first built by the Mint in the Mint yard.[53] As we have seen, however, the number 39 portion of the Front Building, which was pre-existing and renovated, was open for business at least a few days earlier, on September 3.

The warrants issued by the Mint's treasurer to pay contractors offer evidence that supports this view of the proceedings. The first warrant was dated July 15, 1792, and authorized payment to Frederick Hailer for purchase of the first three lots of the Mint. Warrant number three, dated August 4, 1792, pays "Christopher Hart, for 92-3/4 perches of stone for new building."[54] A "perch" is a measurement

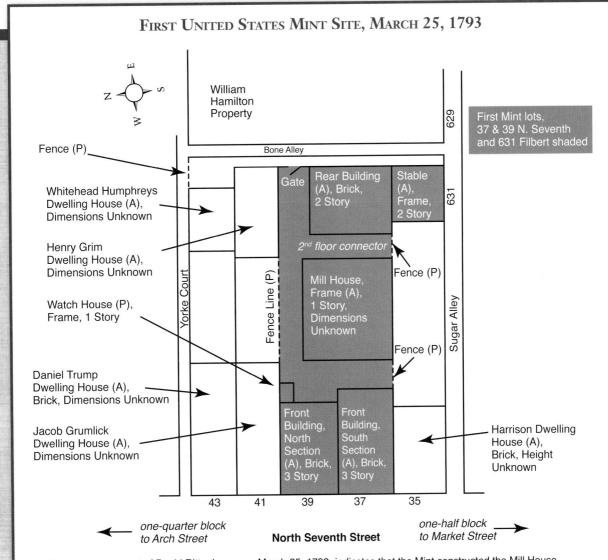

FIRST UNITED STATES MINT SITE, MARCH 25, 1793

First Mint lots, 37 & 39 N. Seventh and 631 Filbert shaded

An expense account of David Rittenhouse on March 25, 1793, indicates that the Mint constructed the Mill House, the Stable, and two brick structures after purchasing the property in July 1792. Since William Barton recalled that there were two contiguous structures (the Front Building) standing when the Mint bought the property, the two brick structures the Mint constructed were the Rear Building and the renovation of #37 North Seventh with a brick façade. While the #37 portion of the Front Building was being refurbished, the #39 portion was open for business as early as September 1, 1792. The reuse of existing structures, and the possible erection of new buildings on existing foundations, would explain why the Mint ended up with clusters of separate structures, rather than a more efficient single- or at least interconnected—structure.

First Mint campus, March 25, 1793.

used to calculate the volume of stone built into walls, piled on the ground, or loaded in freight wagons and cargo ships. The volume varies with each application, but for walls, a perch is 24-3/4 cubic feet.[55] This stone was likely destined for the basement of the number 37 portion of the Front Building, for neither the Mill House nor the Rear Building had basements. In addition, Stewart noted a stone vault built into the basement of the number 39 portion of the Front Building, and the presence of two subterranean stone vaults attached to the rear basements of both halves of the Front Building.[56] The warrants recorded only the purchase of building material without specifying the structures for which the material was intended. Thus warrant number five, to John Nancarrow, for 28 loads of clay for firebricks, could have paid for bricks destined for either the Rear Building or the number 37 portion of the Front Building.[57]

The Rear Building quickly became the venue for important work done at the Mint. When Stewart bought the first Mint yard and its surviving buildings in 1907, he decided that the Rear Building, which he called the Smelting House, was in terrible condition (a fact confirmed by the photographs on pages 63 and 67 of *History of the First United States Mint*), and needed to be taken down immediately. Attached to this brick building was a two-story wooden shack that had been used as the Mint's stable.[58] When these structures were demolished, Stewart discovered that neither had a basement, and they were built atop two wells, one of which served as a cesspool, and the other of which had probably provided water for Shubert's distillery. As Stewart recalled:

> During the destruction of the Smelting House several planchets and coins of copper were found, also a small piece of copper from which a half cent had been struck, two of the planchets which fell down from the overhead joists were of the 1792 silver center cent; the others were of cents and half cents.[59]

The silver center cent planchets provide proof that planchets were being cut in the Rear Building, as early as December of 1792. "The pattern coins of 1792," which included the silver center cents, "were struck very late in the year . . . ,"[60] and it was not until December 18, 1792, that Thomas Jefferson sent George Washington a letter that began, "Th. Jefferson has the honor to send the president two cents made on Voight's [sic] plan by putting a silver plug worth three quarters of a cent into a copper worth one fourth of a cent."[61] This underlines the fallacy of labeling structures by their presumed use, for the first coins struck in the Mint's yard had their planchets punched by a press located in the "Smelting Building."

Although it is probably impossible now to reconstruct the sequence of construction on the Mint's yard in 1792—if indeed there was a discernable sequence—it has not stopped scholars from trying their hands at it. R.W. Julian concluded that the Middle Building was the first to

go up, then "The next building commenced was one of the Front Buildings: (i.e., the front building was actually two—the second [half of this double building] may have been built in 1794). The second building was probably finished in November, 1792."[62]

Julian was correct that the Front Building was in fact a double structure, and constructed in two phases. Before he demolished it in 1911, Frank H. Stewart made the following inside measurements:

> 37 North Seventh Street was 32 feet, 7 inches deep
>
> 39 North Seventh Street was 29 feet, 2 inches deep

The one numbered 39 was probably built before the other.[63]

Julian was only two months off with regard to the completion of the first half of the Front Building (number 39), for we know it was now open for business in early September, but probably incorrect about the second portion of the Front House not being completed until 1794. And Stewart was almost certainly correct that the half at number 39 was the first of the two to be erected.

Don Taxay concluded that "the larger brick building, which fronted on Seventh Street, was not completed until a few months later [after the Rear Building]. Between the two buildings, a frame mill house was built."[64] Taxay was probably referring to the renovation of the existing edifice at number 37 when he wrote of the completion of the Front Building. The wooden Mill House was located between the Front and the Rear Buildings, but it does not appear in Lamasure's *Ye Olde Mint* because, as we shall see, it literally went up in smoke before the time depicted in the painting.

The Julian and Taxay reconstructions are confirmed, in their essentials, if not in their sequences, by two Philadelphia historians' descriptions of the Mint's 18th-century yard. An anonymous author writing in the late 1820s, just as the first Mint was nearing the end of its lifespan, noted: "Early in 1793, the general operations of the establishment were commenced, in a very plain dwelling house, purchased for the object, on the east side of Seventh Street, between High and Mulberry Streets. A rude structure, in the rear of the same lot, was also occupied by a portion of the machinery."[65] Similarly, Philadelphia historian Joseph Jackson wrote: "the first buildings for the first United States Mint were erected in 1792. The Mint proper, or coinage house, at that time was really built on the back part of the Seventh Street lots, 37 and 39 North Seventh Street."[66]

With all due respect to the sequential construction theory espoused by Messrs. Stewart, Julian, and Taxay, the breathtaking speed with which the Mint erected and/or refurbished at least five buildings in less than four months in the autumn of 1792, and probably nine buildings by the autumn of 1795, argues strongly that the Mint was working on all—or at least most—of them simultaneously. The foundation stone had been laid by Rittenhouse on July 31, 1792. Less than four months later, on November 27, 1792, the director wrote President Washington as follows: "Considerable Expenses having since [the warrant for Mint Expenses in July] arisen for Additional Buildings, Furnaces, Horse-mill, and Machines of various kinds, I find it necessary to apply for another warrant for the sum of $5,000 . . . the works are now nearly completed and a particular account of the Expenses shall be made out as soon as the several bills can be got in and paid. . . ."[67] Since the stable, the Rear Building, the Mill House, and the Front Building were constructed and/or refurbished in less than four months, it seems highly unlikely that they were built one at a time. While it is entirely possible that one structure was completed before another, it appears that all must have been under construction more or less simultaneously. Even Frank H. Stewart, as strong a proponent of the "Middle Building First" theory as he was, at one point veered toward the "all at once" point of view. After a close study of the Mint's warrants, he admitted "Evidently two different buildings were erected because bricklayers were employed up to the 22nd of November [1792]."[68] This jibes nicely with Rittenhouse's March 25, 1793, expense account, which records the erection of two new brick structures. In any event, before 1792 was out, the Mint was, as Rittenhouse noted in his letter to Washington, "nearly completed," and poised to begin striking coins in earnest (as they did with the first major delivery of chain cents, February 27–March 1, 1793.[69]

Before proceeding beyond initial years of the first Mint, one other tradition should be examined. Since the time of James Ross Snowden, Mint director from 1853 to 1861, there has been folklore that President Washington took such a close interest in the Mint that he visited it nearly every day in its formative years. (Since he lived only a block and a half away, it would have been very convenient.) Snowden was the first to retail this tradition in print, writing in his 1861 book, *A Description of the Medals of Washington*, that the first president "was in the habit of visiting it daily, as we are informed, and manifested a deep interest in its operations."[70] Stewart was an eager buyer of this story, claiming in his *History of the First United States Mint* regarding the Front Building that "the immortal Washington passed through that doorway many times and stood on that doorstep."[71] No inconvtrovertible evidence of a Washington visit has ever been found, and only a single invitation survives. On December 27, 1792, Rittenhouse wrote Washington's private secretary, Tobias Lear, as follows: "We have begun to Assay some of the European Coins and shall proceed tomorrow, at the Mint, if it will be convenient for the president to attend about 12 oClock [sic]."[72] No record of Washington's response can be located among the president's voluminous correspondence.

One tantalizing piece of evidence, however, suggests that the president might have accepted Rittenhouse's invitation. In 1933, Stephen Decatur Jr., the great-grand-nephew of Tobias Lear, published excerpts from Lear's papers, which he had inherited. Among them were the "cash-books" in which Lear kept Washington's expenses, both official and personal. These were divided into six types: cash transactions; funds received from the U.S. treasury department; household expenses; servants' accounts; stable and carriages; and contingent expenses (defined as any transaction not fitting under any of the five specific categories). The cash-book entry for December 28, 1792, reads: "Do. gave to the men at the Mint, by the President's order, 2-."[73] The "Do." stood for "ditto," and referred to the previous entry, which was classified as a contingent expense.

Decatur annotates this entry as follows: "the President made a tour of inspection of this new government activity . . . and it is quite possible that the visit Washington made to it on this date was the occasion of its first actual operation."[74] Unfortunately, Decatur did not transcribe the cash-book verbatim, so there is no way to ascertain exactly why he concluded that the president made a trip to the Mint on December 28. Decatur was probably unaware of Rittenhouse's invitation from the previous day, which provided a context for such a visit. Even more unfortunately, Lear's cash-books cannot be located today, making it impossible to learn their full contents.

We are left with an assertion that Washington inspected the Mint on December 28, 1792, and circumstantial evidence to support the assertion, but no conclusive data to corroborate it. One thing can be stated with certainty, whether or not the president visited the Mint just after Christmas in 1792: there is no evidence to support Snowden's claim that George Washington visited the Mint on a regular basis.

Mint director James Ross Snowden, as depicted on U.S. Mint medal Julian MT-3.

THE BUILDINGS: 1794–1795

The construction/renovation blitz of 1792–93 created a yard that appeared almost, but not exactly, as Lamasure would depict it in *Ye Olde Mint*. A visitor to the Mint in early 1794 would have found that it contained five buildings on its original three lots numbered 37 and 39 North Seventh, and 631 Sugar Alley, as well as one structure that was offsite, in the Northern Liberties. Approaching from North Seventh Street, the visitor would have first encountered the double Front Building at numbers 37 and 39, appearing just as it did in Lamasure's painting: three stories tall, entirely constructed of brick, dimensions 36 feet, 10 inches wide by roughly 33 feet deep (the half at number 37 was more than three feet deeper than the half at number 39). An enclosed passageway between the two buildings was flanked by offices on either side, both of which faced North Seventh Street, with the counting room and the melting department to the rear; this passageway allowed employees or escorted visitors to gain admittance into the Mint's yard.[75]

A pedestrian walking through the passageway between the two halves of the Front Building would emerge through another door into an 18-foot-wide courtyard paved with bricks.[76] Next, the visitor would encounter the Mill House, a frame building, although its exact dimensions are lost to history, "which contained the horse mill for driving the rolling machines."[77] The southern edge of this Mill House was built right along the Mint's southern border with its neighbors at number 35 North Seventh, but its northern edge did not extend to the neighboring lot at number 41 North Seventh, for there was a gap here where the brick courtyard narrowed into a driveway that gave access to the rest of the Mint's property. However, the eastern edge of the Mill House adjoined the west front of the brick Rear Building.[78]

Warren A. Lapp, in his article on the first Mint in the September 15, 1968, issue of *Penny-Wise*, mistakenly placed the Mill House on the north side of the Middle Building near the Grim house on the eastern portion of number 41 North Seventh. Frank H. Stewart, on page 26 of *History of the First United States Mint*, implied that the Mill House was attached to the rear of the Front Building; it could not have been sited in either of these locations.[79]

In 1816, as we shall see, the Mill House was accidentally set ablaze by the neighbors at number 35 North Seventh; if sited as Lapp depicts it in his diagram, the fire could not have been set in this fashion. The conflagration spared the Front Building but involved the Rear Building. Just the opposite would have been true if the structures had been sited as Stewart believed. There is another compelling reason to pronounce Lapp's placement incorrect: as drawn, his Mill House is approximately four feet wide by 25 feet long. Horse mills, like the one illustrated in Denis Diderot's classic *Encyclopédie*, were square, so that the horses could move the mill by walking in a perpetual circle.[80] Lapp's long rectangular house would have

required the horse to be hitched to the mill, walked through the building, unhitched, led around the structure on the outside, then re-hitched to the mill to begin the process anew. Such a cumbersome system would have been rejected by David Rittenhouse as inefficient.[81]

Attached to the eastern end of the Mill House was the Rear Building. As originally constructed, the Rear Building was a two-story brick edifice, approximately 28 feet wide by 22 feet deep, with its eastern flank squarely on Bone Alley.[82] In this structure, as we have seen, silver center cent planchets were punched, but its main purpose was to house a furnace for smelting. Attached to the southern flank of the Rear Building was a two-story frame shack, 17 feet wide by 20 feet deep, constructed on the lot at 631 Sugar Alley. It was used as the stable for the mill horses, and also housed a horse-powered arrester to grind up worn-out crucibles and dipping cups, from which the Mint recovered traces of silver and gold.[83]

There may have been another modest structure in the Mint's yard in 1794, although the date of its construction is uncertain. Lapp mentions a Watch House built for the Mint's watchmen in front of number 37 North Seventh.[84] This is also in error, for photographs in Stewart's *History of the First United States Mint* clearly show the structure attached to the rear of number 39 North Seventh, at the northeast corner of this structure.[85] Karl Moulton argues that this latter placement was perfect for a watch house, since it provided clear sight lines along the back side of the Front Building and along the front of the Middle Building.[86]

Beginning in September of 1794, the Mint rented, from the estate of William Penn, a structure some distance from the Mint's yard: at the northern terminus of Sixth Street in the Northern Liberties, a frame building that served as a furnace for smelting, and possibly for refining. Once coinage had begun in earnest, the little furnace in the Rear Building was no longer adequate for the necessary tasks. The rented structure remained in use as a furnace until 1802, after which the Mint used it as a storehouse for coke, charcoal, anthracite coal, and wood. The Mint stopped using the building in 1804, after which it was demolished.[87]

Returning to 1794, however, the Mint moved to both enlarge its physical plant and improve the security of its yard by purchasing, on October 4, the Hamilton lot at number 629 Sugar Alley. This narrow but long parcel (20 feet, six inches by 88 feet) offered space for badly needed structures. We know that four modest workshops sat on this lot by 1828, when Mint director Samuel Moore drew his map of the Mint yard and an eyewitness account (about which more will be said later), substantiates that at least one of them was there by 1812. As we will see, however, the four shops were almost certainly in place by 1796. This assertion is corroborated by the big jump in the incidental and contingent expenses in the quarters immediately following the purchase of this lot, offering strong evidence that the space-strapped Mint moved quickly to increase its physical plant.[88] It certainly would make little sense to buy the lot at 629 Sugar Alley and then leave it vacant for years thereafter. Moreover, the purchase of this lot allowed the director to improve the security of the Mint by controlling more of Bone Alley, although that security issue would not be fully resolved until the Mint gained control of the western portions of numbers 41 and 43 North Seventh Street in 1805.

Moore's 1828 map shows four distinct but connected buildings on the lot at 629 Sugar Alley, with the southernmost sitting at the northeast corner of the intersection of Sugar Alley and Bone Alley, and the northernmost standing directly east of the number 41 and 43 North Seventh lots. The southernmost building, and its two companions to the north, were each about the same dimension as the Mint's stable, 20 feet by 17 feet. The northernmost was larger, about 20 feet by 34 feet.[89] In order to facilitate description, these structures will hereafter be referred to as the shops, and numbered from southernmost (Shop 1) to northernmost (Shop 4).

The shops are little-remembered today because they did not appear in Lamasure's *Ye Olde Mint* painting, but they were very much at the center of the Mint's daily

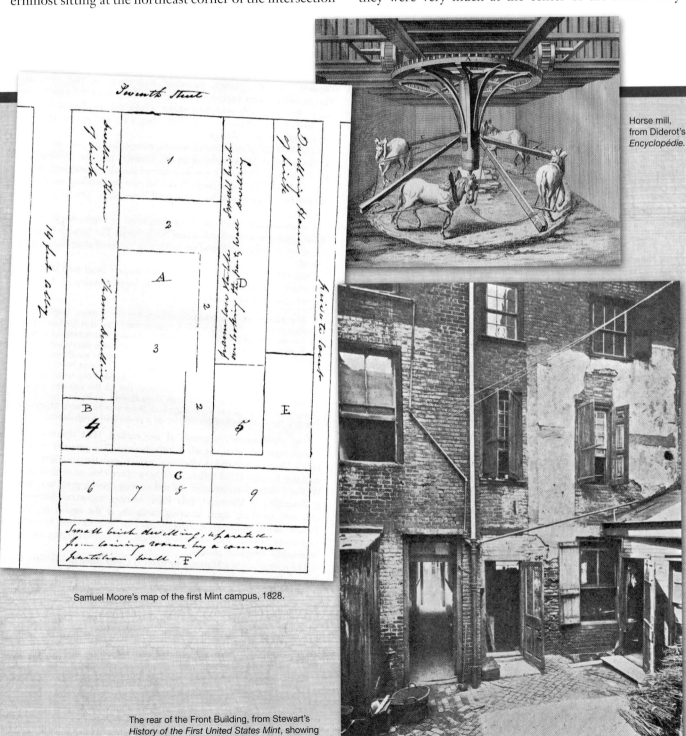

Horse mill, from Diderot's *Encyclopédie*.

Samuel Moore's map of the first Mint campus, 1828.

The rear of the Front Building, from Stewart's *History of the First United States Mint*, showing the Watch House behind 39 North Seventh (right).

operations. Shop 1 (on the corner of Sugar and Bone Alleys), was a two-story frame house; Shop 2, immediately to the north, was a two-story brick building of similar size. Press rooms used for striking coins occupied the first floor of both structures, and the second floor of each contained workshops for fabricating and repairing the Mint's machinery. In 1828, Shop 1 was used to strike silver coins, and Shop 2 to strike copper, but as we shall see, evidence exists that in 1812, Shop 1 struck copper coinage.[90] It is probably the case that the Mint shifted striking duties between shops as demand for silver and copper waxed or waned, or as coinage needs dictated the use of presses of varying sizes. Shop 3 was a rough frame building that con-

tained the Mint's smithy, and Shop 4, another unadorned frame building, was the coal storage house.[91]

The recollections of Henry S. Garrett provide further detail about the shops. Garrett was a long-term employee of the second Mint, but his father had worked in the first Mint, and young Henry started bringing his father's lunches when he was 12 years old. In testimony for the 1888 lawsuit of *Lex v. Kates*, Garrett recalled the coining department as located "in a frame building on the extreme east end of the lot, and between the frame building and the other brick building [Rear Building] that they used as a rolling room, was a cartway [Bone Alley] . . . through [to] what we called at that time Sugar Alley."[92]

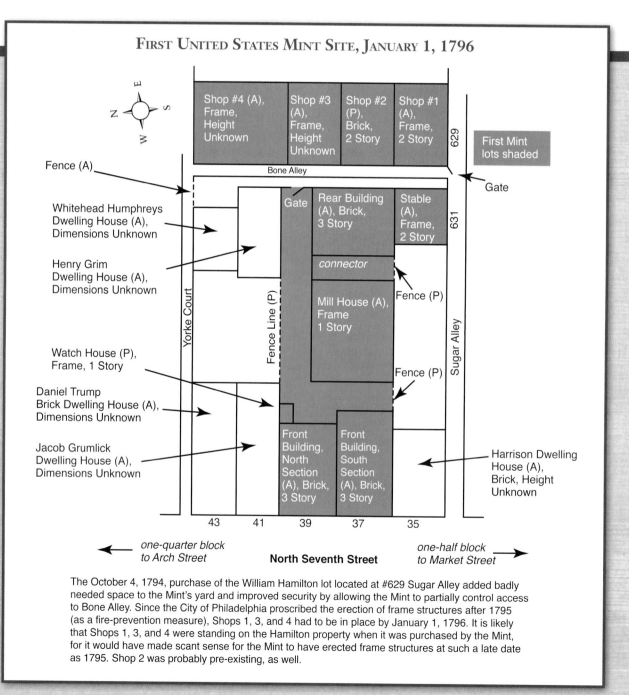

First Mint campus layout, as of January 1, 1796.

Garrett was able to add more detail: "I recollect it distinctly—of this frame building being here, and the coining press here, and four men worked at it."[93]

The three frame shops had to be completely constructed by the end of 1795, because the City of Philadelphia, as a fire safety measure, banned the construction of frame buildings after that year.[94] Once these shops were completed, probably in 1795, the Mint had literally doubled its complement of major structures. More important than the number of buildings, however, was the flexibility that the director gained to shift tasks among them. After the shops became available, for example, the Rear Building, which initially had been used as a furnace, could be converted to house the milling machines and the screw-driven planchet cutters.[95] Similarly, the double Front Building, while serving as the Mint's administrative office, also contained vaults in its cellar, a weighing room, and a press room for striking gold coins on its first floor, with the assayer's office and laboratory on its third floor.[96]

It will be recalled that starting in 1794, the Mint had vainly tried to close Bone Alley by purchasing the adjacent properties of Henry Grim (at the east end of number 41 North Seventh) and Robert E. Griffith (who had acquired the Humphreys parcel on the east side of number 43 North Seventh), but Congress refused to advance the funds to make the purchases. Finally, in June 1805, Elias Boudinot turned exasperation into inspiration, and authorized Adam Eckfeldt, the assistant coiner, to rent these two homes for the benefit of the Mint. Eckfeldt executed his commission to lease Grim's place (by 1805 owned by Jacob Grumlick), on June 6, 1805, and also rented the Griffith property the following December 13.[97] Not only did this create a solution by ridding the Mint of two unwanted neighbors, it also allowed for the closing of Bone Alley to public access. In 1827, the Griffith lot (by then owned by Samuel Yorke), was, according to Don Taxay, purchased on the Mint's behalf by the now chief coiner, Adam Eckfeldt.[98]

Actually, the purchase date was June 2, 1828. Samuel Yorke, who had bought the property from Robert E. Griffith in 1807, died intestate in 1828, leaving his widow and seven mostly adult children. They decided to sell the house and property to Adam Eckfeldt, who bought it personally, for the sum of $1,000, to secure it for the Mint. Later, after the Mint abandoned the North Seventh Street site, Eckfeldt discovered that the Yorke lot had a clouded title, which he eventually cleared, and sold it in 1837 to Michael Kates, a bell hanger about whom more will be said later. Eckfeldt made no profit, selling to Kates for the same $1,000.[99]

As for the use of the Yorke property, Adam Eckfeldt, testifying in an 1847 lawsuit, recalled:

> Mrs. York owned a small house which I bought of her—previous we had paid her $60 a year rent. There was a house hung across the alley [Bone Alley]—the house decayed down, and Mrs. York gave me the privilege of pulling it down. I suppose it was about the year 1818–19. . . . we used it pretty much for a wood yard and store house.[100]

Eckfeldt further recalled that the rental, and later the purchase, of the Yorke property allowed the Mint to open Bone Alley: "We used it getting wood and charcoal in by carts."[101]

As for Jacob Grumlick's property at the rear of number 41, in 1822, his widow, Christiana, sold the land and the house upon it to her son Thomas Cromley for a consideration of $926.66. Thomas Cromley was Jacob and Christiana Grumlick's son, so he must have anglicized his surname. The house and the lot on which it sat remained in the Cromley family until at least 1907.[102] The Mint, however, rented the Cromley house on the property from 1805 until closing operations on North Seventh Street in early 1833, using the house as a furnace. This explains why the next-door Yorke property was used as a wood lot. Finally, it is certain that the Mint was never successful in its efforts to either rent or purchase the parcel at number 35 North Seventh, and the Seventh Street–fronting portions of numbers 41 and 43, as well, for these remained in private hands during the entire time that the Mint was resident in its first location.

The Cromley and Yorke properties had added a rectangle 32 feet by 34 feet to the northeast side of the Mint's yard. When combined with the 1794 Hamilton purchase, the Mint's footprint had increased, but not enormously. Now, instead of covering a mere eight percent of an NFL playing field, the expanded Mint yard covered 13 percent: still an extremely cramped parcel. With these acquisitions completed, some of the Mint's support functions were relocated to buildings on the Cromley and the Yorke lots. The vital heart of the first Mint's operations, however, remained on the four lots that Rittenhouse had acquired during the 1790s, and this was the plot (plus, eventually, the adjoining lot at 35 North Seventh Street), that Frank H. Stewart was to purchase in the far-off 20th century.

Two other eyewitness accounts buttress this reconstruction of the Mint's evolution. The first was from a Portuguese national with the imposing name of Hipólito José da Costa Pereira Furtado de Mendonça, who visited the Mint on February 16, 1799. He noted in his diary, "The Mint here has three windows in front. It is two stories high, 40 feet deep, and has no iron bars or other means of security."[103] The Front Building had four windows in front, so Mendonça could not have referred to that structure. The Rear Building in 1799 had three windows in front (see page 67 of Stewart's *History of the First United States Mint*), but it was only about half as deep as Mendonça estimated. However, the combined depth of the Mill House and the Rear Building was about 40 feet, true to Mendonça's estimate, and since the combined building was not primarily used for coinage in 1799, it would not have needed any extraordinary means of security. Moreover, while the three windows on the second floor of the

Rear Building would not have been visible because of the connection between it and the back of the Mill House, it is entirely possible that the Mill House itself had three windows on its front façade. Ironically, Mendonça seems to have made the same misidentification of the Middle Building as the primary structure in which the coins were struck that Frank H. Stewart would make more than a century later.

The second account comes from George Escol Sellers (1808–1899), an engineer and entrepreneur whose numismatic connections were numerous and enduring. His maternal grandfather, Charles Willson Peale, was among the first to offer numismatic exhibits in his celebrated Philadelphia Museum. His paternal grandfather, Nathan Sellers, was a fast friend of David Rittenhouse. In his youth, Escol's father Coleman Sellers was a partner with the famous engraver Jacob Perkins in a firm that manufactured fire engines. Perkins referred to young Escol as "the boy who asked questions and would have an explanation of everything."[104] But most of all, Escol knew the first Philadelphia Mint. He was born and raised at a house on Mulberry Court, the first court to the south of Sugar Alley (and just north of Market Street). His father (and later he and his brother) were all partners in a firm that sold heavy machinery to the Mint, eventually including steam engines. Mint director Robert Patterson and chief coiner Adam Eckfeldt were frequent guests in Coleman Sellers's home on Mulberry Court.

In his 85th year, George Escol Sellers set down his recollections of the engineering environment in Philadelphia during the era in which he grew up. These appeared in print as a series of articles in the *American Machinist* between 1884 and 1893, but were later abridged in book form by the Smithsonian Institution.

Sellers's memories of the first Mint were exceptionally clear:

> The building used for the Mint had very much the appearance of an ordinary three-story brick dwelling house of that period, the back building and yard extending on the alley. In a rear room, facing on the alley, with a large low down window opening into it, a fly press stood, that is a screw-coining press mostly used for striking the old copper cents. Through this window the passersby in going up and down the alley could readily see the bare-armed vigorous men swinging the heavy end-weighted balanced lever that drove the screw with sufficient force so that by the momentum of the weighted ends this quick-threaded screw had the power to impress the blank and thus coin each piece. They could see the rebound or recoil of these end-weights as they struck a heavy wooden spring beam, driving the lever back to the man that worked it; they could hear the clanking of the chain that checked it at the right point to prevent its striking the man, all framing a picture very likely to leave a lasting impression.[105]

Sellers accurately conveyed the Mint's geography; the "alley" he mentioned was Sugar Alley, and he clearly identified Shop 1—the "rear room" on the corner of Bone and Sugar Alleys—as the place in which the copper cents of his youth were coined. Bone Alley had been closed to the public in 1805, three years before Escol's birth, so the "passerby going up and down the alley" had to be traveling on Sugar Alley: and the only "rear room" with frontage on Sugar Alley was Shop 1. He then related the most charming first-hand account of a coin being struck in the annals of American numismatics:

> One day in charge of my elder brother I stood on tiptoe with my nose resting on the iron bar placed across the open window of the coining room to keep out intruders, watching the men swing the levers of the fly press; it must have been about noon, for Mr. Eckfeldt came into the room, watch in hand, and gave a signal to the men who stopped work. Seeing me peering over the bar, he took me by the arms and lifted me over it. Setting me down by the coining press he asked if I did not want to make a cent, at the same time stopping the men who had put on their jackets to leave the room. He put a blank planchet into my hand, showed me how to drop it in, and where to place my hand to catch it as it came out; the lever and weights were swung, and I caught the penny as we boys called cents, but I at once dropped it. Mr. Eckfeldt laughed and asked me why I dropped it?
>
> Because it was hot and I feared it would burn me. He picked it up and handed it to me, then certainly

George Escol Sellers, 1808–1899, mechanic, who grew up near the first Mint.

not hot enough to burn; he asked if it was not cold when he gave it to me to drop into the press. He told me to look and see there was no fire, and feel the press that it was cold; he then told me I must keep the cent until I learned what made it hot; then I might, if I liked, spend it for candy.[106]

A complementary account appeared in the *American Journal of Numismatics* in 1868:

> I am informed by a friend, who attended school in the neighborhood just previous to the removal of the establishment to its present quarters [referring to the second Mint], that he distinctly recollects stopping at the window, in passing to and fro, to look with longing eyes at the bright pieces as they fell from the press with a ringing sound into the receptacle placed beneath; the only protection from the street being a wire screen across the window.[107]

There is no denying the charm of these tales, but the historian would like to know exactly when they occurred. The Smithsonian reprint of the original articles that Sellers wrote for the *American Machinist* unfortunately edited out the relevant paragraphs, but fortunately, the late Raymond H. Williamson quoted from the originals in a 1951 article in *The Numismatist*. In the Williamson article, Sellers recalled the fate of his cent:

> In this rambling dissertation I have not yet done with my first coined penny that was to have been kept until I learned the cause of its sudden heat. It could not have been many days before I lost it in a manner as strongly impressed on my mind as was its coinage. I dropped it on a flight of rude heavy stone steps and so it rolled into a hole or crevice back of one of the steps, past all hopes of recovery. I was with my grandfather Peale and his wife, visiting a brother of Mrs. Samuel Moore, who we were taught to call Uncle Samuel. [This refers to Mint director Dr. Samuel Moore.] It was at his flour mill on a creek that ran into the Schuylkill some distance above Philadelphia . . . [Mr. Sellers then tells how, many years later, he re-visited this flour mill on business, and remembered losing his copper cent in the crevice between the stone steps. He became interested in recovering it, to verify the date of his visit to the Mint]. . . . It was some time before I could locate the spot, but after pulling up several tufts of grass, a hole was exposed that appeared like what I recollected of the hole into which the penny had rolled. To make the matter certain a crow bar was brought and the step lifted and there lay the once bright cent, thickly coated with the green copper oxide; it bore the date 1812, evidence that I was only about four years of age when the picture of its coinage, loss, and the other incidents were so indelibly impressed on the storehouse of my brain.[108]

Sellers's remarkably detailed recollections are confirmed by genealogical records gathered by William E. DuBois, the long-time assayer of the Philadelphia Mint. Dr. Samuel Moore and Du Bois's father Uriah both married, in 1798, daughters of Robert Patterson, the fourth director of the Mint. After Patterson died on July 22, 1824, he was succeeded by his son-in-law, Dr. Moore. (Ironically, Patterson's predecessor, Elias Boudinot, upon retiring, had failed to secure the Mint directorship for a member of his family.[109]) In 1833, Moore appointed his nephew William DuBois as director's clerk at the Mint. When Dr. Moore left in the Mint in 1835 to take the presidency of the Hazelton Coal Company, his brother-in-law, Robert Maskell Patterson (son of Robert Patterson and another uncle of DuBois), took what was now practically a Patterson family sinecure as Mint director. Even though young Escol was taught to call Dr. Moore his uncle, he was in fact just about the only person in this narrative *not* related to a Patterson. In any case, in his genealogical account of the Patterson family, DuBois mentions that Dr. Moore settled in Bucks County in 1808. "Purchase was made of a considerable tract of land at the junction of the Neshaminy with a tributary creek, on the Easton Road, where there was a good water-power, and a large flouring mill."[110]

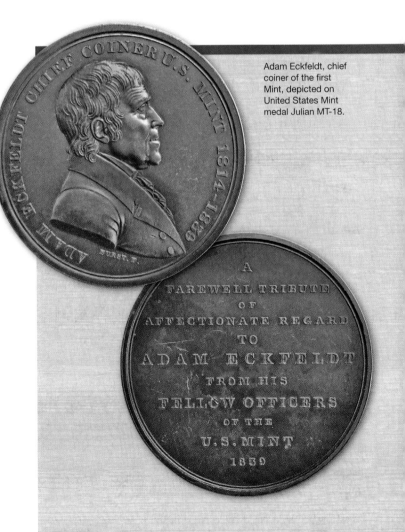

Adam Eckfeldt, chief coiner of the first Mint, depicted on United States Mint medal Julian MT-18.

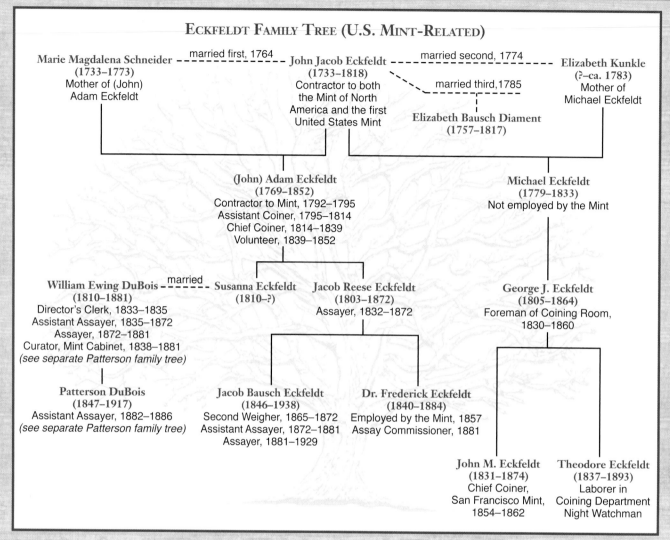

ECKFELDT FAMILY TREE (U.S. MINT-RELATED)

Marie Magdalena Schneider
(1733–1773)
Mother of (John)
Adam Eckfeldt

married first, 1764

John Jacob Eckfeldt
(1733–1818)
Contractor to both
the Mint of North
America and the first
United States Mint

married second, 1774

Elizabeth Kunkle
(?–ca. 1783)
Mother of
Michael Eckfeldt

married third, 1785

Elizabeth Bausch Diament
(1757–1817)

(John) Adam Eckfeldt
(1769–1852)
Contractor to Mint, 1792–1795
Assistant Coiner, 1795–1814
Chief Coiner, 1814–1839
Volunteer, 1839–1852

Michael Eckfeldt
(1779–1833)
Not employed by the Mint

William Ewing DuBois
(1810–1881)
Director's Clerk, 1833–1835
Assistant Assayer, 1835–1872
Assayer, 1872–1881
Curator, Mint Cabinet, 1838–1881
(see separate Patterson family tree)

married

Susanna Eckfeldt
(1810–?)

Jacob Reese Eckfeldt
(1803–1872)
Assayer, 1832–1872

George J. Eckfeldt
(1805–1864)
Foreman of Coining Room,
1830–1860

Patterson DuBois
(1847–1917)
Assistant Assayer, 1882–1886
(see separate Patterson family tree)

Jacob Bausch Eckfeldt
(1846–1938)
Second Weigher, 1865–1872
Assistant Assayer, 1872–1881
Assayer, 1881–1929

Dr. Frederick Eckfeldt
(1840–1884)
Employed by the Mint, 1857
Assay Commissioner, 1881

John M. Eckfeldt
(1831–1874)
Chief Coiner,
San Francisco Mint,
1854–1862

Theodore Eckfeldt
(1837–1893)
Laborer in
Coining Department
Night Watchman

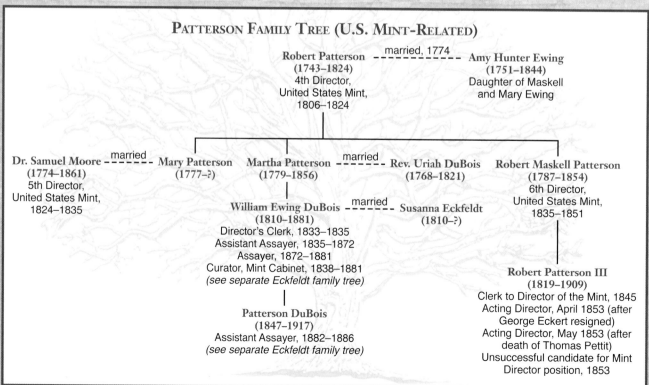

PATTERSON FAMILY TREE (U.S. MINT-RELATED)

Robert Patterson
(1743–1824)
4th Director,
United States Mint,
1806–1824

married, 1774

Amy Hunter Ewing
(1751–1844)
Daughter of Maskell
and Mary Ewing

Dr. Samuel Moore
(1774–1861)
5th Director,
United States Mint,
1824–1835

married

Mary Patterson
(1777–?)

Martha Patterson
(1779–1856)

married

Rev. Uriah DuBois
(1768–1821)

Robert Maskell Patterson
(1787–1854)
6th Director,
United States Mint,
1835–1851

William Ewing DuBois
(1810–1881)
Director's Clerk, 1833–1835
Assistant Assayer, 1835–1872
Assayer, 1872–1881
Curator, Mint Cabinet, 1838–1881
(see separate Eckfeldt family tree)

married

Susanna Eckfeldt
(1810–?)

Patterson DuBois
(1847–1917)
Assistant Assayer, 1882–1886
(see separate Eckfeldt family tree)

Robert Patterson III
(1819–1909)
Clerk to Director of the Mint, 1845
Acting Director, April 1853 (after
George Eckert resigned)
Acting Director, May 1853 (after
death of Thomas Pettit)
Unsuccessful candidate for Mint
Director position, 1853

PORTRAIT GALLERY OF THE FIRST UNITED STATES MINT

John Jacob Eckfeldt, father of Adam Eckfeldt. Contractor to the first Mint, from the Eckfeldt family collection.

Adam Eckfeldt, chief coiner, daguerreotype from the Eckfeldt family collection.

Adam Eckfeldt, painting by Samuel F. DuBois, 1837, Eckfeldt family collection.

David Rittenhouse, first director of the U.S. Mint.

PORTRAIT GALLERY OF THE FIRST UNITED STATES MINT

Joseph Cloud, first assayer of the first Mint.

Jacob Reese Eckfeldt, son of Adam Eckfeldt. Assayer of the first Mint in 1832. Daguerreotype from Eckfeldt family collection.

Henry William DeSaussure, second director of the first Mint.

Elias Boudinot, third director of the first Mint.

PORTRAIT GALLERY OF THE FIRST UNITED STATES MINT

Robert Patterson, fourth director of the first Mint.

Dr. Samuel Moore, fifth director of the first Mint.

Robert M. Patterson, sixth director of the first Mint.

William E. DuBois, grandson of Robert Patterson, and son-in-law of Adam Eckfeldt. Director's clerk in 1833, he may have briefly served in the first Mint. Daguerreotype from the Eckfeldt family collection.

FURNACES AND FIRE CHANGE THE FACE OF THE MINT, 1805–1816

Thus, by 1796, the four shops were an indispensable part of the Mint's operations. A decade later, as has been mentioned, there was also one other building in the lineup, albeit rented (not owned) by the Mint. In Frank H. Stewart's opinion, the Mint razed Thomas Cromley's house, for "it is probable that the Mint erected the one and one-half story brick building facing Bone Alley on the Cromley lot. Its basement construction was similar to the Mint buildings. This building was also used by the Stewart Company for several years prior to its destruction."[111] This structure, whether erected by Cromley or by the Mint, was used as a furnace by the Mint, replacing the rented furnace in the Northern Liberties. The Yorke property next door caused Stewart and Taxay to part company over its use, for Stewart says that the Mint erected a 16- by 36-foot brick building in order to store wood and coal, while Taxay says that the property was acquired mainly to close Bone Alley to the public, and was used as an open-air wood yard.[112] Adam Eckfeldt's previously cited testimony proves Taxay correct in this instance, for the Mint used the Yorke house until tearing it down in 1818 or 1819, utilizing the property as an open-air wood-lot after that. The building Stewart mentions was constructed after the Mint vacated the yard in 1833.[113]

By the end of 1806, therefore, the Mint's physical plant was essentially completed, consisting of the Front and Rear Buildings, the Watch House attached to the rear of the number 39 portion of the Front Building, the Mill House attached to the Rear Building, the stable also attached to the Rear Building, the four shops, the Cromley and (until at least 1818) the Yorke buildings: 10 in all. One note must be added to this accounting, for the Mill House and Rear Buildings were regarded as a single structure, due to their shared wall.

Like an evil genie, the possibility of cataclysmic fire loomed constantly over the Mint. George Escol Sellers vividly recalled one of the reasons why the Mint was at perpetual risk of going up in smoke:

> The little yard in the rear of the old Mint was a very attractive place to us youngsters [with] its great piles of cord wood, which by the barrow load was wheeled into the furnace room and thrust full size in the boiler furnace, which to my young eyes appeared to be the hottest place on earth. There almost daily was to be seen great lattice-sided wagons of charcoal being unloaded, and the fuel stacked under a shed [probably Shop 4] to be used in the melting and the annealing furnaces.[114]

Inevitably, the "hottest place on earth" from time to time spawned uncontrollable flames. For example, the *United States Gazette* of March 18, 1832, reported on a fire "in a small private building adjacent to the Mint, erected for use as a melting room. The building is insured by the

owner. The public property has not been damaged nor the daily operations of coinage imperiled by the occurrence.[115] This fire made but little impression on the history of the institution, for it came just as the government was winding down the operations of the "Sugar Alley Mint," as many Philadelphians fondly called it,[116] and it occurred in a leased structure, the Cromley building.

Another fire occurred on November 15, 1868, long after the government had sold the first Mint, beginning in the Middle Building (which was described as a two-story structure in a newspaper account of the blaze), and spreading to the Front Building. Both structures sustained serious damage, but were later rebuilt.[117] Frank H. Stewart would eventually salvage some of the burnt timbers from this blaze and, as we shall see, one of them has made its way to public exhibition in the current U.S. Mint.

One of these periodic conflagrations, however, permanently changed the face of the first Mint. A Philadelphia newspaper dated January 11, 1816, gave the first account of the disaster:

> The fire broke out in a back building of the United States MINT, in which was erected the rolling mill and some other not very valuable machinery. These were consumed or so much burnt as to destroy their usefulness. Not much other damage was done. There is good reason to believe that the fire was the work of some Incendiaries, in the hope of plunder. In the back building in which the fire broke out the officer's [sic] of the Mint know of no fire since Tuesday morning and in that particular part where the fire was first discovered it is not remembered when any fire was there.[118]

That very morning, Mint director Robert Patterson wrote to President Madison, corroborating the newspaper report in every detail:

> Mint of the United States, January 11, 1816
> Sir, I have the mortification to inform you that this morning, about 2:00, a fire broke out in the mill house, a wooden building belonging to the Mint, which is consumed together with an adjoining building containing the rolling and drawing machines, and also the melting house. The front part of the building, containing the coining presses, the office and the Assayer's Department is uninjured. The manner in which the fire originated is perfectly unaccountable. No fire is even kept in the part of the building where it was first discovered; nor had any of the workmen been there for some days. No loss of gold or silver will be sustained of any consequence, nor will the copper coinage be in the least impeded.[119]

The cause of the fire, as it turned out, was not plunder-seeking "incendiaries," because four days later, Patterson wrote to the president once more:

> On the morning of the 11th I had the painful task of acquainting you with the destruction of a part of the

Mint by fire. At the time its origin was entirely unknown and unsuspected by any of the officers or workmen belonging to the establishment; but on examining a barrel in a neighboring yard partly filled with wood ashes, taken from the hearths of an adjoining dwelling-house, and which had been set in actual contact with the weathered boarding of our mill house, a wooden building, where the fire was first discovered, no doubt remains that here the fire originated.[120]

Patterson's two letters make it clear that the Mill House was located on the west (front) side of the contiguous Rear Building, not the north side, as Warren Lapp believed, for if the "adjoining dwelling house" mentioned by Patterson was the one on the western portion of number 41 North Seventh, it would have been necessary to climb a fence and cross a busy driveway belonging to the Mint in order to place the burn barrel against the Mill House. On the other hand, if the "adjoining dwelling house" was the Harrison home at the front of number 35 North Seventh, it would have been necessary only to place the burn barrel against the wall of the Mill House abutting number 35's back yard.[121]

Hence, it is highly likely that the neighbors at number 35 North Seventh were responsible for setting the frame Mill House ablaze, and that the flames spread from there to the attached Rear Building (the "adjoining building containing the rolling and drawing machines" in Patterson's letter).

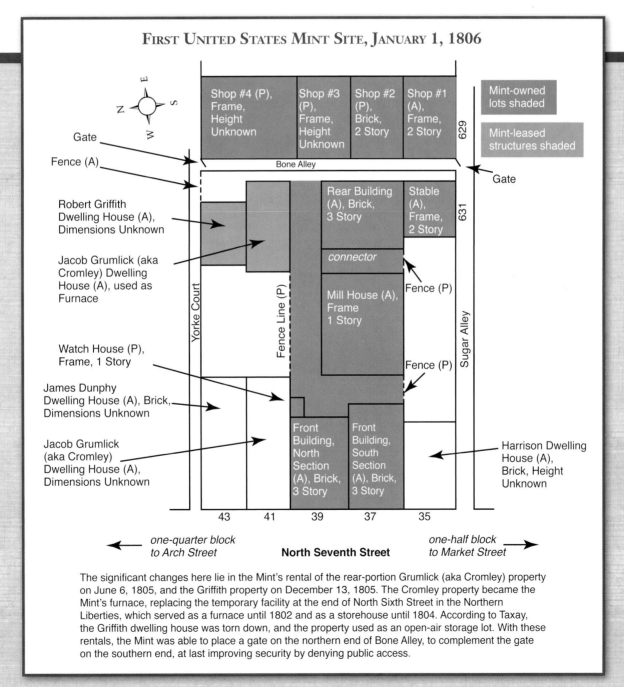

First Mint campus, 1806.

The Front Building, which was not physically attached to the Mill House/Rear Building complex, was left completely unscathed. When the smoke cleared, the frame Mill House was a total loss; the brick Rear Building, as Patterson wrote, appeared to be also "consumed" by the blaze.

The Mint's response considerably altered the yard's appearance, not to mention the source of motive power for the establishment. Director Robert Patterson reported to President Madison on January 1, 1817, that:

> The repairs of the Mint, which you were pleased to authorize, are now nearly completed. A substantial brick building has been erected on the site formerly occupied by an old wooden building; and in the apparatus and arrangement of machinery which have been adopted, many important improvements have been introduced. Among these is the substitution of a steam engine for the horsepower heretofore employed.[122]

The old wooden Mill House was therefore replaced by "a substantial brick building," of three stories, the 30- by 35-foot Middle Building. Patterson's initial judgment that the Rear Building was "consumed" by the fire proved to be incorrect. It was in fact renovated and placed back into service. We know this because it would not have been possible for Stewart to find the 1792 silver center cent planchets there in 1907 had the edifice been entirely razed and rebuilt in 1816. The new Middle Building was the structure that Frank H. Stewart, nearly a century later, would assume to be the Coinage Building. Ironically enough, the edifice that Stewart believed to be the first and most historically significant of all the structures in the Mint's yard was not even constructed until 1816.

Stewart was aware of the fire of 1816, but the newspaper account of it that he quoted said that the fire was in "a part of the back buildings," which led him to believe that it was the Rear Building that was destroyed and later replaced. He noted that the Middle Building had also been damaged by fire, but that he did not know when the fire had occurred.[123] This blaze, occurring after the government had sold the Mint, reduced the height of the Middle Building from three stories to two.

The rear of the new Middle Building was joined, probably during the post-fire construction of 1816, to the front of the old Rear Building, via a roof that connected the second story of each structure. Stewart was unaware of this connector; it was gone by the time he purchased the property in 1907, when he noted that "at the rear was a one and a half story brick building known as the Smelting House."[124] Stewart believed that the alteration from two to one and a half stories was made in 1816, and the evidence for his conclusion is found in the flag that flutters in Lamasure's *Ye Olde Mint.*

In Lamasure's painting, the Rear Building no longer has two stories, but rather a story and a half, indicating that the scene is set after the renovations of 1816 had been completed. The precise date Stewart meant the painting to represent is defined by the version of Old Glory that flaps above the buildings. The first official U.S. flag, from June 14, 1777, to April 30, 1795, had 13 stars. The second, from May 1, 1795, to April 12, 1818, had 15 stars and 15 stripes. The Flag Act of 1818 returned the flag to 13 stripes, and raised the number of stars to 20. This is the flag depicted, quite purposefully, in *Ye Olde Mint,* allowing us to date the time frame of the painting between April 13, 1818, and July 3, 1819. After this latter date, the number of stars was raised to 21.[125]

Stewart's conclusion about the remodeling of the Rear Building is incorrect, for as we shall see, the Rear Building was still two stories tall in 1837. The reduction to a story and a half clearly took place after Michael Kates purchased the old Mint's yard and structures.

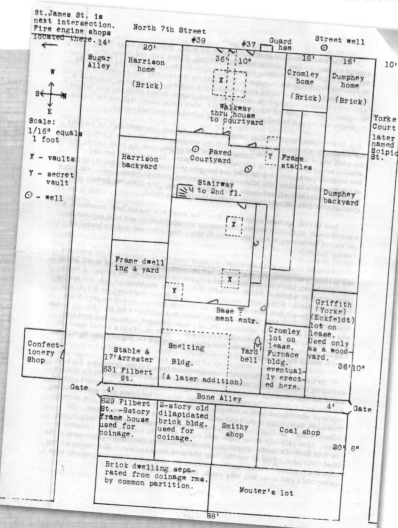

The first Mint campus, as drawn by Warren Lapp in *Penny-Wise,* 1968. Numbers 37 and 39 are inadvertently reversed.

It appears that the finalizing touches were not placed upon the renovation until 1819, for the *Annual Report of the Director of the Mint* for that year includes the following:

> The amount of coinage would have been considerably greater had a sufficient supply of bullion been regularly furnished; but for four or five months, no deposits of any consequence were received. During this interval, however, the men were advantageously employed in completing and improving the buildings and machinery belonging to the establishment.[126]

This work undoubtedly included demolishing the Yorke House, as Adam Eckfeldt had recalled in his previously-cited testimony. By late 1819, therefore, the Mint's yard and buildings had assumed their familiar appearance—the Front, Middle, and Rear Buildings looked as Lamasure would paint them—and the footprint was that as sketched by Director Moore in 1828. As of 1828, after the Yorke house was

Closeup of the U.S. flag from Edwin Lamasure's *Ye Olde Mint.*

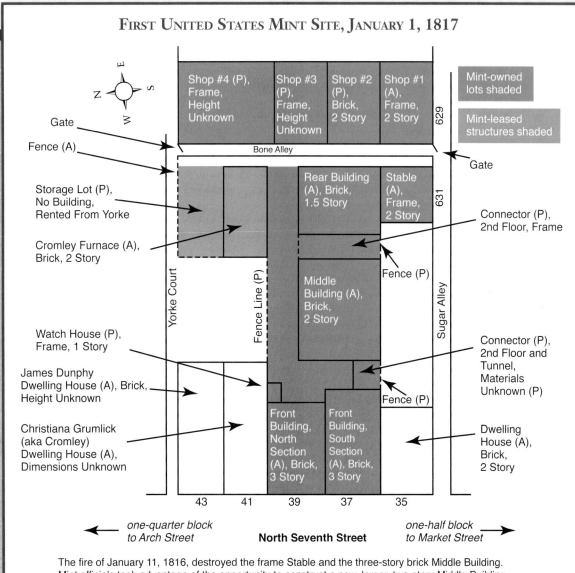

FIRST UNITED STATES MINT SITE, JANUARY 1, 1817

Shop #4 (P), Frame, Height Unknown

Shop #3 (P), Frame, Height Unknown

Shop #2 (P), Brick, 2 Story

Shop #1 (A), Frame, 2 Story

Mint-owned lots shaded

Mint-leased structures shaded

Gate

Fence (A)

Bone Alley

Gate

Storage Lot (P), No Building, Rented From Yorke

Cromley Furnace (A), Brick, 2 Story

Rear Building (A), Brick, 1.5 Story

Stable (A), Frame, 2 Story

Connector (P), 2nd Floor, Frame

Fence (P)

Yorke Court

Fence Line (P)

Middle Building (A), Brick, 2 Story

Sugar Alley

Watch House (P), Frame, 1 Story

James Dunphy Dwelling House (A), Brick, Height Unknown

Christiana Grumlick (aka Cromley) Dwelling House (A), Dimensions Unknown

Connector (P), 2nd Floor and Tunnel, Materials Unknown (P)

Fence (P)

Front Building, North Section (A), Brick, 3 Story

Front Building, South Section (A), Brick, 3 Story

Dwelling House (A), Brick, 2 Story

629

631

43   41   39   37   35

← one-quarter block to Arch Street

North Seventh Street

one-half block to Market Street →

The fire of January 11, 1816, destroyed the frame Stable and the three-story brick Middle Building. Mint officials took advantage of the opportunity to construct a new, larger, two-story Middle Building, which covered most of the footprint of the old Mill House / Middle Building concoction that had formerly stood on that site. It is also probable that they seized the opportunity to construct connectors between the Front and Middle Buildings, and between the Middle and Rear Buildings. It is known that these two connectors were in place by 1837 and 1828, respectively. The Rear Building was also remodeled from three stories to two-and-a-half stories at this time. Finally, the Humphreys/Griffith/Yorke dwelling house had long since been razed in order to create a storage lot.

The first Mint campus, 1817.

demolished, the Mint had 10 buildings, far more than the three depicted in Lamasure's *Ye Olde Mint*.

In order to present a more complete picture of the Mint as it appeared at that time, numismatic historian Pete Smith painted a view of it from the north, as if viewed from a tall building on Arch Street, looking south toward Market Street. The details of this painting have been gleaned from a careful study of surviving evidence, including the insurance surveys. The double Front Building is on the right, with number 37 a bit deeper than number 39. A second-floor walkway connects the rear of number 37 with the front of the Middle Building. The Middle Building, in turn, is connected to the Rear Building by a covered walkway, and the four shops range along the left side of the painting. The roof of the Cromley furnace building occupies the left foreground, partly obscuring the Rear Building, while Mint director Robert Patterson can be seen conversing with an employee in the brick-paved yard. A small portion of the stable's roof can be seen just past the roof of the Rear Building. Smith's painting also sets the Mint in its urban context, for just to the south of the Mint complex we see three houses along Mulberry Court. In the upper left corner, along Market Street, is the President's House, where George Washington lived during the Mint's early years, and to the right, also along Market Street, is the Graff House, where Thomas Jefferson wrote the Declaration of Independence. In the far background, there is Independence Hall with Congress Hall on its right flank, and just to the right, the Episcopal Seminary building. Here for the first time we see the first Mint as it appeared at its zenith, after damage from the 1816 fire had been repaired. A sister image, also by Smith, presents the Front Building's façade as it might have appeared in 1809. Smith adds the following commentary:

A pedestrian passing on Seventh Street might glance with interest at a building on the east side. It is here that the public can exchange foreign coins, gold jewelry or silver flatware for coins of the new nation, The United States of America. This painting catches a mid-day view of activities at the Mint. The doorkeeper, Philip Summers, stands watch over anyone seeking admission. Through the open street level window is seen a Mint clerk weighing a deposit. In the window above, engraver Robert Scot works on a die for coinage. A patient Quaker, assayer John Richardson looks out the third-floor win-

Pete Smith's *Mint Yard*, 2009.

dow to see what is detaining his wife and delaying his lunch. She has paused to chat with the guard.

The fire of 1816 left one other positive legacy for the Mint: The beginning of the process by which horsepower from steam would replace horsepower from horses. On June 24, 1816, in the aftermath of the fire that had consumed the Mill House, the Mint installed a 10-horsepower steam engine purchased from Oliver Evans, a Philadelphia pioneer of steam engine technology. The engine displaced horses as the power source for rolling and drawing machines, and at least one of the planchet cutters. Human muscle, however, was still employed to strike all of the coins. Complete utilization of steam technology would have to wait for the completion of the second Mint, in 1833. The arrival of the steam engine made the Mint's horses superfluous, and the stable was given over entirely to other uses, such as the operation of the arrester.[127]

THE BUILDINGS: 1813–1907

At the "Sugar Alley Mint," in doll's house buildings sprouting from an inadequate sliver of land, the men of the first Mint soldiered on, with only partial assistance from the steam power (and that only after 1816), for four bone-wearying decades of 11- to 13-hour days. That even

Pete Smith's *Philadelphia Street Scene 1809*, 2009.

in spite of these gargantuan efforts, they could not meet the growing national demand for coinage, is hardly surprising. The wonder is that they were able to do as well as they did, for as long as they did, with as little as they had. By the end of the 1820s, however, no amount of heroic exertion in this tiny and technologically backward facility could come anywhere close to satisfying the ravening appetite for coinage in the rapidly growing American republic. Something had to be done, and soon, or the already embarrassing reliance on foreign coinage to keep the wheels of commerce turning would swell to humiliating proportions.

During the late 1820s, Director Samuel Moore considered enlarging the footprint of the first Mint's site by purchasing the lot to the south (35 North Seventh) and the lots to the north (41 and 43 North Seventh), to provide a yard 90 feet wide by 150 feet deep. Clearly, changes must be made. Visitor B.L.C. Wailes noted in his journal for December 28, 1829, "Visited U.S. Mint. The Establishment is carried on in a very *mean* house."[128] Not even Director Moore was an advocate for retaining the miscellaneous array of brick and frame buildings, certainly because they were too small, but also "on account of the repulsive aspect which the group of buildings appropriated to the Mint presents." Ultimately, Moore conceded that the site was completely inadequate, for he judged that only one of the Mint's structures—the relatively new Middle Building—was worthy of retaining.[129]

On May 31, 1830, Congress bowed to the inevitable, and authorized the president to sell the Mint, its property and improvements, at such time and under such terms as he deemed most advantageous to the United States.[130] That time arrived in 1832, when from July 2 through July 19 an advertisement offering the Mint and its machinery to the highest bidder ran in *Poulson's Daily Advertiser.* Apparently, no bid was received, or at least none that was deemed satisfactory, for neither property nor improvements were sold.[131]

The second Philadelphia Mint, a lovely marble Greek Revival temple of numisma, opened for business in late January of 1833 at the corner of Juniper and Chestnut Streets. Interestingly, just as David Rittenhouse had chosen the site for the first Mint four decades previously that was a mere half block from his home, so Adam Eckfeldt, by now the venerable chief coiner, suggested a location only six blocks from his residence at Juniper and Vine Streets.[132] When the second Mint was constructed, it was furnished with entirely new machinery, so that the first Mint could continue operating at full capacity until the new one was ready for operation.[133] Rittenhouse's "Sugar Alley Mint," continued at speed until early 1833, and may have remained in operation at some level even after its

The second United States Mint, engraving from drawing by William Strickland, architect of the building.

successor opened for business.[134] When it finally closed for good, a mere 36 employees were transferred to the new Mint at Juniper and Chestnut.[135]

By the autumn of 1835, the U.S. government was ready to place the first Mint on the auction block once more. The sale was scheduled for October 8, 1835, at the Philadelphia Exchange, according to advertisements run in the *United States Gazette* and the *American Sentinel*.[136] This time, the offering was more productive. The three original Mint lots (37 and 39 North Seventh and 631 Sugar Alley), and the buildings on them, were sold to Michael Kates, a bell hanger, for the price of $8,100, subject to the old ground rent of 21 pieces of eight per annum. Frank H. Stewart had in his possession, as of 1924, the deed of sale, dated January 12, 1836, and signed by President Andrew Jackson.[137] As we shall see, that deed today resides at the fourth Philadelphia Mint. The Mint's fourth lot, across Bone Alley at 629 Sugar Alley, was sold for $2,000 to the firm Tower and Lunt, which could not consummate the sale, so the property went to the underbidder: Michael Kates, subject to a ground rent of six and one half pieces of eight per annum. The deed for this lot was dated November 22, 1837.[138] In the meantime, Kates had also purchased, on July, 20, 1837, the old Yorke lot owned by Adam Eckfeldt.[139] The machinery of the first Mint was sold separately from the land and buildings, mostly as scrap metal, while some of the functioning works went to the Mint's old neighbor, George Escol Sellers, who purchased the rolling mill department with its shafting and connected machinery for his engineering firm. This foreshadowed the exploits of George Soley, who was destined to buy, as we shall see, the first steam press used by the U.S. Mint. Sellers had other connections with the Mint, as well, for his uncle Titian Peale designed the reverse of the Gobrecht dollar, and another uncle, Franklin Peale, was by 1835 a Mint employee, and from 1839 to 1854 the chief coiner.[140]

Michael Kates proved to be no mere speculator, seeking only to sell the Mint property for a quick profit. Quite to the contrary, he and his relatives owned the land and preserved the buildings for 72 years, nearly twice as long as the U.S. government had been the proprietor. Michael died, unmarried and childless, in 1861, and bequeathed the property to his sister, Louisa S. Kates. She died on August 20, 1884, also unmarried and without issue. Her will directed that the property be disposed of by public sale, at which the purchaser was John L. Kates, nephew of both Michael and Louisa.[141] Eventually, the old Mint's land and buildings passed by inheritance to John L's son, J. Louis Kates, who finally sold them to Frank H. Stewart in 1907. During their long ownership, the Kates family were landlords to a variety of worthy tenants. Among the first was the Apprentices Library of Philadelphia, which attempted, in late October of 1835, to provide Michael Kates a tidy profit, by offering $10,000 for the lots and the buildings he had just purchased at auction for $8,100. Kates refused,

but he did let out the first floor of the Front Building to the library from January 1836, to May 1841.[142] The library's managers reported, "The locality is central, and *the rent is not high*."[143] This candor came back to haunt them, for in 1837 Michael Kates raised their rent from $125 to $150 per annum.[144] The library found that "the building was a mere factory, and without artificial lighting," so by March 12, 1838, they had paid for the installation of gas lighting fixtures.[145] After 1845, the Front Building was occupied by the Laboratory and School of Analytical Chemistry, which had as a student William H. Gobrecht, the son of Mint engraver Christian Gobrecht.[146]

Part of Michael Kates's stewardship of the old Mint property was to properly insure the main buildings of the complex. To that end, the Franklin Fire Insurance Company of Philadelphia performed a thorough survey of the buildings and grounds on February 16, 1837, providing

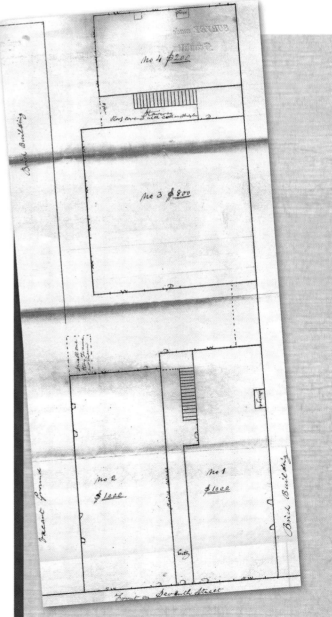

Franklin Fire Insurance Company survey of the old Mint yard, 1837.

the owner with a detailed written description and a thorough diagram of the old Mint's yard and buildings. This recently discovered document was unknown to Frank H. Stewart, and would have altered the appearance of *Ye Olde Mint* had he been aware of it.

The diagram accompanying the survey focuses on the buildings sitting on numbers 37 and 39 North Seventh Street, namely the double Front Building, the Middle Building and the Rear Building, although it also shows the Cromley Furnace on the eastern segment of number 41 North Seventh. On the diagram, the portion of the Front Building at number 37 is labeled no. 1, while the portion at number 39 is labeled no. 2. The Middle Building is labeled no. 3, and the Rear Building is labeled no. 4. Each of the Front Buildings, nos. 1 and 2, are insured for $1000. The Middle Building is insured for $800, and the Rear Building is insured for only $200. The Cromley Furnace, though depicted on the diagram, is not insured; the old stable adjoining the Rear Building to the east is mentioned in the written description, but not illustrated on the diagram, and the four shops at 629 Sugar Alley are neither mentioned nor depicted. It is probable that this map was meant to show only those buildings on the lots at numbers 37 and 39 North Seventh, but it is also possible that since Kates owned property at 631 and 629 Sugar Alley as well, and chose not to insure them, that he valued them substantially less than the structures on numbers 37 and 39.

The diagram both confirms things known from other sources and reveals new facts of interest. For example, the diagram confirms the existence of the Watch House at the northeast corner of the Front Building at 39 North Seventh, as well as the street-level passageway between numbers 37 and 39 that led to a stairway at the rear of number 37. To the rear of the yard, the covered walkway connecting the Rear and the Middle Buildings is shown in more detail as a roof covered with cedar shingles that joins the two structures, sheltering a stairway that led to both the full second story of the Rear Building and the full second story of the Middle Building. A completely new fact also emerges: a heretofore-unknown connection between the number 37 half of the Front Building and the Middle Building. The written description also reveals significant new facts about the interior of the Front Building.

According to the written description, although numbers 37 and 39 were separated on the ground floor by the passageway, "the second and third stories of both houses has the wall taken down in the centre between the houses about 18 feet from the front wall, the joist over the opening in each story being supported by a girder with turned columns under it in each story."[147] Thus, the second and third stories of numbers 37 and 39 were opened as if they were a single building. On the second floor of number 37 (or no. 1 in the diagram) there was also "a doorway leading onto a platform to Building no. 3."[148] In other words, a second-story passageway existed between the back of the

number 37 portion of the Front Building and the front of the Middle Building. Moreover, "the cellar of each house has been vaulted, and a passage under the yard back into no. 3, which is a two story Brick Building 30 feet front by 35 feet deep."[149] There was, therefore, a tunnel directly under the second-story passageway, making for a double connection between the Front and Middle Buildings.

Frank H. Stewart found one opening of this tunnel when demolishing the Front Building. In the southeastern corner of the basement of number 37, after punching through the stone wall of the cellar, workmen discovered

> a brick wall bisecting it about five feet from the wall of 35 N. 7th, and parallel with it . . . also a brick pavement between these walls, which at first led me to think there had been a brick walled passage between the coinage building basement, and the front building, but very much to my surprise, another brick wall was uncovered, which showed that a vault or annex basement to the one under 37 had once existed, and been filled up after the rear basement wall had been closed.[150]

Stewart mapped this "filled vault" in his *History of the First United States Mint.* His first impression, however, was the correct one, for the tunnel was filled in by the Kates family, which, with different tenants in the different buildings, would have had no need to connect the Front and Middle Buildings.

The big picture that emerges from this description is not that of separate structures, as implied in *Ye Olde Mint,* but rather that of buildings interconnected by passageways and a tunnel to make a single unit. The diagram and description make it clear, for example, that it was possible to walk from the second floor of any building on numbers 37 and 39 North Seventh, to the second floor of any other structure on those two lots, without ever going outside. In short, the Mint had done all it could to integrate its disparate physical plant into a single entity.

It is curious that Mint director Samuel Moore's 1828 diagram of the Mint's yard and structures makes no mention of either the tunnel or the second-floor passageway connecting the Front Building with the Middle Building. One explanation might be that neither tunnel nor passageway existed in 1828, but were added by the Michael Kates family after they purchased the property in 1835, but prior to the insurance survey in 1837. This seems nonsensical, for the Mint, being an integrated operation, needed the connections, while the Kates family, with different tenants in different businesses, did not. A more plausible explanation is that the tunnel was excavated after the Mint fire of 1816, in order to gain access to the steam engine installed in the Middle Building, but Moore did not include the tunnel in his diagram because it was below the grade of the Mint's yard. The second-story passageway could have been added after 1828 as the Mint attempted to maximize the usefulness of its buildings.

The record of miscellaneous expenses offers some support for the notion that both the tunnel and the second-floor passageway were added in 1828 or later. In 1828 and 1829, warrants were issued for $468.03 in construction bricks, and $235.53 worth of boards and scantling. In addition, in 1829, the Mint spent $16.00 for "stone paving of yard," perhaps to cover the top of the tunnel.[151]

The diagram reveals a final irony. By 1837, the neighboring dwelling house on the western portion of number 41 North Seventh had been demolished, leaving precious vacant ground in its wake. By then, however, the Mint's ongoing search for additional space had led them to the southwest, to Juniper and Chestnut Streets, and the Sugar Alley Mint was no more.

In 1858, the Hexamer Insurance Company created a map of the first Mint buildings and yard. The primary value of this newly discovered map is to reveal what was still standing—and what had been built—during the 28 years since Michael Kates had purchased the property. Still standing were the four shops, although Shops 3 and 4 had been combined into a single unit. The connectors between the Front and the Middle Buildings and the Middle and the Rear Buildings were still in place. The map is ambiguous as to whether the Cromley Furnace still stood (if so, it was still owned by Thomas Cromley). The map, however, clearly does show a brick structure erected on the Yorke lot, replacing the Mint's open-air wood lot. Another value of the map is that it confirms the materials of which the lesser-known buildings were constructed, including frame for the stable and shops, excepting brick for Shop 2. A final useful note is that the Watch House is correctly placed on the northeast corner of number 39.[152]

The earliest known view of the Middle Building, an engraving published in the *Philadelphia Inquirer* of February 7, 1898, shows that the overhead connector between the Front and Middle Buildings had been altered to restrict access; now a stairway leads from the ground level to the second floor entrance of the Middle Building.

The first Mint property was still in the hands of Michael Kates in 1854, when the earliest known photograph of any of its buildings was created. The photographer, Frederick Richards, went uncredited in the article, probably by Benjamin Betts, which accompanied the illustration.[153] Richards's albumen print holds the distinction of being

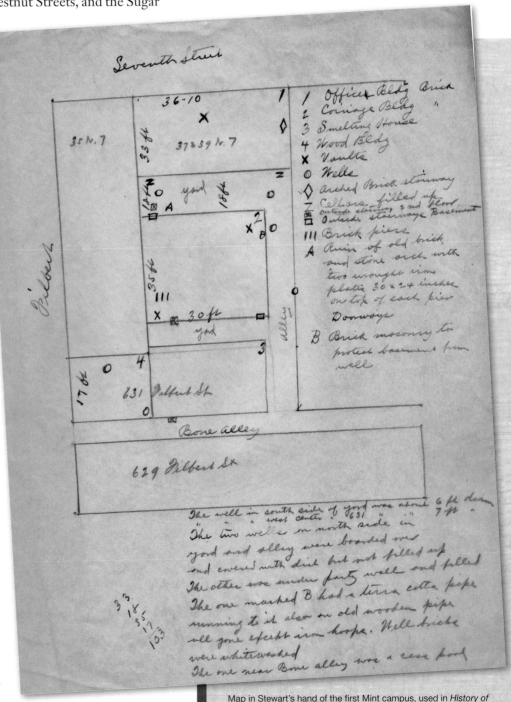

Map in Stewart's hand of the first Mint campus, used in *History of the First United States Mint*. The vaults are marked with an "X."

the first photograph published in the *American Journal of Numismatics* (in 1868), as well as the earliest known image taken of any of the Mint's structures. Although the government had sold the Front Building nearly 20 years before the photograph was taken, it was little changed, except for the addition of bow windows. The fact that it was in actuality two structures is evident in this photo, for the differing heights of the door jambs, and the seam sep-

arating the two halves of the structure, are both clearly visible. The old street-level passageway to the Mint yard was still in evidence, for a gentleman lounges in its entrance. In the background, south of the Front Building, is an adjoining three-story edifice at 35 North Seventh Street, the south side of which faced Sugar Alley (by 1868, called Filbert Street), a lot and building that the Mint never owned. In the accompanying article, Benjamin

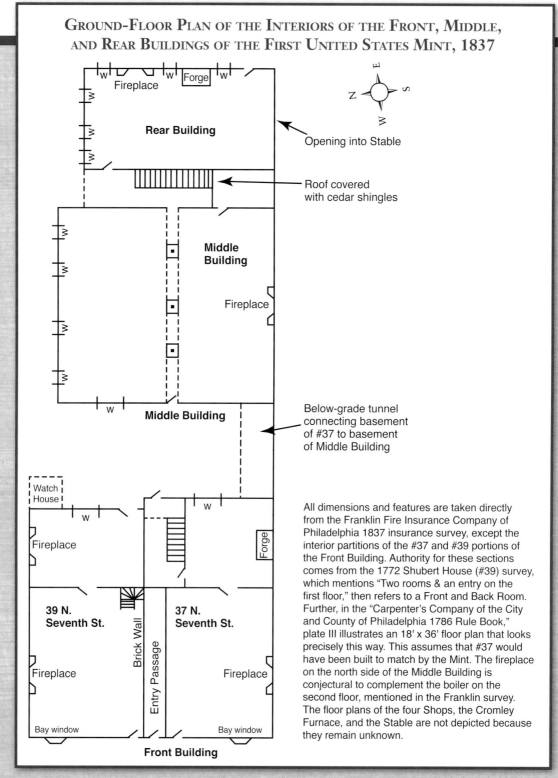

GROUND-FLOOR PLAN OF THE INTERIORS OF THE FRONT, MIDDLE, AND REAR BUILDINGS OF THE FIRST UNITED STATES MINT, 1837

All dimensions and features are taken directly from the Franklin Fire Insurance Company of Philadelphia 1837 insurance survey, except the interior partitions of the #37 and #39 portions of the Front Building. Authority for these sections comes from the 1772 Shubert House (#39) survey, which mentions "Two rooms & an entry on the first floor," then refers to a Front and Back Room. Further, in the "Carpenter's Company of the City and County of Philadelphia 1786 Rule Book," plate III illustrates an 18' x 36' floor plan that looks precisely this way. This assumes that #37 would have been built to match by the Mint. The fireplace on the north side of the Middle Building is conjectural to complement the boiler on the second floor, mentioned in the Franklin survey. The floor plans of the four Shops, the Cromley Furnace, and the Stable are not depicted because they remain unknown.

Authors' recreation of floor plans of the Front, Middle, and Rear Buildings of the first Mint.

Betts notes that Michael Kates had also preserved the character of the Front Building in another way: "it is tenanted (as it always has been since I first knew it) by workers in metals—a plumber, a metallic roofer, a silver plater, and an engraver occupy the premises."[154]

Another image of the Front Building, taken 35 years later, and published in James Rankin Young's *The United States Mint at Philadelphia*, shows a few changes. A new,

taller building now occupies number 35 North Seventh next door, and the old Front Building has both new tenants (Chambers Umbrella Factory and Fauth & Ogden's "Cosmos" Cigars), along with modern amenities (two sidewalk elevators are visible and open for business in front of the structure).[155]

More than 40 years after Richards's 1854 photo of the Front Building was fixed for posterity, Frank H. Stewart

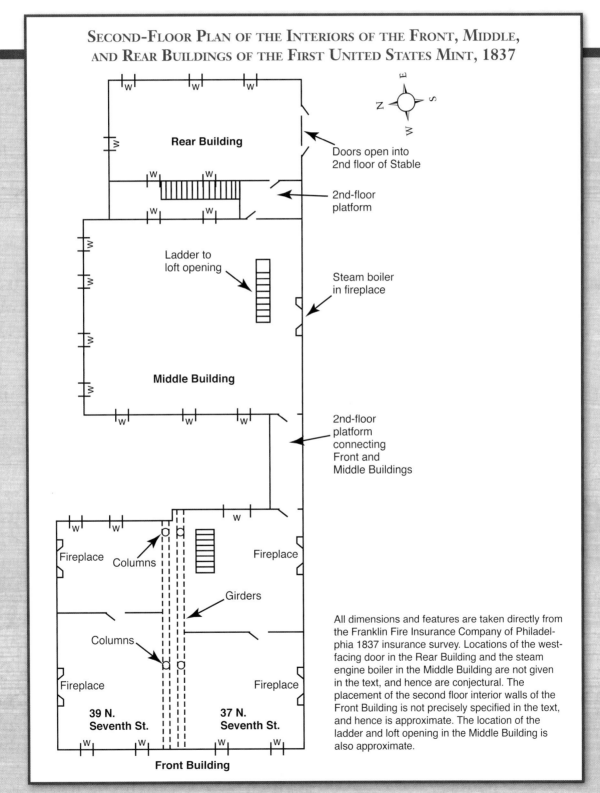

SECOND-FLOOR PLAN OF THE INTERIORS OF THE FRONT, MIDDLE, AND REAR BUILDINGS OF THE FIRST UNITED STATES MINT, 1837

Rear Building

Doors open into 2nd floor of Stable

2nd-floor platform

Ladder to loft opening

Steam boiler in fireplace

Middle Building

2nd-floor platform connecting Front and Middle Buildings

Fireplace   Columns

Fireplace

Girders

Columns

Fireplace

Fireplace

39 N. Seventh St.

37 N. Seventh St.

All dimensions and features are taken directly from the Franklin Fire Insurance Company of Philadelphia 1837 insurance survey. Locations of the west-facing door in the Rear Building and the steam engine boiler in the Middle Building are not given in the text, and hence are conjectural. The placement of the second floor interior walls of the Front Building is not precisely specified in the text, and hence is approximate. The location of the ladder and loft opening in the Middle Building is also approximate.

Front Building

Authors' recreation of floor plans of the Front, Middle, and Rear Buildings of the first Mint.

THIRD-FLOOR PLAN OF THE INTERIORS OF THE FRONT AND MIDDLE BUILDINGS OF THE FIRST UNITED STATES MINT

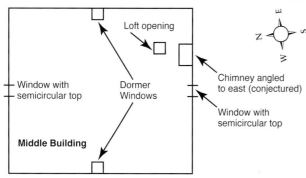

Loft opening

Window with semicircular top

Dormer Windows

Chimney angled to east (conjectured)

Window with semicircular top

Middle Building

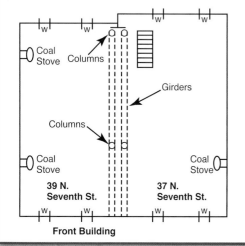

Coal Stove

Columns

Girders

Columns

Coal Stove

Coal Stove

39 N. Seventh St.

37 N. Seventh St.

Front Building

All dimensions and features are taken directly from the Franklin Fire Insurance Company of Philadelphia 1837 insurance survey. Exact locations for the loft opening, dormer windows, and semicircular windows in the Middle Building are not specified in text, and so are approximate. Semicircular dormer windows were likely centered in the north and south gable ends, so it is possible that the route of the chimney was angled to the east. The opening between the two halves of the Front Building was said to begin 18 feet back from the front of the house; exact dimensions are thus conjectural. Also, exact locations of the coal stoves are not specified in text, and therefore are approximate.

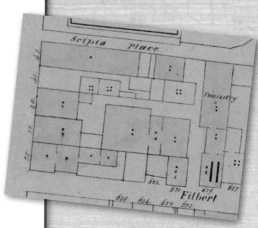

Hexamer Insurance Map of the former Mint campus, 1858.

Authors' recreation of floor plans of the Front, Middle, and Rear Buildings of the first Mint.

GARRETT-LEVEL FLOOR PLAN OF THE INTERIOR OF THE FRONT BUILDING OF THE FIRST UNITED STATES MINT

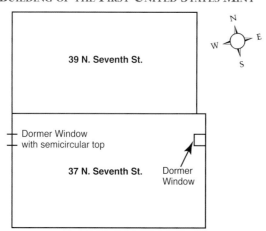

39 N. Seventh St.

Dormer Window with semicircular top

37 N. Seventh St.

Dormer Window

Front Building

All dimensions and features are taken directly from the Franklin Fire Insurance Company of Philadelphia 1837 insurance survey. Exact locations of the dormer windows are not specified in the survey, although only one of each is specified. The locations of the dormers are thus approximate.

Engraving depicting the front of the Middle Building, 1898.

was looking for a new home for his rapidly growing electric company. In 1895, he rented the building at 35 North Seventh Street (probably the one pictured in the 1854 photograph), to be his headquarters.[156] Over the ensuing decade, as his business continued to prosper, he outgrew this building, and moved into the modern four-story structure (probably the one pictured in the 1903 photograph) on the spot.[157] Finding that he needed more room still, his attention naturally fell on the tract to the north and east of number 35, the land still in the Kates family holdings, but which, more than a century before, comprised David Rittenhouse's three original lots. Frank Huling Stewart was about to become the "Master of the Mint," an act with profound consequences for the history of numismatics—and the art of numismatics—in the United States. The rest of this book will recount, for the first time, how this saga unfolded.

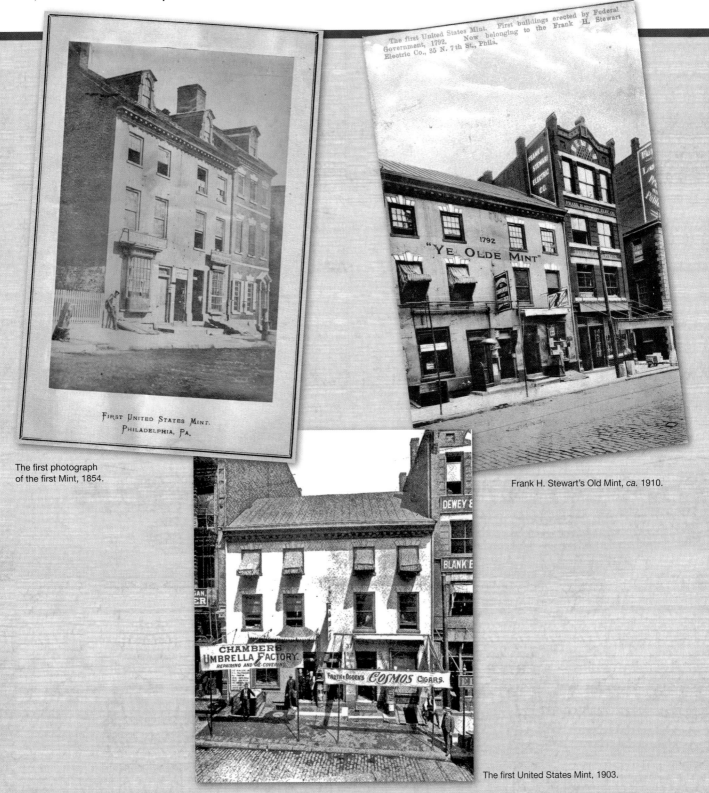

First United States Mint.
Philadelphia, Pa.

The first photograph of the first Mint, 1854.

The first United States Mint. First buildings erected by Federal Government, 1792. Now belonging to the Frank H. Stewart Electric Co., 35 N. 7th St., Phila.

Frank H. Stewart's Old Mint, ca. 1910.

The first United States Mint, 1903.

Cornerstone laying of the Stewart building, January 27, 1912. Holding the gavel is likely Wilfred Jordan, Independence Hall curator. To his left is Frank H. Stewart.

Chapter 4

The Frank H. Stewart Collection: Relics of the First United States Mint

Frank H. Stewart became the "Master of the Mint" on April 20, 1907, for on that day he purchased the old Mint property for the sum of $45,000.[1] By this time the old Mint was a stranger to public recollection. The Philadelphia *North American* observed that the buildings were "for the most part unnoticed and forgotten by passersby . . . occupied by various tenants for the last seventy-five years."[2] Most Philadelphia residents, the *North American* thought, mistakenly believed that the first Mint was actually at Chestnut and Juniper streets, this of course being the site of the second Mint which opened in 1833 and had been demolished only a few years previously, in 1903. Even the North Seventh Street locals were uninformed, as Stewart wrote in 1909:

> the people of the neighborhood in a great many instances were unaware of the fact that for a period of forty (40) years all of the United States coins were made so near at hand. Those who daily walked past the buildings had nothing to direct their attention to them.[3]

The Numismatist further weighed in, calling the buildings "for probably more than two generations unmarked and unrecognized in the business district of Philadelphia."[4] A trade magazine offered that "'Ye Olde Mint' has passed so far into the limbo of forgetfulness that outside of the present owners of the property few of the business men [sic] in its vicinity are aware of its identity."[5]

Devoid of public respect and blocking the path of almighty commerce, it was no surprise when the *North American* reported in September 1907 that "within a few days the first United States Mint will be demolished, to make room for an up-to-date building."[6] Though the *North American* headline suggested the imminent demise of the entire site, only the Rear Building was taken at first, while the Front and Middle buildings stood until 1911. Stewart was no trained archaeologist, but he did have some experience digging Indian sites in southern New Jersey, thus following in the footsteps of Montroville W. Dickeson, the 19th-century numismatist who likewise excavated Indian burial mounds.[7]

Within the numismatic community, no one knew what might be unearthed in the first Mint excavation, but the possibility of fortune piqued interest. Thomas Elder, the New York City coin dealer, met Stewart in person in Philadelphia and

71

later reminded Stewart to "not forget me if you come across any coins at the old mint. Hope you find some."[8] Farran Zerbe, president of the American Numismatic Association, and Edgar H. Adams, coin columnist of the *New York Sun*, also paid their respects.[9] Howland Wood, an ANA governor, met Stewart in Philadelphia.[10] T.L. Comparette, curator of the Mint Cabinet, received a personal tour of the old Mint from Stewart.[11] No doubt all were interested in first Mint relics, but the strongest "play" seems to have been made by one J.C. Mitchelson, a Connecticut numismatist. He first wrote to Stewart on November 16, 1908:

> Our mutual friend Mr. Nash of Hartford and I were talking today about coins. He gave me your Postal [unclear, probably a reference to a Frank H. Stewart Electric Co. postcard] with pictures of your building including the Old Mint which I have read so much about. I have been an ardent collector of coins and American Moneys ever since I was at Philadelphia in 1876 to attend the Centennial. . . . Since then I have been at Philadelphia almost yearly looking for coins. . . . If you have anything from the Old Mint any dies they used to make coins from or any good pieces in nice condition I would buy or exchange for them if you are interested. . . . I would like very much to get something that was used to make coins from the Old Mint.[12]

Stewart hadn't yet found such a die, but his time was coming.

FIRST MINT DIES

Coining dies are the Rosetta Stones of numismatics, keys to translation between the technology and the art of the engraver. They necessarily exist in minute proportion to surviving coins, some having been discarded as worn out scrap, others defaced at the end of their useful life in order to thwart unauthorized use. Information about dies is closely held, as described by R.W. Julian, a long-time denizen of the National Archives:

> There once existed a die record book covering 1844–1925. In 1963 I saw this book at the GSA [General Services Administration] in Philadelphia and made formal application at Mint Director Eva Adams' office to use it. I had a meeting with her assistant who indicated that I must be a front for a counterfeiting gang, as otherwise I would not have asked to use it. He also indicated that if I went to the trouble of getting a court order he would destroy the book immediately. In 1970, at my request, Mint Director Mary Brooks had her staff make a search for this volume but nothing was found.[13]

During Stewart's excavation of the Mint, most likely in 1911, a "die of the eagle side of a half dollar" was uncovered, and sent to the Secret Service in Washington "by request."[14] The lure of first Mint dies extended as far back as 1795, as Stewart noted in *History of the First United States Mint:*

> In 1795 an attempt was made to steal the Mint dies. William Hodgins and Charles McNear were arrested but escaped indictment because the evidence was insufficient.[15]

Montroville W. Dickeson, posing with an Indian.

The first United States Mint, from the *North American,* September 1907.

Apart from thievery and excavation, there are several discussions in the literature that describe how dies escaped the first Mint. The first of these was authored *ca.* 1860, probably by Montroville W. Dickeson. The account, found in a manuscript volume in the American Numismatic Society, was uncovered by Walter Breen:

> In digging out the rubbish from the cellar of the Mint which was destroyed in 1815 [likely referring the fire of January, 1816], a small vault was found under the pavement bricked up with the exception of a small hole, and tearing away the wall a number of dies were found in this inclosure, there were about one bushel, they were picked out by workmen and finally sold as old steel to a worker in this metal. Some time after their disposition Mr. James [sic] J. Mickley hearing of them endeavoured to obtain them, but most of them had been worked over, they being of the very best kind of steel, a number of them are now in his cabinet, among which is that very scarce number, the halfpenny of 1811.[16]

This account places Joseph Mickley, and by implication, Montroville W. Dickeson, "at the scene of the crime." We shall hear more from both. The second account was related by Charles K. Warner, a Philadelphia coin dealer, who told his story in the December 1910 issue of *The Numismatist*:

> My father, the late John S. Warner, who from 1823 to 1868 was the oldest established medallist in the United States, was well acquainted with a certain William Sellers who for many years conducted business of a silversmith in the old mint building. He occupied the first floor and a greater part of the basement. In the latter part of 1857 Mr. Sellers gave to my father a large number of old coin dies which were a part of a great lot of obverse and reverse dies for all the silver and copper denominations that Sellers found in the old building when he first occupied it years before. It was stated at the time that these were found among general rubbish when the basement was cleaned. Most of the dies were considerably rusted, chipped on the edges, or cracked across the face. My father, having no use for the old dies gave them to a particular friend of his, the then Chief Coiner of the mint [George K. Childs, from 1855 to 1861], which was then located in Chestnut Street near Broad.
>
> As a lad I frequently visited the old Mint building on errands to Mr. Sellers for my father and often played about the building with a son of Sellers, who was about my age. I well remember the old vault. I could have easily explored the vault, and no doubt could have found many things which, if preserved, would be of great interest today, but lad that I was, I had no interest in such things.[17]

Joseph J. Mickley, Philadelphia numismatist.

Howland Wood and T. Louis Comparette, first Mint visitors.

Charles K. Warner, June 1867,
auction sale catalog (rear cover).

Charles K. Warner store cards.

William Sellers was a cousin of George Escol Sellers, and the founder of William Sellers & Co., which, as Warner indicates, was a tenant of the Kates family in the old Mint buildings. Both of these accounts may refer to the same finding. Both make reference to a cellar vault and to "rubbish" in the basement. Conversely, the first account seems to date itself to the 1816 fire, while the second account clearly takes place after the Mint exited the premises in 1833. Also, the first account indicates that the dies were sold as scrap, while the second account indicates that they passed directly from Sellers to Warner and then back to the Mint. What is certain is that first Mint dies got into public hands, and that they were quite desirable to collectors. The matter remained quiet, or at least clandestine, until 1878.

In February of that year renowned collector Joseph J. Mickley passed away, and his estate made the decision to sell the first mint dies that remained in the Mickley cabinet. Curiously, the Mickley dies had not appeared in Woodward's 1867 sale of the principal part of his collection. The dies, apparently all from the first Mint, were thus consigned by the estate to Ebenezer Locke Mason Jr.'s sale of November 1878, and cataloged as follows:

> Lot 909 1806 Hub; *obv.*, United States Dime, *very good.*
>
> Lot 910 1806 Hub; *obv.*, United States Silver Twenty-five Cent Piece, *good.*
>
> Lot 911 1807 Hub; *obv.*, Half Eagle, *good.*
>
> Lot 912 1811 2 Hubs; *obv.* and *rev,* United States Half Cent; *rev.* slightly damaged on edge.
>
> Lot 913 1816 2 Hubs; *obv.* and *rev.* United States Cent, *fair condition.*
>
> Lot 914 1817 2 Hubs; *obv.,* and *rev.* United States Cent, *good condition.*
>
> Lot 915 1820 1 Hub; *obv.*, Half Eagle, *good.*
>
> Lot 916 1 Hub; *rev.*, United States Twenty-five Cent Piece, about 1820.
>
> Lot 917 Miscellaneous Lot Dies and Hubs; *obvs.* and *revs.* of American coins, 8 pieces, *broken, and in poor condition.*

Although Mason cataloged the items as hubs, O.C. Bosbyshell, the Mint coiner, reported that they were in fact dies.[18] The Mint got wind of the sale, "acquired" the dies, and is said to have destroyed them on October 19, 1878.[19] The *American Journal of Numismatics* took a dim view of the affair, and reported in its January, 1879, issue:

> The statement that the dies, hubs, & c., of U.S. Coins, advertised for sale with the Mickley Collection, were seized by the United States authorities,

has given rise to a great deal of comment. We have received from a gentleman in Philadelphia [Robert Coulton Davis] the following account of the affair.

A few days previous to the sale, the United States authorities claimed the above, viz: Some 20 obverse and reverse dies of the U.S. Coinage, mostly in a damaged and corroded condition, the same having been condemned by the Mint authorities above "half a century ago," and as tradition says was the custom in those days, "sold for old iron," and as then we have grown more *artful*, and it has been deemed politic under existing laws, that the whole multitude of dated dies should be annually destroyed in the presence of three designated officers of the Mint. In the above described lots in the catalogue, there was not a complete *pair* of obverse and reverse dies. Even the obverse die of the half-cent of 1811 was muled with the reverse die of a different year. We cannot conceive by what authority the government, after making sale of its "refuse material," could seize upon the same property without tendering some compensation. There is scarcely a numismatist in the United States, but who is aware of the existence and whereabouts of similar dies, and who is also aware of the many "re-strikes,"—*known to be such*—being made from the dies, say of the 1804 cent, the 1811 half-cent, and of the 1823 cent, *outside* of the Mint.

Philadelphia, December, 1878. "COULTON."

From what we have seen in the public prints in reference to this matter, we infer that the government authorities were somewhat hasty in their action, and claimed the property without first satisfying themselves as to the ownership. No one would for a moment suspect Mr. Mickley of any wrong doing in the matter. The affair was settled, we believe, by a payment to the family of the estimated value of the dies, which were then presented to the Mint, and subsequently destroyed.[20]

"Coulton's" recollection of dies "sold for old iron," echoes the Dickeson description of "sold as old steel," and as Dickeson lived until 1882,[21] it is possible that the two Philadelphia collectors had discussed the subject. As for the seizure of the dies, the copy of the Mickley catalog at the American Numismatic Society contains a notation around the lots in question indicating "Sold to U.S. Mint," with no indication of the price paid.

Though the dies were surrendered to the Mint, it was Mickley who perhaps had the last laugh, for he may have used the dies to create restrikes of certain issues. Mickley was quite familiar with such esoterica, as described by the Philadelphia collector John Story Jenks in 1908:

Mr. Mickley was a very old friend of mine and a very dear man. He . . . had excellent facilities for getting pieces, being friendly with the officials of the Mint, and thus obtained coins otherwise unobtainable. . . .

He had a valuable collection of old coins. Mr. Mickley's customers were his old friends, and they would assemble on Sunday afternoons and he would show them his coins. He had them in nearly every drawer and closet in the house, and a great many were lost in this way.[22]

The 1811 half cent restrikes, probably executed by Mickley in the late 1850s per R.W. Julian,[23] are today highly prized and have even attained the status of a listing in the *Guide Book of United States Coins*, albeit as "unofficial restrikes." Similarly, examples of 1804 and 1823 large cents, also "unofficial restrikes" per the Red Book, seem to have appeared on the scene about the same time. The coiners of the 1823s could not help themselves, and struck off a few examples in silver while they were at it. The 1810 large cent, as noted by "Coulton," is additionally found in restrike form.[24] *Pièces de caprice* seemed to trade openly, such as these two examples in tin appearing in Woodward's sale of June, 1883:

Lot 804–1804 half eagle in tin, struck outside of the mint; from genuine dies. [Realized 12 cents]

Lot 805–1804 Cent; obv from a genuine die; rev. from a die in the [eighteen-]twenties; struck outside the mint; tin, fine. [Realized 10 cents]

The 1804 and 1823 large cents restrikes, while widely appreciated in the current era, created consternation in their own time, as evidenced by this note written by Pennsylvania dealer Charles Steigerwalt in the April 1907 issue of *The Numismatist*:

A certain kind of 1804 and 1823 cents have appeared in sale catalogs for years as "Mint Restrikes." The recent cataloguers may be excused on the plea of ignorance, but when these rank counterfeits are sold by those who have been doing so for years, it is time collectors knew their true character.

While at a recent sale, the lacking information regarding the 1823 was given by an aged collector, who told how, years ago, he had found the dies in New York, probably sold with old iron from the mint, brought them to Philadelphia, had a collar

1811 half cent, Mickley Restrike.

made, which was lacking, and the coins struck by a man named Miller on 7th St., that city.

Later, the dies came into possession of a then leading dealer there and, when his store was sold out in 1885 [the "leading dealer" is likely John W. Haseltine, who moved from Philadelphia to New York in that year], the writer finding them among a lot of old dies purchased, they were at once destroyed so effectually that no more will come from that source. These coins never saw the Mint, and are counterfeits pure and simple.

It was supposed the 1804 came from the same source as the 1823, but the originator of those disclaimed any knowledge of the 1804. An effort was made in a recent sale catalogue to throw an air of mystery around the 1804. That is simply ridiculous. The obverse has been identified as an 1803, but as that date was too common, a crude 4 was cut over the 3 and a reverse of the period after the fraction was omitted, probably of about 1816 or later, was used in striking those abominations. By whom struck is unknown, but it was a period long after, when the dies were rusty, and certainly not in the Mint.[25]

Apart from early cent dies, the Mickley estate also possessed a John Adams medal die which presented certain problems for the Mint, for their own records proved that it was privately held! "COULTON," collector Robert Coulton Davis, picked up the story in the *American Journal of Numismatics* in 1879:

Immediately upon the announcement that this die would be sold in the "Mickley Collection," the Government caused the history of the die to be investigated, presuming that as Medals struck from the die had been executed at the Mint, and that the reverse was taken from the series of the Presidential or Peace Medals, it was government property. In [the] course of investigation, "The List and History of the National Medal Dies," which had been kept by Mr. Franklin Peale, Chief Coiner of the United States Mint for nearly twenty years, was examined, when the following entry was found in his handwriting, under date of 1841:—"There is an obverse die engraved by Fürst, with the Portrait of John Adams. It is the property of Mr. Adam Eckfeldt and in his possession. It is a good likeness, and is very desirable to complete the series of Presidential Medals." This being conclusive evidence that it was the original property of Mr. Eckfeldt, afterwards coming into the possession of his nephew, Mr. George Eckfeldt, (die-hardener, U.S. Mint,) after his death sold by his (George's) son-in-law, Mr. John Pedrick [sic, Pedrick is correct], to the late Joseph J. Mickley, there was but one course to pursue, and the Government entered into negotiation for its purchase from the estate of the decedent, which was done.[26]

R.W. Julian, writing in *Medals of the United States Mint*, put the price paid at $40.[27]

Besides the Adams medal, an obverse die for Peale's Museum token (Julian UN-22, UN-23) also seems to have escaped the confines of the first U.S. Mint. Featuring a bust of Charles Willson Peale (the father of the Franklin Peale, above), the piece served as an admission token to Peale's Museum, located in Independence Hall. The museum, opened in 1786, housed all manner of scientific and natural curiosities, even a coin collection, though unfortunately today no catalog of this very early American collection is known. The token dies may have rightfully belonged to the Peale family, but in any event, the Peale obverse, now with severe die breaks, was muled with a Washington bust, a "mint sport" probably executed by Robert Lovett Jr., *ca.* 1860. One impression is known, in white medal, cataloged as Baker J-220.[28]

The disposition of the Peale die is unknown, but much later, in 1962, more trouble arose with the government in regards to another first Mint die, this time a Capped Bust dime reverse of the year 1814. First reported by Walter Breen in 1966,[29] David Davis and others related the full story in their standard work, *Early United States Dimes 1796–1837*:

It is alleged that the reverse die was sold by the Mint as scrap in the 1830s, probably at the time of its move to a new location. It was held by unknown individuals until 1962, when it was acquired by Robert Bashlow, a New York City dealer. He took the reverse die to the Kirkwood firm of Edinburgh, Scotland and had 536 impressions struck in various metals, some with a fantasy obverse and some uniface on larger than normal planchets of varying thicknesses. Upon returning to the States, Bashlow was detained by Customs, forced to surrender both the die and all of the impressions, and fined $100.00. Everything was destroyed by Treasury agents, despite pleas from the curator of the Smithsonian [Vladimir Clain-Stefanelli] to save this historic die. Recently [this, written in 1984], a uniface specimen on a white metal alloy planchet, weighing 6.6 grams and measuring 26.5mm in diameter, has surfaced. Reportedly, it was obtained in Scotland from a man who acknowledged seeing a handful of others in that country.[30]

The 1814 die, "held by unknown individuals" between 1814 and 1962, suffered a fate similar to two pattern dies that survived in the collection of the Boston Numismatic Society until seized by the Secret Service about 1954.[31]

Apart from the genuine article, a privately made die has masqueraded as a first Mint product. Montroville W. Dickeson, author of the first comprehensive guide to U.S. coinage (1859), chanced upon a revenue stamp die depicting an eagle perched on a rock, and, mistaking it for an early Mint pattern, executed a small number of restrikes using a newly produced obverse: TRIAL PIECE

/ DESIGNED FOR UNITED STATES / CENT. / 1792. Dickeson made extensive use of the Mickley collection for his 1859 work, *The American Numismatical Manual*, and Joseph Mickley in return, who possessed *real* dies of the first Mint, thought enough of the Dickeson fantasy to acquire one of the restrikes. W. Elliot Woodward cataloged in the piece in 1867 as follows: "Pattern Cent, 1792; eagle on a rock; rev, 'Trial Piece,' &c., said to be from an original die; copper proof, scarce." The public was not fooled, bidding this piece up to 50¢, while an unquestioned pattern cent of the same year sold for $155.[32] B. Max Mehl eventually came into possession of Dickeson's "wishful thinking" obverse die and used it as a paperweight. Later, a young Q. David Bowers auctioned the same die along with one of the trial strikes.[33] Both were purchased by a Mr. Weber in San Francisco, but lost in an insured mail shipment.

Interestingly, while the Dickeson "pattern" dies were a complete fantasy, the Dickeson eagle was also muled with a genuine obverse die of an 1805 quarter, the Browning-2 variety. This concoction most recently traded hands in 1997, at a price of about nineteen hundred dollars.[34] Other bizarre bust quarter mulings are known, including an 1806 Browning-5 obverse die mated with an 1800 Sheldon-207 large cent reverse die, as well as an 1818 Browning-2 obverse die paired with an 1818 Newcomb-8 large cent reverse die.[35] The last is particularly intriguing as the *tout ensemble* was overstruck on an 1860 Liberty Seated quarter. As the latter piece sold at auction in 1862, it seems possible that much of the restrike and muling mayhem discussed above occurred during the period 1860–1862. Also known are two other bust quarter dies that somehow escaped the first Mint—an 1821 Browning-1 obverse die, in addition to an incomplete reverse die of the period 1820–1828.[36] The Judd pattern reference similarly makes multiple references to "private restrikes" executed from first Mint dies.[37]

Certain first Mint dies today are preserved in the collection of the American Numismatic Society, which holds an 1803 $10 gold obverse die (apparently unused as no extant varieties match), 1805 Overton-102 half dollar obverse die, 1806 half dollar obverse die used for Overton-123 and Overton-124, 1805 Browning-2 quarter obverse die, and an 1818 Newcomb-9 large cent obverse die.

The American Numismatic Association collection includes an 1820(?) half eagle obverse die, as well as the dies used for the 1823 large cent restrike, which are currently on loan to that institution.[38]

Other Mint dies, not of the first Mint but from others, remain extant in a variety of institutional collections. The Fort Jones Museum in California, for example, possesses an obverse die for the 1878 quarter, and two obverse dies for the 1878 trade dollar. The three dies, all cancelled, were acquired by the museum in 1947 and appear to have

Peale's Museum admission tokens. The numbered token is thought to have been a permanent pass, while the ADMIT THE BEARER variety would have been sold and redeemed on a daily basis.

Dickeson pattern cent, from the Frank H. Stewart collection at Independence Hall.

originated from the family of John Daggett, one-time superintendent of the San Francisco Mint.[39] Elsewhere, the American Numismatic Society holds cancelled dies for an 1883 Carson City Morgan dollar,[40] while Larry Briggs in 1991 presented a set of 1872 Carson City quarter dies, unused but cancelled, in his standard work on the seated quarter series.[41] In 2010, an 1885 Carson City $10 obverse die, with two associated splashers, appeared on the market.[42]

In 1969, a number of dies escaped the San Francisco Mint as scrap metal. The story is captured in 1972 correspondence from Mary Brooks, director of the Mint:

> The dies that had been mutilated in 1969 were sold by GSA [General Services Administration] to the highest bidder as scrap steel. The buyer was approached by a coin dealer who called himself "The Little Mint of San Francisco." The dies were sold to the dealer [Wayne Pratali] who advertised them for sale to collectors. We had the United States Secret Service check the dies at the "Little Mint of San Francisco." It was reported by Secret Service that they were not in contravention of law and all were sold to the public. There have been no sales of dies to anyone since, the dies being completely melted and cast into a form that would make their sale as scrap perfectly appropriate.[43]

Apparently questions kept arriving at Ms. Brooks' desk, for in 1973 she clarified further:

> Your letter of January 16, 1973, addressed to the United States Secret Service, has been referred to this office for reply. You have enclosed a clipping from [the] January 3, 1973 issue of *Coin World*, which contains an advertisement by the New England Rare Coin Galleries, Framingham, Massachusetts, offering for sale items there described as "Genuine United States Mint Coin Dies."
>
> In later 1968, mutilated die bodies, remaining from the defacement and destruction of worn or otherwise retired dies at the San Francisco Mint, were included in scrap steel sold by the Mint through the General Services Administration. GSA sold it as public sale. A West Coast scrap metal dealer purchased it, and in turn sold the included mutilated die bodies to a West Coast dealer. In turn, that dealer is said to have sold some of the mutilated die bodies to other dealers throughout the United States. Apparently the advertisement you cite is for some of those items.
>
> When the items were first offered for sale to individuals in San Francisco in January 1969, the matter was investigated by the Department. The scrap steel die bodies were examined by a Treasury representa-

1803 $10 gold obverse die (image reversed), ANS collection.

1806 half dollar obverse die (Overton-123 and Overton-124, image reversed), ANS collection.

1805 half dollar obverse die (Overton-102, image reversed), ANS collection.

1805 quarter dollar obverse die (Browning-2, image reversed), ANS collection.

tive, who concluded that some of them had been defaced and destroyed and that none were usable for stamping coins. The scrap metal die bodies had been mutilated to such an extent (by grinding off and them puddling with a welder's torch) that private possession of them presented no threat to the Treasury's responsible interest in the matter—the detection and suppression of counterfeiting. Since this occurrence, regulations provide that the scrap steel remaining from die destruction be delivered under security into a steel melting furnace and there melted.[44]

Former mints continue to give up secrets, as Carson City dies were unearthed in 1999 and today reside in the collection of the Nevada State Museum. Indeed, the old Carson City Mint building itself belongs to the Nevada State Museum, a connection which proved most fortuitous when a landscaper working the old Mint grounds located a cache of dies, about 100, in a "shallow hole." A ground conductivity study, searching for ferrous material, later uncovered the mother lode. As of 2003, several hundred additional dies had been excavated from this pit, adjacent to the former site of the Carson City Mint black-

smith shop. A number of "test strikes" from these dies have been made in various media, in some cases raffled at the museum's annual coin show. These include impressions of an 1876-CC seated half dollar, 1876-CC half eagle, and others. *Coin World* reported in 2003 that "a canceled Morgan die was used to produce about 100 money clips at one of the coin shows. Production was stopped after concerns were raised about whether the die might be about to bend or break."[45]

As for Stewart's half dollar die of the first Mint, there is no indication that it was ever returned by the government, or that Stewart, unlike Mickley's estate, received compensation for the die. Stewart was 70 years too late to find the Warner hoard of abandoned first Mint dies, which like the Carson City group, might well have waited for Stewart had they been discarded into a pit, instead of a cellar. Conversely, Stewart was about 70 years too early to deal with the reasonable Mary Brooks, who had little problem with Mint dies in public hands as long as no counterfeiting threat existed. Ever the marketer, Stewart surely would have loved to have made a few restrikes, perhaps with the "Old Mint" logo of the Frank H. Stewart Electric Co. on one side of the coin.

1818 large cent obverse die (Newcomb-9, image reversed), ANS collection.

1823 large cent dies (N-2 obverse, Sheldon-293 reverse), images reversed, currently on loan to the ANA.

Early half eagle obverse die (image reversed), possibly 1820, although the die is sufficiently corroded to prevent a definite attribution. ANA collection.

Cancelled dies (image reversed) for an 1884 Carson City Morgan dollar.

Marketers themselves, the U.S. Mint has of late gotten in on the act, selling approximately 3,000 dies associated with the 1996 Olympic Games in Atlanta. Collectors snapped up cancelled dies for commemorative silver dollars and half eagles, with good detail remaining, at an issue price of $49.95. The Mint stock was exhausted after only eight days. A few years later, California dealer Fred Weinberg reported that specimens were selling for as much as $1,000, and that he could only obtain "a fraction of the dies he could place with serious collectors."[46] Currently, the U.S. Mint continues to sell dies that have been completely defaced, in order "to prevent unauthorized reproduction of U.S. coinage."[47] Priced at $34.95, a smooth, blank die is delivered along with an example of a coin struck by such a die, and a numbered "Certificate of Authenticity," presumably sufficient documentation to protect present collectors from future authorities.

First Mint Timber

While Stewart was not allowed his first Mint die, there remained much to be reclaimed from the demolition. Modern construction sites in the big city are liberally draped in protective plywood curtains, but 100 years ago it was not so, and certainly not at 37 and 39 North Seventh Street in Philadelphia. Stewart's demolition was wide open to the public, who were free to wander the site in search of treasure. Stewart thought enough to capture a photo for posterity. "People from off street at noon time—digging for relics," he wrote on the reverse.[48] To this pictorial record Stewart added the following commentary:

> Every noontime, while the workmen were eating their luncheon, a crowd of boys would search the dirt for relics, and the finds made by these boys will unquestionably be saved by them. Scores of pieces of iron, brick, stone and wood were taken away and curiosity was unhampered to the fullest extent.[49]

Despite Stewart's prediction that the various bits would "unquestionably be saved," few such finds have survived. Today the most widely known relics of the first U.S. Mint are various items constructed from first Mint timber. During the demolition Stewart noted that he saved "some heavy pine timbers and oak joists, all from the coinage building,"[50] and further that "a great many requests for old timbers have been granted."[51] More specifically, Stewart salvaged the roof supports of the Middle Building, as explained in a photograph caption:

> Taking out the . . . thing made of two planks bolted together. . . . This supported the roof of the coinage [Middle] building and took the place of the original which was burned off. The end was left in wall after being sawed off and I saved it to make souvenirs. It shows strong evidence of fire.[52]

Further clarification was offered regarding the fire:

The first building back of the Seventh street [Front] buildings, which I have always called the coinage building . . . was . . . seriously damaged by fire, but when I do not know. It at first had a peaked roof, but after the fire an inclined flat roof replaced it. When it was demolished an immense square timber that had been burned off entirely was found imbedded in the North wall at its center where the floor joists of the attic or third floor were originally placed.[53]

With timber in hand, Stewart set about putting it to work. A beam donated to Independence Hall was evidently quite a hit with the public, as the curator mentioned in correspondence to Stewart:

> We would also like to have a case made for the exhibition of the large beam which you presented to us. We find that in exhibiting it, as heretofore, on a pair of wooden trusses that the visitors have from time to time chipped pieces from it to carry away as souvenirs. While it is too large in its present size to have a case made for it, with your permission we would like to cut a section of it to be placed in a case. . . .[54]

Stewart approved the "rightsizing" of the timber in a letter dated the following day.[55] Today a section of timber, exhibiting fire damage, is on display at the fourth U.S. Mint in Philadelphia, on loan from Independence Hall. Apart from the raw beam, a number of other pieces from First Mint timber are known, including two chairs and a bench, all similarly styled. Stewart commented in 1913:

> The bench and chairs . . . were made of oak joists from the Coinage building. These timbers were so hard that the cabinetmaker claimed extra compensation for his work. One hundred and twenty years of seasoning gave the wood an obstinacy which even a novice would suspect if he were to feel the weight of the furniture. The bench has a suitably engraved brass plate screwed on the top piece. These three pieces of unique furniture are now part of our office equipment.[56]

Stewart also found pine, which he apparently discarded. "I intended to save some of the big timbers in the basement of the coinage [Middle] building," he wrote, "but found them to be yellow pine."[57] As for the obstinate oak, it had already made its presence felt some years earlier, as Stewart recalled in *History of the First United States Mint*:

> After I established my business at the Northeast corner of Seventh and Filbert Streets (35 North Seventh street) in 1895, there were several serious fires in the neighborhood and nearly every instance of flying embers set fire to the shingle roof of the Old Mint [Front] building facing Seventh street. The last time, the firemen damaged the roof beyond repair, which damage I think was intentional on their part.

The owner of the building then decided to change the mansard peaked roof to an inclined flat roof, but when the workmen started to saw off the century old oak rafters they found it too difficult, which resulted in placing a new tin roof over the damaged one with its original rafters intact.[58]

Stewart offered one of the chairs to Independence Hall, but this gift was apparently not consummated.[59] The location of the two chairs is today unknown, although based on a surviving image they appear quite similar in construction to the bench. Harry Forman and Catherine Bullowa, longtime Philadelphia coin dealers, were both unaware of these pieces.[60] The bench resides at the Gloucester County (New Jersey) Historical Society. Affixed is a brass plate with the inscription:

> This Bench was made from the original timber taken from the Coinage Building of the First United States Mint, erected 1792, and presented to Frank H. Stewart, Christmas, 1911, by the officers and employees of the Frank H. Stewart Electric Company.

Stewart commissioned two other souvenirs at the same time: paperweights and gavels. "About two dozen gavels and the same quantity of paper weights made of the same wood as the bench and chairs were made for us by Mr. James Barton, of Camden, N.J.," Stewart wrote. "These rare mementos were nearly all distributed at the cornerstone laying [of Stewart's "Old Mint" building in 1912] to those participating and a few special guests."[61] At least three of the paperweights today reside in the collection of the Stewart Room at Rowan University in Glassboro, New Jersey.[62] Another example was placed with the Salem County (New Jersey) Historical Society, which acknowledged receipt of the item on March 10, 1914, more than two years after Stewart's cornerstone laying.[63] Yet another was given to Jacob B. Eckfeldt of the Philadelphia Mint (Adam Eckfeldt's grandson), and was on display in the Eckfeldt home as of 1915.[64] The Gloucester County (New Jersey) Historical Society also retains an example.[65]

Of the gavels, one is currently located in the display case of the Stewart Room, at Rowan University, a second is on display at the fourth Mint in Philadelphia,[66] and a third was placed in the cornerstone of Stewart's "Old Mint" building, of which more will be said later. A fourth

Section of fire-damaged timber, preserved by Frank H. Stewart.

Roof support from the Middle Building, facing east.

Frank H. Stewart's snapshot, depicting the public at work following the Mint demolition. Scaffolding from the Seventh Street frontage is seen to the left.

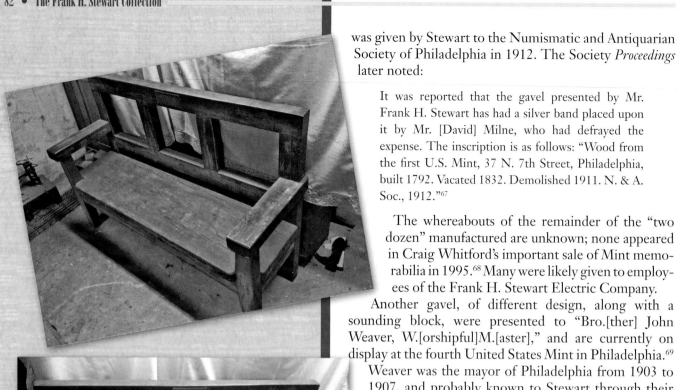

First Mint timber bench, currently in storage at the Gloucester County (New Jersey) Historical Society.

First Mint timber chairs, as depicted in Stewart's *Our New Home and Old Times,* 1913.

was given by Stewart to the Numismatic and Antiquarian Society of Philadelphia in 1912. The Society *Proceedings* later noted:

It was reported that the gavel presented by Mr. Frank H. Stewart has had a silver band placed upon it by Mr. [David] Milne, who had defrayed the expense. The inscription is as follows: "Wood from the first U.S. Mint, 37 N. 7th Street, Philadelphia, built 1792. Vacated 1832. Demolished 1911. N. & A. Soc., 1912."[67]

The whereabouts of the remainder of the "two dozen" manufactured are unknown; none appeared in Craig Whitford's important sale of Mint memorabilia in 1995.[68] Many were likely given to employees of the Frank H. Stewart Electric Company.

Another gavel, of different design, along with a sounding block, were presented to "Bro.[ther] John Weaver, W.[orshipful]M.[aster]," and are currently on display at the fourth United States Mint in Philadelphia.[69] Weaver was the mayor of Philadelphia from 1903 to 1907, and probably known to Stewart through their Masonic association.

Beyond these Stewart-flavored first Mint timber items, a second grouping of first Mint timber objects appeared on the scene *ca.* 1959–1960, with a provenance stretching back to the demolition of the first Mint. In a December 7, 1962, article in *Coin World,* George B. Cucore, who was a woodworker in addition to being a numismatist, told the story as follows:

In the year 1911 J.P. Hallahan, a noted builder from the City of Philadelphia, with permission from the owner, Frank H. Stewart, removed pieces of timber from the [Mint] building. These pieces of timber were saved and preserved by his son, Dr. John D. Hallahan of Media, Pa. Utilizing this piece of historical timber, Mr. Hallahan had a replica copied from the original gavel that had been in constant use at Carpenter's Hall since 1774. The turning of this gavel was done by an inmate of the Eastern State Penitentiary. It was later presented to President Eisenhower with an inscription that read: "To President Eisenhower From a Fellow Angler, John P. Hallahan, Lansdowne, Pennsylvania, Gavel of Timber from First United States Mint, Philadelphia, Pennsylvania."[70]

Cucore's account is confirmed by a story in *The Numismatist* from November 1960, which described "a beam removed with permission of the owner [Stewart] in 1911 by John P. Hallahan, a Philadelphia builder. His son . . . gave a piece of the joist to George B. Cucore."[71] This was not Cucore's only source of first Mint timber, for he recalled:

In April 1960, the Philadelphia Coin Club was holding its monthly meeting at the Benjamin Franklin Hotel and a large piece of the timber from the old Mint was exhibited by John Harris, a member of the club. This aroused quite a discussion and the question "What can be done with this historical piece of timber?" was the main topic. After many pros and cons the writer was instructed to create a gavel and a sounding board for the use of the Philadelphia Coin Club. The original bark was still attached, and after sawing through the center of the beam, I counted the growth rings which totaled 190.[72]

Warren A. Lapp, M.D., writing in 1969, confirms the essentials of Cucore's account, although Lapp gives the name of the wood donor as "John Harrison," and says that the gavel was presented to the Philadelphia Coin Club on March 17, 1959.[73] Cucore made other first Mint relics, as well:

Gavel from first Mint timber, Stewart Room at Rowan University.

The First United States Mint
1792–1832
This paper-weight was made from wood removed from the mint when it was demolished in 1907. At this time Mr. Stewart offered the building to the city of Philadelphia to be removed to another site as a museum and shrine, but he was unsuccessful. However, measurements and photographs were made.

First Mint timber paperweight, Stewart Room at Rowan University. The reverse is marked "Old Mint Wood 1792 1911," probably in Stewart's hand.

After completing the gavel for the Philadelphia Coin Club, the writer had the pleasure of making and presenting gavels and sounding boards from the same piece of oak to the following coin clubs: Delaware County Coin Club, American Numismatic Association, Middle Atlantic Numismatic Association. If you attend any meeting held by the above organizations you will hear [in] the sound of the gavel and sounding board the tones which are the "Echoes of Ye Olde Mint."[74]

Cucore was well-qualified to create the wooden relics, for he was a manufacturer of wooden patterns for steel castings, based in Lansdowne, Pennsylvania.[75] Of the four gavels and sounding boards that Cucore crafted, only the gavel belonging to the American Numismatic Association can be traced today, and that one is missing its sounding board.[76] It was donated to the American Numismatic Association at its 1960 Boston convention. An attached engraved plate reads:

THIS GAVEL AND SOUNDING BOARD MADE OF TIMBER TAKEN FROM THE FIRST UNITED STATES MINT BUILDING IN PHILADELPHIA ARE HEREBY PRESENTED TO THE AMERICAN NUMISMATIC ASSOCIATION BY THE PHILADELPHIA COIN CLUB, 1960.[77]

In addition to the gavels, a piece of scrap was preserved from the Cucore shop, cataloged by Craig Whitford in 1995:

Masonic block and gavel of first Mint timber, presented to Philadelphia Mayor John Weaver.

Piece of wood, 1 3/4" x 6 1/4", from the original U.S. Mint building . . . Scrap from George Cucore's shop where he made gavels from blocks, c. 1959. . . . With a letter, signed by past ANA president Arthur Sipe related to this relic.[78]

A second Cucore scrap seems to have passed through the hands of Alexander Kaptik. Kaptik, like Sipe, was a member of the Philadelphia Coin Club in the 1960s.[79] Eric Newman, the St. Louis collector well known for his studies of early American numismatics, reported the Kaptik scrap, which is accompanied by a typewritten card that indicates "Cross section of the Original Beam from the First United States Mint at 7th and Filbert Streets, Philadelphia / Gift of Alexander Kaptik."[80]

Gavel from first Mint timber, ANA collection.

Cross section of oak beam from the First Mint.

Paperknife from first Mint timber, fashioned by Cora Frieman.

Frank H. Stewart Electric Company ruler.

Included in the set of first Mint timber items is a letter opener, referred to as a "paper knife" at the time of its construction. Cora Frieman, of Terre Haute, Indiana, first contacted Stewart in December, 1909, requesting any relic of Stewart's choosing for her personal collection.[81] Stewart evidently complied with the request, for in February of the following year Ms. Frieman acknowledged receiving a block of timber.[82] The relic came full circle in May, 1910, when Frieman sent the "paper knife" to Stewart. The letter of transmittal, along with the knife, is preserved in the Stewart Room at Rowan University:

> Dear and Kind Sir:
> The piece of timber from the "Ye Olde Mint" which you sent me some months ago I had shaved into thin sticks, and from one of them I made the paper knife which I am sending you by registered mail. I did all the work myself even the lettering, and you can see that I am not an expert at such work. However I feel sure that you will appreciate it and trust that you may place it on your office desk or with your collection of relics from the old mint. If not too much trouble I would like to hear from you as to whether you get it all right. With my best wishes to you I am,
> Very Respectfully yours,
> Cora Frieman[83]

Another item of first Mint timber was similarly constructed for Stewart as a gift. John McDowell, carpenter and one-time tenant of the Middle Building of the first Mint, presented a picture frame to Stewart sometime before February, 1915. McDowell took great interest in the Mint property, and we shall hear more from him later.[84] Like much of the first Mint timber, the location of Stewart's picture frame is today unknown.

Apparently Stewart's picture frame was not unique, for McDowell's friend Ben R. Browne recalled, "One of the last things he [McDowell] was working on were picture frames made from the original oak girders of the first Mint."[85]

A final candidate for inclusion in the first Mint timber fraternity is a wooden ruler used as a promotional item by the Stewart Electric Company. The address given on the ruler is 35 North Seventh Street, thus dating the item prior to the construction of Stewart's Old Mint building at 37–39 North Seventh. While it has been speculated that this item might be constructed of first mint timber, no documentary evidence has been located to support this theory. In light of the difficulty in fashioning first Mint timber artifacts, it seems more likely that the ruler originated with an advertising house, customized for promotional purposes. Further, the ruler is thought to be maple, not oak or pine as Stewart mentioned.[86] In any case, Stewart was likely pleased with his first Mint timber creations, and later was involved in the distribution of other wooden artifacts, fashioned from the "Tatum Oak," in conjunction with the Gloucester County Historical Society.[87]

MORE RELICS

Apart from certain first Mint timber, a doorsill of the first U.S. Mint survived the demolition. As Stewart noted, "if any relic hunter had wanted some things which had felt the tread of Washington they could have been had for the expense of carting them away. . . . John C. Curry, D.D.S., of Woodbury, New Jersey, took away to the lawn of his residence the doorsill of the middle doorway of the Seventh Street front building."[88] Curry's son in turn donated it to the Gloucester County Historical Society in 1960.[89] At the same time the Delaware Valley Coin Club of Woodbury commissioned a bronze marker inscribed

"DOORSILL FROM FIRST / UNITED STATES MINT / ERECTED 1792 / DEMOLISHED 1911." The marker and doorsill remain with the Gloucester Society to the present day, where the doorsill has resumed its former duties as a footstep, into the Society's library.

Stewart, of course, dug in other sites besides the first Mint, looking for information anywhere it could be found. In the process he struck up a friendship with the Jacob B. Eckfeldt family. Jacob was the grandson of chief coiner Adam Eckfeldt and represented the third generation of the family to serve the U.S. Mint. All told, the family worked in the Mint for an uninterrupted string of 130 years, with Jacob B. himself putting in over 60. His service had started on April 15, 1865, a "memorable" date according to his wife, for President Lincoln passed away the same day.[90] Stewart attended Eckfeldt's 50th anniversary celebration in 1915, and was invited to the 60th.[91] Jacob B. possessed tongs and a shovel of the first U.S. Mint, and two chairs besides.[92] Today the whereabouts of the tongs and shovel are unknown, while one of the chairs was reported in the family as of 2007.[93] Unrelated to Eckfeldt was yet another chair of the first Mint, said to be in the family of Patterson DuBois, who along with his father, William E. Dubois, was an assayer in the Mint.[94]

Doorsill of the first U.S. Mint, Gloucester County Historical Society library.

50th anniversary silver cup presented to Jacob B. Eckfeldt, 1915, Eckfeldt family collection.

Stewart located also a number of test cups in "one of the wells that had been filled," "mixed with . . . a lot of large and small broken crucibles."[95] Fire-resistant vessels formed of calcined bone, the test cups were—and still are—used in the assaying process, allowing metal to be heated to a very high temperature at which point base metals separate. Multiple examples of these test cups remain in the Stewart collection at Rowan University in Glassboro, New Jersey, and a number were donated by Stewart to Independence Hall.[96] A Philadelphia journalist, touring the third Mint about 1915, explained the bone cups further:

> In a neat little row of furnaces set into a tiled wall I was shown some queer little cups heating to 1700 degrees in a rosy swirl of fire. These little "cupels," as they call them, are made of compressed bone-ash and are used to absorb the baser metals in an alloy. Their peculiar merit is that at the required temperature they absorb all the copper, lead, or whatever other base metal there may be and leave in the cup only the gold and silver. Then the gold and silver mixture is placed in nitric acid, which takes out all the silver and leaves only the globule of pure gold. The matter that puzzles the lay observer is, how do you find these things out in the first place?[97]

A boot scraper was located alongside the steps of the Middle Building; Stewart speculated that Washington himself had made use of it. Recovered on August 14, 1911, this drew the attention of the local media, which reported that "it is, without doubt, the one used by every celebrated personage who visited the place."[98] The scraper was donated to Independence Hall and is currently on loan to the fourth U.S. Mint in Philadelphia and there displayed. Other miscellaneous items included bricks, a door lock of the Middle Building, and a set of iron bars to protect a basement window facing Seventh Street. The iron bars were returned by Independence Hall to Stewart in 1920, considered too large for display purposes.[99] Their location is today unknown. Stewart also preserved a large number of small bits, including nails, bolts, hooks, and pins, all of which were donated to Independence Hall.[100]

Interestingly, Stewart played "finder's keepers" with the excavation crews, allowing them to sell scrap materials on the side, while rewarding them for the more interesting finds. Stewart told the story later:

> Pieces of sheet lead evidently placed to make the floors tight in certain places and other metal scrap were sold by the workmen for their own benefit to the ever present junkmen . . . I stood around as the work progressed for a period of four weeks and when a coin or planchet was found I got it by liberal use of modern money which was unquestioned at the grocery store.[101]

The tale reveals Stewart's character, for the enterprising businessman might have rightfully claimed everything for himself. Stewart worked hard but was not hard-nosed.

CORNERSTONES OF THE UNITED STATES MINT

Relics come in multiple flavors. Some, like Stewart's boot scraper, are organic parts of an archaeological site, ordinary items indicative of their milieu. Cornerstone relics are quite different—deliberately cached and reflecting the ceremonial intentions of the depositors. Coins and cornerstones are a natural combination; coins are dated, durable, easily stored, and provide a tactile connection with the past. The idea of cornerstone coins dates back to at least Roman times,[102] and when one adds the idea of antiquity to the romantic notion of forgotten treasure idly waiting to be discovered in an ancient cornerstone, the stuff of legend is born. Pleasantly, American numismatics is no stranger to the cornerstone coin. For example, the Carson City, Nevada, Capitol building cornerstone was laid in 1870, and what could have been more natural than to deposit a few lustrous examples of the newly opened Carson City Mint coinage? Sure enough, a "CC" quarter, half dollar, and dollar of that year were encased therein; all three today prized rarities.[103] And even better, so as to dispel all rumor, the coins of the Carson City cornerstone were displayed over 100 years later at the Nevada State Museum for all to see.[104]

Boot scraper from the first U.S. Mint.

BRICKS FROM WELL OF FIRST U.S. MINT ERECTED 1792

Brick from the first U.S. Mint.

Equally prized might be the cornerstone of the second U.S. Mint, laid July 4th, 1829. The 300-pound stone protecting a candy jar with its contents was unearthed circa 1903 and reported in *The Numismatist* that year.[105] The find reportedly included an 1829 dime, an 1829 half dime, said to be the very first struck in that year, and an unidentified coin of the first year of the Mint, "one of the very few executed in the year 1792,"[106] probably a half disme. Another account mentioned an 1828 cent and half cent, and a "valuable penny," possibly a 1792 Birch or silver center cent.[107] Curiously, one of the workers put his hand in the candy jar and quietly made off with the precious jug during the excavation. Later reported to authorities, one Thomas O'Brien escaped prosecution on the grounds that the government could not produce a definitive inventory of the cornerstone contents, and to this day none has been located outside of inconsistent press accounts. O'Brien in fact returned some of the loot, but no one could prove what did or did not remain from the original cache.[108]

Likewise, cornerstone coins were laid at the Bank of the United States in Philadelphia on April 9, 1819. "Enclosed in the stone was deposited, secured in a leaden case, a glass vase, containing several of the gold, silver, and copper coins of the United States," *The American Journal of Numismatics* related much later.[109] A branch bank of the United States located in New York was not so regally commemorated. Opened in 1874 at the corner of Wall and Nassau streets, the vault contained, among other things, "a quart bottle filled with what was subsequently found, by analysis, to be an excellent quality of Jamaican rum, . . . a peck measure filled with hickory nuts," and a New York city directory of the year 1821. A U.S. dime, of the year 1820, was the only coin found. A memorandum in the vault described the deposit. "Deposited on the 23rd May, 1823. If it should be the fate of these papers to be discovered many centuries hence by the descendants of the present inhabitants of New York, for the gratification of reading the description of the present state of this aspiring City, they will be indebted to persons who feel the same interest in its prosperity as if they were to occupy it forever." Lofty intentions to be sure, for a cache that remained undisturbed barely for half a century.[110]

Year sets have been popular cornerstone items. A complete 1888 set, including U.S. copper, silver, and gold was placed in the Philadelphia Methodist Hospital on June 21, 1888, and sold for $3500, *ca.* 1965, following the building demolition.[111] In 1957, a full set of 1882 coinage was reported when the cornerstone of the New York Produce Exchange building was opened.[112] More recently, American Numismatic Rarities sold an 1867 proof set, from the Agricultural Hall cornerstone in Hingham, Massachusetts.[113] Perhaps the most famous cornerstone date set is that of the 1870 San Francisco coinage, deposited in the cornerstone of the second San Francisco Mint. An inventory of the set was uncovered by researchers

Richard Kelly and Nancy Oliver and disclosed to the numismatic community with much excitement in 2004. Among the more tempting morsels was a unique 1870-S quarter.[114]

The ultimate numismatic cornerstone, of course, would be that of the first U.S. Mint. Collectors of Stewart's time recognized the potential, as *The Numismatist* noted that "there is good reason for speculation as to probable finds, particularly should the original corner-stone be located."[115] A local newspaper added,

> Of great interest to antiquarians will be the contents of the corner-stone of the building. A careful search will be made for it by the workmen who are to demolish the building. It is probable also that coins minted in the building will be found on the premises, and some of these are very rare. Dollars made in 1804 in this Mint have sold at the record price of $3600. Other rare coins much sought for by numismatists were minted in this building.[116]

J. Louis Kates, who sold the property to Stewart, certainly believed in the existence of the cornerstone and related as much to Stewart in 1915:

> The middle one or the second building East of 7th Street, had an additional value and interest realy [sic] more than any of the three buildings as the corner stone was placed in this building and set by George Washington, within which was placed some coins and newspapers of that day, which today would be of great value. . . . I have never been able to find it to carry out the instructions or wishes of my Father John L. Kates, Dec'd as it was his desire that this corner-stone and all its contents should be given to the Historical Society of Penna [sic], as he had promised it to them during his life, the property was the first property owned by the United States Government and was the original Mint and as I state the cornerstone was laid by George Washington, President of the United States.[117]

The Kates family had been searching for the cornerstone since at least 1898, as indicated in the *Philadelphia Inquirer* of that year:

> T.F. Nealis, a well-known real estate man, who, having been employed by the heirs of J.J. Kates, relatives of former owners of the Seventh Street United States Mint site, is able, by reason of long familiarity with the properties of the neighborhood, to throw a pretty certain light upon the original Mint building and the probable location of the corner-stone laid by David Rittenhouse in 1792. . . . Mr Nealis, after many critical examinations of this "two-story plain brick building [the Middle Building]," thinks that the cornerstone, which is to be bequeathed to the Historical Society when found, is located at the northeast corner of the building. His reason for thinking so is that

it is the site which dignity and safety would have suggested in view of the approaches to the Mint and the inside arrangements for mechanical purposes.[118]

Despite the oral tradition of the Kates family, supplemented by the opinion of Nealis, Stewart noted that Washington "was not in Philadelphia the day on which it [the cornerstone] is supposed to have been laid."[119] While good evidence connects the Mint director David Rittenhouse with a "foundation stone," the Washington story is unsubstantiated except by Kates's recollection. The notion of an artifact-laden cornerstone seems also to have originated with Kates. Stewart summarized the situation in *History of the First United States Mint*:

> It has often been stated that a cornerstone was laid, but I have not found any evidence of it in manuscript or printed records of the time. The 'foundation stone' laid by Rittenhouse, 10:00 A.M., July 31, 1792, has undoubtedly been confused with 'cornerstone' although a certain person claimed that he had some of the contents of the cornerstone, but declined to substantiate his statement.[120]

Not reported in Stewart's *History* were the juicy details regarding his "certain person." The newspapers were not so shy:

> When Mr. Stewart purchased the property to enlarge his electrical plant at 35 N. 7th st. there was a clause in the deed that the cornerstone and its contents should go to the Society [Historical Society of Pennsylvania] for preservation. Yet despite a most diligent and painstaking search during the demolition process, the cornerstone was not found. . . . John W. Jordan, librarian of the Historical Society, stated that while he had no official information that there was a cornerstone and that it had been willed to the Society, he had been told that such was the case. He had also been informed, he said, that the stone was in the possession of Joseph D. Ellis, who has an office on the eighth floor of the Provident Life and Trust Building. This Mr. Ellis emphatically denied. He said that he did not have the stone and did not know who had. He admitted, however, that he had an old penny that was taken from the corner stone, but refused to say how or under what circumstances it came into his possession.[121]

J. Louis Kates had a theory as to the origin of the supposed Ellis coin:

> At the time [*ca.* 1885] Dr. Wilson raised the adjoining property to the South being number 35 N. 7th Street, and during the excavation or deepning [sic] of [the] cellar to his property there was considerable rainfall for several days which inundated the old party wall on south line, Mint property, and the cellar wall and part of the inner Court Yard to the Mint

property caved in and fell over into the excavated cellar of 35 N. 7th Street, and I have every reason to believe that the corner stone and its contents was either lost or stolen at that time.[122]

With only hearsay to go on, Stewart declined to take any action against Ellis, as he indicated to a reporter:

> Mr. Stewart said, when asked what further action he was going to take, that he would notify the Historical Society that the corner-stone has not been found, and then they could take whatever measures to recover the relic that they might see fit.[123]

Stewart, good as his word, put closure to the situation following the excavation, writing to the Historical Society of Pennsylvania:

> This is to advise you that no corner stone was found under the Old mint buildings, which I purchased from the Estate of John L. Kates. When I bought the property, I was required to deliver the corner stone and contents when found to you, in accordance with the will of Mr. Kates. I watched the work and am positive no corner stone was under the buildings when demolished, and from rumors I have heard I am inclined to believe it was taken out years ago when the adjoining buildings were erected. If you want something from the Old Mint as a curiosity, I shall be glad to accommodate you.[124]

Despite Stewart's 1911 letter, he was still seeking information 14 years later, for in 1925 he discussed the matter on local radio, suggesting that "If any listener-in [sic] has ever heard anything about the cornerstone or its contents, it is hoped that he will communicate with the Frank H. Stewart Electric Company, now on the site."[125]

Frank H. Stewart, ever the historian, felt it was proper that his new building should have the cornerstone he failed to find, and so he buried a lead box inside the cornerstone of the Old Mint Building erected at the first U.S. Mint site. Stewart chose Wilfred Jordan, the curator at Independence Hall (which of course housed Stewart's "Old Mint" collection), to lay the lead box inside the cornerstone during the ceremony held on January 27, 1912.[126] The Frank H. Stewart Electric Company cornerstone held any number of goodies, and the treasure trove was enumerated in Stewart's *History of the First United States Mint*.[127] The numismatic items included:

> Pictures of the Old Mint.
>
> "Ye Olde Mint" booklet.
>
> A gavel made from the old Mint wood.
>
> Eight silver dollars, dates 1795–1803.
>
> Nine half dollars, dates 1795–1817.
>
> Five quarter dollars, dates 1815–1825.
>
> Five dimes, dates 1821–1831.

Ten cents, dates 1794–1829.

Seven half cents, dates 1793–1828.

Four coins dated 1911.

Columbian half dollar, 1892.

Coin, silver dollar size, of Ludwig the 16th, dated 1775.

Stewart also enclosed a note asking any future finder of the box to replace it within any new structure built on the site. The *Numismatic Scrapbook Magazine* disclosed the fate of Stewart's precious box in 1965:

> Now Stewart's 1912 building (which he named Olde [sic] Mint Building) has been torn down to make way for a new Federal courthouse. In the cornerstone workmen of the Cleveland Wrecking Co., found a lead box which contained a biography of Stewart and history of first Mint—along with 50 coins struck at the original Philadelphia Mint. A letter in the box asked that the contents of the box be placed in a future building, however, under the wrecking contract the contents belong to the demolition firm.[128]

An unattributed news clipping found in the Stewart collection at Rowan University added a few more details. Francis J. Lammer, the executive director of the Redevelopment Authority of Philadelphia, enjoyed the privilege of opening the box with a hacksaw and being the first to see the contents. Lammer confirmed the ownership of the antiquities:

> In a letter to the future, Stewart, who died in 1948 at the age of 75, asked that the contents of the box be placed in the cornerstone of any future building. Lammer says, however, that he won't get his wish. The coins, probably being very valuable, belong to the wrecking company. The gavel will probably be given to the new mint.

Sadly, the contents of Stewart's cornerstone are today lost to the numismatic winds, and perhaps rightfully so, echoing the unfound "foundation stone" of the first Mint. Just as John L. Kates could not successfully bequeath his cornerstone to the Historical Society of Pennsylvania, so Frank H. Stewart lost the posterity of his as well.

Besides the cornerstone, Stewart placed a bronze tablet upon the Old Mint Building at the first U.S. Mint site, reading "ON THIS SITE / WAS ERECTED / THE FIRST U.S. MINT / A. D. 1792 / FIRST / PUBLIC BUILDING / AUTHORIZED / BY CONGRESS. / COINAGE CONTINUED / HERE 40 YEARS. / BUILDING RAZED / A.D. 1911."[129] Unlike the cornerstone, the fate of the bronze marker is well known:

> A short time ago [*ca.* 1930] the writer ordered the very fine bronze sign tablet of the concern he founded in 1894 [the Frank H. Stewart Electric Company], the first one of its kind in the city of Philadelphia, to be buried beneath the concrete basement floor near the freight elevator of the Old Mint Building in Philadelphia, now occupied by the Franklin Institute. . . . The writer guesses that maybe a century from now some workman will dig up the heavy bronze business tablet and sell it for old junk. It certainly cannot be broken up with a hammer.[130]

While the cornerstone of Stewart's enterprise is long gone, other Stewart cornerstones may still exist, for in April, 1925, *The Numismatist* reported that Stewart interred New Jersey colonial coins and paper money in a Gloucester County building cornerstone in the city of Woodbury, New Jersey.[131] The cache included six New Jersey cents, in addition to a Mark Newby copper. And, in 1908, Stewart deposited a 1795 dollar at the Pitman (New Jersey) Grammar School.[132]

Cornerstone laying of the Stewart building, January 27, 1912. Holding the gavel is likely Wilfred Jordan, Independence Hall curator. To his left is Frank H. Stewart.

FIRST MINT GOLD

While Stewart excavated numerous first Mint relics, and created still others through the ceremonial act of cornerstone deposit, the ancient lure of the treasure hunter—gold—remained in his imagination. Gold was no less on the mind of the first minters of the 18th century, for if a domestic coinage mill was a sign of sovereignty, then one that processed and struck gold was even better. Rittenhouse, the first director, was not able to extract yellow metal from the primitive structure, but his successor, Henry William De Saussure, proudly asserted in a 1795 report, "The enclosed documents, marked B and C, will shew the quantity of precious metals which have been worked up and coined; partly under the direction of Mr. Rittenhouse, partly under mine. The gold, wholly under mine."[133]. The back story of De Saussure's achievement was not documented until 1841, by his biographer:

> General Washington, whose habit was to see the heads of departments every week at his table, upon one of these occasions, expressed to the director of the mint [De Saussure] his satisfaction at the activity which had been introduced into the silver coinage, and added, "I have long desired to see gold coined at the mint, but your predecessor found insuperable difficulties. I should be much gratified if it could be accomplished before I leave office." "I will try," was the reply; and the director went to the mint, summoned the officers, ascertained the wants and difficulties of each department, and by great diligence, speedily removed all obstacles. In six weeks he carried to the President a handful of gold eagles [sic, half eagles were struck first], and received his thanks and approbation.[134]

Washington's golden twinkle captured Stewart's eye. A friend of Stewart's, who "borrowed some money which he still owes me,"[135] made the observation that perhaps some stray bits of gold could be extracted from the old Mint structure. The public got wind of the idea quickly, for only a week after Stewart's purchase of the property the *Philadelphia Record* reported:

> There is a possibility that Mr. Stewart may realize several thousand dollars when he demolishes the building by scraping the chimneys and roof for particles of gold that escaped in the crude methods of refining a century ago. Great care will be taken in the destruction of the building to insure the saving of any such hidden wealth.[136]

Stewart had several chimney bricks of the Middle Building refined and assayed, with the thought of perhaps manufacturing souvenirs from the recovered bullion. Stewart had done enough research to calculate the gold and silver wastage during the operation of the first Mint—some $100,000[137]—and the prospect of undertaking a gold "dig" in the possibly fertile fields of downtown Phil-adelphia was more than a little bit exciting. Even in the early days of the first Philadelphia Mint, the accumulation of detritus was recognized as valuable. Elias Boudinot, mint director from 1795 through 1805, or someone in his administration, had the bright idea to recover bullion from the Mint ashes. Boudinot proudly reported his success to President Adams in 1801:

> The Director has particular satisfaction in informing the President that there has been received from the test bottoms and ashes, accumulated before his administration of the mint [possibly a shot at Boudinot's predecessors, David Rittenhouse and Henry William de Saussure], four hundred and twenty-eight dollars and forty-seven cents . . . and that there is still a quantity of ashes remaining to be cleansed and refined.[138]

Of course there was more than one way to get gold out of the Mint, and such an idea to begin with is pregnant with rumor and mythology. In 1832, or some time before, the story arose that gold had been mixed into the copper alloy used to strike 1814 cents. A Boston newspaper told the story:

> NEW SPECULATION!—Within a few days there have been runners in most of the towns in this vicinity, gathering up cents coined in 1814. They find but few and buy them as they can, giving 2, 4, 6, 10, 12 or 17 cents each; and we have heard of 75 cents being given for a single cent. 12 1-2 cents have been offered in this town. The story is that in 1814 some gold was accidentally mixed with the copper at the United States Mint, and that the cents of that year contain gold. We verily believe that the whole affair is a humbug, and that the cents of 1814 are of no more intrinsic value than those of any other year. It has been suggested that the speculation originated in the following manner. Copper was very scarce in 1814, on account of the war, and but few cents were coined at the mint during that year. Some virtuosi, who were desirous of laying up in their cabinets specimens of the coinage of every year, could not find any cents coined in 1814, and offered certain toll-gatherers a dollar or two to collect for them a few cents of that year. This offer led others to suppose that the cents of 1814 contained gold.—We know not whether this be a true explanation of the mystery.[139]

The cent mintage of 1814 was indeed lower than average, and none at all were coined with the date of the following year. The Mint report for 1815 clarified the matter, indicating hard metal was just plain scarce, whether gold, silver, or copper:

> The high price of gold and silver bullion, for some time past, in the current paper money of the country, has prevented, and, as long as this shall continue to be the case, must necessarily prevent, deposites [sic]

of these metals being made for coinage, to any considerable amount. But a fresh supply of copper having lately been received at the mint, we have again resumed the coinage of cents [this, written early in 1816].[140]

Regardless, the myth reared its head again in the May 1858 issue of the *Historical Magazine*.[141] Later, Ebenezer Locke Mason Jr., Philadelphia coin dealer, recounted the tale in the March 1881 issue of *Mason's Coin Collector's Herald*:

> Some time ago a . . . story was circulated with reference to the coinage of cents in the United States Mint in 1814. It was alleged that in that year there was a dishonest workman, who was detected in the act of stealing a quantity of gold. In order to screen himself from punishment and dispose of the evidence of his crime, he hastily threw his stolen gold into a crucible of molten copper that he was passing. The story ran that the workman's secret had become known, and that the pennies of 1814 were being bought up to extract the gold from them.

The story mutated, as an Indianapolis reader inquired of Mason in the June 1884 issue of his current house organ, *Mason's Coin Collectors' Magazine*:

> Noticing an article in one of our city papers on the subject of old coins and their value, I take the liberty to inquire of you the value of a *few* coins which I happen to have in my possession. . . . nickel cents (twenty-four in number) bearing date 1857 and 1858. In the composition of the metal used in the coinage of these issues you, perhaps, remember there was gold used instead of other metal (by mistake). Hoping to hear from you as early as convenient.

The golden penny gathered traction once more in 1903, as reported by *The Numismatist*:

> Recently some wag—or liar—started a story in New York, which floated all over the country as New York lies generally do, to the effect that in the mint a bar of gold fell into a pot of molten copper and entered into the composition of a job lot of pennies later deposited in the New York sub-treasury. Straightaway collectors and greedy persons began bombarding the sub-treasury with pecks of letters begging for a few bushels of those pennies. So intense and widespread has the demand for the coins become that the officials have issued five or six explicit and emphatic denials of the assertion that any gold has crept into the pennies. They say the report is a Rotterdam lie and that persons applying for the coins are wasting money they spend for postage stamps.[142]

Remarkably, the same idea captured public attention in Calcutta, India, as *The Numismatist* described in 1907:

> An amusing swindle occurred in Calcutta a short time ago. A considerable number of the local fakirs have been busy for some months at hoarding the small copper coins of the year 1907. Then a rumor was suddenly circulated that the workmen at the native mint had made an error in proportioning the alloy, and that a large amount of gold had been accidentally mixed with the copper, and the government would take prompt steps to repurchase them, with a view to re-melting them.
>
> At the same time the swindlers began to buy up all of these coins at double and triple their values. The rumor of course circulated rapidly and it seems to have created an active business in these coins in the bazaars and streets of interior, some of the prices paid for the coppers running as high as a shilling.
>
> Of course, the swindlers seized upon this opportunity to dispose of their stock at a handsome profit, and the credulous buyers are the sufferers.[143]

The Numismatist followed up in 1924, relating the story of yet another "golden penny":

> George I, King of England and Elector of Hanover, on the occasion of one of his visits to Hanover, invited a certain Miss Von J. to play a game of cards with him. The lady excused herself with the explanation that she had no money to spare for games of chance, as she belonged to a family of very limited wealth. The King replied that this would make no difference and that they would only play for pennies. The card game was played and the King managed to lose, and on the next day he sent to the lady her winnings in golden pennies, for the striking of which he had given a rush order to the Mint at Hanover. These ducats on the obverse show the well-known Wild Man of Brunswick, Luneburg, and on the reverse, the inscription: "1 Pfenning Scheide Muntz 1726." These coins can still be had, but today are of considerable numismatic rarity.[144]

The "golden cent" was seemingly pure hogwash, mythology passed by word of mouth throughout an ignorant populace and occasionally reported in the numismatic press. But, like a good legend, there was a nugget of truth to the story, and no less than the assayer of the U.S. Mint personally made "several interesting examinations . . . as opportunities of leisure would allow." The results, reported in the *American Journal of Numismatics* in 1885, revealed that in fact there was a slight amount of gold contained in the nation's copper coinage:

> Copper was tried in various forms. A cent of 1822, the material for which was imported from England, showed gold equal to one part in 14,500, which is one cent's worth in 20 cents...A cent of 1843, of American material, was found to contain one cent's worth of gold in 14 cents. The result brings to mind

the old story of the golden cent of 1814. In that year, as was idly reported, the melters at the Mint carelessly emptied some gold into a pot of copper from which the cents were coined. It gave some trouble at the counter of the Mint for many years afterwards, in consequence of numerous inquiries and offers to sell. It turns out to be pretty certain that every cent we have coined contains gold, effectually locked in.[145]

Some thought has also been given to the idea of gold being mixed in with silver. A Carson City quarter dollar of the year 1872 is known with the counterstamp "GOLD."[146] An enterprising researcher thought perhaps that similar shenanigans were in play at Carson City, and with the idea that gold might have been surreptitiously mixed into the silver alloy, submitted the coin for analysis to a research firm.[147] A good try, but no gold was found in the sample!

Stewart was more likely inspired by the story of a successful gold recovery undertaken at the San Francisco Mint in 1885, as reported by the *American Journal of Numismatics*:

1872-CC Liberty Seated quarter, counterstamped "GOLD."

A precious carpet has been destroyed in San Francisco. It had covered the floor of one of the rooms of the Mint, and had been used for five years. The dust of the precious metals used in the coinage had, during that period, daily fallen upon it, and when it was taken up the authorities had it cut in small pieces and burned in pans. The ashes were subject to the process employed with mining dust, and they realized $2509. Thus the carpet after years of wear was more precious than when it was new.[148]

Equally promising was the 1903 recovery conducted at the U.S. Assay Office in New York. *The Numismatist* explained:

Uncle Sam started his yearly house cleaning at the assay office a few days ago. It is expected that from $1,500 to $2,000 will be collected in little flecks of gold that have escaped from the retorts and smelting pots within the last year. The iron flooring of the refining room will be removed, the dust collected and the gold dust melted down. Much gold escapes with the fumes from the refining furnaces, and goes up through the chimney, falling upon the roof of the building. The roof has been swept of the dust which collected during the year. The big chimney is lined with steel, and in sections. Each one of these sections will be removed, the dirt and accumulations scraped from them and put into the melting pot. They will then be replaced. The dust has been collected from the roof of the sub-treasury and the building adjoining the assay office in Pine Street.[149]

Technology progressed, and by the 1930s the Mint could extract precious metal from smoke, as reported in a local newspaper:

Bits of metal used to fly away with the smoke out of the Mint's chimney. Now, the settling chamber catches most of the valuable dust before it gets out. A year's accumulation in one of these chambers might yield a bar of silver weighing 1141 ounces, worth $570.[150]

Stewart had some history on his side, but alas, his assayer's report, like that of the 1872-CC "gold" quarter, revealed no traces of the yellow metal, and in *History of the First United States Mint* Stewart expressed regret that he had not tested the chimney bricks of the Rear Building as well.[151] Left unexplained was Stewart's interest in the rear building. The answer was revealed in a 1915 article in *The Philadelphia Rotarian*:

I bought the property in 1907 and immediately tore down the rear building, then used as a rag and paper warehouse. Mr. Riley, of Rea & Riley, Carpenters, told me that the first floor of this particular building was known as the "gold room" and that some gold was found in the old chimney when partially torn down by him during his occupancy of the building, as a carpenter shop.[152]

The "gold room" attribution was further corroborated by Joseph F. Meredith, who had worked in the building as a boy.[153] Stewart, the promoter of the "Old Mint Gold Standard," thus apparently failed in his quest for first Mint gold, which he sought for the purpose of manufacturing a few souvenirs.[154] Yet, Stewart's will contains a tantalizing clue. One "Gold Ring, Marked Old Mint" is listed in the inventory.[155] Valued at $10, no mention is made as to the origin of the gold, and Stewart seems not to have made mention of it anywhere else, either. If the ring was indeed fabricated from first Mint gold, Stewart took the secret to the grave. Far more certain is that the excavation of the first Mint yielded other items of great interest to treasure hunters, enabling the Master of the Mint to make any number of pleasant additions to his growing coin collection.

The U.S. Assay Office in New York City, *ca.* 1892.

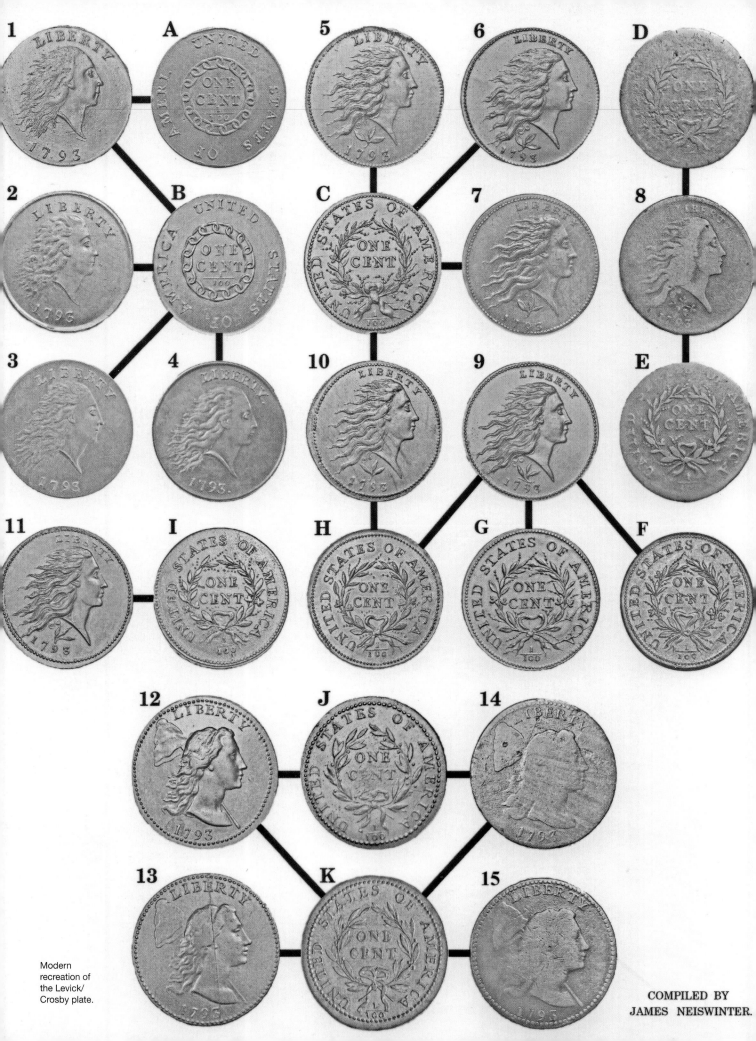

Modern recreation of the Levick/Crosby plate.

COMPILED BY JAMES NEISWINTER.

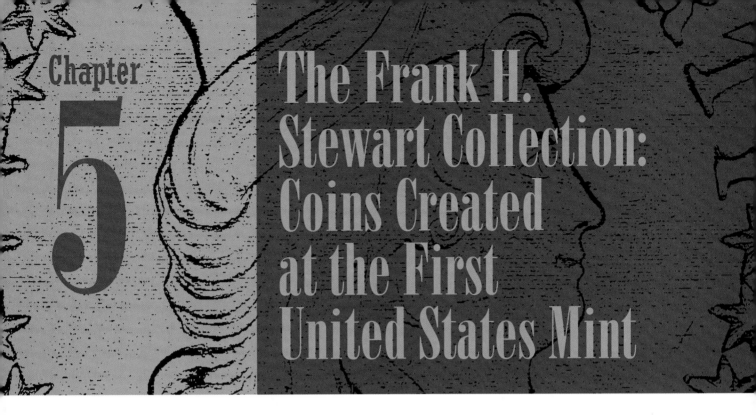

The Frank H. Stewart Collection: Coins Created at the First United States Mint

tewart's interest in numismatics appears to have been a fortuitous combination of his location on Seventh Street in Philadelphia and his natural inclina-
tion for all things historic. Even before he purchased the Mint property in
1907, Stewart was well aware of the building's significance, even if he didn't have
all the facts quite right:

> You will notice on the cut of our building the small three story building adjoining
> us. This property is one of the historical buildings in Philadelphia and the first
> bought by the United States Government. The plot of ground was purchased by
> special act of Continental Congress in 1792. The corner stone was laid the same
> year and the building was used as the sole U.S. Mint from 1793 to 1835. The
> 1804 dollar, now worth Two Thousand Dollars each, was coined there as well as
> the Washington cent and other coins now very rare.[1]

Stewart recorded that his coin collection was launched after purchasing the old
Mint.[2] In September of that year, the *North American*, a Philadelphia newspaper,
reported that "Frank H. Stewart, whose proximity to the neglected first Mint has
made him interested in the early coins, has quite a collection."[3] By this time Stewart possessed a run of silver dollars from 1795 to 1803 (more will be said later of
the elusive 1794 and the celebrated 1804) as well as a 1793 half cent, a Chain
Reverse large cent, and a Liberty Cap large cent, all three desirable early copper
issues. About the same time, Stewart possibly participated in a number of auctions
conducted by the brothers Chapman in Philadelphia (see appendix B). He attended
the American Numismatic Association convention in 1908,[4] joined the ANA later
that year,[5] and furnished illustrations for *The Numismatist* shortly thereafter.[6] Later
he would contribute a number of articles as well. Stewart also authored articles for
coin dealer B. Max Mehl's house organ, *Mehl's Numismatic Monthly*. Stewart was
invited to join the American Numismatic Society in 1918 but seems to have
declined the offer.[7]

Stewart's locale on Seventh Street notwithstanding, numismatic seeds had been
planted in his youth, for he recalled having found New Jersey state coppers while
at work on his parent's farm, *ca.* 1885 through 1888.[8] A friend recalled, "All his life
he had been a collector of coins . . . and his acquirement of the Old Mint buildings

Frank H.
Stewart,
numismatist,
about 1932.

to convert American know-how into hard money while separated from European expertise by considerable space and time. A $10 gold piece from its first year of issue, 1795, is certainly a fine thing and highly desirable. But its mintage of only a few thousand specimens is dwarfed by large cent emissions in the hundreds of thousands. Clearly, the first days of the first Mint were primarily focused on the red metal.

Moreover, large cents, struck from 1793 to 1857, were the first issue to capture the fancy of the American collecting public. The appearance of small cents beginning in 1856 (and to a greater extent in 1857) created a numismatic frenzy of sorts focused on the now obsolete large coppers. Fascination with the early days of the Republic was not limited to coin collectors, for the Centennial, 20 years in the future, induced a colonial revival throughout the country, causing the citizenry to reflect upon and reinterpret the revolutionary era. For now, collectors chased large cents, and the more discerning among them quickly recognized that the earliest of them could be collected in hundreds of varieties, each one a glimpse of an engraver working a die by hand in the Seventh Street coinage factory. Among cents dated 1794 alone, one finds 76 distinct obverse and reverse dies.

By Stewart's time, approximately 50 years into the American coin collecting boom, copper remained king among the cognoscenti, and its influence is easily seen in Stewart's cabinet, which started out with a generous helping of large cents of the year 1793. The first year of regular issue large cent production, 1793s were among the earliest documented American varieties, notably depicted by the Levick plate published in the *American Journal of Numismatics* in 1869.[11] Joseph N. T. Levick, smitten with 1793 fever, corresponded with the premier collectors in order to construct a comprehensive photographic record of high-grade 1793 varieties. Levick performed the legwork, coordinating specimens and photography, while Sylvester Sage Crosby executed the cataloguing. The result was a *tour de force* which documented 14 of the 16 Sheldon varieties for the date. Crosby himself discovered the final two, one in 1870 and the last in 1879.[12] Auction catalogers rapidly adopted Crosby's 1793 attribution system, and by the Stewart era the idea of assembling a 1793 large cent variety set had captivated many a numismatist.

Stewart accumulated at least six different Sheldon varieties of the year 1793, including two Chain Reverse cents (S1, S2) and three Wreath Reverse cents (S8, S10, S11a). No 1793 Liberty Cap cent (S12 through S16) is currently found in the Stewart collection, though per the *North American* (cited above), Stewart owned such an example in 1907. However, Congress Hall accession records do not include a 1793 Liberty Cap cent, so it seems that Stewart either retained this coin or otherwise disposed of it.[13] Stewart's 1793s are charitably described as passable examples, but more accurately as "scudzy" in the parlance of modern copper collectors. Stewart was no coin connoisseur, and

further increased his interest in numismatics."[9] Stewart was no mere accumulator, and sought to discover the history behind his coins. His *History of the First United States Mint* demonstrates a familiarity with sources such as the *American State Papers* and the work of numismatic authors Sylvester Sage Crosby and George Escol Sellers. In his personal notes are found citations to *The Numismatist*, the *American Journal of Numismatics*, and Scott's *Coin Collector's Journal*. He was aware of bibliographic resources that were missing, most notably the inaugural account book of first Mint chief coiner Henry Voigt.[10] Today, Stewart's collecting activities are known to us by the collection he bequeathed to Congress Hall, which now is administered by Independence National Historical Park. Stewart's cabinet included the coins unearthed during the first Mint excavation, in addition to pieces acquired privately. The circumstances of Stewart's eventual gift to Congress Hall shall be discussed later; for now, let us meet the coins.

THE SEVENTH STREET COPPERSMITHS

Of all the issues of the first U.S. Mint, none has exerted more force in numismatic circles than the early coppers. The reasons for this are legion. The copper cent and half cent were the first denominations produced in large quantity, they were struck in an astounding number of varieties, and today survive in sufficient number to maintain a sizable collector base. Produced by hand with primitive technology, early copper best captures the romance of the early days of the first Mint, men and machines struggling

TYPES AND VARIETIES OF THE U. S. CENT, 1793.

Pub. 1869 by the Am. Numismatic & Archæological Soc. New York.

The Levick/Crosby plate of 1793 cents, from the *American Journal of Numismatics*, 1869.

the fussiness which characterized similarly endowed collectors seems to have escaped the Stewart cabinet. The *tout assemblage* is an eclectic mix, for Stewart literally had firsthand access to the first Mint, and extracted any number of delicacies from its ruins. These prizes came to be surrounded by lesser brethren—but from Stewart's apparent point of view, the history was the same either way. Still, 1793 cents are today coveted in any condition, and most numismatists would be pleased to be possessed of Stewart's 1793 "starter set."

1793 LARGE CENTS FROM THE FRANK H. STEWART OLD MINT COLLECTION

The 1793 large cent, Sheldon-1, marked with Independence Hall inventory number 9264. This type is distinguished by the AMERI. abbreviation on the reverse.

The 1793 large cent, Sheldon-2. The Sheldon-2 variety is marked by the wide spacing of LIBERTY on the obverse.

The 1793 large cent, Sheldon-8. The Sheldon-8 variety features a nearly triangular bow on the reverse, along with a curved fraction bar.

The 1793 large cent, Sheldon-10. On the Sheldon-10, the left and middle leaves of the obverse sprig are at close to a right angle.

The 1793 large cent, Sheldon-11a. The Sheldon-11 variety is distinguished by the reverse fraction to the far right. This example is more particularly designated as Sheldon-11a, due to the vine and bars device impressed on the coin's rim.

While the 1793s are enumerated by 16 Sheldon varieties, the situation mushroomed in 1794. Of all American coins, perhaps more ink has been spilled on the subject of 1794 large cents than any other issue—indeed, one could fill a shelf full of references dedicated to 1794 large cent varieties. Some 56 Sheldon numbers in all, Stewart's lone representative is a chocolate brown example of the common S65. A second lot of eight 1794s appears in the Congress Hall accession records; unfortunately these today are missing. Beginning in 1795, the Stewart collection included but one example of each year despite large numbers of collectible varieties. Stewart seemed content to form a date set concluding with the 1832 large cent, after which operations moved from the first U.S. Mint to the second. Stewart apparently had no interest in coins of the second Mint, and today none are found in the Congress Hall collection.

Stewart's half cents likewise form a date set beginning in 1793 and concluding in 1832. A long-forgotten denomination, the half cent was a not inconsiderable sum in 1793, when the pay of a common laborer at the Mint was on the order of a dollar per day. The half cent of 1793 thus equates to about 50¢ in modern terms, approximately the purchasing power of a postage stamp. Alexander Hamilton provided the rationale for the denomination, stating that "in a great number of cases, exactly the same things will be sold for half a cent, which, if there were none, would cost a cent."[14]

Stewart's 1793 half cent (Cohen-3), like the 1793 large cents, is in somewhat dreadful condition, reasonably detailed but highly corroded. The other date of most interest to half cent collectors is the 1796, minted to the extent of 1,390 pieces with perhaps 50 surviving today. Stewart's 1796 is today somewhat of a mystery, as the museum records are inconsistent in the description of the coin. In some places it is referred to as a "1796 over 1795," suggesting that it was a 1795 half cent with the "5" altered to a "6."[15] 1796 half cent fakes were certainly no stranger to Stewart's era, mentioned as early as 1866 in the second issue of the *American Journal of Numismatics*, which, in its

opening salutatory of the premier issue, had condemned "nefarious and improper acts . . . in the manufacture . . . of coins," clearly an early shot at the forgery of collectable coins.[16] Despite the *AJN* condemnation of facsimiles as an "unjustifiable practice," Philadelphia dealer Charles Warner was undeterred as he sold a pair of 1796 half cent electrotypes in his June 1867 sale, one for 25¢ and a second for 30¢.[17] Later, the Secret Service began scoping out auctions and seizing such electrotypes.[18] Besides electrotypes, coin dealer Édouard Frossard made mention of struck copies in 1879.[19]

However, the story does not end there, for Stewart's 1796 half cent is alternately cataloged as a "1796 re-struck with die of large cent."[20] Elsewhere, in museum records, the coin is referred to as a "freak," an old term used to describe all manner of striking anomalies.[21] The specimen was loaned to the U.S. Mint in 1969 for exhibition in the newly built Mint at Fifth and Arch streets, and officially remains on loan to that institution. Cataloged alternately as no. 9278 (Independence National Historical Park catalog number) or no. 37019 (U.S. Mint), the coin presented today under those numbers is an unstruck copper planchet, possessing a diameter consistent with a large cent (27mm) and a weight of 10.6 grams, which is neither consistent with a half cent (6.74 grams) or a large cent (13.48 grams). Clearly something is amiss: this planchet is neither a fake 1796 half cent, nor a half cent-large cent "freak."

If the coin in question was indeed a combination of half cent and large cent strikings from 1796, it may have resembled a 1796 large cent consigned to Bowers and Merena Galleries on October 17, 1994, and auctioned as lot 2307 in that firm's March 1995 auction. Described at length in the auction catalog[22] and later in Breen's large cent Encyclopedia,[23] the latest thinking on this enigmatic chunk of copper seems to be that it started life as an off-center 1796 Sheldon NC-7 large cent (a quite rare variety in its own right), was then cut down in diameter in order to recoin the error as a half cent (a common practice at the time), then restruck with 1797 Breen-3a half cent dies. The half cent strike did not completely impart the

The 1794 large cent, Sheldon-65.

The 1793 half cent, Cohen-3.

design to the planchet, a portion of which was thinner than the whole. The most notable remaining legends are the "1796" date from the large cent, and "HALF CENT" from the half cent dies. The piece attracted considerable debate, with some considering it a large cent restruck with half cent dies, while others believed it was a half cent restruck with large cent dies. A similar piece, a 1795 half struck over an off-center 1795 large cent, appeared in the Goldberg Auctioneers Davy Collection sale of September 2010, lot 29.

Something of this nature once was in the museum collection, for Stewart described his coin in 1916:

> There is a freak 1796 half cent in the Congress Hall collection, Philadelphia. It is stamped over a 1795 half cent. The date 1796 is perfectly plain. I gave $75 for it and gave it to the city of Philadelphia.[24]

Unfortunately, no photograph of Stewart's coin is known. If the coin was eventually determined to be an alteration of a 1795, one can imagine Stewart's embarrassment at having paid a large sum, and a resulting desire to dispose of the matter quietly.

STEWART'S SMALL BEGINNING

While the half and large cent coppers flowed out of the Mint, silver and gold came only in a relative trickle. Ironically, presidential recognition of the silver came first. Washington laid the groundwork in his October 1791 third annual address to Congress:

Off-center Sheldon 1796 NC-7 large cent, cut down and restruck with Breen-3a half cent dies,

The disorders in the existing currency, and especially the scarcity of small change, a scarcity so particularly distressing to the poorer classes, strongly recommend the carrying into effect the resolution already entered into concerning the establishment of a mint. Measures have been taken, pursuant to that resolution, for procuring some of the most necessary artists, together with the requisite apparatus.

A year later Washington was able to report further progress on the subject of "small change," in his fourth annual address to Congress on November 6, 1792:

> In execution of the authority given by the Legislature measures have been taken for engaging some artists from abroad to aid in the establishment of our mint. Others have been employed at home. Provision has been made of the requisite buildings, and these are now putting into proper condition for the purposes of the establishment. There has also been a small beginning in the coinage of half dimes, the want of small coins in circulation calling the first attention to them.

Washington's "small beginning" referred to the 1792 half dismes, of which much more will be said later. They were perhaps Stewart's favorite coin, for he had two of them, and chose not to systematically pursue the remainder of the half dimes coined in the first Mint. Thus, it is no surprise that the mega-coin of the early half dime series, the 1802, is absent in Stewart's collection. Indeed, even the easily acquired issues of the early 1830s are not to be found. On the plus side, Stewart's 1794 half dime, Logan/McCloskey-1 (Valentine-1), represents a very difficult (Rarity-6) die variety. Such niceties were probably lost on Stewart, for although the first reference to half dime varieties appeared in 1883, variety collecting in Stewart's time typically tended to attract the early copper aficionados. Stewart got less lucky on the 1795 half dime, a common variety attributed as Logan/McCloskey-8 (Valentine-5). Similarly, the 1796 is the common Logan/McCloskey-1 (Valentine-1). Like the large cents, Stewart's early half dimes exhibit any number of problems—scratches, gouges, or old cleanings. And yet, these primitive souvenirs of the first Mint, warts and all, remain highly desirable to modern collectors.

Stewart's early dimes are similarly incomplete, the most notable specimens present being those of 1796 and 1804. Stewart's 1796 (JR-1) represents the first year of issue, and though worn smooth, presents nicely with attractive toning. A distinctive cud at the first star is an ever-present reminder of the difficulties of die preparation and coinage production in the first Mint. Such examples would find it difficult to escape today's Mint, but in 1796 the situation was much different, quality control taking a backseat to production demands. Stewart's 1804 dime is the curious 14-star (JR-2) variety, an error which presages the 12-star half cent of 1828. The 14-star reverse die was reused on the 1804 quarter eagle, certainly an economy reflecting the labor invested in crafting dies by hand in the first Mint. The idea of sharing dies across multiple denominations is an intriguing one, and the reader is referred to the Ed Price collection presented by Heritage Auction Galleries in July 2008, a fascinating exposition of the concept.

The early quarters in Stewart's collection are represented to the extent of only four pieces, including the 1796 (Browning-2), 1806 (Browning-2), 1818 (Browning-2), and 1821 (Browning-3).[25] The 1796 is the most compelling of the group, and, like the other denominations, Stewart acquired an example of the first year of issue in his collection. A mid-grade specimen, Stewart's 1796 is easily a five-figure coin today. Stewart probably paid less than $10 himself—a similar specimen sold for $5 in a Philadelphia auction in 1906.[26] The keys to the early quarters, the 1823 and 1827, are not to be found here. Stewart had the means to pursue such delicacies, but seemed content to collect representative examples of the coins of the first Mint, and even then preservation seems to have been less important than historicity.

The 1794 half dime, Logan/McCloskey-1.

The 1795 half dime, Logan/McCloskey-8.

The 1796 half dime, Logan/McCloskey-1.

The 1796 dime, JR-1.

The 1804 dime, JR-2.

Stewart's half dollars follow suit. The first year of issue, 1794, is present while the keys of 1796 and 1797 are not. Curiously, Stewart is elsewhere credited with donating a 1796 half valued at $75 in 1915, but this coin does not appear in the Congress Hall accession records.[27] Stewart's 1794 is a low grade example with reverse damage which, nonetheless, is a valuable coin from a collector's standpoint. A fairly complete date run follows through 1832. Many of these were likely acquired for face value or at small premiums. Early half dollars were struck by the first Mint in greater quantities than other silver denominations, in part because dollars were discontinued in 1804.[28] Today they survive in large numbers and are avidly pursued by specialists who have many varieties from which to choose. In Stewart's time they were not so highly prized and there were many opportunities to acquire these for little more than 50¢ each. The situation of a coin being auctioned for its face value seems odd to modern collectors, and yet this was a common occurrence in sales of the late 19th and early 20th centuries, which coin dealers probably considered a service to the hobby if nothing else.

STEWART AND THE KING

The "King of American Coins," an 1804 silver dollar is the stuff of American numismatic legend, inspiring all manner of mythology, misinformation, and masterful

The 1796 quarter, Browning-2.

The 1794 half dollar, Overton-104.

research. The only date not represented in his early silver dollar collection, Stewart felt compelled to offer his own spin on the 1804, though doing little to hasten the untangling of this issue, ultimately sorted in 1962 by Eric Newman and Ken Bressett in *The Fantastic 1804 Dollar*. Stewart stated the facts as well as he knew them, but did not possess numismatic insight sufficient to advance the investigation. Newman and Bressett, for example, clearly demonstrated the practice of the Mint in employing dies not bearing current dates, while Stewart could only speculate as to this possibility.

At the same time, Stewart must be given credit for doing everything he knew how to do. In the case of the 1804, he used an "inside connection" at the Mint during his research. Ellis Pugh, adjustor of scales, left behind a notebook today preserved in the Stewart collection at Rowan University.[29] Pugh seems to have been dispatched to investigate the 1804 dollars, and recorded silver deposits, warrants, coinage, and assay data for 1803, 1804, and 1805.

Stewart was obviously acquainted with the rarity of the 1804,[30] and certainly had his chances to acquire an example. The well known Philadelphia dealers Samuel and Henry Chapman handled at least five of the 15 known 1804s during their illustrious careers.[31] Stewart's best opportunity came in May 1913, when Samuel Chapman sold the impaired Adams-Lyman specimen at the bargain price of $340. Nicer examples had sold for more than 10 times as much, but Stewart may have been put off by the fact that this particular example was a class III restrike.[32] Although the full story on the 1804 dollars was unknown at the time, it was clear even in 1913 that this specimen was not an "original," and Chapman admitted as much in the catalog description. Later research indicated that even the class I coins were not struck in the first Mint, but in Stewart's time the lack of an 1804 constituted a hole in a collection of coins thought to have been struck on North Seventh Street.

Despite lacking the confidence, or ambition, to step up to the plate on the 1804 dollar, which he clearly had the means to purchase, Stewart still had a working understanding of the coin trade. Perhaps writing about the Chapman brothers, Stewart made the following observation:

> There are literally tens of thousands of old coins, particularly the old-fashioned large copper cents, mixed with tokens and foreign coins, practically all of no market value, that were hoarded by persons long since deceased . . . . there is little to be gained by their possession, but in order to avoid any possible chance of being careless with an item of extraordinary value they should be taken to an old established, reliable and respectable coin dealer for inspection and appraisal . . . . the long established dealers with a place of business [the Chapmans had opened their doors in Philadelphia in 1878] are as a rule entitled to confidence and worthy of their profession, but they have to buy so that they can sell at a profit. Some

of them hold sales at auction on regular commission, and a person unfamiliar with such sales would be amazed at the totals realized when a really fine coin collection is sold under the hammer.[33]

Stewart himself marveled at the $3,600 price that a class I 1804 had fetched in 1907[34] and thought that it would be a pleasant thing if perhaps a few were discovered during the excavation of 37 and 39 North Seventh Street. "If a few 1804 dollars should be found in the buildings," he wrote, "their removal would be rendered easier." Always the practical businessman, Stewart knew it was unlikely. "But this is highly improbable," he added, "although there will undoubtedly be a few [other] coins discovered."[35] A local reporter listened to Stewart's story, and perhaps trying to sensationalize the import of the moment reported precisely the opposite. "It is expected," he wrote, "with some degree of confidence, that there may be discovered a few of the rare and highly prized silver dollars of the coinage of 1804, and which are reckoned by numismatists to be worth between $3,600 and $3,800 each."[36]

Stewart's expectation that *some* coins would be found was more than reasonable. He was aware, perhaps, of an excavation effort at nearby Independence Square, which in 1876 had unearthed a number of American, German, and Russian coins dated between 1778 and 1803.[37] The Independence Square campus was the gift that kept on giving, for, at the advanced date of 1968, excavators working the site uncovered an 1834 U.S. $5 gold piece, and an 1815 five-thaler German gold coin.[38] In addition nearly 100 other coins were found, ranging in date from 1723 through the 1900s.[39] But, as Stewart anticipated, no 1804 dollars were unearthed at the first Mint site, and Stewart never acquired an example on the secondary market.

Lacking the 1804, the next focus of an early dollar collection is the 1794, the first year in which silver dollars were struck. Stewart's 1794 dollar is an alteration similar to his 1796 half cent, the catalog record indicating "altered date."[40] The 1794 clearly shows discoloration around the 4 in the date and is in fact an altered 1795 (Bowers/Borckardt-27). W. David Perkins, early dollar expert, commented that "for 26 years I've read about 'many dollars altered to 1794 dated dollars.' This is the first I've seen."[41] Fake 1794s were more familiar to the collectors of Stewart's day. *The Coin Collector's Journal*, for example, in March 1877 noted a "fine electrotype forgery" which had recently sold for $2.50.[42] Today, the risk involved in producing an altered 1794 is considerable—not only may an otherwise valuable 1795 dollar be defaced to accomplish the forgery, but the perpetrator must be reasonably sure of a profitable sale, a challenging task when nearly all 1794s are today authenticated and entombed in plastic holders. In Stewart's time a 1795 could be acquired for several dollars—today the figure is several thousand. Besides the altered coin, a second 1794 dollar appears in the Congress Hall accession records, with the notation "stolen from calssroom [sic] 9/28/61."[43] The fact that the

altered coin was left for another day suggests that Stewart might have owned a genuine 1794 after all.

Stewart's remaining early dollars present better than other portions of this collection. While they are not completely problem-free, they are reasonably detailed, and a number exhibit attractive toning. Stewart pursued a date set, which, along with the exception of the 1794 and 1804 discussed above, is missing only the 1796.

This 1804 dollar, sold for $3600 in Henry Chapman's sale of the Stickney collection in 1907, captured Stewart's imagination.

THE KING OF UNITED STATES COINS!

849 1804 Original. Upper right hand star almost touches the letter Y. R. The words STATES OF evenly spaced between the eagle's wings. Borders are beaded as are the dimes of this year. Letters on edge are lightly struck, some almost invisible as is all the other five examples there being but the six known—as follows—No. 1 U. S. Mint, Philadelphia, weight 415 40/1000; No. 2 Appleton collection in N. E. Hist. So., Boston; No. 3, Byron Reeed now in City Museum, Omaha (formerly in Parmelee Collection); No. 4, W. F. Dunham, Chicago, (from S. H. & H. Chapman 1885 to J. V. Dexter, to M. A. Brown to Mr. Dunham) weight 415 307/1000; No. 5, J. H. Manning, Albany, (from Wetmore, Adams, Parmelee, Cohen collection) weight 410 750/1000; No. 6 the present piece which Mr. Stickney received May 9, 1843 from the U. S. Mint at Philadelphia, it being a duplicate, in exchange for other coins one of which was an impression in *gold* of the 1785 Immune Columbia and which coin has remained to this day as the *only* example known. This 1804 dollar has never been out of Mr. Stickney's possession and so carefully guarded by him that few persons were ever even allowed to see it.

The 1804 dollar description from the Chapman catalog of the Stickney collection.

The 1794 dollar from Stewart's Old Mint collection, more precisely an example of a 1795 (Bower/Borckardt-27) with an altered date.

The 1795 dollar, Flowing Hair type, Bowers/Borckardt-27.

The 1795 dollar, Draped Bust type, Bowers/Borckardt-52.

The 1797 dollar, Small Eagle reverse, Bowers/Borckardt-71.

The 1798 dollar, Heraldic Eagle reverse, Bowers/Borckardt-122.

The 1799/8 overdate dollar, Bowers/Borckardt-143.

The 1800 dollar, Bowers/Borckardt-196.

The 1801 dollar, Bowers/Borckardt-213.

The 1802 dollar, Bowers/Borckardt-241.

The 1803 dollar, Bowers/Borckardt-255.

STEWART'S "FIRST" COIN OF THE FIRST MINT: THE 1792 HALF DISME

The half disme of 1792 is unique in the literal sense of that oft-misused word. As the first coin issued under the federal Constitution, it takes precedence over all emissions that followed. It is one of only two circulating U.S. coins (Fugio cents being the other) that were not struck at a Mint facility, for all 1,500 of them were created before the construction of the buildings on North Seventh Street had even begun. It remains the only U.S. coin that is widely considered to be a pattern, despite the fact that most of the 300 or so survivors show evidence of heavy circulation. And of course, with the exception of the 1792 pattern disme, it is the only U.S. coin ever to bear the French spelling of "disme." Frank H. Stewart regarded the half disme as a pivotal symbol of the first Mint, as demonstrated by his making it the centerpiece of John Ward Dunsmore's painting, *Washington Inspecting the First Money Coined by the United States*, and also his gathering of two examples for the Old Mint collection.

A coin of such distinctiveness must be of abiding interest to numismatists, and this observation is amply borne out in the marketplace. Every one of the surviving half dismes, no matter how dismal their state of preservation, is eagerly sought by collectors. Adding to the allure of these diminutive pieces of silver is the assertion by chief coiner Adam Eckfeldt, as recorded in a memorandum by Philadelphia numismatist John A. McAllister Jr., that President George Washington deposited silver "Bullion or Coin" in the amount of $100, from which all of the half dismes were struck.[44] The McAllister memorandum lacks independent corroboration; thus, there is no way of knowing whether the "Martha Washington half disme," as it was known even before McAllister's memorandum surfaced, truly owes its provenance to the first president or to someone else entirely.

What is known beyond dispute about these intriguing inaugural products of the Mint comes from the pen of Secretary of State Thomas Jefferson, to whom President Washington initially gave responsibility for the nascent U.S. Mint. On July 11, 1792, Jefferson noted in his Memorandum Book: "Delivd. 75 D. at the Mint to be coined."[45] The "Mint" to which Jefferson referred was the basement of a building occupied by John Harper, saw manufacturer, located at North Sixth and Cherry Streets in Philadelphia, which temporarily housed the Mint's first machinery until the facilities on North Seventh Street were ready for use.[46] A mere two days later, Jefferson recorded, once again in his Memorandum Book: "Recd. from the mint 1500. half dismes of the new coinage."[47]

After this, however, the certainties about the 1,500 half dismes quickly evaporate. We know that Jefferson left Philadelphia for Monticello on July 13, shortly after accepting delivery of the new coinage, and that he paid a visit to President Washington at Mount Vernon on October 1, 1792, but neither Washington nor Jefferson, or indeed anyone else, recorded what became of the first products of the infant U.S. Mint.[48] Eckfeldt's reminiscences, as recorded in the McAllister memorandum, claim that Washington handed out the half dismes as gifts to friends and relatives, both in Virginia and abroad. No evidence has been found to corroborate this statement, however, and since most surviving specimens are heavily circulated, it is very likely that most of the half dismes were released into the channels of commerce. This supposition seems to be confirmed by a passage in President Washington's Fourth Annual Address to Congress, November 6, 1792, which reads: "There has also been a small beginning in the coinage of half dismes; the want of small change in circulation calling first attention to them."[49]

A number of half dismes were indeed saved as souvenirs, although none can be traced to Washington. In Henry Chapman's 39th catalog (the October 4, 1919, American Numismatic Association sale), lot 249 was a 1792 half disme described as uncirculated, with file [adjustment] marks. Chapman added: "This specimen has an interesting history, being one of four that belonged to David Rittenhouse, the astronomer and first Director of the U.S. Mint, 1792 through 1795, and has never been out of the family until now."[50] Apparently, Rittenhouse at one time had owned a significant number of the half dismes, for Frank Stewart received the following letter, dated June 12, 1915, from a Philadelphia physician named George S. Gerhard:

David Rittenhouse, engraving by Christian Gobrecht, 1835, derived from painting by Charles Willson Peale.

The David Rittenhouse silver 'Half Disme' (never in circulation) came into my possession many years ago having been given to me by my half uncle, David Rittenhouse Sergeant, a son of Jonathan Dickinson Sergeant (my great-grandfather) by his second wife Elizabeth Rittenhouse. David Rittenhouse Sergeant, when I was a young boy, had a number, perhaps eight or nine, of these coins which he had inherited from his mother and what has become of them, I do not know.[51]

Elizabeth Rittenhouse was David Rittenhouse's daughter, which would explain how she came into the possession of eight or nine half dismes. As for Dr. Gerhard's specimen, Stewart notes that it went missing from his estate shortly after his death.[52] Stewart wrote to Albert P. Gerhard, probably a son, on December 13, 1920:

I thank you for your letter of the 6th instant and regret to learn that you have not located the Washington half-dime [sic]. Dr. Gerhard I judge put it with his most prized relics because when he showed it to me it was wrapped in tissue paper and because of its traditions was of great personal interest to him.[53]

We do know of one other half disme that was reserved at or shortly after the time of striking. In Thomas Elder's

The 1792 half disme from the Old Mint collection.

A second 1792 half disme from the Old Mint collection.

197th sale (October 9 through 11, 1924), he offered a collection of coins belonging to Edward H. Eckfeldt Jr. of Orange, New Jersey. Elder stated: "Mr. Eckfeldt is of the fifth generation descended from Adam Eckfeldt, the first coiner [sic] of the U.S. Mint, and includes among the highlights of the collection . . . a Martha Washington Half Disme of 1792 in almost proof condition, one of the very first impressions, and inherited by the present owner from the well known Mr. Eckfeldt of American numismatic and Mint history."[54] Actually, Edward Hooper Eckfeldt Jr. was descended from chief coiner Adam Eckfeldt's half brother, Michael (1779–1833).

Clearly, Mint Director David Rittenhouse and Adam Eckfeldt, who in 1792 was not yet employed by the Mint, but was a contractor for it, reserved a portion of the half disme mintage, amounting to about one percent of the total, as keepsakes. Whether Washington or Jefferson did the same is an imponderable at this point. It is certain that the bulk of the issue of 1,500 half dismes went into circulation, and began to meet, as President Washington noted, the desperate need for small change in the early American republic.

In Frank H. Stewart's heyday, the early decades of the 20th century, the McAllister memorandum had yet to be discovered (the first of its three versions was not revealed until 1943), but the stories of the 1792 half disme being struck from the Washingtons' silver tableware and of Martha Washington serving as the model for Miss Liberty were well established, having first appeared in print in 1846.[55] Despite this stellar pedigree, however, half dismes were not valued as highly as comparable rarities, such the 1794 silver dollar, mainly because the first coins struck by the Mint were considered to be patterns, and patterns were not as highly prized then as they are now. In the celebrated 1867 Mickley sale, a high-grade 1794 silver dollar sold for $75, while an uncirculated 1792 half disme, cataloged as a pattern, garnered only one tenth as much.

Frank Stewart bucked this tide of relative indifference. He directed that a tray of freshly struck half dismes would be the focal point of John Ward Dunsmore's *Washington Inspecting* in the (mistaken) belief that these were the first coins struck at the North Seventh Street Mint. For Stewart, the connection was highly important: the 1792 half disme represented the first emission of the first Mint, of which he was the last owner. Other coins may have been more expensive in his day, but there were none in his eyes that were more significant.

Stewart's, and all the 1792 half dismes, were all struck from a single pair of dies, so there are no varieties. Variation exists, however, in the centering of the strike upon the planchets. The dentils surrounding the edge of the coin in some examples, presumably those struck later in the press run, pull away from the edge of the coin on both the obverse and the reverse. This results in blank space between the dentils and edge, and in extreme cases, the loss of small portions of the lettering that surrounds the main devices on both the obverse and reverse.

Frank Stewart purchased a pair of half dismes for the Old Mint collection, which was unusual in that he was satisfied with single specimens of most other coins. Both have sustained heavy circulation, but are readily identifiable in their main design elements. The first (Independence National Historical Park no. 9245) displays a well-centered strike with evidence of uniform wear. Devices and lettering, though worn, are all legible. A few small scratches on both sides, especially over the "RY" of "INDUSTRY" on the obverse, serve to hallmark the piece, as does a smattering of discolored spots around the bust of Miss Liberty. Unfortunately, some vandal attempted to hole the piece in the space between "LIB. PAR." on the obverse, and the damage has been crudely repaired. Overall, this specimen merits a grade of Very Good-8.

The second half disme (Independence National Historical Park no. 9244) displays neither a well-centered strike nor evidence of uniform circulation. The dentils pull away from the edge, most notably around "INDUSTRY" on the obverse and "AMERICA" on the reverse, and a few obverse letters are affected. The reverse shows much greater evidence of wear than does the obverse. The eagle on the reverse, although still identifiable as such, has lost most of its detail, the words "HALF DISME" beneath it are simply obliterated, and much of the lettering around the denticles is lost. The obverse has sustained several scratches, particularly on and in front of Miss Liberty's nose, and discolored spots are both above and behind the bust. Overall, the piece merits a split grade of Good-4 for the obverse and About Good-3 for the reverse. Like most of Stewart's coins, the pair exhibits a greater appreciation for the history of the Mint than for the *products* of the Mint. Yet, today both are highly desirable as representatives of the seminal year in American numismatics, even if less so as pristine artifacts, which they certainly are not.

Thus, while they certainly do not rival the half dismes set aside by Rittenhouse or Eckfeldt in terms of condition or historical significance, the half dismes of the Old Mint collection are still important specimens in their own way. Besides being examples of the inaugural effort of the U.S. Mint, they represent nearly one percent of all of the survivors of our nation's "small beginning" in coinage, pieces that were personally delivered, as possibly planchets, to Harper's cellar, and personally received, as coins, by Thomas Jefferson. Then there is the legend, unconfirmed but persistent, of the connection to George Washington. Despite their cuts and scrapes in the service of commerce, these two half dismes are centerpieces of the Old Mint collection, the heralds of a new dawn in the history of coinage in the United States, and talismans for Frank Stewart's devotion to the heritage of the first U.S. Mint.

THE 1792 PATTERN DISME

Beyond the half disme, Stewart used "1792" as a logo both within his company letterhead and upon the façades of the old and new buildings at 37 through 39 North Seventh Street. The year "1792" shows up in other Frank H. Stewart Electric Company literature, for example on the cover of his booklet *For the Man Who Buys Electrical Supplies.* Stewart thus employed the "1792" number as a brand, much as a modern auto manufacturer might use model numbers as part of an overall marketing strategy. As such the number represented much more than the first year of the first Mint—to Stewart it further symbolized the vitality of the Frank H. Stewart Electric Company, which was of course, merely a proxy for the man himself.

Stewart would thus have been bitterly disappointed to learn that his 1792 half dismes were in fact not struck in his first Mint buildings. The pride and joy of his collection, Stewart's half dismes were not quite the embodiment of historicity that he made them out to be. In short, Dunsmore's painting falls down the slippery slope in this regard, at best mythology and at worst fraud. Genuine products of 1792 they might be, but coins created in

Cover of Frank H. Stewart Electric Company promotional booklet. The year 1682 marked Penn's arrival in Pennsylvania; 1792, the construction of the First Mint; 1894, the founding of the Stewart Electric Company; and 1910, the year of publication.

Stewart's "Sugar Alley" Mint they are not. Whether Stewart was aware of this when the painting was conceived, or came to be aware over time, is unknown. The most pertinent bibliographic resource in Stewart's era would have been Sylvester Sage Crosby's *The United States Coinage of 1793*, published in 1897, which contains some discussion of 1792 issues and indicates that the half dismes were struck in Harper's cellar, as noted above. Stewart was familiar with Crosby's masterwork, *The Early Coins of America*, which is mentioned in his 1947 pamphlet on the Mark Newby St. Patrick coinage. Whether he fully comprehended the lesser known *Coinage of 1793*, or perhaps chose to ignore it, can only be left for speculation.

Stewart possessed other issues of 1792, and these too are shrouded in archival mist. The counterpart of the 1792 half disme is the 1792 disme, which comes in several varieties and is represented in the Stewart collection by a reeded-edge copper specimen (Judd-10, Independence Hall National Park no. 9267). Congress Hall accession records offer conflicting evidence as to whether or not this piece was uncovered during the excavation of the first Mint. The point is important, for it is not clear whether the 1792 disme was, like the half disme, struck in Harper's cellar, or whether it was struck in the first Mint. The design of the coin bears some similarity to the half disme, and it is reasonable to speculate that both were coined about the same time. Ebenezer Locke Mason Jr., in 1885, went so far as to ascribe to the 1792 disme the same mythology surrounding the half disme:

> It is recorded that Washington resorted to this mint for the private coinage of 1792 silver dismes and half dismes, which were coined from a portion of his old silver plate, and presented by him to friends of the family.[56]

Mason conveniently failed to note where "it is recorded," nor does he touch upon the fact that only three of the silver dismes are known; the remainder of the issue was struck in copper. If Mason didn't cover the copper end of it, William

H. Sheldon later did, suggesting that Washington donated a copper tea kettle for the coinage for 1793 cents.[57]

Regardless of the origin of the bullion, Stewart's coin reveals a clue about its excavation status, for it exhibits significant signs of circulation and warrants a grade of About Good-3. A specimen struck within the Mint and misplaced should bear substantially more detail, so it seems more likely that Stewart's coin came from the secondary market and not from the Mint itself. Further, he made no mention in his writings of having found the 1792 disme during the excavation, surely a notable event if in fact such was the case. Other low-grade examples of the 1792 disme exist, reinforcing the idea that some number of these coins entered circulation and ultimately landed in the hands of dealers and collectors like Stewart.

In recent times, the 1792 copper reeded-edge disme has captured the imagination of collector Ed Price, who amassed a mini-hoard of six specimens.[58] Price was "interested in understanding how many of these existed" and came to the conclusion that the number was on the order of 20 or 25. Price's high-grade NGC Proof-62 Brown specimen auctioned in July 2008 for $690,000.[59] By contrast, Stewart's lowly About Good example, while of course not approaching the $1,000,000 mark, would still merit a five-figure bid at public sale.

THE 1792 SILVER CENTER CENT PLANCHETS

Next in Stewart's "1792" parade is a pair of silver center cent planchets. Unlike the 1792 pattern disme, these two planchets were unquestionably found in the Rear Building and proved to be Stewart's most exciting find from a numismatic perspective. The planchets represented a quick return on Stewart's investment, for they were found in 1907 shortly after he purchased the old Mint, when the Rear Building was demolished. Stewart noted that the planchets "fell down from the overhead joists," along with a number of cents and half cents.[60]

The silver center cent, as opposed to much of the other 1792 coinage, carries a strong documentary trail. Henry Voigt, the Mint coiner, noted in his account book that on December 17th, 1792, he "struck off a few pieces of copper coins."[61] The next day, Thomas Jefferson followed up with the President:

> Th. Jefferson has the honor to send the President 2 cents made on Voigt's plan by putting a silver plug worth 3/4 of a cent into a copper worth 1/4 of a cent. Mr. Rittenhouse is about to make a few by mixing the same plug by fusion with the same quantity of copper. He will then make of copper alone of the same size and lastly he will make the real cent as ordered by Congress 4 times as big. Specimens of these several ways of making the cent may now be delivered to the Committee of Congress now having the subject before them.[62]

The 1792 disme from the Stewart Old Mint collection at Congress Hall.

"Voigt's plan" had the advantage of creating a smaller and more manageable coin than the eventual large cent. Conversely, the production of the silver center cent was considerably more complicated, requiring the insertion of a silver plug into a hole formed in the middle of the copper planchet. The Mint had enough problems to deal with, and only a few samples were coined. P. Scott Rubin identified 11 distinct specimens in 1984.[63] The silver center cents are known both with and without reeding, and Stewart's pair of planchets represents a complete set, for one exhibits a plain edge while the other presents an "imperfectly milled edge."[64] Yet another variant, Rittenhouse's "fusible alloy," did away with the silver plug entirely and mixed the silver and copper into a single planchet.

Stewart's two planchets are otherwise unremarkable in appearance—blank copper disks with a center perforation. But in locating the planchets during the excavation, Stewart demonstrated that the silver center cents were in fact manufactured within the new Mint, and further that the newly created coinage factory was operable by December of 1792. Stewart's planchets taken as a pair are unique, and none others have come to light in the century since. Stewart was proud of the significance of his find, as he wrote in a prospectus for his book *History of the First United States Mint*: "It will also prove that the 'Voigt' cent as named by Mr. Stewart was the first copper coin struck at the Mint. This is commonly known as the silver center cent."[65]

In 1947, he again referred to the pair of planchets, in the context of his research on the enigmatic Mark Newby coppers:

> The writer hopes that some time in the future a researcher who has better ability, better facilities and perfect specimens may contribute to the Numismatist additional information about Mark Newby and his coins. While the problem may mean hard work it will be no greater than the successful effort to prove that the Voight [sic] silver center cent was a product of the First U.S. Mint.[66]

While Stewart was undoubtedly engaging in a bit of chest puffing towards the end of his life, the silver center cent planchet find was duly recognized in its day. Edgar H. Adams and William H. Woodin noted in their 1913 work *United States Pattern, Trial and Experimental Pieces*:

> When excavations were made alongside the old Mint building on Seventh Street a short time ago there were found several specimens of these odd little copper pieces, with perforated centres, both with reeded and smoothed edges. The small plug of silver inserted in the centre [sic] evidently was intended to bring the intrinsic value of the coin up to the exact value of one cent.

More excited was the Connecticut collector J.C. Mitchelson. When we last met Mitchelson, he was putting his

High-grade 1792 silver center cent.

Silver center cent planchet, with plain edge. 5.6 g., diameter 22.mm. Currently on loan from Independence Hall (INHP no. 9249) to the U.S. Mint, and bearing U.S. Mint inventory number no. 37017. The adhesive is probably from an old museum label.

Fusible alloy version of the 1792 cent.

Silver center cent planchet, with partially reeded edge, 4.9 g., diameter 21 mm. On loan from Independence Hall (INHP no. 9250) to the Mint, inventory no. 37018.

name in the hat for any first Mint dies that Stewart might make available. Stewart evidently responded shortly after Mitchelson's initial inquiry in November 1908, apparently describing his 1792 pattern disme in copper, and Mitchelson took the bait, making a dubious trade offer in return:

> I think your disme must be a pattern piece. I have seen several of them. I have not gone into pattern coins until lately so am now just getting worked[?] up on them. You know of the Half Disme struck in silver they are not rare. I have a couple of them they have the head of Martha Washington and tis said she gave $100.00 worth of her old silver to make into half dismes these are truly the first coins struck at the Mint your place of business. If your pattern piece is in good shape I will exchange you one of my half dismes in silver for it. . . . Did you find any of the old dies laying around or buried near your establishment I would like very much to get hold of any old tools used in the Original Mint for keep sakes. . . . I have a good many duplicates. . . . I will trade you some of these for your copper disme if you wish.[67]

Stewart's 1792 copper disme was a dozen times more scarce than the half disme Mitchelson offered in return and yet Mitchelson, the self-confessed pattern neophyte, claimed to have seen several of them. Mitchelson was in truth no beginner, having joined the ANA some years previous.[68] And while Stewart may not have been an ace numismatist, trading skill was quite another matter. The two gentlemen eventually agreed to meet in Philadelphia. Many years later, Stewart described Mitchelson's quest for a silver center cent planchet:

> The late J.C. Mitchelson offered a fifty-dollar California "slug" then worth three times that much for one of the two planchets now at Congress Hall. The writer called them "buttons" and the genial fellow from Tarriffville [sic], Connecticut, "played ignorant" but he was much disappointed. We never met after we parted at Mahlon Newton's, Green's Hotel, 8th and Chestnut Streets, Philadelphia, a long time ago.[69]

A slightly different version, again written by Stewart, appeared in The Numismatist:

> The story of the find [of the silver-center cent] was published in the metropolitan newspapers, and a gentleman who has since died and who bequeathed his collection to the State of Connecticut, came all the way to Philadelphia and made me what some would consider a fabulous offer for what I, to tease him, called a copper button.[70]

Stewart's true feelings were revealed in an early draft of *History of the First United States Mint*:

> Mr. J.C. Mitchelson of Tariffville, Conn., a very congenial gentleman, with a very strong sense of humor,

visited me shortly after the demolition of the smelting house building, and offered me a $50 hexagonal California slug for one of the silver center cent planchets. After considerably joking, I declined the trade on the grounds that the findings of the old Mint should be kept in Philadelphia.[71]

Mitchelson struck out at the first Mint, but did better with the third, being friendly with Thomas L. Comparette, the Mint Cabinet curator. Comparette was instrumental in placing coins from the annual pyx into the Mitchelson collection, today housed at the Connecticut State Library.[72] The collection includes a significant group of pattern pieces, numbering nearly 400 specimens.[73] Despite failing to accomplish a deal, Mitchelson and Stewart seem to have stayed on good terms, for Mitchelson later wrote of Stewart's research, "No one appreciates your good work more than I."[74]

Stewart's "1792" collection thus consisted of the pair of silver center cent planchets, a pair of 1792 half dismes, and one 1792 disme. While incomplete (other cents and a quarter dollar are known), the five-piece assemblage is the highlight of the Stewart collection, the two half dismes being particularly significant in terms of the Stewart pedigree and their visceral connection to the iconic painting by John Ward Dunsmore. Indeed, Stewart's visual mythology of the first Mint flows directly from these two tiny pieces of silver, and as such the two coins carry a special significance which far outweighs their deficient state of preservation.

Beyond legitimate 1792 issues, Stewart also owned an example of the Dickeson 1792 pattern cent fantasy, discussed earlier. The acquisitive J.C. Mitchelson fancied the issue as well, both collectors perhaps covering the bases "just in case" the coin turned out to be something important. Wishful thinking may have also come into play, for a "cent, copper trial piece, 1792" appears in the Congress Hall accession records. The catalog here almost certainly refers to the Dickeson fabrication, made from an embossed revenue stamp for documents, which bears the inscription "TRIAL PIECE / DESIGNED FOR UNITED STATES CENT / 1792," and which almost certainly was not found during the Mint excavation.[75]

Some 100 years after Stewart excavated the pair of silver center cent planchets, a northern California collector similarly hit pay dirt with the acquisition of a struck silver center cent. Purchased out of a police auction for $400 in 2006, the collector came to question the authenticity of the piece and "had given up on it," before submitting the coin for professional authentication in 2008. The coin was indeed genuine, the 14th known, with one expert suggesting that it "was likely an excavation find." How the coin got from the first Mint in Philadelphia to California was anyone's guess. In any case, the lucky bidder passed on a potential six-figure payday, indicating that "I have a great piece of history to share. I'll relish holding it for a while. I didn't become a coin collector because of money."[76] Much the same could be said of Stewart himself.

Gold Coins in the Stewart Collection

For whatever reason, Stewart did not systematically seek the gold coins struck in the first Mint. Based on the resources allocated to the remainder of the collection, it is fair to say that Stewart may not have perceived a commensurate historical value in the gold coinage. Stewart referred to the idea, obliquely, around 1913:

> Individual examples of each of the gold, silver and copper coins made in the U.S. Mint in perfect condition would bring more at auction than it cost to erect our new building, and that is no small sum [about forty thousand dollars at the time]. We have a modest collection sufficiently large enough to enthuse those interested in old and rare coins, some of which were found on site of the old mint building.[77]

Stewart's "Old Mint" collection thus included only gold half eagles of the year 1804 and 1806, and a third, more interesting specimen of the year 1803. Stewart's 1803, unfortunately missing from the collection today, was struck in copper and is cataloged within the United States pattern series as an off-metal strike (Judd-27). The Judd pattern reference describes this issue as a private restrike, created from dies which escaped the Mint. The uspatterns.com website speculates that this concoction was another Dickeson fantasy, produced *ca.* 1860. If so, it is a fitting companion to the Dickeson 1792 cent earlier discussed.

Coins Discovered in the First Mint Excavation

Along with the two silver center cent planchets, Stewart uncovered a number of other coins and planchets during the Mint excavation. Congress Hall records are somewhat inconsistent on the exact list of these—following is the authors' list based on analysis of the available records. A number of these pieces are currently on loan from Independence National Historical Park (INHP) to the U.S. Mint in Philadelphia, where they are displayed in the exhibition area.

Half cent planchets (3?), copper (INHP no. 9260). Accession records alternately indicate one, two, or three half cent planchets, and further that this item is on loan to the Mint (Mint inventory no. 37023). The specimen at the Mint is 6.6 g, 22 mm. Stewart noted three examples in *History of the First United States Mint.*[78]

The Stewart collection also contains a fragment of half cent scissel which remains at Independence Hall. This is no doubt the same piece plated in Stewart's *History.*[79] The diameter of the void is 22 mm.

1825 Half cent (INHP no. 9277). 4.4 g, diameter 23 mm. Corroded. Probably the same as plated in Stewart's *History.*[80]

Silver center cent planchets (2), copper (INHP nos. 9249, 9250). INHP no. 9249 is 5.6 g, diameter 22 mm, and on loan to the Mint (inventory no. 37017). This piece

The 1804 half eagle from the Stewart Old Mint collection.

37023

Half cent planchet from the Mint excavation. (INHP no. 9260)

Half cent scissel from the first Mint excavation.

exhibits a plain, but not smoothed, edge. INHP no. 9250 is 4.9 g, 21 mm, and also on loan to the Mint (inventory no. 37018). This planchet is partially reeded. (Both are illustrated in the previous section.)

Large cent planchet, copper (INHP no. 9251). 13.6 g, diameter 27 mm. The *Philadelphia North American*, on August 15, 1911, reported the finding of a large cent planchet, with edge lettering ONE HUNDRED FOR A DOLLAR.[81] Stewart appears to have referred to this piece in *History*, describing a planchet "with the letter A stamped thereon."[82] On loan to the Mint (inventory no. 37011).

Large cent planchet, copper (INHP no. 9252). 13.3 g, diameter 25 mm. Vine and bars edge device. On loan to the Mint (inventory no. 37015).

Large cent planchet, copper (INHP no. 9254). 10.8 g, diameter 27 mm. On loan to the Mint (inventory no. 37020).

Large cent planchet, copper (INHP no. 9255). 10.3 g, diameter 28 mm. On loan to the Mint (inventory no. 37021).

Large cent planchet, copper (INHP no. 9256). 13.2 g, diameter 26 mm. On loan to the Mint (inventory no. 37022).

Large cent, corroded (INHP no. 9273). 10.1 g, diameter 28 mm. The date is unreadable.

Large cent, corroded (INHP no. 9275). 7.6 g, diameter 28 mm. Currently on loan to the Mint (inventory no. 167001). The date is unreadable.

1816 Large cent (INHP no. 9270). 9.7 g, diameter 28 mm. Possibly the same as referred to in Stewart's *History*.[83]

1818 Large cent (INHP no. 9272). 10.1 g, diameter 28 mm.

1826 Large cent (INHP no. 9271). 10.4 g, diameter 28 mm. Probably the same coin plated in Stewart's *History*.[84]

1832 Large cent (INHP no. 9269). 10.7 g, diameter 29 mm. Probably the same coin plated in Stewart's *History*.[85]

1834 Large cent. This coin is unnoted in Independence Hall records and not present in the collection today. However, Stewart depicted the 1834 large cent in *History of the First United States Mint* (1924), and indicated that it was found at the first U.S. Mint site.[86] Stewart demarcated 1832 as the terminus of first Mint coinage, and may not have considered this coin to be properly associated with the first Mint. The plate including the 1834 was originally prepared about 1909 for inclusion in Stewart's *Ye Olde Mint* pamphlet. Stewart likely reused the plate simply as a matter of convenience.

Half dime planchet, copper (INHP no. 9258). 1.4 g, diameter 16 mm.

1795 half dime in copper, Judd-21 (INHP no. 9268). 1.3 g, diameter 16 mm, bent. Normally struck in silver, this off-metal striking was probably intended to test the die pair (Logan/McCloskey-9, Valentine-6[87]) before coinage of the more valuable metal commenced. The coin has been defaced, likely to prevent its circulation as a "normal" half dime. The uspatterns.com website notes two specimens, Stewart's and a second "pierced and plugged" example appearing in John Haseltine's April 1870 sale and making a probable subsequent appearance in Mason & Company's June 1870 sale.

Two half-dollar planchets, silver (INHP no. 9247, no. 9248). The first is 13.2 g, diameter 31 mm, currently on loan to the Mint (inventory no. 37016). The second is 13.5 g, diameter 32 mm, also on loan to the Mint (inventory no. 37024).

1803 half eagle, copper (INHP no. 9266). As previously noted, Independence Hall records note this piece missing as of 1969. Stewart indicated an 1804 half eagle in copper was found in the excavation,[88] but this piece is not cataloged in the Independence Hall collection. The 1804 half eagle, like the 1803, is known in copper (Judd-29 to Judd-32).

The 1825 half cent from the first Mint excavation. The existing label is dissolvable in acetone, consistent with modern museum practice. (INHP no. 9277)

Large cent planchet from the first Mint excavation, counterstamped, with lettered edge. (INHP no. 9251)

Large cent planchet from the first Mint excavation, exhibiting vine and bars edge device. (INHP no. 9252)

Large cent planchet from the first Mint excavation. (INHP no. 9254)

Large cent planchet from the first Mint excavation. (INHP no. 9255)

Large cent planchet from the first Mint excavation. (INHP no. 9256)

Large cent from the first Mint excavation, date unknown. (INHP no. 9273)

Large cent from first Mint excavation, date unknown. (INHP no. 9275)

The 1816 large cent from the first Mint excavation. (INHP no. 9270)

The 1818 large cent from first Mint excavation. (INHP no. 9272)

The 1826 large cent from the first Mint excavation. (INHP no. 9271)

The 1832 large cent from first Mint excavation. (INHP no. 9269)

The 1834 large cent, as depicted in *Ye Olde Mint* and *History of the First United States Mint.*

Half dime planchet in copper, recovered from the first Mint site. The number in red is an old Congress Hall accession marking. (INHP no. 9258)

The 1795 half dime, copper, from the first Mint excavation. (INHP no. 9268)

Half dollar planchets, silver, from the excavation of the first Mint. (INHP no. 9247, no. 9248)

Frank H. Stewart and Congress Hall

Sometime around 1910, Stewart conceived the idea of exhibiting his collection, in conjunction with the "Old Mint" marketing brand of the Frank H. Stewart Electric Company. Stewart cast his electric eye two blocks south and happened upon Congress Hall. This building lies on the west side of Independence Square in Old City Philadelphia, part of the Independence Hall complex, a few steps south of the iconic Liberty Bell.

Stewart was attracted to using Congress Hall for exhibition for a number of reasons, including the fact that the Mint Act of 1792 was passed in the same building.[89] While private collectors vied to acquire the Stewart first Mint desiderata,[90] Stewart also considered donating the collection to the U.S. Mint, then in its third location.[91] The third Mint was an attractive site, recently constructed in 1901, decked in Italian flooring and glass installed by the firm of Louis Comfort Tiffany.[92] A two-story rotunda housed the U.S. Mint coin collection which contained such delicacies as two 1804 dollars, a Brasher doubloon, the unique 1849 double eagle, an ultra-high relief $20 gold piece from 1907, and many other tempting morsels.[93] Surrounding the exhibition room were encaustic (molten beeswax) panels executed by William B. Van Ingen, a Tiffany apprentice whose work graced the Library of Congress as well.[94] Stewart would have been further impressed by the adaptation of electricity in the building, and the self-sufficient nature of the Mint's on-site electrical generators.[95] The venue was highly desirable, but Stewart was driven more by history than modern opulence.

Stewart certainly knew that Congress Hall was the seat of American government from 1790 until 1800, the equivalent of the present day Capitol in Washington, D.C. Presidents Washington and Adams were inaugurated in this historic edifice, but after the turn of the 19th century the structure reverted from federal to municipal use and was eventually abandoned in 1895.[96] Gradually, the public began to recognize the legacy of the structure, and a cry was heard to restore Congress Hall. Elizabeth McClellan, "chairman of the Committee of Thirteen" of the Pennsylvania Society of the Colonial Dames of America, in 1898 penned a letter to the *Pennsylvania Magazine of History and Biography*[97] calling for research and restoration of the edifice. Many years later, Frank H. Stewart claimed credit for having similarly advocated the renovation.[98] By 1913 the work was complete, and President Woodrow Wilson participated in the dedication ceremonies,[99] elegantly linking in a dignitary fashion the first and his own presidencies.

The resurrection of Congress Hall surely appealed to Stewart. Congress Hall and the Frank H. Stewart Electric Company were Old City Philadelphia, while the third U.S.

The third U.S. Mint, from an old postcard.

Mint, oozing with grandeur or not, was little more than the upstart newcomer, and outside the downtown area at that, to the northwest at North 16th and Spring Garden. Wilfred Jordan, Independence Hall's curator, impressed upon Stewart his desire to display items related to the Congressional acts passed in the Congress Hall building, and Stewart was sufficiently convinced to begin a series of donations beginning in 1910 and ending in 1919.[100]

Stewart was concerned that his collection be preserved *in toto* as a separate entity, and donation to the U.S. Mint Cabinet would have merely incorporated his treasures among greater treasures. In 1913, while the bulk of the Stewart collection was already on display at Congress Hall, Stewart expressed his desires to the Curator Jordan. "All of the above," Stewart wrote, "subject to the understanding and acceptance that the old collection be known and labeled as the 'Old Mint Collection,' to be kept intact at Congress or Independence Hall, and open to the public view. In other words, it is not my object to give this rare, historical collection away to find it, at some future time, packed away in boxes or closets."[101]

Stewart conveniently failed to mention that he was using "Old Mint" as a trademark term for his electrical business, but that small bit of commercial interest notwithstanding, Stewart had strong convictions about public accessibility and preservation of archival knowledge. In his personal papers he angrily described a situation where he had donated documents to a local library, only to have an academic acquaintance "treated like a thief" when later calling for the same items.[102] Moreover, Stew-

art's eventual decision to leave his personal collections to Rowan University instead of the Gloucester County Historical Society is rumored to have arisen from the removal of Stewart donations from a fireproof safe.[103] Stewart, who had supported the Society to the extent of $40,000,[104] was apparently displeased with the perceived lack of curatorial competence. Stewart took preservation seriously, as he himself was a victim of archival mismanagement, reported in autobiographical papers:

> Two carloads of ancient records of our business, including my first sales books were deliberately sold for old paper without my sanction or my personal knowledge by a person who had no right or privilege concerning them. They had been promised to a great university but unfortunately there was considerable delay in their acceptance.[105]

Much later, Stewart reflected on his choice of Congress Hall as opposed to the Mint Cabinet:

> Some years ago the excellent[?] coin collection in the Philadelphia Mint was transferred bodily to Washington. It had gradually grown in importance from the days of Adam Eckfeldt by donation and purchase until it vied with everything else in Philadelphia as a mecca for visitors. If I had been unfortunate enough to have given my collection to the Mint instead of the City of Philadelphia which placed in on exhibition in Congress Hall, where the Mint Act was passed in 1792, I should have been very much chagrined by

North view of Congress Hall, which lies on the west side of the Independence Hall complex.

the subsequent transfer. . . . the coin collection of our Philadelphia Mint now in Washington . . . [is] probably forever lost to Philadelphia.[106]

In any case, with Stewart's "Old Mint" collection now comfortably on public display at Congress Hall, the creative businessman began thinking about a new way to promote the "Old Mint" brand. In doing so, Stewart commissioned the indelible pictures of the first U.S. Mint, the iconic works today far better known than Stewart himself. Stewart probably well understood that imagery, "being worth a thousand words," might well eclipse any commercial legacy that he would leave behind. "No person now alive knows the name of the greatest merchant of Philadelphia in the year 1800," he wrote in the early 1930s, shortly after his retirement.[107] And today, perhaps only one person in 1,000 who has seen these pictures of the first U.S. Mint connects them to the man ultimately responsible for their creation, Frank H. Stewart.

Modern views of Independence Hall (south side).

Edwin Lamasure's *Cradle of Liberty*.

Frank H. Stewart's Commissioned Artworks: Edwin Lamasure's *Cradle of Liberty* and *Ye Olde Mint*

A small, frail piece of cardboard, carrying a delicate wash of watercolors, conveys the most familiar image of the long-departed first Mint of the United States. Over the years, this famous painting has been exhibited under less than ideal conditions, and stored under worse; the resulting damage has not always been promptly or properly restored. Even when reproduced for publication—as it has been thousands of times—the image has suffered indignities due to mislabeling, crude croppings and repeated misspellings of the artist's surname. As if these accumulated misfortunes were not enough, critics have assailed Edwin Lamasure Jr.'s painting for the artistic liberties he took and the historical inaccuracies he portrayed within it. Yet, despite all of the difficulties—the fragility, the damage, the mischaracterizations, the aesthetic and historical licenses—*Ye Olde Mint* succeeded as a work of art far beyond the most optimistic imaginings of its creator and its patron. The myriad published reproductions of the painting have spread its fame— quite literally—across the globe, and if there is a single iconic image in the field of the numismatics of the United States, it is, beyond any dispute, Edwin Lamasure Jr.'s rendering of *Ye Olde Mint*.

As with so many other facts and circumstances surrounding Frank H. Stewart and the first U.S. Mint, however, the whole story is far more complex than it appears to be. Before Edwin Lamasure Jr. entered the picture, there was another artist, a Philadelphian by the name of Frank Hamilton Taylor, who made preliminary drawings. Before Taylor, there was Stewart himself, who made measurements and photographs of the Mint buildings prior to razing them. Before the Master of the Mint came a number of mostly anonymous photographers, who began taking shots of the Front Building as early as 1854; and, there was an unnamed engraver in Philadelphia who captured the façade of the Front Building during the Gilded Age. None of these antecedents diminishes Lamasure's accomplishment in painting *Ye Olde Mint*, but there is evidence that Lamasure relied on some of them, especially Taylor's sketch, Stewart's photographs, and the 1854 photo by Frederick Richards, in order to compose his own image. *Ye Olde Mint*, therefore, must be understood in its context as the latest in a long line of efforts to fix the image of the "Sugar Alley Mint" for posterity.

Frank H. Taylor's Predecessors: Pictures of the First United States Mint

1854: The oldest known image of the first Mint, as has been discussed previously, is the photograph of the Front Building taken in 1854 by Frederick De Bourg Richards, and first published in the November 1868 issue of the *American Journal of Numismatics*.[1] The *Journal* included actual prints, tipped in. A copy of the photograph in the Free Library of Philadelphia (depicted here) indicates that the image as published in the *American Journal of Numismatics* was cropped. The catalog of the Library Company of Philadelphia lends additional context to the photograph:

> One of images originally part of a series of eleven scrapbooks compiled by Philadelphia antiquarian Charles A. Poulson in the late 1850s entitled *Illustrations of Philadelphia*. . . . The scrapbooks contained approximately 120 photographs by Philadelphia painter and pioneer photographer [Frederick De Bourg] Richards of 18th-century public, commercial, and residential buildings in the city of Philadelphia commissioned by Poulson to document the vanishing architectural landscape.[2]

The first photograph of the first Mint, F.D. Richards, 1854.

It is almost certain that this image was used by Lamasure in preparation of *Ye Olde Mint*, as will be discussed later.

1883: The Richards photograph was followed by an engraving that appeared in 1883 in *Dye's Coin Encyclopedia*.[3] Ebenezer Locke Mason Jr. reused this image in an 1884 issue of his house organ[4] and the same engraving reappeared yet again in the 1892 edition of George Evans's work, *Illustrated History of the United States Mint*, artist unnamed, but possibly the work of the Electro-Tint Engraving Company, 726 Chestnut Street in Philadelphia.[5] Stewart was aware of this image and commented in 1914, "The oldest print, and the only one I have ever seen, is in Evan's [sic] history of the United States Mint. That shows part of the front building and is incorrect, because there were only two windows on the ground floor. The print shows four."[6] The engraving is also incorrect in that it depicts only two doorways, omitting the center passageway between them. Stewart's use of the word "print" is careful, and we shall later learn that he was aware of the 1854 photograph.

1898 or earlier: This photograph is known only through an unattributed news clipping, with the notation "Levytype Co. Phila." at the lower right corner.

1898: This engraving depicts the front (west) side of the Middle Building and appeared in the *Philadelphia Inquirer* of February 7, 1898.

1898: This is the third earliest photograph of the first Mint, and the second for which actual prints are known. An example in the Stewart collection, donated by Frank H. Taylor, is stamped in blind at the lower left corner "PHOTO BY R. NEWELL & SON." A wallpaper merchant resides at 39 North Seventh, while at 37 North an advertisement for "Show Cards / Signs / Canopies" is posted in between the second story windows. The drab appearance of the building suggests that this vendor did not do much business at the location, or at least did not do a very good job. Broken windows and peeling paint indicate a lackadaisical landlord, and the sign above the middle doorway, "THIS PROPERTY / FOR SALE / APPLY TO / 1606 ARCH ST.," completes the picture of urban disintegration. A close copy of this image appeared in George F. Kolbe's sale of the Stack Family Library in January 2010. These two photographs were probably taken at the same time, in 1898.[7] Several differences suggest this pair chronologically follows the Levytype (above) image—the ground level of the façade is freshly white, while the "39 WALL PAPERS 39" sign now exhibits a tear at the left. The Levytype image depicts a chimney on the north side of 39 North (removed here), and a shorter building at 41 North (here built much higher than 39 and 37 North).

Engraving of the first Mint façade, first published in 1883.

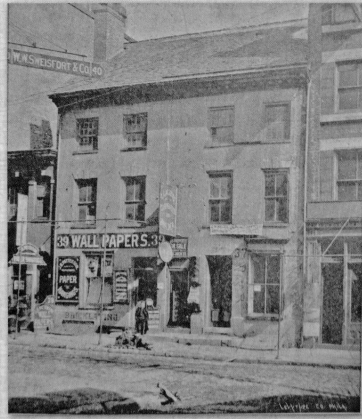

Early photo of first Mint, probably taken by the Levytype Company in Philadelphia.

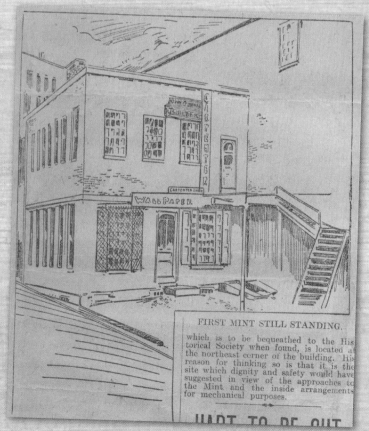

Engraving of the
Middle Building
from 1898.

FIRST MINT STILL STANDING.

which is to be bequeathed to the Historical Society when found, is located at
the northeast corner of the building. His
reason for thinking so is that it is the
site which dignity and safety would have
suggested in view of the approaches to
the Mint and the inside arrangements
for mechanical purposes.

HADT TO BE OUT

Interestingly, the print in the Stewart collection may be a retouched version of the Stack Family photograph. In addition to the absence of the man walking south, the Stewart version exhibits a roofline parallel with that of the building at 35 North, while in the Stack Family photograph, the building at 35 North clearly peers over the 37 North and 39 North roofline.

1899–1907: From the period between 1899 and 1907, when Stewart purchased the property, one engraving and a number of lower-quality halftones survive. Original prints are unknown for any of the halftones. The *Philadel-*

phia Inquirer published an engraving of the Front Building on March 19, 1899.

This engraving appears to be based on the following photograph from an unattributed news clipping, dated May 13, 1900. The most prominent feature is the addition of a sign placed between the third-story windows of 37 North which reads in part "AWNINGS TENTS / 37 39 / FLAGS TO ORDER." The same image appears to have been republished on the cover of the *Youth's Companion* of July 11, 1901.[8] The most telling feature is the shadow of the 35 North Seventh building, cast upon the roof of the first Mint.

Newell photographs of the first Mint, *ca.* 1898.

The next image in the sequence appears to be that which appeared in James Rankin Young's *The United States Mint at Philadelphia*, published in 1903.[9] Now, Chambers's Umbrella Factory is prominently doing business at 39 North Seventh, while a cigar emporium holds forth at 37 North. Stewart's brother Burnett referred to this space as the "cigar store" as late as 1911, suggesting that the business survived at least several years in the storefront.[10] Likely published about the same time as Young's volume, an unattributed news clipping similarly depicts both the umbrella factory and cigar outlet. In addition, two business names appear on the façade between the second and third floors: "39 EXCELSIOR KNIT[TING?] MILLS SUPPLY CO. 37."

The Old Mint Building as It Looks To-day

Engraving from the *Philadelphia Inquirer*, 1899.

First U.S. Mint, from an unattributed news clipping, dated May 13, 1900.

Front cover of the *Youth's Companion*, July 11, 1901.

1907: After Stewart's purchase of the property in April 1907, a number of photographs quickly appeared in the local press, probably in response to Stewart promoting the historic nature of his latest acquisition. As was discussed in chapter two, "YE OLDE MINT" was applied to the façade sometime between April and November of 1907. This group of pictures, devoid of "YE OLDE MINT," thus dates before November of that year. Stewart's purchase was consummated April 20th (a Saturday), and the Philadelphia *Evening Bulletin* on April 24th weighed in first, using a stock photograph from 1906.[11]

The *North American* also published a photograph on April 24th, and the caption gives some idea of the information that Stewart was feeding the press:

OLD UNITED STATES MINT TO BE TORN DOWN

This building is situated at 37 and 39 North Seventh street. It was purchased in 1792 by the Continental Congress, and for several years used as a Mint. It has been sold, and will be torn down shortly. A four-story warehouse is to be erected in its place.

First U.S. Mint, from James Rankin Young's *The United States Mint at Philadelphia*, 1903.

First U.S. Mint, from an unattributed news clipping, *ca.* 1903.

Only a portion of the site was "torn down shortly," but that didn't seem to get in the way of Stewart's story. As for the existence of a Continental Congress in 1792, this seems to be fiction perpetuated by Stewart himself, as quoted above (see the beginning of chapter five). This photo similarly depicts the triangular awning frame as seen at 37 North in the *Evening Bulletin* photograph above.

The triangular awning is also the most readily identifiable characteristic of an image from the Library of Congress, previously unpublished to the authors' knowledge.[12]

The last news clipping in Stewart's initial publicity campaign appeared in the *Record* on April 28th.

As a whole, this set of images just prior to November 1907 depicts buildings with minimal external signage and no readily discernable indication of the buildings' function. The Kates family had wanted to clear out for some time and let the new blood take over. The property "has been in the market for several years," per one account from 1907.[13] Indeed, the 1898 Newell photograph, above, indicates that the property was for sale even before the turn of the century.

Evening Bulletin photograph of the first U.S. Mint, 1906 and 1907.

North American photograph of the first Mint, 1907.

1907–1911: These images are distinguished by the words "1792 / Ye Olde Mint" now neatly painted upon the façade of the Front Building. As previously mentioned, Stewart applied this appellation sometime between April and November of 1907. The exact emission sequence is unclear, but in any event, a number of images are dated between this period and August 1911, when the building was demolished.

The best-known image from this period, depicting the first Mint façade with a touring car to the right, is attributed to Robert Newell of Philadelphia and has been published widely.[14] Chambers Umbrella Factory is at 39 North Seventh, as in the earlier (1898) Newell photograph, while the Lipschutz "44" Cigar Company appears to be at 37 North Seventh.[15]

First U.S. Mint, now with *Ye Olde Mint* on the façade, from an unattributed news clipping.

First Mint façade, from the Library of Congress, *ca.* 1907.

The first U.S. Mint, from the Philadelphia *Record,* 1907.

The best-known photograph of the First Mint. The example shown is from David Sklow sale no. 5, 2008.

The Stewart marketing machine also produced a number of postcards during this period. The first two are clearly identified as Stewart emissions while the attribution of the next two is tentative. Further discussion is found in appendix B (AO-401 to AO-404).

The last known picture of the first Mint intact (Stewart took photos during the demolition process), from 1911, was almost certainly taken by Stewart himself and currently resides in the Stewart Collection at Rowan University. A note in Stewart's hand is found on the reverse:

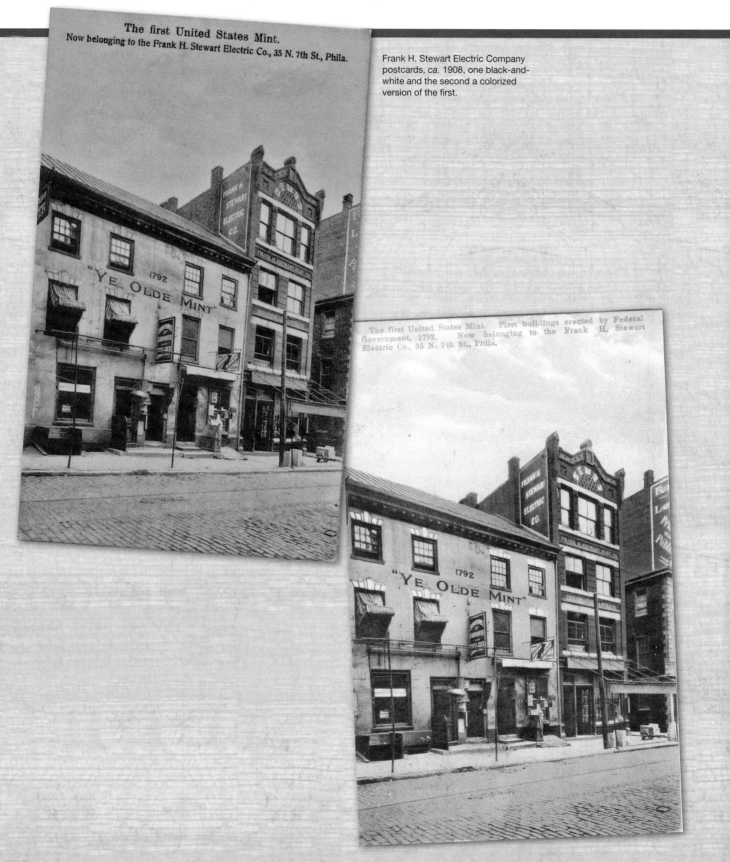

Frank H. Stewart Electric Company postcards, *ca.* 1908, one black-and-white and the second a colorized version of the first.

Picture of front buildings taken about 1 P.M. Friday Aug 4th [1911] just before I left for Ocean City [where Stewart maintained a summer residence] to visit Fisher. When I saw the buildings again on Tuesday Aug 8th the roof was off and buildings were down to the 3rd floor boards.

Additional postcards depicting the first Mint, versions possibly rejected by Stewart.

Finally, there were a series of photos Stewart commissioned to document the interior and exterior appearance of the Front, Middle, and Rear Buildings, which Stewart published in his 1924 *History of the First United States Mint*. These images he donated to Congress Hall. This set of photos was lent to the U.S. Mint and, sadly, has been missing since 1969.[16] Independence Hall records alternately state the number of photographs in the collection as 21 or 22. As 22 photographs of the building and associated first Mint artifacts are found in Stewart's *History of the First United States Mint*, it is possible these photographs were the originals used for Stewart's book. Beyond the commissioned photos, Stewart himself took snapshots (appendix E).

Despite this comparative wealth of graphic resources, Stewart wrote in 1924: "Sometime after the Mint buildings were destroyed [1911], I was compelled to give up hope of ever finding an old print or sketch of them."[17] He concluded that "no local artist ever made a sketch of it outside of Captain Frank H. Taylor, who made one at my request from my description."[18] This seems a bit curious, since Stewart clipped a number of newspaper articles illustrated by photos of the first Mint, several of which appeared when he purchased the property in 1907. Then, too, were the photos he had commissioned. Certainly, he was aware of the 1892-vintage engraving of the Front Building, since he owned a copy of George Evans's *History of the First United States Mint at Philadelphia*, which resides today in the Stewart Collection at Rowan University.[19] Perhaps the best explanation is that Stewart considered none of these

images, the earliest of which was made in 1854, as satisfactory, since they were all created long after the Mint had left the premises in 1832. This would explain why he said that he had not found "an old print or sketch of them," for practical photography was still more than a decade in the future when the "Sugar Alley Mint" closed its doors for the last time in 1832. Stewart clarified his thinking in a 1914 letter to the editor of *The Numismatist*:

> If any of the readers of THE NUMISMATIST wants to do something at odd times I know of nothing more hopeless than a search to uncover an old print or description of the first United States Mint published prior to, say, 1832. . . . It may be that some magazine or newspaper or book still in existence shows a picture of the first United States Mint before the days of photography. . . . This letter is sent to you with the slight hope that you may do something that will bring to light the long-sought picture or visitor's description of Ye Olde Mint.[20]

It is clear that Stewart believed no authentic, contemporary image of the first Mint, "before the days of photography" had ever been captured, and so, shortly after tearing down the last of the Mint buildings in 1911, he sought to create one, and later stated that "to the best of my knowledge, there is no other known print of the First Mint Buildings; that is the reason why I had this one made."[21]

Frank H. Stewart was no artist himself, as a sketch he later made of Ye Olde Mint hanging in his office readily

The last picture of the first Mint, most likely taken by Stewart himself.

demonstrates.[22] And, of course, he was not only the Master of the Mint, but also its destroyer, for he had torn down the Rear Building in 1907, and the Front and Middle Buildings in 1911. Nonetheless, as previously mentioned, he was careful to preserve measurements of the structures, and document their interior and exterior appearance with photographs before he ordered the wrecking balls to swing. Thus, when he turned to Frank H. Taylor as the artist to immortalize the first Mint, he had plenty of solid data to share with a "special artist" who had done his fair share of immortalizing people, places and events. Taylor's resulting pen-and-ink sketch, which we shall see later, was executed after the buildings came down in 1911, according to Stewart[23], "from the information at hand," which likely included Stewart's data trove. Taylor, however, had lived in Philadelphia since 1865, and kept an office near the Mint's old North Seventh location, so he likely had first-hand knowledge of the Front Building's appearance.[24] While the sketch, preserved in the Stewart Collection at Rowan University, is unsigned, it was obviously important enough to Stewart to save. It is a "pen and ink sketch" as noted by Stewart, and that Stewart asked Taylor to create such an image in the first place is clear. Stewart had any number of reasons to choose Taylor as the first artist of the first Mint, as we shall now learn.

Frank H. Stewart's own adaptation of Lamasure's *Ye Olde Mint*, from the *Ocean City Fishing Club 1919 Year Book*.

FRANK H. TAYLOR: THE FIRST ARTIST OF THE FIRST MINT

Taylor (1846 through 1927)[25] was a "special artist," an occupation unique to his era. With the advent of mass-produced periodicals relying on wood engravings for illustration, offerings such as *Frank Leslie's Illustrated Newspaper* (1855) and *Harper's Weekly* (1857) created a need for artists who could quickly and accurately render the "pictorial journalism" that readers increasingly demanded. To be blunt, Taylor was the 19th-century equivalent of the modern paparazzo, traveling throughout the country and supplying news images to the popular media, albeit with primitive technology and certainly not, at least in Taylor's case, given to the journalistic excesses of the present time. The "special artists" were superseded by photographers within a generation, but Taylor had no quibble with new technology. "Those who despair have failed to adapt their methods to modern conditions," he noted.[26] Taylor practiced what he preached, winning a bronze medal from the Franklin

Institute in 1874 for an exhibit demonstrating advances in photolithography.[27] Stewart was similarly realistic. "The inexorable tide of business always overflows every human sentiment and achievement," he once wrote.[28]

Taylor and Stewart had much in common and were acquaintances, as demonstrated by correspondence in the Stewart papers that discusses fishing and Seventh Street history.[29] The pair were conversant in numismatic matters, for Taylor wrote to Stewart describing the Saxton daguerreotype shot from the second U.S. Mint in 1839.[30] Taylor also furnished Stewart with two Mint-related photographs, one of the Mint exhibit at the 1864 Great Central Sanitary Fair in Philadelphia,[31] and a second of the first U.S. Mint, by Robert Newell & Son, *ca.* 1898 (discussed above).[32] Stewart and Taylor maintained offices in close proximity, Stewart of course at the First Mint site while Taylor was a stone's throw away at 718–724 Arch Street.[33] The two had deep American roots, Taylor counting himself as a Mayflower descendant[34] while Stewart traced his family back to the same era, identifying one Joseph Steward as an ancestor who emigrated in 1682 on one of William Penn's three ships.[35] Beside the personal history, the two men were chroniclers of local lore, with numerous publications to the credit of each. Stewart used Taylor's engravings on at least one of these projects, namely *Notes on Old Gloucester County, New Jersey*, compiled by Stewart and published by the New Jersey Society of Philadelphia in 1917. The two envisioned writing a history of Seventh Street, and although this project never came to fruition, there are surviving fragments in the Taylor papers at the Historical Society of Pennsylvania and in the Stewart papers at Rowan University.

Taylor and Stewart were both fishing fanatics. Stewart served as the club historian of the Ocean City (New Jersey) Fishing Club and dedicated much vacation time pursuing his passion in Florida and California.[36] Indeed, as with the imagery of the First U.S. Mint, Stewart commissioned artwork reflecting his angler's passion and distributed it freely among friends. *The Biggest One Got Away*, depicting young boys excitedly inventing tall tales of the bait and tackle, was drawn by one Louis R. Dougherty at Stewart's request.[37] Taylor likewise extolled the glories of the rod and reel in a tourist guidebook:

> The desire to catch a fish rests dormant in every human breast, only requiring favoring circumstances and ample leisure time to arouse the impulse honestly inherited from remote ancestors of nomadic tendencies. The question of liking or disliking fish as an article of food has little bearing upon the matter of ensnaring the victim, for having once captured, rejoiced over and exhibited the creature, all interest in its subsequent disposition ceases. At least in most instances. The element of uncertainty attending every phase of angling doubtless accompanies the pleasure of the undertaking.[38]

Moreover, Stewart and Taylor both believed in the value of history while pushing forward into modernity. Taylor spent much of his later years executing Philadelphia street scenes, noting in a 1926 letter to the Philadelphia Sketch Club, "Long after I am forgotten [my sketches] will remain to tell other generations that I once lived and added something to help future Philadelphians to visualize our city of today."[39] Stewart could have made the same observation of his own writings, such as *Reminiscences of Sharptown*, a monograph that captured glimpses of life in 19th-century New Jersey. At the same time, the pair were no dinosaurs. Taylor's biographer sums it up:

> There was a realization and appreciation, even a glorification of industrialization in America, while simultaneously, the agrarian values espoused by Jefferson still remained important. Taylor and others [Stewart, for example] seemed to justify this dichotomy through active participation in outdoor activities and, if possible, through living a part of their lives in each world, appreciating the cultural values of both.[40]

United States Mint exhibit at the 1864 Great Central Sanitary Fair in Philadelphia, photograph presented by Frank H. Taylor to Frank H. Stewart.

Jacob R. Eckfeldt fair pass, Eckfeldt family collection.

Like Stewart, Taylor also had some interest in coin collecting, or at least enough to transcribe a numismatic tale related to him by an acquaintance, Porter F. Cope, preserved in the Taylor papers at the Historical Society of Pennsylvania. "My friend," Taylor wrote, "fingered in his vest pocket a moment and produced a very old sample of Portuguese money. The centre of the obverse side had been ground out and engraved thereon is the name 'Caleb Cope' and date, 1745. 'This luck piece' said Mr. Cope, 'leads to a rather interesting story. Briefly, it is this:'"

> Among the British officers captured by the American colonial force operating in Canada in 1775 was Capt. John Andre. With some other prisoners he was sent to Lancaster, PA. These captives were allowed considerable freedom of movement in and about the town but faced much difficulty in securing quarters. Young Andre—he was then but twenty-four years old—was offered shelter and food by my great-grandfather, Caleb Cope, who was, like most Quakers of the time, opposed to the growing Revolutionary sentiment. Andre was the son of a Swiss father and French mother but was born in England. Naturally vivacious and talented he became the hero companion of the two Cope boys John and Thomas, and instructed the eldest John in drawing and painting.
>
> The Cope family was much abused by the townspeople for harboring one or more "enemies" but were indifferent to the clamor. When after several months of most enjoyable captivity Andrew and his fellow prisoners were sent to Carlisle [Pennsylvania]. Caleb Cope gave him this coin saying that whoever should at any future time bring it to Lancaster would be welcomed by his family. Five years later John Andre, then ranking as a major died the death of a spy at Tappan [New York] on the Hudson river. You know the details of that tragic moment, the shadow of American's most sinister character. Benedict Arnold had for a second time spread across the pathway of the young Briton and he fell a victim of mistaken zeal for his flag and King. [Involved in a scheme with Arnold to secure West Point for the British, Andre was captured by the Americans while Benedict escaped to England.] After the execution Andre's effects were sent to his relatives in England.
>
> Recently a friend interested in numismatics told me, one day, that Mr. Chapman, the [Philadelphia] coin dealer, had, among a lot of coins bought at a sale in London, one bearing the name of Caleb Cope. I lost no time in securing it. When, in 1904, the old Cope homestead in Lancaster was sold for removal, the occasion was marked by a notable celebration in the course of which I showed

the coin and claimed its promised hospitality. I certainly secured the best the town could provide!

> Two bricks were saved from the old house, one of them bears the initials "I.A.," this being the old style for those of John Andre who had cut them there as a memento of his stay. The other brick contains the initials of Thomas P. Cope, the date being 1782, at which time he was fourteen years old.[41]

While Taylor engraved away throughout the United States, traveling in pursuit of the latest news and the occasional numismatic tale, another family of engravers stayed close to Washington, intimately involved with the production of our nation's paper money at the Bureau of Engraving and Printing.

Stewart with prize catch, Catalina Island, 1920.

EDWIN LAMASURE AND THE BEP

The Bureau of Engraving and Printing (BEP), the economic sister of the U.S. Mint, traces its roots to 1862, 70 years after the opening of the first U.S. Mint, in a decidedly different milieu. The first Mint heralded the birth of a nation, the infant Hercules so gloriously depicted by Dupré's *Libertas Americana*, now empowering itself to create the lifeblood of commerce, a medium of exchange. In contrast, the Bureau of Engraving was essentially opened as a loan office for the divided and financially struggling United States, trying to convert the burning faith of Lincoln into cold cash. Congress authorized the issuance of $250 million of federal currency[42], and the "greenback" was born.

The nascent currency had a troubled childhood. Some thought the whole idea of the federal government issuing paper money in the first place was unconstitutional, and even those who accepted the bills generally did so at a discount to gold. Indeed, the new legal tender notes fell to 92¢ on the dollar within two months of issue[43], and traded as low at 35¢ at the height of the Civil War.[44] Compounding the situation was public suspicion of all forms of paper money, as reported by the *New York Times* on July 30, 1862:

> There are very few persons, if any, in the United States, who can truthfully declare their ability to detect at a glance any fraudulent paper money. So numerous are our Banks, and so varied the tricks of the counterfeiter, that even professional detectors of bad bills, brokers, bank tellers and others in the constant habit of handling large sums of money, are frequently imposed upon. Our "Counterfeit Detectors"[45] have, within the last few years, increased in size, until their proportions rival our Family Bibles, and generally compel much more studious perusal. If a man offers a bill in payment for anything, it is a signal for the production of the inevitable volume. The merchant wades through the long list of "altered," "counterfeit," "spurious," "old plate," "broken bank," and a hundred other frauds, and if he fails to find a description of the proffered given, the purchaser must borrow the book and go through the same tedious process, in his turn, to prevent being imposed upon. So rapidly are these frauds in paper money produced, that in all our large cities the aid of the police and the telegraph is called into requisition to protect the merchant. Even the types and the printing-press, the police and the telegraph, are frequently too late for the shrewd counterfeiter, and in defiance of them all, the City is often flooded with a worthless issue before citizens can be put upon their guard. In spite of all precautions, every merchant has his pile of counterfeit money, and his hourly fear of having it increased. Our wives and daughters accept a banknote from a stranger with fear and trembling, and the memories of our servants are taxed to recollect who gave that last "bad bill." The poorer people are, the less likely are they to be able to avoid taking counterfeit money, while the poorest apple-woman is as good a judge as the best, of all the coins; it is only a privileged class who can rely to any extent upon their judgment of the genuineness of our paper currency.

Sir Thomas Gresham's law, that "bad money drives out good," was once again operative, and hard coin quickly departed everyday circulation. Indeed, a house in New York City reportedly collapsed due to the weight of the coins hoarded therein.[46] Even the three-cent silver pieces, debased since their time of issue in 1851, were no longer seen in daily commerce.[47] Ironically, this was a boon for the Bureau, which now started manufacturing fractional currency to replace the coins that had disappeared in part because of the new legal tender notes! But from the Bureau's point of view, work was work, and considerable talent was attracted to the basement of the Washington, D.C., Treasury Building—today featured on the reverse of the $10 bill—where the Bureau operated. The young Bureau won an award at the Vienna International Exhibition in 1873 for engraved portraits and vignettes, and followed suit in Paris in 1878.[48]

Along with these early successes, the Bureau had its share of growing pains. Facilities were a constant thorn as operations grew quickly. Within three years of opening shop, the Bureau employed over 500 employees[49], all crowded into the basement and now attic of the Treasury Building. By the mid-1870s, a completely new structure was inevitable, and a four-floor behemoth with a half-acre footprint was constructed a stone's throw south of the Washington Monument. Even this was not a long-term solution, and by 1914 yet another palace of paper was in operation, adjacent to the existing site. This location has survived to the present time, along with the Western Currency Facility in Ft. Worth, Texas—the BEP's version of a "branch mint"—which was opened in 1991.

Like the first Mint, the BEP also experienced a slow transition to steam power. The technology did not sit well with the hand press operators, who insisted that the old ways were necessary to prevent counterfeiting.[50] One was reminded of the analogous situation in the Mint some 50 years prior, when the engraver Gobrecht complained that the new Contamin lathe produced results inferior to hand-engraved dies.[51] In actuality, job protection was the watchword of the day, and the unions were not the least bit subtle, demanding in 1888 that the government print all securities using hand presses.[52] Edwin Lamasure Sr., father of the painter, of whom more will be said later, summed it up:

> They [the labor interests] were so far-reaching and had such power with Members of Congress, especially about election times, that he [the chief of the BEP]

was kept in almost constant fear of being removed from his place through the agency of the printers and others who were opposed to the steam presses, which at that time we knew ourselves were doing better work than the average printer could do.[53]

Only in 1923 did organized labor finally lose its grip, when unrestricted use of power-driven presses was allowed within the BEP.[54] Despite attachment to "old ways," the BEP was thought in 1927 to be "the world's premier printing establishment," at least according to a group of Washington, D.C., businessmen.[55]

Technology brought motorized vehicles as well, giving rise to a mascot of the BEP, a horse named Prince, which was sold in 1920 as the last of the BEP stable.[56] Like the BEP, the early Mint used horse power as well, to drive the drawing and rolling mill machines.[57] That horses were used is clear from early Mint reports,[58] and in the 1816 Mint report Robert Patterson was proud to announce to President Madison that the Mint was finally to be rid of the high-maintenance beasts:

> The repairs of the Mint, which you were pleased to authorize, are now nearly completed. A substantial brick building has been erected on the site formerly occupied by an old wooden building; and in the apparatus and arrangement of machinery, which have been adopted, many important improvements have been introduced. Among these is the substitution of a steam-engine, for the horse-power heretofore employed. A change which, it is believed, will not only diminish the expenses of the establishment, but greatly facilitate all its principal operations.[59]

The BEP horses persisted into the 20th century, consuming all manner of bureaucratic attention. In 1908, the BEP director wrote the following to the secretary of the treasury of the United States, presumably a world power at the time:

> Sir:
> I have the honor to state that the gray mare, 'Maude', belonging to this Bureau is unfit for further service and to recommend that a committee be appointed to determine what disposition shall be made of her.
> Respectfully,
> J[oseph].E. Ralph, Director.[60]

The irony, of course, is that the old, broken-down horse was probably more nimble than the plodding, committee-building administration. In any case, Prince and Maude thus joined the watchdog of the first U.S. Mint, Nero,[61] in the zoo of American numismatics. Not be left out is Peter, the Mint eagle, who was first introduced to the numismatic public by Elizabeth Johnston in 1876:

> An old citizen of Philadelphia is authority for the following story: On one fourth of July "Peter," making a longer flight than was his custom, sat upon the topmost bough of a large tree, corner of South and Broad Streets, attracting and amusing a large crowd by his demonstrations—of course the result of excitement from the unusual noise in the streets. Soon, however, an Irishman, who fed him in the Mint, came under the tree and called, "Peter, coome down!" The crowd jeered, but the Irishman averring "Sure he looves me as if he were me own son," repeated "Peter, coome down!" and the bird came swooping down to the shoulders of the delighted Patrick, rather to the sudden terror of the lesser element in the assemblage.[62]

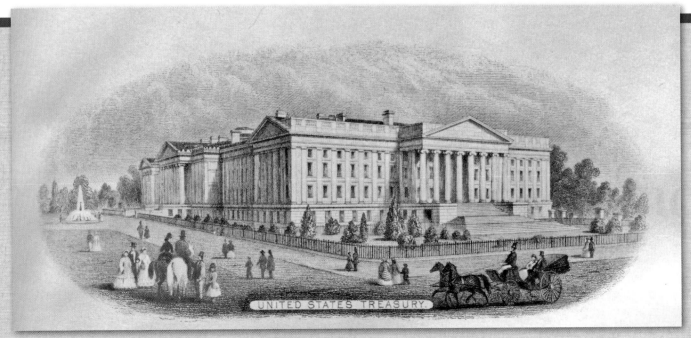

The United States Treasury, home of the Bureau of Engraving and Printing from 1862 through 1880.

Peter's end was far less pedestrian than that of Prince, the beast of the BEP. George Evans told the tale while describing a visit to the U.S. Mint Cabinet in the late 19th century:

> Near the exit door of the Cabinet, in a large glass case, is a magnificent American eagle, which is worthy of the visitor's attention. It is superbly mounted, with grand breadth of wing and wondrous piercing eyes.... "Peter," the name which the noble bird recognized, was an inhabitant of the Mint six years. He would fly about the city, but no one interfered with the going or coming of the "Mint bird," and he never failed to return to his daily exercise before the time for closing the building. In an evil hour he unfortunately perched upon a large fly wheel, and getting caught in the machinery, received a fatal injury to his wing, and this ended rather an unusual career for an eagle.[63]

Black Diamond, the final member of our zoo, and likely model for the reverse of the Buffalo nickel, did not fare much better, being slaughtered in 1915 and served up to New York gourmands.[64] Today a bronzed version of Peter is on exhibit at the fourth U.S. Mint, while Nero is memorialized in Edwin Lamasure's *Ye Olde Mint*. Edwin Lamasure brought the zoo full circle, for, along with other family members, he had worked at the BEP in the 19th century.

THE LAMASURE FAMILY: THE ECKFELDTS OF THE BEP

Along with the "greenbacks" of the early 1860s, the financiers of the Civil War, namely, the Northern government, had another idea for the Bureau. On July 1, 1862, the Internal Revenue department was born, and while Lincoln fought to preserve the Union, this new part of the government ensured that the federal bureaucracy would be awarded a perpetual portion of the spoils. By 1870 Internal Revenue was asking for over 30,000,000 tax stamps a year, and the number ballooned to over 200,000,000 a mere three years later.[65] Liquor, tobacco, playing cards, and cosmetics, all items of sin in a Victorian age, required tax stamps. Even medicine came under the eye of the authorities, determined to replenish the coffers of the exhausted war-torn government. The young BEP could not keep up with the demand, and so private firms were engaged to cover the shortfall. One of these firms, in Philadelphia, was Butler and Carpenter.

Messrs. Butler and Carpenter were quick to the game, opening up shop in 1862. Edwin Lamasure Sr., the father of the painter, was not far behind, joining the firm in 1864.[66] He remained with Butler and Carpenter until 1877, at which time he secured employment with the BEP. The BEP director, William M. Meredith, summed up Lamasure's service to the BEP many years later:

> Mr. [Edwin] Lamasure entered the Bureau November 1, 1877, at the expiration of contracts held by Mr. Joseph R. Carpenter, bank note engraver and printer of Philadelphia, Penna., for manufacturing internal revenue stamps and printing fractional currency for the Treasury Department, after having held a managering position of great trust and responsibility in Mr. Carpenter's establishment for thirteen years, and I am assured at a very much larger salary than he now receives. On entering the service here he was equipped by experience with a general knowledge of the bank note business, and furnished letters from Mr. Carpenter, and the late Hon. William D. Kelly [sic], attesting his high qualifications, which letters were instrumental in securing his appointment in the Bureau.[67]

Lamasure's recommendations were critical, as most employees entering the BEP at this time were accompanied by similar high-level recommendations[68]. William D. Kelley was a longtime U.S. Congressman from Philadelphia, and coincidentally the chairman of the congressional committee on Coinage Weights and Measures from 1867 to 1872.[69] Lamasure also carried a recommendation from A.E. Borie, the secretary of the Navy in the Grant administration.[70] Whether Lamasure knew either personally is unknown, but in any case he was connected enough to secure the appropriate letters. Lamasure also had an "in" with his good friend Elverton R. Chapman, chief of the stamp division of the Internal Revenue department, precisely the same person who had overseen the work of the firm of Butler and Carpenter with which Lamasure was associated. The pair were, according to Lamasure, "on very friendly terms always," and Lamasure had known Chapman's wife prior to her marriage.[71] Altogether it was sufficient enough to gain employment in the BEP, and then as now, connections are key.

Lamasure Sr. quickly gained respect at the BEP, and within a year of his employment was appointed onto committees entrusted with witnessing the destruction of U.S. notes and securities.[72] By 1883, he was considered third in command at the BEP, and was periodically designated to act as the BEP chief in the absences of the chief and assistant chief.[73] Lamasure served in various capacities in the BEP office, primarily in accounting, and eventually assumed the role of what today would be called the chief financial officer of the enterprise. An 1897 Congressional inquiry into the BEP operation heaped praise upon Lamasure, describing him as "a gentleman of large business experience and unusual capacity for affairs, and who, so far as our examination enables us to judge, performs his varied and responsible duties with intelligence and efficiency."[74] Lamasure remained in the BEP until his death in 1910, at the age of 77.[75] On March 23, 1910, the BEP director reported his passing to the secretary of the treasury, noting, "Mr. Lamasure . . . has rendered faithful and valuable services to the Government."[76]

Lamasure Sr. had two sons who also worked in the BEP as engravers, Edwin Lamasure Jr. and Frank Lamasure. Frank began at the BEP in 1896, starting as a plate cleaner in the engraving division at the salary of $700 per year.[77] In 1901 his title was officially changed to engraver, in which capacity he remained until 1906, thereafter moving into private industry for a period of about two years.[78] He was rehired at the BEP in 1908 at a salary of $2,100 per year, where he remained, like his father, until his death in 1938.[79] Unlike his father, the chief accountant of the office who was counted among the inner circle of the BEP establishment, Frank was the "talent," the highly skilled engraver whom the BEP desperately needed, but conversely had to compensate. Indeed, the salaries for the engraving division consumed nearly 75 percent of the BEP payroll.[80] The BEP archives hint at some of the friction between the management and the engraving team.

In 1908, the BEP director addressed a letter to Frank Lamasure and the Washington Society of Bank Note Engravers, in response to a complaint regarding overtime pay. The director's reply appealed to the conditions of the federal bureaucracy, as intransigent one hundred years ago as today. "As no charge of this kind was submitted in the estimates to Congress on which the appropriations for the current year were made," BEP Director Joseph E. Ralph wrote, "if such an additional rate were established for the Engraving Division it would necessarily have to be allowed for all the other employees working overtime, and the result would be a deficiency, which is directly prohibited by law."[81]

Labor strife flared again in the World War I era, with the production of over 100,000,000 Liberty Loan bonds. The BEP moved onto a 24-hour daily schedule necessitating an increase of 1,200 workers.[82] The engravers were forced to work in congested conditions, and with poor lighting to boot. Even the BEP director admitted that "it was almost criminal to place these engravers in their present position and surroundings."[83] The official treasury report put quite a different spin on the matter, claiming that "the task was carefully and cheerfully performed by employees of the bureau, who worked uncomplainingly in day and night shifts."[84] The overworked engravers voted with their feet, and by 1923 over a third of the engraving force had left the BEP, "to fill positions elsewhere at larger salaries and there exists at the present

Family of Edwin Lamasure Jr.: Bertha, his wife, and son Edwin.

time such a spirit of murmuring and discontent on account of the positions offered and salaries paid for like services by outside establishments that more men are tempted to resign," wrote the Superintendent of the Engraving Division.[85] Frank Lamasure soldiered on, although two suspensions (reasons for which are unrecorded) are noted in his personnel records in 1931 and 1937. Frank passed away the following year.[86] Today he is remembered among stamp collectors as supplying lettering and numerals on any number of issues.

Jules Demonet, a grandson of Edwin Lamasure Sr. and nephew of Frank Lamasure, related in 1945 the following tale of derring-do regarding his relatives in the BEP:

> On a day in 1903, in Washington's Bureau of Engraving and Printing, the chief accountant of the Bureau [Lamasure Sr.] paced the floor, musing to himself. Suddenly he summoned the secretary and ordered: "Send my son to my office immediately." His son, Frank Lamasure, was an engraver, one of the men who make the engravings from which is printed the money of the United States. When he arrived, his father explained that the Treasury Department's Secret Service had asked for his help in their search for a certain counterfeiter. "Let me see his work," said Frank. "It won't do you any good this time, Frank," replied Lamasure Sr. "I know that you can recognize the work of many counterfeiters. But in this case we can't identify the phony bills except by chemical analyses of the paper and double checking the serial numbers. The copies are just about perfect."

In a subsequent conference with Treasury officials, Frank was shown a large map. The map was decorated with red-headed pins, indicating each city in which one or more of the spurious bills had been found— and the pins clustered about the little town of Bismarck, North Dakota. "That's where the bills must be made," said Frank. "Okay, now find the man who made them," directed the Treasury chief.

So Frank journeyed to North Dakota, posing as an artist. Visiting farms throughout the area of Bismarck, he kept his eyes peeled for the usual sign of a counterfeiter—ink stains. After weeks of fruitless search, he was one day packing away his paintings and preparing to move on to the next farm, when he noticed a peculiar odor. "What's that?" he asked the farmer. "Oh, just some chemical my crazy kid spilled while making photographs in a cave down by the river," replied the old man. "He's crazy about photography. I've bought him a heap of chemicals and metal plates." Metal plates! Lamasure knew this might well be the clue he had been looking for.

When Treasury agents descended upon the cave, they found there a much thumbed chemistry book, a farm boy with little better than an eighth grade education and the finest set-up for duplicating money they had ever seen. The means were crude, but the quality of the work and the low cost of operation were superior to anything the Treasury's own experts had been able to devise. The boy had netted only three thousand dollars for his work, having sold the spurious bills to "spenders" for as little as 10 cents on the dollar. Had he taken his new process to the Treasury Department or any reputable engraving company, he could well have become a wealthy man, and won renown as an inventor.[87]

Whether or not the grandson's tale was invented (the idea of dispatching a busy engraver into the field to chase counterfeiters invites skepticism, especially in light of the fact that the Secret Service had agents dedicated for this purpose), clearly the family took pride in their history of service to the BEP.

Edwin Lamasure Jr., the painter, also took a short turn in the BEP, but lacked the staying power of his brother and father. He was hired in July, 1884, at the age of 17, as an engraving apprentice for the princely sum of $1.25 per day.[88] The next month, the acting superintendent of the engraving division reported that Lamasure "is doing well at his work, and the Committee recommended his permanent designation as an apprentice in that division."[89] Lamasure's budding career as an engraver, however, was cut short the following July when he was taken off payroll. Hoping a paid position might be restored, Lamasure labored on as an apprentice until December 1885, when he officially resigned from the BEP, leaving the family business to his father and brother.[90] George Casilear, a superintendent of engraving at the BEP[91] recalled the sit-

uation: "He [Lamasure Jr.] had considerable ability . . . and was turned out by O'Neil [BEP chief engraver]."[92] Casilear added further commentary regarding O'Neil's ability to manage engravers, none of it charitable, and but for this lack of management acumen, young Lamasure might have spent much more of his career at the BEP.

Some time after this Lamasure returned to Philadelphia, the city of his birth, where he worked as an engraver for the firm of Bailey, Banks & Biddle.[93] "This work did not satisfy his tastes, and he decided to devote all his time to the painting of water colors," a newspaper reported some years later.[94] While still in Philadelphia, Lamasure probably spent some time in area art schools. A biographical piece accompanying a reproduction of his work added that Lamasure

> entered the National Engraving Bureau [sic] at Washington, where he developed a fineness and surety of touch in drawing, while still other years passed in the art schools of Philadelphia opened out and broadened the talents disclosed by his previous training.[95]

By 1894, Lamasure was back in Washington, teaching and executing watercolors.[96] He was married shortly thereafter[97], and from this time forward seems to have worked exclusively in watercolors, selling primarily to mass market lithographers. The commercial nature of his work irritated at least one critic, who noted in part:

> His work is wanting in certain technical qualities and is "finished" to a fault, so that the effect in some instances is scarcely that of original watercolor work. The impression one receives is that he works too evidently to please the general public and not enough to reach those standards toward which an artist should strive without considering the opinion of the average possible buyer, even though in the process he narrowly escapes starvation.
>
> With a little more vigorous independence, a higher standard, and serious study the ability which Mr. Lamasure possesses might rank him much higher among his brother artists than he is at present. That his work, however, possesses many pleasing qualities is evidenced in the fact that already a number of his things are marked "sold," and among the collection are several well composed, nicely seen little bits that any one might be glad to own.[98]

Lamasure's work focused on nature scenes, landscapes, and country settings, all with a liberal infusion of nostalgia set amid romantic yearnings of a former time. The appeal to Frank H. Stewart was obvious, a man who was to pen works such as *Our New Home and Old Times, Reminiscences of Sharptown, N. J.*, and *Salem a Century Ago*. The titles of the Lamasure works, nearly formulaic, evoke the same sentiments. *The Old Barn, Bring Back the Days of Long Ago, The Old Homestead, Where the Old Folks Live, The Old Spring House*, etc., are but a few examples of the hundreds of watercolors executed by Lamasure in a similar vein. Viewed against this backdrop, it is quite understandable that Lamasure's *Ye Olde Mint*, as will be seen, set the first Mint in a verdant Philadelphia meadow, a peaceful easy setting paradoxically placed in a bustling city. Lamasure thus did not betray the overall tone of his oeuvre, and one suspects that Frank H. Stewart wanted it that way.

Regular exposure to nature was necessarily the lifeblood of Lamasure, and he drew inspiration from the countryside surrounding Washington, D.C., as noted in a brochure accompanying a 1912 calendar depicting his *Mount Vernon at Sunset:*

> For many years he has resided in Washington, where is a member of the leading art clubs, a situation which is conveniently near the Blue Ridge region of Virginia, where he finds those picturesque landscapes that have made him famous.[99]

Lamasure evidently spent summers out of the city, for the social column of a Washington newspaper reported that "Mr. and Mrs. Edwin Lamasure have a cottage near Round Hill, Va., where Mr. Lamasure is doing some excellent pictures and sketches."[100] Another year the couple are placed at the "Blue Ridge Inn," along with Lamasure's sister and brother-in-law.[101]

Lamasure engaged any number of clients, including Louis Prang,[102] the Boston lithographer and "father of the American Christmas card."[103] Like Frank H. Taylor, who crafted Stewart's first sketch of the first U.S. Mint, Prang cut his teeth carving wooden blocks for engravings,

The artist Lamasure at work.

Lamasure's *Mount Vernon at Sunset,* from a 1912 calendar.

and eventually enjoyed much success in the lithography business, reproducing fine art, album cards, color advertising, and the like. Color reproduction technology met Lamasure at the right time; a popular medium in need of popular artists. Lamasure's work today is most remembered for his calendar art, which was reproduced by any number of calendar printers, including Brown and Bigelow,[104] the Thomas D. Murphy Company of Red Oak, Iowa,[105] and the Osborne Company of New Jersey. Lamasure's "Murphy period" seems to have begun around 1906,[106] while his relationship with Osborne began before 1900 and lasted until his death in 1916.[107]

Osborne apparently thought highly enough of Lamasure to send him to Panama in 1913 to capture a visual record of the Panama Canal construction. The voyage to Central America, and to a worksite where malaria and other tropical diseases claimed a staggering 20,000 human lives, was much in the tradition of Frank H. Taylor, dispatched to deliver sketches of major news events. Lamasure's Panama Canal drawings were copyrighted in December 1913 and appeared as a set in a monthly calendar of 1915.[108] The series highlights Lamasure's ability to render drawings of a technical nature, as opposed to the landscapes and nature scenes for which he was more popular. Frank H. Stewart, in *Ye Olde Mint*, would come to appreciate Lamasure's capacity to deliver both nostalgia and detailed accuracy.

EARLY CALENDARS OF THE FRANK H. STEWART ELECTRIC COMPANY

Stewart's first known association with Edwin Lamasure Jr. came in the form of the Frank H. Stewart Electric Company 1914 calendars. The art calendar was in its heyday, and as lithographic color reproduction had become viable, millions were distributed each year for promotional purposes. Stewart worked primarily with the Osborne Company in Newark, New Jersey, to produce a number of calendars for his firm. Osborne was a major player in the art calendar business; indeed, Edmund B. Osborne, the company founder, is credited with the creation of the art calendar in the 1880s.[109] Along with the Osborne concern, many other American art calendar manufacturers chased the public fancy and sought artists capable of satisfying the demand for appealing images of attractive young women, Indian maidens, landscapes, hunting and fishing, and other popular genres.

Stewart's earliest known calendar dates to 1910, and depicts a wooden door upon which is hung a bundle of decorative cornstalks. The piece is entitled *King Corn*, copyrighted by Woodward and Tiernan, a St. Louis printing company.[110] Stewart continued the calendar series in 1911, and made brief comments in his pamphlet *For the Man Who Buys Electrical Supplies*:

> Our calendars for the year 1911 are reproductions of works of art by famous artists, and are subjects which

patriotism and appreciation will cause many to frame after they have served their purpose as calendars at the close of the year.[111]

A single example of a 1911 Stewart calendar survives in the Stewart Collection at Rowan University. Depicting *Washington in Time of Peace*, Henry Mosler's illustration imagines George Washington playing the flute at Mount Vernon with his step-granddaughter Nelly Custis accompanying on the harpsichord. Washington seems to have had a resonance with Stewart, who distributed portrait prints of the first president during at least one holiday season.[112] Stewart's statement regarding the 1911 calendar further suggests that the company would issue more than one per year, and this would happen again in 1914. For the year 1912, there are no records of Stewart calendars, though it seems likely that these are waiting to be discovered. In 1913, the Stewart company distributed *In the Gloaming*, an image apparently named after a popular song of that era, identifying the artist as "Bryson."[113] While this work remains unlocated by the authors, J. Ross Bryson was a calendar artist known for images of Victorian women. The copyright entry for *In the Gloaming* describes it thus: "Young woman in low-neck, white gown, lace fichu thrown over shoulder, seated, gazing out the window."[114] Bryson created this work for the Thomas D. Murphy Company of Red Oak, Iowa. Bryson was a regular member of the Murphy "stable," producing over 100 works in the early 1900s, including titles such as *Matinee Girls*, *Queen of the Vaudeville*, *Coquette*, and so on.[115] Stewart acquired the original art for *In the Gloaming*, as reported by a publication apparently aimed at the sales force of the Murphy Company:

> The sale of Bryson's star subject *In the Gloaming* by A.B. Getty, shows how important it is to make an outright sale instead of a sale on approval, and it also shows how fast and furious is the sale of our most attractive pictures. At 8:15 a.m., we received a telegram from Mr. Getty reporting the absolute sale of *In the Gloaming* to one of our customers, a man of unquestioned financial standing. At 8:27 a.m., we received from R.S. Perry [probably another Murphy salesman] another telegram selling the same subject on approval. . . . We feel that we made a mistake in letting this, the best thing Bryson ever did, go at the same price as the rest of his pastels. However, it's our own fault—we'll have to take our medicine and Getty and Getty's customer get the benefit.[116]

For the 1914 calendar, Stewart presented Edwin Lamasure's *Peak on Peak Against the Turquoise Blue*. An accompanying brochure described the work. "A cluster of peaks, rising one upon the other—more than the eye can count— some snow capped; others crowned with straight, narrow shafts of evergreens; and over all the cloudless, turquoise sky—this is one of the delights that greet the traveler in the wonderful Yosemite." While this particular tableau

COMPLIMENTS OF

Frank H. Stewart Electric Co.

35 N. SEVENTH
STREET

STEWART'S
OLD MINT
GOLD STANDARD

PHILADELPHIA

ELECTRICAL SUPPLIES

1911	January					1911
SUN	MON	TUES	WED	THUR	FRI	SAT

Early calendars of
the Frank H. Stewart
Electric Company.

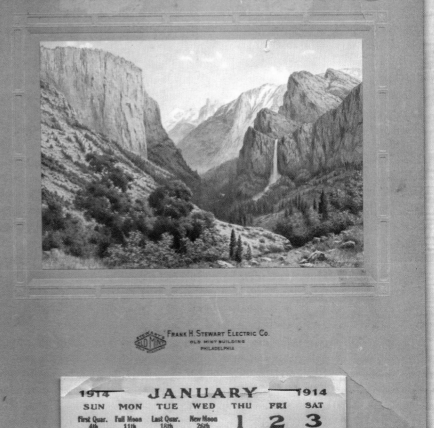

STEWART'S
OLD MINT

FRANK H. STEWART ELECTRIC CO.
OLD MINT BUILDING
PHILADELPHIA

1914	JANUARY					1914
SUN	MON	TUE	WED	THU	FRI	SAT
First Quar. 4th	Full Moon 11th	Last Quar. 18th	New Moon 26th	1	2	3

was quite typical of the art calendar era, the image resonated with Stewart for other reasons. Beginning in 1912, Stewart left Philadelphia during the cold months[117] and traveled widely, though most frequently to Florida. Later Stewart described himself as a traveler from "Golden Gate to Golden Horn."[118] In 1913, Stewart trekked to California, and in the process won a fishing prize for a catch made off of Catalina Island.[119] It seems likely that Stewart visited Yosemite on the same trip, hence the appeal of Lamasure's *Peak on Peak*. That Stewart visited Yosemite at least once is certain, as he later wrote:

> In the [Sharptown, New Jersey] school geography, which was the text-book of largest dimensions, there were illustrations of Niagara and Yosemite falls and the three noted pyramids of Egypt. These points of interest created, in the writer's mind, at least, the idea that they were the most important faraway places in the world and as a result his travels took him to those places at the first opportunity.[120]

Apart from the *Peak on Peak* calendar, Stewart thought enough of the work to purchase the original art[121], just as he had done for *In the Gloaming*.[122]

Stewart's second calendar for 1914 was based on Lamasure's *Cradle of Liberty*, a depiction of the Independence Hall complex. Lamasure assigned copyright of both *Cradle of Liberty* and *Peak on Peak Against the Turquoise Blue* to the Osborne Company on December 27th, 1912,[123] and as had been the case with *In the Gloaming* and *Peak on Peak*, Stewart acquired the original art.[124] The present location of these pieces is unknown by the authors, but they do not reside in the substantial collection of Lamasure works currently held within the Lamasure family. In any case, while *Peak on Peak* evoked, for Stewart at least, memories of a pleasant journey to the West, *Cradle of Liberty* was closer to home, and represented an evolution towards the masterpieces that Stewart would commission for his 1915 and 1916 calendars.

Cradle of Liberty depicts the three buildings of the Independence Hall complex. Congress Hall lies to the west while the Old City Hall is found on the east. In the center lies Independence Hall proper, in whose tower the Liberty Bell hung for many years (the Liberty Bell is currently located nearby at the recently founded Liberty Bell Center). Lamasure's view shows the entire set of buildings. Stewart was fascinated with the image. "Our admiration for Mr. Lamasure's skill as an artist," he wrote, "coupled with our love for the historical, simply compelled us to purchase another one of his artistic gems, entitled, *The Cradle of Liberty*. This original picture is a

Edwin Lamasure's *Cradle of Liberty*, subject of the Frank H. Stewart Electric Company 1914 calendar.

copy of Independence Hall from the Walnut Street [southern] side. We are not positive, but think that this is the first time an artist with the reputation of Lamasure has ever painted Independence Hall from the rear."[125]

Stewart had been making donations to the Congress Hall collection since 1910 and had no doubt formed a collegial relationship with the administration. Wilfred Jordan, the curator of Independence Hall, had been chosen by Stewart to deposit a lead safety box during the cornerstone ceremony for the new Stewart Electric Company building[126]. The reconstruction of Congress Hall in 1913, marked by a visit from President Wilson, further drew attention to Stewart's "Old Mint" collection, and Stewart likely calculated that whatever was good for Congress Hall was good for Stewart Electric, removed by foot only a few minutes to the north. In any case, Stewart added to the publicity by displaying *Cradle of Liberty* at Congress Hall along with the rest of his "Old Mint" collection.[127] Lamasure's idyllic interpretation of Independence Hall, viewed from the park to the south of the buildings on a bright fall day, illuminated the proverbial light bulb in the mind of the electric entrepreneur. Stewart was ready to focus his incandescence on American numismatic history.

Ye Olde Mint: The Painting

In 1915, the Master of the Mint issued his sixth Frank Stewart Electric Company calendar, and with it, he hit the sweet spot in the merger of memorializing the old Mint

and marketing his company. Naturally, he turned to his favorite artist to produce the composition: Edwin Lamasure Jr. As before, Lamasure assigned the copyright to the Osborne Company, and Stewart bought the painting. Nothing could be more appropriate, for the subject was the old Mint itself, composed according to photos and other data supplied by its final master. Stewart did not act unintentionally, and well understood the power of art to preserve and interpret history; indeed, he gave it consideration even within other contexts. In one of his numerous historical pamphlets Stewart lamented of his great passion, Gloucester County (New Jersey) military history:

> No painter has ever painted a battle scene of Old Gloucester County. No sculptor has ever carved anything in likeness of any happening hereabouts. . . . I venture to express the hope that the past may not continue to be carelessly forgotten to the extent it has heretofore.[128]

In short, Stewart knew precisely what he was doing. Yet, for a work of art that was fated to have such an enormous impact, the physical aspect of *Ye Olde Mint* can be described only as "unprepossessing." The paint is not oil, but rather watercolors.[129] The surface is not canvas, but rather cardboard.[130] The dimensions, 24 inches high by 34-7/8 inches wide, are more modest than imposing.[131] Nothing about *Ye Olde Mint* suggests an exalted status, but its humble nature notwithstanding, it has become an icon of American numismatics.

The Osborne Company reserved the rights to *Cradle of Liberty* and here incorporated the image into an advertising card for the Chicago Gravel Company.

The image itself, presumably at Frank Stewart's behest, offered an unprecedented way of looking at the "Sugar Alley Mint." Every previous image, whether photographic or lithographic, had viewed the Front Building only, and from a head-on (or nearly so) perspective, as if the person looking at the image was standing on the west side of North Seventh Street, directly across from the Front Building. Lamasure's perspective was different; he placed the viewer smack in the middle of North Seventh Street, and well to the north of the Mint yard; indeed, almost all the way to North Seventh's intersection with Arch Street. Perhaps not coincidentally, this would have been the view that David Rittenhouse beheld as he walked to work each morning. This perspective allowed Lamasure to paint the full northern flanks of the Front, Middle, and Rear Buildings; the full western façade of the Front Building, and partially obscured views of the western façades of the Middle and Rear Buildings. Thus, for the first time, the principal structures of the Mint (or at least those Stewart believed to be the principal structures) were depicted as a coherent group (the stable, attached to the southern flank of the Rear Building, was not visible from this perspective, and hence not included).

This view could be presented only because of a significant exercise of artistic license on Lamasure's part (again, probably at Stewart's direction). The structures surrounding the Mint (especially the dwelling houses to the north at numbers 41 and 43 North Seventh) in actuality would have made this view impossible by blocking the sight lines to the Mint buildings: an obstruction that existed for all 41 years of the Mint's tenure on North Seventh Street. Lamasure solved this problem by simply omitting these two dwelling houses, as well as one at number 35, on the south side of the Mint. In fact, he omitted literally every building on the east side of North Seventh, including those attached to the Mint, such as the Cromley Furnace, as well as the four shops along Bone Alley. As earlier noted, the tableau Lamasure painted strongly suggests that the first Mint was located, not in bustling downtown Philadelphia at all, but rather at some bucolic address in rural Pennsylvania.

The painting is also chockablock with details emanating from Stewart's research, included to create an air of verisimilitude, but sometimes tending toward the opposite effect. A flag pole, for example, sprouts from a cupola atop the Middle Building. Stewart was informed of the alleged one-time existence of this cupola (it was not in evidence when he bought the structure in 1907) by one of his tenants, a carpenter named John McDowell, who in turn had been told of it by "a man named Campion who had been a tenant in the second floor some 40 years before…."[132] There is no other evidence that a cupola ever graced an early Mint building. Nor does it seem sensible for the Mint to have placed a cupola on the Middle

Edwin Lamasure's *Ye Olde Mint,* photographed by Jeremy Katz, 2009. The watercolor, as currently framed, is cropped on all sides.

Building when it was constructed in 1816, since the bulk of the Front Building would have rendered such an embellishment invisible from North Seventh Street. Indeed, if a "numismatic cupola" exists at all, it is that which sits atop Independence Hall—designed by the same William Strickland who was the architect of the second U.S. Mint and the 1835 branch Mints in Charlotte and New Orleans. Lamasure apparently worked directly from McDowell's description, as Stewart stated:

> John McDowell, carpenter, was a tenant of the coinage [Middle] building of the first Mint for a considerable length of time, and the roof and cupalo [sic] of that building appearing in the coinage [Middle] building of the group picture of the Mint by Lamasure was in accordance with his observation and description, based on the interior and exterior construction of the walls.[133] McDowell's Carpentry Shop was on the second floor of the Middle Building. A drawing of the structure, published in the *Philadelphia Inquirer* for February 7, 1898, reveals that the doorway to his shop was at the south side of the second floor, where the overhead walkway had once connected the Front and Middle Buildings. That walkway had been demolished by 1898. So access to McDowell's shop was gained by climbing two sets of rickety stairs from the courtyard between the two structures to a platform outside the second-story door. McDowell's friend Ben R. Browne remembered him as "a quaint old North of Ireland man, a good scholar, well read, a great reader and a fine Bible teacher."[134]

Returning to *Ye Olde Mint*, to the north side of the front building is a dog, none other than the celebrated Nero, the first Mint's fearsome canine protector. In reality, Nero was a "savage brute" who was allowed outside only at night, and only within the confines of the Mint's fenced yard.[135] In the painting, we see Nero gamboling in broad daylight in an unfenced Mint yard. On the other side of a partial picket fence from Nero sits a lady engaged in selling small articles; according to Stewart, she was the "molasses candy lady" who frequented the neighborhood.[136] This story has some basis in fact; George Escol Sellers, in his recollections, says that a shop selling the best molasses candy in Philadelphia was located on Sugar Alley during the early part of the 19th century, but he makes no mention of its proprietor plying her wares in front of the Mint. In fact Sellers makes no comment on the proprietor's gender.[137] After Stewart distributed the Lamasure picture, further corroboration arose:

> I will thank you for the beautiful picture . . . of the old Mint as it was in those days, with the Candy Woman sitting there with her basket of Apples and Candy. Many Children went there with their pennies as I myself did and enjoyed the trips, in those days Candy stores were very scarce. . . . I started going to Zane St. Grammar School [*ca.* 1849] now called Filbert St. until my 14th year [*ca.* 1853].[138]

Stewart's analysis is nowhere completely spelled out, but it may very well be that Lamasure's "Candy Woman" came about as a result of Stewart's interviews with neighborhood residents, who might have been children in the 1850s, but probably not during the 1820s, when the Mint was operational. The latter case would have required a surviving centenarian.

The suspect details, however, should not overwhelm the valuable historical data presented by *Ye Olde Mint*. One of the pumps used by the Mint, for example, is depicted where Stewart's excavations determined it was placed in the original yard. Lamasure clearly made a close study of the photographs Stewart provided, and carefully transferred key details to his painting. The best example of this can be found in a side-by-side comparison of Lamasure's painting with Frederick Richards's 1854 photograph of the Front Building and its immediate environs. In the Richards photo, we see a short section of picket fence attached to the northwest corner of the Front Building, and immediately in front of the fence, the stump of a tree. In *Ye Olde Mint*, the same short section of picket fence is in exactly the same location, and a young tree sprouts where the stump appeared in the picture. Further, the Richards photo depicts an illegible sign at the doorway of the number 39 section of the Front Building; Lamasure similarly places a sign with nonsense lettering at the same location. Stewart left behind a cryptic statement regarding Lamasure's use of a photograph:

> There are no prints of pictures of the first U.S. Mint known prior to the Newell photograph of 1855. This photograph was used as a basis for the 7th Street front in the Lamasure painting of the Mint.[139]

Stewart apparently erred on two counts, substituting Newell, another Philadelphia photographer, for Richards, and further changing the date from 1854 to 1855. A concerted effort by the authors has not uncovered the supposed Newell 1855 photograph. Stewart was almost certainly aware of the Richards 1854 photograph as published in the *American Journal of Numismatics* in 1868, and perhaps did not have that particular issue at hand when writing the above.

Stewart also dated the painting in time, although not with a caption. The flag that flutters above the cupola on the Middle Building clearly carries 20 stars. This arrangement was possible only from July 4, 1818, until July 3, 1819.[140] Since the painting also depicts the Middle Building with two stories and the Rear Building with one and a half stories, Stewart must have meant *Ye Olde Mint* to represent the structures during a time from 1817, after the post-fire repairs were completed, up through mid-1819. During this time frame, the new Middle Building had been erected, and the repairs to the Rear Building had been completed.[141] Stewart apparently considered this year to mark the apotheosis of the "Sugar Alley Mint."

THE EVOLUTION OF *YE OLDE MINT*

Edwin Lamasure's *Ye Olde Mint*, as we have seen, is not a perfect rendering of the appearance of the first Mint's buildings, but this was not for want of effort on Frank Stewart's part. Lamasure was given very clear direction by Stewart as to how he wanted the finished product to appear, as this excerpt from *History of the First United States Mint* demonstrates:

> Some time after the Mint buildings were destroyed [1911], I was compelled to give up the hope of ever finding an old print or sketch of them, and it occurred to me that would be a job worthy of one of America's foremost artists. With that thought in mind I made an arrangement through the Osborne Company to have Edwin Lamasure paint the picture after I had obtained all of the data available. From the information at hand a pen and ink sketch was made under my direction and from that sketch Lamasure, who has since deceased, painted the group of three buildings known as "Ye Olde Mint" [1914]. The Osborne Company made color plates which were duly copyrighted. Later, I had Captain Frank H. Taylor, of Philadelphia, make a revised sketch showing a Conestoga wagon.[142]

The "pen and ink sketch" that served as Lamasure's guide (in part) is likely the Taylor emission previously discussed. Stewart's efforts to obtain "all the data available" about the appearance of the first Mint, consisting of letters and sketches from at least two correspondents, are today found in the Stewart Collection at Rowan University. Enough information can be gleaned from these materials to form a provisional chronology of Stewart's research into the Mint's appearance, culminating in Lamasure's famous painting.

In his quest for reliable data, Stewart turned to people who possessed firsthand knowledge about the departed buildings of the first Mint. Stewart's initial contact—or at least the first person to have responded to his inquiries—was John McDowell, a carpenter by trade, who had been one of the Kates family's long-time tenants in the Middle Building.[143] In a letter to Stewart dated March 26, 1913 (with the printed address of 37 North Seventh Street scratched off the letterhead, replaced by number 832 Arch Street), McDowell states he had been a tenant on the second floor of the Middle Building for "some years."[144] He called Stewart's attention to the "floor timbers . . . also the charred end of a beam or girder that had served to support floor joists, for a third story, or garret at one time."[145]

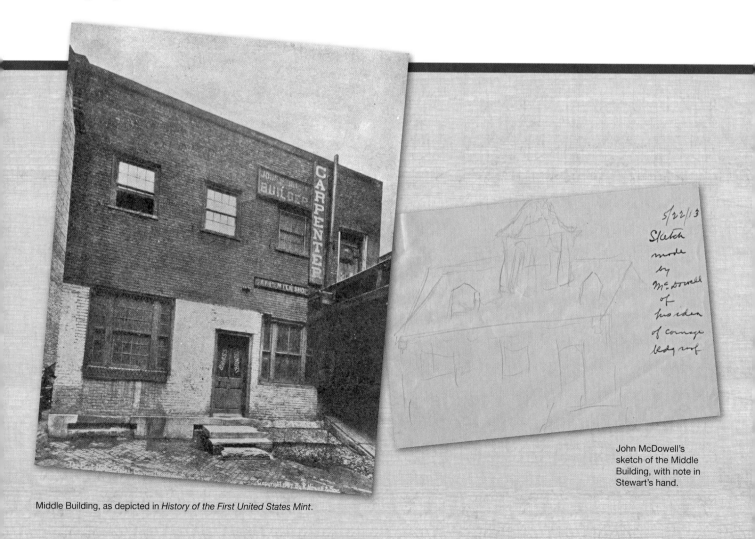

Middle Building, as depicted in *History of the First United States Mint*.

John McDowell's sketch of the Middle Building, with note in Stewart's hand.

Moving from direct observation, McDowell then shared some hearsay evidence: "Now there had been a cupola on the first roof, I was informed by a man named Campion, who had been a tenant on the second floor some forty years before, also dormer windows, as was the custom at the time of its erection by the United States government for a Mint."[146] McDowell goes on to say, "From this data we may form some idea of what the upper part was like, at first. The accompanying sketch is a suggestion."[147] McDowell's sketch depicts the Middle Building from the second floor up, topped by a half third floor, surmounted by a large cupola in the middle, flanked by a dormer window on either side.

Just how influential McDowell's and Campion's ideas were can be seen from a glance at the *Ye Olde Mint* painting. Lamasure depicts the Middle Building as having two and a half stories, capped by a large flagpole-bearing cupola, which is flanked by dormer windows. But just how accurate was this information? Neither dormer windows nor cupola are in evidence in the photograph, *ca.* 1909, of the Middle Building published in Stewart's *History of the First United States Mint*.[148] If there had been a cupola and dormers on the "first roof," as Campion remembered, they would have been consumed in the fire of November 15, 1868, when "the roof was destroyed and the building burned down to the second story."[149] McDowell's account of Campion's tenure does not place him as a tenant until 1873, five years after the original roof of the Middle Building had been destroyed. How did Campion have a personal reminiscence of features that were not there when he became a tenant?

McDowell was correct that there was once a half-story above the second story, for the support structure existed for it and the 1868 newspaper account mentioned the fire burning down to the second story. Campion's assertion that the structure once boasted a cupola and dormers, however, is a much less certain proposition; even Stewart had to admit: "Kates had no knowledge of the cupola I had placed on top of the Coinage Building in the pen and ink sketch because of the tradition handed down to me by old tenants of the building, particularly John McDowell, carpenter."[150] The cupola itself was a concoction, as Stewart readily admitted: "The cupola placed on the Coinage Building was sketched from one of the same period on the old City Hall, corner of Fifth and Chestnut Streets, and naturally differed somewhat from the sketch of John McDowell."[151] From all of the evidence that can be assembled at this late date, therefore, Campion's claim that the Middle Building once sported a cupola seems questionable, at best. Moreover, the Franklin Fire Insurance survey of 1837, which does not mention a cupola, does say that there was a single dormer window— not two—on the east and west sides of the roof.

Armed with this information from John McDowell—as well as the apparent misinformation from Campion—Stewart then turned to an artist to do more detailed renderings of the Middle and Front Buildings. The identity of this artist is unknown. The quality of the sketches appears to be beyond what Stewart himself was capable of achieving. One possible candidate is Frank H. Taylor, whom Stewart hired to do sketches of the Mint both before and after his commission to Lamasure. Taylor's

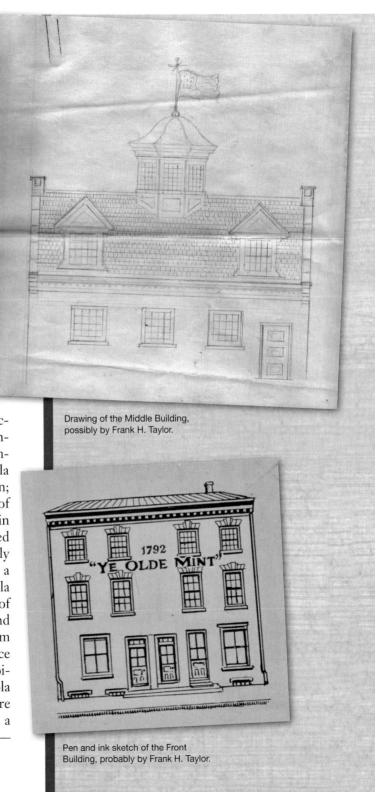

Drawing of the Middle Building, possibly by Frank H. Taylor.

Pen and ink sketch of the Front Building, probably by Frank H. Taylor.

trademark style, however, was rather soft-edged, as if the structures were being viewed in soft evening light. The two sketches in question are rendered in hard, distinct lines, as if in an architectural scale drawing. Perhaps it was Lamasure himself who created these as preliminary drawings; at this point, there is no way of knowing. The attribution of the Front building sketch is more definite, for Stewart confirms in *History of the First United States Mint* that Taylor executed it.[152]

One thing certain, however, is that the sketch of the Middle Building closely reflects the outlines of McDowell's influence. Just as in McDowell's 1913 sketch, it depicts the structure only from the second floor up. A large cupola, topped by a flagpole, dominates the center of the roof, and it is flanked by two substantial dormer windows. On the right side of the second floor is a very incongruous-appearing "doorway to nowhere." This is not a fantasy of the artist, for it can be clearly seen in the 1909-vintage photograph of the Middle Building in *History of the First United States Mint*.[153] This doorway was part of the second-floor connector that attached the front of the Middle Building and the rear of the Front Building when the first Mint occupied the site. Therefore, incongruous as it appears on the sketch, this doorway belongs there.

The sketch of the Front Building was definitely done from direct observation, as can be confirmed by the well-known photograph of the Front Building (with touring car to the right), published in Stewart's *History of the First United States Mint*.[154] The roofline lacks the dormer windows that found their way into *Ye Olde Mint*, and the façade sports the wording: "1792 Ye Olde Mint" that Stewart had painted onto the street front of the structure in 1907. There is also the question of color—the "pen and ink" sketch was black and white, and while Lamasure's façade is gray, a 1907 account of the front buildings describes them as "yellow-plastered."[155]

Whether the artist was Taylor, Lamasure, or someone else entirely, these two sketches portrayed only the Front and Middle Buildings, leaving the Rear Building undepicted. At some point, therefore, Stewart turned to another of the Kates's long-term tenants to fill in the blank. In *History of the First United States Mint*, Stewart mentions the tenant's name, but curiously, he does not share any of the observations: "Joseph F. Meredith, a carpenter, who had spent a large part of his business life working for Riley, 627 Filbert Street, and others in the same place, was also interviewed for his opinion about the changes that had taken place."[156]

Meredith, in fact, supplied detailed information as to his recollection of the Rear Building, including a pair of sketches. Stewart, on October 15, 1923, wrote the following note on Meredith's sketch of the Rear Building: "This was drawn by Meredith after the [Rear] building was down several years [Stewart had demolished it in 1907]. . . . Meredith worked in the building as a boy and had to close the shutters. He must have been 60 years old when he

sketched this about 1913."[157] Meredith's sketch depicts a structure fronting Filbert Street (formerly Sugar Alley), noting, "front set back 20' from Filbert Street."[158] The structure in the sketch is two full stories tall, whereas the corresponding building in *Ye Olde Mint* is a story and a half. Stewart notes another discrepancy: "This building was of brick on Bone Alley and had an outside stairway that entered where the 2nd story window to the left of the chimney is shown." The Rear Building bordered on Bone Alley as well as on Sugar Alley, but Meredith had forgotten about the outside stairway and its corresponding second floor doorway. The chimney in the Meredith sketch is also far shorter than that in *Ye Olde Mint*.

The other Meredith sketch shows a single-story, windowless structure with a two-story building standing in the immediate background. Stewart's notes indicate that: "The 'old rag shop' was in front of it [the Rear Building] and I never saw any windows or doors in its front. My recollection is that the front was out."[159] This was none other than the first Mint's Stable, which sat on the 20 feet of space between the Rear Building and Sugar Alley, with its front on the Alley itself, and its back abutting the south side of Rear Building. By Stewart's time, it is entirely possible that the front of it was open to the elements, for it had never been a very substantial structure to begin with.

Interestingly, Meredith's sketches suggest that the Rear Building's orientation followed that of the lot on which it sat; that is, the structure faced Sugar Alley. This would set the building at a 90-degree variance with the Front and the Middle Buildings, both of which fronted North Seventh Street. Of course, the frontage of the Rear Building was obscured by the stable, which sat between it and Sugar Alley, but nonetheless, the Mint's three principal structures were L-shaped, following the contours of the three lots on which they sat.

It seems likely that Stewart did not quote from Meredith's sketches in *History of the First United States Mint* for a variety of reasons, including error, disagreement, and what might be called "an inconvenient truth." Meredith had erred in replacing the second story doorway with a window. Stewart disagreed with Meredith about the height of the chimney. Nor, apparently, was Stewart in accord with Meredith's handwritten note on the sketch of the Rear Building: "the first floor of this building was known as the gold room."[160] Perhaps these issues gave Stewart pause about the accuracy of Meredith's memory. But the most important reasons seem to be the inconvenient truths that Meredith provided: the Rear Building was two stories tall and faced Sugar Alley. These facts would disrupt one of the primary compositional harmonies of *Ye Olde Mint*, which depicts three buildings, all facing in the same direction, progressing, in neat stair-step fashion, from one and a half to two and a half to three and a half stories, as one looks from left to right across the canvas. To depict the Rear Building as it originally was—a full two stories and facing Sugar Alley—

would seriously compromise the pleasing composition of the painting. Meredith's contribution, therefore, was left on the cutting room floor.

Having gathered all of this material from McDowell, the mystery artist, and Meredith, Frank Stewart could not resist adding some nuances himself. In a sketch entitled *Painting Data*, Stewart himself drew a flag-bedecked cupola, but added to it an element heretofore unmentioned: a clock prominently set into the face of the cupola. This flight of fancy—after all, both a cupola and a clock set into it would have been almost totally obscured by the nearby Front Building—was happily not long-lasting. It did not make it into *Ye Olde Mint*, for its cupola is surrounded by arched windows. A different absurdity, however, was translated onto *Ye Olde Mint's* canvas: the flagpole planted directly atop the cupola. As depicted, the only way to raise or lower the flag would have been for a workman to clamber out onto the steeply pitched roof of the cupola, a well-nigh suicidal act that would have been necessary every morning and every evening in an era when flag etiquette was more strictly observed than it is today.

If Stewart did not get his cupola clock, however, he did get almost everything else he wanted into *Ye Olde Mint*. His handwritten checklist survives, with elements that made it into the painting checked, and those that were ultimately abandoned crossed out. The level of detail is high; not only did Stewart want a watchdog, he wanted a big one, and not just Old Glory, but an "1820 (old style)" flag.[161] Modern trap doors (sidewalk elevators) were appropriately ruled out of bounds, but cellar windows, covered by iron security bars, were stipulated for the Front Building. A yard bell was to be included, the pump to be changed, and the chimney on the Middle Building to be moved. The Mint clock and a "red brick front" were among the items that were eliminated.[162]

There can be no question but that Stewart kept a careful watch over the evolutionary process that resulted in *Ye Olde Mint*. What is not known is whether this checklist specifically referred to an initial sketch or color cartoon of the painting by Lamasure. All of this material—from McDowell, the mystery artist (possibly Frank H. Taylor), Meredith and Stewart—went into the creation of the now-missing pen-and-ink sketch that was Edwin Lamasure's definitive model for painting. It is possible that there was more besides this material that did not survive, but the authors were not able to locate any further evidence. In any event, Lamasure was well-prepped to do the painting, and he did a fine job of creating the ensem-

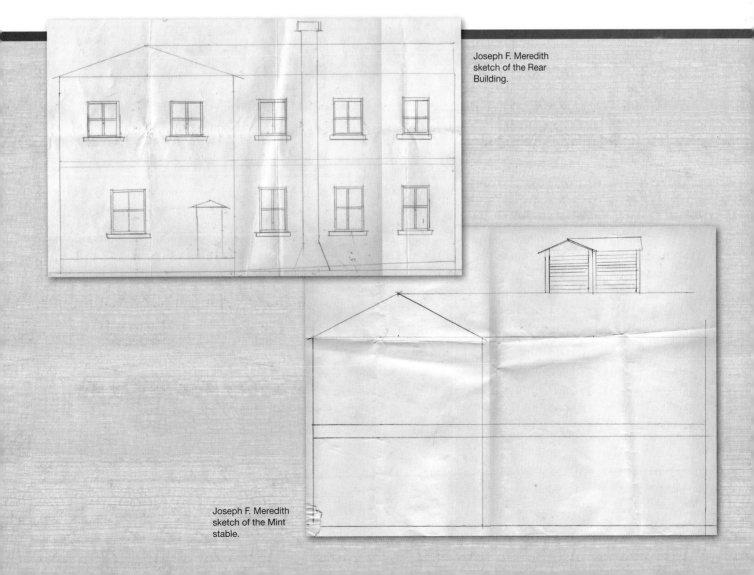

Joseph F. Meredith sketch of the Rear Building.

Joseph F. Meredith sketch of the Mint stable.

ble to Frank H. Stewart's satisfaction. The completed work was probably registered with the copyright office in December 1913.[163]

In its final, painted form, *Ye Olde Mint* literally solves a number of problems by the perspective chosen by the artist, and presumably by its patron, as well. The choice was to view the Front, Middle, and Rear buildings only, and from a point to the northwest of them. From this viewpoint, the Front Building partially obscures the Middle Building, including half of its cupola and all but one of its dormer windows. This meant that the exact appearance of the concocted cupola and the precise number of dormers could be fudged. This perspective also neatly obscured the historically correct (but completely incongruous-appearing) "door to nowhere" on the second floor of the Middle Building. (The second floor connector was still in existence when Stewart bought the property, as shown in the picture on p. 151 of *History of the First United States Mint*, but nowhere does Stewart mention it in his writings, probably because he believed it to be a Kates family addition, not a Mint-built feature.) Similarly, the Rear Building's placement conveniently prevented viewing of both the ramshackle workshops to the east of Bone Alley and the unsightly Stable fronting Sugar Alley. And, of course, by rotating the Rear Building to face west, and

by foreshortening it by half a story, the aesthetically pleasing (but historically inaccurate) proportion of 1.5:2.5:3.5 was successfully achieved.

However the final decisions were made, there is no doubt but that the process used to arrive at them was thoughtful and carefully executed. Stewart interviewed men who had spent their careers in the old Mint buildings, and for the most part heeded their testimony. Stewart himself paid close attention to detail, and minutely reviewed successive drafts. Even when an item was added beyond incontrovertible historical evidence (such as the cupola), care was taken to make its design as contemporary to that of the first Mint as was possible. *Ye Olde Mint* is a composition, it is true, neither complete nor historically impeccable, but it is nonetheless a composition based upon sources that possessed first-hand knowledge. *Ye Olde Mint*, therefore, is and was a composition with credibility, a work of art that, for all of its flaws, points to a larger truth. Without Frank H. Stewart's careful research and thoughtful weighing of the results, this would not have happened in 1914, and not many years thereafter, such fact-finding ceased to be possible at all. We owe the Master of the Mint our thanks for saving as much as he did, as comprehensively as he did, in the crucial window of time during which he chose to do it.

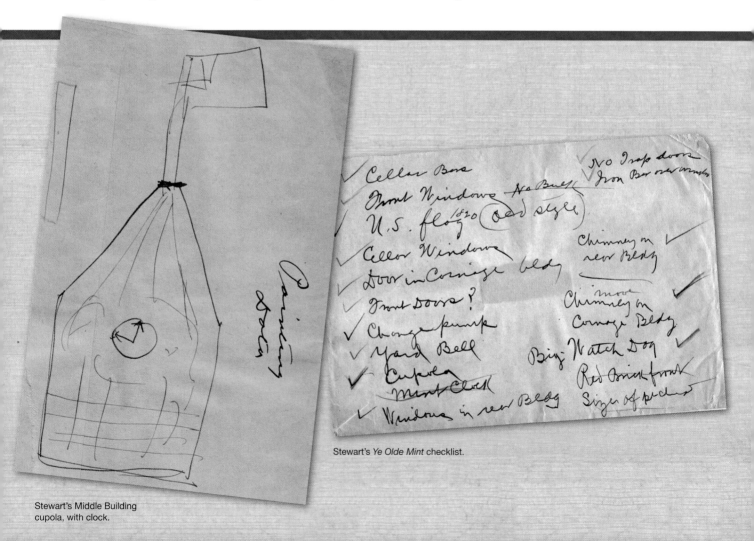

Stewart's Middle Building
cupola, with clock.

Stewart's *Ye Olde Mint* checklist.

YE OLDE MINT: THE CALENDAR

The sixth Frank H. Stewart Electric Company calendar, for the year 1915, translated Lamasure's *Ye Olde Mint* into a strikingly vivid color lithograph. The result clearly delighted Stewart, who distributed the calendars widely. Indeed, Stewart invested $3,000 in the *Ye Olde Mint* project, covering Lamasure's fee as well as calendar printing and distribution.[164] This equates to over $60,000 in current terms—a substantial marketing budget for a commodity business. The Stewart Collection at Rowan University today retains what was probably the first *Ye Olde Mint* calendar, dated November 1914, and likely submitted to Stewart as a sample prior to the final printing. On cardboard stock, the overall size is 8-7/8 by 11-1/8 inches,

with the image sized at 6-1/8 by 4-7/8 inches. A calendar for a single month, November, is glued directly to the board.[165]

Following this single sample, *Ye Olde Mint* was issued in large- and small-format calendars, as well as large- and small-format lithographs (see appendix A). Thanks to Pete Smith, who owns an original Frank H. Stewart Electric Company calendar for 1915, we are able to describe the appearance of the small-format final version in detail. It consists of five layers, the topmost of which is the calendar proper, with 12 monthly tear sheets, each measuring 5-1/2 by 3 inches. The layer immediately below is a tan paper measuring 16-1/2 by 14-1/2 inches. A 12 by 7-inch rectangle is cut out at the top of this piece; the tear

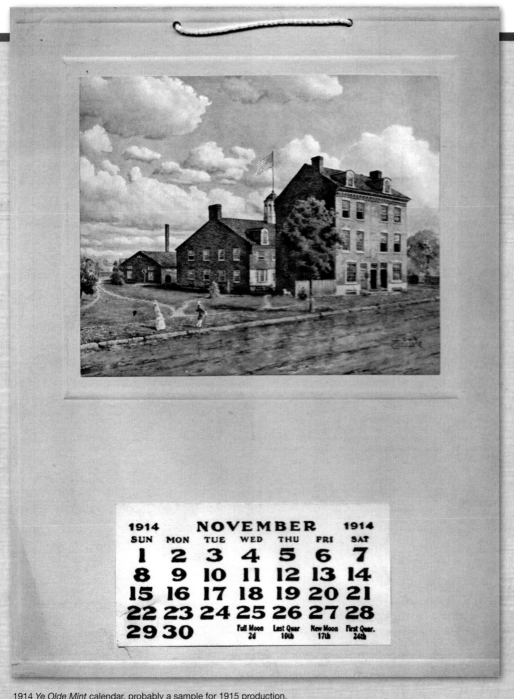

1914 *Ye Olde Mint* calendar, probably a sample for 1915 production.

sheets are attached below this opening. The calendar's third layer shows through this 12 by 7-inch opening: it is the lithographed illustration of *Ye Olde Mint*. The opening in the second layer frames the illustration, covering about a half inch of it on all four sides. The fourth layer is a green sheet, only slightly larger than the tan second layer. This green paper forms the backing sheet to which all of the three layers described above are attached. The fifth and final layer is a 6 by 11-inch text block, printed on both sides, which is attached to the green fourth layer.[166] This essay, unsigned, but presumably written by Stewart, contains a wealth of useful information, including a photograph of Edwin Lamasure Jr. and the story of *Ye Olde Mint*'s creation.

Stewart's commentary is headed "YE OLDE MINT," and the subhead gets right down to business: "Reproduced by color photograph from an original painting by EDWIN LAMASURE now owned by FRANK H. STEWART of Philadelphia, published by THE OSBORNE COMPANY, Newark, New Jersey."[167] This sentence clarifies an interesting distinction in ownership. Stewart paid Osborne the commission for Lamasure's *Ye Olde Mint*, and bought the painting, but the Osborne Company owned the copyright on the image itself, and thus made its profits by selling permissions to reproduce that image. Stewart was

incorrect, however, when he stated that the calendar illustrations were reproduced by color photograph. The calendar images are in fact the product of color lithography. This rather technical distinction was not Stewart's only error, for he went on to say:

> Apparently no artist ever painted and no engraver ever engraved the group of buildings known as the "First United States Mint Buildings," until the Osborne Company secured the data from the present owner of the Mint site, and made arrangements with Lamasure for this picture which must for all time be the accepted authentic picture of the buildings as they stood in the first quarter of the last century.[168]

Stewart chose his words carefully here, for it was true that no painting or engraving of the buildings "as a group" had ever previously been created. But his claim of authenticity in perpetuity rings hollow, since he directed Lamasure to omit two-thirds of the Mint's structures, not to mention the other inaccuracies discussed earlier.

Stewart concluded his commentary by announcing that "the original picture of *Ye Olde Mint* and the *Cradle of Liberty* are on exhibition in the office of the Frank H. Stewart Electric Company in its new home on the site of the U.S. Mint."[169] Stewart was obviously proud of his accomplishments, both in building a new temple of commerce, and in commissioning a first-rate artwork to commemorate the old factory of coinage. It must have been sweet, indeed, to invite the public to admire both of these achievements at the same time.

1915 *Ye Olde Mint* small-format calendar (fifth-layer text block not displayed).

THE MINT AND THE CONESTOGA WAGON

Stewart did truly cherish the images that he had commissioned Lamasure and Dunsmore to create, but to be fair, he did not consider them to be sacrosanct. In fact, the Master of the Mint himself commissioned a variant version of *Ye Olde Mint*. "Later, I had Captain Frank H. Taylor, of Philadelphia, make a revised sketch showing a Conestoga wagon," Stewart recalled.[170] Stewart's simple statement hides a substantial reworking, at least philosophically, of *Ye Olde Mint*, which occurred sometime between Lamasure's death in 1916 and Taylor's death in 1926. Taylor was a natural choice for Stewart, since Lamasure had worked from Taylor's sketch to begin with when *Ye Olde Mint* was originally created.[171] Furthermore, Taylor was well known for his Philadelphia street scenes interposing the architecture of the city and the daily life of its inhabitants. It was this capability to which Stewart was drawn.

Taylor, working from a lithograph copy (the work is signed "Frank H. Taylor / from lithograph") made a number of modifications to the original version of *Ye Olde Mint*. Lamasure's whimsical depictions of the Mint watch-

dog and the "molasses-candy lady," no doubt both specified by Stewart for the original, were removed. The molasses lady dated to about 1815, being mentioned by George Escol Sellers as a pleasant childhood memory.[172] Nero, the "First Dog" of the Mint, was purchased by chief coiner Henry Voigt on January 7, 1793, for three dollars.[173] The molasses vendor probably survived to that period while Nero's fate seems much less assured. In any case, Taylor removed both, and a fence adjacent to these two characters, extending from the north side of the Front Building, also met Taylor's eraser. Two other figures, walking in opposite directions on the footpath in front of the Mint, were similarly effaced.

As mentioned, Taylor worked from a lithograph, and Stewart distributed black-and-white, sepia-toned, reproductions of Taylor's work. Stewart did not own the color reproduction rights. *History of the First United States Mint*[174] notes of the original, "the Osborne Company made color plates which were duly copyrighted." Similarly, of Dunsmore's *Inspecting*, Stewart wrote, "It is copyrighted and the contract was that it could be used historically. The Osborne Co. reserved the rights to use it in color prints."[175]

The First United States Mint, Frank H. Taylor's re-rendering of *Ye Olde Mint*.

Besides the modifications noted above, Taylor added a number of other figures. A Conestoga drawn by horses is noted to the left (north) of the Mint. The Conestoga was indeed contemporary, thought to have been introduced by Pennsylvania Amish sometime around 1725.[176] A similar wagon appears in Taylor's drawing of Fifth and Sansom Streets[177], depicting the Library Company of Philadelphia in its early days. Taylor has widened Lamasure's footpath and graded the street, in order to allow the wagon to access the Middle and Rear buildings of the Mint. A mother holding a parasol walks with her young daughter on the sidewalk, while close by two gentlemen, one mounted on horseback, engage in conversation. A dog in the surrounding area appears to wait for his owner, probably one of the two gentlemen. Two other pairs of figures are similarly engaged at the front entrances of the Front and Rear Buildings. At the southern corner of the Front Building's façade, Taylor adds a hitching post and trough. All of these figures were not chosen haphazardly. "Taylor's drawing also includes the local citizenry as well as contemporary modes of transportation," Taylor's biographer wrote of his *A Southwestern View of Washington Square*, and the same could be said here. Taylor's modified view of *Ye Olde Mint* demonstrates conveyance by foot, by horse, and by wagon, and shows us a number of individuals at work or at play. Finally, Taylor has obfuscated the stars on the cupola flag, apparently an attempt to remove any strong correlation with a specific date.

Thus, the idea behind Stewart's re-commissioning of *Ye Olde Mint* seems to have been one of removing characters related to trivial points of Mint history, and replacing them by a set of contemporary figures intended to demonstrate the quotidian existence of Philadelphia in the early Federal period, when the city reigned as the capital of the new republic. In short, Stewart and Taylor wanted to set *Ye Olde Mint* into the context of the greater American community, as opposed to bathing the Mint in the hundreds of arcane facts that Stewart carefully researched and documented in his *History of the First United States Mint*.

Taylor clearly intended to refocus attention on the hustle and bustle of the Philadelphia city street, for his cloudless sepia-toned version effaced Lamasure's compelling contrast between earth and sky. The effect creates a dynamic interplay between the activity of the street and the activity of the Mint, as opposed to Lamasure's staid impression of vacant doorways and solitary figures. In short, Lamasure was of the country and Taylor of the city, and, echoing the arc of Stewart's own life, *Ye Olde Mint* here evolves from a rural to an urban existence. As a final touch to emphasize the city locale, Taylor partially effaced a tree and presented additional detail in the formerly occluded building bordering the Mint to the east. While Stewart and Taylor were most deliberate in their reinterpretation of *Ye Olde Mint*, history has not embraced the evolution, and today the original version of the Lamasure

Medallic realization of the Taylor version of *Ye Olde Mint*.

has been far more reproduced than the latter. There is one notable exception, in the form of a commemorative plaque placed at the former site of the first U.S. Mint in Philadelphia. The plaque is clearly based on the Taylor interpretation of *Ye Olde Mint*, as it adds the wagon and additional characters to the original Lamasure.

Beyond the re-rendering of *Ye Olde Mint*, Stewart may have had in mind a series of Mint-themed images for Frank H. Taylor to execute, perhaps as illustrative material for his *History of the First United States Mint*. At the time Taylor was engaged in an "Old Philadelphia" series which ultimately consisted of over 400 numbered prints, mostly Philadelphia street scenes. A handful of these are suggestively coincident with the interests of Frank H. Stewart, and these all happen to be bunched closely together within the overall series.[178]

The first, *A Bit of Old Philadelphia at Seventh and Filbert Streets*, number 56 in the Taylor series, depicts residential structures at the southwest corner of Seventh and Filbert, directly opposite the U.S. Mint at the northeast corner. Stewart, who earlier set up business on this side of the street, at 20 North Seventh, made reference to the area in his autobiographical papers:

> Most of the houses on the West side of Seventh Street, north and south of no. 20, were fine old dwellings of the days when that district was a residential section. . . . On the first floor [of number 20] was Weber's Barber Shop. . . . David Bispham, the celebrated Quaker singer, was born within a couple numbers.[179]

The next print of interest in the series, as depicted above, is number 60, Taylor's adaptation of *Ye Olde Mint*, more precisely entitled *The First United States Mint* by the artist. Taylor included the following text with the print:

THE FIRST UNITED STATES MINT

The great historical interest relating to the group of old structures upon North Seventh Street (Numbers

A Bit of Old Philadelphia at Seventh and Filbert Streets by Frank H. Taylor.

37 and 39), which were the first buildings ever erected under authority of Congress for national purpose and which were used forty years as the first United States Mint, was fortunately, fully realized by Mr. Frank H. Stewart, who bought them in 1907 and removed them to make room for a modern business edifice in 1911. The Frank H. Stewart Electric Company thus became the third title-holder of the site from the original sale by William Penn. This drawing has been made from a painting by Edwin Lamasure, based upon careful research for all exterior details of construction.

The middle building, first of the group erected, housed the coinage department. During the incumbency of his friend, David Rittenhouse, 1792–95, the first Director, George Washington was a frequent and enthusiastic visitor. Practically every rare coin bearing the United States stamp was made in this building, including the silver-centre cent of 1792 and the silver dollar of 1804.

Steam power was introduced into the Mint in 1816 for heavy work. The treasure vaults were located beneath the front building. The coinage building also contained bullion vaults. The rear building contained the smelting and refining department.

In 1832 [sic, 1833 is correct] the Government removed its Mint to the handsome and spacious building then just completed for the purpose at Chestnut and Juniper streets. Thereafter the old

buildings were occupied by industrial concerns until secured by the present owner of the site.

Taylor's very next print in the series, number 61, based on an old photograph and entitled *Where Thomas Jefferson Wrote the Declaration of American Independence*, depicts the Declaration House at Market and Seventh Streets, the destruction of which had of course made a deep impression upon Stewart. Shortly thereafter, Taylor produced *The Mint on Chestnut Street*, a rendering of the second U.S. Mint at Chestnut and Juniper Streets, number 68 in the series. The final mint-related image, *The First Photograph Made in America*, number 77, recreates America's first photograph. In 1839, a Mint employee, Joseph Saxton, stood in a second-floor rear window of the second U.S. Mint and shot a picture of the Central High School on the opposite corner of Juniper and Olive Streets in Philadelphia. It is possible that Saxton employed a silver coining strip from the Mint, polished to serve as a photographic plate.[180]

While perhaps all five of these Taylor images were inspired, or even commissioned, by Stewart, no unifying project seems to have emerged from the collective set, and today Taylor's other Mint-related images are even less recognized than his adaptation of *Ye Olde Mint*. Stewart's "Old Mint" marketing machine was instead working with yet another artist, this time not a local Philadelphian, but a historical painter of national repute, whom we shall meet in the next chapter.

The Mint on Chestnut Street by Frank H. Taylor.

The First Photograph in America by Frank H. Taylor.

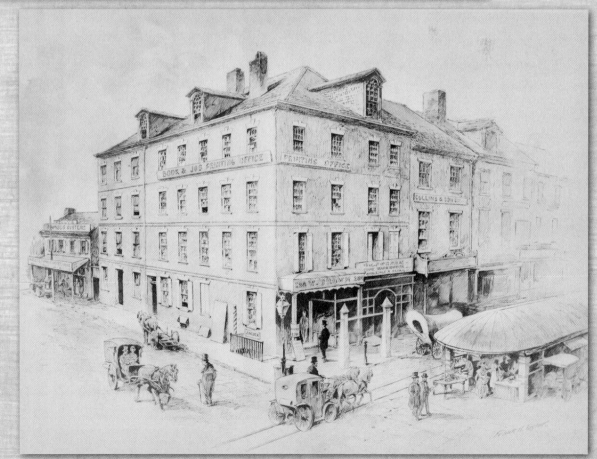

Where Thomas Jefferson Wrote the Declaration of Independence by Frank H. Taylor.

John Ward Dunsmore self portrait, 1897. Collection of the New-York Historical Society, accession no. 1945.358.

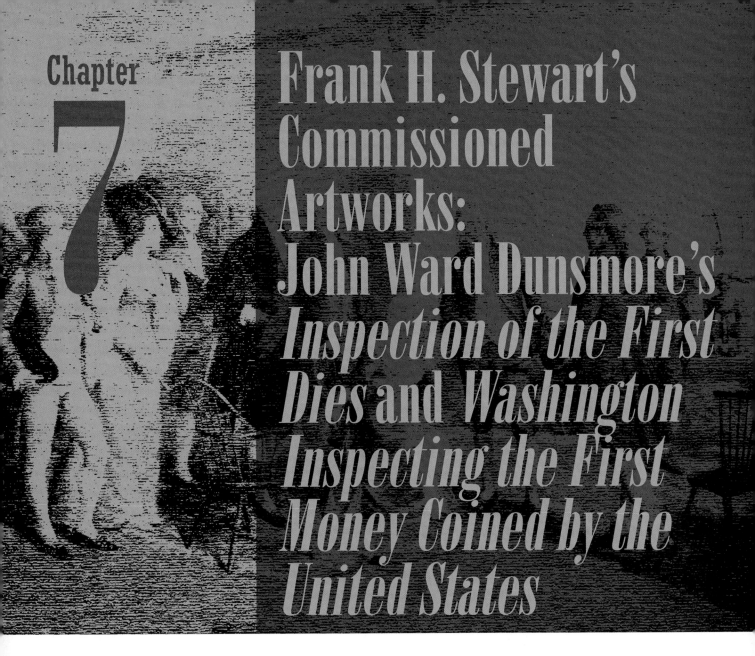

Chapter 7

Frank H. Stewart's Commissioned Artworks: John Ward Dunsmore's *Inspection of the First Dies and Washington Inspecting the First Money Coined by the United States*

John Ward Dunsmore boasted the rarest of birthdays, February 29, and was born in the year 1856 in Riley, Ohio,[1] the first child of Joseph Pollock Dunsmore and Margaret Anette (née Ward) Dunsmore. Dunsmore's father was born in Scotland, while his mother's family had been in America as early as 1633.[2] The young Dunsmore's feet were to be planted in Europe as well as in the new country, and in time he would prove equally adept at operating in both environments. Family connections certainly did not hurt the cause, as Dunsmore's great-uncle, one Hugh Pollock, was the finance officer of the Ulster government in Ireland. "When my father went back there in 1851," Dunsmore noted, "he [Pollock] introduced him to Queen Victoria."[3] The introduction to the sovereign of arguably the most powerful nation on earth was clearly noteworthy, but overshadowed in Dunsmore's recollection is the fact that his father had made at least one voyage from America back to the homeland, an unusual situation in the American immigrant experience, and typically limited to those endowed with both wealth and leisure time.

Dunsmore lived only briefly in Riley, then a few years in Cincinnati, and primarily grew up in Greensburg, Indiana, a farming town of several thousand inhabitants. A reversal of family fortune seems to have initiated the move west. His father "was a merchant in Cincinnati and had a partner who cleaned him out. He went to a smaller place," Dunsmore recalled.[4] Dunsmore's father is listed as a "horse dealer" in the 1870 census,[5] and by that time had sufficiently revived his business affairs to the point that he was able to support his son's artistic career. Dunsmore had taken to art early. "I can't remember just when I first began to draw and paint," he said.[6] "It was when I was very young. I do remember, from those days so long ago, that on account of my persistent attempts I was given a small box of water colors, and to show me how to begin, my mother painted a moss rose with its stem and leaves. The fact that she could do that amazed me as much as the paints gave me pleasure, for I never dreamed that she knew how to do it." Dunsmore continued, "When, at the age of seventeen, I was preparing for college with one side of my head full of Latin and the other side dreaming of pictures, my father remarked that he was willing to have me enter the Art School in Cincinnati, I received the second greatest pleasure shock of my existence. I dropped Virgil at once, and never again looked into it."

Until his teenage years, Dunsmore was largely self-taught, isolated as he was in a rural area devoid of cultural resources. His mother "could paint, like a lady who had learned to paint in drawing school or college,"[7] but apart from this Dunsmore cited only influences such as *Godey's Lady's Book*, a popular American women's magazine, which featured hand-colored copper and steel engravings. Dunsmore was not the least bit deterred by the minimal stimulation. "I was always painting, and interested in engravings, etc.," he said. "It was the drawing and learning how to paint. That enthusiastic art I had it strong from the time I was a very small boy. . . . I have always had this painting idea."[8] Dunsmore's first lessons in Greensburg, under Will Woodward, began sometime around Dunsmore's high school years. Woodward was only five years older than Dunsmore, but had already enjoyed at least one European tour, studying in Antwerp.[9] The Woodward family was locally prominent, the father serving as the county sheriff while the mother had the privilege of a domestic servant.[10] That two young artists could land together in the small, southern Indiana farming town was something of a coincidence, and one of which Dunsmore would take full advantage.

Dunsmore's father apparently decided that what was good enough for the scion of the sheriff was good enough for his family as well, and so it was that young Dunsmore and Will Woodward headed to the University of Cincinnati in 1873, where the two roomed together. Woodward was an instructor at the University, while Dunsmore studied under Thomas S. Noble.[11] In 1874, the Greensburg elite sent another of their member to Cincinnati, namely Henry A. Bunker, the son of a physician,[12] with whom Dunsmore lived in that year. Bunker would become a prominent New York physician. It appears that Dunsmore and Bunker remained lifelong acquaintances.[13]

Dunsmore's instructor, Noble, had spearheaded the formation of the art department at the University of Cincinnati several years prior, in 1869.[14] The value of the fine arts in an agricultural economy was naturally questioned. "Now what good would the study of art be to a farm boy?" he was asked during his interview. "It would help him to dig a better ditch and plough a straighter furrow," Noble ventured. The answer was good enough for the committee, and so Noble, who was born in Kentucky and had lived in both Paris and New York, came to Cincinnati. Dunsmore's own professional path would follow closely that of his teacher—from rural America to large cosmopolitan cities, and back again. Moreover, a thematic connection was to emerge. Noble was a historical painter and obsessed with detail. Noble's biographer wrote of *John Brown's Blessing*, which recreated the execution of the abolitionist who raided Harper's Ferry:

> The picture is historically correct, showing the Virginia National Guards in their Continental uniforms. The representation of the guard standing behind John Brown caused . . . the editor to ask if he had been present at the execution. Answered in the negative [the editor] exclaimed: "But that is an exact likeness of the lieutenant who stood there. I was there and saw him."[15]

The seeds of history were thus sown, and after two years at Cincinnati, it was decided that young Dunsmore, then all of 19 years, should continue his studies on the other side of the Atlantic. The young American thus headed to Paris in the autumn of 1875, carrying a letter of introduction to the artist Thomas Couture, who in turn had been the teacher of Noble in the 1850s.[16] The artistic life of that city had been notably celebrated in 1849 with the publication of Henri Murger's novel, *Scènes de la vie de Bohème*, which in 1896 became the basis for Puccini's operatic masterpiece *La Bohème*. Dunsmore embraced his role on the artistic stage of the Left Bank, reasonably assured that an American patron, namely his father, would spare him the fate of Puccini's penniless cast.

Dunsmore and his father together made the trek from the Midwest to the port of New York, by automobile. "We drove through the country to get there," Dunsmore said. "It was not built up then."[17] Joseph Dunsmore saw his son off, and 10 days later young Dunsmore arrived in London. He made an impression on a wealthy English art collector during the voyage, "one of the stockholders of the Cunard Line," Dunsmore noted, enough so that Dunsmore was invited to visit the gentleman upon his arrival in London.[18] Dunsmore remained in that city only a week, seeing the usual tourist sights and taking in the art museums. "Of course, I did not appreciate it as much as I did four or five years later," he said of the National Gallery. A few days later he removed to Paris and was met there by his old friend from Greensburg, Will Woodward.[19]

Shortly thereafter Dunsmore was set up in a studio at 22 Rue M. le Prince in the heart of the Latin Quarter.[20]

Once in Paris, Dunsmore maintained an active correspondence with his local newspaper, the Greensburg, Indiana, *Standard*, and this record does much to illuminate the life of the young artist in a strange new land.

> On my arrival in Paris I was struck by the clean appearance of everything, which was the more perceptible coming direct from London, where everything is dark and gloomy. . . .
>
> Every Englishman, or American, who has been a student in Paris, knows something of the Bohemian life of the Latin Quarter. Here you meet with students of every kind, but the Americans here are mostly artists. The day of my arrival I was introduced to quite a number of them. A jolly set of fellows they are, too, some of them, without a cent in their pockets, work hard all day, trying to paint something that will sell, and bring them a little money, but when evening comes you find them all gathered around the table at a restaurant eating good warm dinners, (for all of them have credit there), telling stories, laughing, talking, and enjoying themselves. . . .
>
> It has been discovered, lately, that there is a great deal of musical talent among the students of the Quarter, and we have had two or three meetings in some of the studios, which succeeded very well at keeping all the neighborhood awake until after midnight. . . .
>
> You hear the expression, "There is only one Paris," and truly there is no other place that will compare with it. It is the center of the life. It is here that all the fashions are originated, and yet here you see a greater variety of fashions than anywhere else. On the streets you meet with people from all parts of the world. And asking it altogether, it is the most desirable place in the world to live.[21]

Dunsmore clearly enjoyed Paris, and the 19th-century tourist traps as well:

> I have always had an intense desire to visit the catacombs and on my arrival in Paris I immediately inquired how I could get permission to visit them. [Dunsmore notes that the public was allowed to visit only four times per year, with government guides. Visitors had to carry candles.] Many of us marked our initials on the ceiling with the smoke from our candles. . . . I marked several coming through the passage. . . . the guard at the entrance takes the number of all who go down, and they are counted as they return. . . . Someone remarked, "What a commotion there would be, on the Resurrection Day, when every skull will be hunting around for its own bones." One man, disregarding the rules, wanted to carry off a tooth from one of the skulls, but in his attempts to

John Ward Dunsmore, ca. 1870.

extract it he tumbled down three or four others. He was successful, however, and carried off his prize.[22]

Apart from exploring *Les Catacombes*, Dunsmore in Paris studied under Thomas Couture and Aimé Millet.[23] Couture (1815–1879) was a painter of portraits and historical genre, a theme that would come to dominate Dunsmore's oeuvre. Dunsmore had already been influenced in this regard by Noble, but there was family history besides. "It was during my first year in art school in Cincinnati that I made up my mind to paint the Revolutionary War," he said,[24] and again in another interview, "My grandmother was always telling me stories of her grandfather who was in the Revolution and when I was in Cincinnati I made up my mind that I was going to paint the Revolutionary War."[25] Dunsmore related one of his great-great-grandfather's adventures:

> It was the custom during the Revolution [sic] War that between the battles the volunteers went home, and then they would turn out again. He happened to be home on a furlough . . . when the British came over from Staten Island as they were prowling around, and they came to the house. They rushed over his wife and they asked him if he had any arms there, and he said 'no', but they hunted around then they found his musket up the chimney and one

suggested that they settle [execute] him right there, and the other said "no", and they compromised by breaking the musket over his head and setting fire to the house. But when they went away, he escaped and he lived to be ninety-one years old. He was in the Battle of Valley Forge, and all those early battles.[26]

Dunsmore carried a letter of introduction from Noble to Couture on his voyage from America, a useful document that he no doubt guarded closely.[27] Shortly after arriving in Paris, Dunsmore and Woodward headed for Couture's estate in the northern suburb of Villiers-le-Bel. The two probably traveled by train; Dunsmore's sketchbook from this period includes a handwritten copy of the train schedule between Paris and Villiers-le Bel.[28] He recalled the meeting many years later:

> We went up to the gate, pulled the bell rope and waited a little while. For some time there was no response, finally there was a clattering of wooden shoes inside and an old Breton peasant came and peeked through the gate. We asked to see the master and she took us into the house. Finally the old man

appeared. When he heard I had come from Noble he was exceedingly cordial for he had been very fond of Noble. He took us all over his place. He had a fine big estate out there but he never completely restored it since the Franco-Prussian War [1870–1871]. It had been occupied by troops during the siege of Paris.[29]

Couture made a tremendous impression on Dunsmore, and two years later Dunsmore wrote as perhaps only a young man can, smitten with his first professional mentor:

> Cincinnati is fast becoming one of the first art cities of America, and her citizens are very much interested in foreign pictures, among others those of Couture, the greatest of modern painters. It would be, perhaps, interesting to know something of the private life of this great master, who for so many years has charmed the artistic world with his pictures, which not only stand unrivaled in modern times, but are the connecting links between the pictures of the old masters and the would-be masters of to-day. His picture of the "Decadence des Romans" is considered the grandest picture painted since the time of Rubens; but it is useless to speak of his works here. They are well known to a great portion of your readers, and I am proud to say Cincinnati possesses some superb specimens of his work. . . .
>
> For more than two years I have enjoyed the pleasure of an intimate acquaintance with Couture; a great part of the time I have worked with him, and under his immediate charge. His manner of painting is at once the simplest, and the most difficult of all manners—i.e., to put the paint on the canvas just right at the first touch, and leave it there. He says: "Work careful; look four times at your model to one at your canvas; be sure that your drawing is correct before you begin to paint, and then be sure that each touch of color is the right one before you put it on the canvas." The best lesson in painting I ever had was the first time I saw Couture paint. He never made a single line or placed a single touch which had no meaning, and the carefulness with which he did it was almost as surprising.[30]

Aimé Millet (1819–1891), the other of Dunsmore's teachers in France, exerted less influence. Millet was a sculptor, and while Dunsmore had some interest, his first love remained historical painting. "When I was in Cincinnati," he said, "I took up etching and wood carving, but I never did much except for myself. I have a desk over at the house with carved designs on it."[31] Dunsmore also used plaster to model figures before painting. In between the pleasures of youth and professional instruction, Dunsmore began to experience the delicate balance between the demands of art and commercial viability. In May 1876, he wrote to his father:

John Ward Dunsmore, *ca.* 1880.

I hate to say anything about sending me any *more* [original not italicized] money yet, but I wish you should send me some about the first of July, so I can get it about the 15th of July, for I have to pay for three months rent on the 15th and it will take all the money that I have. I have had to get a good many paints and canvas since I came back, for while I was in Corsica I used up nearly everything I had.[32]

Dunsmore, who had spent the winter of 1875–1876 in Corsica, a more temperate climate than Paris, perhaps realized that this might not be the best forum in which to further elaborate upon his winter trip through the south of France. Instead, he offered some hope of future business success:

I think I will have a chance to sell some pictures next winter, for the pictures like the one I took to show Couture are the kind to sell, and the only way to sell pictures is to go to parties and receptions given by wealthy Americans & English, and invite them to come to your studio and see your pictures. They have most all gone to the country for the summer, but will be back in the winter. It does not cost anything to go. It is only necessary to have a good suit of clothes, etc. It is easy enough to get invitations. I went with Will Woodward to call on a lady one evening and she asked me to go with her, to see this Indian Prince. . . . I had the honor of calling upon the Prince of India who is at the Grand Hotel with a [wondrous?] suite. He has been in Paris for two or three weeks, but the first day after his arrival, His royal Highness slipped down stairs and had been confined to his room until a few days ago. He is going to London in a few days (where he will be the guest of the Prince of Wales).[33]

It is safe to assume that Dunsmore did not sell a painting to the Prince, but in any event he was clearly charming enough to be invited into high places. In other recollections he mentioned meeting the wife of the Austrian ambassador to Italy[34] and the writer Robert Louis Stevenson.[35] In all he spent five years in Paris, the high point no doubt being the exhibition of his *Reverie* at the 1878 Salon, a periodic exhibition of the *Académie des Beaux-Arts*, which was at the time the foremost showplace of the artistic world.[36] Dunsmore's mentor, Thomas Couture, died the following year. Dunsmore may well have been present when his master expired, for several years later he exhibited "a sketch of the face of Couture after his death."[37] Following Couture's passing, Dunsmore visited Italy and authored a travelogue printed in the Kokomo, Indiana, *Tribune*, a letter more noteworthy for the editor's introduction than for the text itself:

"A Day in Rome," contributed to the Home of this issue, was written by John W. Dunsmore, a son of J.P. Dunsmore, well known to many of our readers.

The writer has been abroad several years, returning last month. He is an artist of much more than ordinary reputation, and several of his pictures now on exhibition at the Cincinnati Exposition, have been highly complimented by the press and public. Mr. Dunsmore has also written foreign letters for a leading Boston paper, and is a thorough scholar and master of several languages. He has opened a studio in Cincinnati, and will make that city his home for the present.[38]

Dunsmore stayed in Cincinnati only a few months before settling in Boston in 1880.[39] He went to that city at the encouragement of Frank Millet,[40] whom he had met in Paris. Millet, like Frank H. Taylor, the "special artist" engaged by Frank H. Stewart to execute the pen-and-ink sketch of the first U.S. Mint, had traveled widely and reported on world events through drawings and writing. Millet was numismatically connected—he designed the 1907 Civil War Campaign Medal, and was friends with Augustus St. Gaudens. While in Boston as a painter and teacher[41] Dunsmore married Corinne M. Buffington in 1882. She was from an old Boston family, said to be descendants of the fourth duke of Marlborough, thus making Dunsmore's wife a fourth cousin of Winston Churchill, the future English prime minister.[42] Their only child, Malcolm Ward Dunsmore, was born May 23, 1883.[43]

Dunsmore's *chef d'œuvre* in Boston was *Macbeth and the Witches*, evoking his own Scottish heritage. Shakespeare's supernatural tale mixing fate and a lust for influence made for a powerful palette that attracted not only Dunsmore but artists of all disciplines. Giuseppe Verdi's *Macbeth* appeared on the operatic stage in 1847, while Richard Strauss, in the late 1880s created a symphonic tone poem of the same name. The initial reviews of *Macbeth* were not favorable:

while Mr. Dunsmore has not only made the mistake of undertaking to render a poetic idea in a realistic manner, but he has also failed emphatically in the performance of his self-imposed task. His witches are such hideous, mammoth creatures, not veiled mysteriously or shadowed in the least, that no expression to Macbeth could begin to express fear or awe adequate to the situation. The whole work is misconceived in composition and crude in execution, and ought to serve as a warning to young painters not to seek to do great things except by the slow stages by which they may achieve through the necessary successive steps the desired goal.[44]

The artist seems to have taken the criticism to heart, for he reworked the piece and exhibited again several years later. This time the critics were kinder, noting, "This, however, has been repainted, made lighter in tone, and greatly improved since it was publicly exhibited."[45]

Dunsmore was awarded a medal for the work by the Ohio Mechanics Institute in Cincinnati.[46]

Dunsmore successfully sold a number of paintings in Boston.[47] Late in 1883 he left with his family for a second tour in Europe.[48] A sales catalog of Dunsmore's work from that year offered to the Boston public *Macbeth and the Witches*, among other pieces.[49] The family sailed for France, and remained there a year before settling in England until 1888. Dunsmore seems to have enjoyed commercial success in London, where "many of his best works were readily appreciated by English connoisseurs, and sold for a good price,"[50] according to one biography. Among his patrons was Sir Stuart Knill who later became the lord mayor of London.[51] Dunsmore also worked as a staff illustrator for *Pictorial World*.[52] In 1888 he was invited to join the Royal Society of British Artists, on the strength of his painting *La Duchesse de Polignac á Versailles*.[53] Dunsmore had originally thought that he would permanently settle in England,[54] but returned to America at the end of 1888, accepting a position as director of the newly formed Detroit Museum of Art.

Dunsmore in Detroit was a stranger in a strange land. Virtually his entire adult life had been spent in London, Paris, or Boston, all three old cities oozing art and artists, crammed full of museums, galleries, and enthusiastic patrons. Dunsmore's task in the midwest was to duplicate the artistic culture of the more sophisticated cities, and starting from scratch at that. Here was a challenging task calling for a high level of personal charisma, political skill, and organizational ability, not to mention artistic talent! Dunsmore recalled the introductory meeting many years later:

> My first interview with the Trustees was very funny. I had been brought there to direct that institution, and their idea of running the institution was like managing a country fair with the cattle left out. Senator Palmer was President of the Board, James McMillan was Vice President (afterwards United States Senator), who in themselves were fine gentlemen, but they never had any connection with an institute of that sort. They probably would not want to open on Sunday. I said "This institution should be kept open every day in the year. Sundays too." "How will you get the exhibits?" [they asked]. "You can get exhibits if you furnish the money," [Dunsmore replied]. They said "Go to it." I organized the institution as a real museum and the art school as a good working school with a corps of instructors and everything. It took six months to get it started, but I did it.[55]

Dunsmore got it from both sides. While tuning up the administration on the proper way to run a museum, he faced a rebellious clique of young women in the classroom:

> Detroit has an art school, the principal beneficiaries being a class of young women. The conductor of the school is Professor John Ward Dunsmore, from England. Recently Professor Dunsmore issued an order that all pupils must be punctual in attendance, or submit written excuse for their absence. This worried the young ladies, but they bore the wrong in dignified silence. More recently Dunsmore issued another law. No pupil should be allowed to chew gum during the sessions.
>
> This assault upon the free born American's dearest fad was too much, and an indignation meeting was held. The boss gum chewer of the class was made president, and she declared that the object of the meeting was to protest against British tyranny. By a unanimous vote the young ladies decided that Professor Dunsmore must go or they would desert the school in a body. The directors of the Museum of Arts have not less than $200,000 invested in the enterprise, and have a long time contract with Professor Dunsmore. The action of the young women places them in an unpleasant predicament. If the professor is retained the class will desert. If he is removed he will appeal to the courts to enforce payment of his salary during the time for which he was employed.[56]

A few weeks after the chewing gum uprising, Dunsmore resigned the position. "His reason appears to be that another official, a lady, has undertaken to override his authority, and his demands for a proper management have not been listened to by the Trustees," reported the *New York Times* in May 1890.[57] Dunsmore went on to form the Detroit School of Art where, in a promotional attempt to lure students, he played on the public fascination with the aesthetic life of Paris, forming a club called "The Bohemians," of which Dunsmore was the first secretary. The local paper explained it:

> The purpose of the society is to furnish club parlors easy of access to the members, where regular entertainments of a varied character may be enjoyed, where informal receptions to visitors of note may be held, and where the members may repair at all times to peruse the art, literary, music and scientific reading which will be on file and chat over and discuss themes of a kindred nature.[58]

Dunsmore remained four years at the Detroit School of Art, employing instructors and evincing a rising level of administrative capability while yet in his thirties. In 1893 he found time to attend the Columbian Exposition in nearby Chicago. He moved in 1894 to Cincinnati, where he set up his studio in the Pike Opera House and lived in "the oldest house in city," next to his old teacher Thomas S. Noble, the head of the Cincinnati Art School.[59] The fact that Dunsmore happened to land in the Kemper Lane house next door to his old professor can be no mere coincidence; no doubt Noble thought highly of Dunsmore and was probably instrumental in attracting the young artist to the Queen City. Indeed, Noble's granddaughter described Dunsmore as a "dearly loved friend" of her grandfather's.[60]

Dunsmore's time in Ohio was much given to portrait work, producing over 100 pieces in seven years, including that of his neighbor Mr. Noble in 1896.[61] A local newspaper commented: "Mr. John Ward Dunsmore has just finished a carefully executed portrait of Mrs. Truitt. It is a faithful likeness, and he has caught her very pleasing expression. The dress is a rich study in brown, with gold thread running through."[62] Dunsmore gained also the presidency of the Cincinnati Art Club and substantially grew the organization during his tenure.[63] Some time around 1901, Dunsmore was called to the New York area on a portrait commission for the president of the Aetna Life Insurance Company.[64] Noble was not far behind, and also moved to New York, in 1905, where he died two years later.[65]

Following the Aetna portrait commission, Dunsmore spent two years illustrating sets of the collected works of authors Tobias Smollett, Henry Fielding, and Daniel Defoe, published by the University Press in limited editions. After this last overtly commercial endeavor, Dunsmore dedicated himself primarily to the study of the American Revolution and its depiction through fine art. By now Dunsmore was apparently secure financially, either through his own efforts or through marriage, a fortunate circumstance as his historical work did not sell well. "I have not found such a demand for it, for I have the biggest collection of my own pictures in existence," he remarked in 1927.[66]

Besides accumulating his own art, Dunsmore collected antique clothing and military uniforms that were used as models for his historical work. He understood the collector's mentality well. "The principal thing in collection things is to know what you want to get, because they have things and they don't know what they have," he observed,[67] adding that one of his favorite sources was to buy from stage productions closing up shop at the end of a run. What he couldn't buy, he duplicated himself. Dunsmore charmed a Smithsonian curator into allowing him to handle one of George Washington's uniforms, taking large sheets of paper and tracing the outlines of a national treasure.[68]

Beyond the characters and costumes, Dunsmore strived to recreate the physical settings represented in his historical paintings. Now based in New York, Dunsmore could easily travel to Boston, Philadelphia, or his favorite haunt, Mount Vernon. In 1905, he spent two weeks at Washington's home, executing sketches

Dunsmore's Columbian Exposition pass, 1893. Collection of the New-York Historical Society, negative no. 80603d.

Photograph from Dunsmore's Columbian Exposition pass, 1893. Collection of the New-York Historical Society, negative no. 80604d.

that were later referenced in the preparation of certain of his works. Dunsmore noted of his Paul Revere pictures, "I went to Lexington, made my sketch from the old North Church—from the spot where Paul Revere landed. I went all over the field from several angles." Even the timing of the visit was important to Dunsmore. "I went down to Yorktown in midwinter and spent the Christmas there so as to know what the soldiers were up against when they were there," he said, referring to the military campaign in the fall of 1781.[69]

Now fully settled in his *raison d'être*, Dunsmore suffered the death of his wife in June, 1908[70] and the next year found himself afflicted by ptomaine poisoning and typhoid fever. In the absence of his wife, and apparently that of his son as well, by now in his mid-twenties, Dunsmore was forced to rely on outside help:

> It reduced me so; paying a fellow for coming while I was laying on the couch and not able to work. I was two months in the hospital. When I came out of the hospital I went up in Connecticut for a short time and then went to work. I did not work with very

much vigor, after a siege like that it was fully six months before I was in real trim. I then painted some pictures while I was in the hospital.[71]

Dunsmore was an invalid, and a widower at that. It was an appropriate time in his life to get outdoors and meet new friends, and that is precisely what he did. Responding to a letter from William. L. Calver, an acquaintance and amateur archaeologist, he explained what happened next:

> When I was able after I had returned home from the hospital I went one night to his house [referring to Calver]. And the things they had been digging up the results of their exploration were more interesting and exactly along the line and fitted in exactly with the work that I was doing—being buttons and military equipment of the date of the Revolutionary war. From that time I was a part of the exploring society. I never miss a Sunday during the whole year weather will permit that I do not work with them. In the winter we work up until Christmas, or until the ground was so hard that it was impossible to cut it with a shovel, or dig with an axe.[72]

John Ward Dunsmore atelier, ca. 1925. Collection of the New-York Historical Society, negative no. 80606d.

So it was that Dunsmore joined the Field Exploration Committee of the New-York Historical Society. Beyond his study of Revolutionary-era fashion and physical settings, Dunsmore now had the opportunity to add an even higher degree of authenticity to his historical depictions through the firsthand study of artifacts unearthed at sites of military encampments in and around New York City. Another of the committee's members, Reginald P. Bolton, explained their passion in his 1916 work, *Relics of the Revolution:*

> The work has been conducted for its own reward, the establishment of historical fact, the preservation of valuable remains, and the enjoyment and instruction of the public. The work has been productive, as we have reason to believe, of practical and far-reaching value in the interest it has awakened in the historic past of our city in a large number of our citizens, old and young, an interest which cannot fail of beneficial effects in promoting the growth of patriotism and good citizenship. The work has attracted hundreds of visitors, has interested and informed numbers of children, has provided a theme for many newspaper articles, and the exhibition of poor rusted objects in public places has proved a source of keen interest to thousands of visitors from all parts of our country.[73]

Youngsters in particular were fascinated with the excavations:

> To children, such work always appeals, their imagination generally begetting extravagant ideas of its possible results. "What yer lookin' for, Mister?" is a stereotyped inquiry, humorously developed in the searching question by one future humorist, "What d'yer *think* yer lookin' for?" The commonest demands are whether Captain Kidd's treasure is being sought, or gold, or worms for bait. No little aid is given by the willing schoolboy in the lighter work of sorting or searching, and often to practical effect, in conveying needed supplies of ginger ale or sarsaparilla, copious draughts of which assuage the heat of labor under the summer sun.[74]

The group unearthed all manner of military detritus including buttons, badges, cannon balls, glass, chinaware, and pottery. Sometimes there was difficulty:

> Speculation and imagination are brought into play when some new or unusual object is found. Often these objects are incased in a mass of caked rust and sand, and ere [before] shape can be determined the crust must be picked away with some hand tool. One worker's expertness in this direction has become a

John Ward Dunsmore at work as an amateur archaeologist. Dunsmore is the central figure, facing left.

standing joke with his fellows, who maintain that out of a given shapeless block he may fashion the result "to order." And when partial disclosure of some buried object has been made, the excitement and interest are communicated to explorers and visitors alike, as with knife and scraper, trowel or gouge the material is dug away and the whole of it is tenderly lifted to daylight.[75]

While Dunsmore and his friends were clearly focused on historical preservation, the owner of one privately held site remained suspicious:

> There was always a legion [sic, *legend* is likely intended] that the soldiers had buried money on the hill side and this man thought that was what we were after. He did not want anybody to get what he owned. They had certain vague stories afloat in the neighborhood that some workman employed there had gone up and explored that hillside and had found money and skipped out. It was ridiculous.[76]

Dunsmore's work as an excavator was no whim; starting in 1909 he continued until at least 1927. Beside his intense historical curiosity, Dunsmore thought the task good for his health. "Each man on the committee has found that the work benefitted his health," reported the *New York Times* in 1919. "It has relieved some of too much fat and hardened their flesh, and has strengthened the muscles and sinew of others."[77] Today, many of the relics he recovered reside in the collection of the New-York Historical Society, which he officially joined in 1921 upon the recommendation of fellow member and field explorer Reginald Bolton.[78] Dunsmore was regarded highly, enough so to be invited to lecture at the Society on the subject of the Revolutionary War.[79]

Dunsmore remarried in 1910. His wife might have been grateful that Dunsmore was getting some constructive exercise on his weekly excavations, "instead of playing golf on Sunday afternoons," as one reporter put it .[80] Dunsmore's second wife was one Margaret Ney, a great-great-niece of Marchel Michel Ney,[81] a commander under Napoleon, ultimately executed for having been unfaithful to the French monarchy. Dunsmore had thus married into history for the second time, but there was apparently some bad blood between his second wife Margaret and Dunsmore's son Malcolm. "We are not happy having John's son around. . . . We were for years paying old debts that he had contracted," she later wrote to Dunsmore's good friend Oscar Barck.[82]

Apart from links to old European nobility, Dunsmore made his own connections in America. In the spring of 1918 he was chosen to paint a portrait of President Wilson, who sat for Dunsmore in his New York studio.[83] Dunsmore's work echoed that of his old Cincinnati teacher, Thomas S. Noble, who painted President McKinley. Indeed, McKinley's wife remarked that it was best likeness of her husband.[84] Later, Dunsmore had connec-

tions to the Coolidge administration as well, for in 1925 he casually remarked in a letter, "On Friday last I was at the White House and had a very pleasant call on Mrs. Coolidge."[85] Dunsmore also crossed paths with the work of Gilbert Stuart, the celebrated Washington portraitist. Stuart is of course known for three iconic images of Washington identified as the Landsdowne, Vaughn, and Athenaeum types, the last of which graces the modern dollar bill. It was a lucrative franchise for Stuart, who produced any number of copies of the tremendously popular Washington portraits. In any event, Dunsmore was called upon to restore the Athenaeum portrait held by Robert L. Pierrepont, an important copy painted by Stuart at the same time as the original, with Washington said to have alternated sittings for the two.[86]

Full of the history of the Revolutionary War, Dunsmore probably never imagined himself taking a role in a far bloodier conflict, but fate had different ideas, and with the entry of the United States into the first World War there were opportunities for patriots of all ages. Dunsmore explained it:

> [The] Sons of the Revolution [of which Dunsmore was a member] sent messages to every one of their members urging them to join the Veteran Corps of Artillery in spite of the fact that they might be over military age. I was considerably over military age [61 at the time], but my inclinations were in that direction so I went to the Veteran headquarters and interviewed the Colonel. He said "see what the doctor says." The doctor said "Come on in it will do you good." So I went in.[87]

Dunsmore eventually became involved in hospital administration for the Army, rising to the rank of Major. He longed to be dispatched to the European front, but appealed in vain to the secretary of war. In 1919 he was given charge of a large hospital, 1,500 beds, on Staten Island. Even though the Great War ended in November 1918, one must remember its price—20,000,000 dead, 20,000,000 wounded, and the United States had its share of both. Dunsmore was effective, or at least effectively admired by his superiors:

> They were all very glad to see me when I came, and after I had been there awhile they wished some one else had come. They sent me to clean house. I personally discharged more workers than anybody else in the service. It is a funny thing the workers do not like to be kept to rules, but the organization does approve of it. I was there until that hospital closed October 1st, 1920. I was offered the biggest army hospital in the country if I would take it over—the Walter Reid [sic] Hospital at Washington.[88]

Dunsmore turned down the offer, more content to return to his studies of the Revolutionary era. In 1922 he delivered a painting of Washington leaving a memorial service following the victory in Yorktown in 1781. Dunsmore continued to play the part of the researcher:

> The first thing is to dig out the historical end of it. Go through every blessed thing that you can find on the subject. I found out that Washington and his staff with the President and members of Congress attended this service on the 6th day of December, 1781, at Christ Church, Philadelphia—I found this data partly in New York and partly in Philadelphia. Of course, the painting of the picture is just painting. You make your sketch, then you work around that for composition, and in this particular picture you had the fixed lines of the church itself, which had to play its part.[89]

Dunsmore took the time to do the research, but unfortunately was not careful with his documentation. "I have never had the habit of writing down where I got my authority," he said in 1927.[90] The copyright office registration for the above work gives the title as *Memorial Service in Honor of Victory at Yorktown, December 13th, 1781*,[91] and clearly in this case Dunsmore got the date wrong in at least one place. Certainly it was not for lack of trying, as Dunsmore explained another 1922 work:

> The next picture was the Captured Flags from Yorktown in 1922. That was the big picture which was in the Academy [probably referring to the National Academy, to which he was made an Associate in 1925]. That picture took a tremendous amount of work. I had to find out the particular men who were in Congress at that time and get their portraits but I had to determine the designation of flags and some of them had never been determined up to that time. The records of Congress tell you there were six English flags, ten German flags, and six Hessian flags. I had to get pictures. I have original negatives of every flag in existence. The six British flags were two from each regiment surrendered, one the King's colors, but the other were regimental flags. The German flags were easy, they were Anspacher's [unclear] and there were four of those up at West Point; but the Hessian flags were the most difficult, and it was not known to anybody until that time what the flags at Yorktown were. The designation is the same on all Hessian flags, and while each regiment carries five flags, there is quite a little variety in them.[92]

Dunsmore's output seems to have ebbed in the late 1920s, and his latest entry in the Copyright Office is dated 1933.[93] Dunsmore's retirement was funded through the generosity of George A. Zabriskie, the president of the New-York Historical Society. Dunsmore donated his collection of Revolution-themed paintings to the Sons of the Revolution in 1936 in exchange for a payment of $2,000

John Ward Dunsmore, ca. 1930. Collection of the New-York Historical Society, negative no. 80605d.

per year, not to exceed 15 years or Dunsmore's lifetime.[94] The paintings reside today at the same location, the Fraunces Tavern Museum in New York City. The first payment was made in 1936. Dunsmore closed down his studio in 1941[95] and on April eighth of that year donated to the New-York Historical Society much of the material still in his possession, including personal papers, studies, artifacts from the Field Exploration Committee, and old sketchbooks. The drawings today are highly unorganized, and were probably even more so at the time of the accession. Dunsmore suffered mental illness at least by 1942, and may not have been able to systematically dispose of his studio. Ironically, this may be the reason why so much of this material has been preserved.

In 1942, Dunsmore's wife reported to Oscar Barck, a friend of Dunsmore's, that Dunsmore had lost his memory and had gone missing on several occasions, wandering out of the home.[96] Shortly thereafter she related that he had suffered from falls and required constant attention. Compounding the strain was Dunsmore's son, whom she suspected of stealing checks intended for his father and personally endorsing and cashing them. "We will never be able to trust . . . Malcolm again," she wrote, adding, "for although he is over 60 he has not improved with the years."[97] She was particularly suspicious that Malcolm had been visiting his father more frequently, as his yearly check from the Sons of the Revolution was coming due, and thus communicated explicit directions regarding delivery of that year's check. Margaret herself took sick in 1945, and, apparently not having a caretaker in the New York area, went to be with a sister in Cincinnati. Dunsmore died on September 30th, but the news was withheld from his wife upon medical advice.[98] She passed on November 22nd. She had apparently taken only one personal item of Dunsmore's to Cincinnati, a Masonic medal awarded to him in 1934.[99] A sister sent it to Barck with the note, "She [Margaret] was always confident the medal in your hands would be properly placed."[100] Barck was up to the task. The medal, annually awarded to the American Mason who had made the most significant artistic contribution to the world, today resides in the collection of the New-York Historical Society.

The Evolution of *Washington Inspecting the First Money Coined by the United States*

Most numismatists are familiar with the oft-reproduced oil painting by John Ward Dunsmore, *Washington Inspecting the First Money Coined by the United States*. Very few of these numismatists, however, are aware that Dunsmore's celebrated canvas does not stand alone, but instead was a culmination of a long process of artistic evolution, in the form of seven sketches: two roughed out in pencil, two in pastels, two in watercolors, and one in oil. Taken together, this series illustrates a thoughtful development from rough idea, to a couple of dead ends, to fresh starts, to finished iconic work. Three of the seven sketches are completely different from the final painting, being set outside of the Mint's front door. Two of the seven move inside of the Mint, but focus on a very different subject, namely an engraver hard at work on the first coinage, the half dismes. The remaining two sketches depict the evolution of *Inspecting* in the artist's mind, and lead very clearly from initial concept to finished painting.

Before analyzing the sketches, some clarification should be made regarding the precise title of the painting, as even Stewart referred to it inconsistently. The confusion begins with the title as registered in the copyright office, for two different versions are given on the copyright entry—one being *Washington Inspecting First Money Coined by the United States*, while later the word "the" is added: *Washington Inspecting the First Money Coined by the United States*.[101] Dunsmore, when assigning the copyright to the Osborne Company, used the latter title.[102] This version seems less awkward and is used in the present text, and further matches the title as reproduced by Osborne on the Frank H. Stewart Electric Company calendar of 1916. The painting itself today bears a nameplate, probably furnished by Stewart, which reads simply *Inspecting the First Coins*.[103] Conversely, Stewart also used the title *Inspection of the First United States Coins*.[104]

The Dunsmore sketches are completely unfamiliar to numismatists because they have never before been published. As preliminary, rough designs, they were probably shared with Frank H. Stewart, but not with anyone else, and once they had served their purpose, they receded back into the collection of studies that Dunsmore kept at his studio. The artist was an inveterate painter of Revolutionary-era subjects, so it is plausible that he referred to them as he tackled later commissions. After his death, the sketches were bequeathed to three different institutions with which he had close connections: the New-York Historical Society (Dunsmore was a member of the Field Exploration Committee); the Fraunces Tavern Museum (Dunsmore was a member of the Sons of the Revolution, which owned and operated this lower Manhattan museum); and the Wagnalls Memorial Library in Lithopolis, Ohio (Dunsmore was a fast friend of Mrs. Wagnalls, who endowed the library).

The seven sketches, all published here for the first time, tell a tale of a developing artistic vision, but they do so only grudgingly. Only four of the seven are labeled in any fashion, and only one of them is dated. No correspondence between Frank Stewart and John Ward Dunsmore about these sketches—or indeed, about their artistic dealings in general—is known to exist. While it is therefore impossible to place them, with certainty, in a sequence of creation, the authors have pieced together a speculative sequence that, until a more definitive interpretation comes along, will serve to suggest the way in which Dunsmore and Stewart shepherded the concept for *Washington Inspecting* from rough idea through dead ends and fresh starts, to the finished painting.

The final version of *Washington Inspecting*, is set inside the "Coinage Building" (Middle Building) of the first U.S. Mint. We now know that this structure was not in fact built until 1816, but Stewart was unaware of that fact. This suggests, therefore, that the three sketches set out of doors hard by the front door of this building may have been Dunsmore's first essays toward the creation of the work. Of the three outdoors renderings, the roughest, and hence probably the first, is the pencil sketch found in the New-York Historical Society's Dunsmore Collection. This is not only a crude version of the scene, but also the only one of the seven that contains inaccurate details about the buildings and equipment of the Mint: another reason to believe that it was the first to be created. In the sketch, a tall figure on horseback (presumably President Washington), with one mounted companion, approaches a fenced-off building in the left background that is guarded by a rifle-toting sentry. This small party is met at the gate by an older gentleman (presumably Mint Director David Rittenhouse), who is bowing at the waist and doffing his hat. The head of another man, who seems to be tending to Washington's companion's horse, is visible over the hindquarters of Washington's steed.

While the presence of Washington and Rittenhouse in this sketch is plausible, the rest of its elements are all wrong. The building in the background, with its entrance to one side of the structure, sheltered by a small entry roof, looks nothing like any edifice occupied by the first Mint. History records no flintlock-bearing sentry standing in its yard, and no fence was located directly in front of any of the Mint's structures. Perhaps most glaring of all is the background, in which trees seem to be issuing from large boulders, a most startling development on Philadelphia's highly urbanized North Seventh Street! All in all, it seems that this sketch was completed very early in the creative process, after Stewart's initial contact with Dunsmore, but before the Master of the Mint had the opportunity to share with the artist any of the facts about the Mint and its physical setting.

The second sketch in the "outside" set, which resides in the Wagnalls Library, represents a significant improvement in both accuracy and artistic quality over the pencil sketch. As a watercolor, it is much more polished than the initial effort. The building that dominates the left half of the composition is well-rendered, and quite clearly represents the "Coinage" (Middle) Building of the first Mint. Most impressively, the two horsemen of the pencil sketch have given way to a carriage manned by two liveried coachmen, discharging six passengers in front of the Mint. Greeting them is a blue-coated David Rittenhouse, bowing as he was in the pencil sketch, but this time with his back to the viewer. The Mint director is offering his hand to Martha Washington, resplendent in a purple dress, with the president standing tall behind her. Two gentlemen, the taller of whom may be Thomas Jefferson, walk behind the Washingtons. Behind them, a man is helping a woman from a carriage; they are probably meant to represent Alexander and Elizabeth Hamilton. On the Mint side of the picture, two men stand in the doorway, while a third takes a post beside the steps. Beside the building, a group of three citizens standing around the Mint's water pump gawk at the arriving presidential party. At the corner of the building stands a large dog, presumably Nero, the Mint's faithful guardian.

The final version of *Washington Inspecting the First Money Coined by the United States*, from a lithograph.

Dunsmore outdoor rendering pencil sketch for *Washington Inspecting the First Money Coined by the United States*. Collection of the New-York Historical Society, accession number INV.14700.

Quite clearly, Dunsmore crafted this sketch after having had the benefit of seeing Edwin Lamasure's *Ye Olde Mint*. The structure is certainly copied from the Middle Building in that painting, from the flag-bedecked cupola to the configuration of the ground-floor windows, to the placement of the water pump, to the presence of Nero. If the physical setting is much improved, however, there is still much in this version that is wanting. It is not known whether Stewart offered suggestions for changes, or if the impetus was self-criticism on Dunsmore's part, but there was much to criticize in this second version of the "outside" set. The sketch is dominated on the left side by the massive bulk of the Middle Building, and on the right side by the long expanse of the horse and carriage, leaving scant room for the 15 human figures in the painting. The humans are therefore, of necessity, minuscule in dimension, and some, like Rittenhouse and one of the visitors, have their backs turned upon the viewer. The greatest objection, however, must have been the generic nature of the scene as painted. While viewers probably would recognize the Washingtons, there is nothing else in the sketch, especially with Rittenhouse's back turned, to suggest that the building was a part of the U.S. Mint, or that coins were the theme of this composition. And the background beyond the carriage, though improved by the removal of the boulders found in the pencil sketch, now features a small forest, still far too pastoral for North Seventh Street.

The third and final sketch in the "outside" set solves nearly all of these problems. This oil-on-linen depiction, which resides in the New-York Historical Society's Dunsmore Collection, carries the following label: "*Sketch for a Visit to the Mint by Pres. Washington & Party in 1792* [signed] John Ward Dunsmore." Of the three "outside" sketches, it is by far the most finished composition, with detailed, recognizable faces painted in as opposed to the gauzy facial renderings of the other two. Dunsmore seeks to capture the same moment as in the second sketch: the arrival of the presidential party at the Mint's front door. Now, however, Thomas Jefferson is standing by the front steps, apparently part of the greeting party, flanked by David Rittenhouse, still in blue, still bowing, but now turned to face the viewer. President and Mrs. Washington stride from the carriage; Alexander Hamilton stands behind them, while a man in a green coat, possibly Tobias Lear, Washington's secretary, hands Mrs. Hamilton down from the carriage. One person still stands in the doorway of the Mint, and a total of six onlookers are distributed behind the carriage and in front of a brick wall that has been added to demarcate the Mint's property from that of the two houses visible amongst the trees in the distant background.

John Ward Dunsmore had certainly improved the composition immensely, and the fact that he inscribed it suggests that he may have been rather proud of his efforts. By depicting only the front façade of the Middle Building

and by rotating the carriage so that it faces the viewer, he opened up the central space, allowing the human figures to be painted much larger, and also to take center stage. On the Mint's façade itself, he placed both a plaque and a hanging sign, complete with a spread eagle, which reads "United States Mint." Now every viewer would know the function of the structure that graced the picture. Finally, the background recognized the fact that the Mint had neighbors on North Seventh Street.

Despite all of the improvements, though, it is easy to see why Stewart (or possibly Dunsmore himself), ultimately rejected this version. To begin with, historical details were definitely wrong. The real Middle Building is not known to have had a hanging sign identifying it as the Mint, and since it was in the interior yard of the institution, not open to the public, there was no reason for having such. There was only a cramped, enclosed brick courtyard in front of the Middle Building, not the large open space depicted here. The Front Building cut off the Middle Building from access to North Seventh Street, so there was no driveway, as shown in the sketch. The neighboring houses were not set in arboreal parks, as suggested in the watercolor, nor was there ever a high brick wall between the Mint and adjoining properties. All of these inaccuracies would be very objectionable, but one other very significant problem remained from the second sketch: there still were no coins or coinage equipment on view. Ultimately, this third sketch showed a party of important people *arriving*. It did not reveal why they had come; and most problematically, it had nothing directly to do with the first coinage of the United States. At some point, either patron, artist, or both together, must have come to the conclusion there was no way to adequately depict the first coinage theme if the protagonists were standing outside of the Mint: the setting must be moved within its walls.

The four "inside" sketches divide themselves into two sets. Two of them closely foreshadow the final form of *Inspecting*. The other set of two look nothing like the finished painting, which strongly suggests that they were earlier, and ultimately rejected efforts. No pencil sketch has been found for this earlier set, but a good guess can be made as to which came first. The oil, which resides in the New-York Historical Society's Dunsmore Collection, is unique among the sketches in that it portrays a solitary person. It depicts an engraver in profile, sitting on a stool in front of his engraving bench, which holds an assortment of the tools of the trade. The engraver's cloak is hung behind the bench, near a window that provides him with natural light. Toward the back of the room, sitting on a sturdy bench, is a coin press, modeled after the so-called "first press" of the U.S. Mint.[105]

The problem of "nothing to do with coinage" is addressed here, for the viewer sees an engraver working on a die, and in the background, the very machine that strikes coins. What has been lost, of course, is the centrality of

Dunsmore outdoor rendering watercolor for *Washington Inspecting the First Money Coined by the United States.*

Sketch for a Visit to the Mint by Pres. Washington & Party in 1792, John Ward Dunsmore. Collection of the New-York Historical Society, accession no. X.704b.

Inside sketch, engraver in profile, John Ward Dunsmore. Collection of the New-York Historical Society, accession no. X.704c.

George and Martha Washington, along with accompanying dignitaries, in the picture. Clearly, there is limited utility in turning the spotlight upon a solitary engraver; Dunsmore would have to expand upon this insufficient beginning.

Expand he did, and the next version seemed to satisfy the artist. By painting it in oil, he appears to have had considerable confidence that this version would meet his patron's approval. The title, as written on the frame, is long and ponderous: *Sketch for* [illegible] *Engraving Die for 1st Silver Coins Struck in the Philadelphia Mint 1792.* The illegible portion may have contained the name of the engraver depicted in the painting, in which case it probably would have been Chief Engraver Robert Scot. The subject of the painting, which resides in the Fraunces Tavern Museum (where it was repaired and cleaned in 2008), is exactly the same as that of the previous sketch: the engraver at his bench, with his cloak hanging on the wall, with the "first press" standing in the background. To this tableau, Dunsmore added four additional figures; to the left side of the painting is David Rittenhouse, standing in a supervisory mode; to the right side, George Washington, Thomas Jefferson, and Alexander Hamilton, all peering over the engraver's shoulder, or at least trying to peer; the diminutive Hamilton is challenged to see anything but the shoulders of strapping specimens like the president and the secretary of state. In the foreground, with Washington's left hand resting upon it, is a Windsor chair

Sketch for [illegible] Engraving Die for 1st Silver Coins Struck in the Philadelphia Mint 1792, John Ward Dunsmore.

painted after an example from the U.S. Mint.[106] An Adam Eckfeldt descendant reported in 2007 that a similar chair remains in the family and that oral tradition places its origin in the first Mint.[107] More contemporary to Stewart, a chair owned by Patterson DuBois, "that is a duplicate of one in the picture," was reportedly purchased "of the Mint sale," presumably referring to the sale of the first Mint property.[108] DuBois and his father, William Ewing DuBois, both served as assayers in the Mint.

Why was this oil painting ultimately rejected and forgotten? It is, after all, located within the Mint, it depicts the process of designing a coin, includes a coin press, and features four important dignitaries. Yet, there were many reasons to consign it to the "unacceptable" file. One is the focal point of the painting, which is the anonymous engraver; as a result, his four famous visitors are viewed only in profile. Worse, other dignitaries, including both Martha Washington and Elizabeth Hamilton, are eliminated from *Sketch for . . . Engraving Die*, which also robs the painting of splashes of vivid color. Like the first set of sketches, unacceptable because the focus was upon dignitaries *arriving*, this set was probably deemed unacceptable because its subject was a workman *engraving*. The spotlight needed to fall more directly upon the coins and the dignitaries in order for the tableau to satisfy Stewart. So the engraver was not a suitable subject, but some of the sketch's elements—the "first press," the Windsor chair, even the hanging cloak—would survive into the final version of *Washington Inspecting*.

About this time, Stewart weighed in on the progress of the project, and, in a letter to the Osborne Company on May 11, 1914, outlined any number of elements which are clearly seen in the final version:

> Gentlemen:-
> Regarding the contemplated picture of *Washington at the Mint* or *Beginning of our National Coinage.*
> David Rittenhouse was the first Director of the Mint and was appointed April 14, 1792. Henry Voight was an employee of Rittenhouse as a clock maker and unquestionably was associated with Rittenhouse at the Mint from its beginning. He was appointed Chief Coiner January 29, 1793.
> Adam Eckfeldt was engaged to construct machinery for the Mint and in a law suit, Wood vs. Kates, in this city, on February 23, 1847, testified,—"I was employed at the Mint on Seventh Street; began there with it—began in '92."
> Tobias Lear was Washington's private Secretary, and at the time a distinguished man. Alexander Hamilton and Thomas Jefferson both had a great deal to do with the establishment of the Mint.
> The first coins made at the Mint had always been known as the Washington Half Dime and the head thereon was supposed to represent Martha Washington, who is said to have sat to the artist while he was

designing it. The coins are said to have been made from private plate or bullion contributed by Washington. He referred to the coins in his annual address of October, 1792.

The following publications are worth inspection:—

Page 116, Ancient & Modern Coins, by J. Ross Snowden, Director of the Mint, printed by J.B.Lippincott & Company, in 1860. [Snowden gives a description of the 1792 half disme, and suggests that Washington provided the silver for this issue.]

Current Gold & Silver Coins of All Nations, by Ivan C. Michaels, published by R.S. Menamin, Philadelphia, 1880. [On page 6, Michaels cribs from the Snowden account.]

Coins & Coinage, by A.M. Smith, Philadelphia, 1881. [On page 6, Smith also borrows from Snowden.]

American Numismatic Manual, page 229, by M.W. Dickeson, published 1865. [Dickeson states that Washington was "almost a daily visitor" to the Mint, and that he provided bullion for the 1792 half dismes.]

Life of David Rittenhouse, by William Barton, wherein Mr. Lear, Mr. Voight, Jefferson and Hamilton are mentioned in connection with the Mint.

I have no doubt that there are records prior to those above mentioned, but there has been no question in my mind that the first silver was delivered by Washington, because the first regular coinage of silver did not begin until 1794 and there is a Mint record of who delivered the bullion for coins of that date.

The picture should contain an antique clock, either a Rittenhouse or a Voight, of which there are many still in existence; the old Mint scales, which are still in existence; a chair from the old Mint, now in the new Mint in Philadelphia; George Washington's white haired, old, Negro servant carrying the coffee pots,—and other household utensils for coinage purposes; and possibly Martha Washington, or her portrait, should be considered.

There are portraits of Tobias Lear still in existence, but I am not so sure about Adam Eckfeldt or Henry Voight, although it is quite likely there are several of Mr. Eckfeldt, as he lived to be a very old man and I an informed that there has been an Eckfeldt in the Mint from its establishment in 1792 down to the present day.

Henry Voight was a noted man and it is possible there is a likeness of him somewhere.[109]

Stewart's critical thinking aside (suggesting that lack of Mint documentation proves Washington provided the 1792 bullion is a particularly egregious leap, not to mention the suspicious nature of two of the accounts being lifted directly out of Snowden without independent verifi-cation), this correspondence does much to clarify the final version of the painting, as we shall see. Before proceeding to the ultimate state of the painting, however, mention should be made of the date in the lower left corner of *Sketch for . . . Engraving Die.* As can clearly be seen, the sketch is marked "J.W.D. 1916." This date does not fit with the known chronology of *Washington Inspecting*, which was copyrighted in 1915 and reproduced on the Frank H. Stewart Electric Company calendar in 1916. The attribution is marked in pencil on the sketch, and Dunsmore's practice of signing sketches is inconsistent. As has been noted, most others in this series are undated. The authors theorize that this sketch was signed some time after 1914, perhaps relying on the artist's memory for a date. Ultimately donated by Dunsmore's friend Oscar Barck to Fraunces Tavern, the artist might have signed it just before presenting it to Barck. Dunsmore seems not to have maintained a *catalogue raisonné* which might clarify the issue.

This brings us to the last set of two sketches, both of which are clearly precursors to *Washington Inspecting the First Money Coined by the United States.* The first in this set is a pencil drawing found in the New-York Historical Society's Dunsmore Collection, labeled *Sketch for Mint Picture,* and dated "June 1914." Since the final painting of *Washington Inspecting* was dated by Dunsmore to 1914, it seems clear that this set comes last chronologically in the series of seven. This pencil drawing will be instantly recognizable to anyone who has seen the finished version of *Washington Inspecting.* The arrangement of the dignitaries in this version is nearly identical to that in the final painting.

On the left, Alexander and Elizabeth Hamilton view the tray of half dismes, with Tobias Lear standing behind them. The central grouping of four figures is dominated by the tall figure of Washington on the left, with Jefferson just behind the president, while to the right of them, Martha Washington, lorgnette in hand, bends forward to view the tray of newly minted half dismes, and just to her right, David Rittenhouse, retaining that half-bow from earlier sketches, explains what she is seeing. On the right side of the sketch is chief coiner Henry Voigt, holding the coin tray, and behind him, Adam Eckfeldt stands at his post, manning the "First Press," while intently observing the action. The one major difference between this sketch and the finished painting is at the far left, where a very roughly drawn figure, perhaps "Washington's white-haired, old, Negro servant" described in Stewart's May 11, 1914, letter, stands holding a tray loaded with crockery, presumably bearing refreshments for the Mint's honored guests.

It is striking just how near Dunsmore came, in this initial pencil sketch, to the finished version of *Washington Inspecting.* In both of the previous sets of sketches, there was considerable evolution between the first essay and the last essay in the set, but in this case, Dunsmore's inspiration seems to spring onto the paper almost fully formed. It seems that the lessons that he had been learning in his five previous essays all came together in this pencil sketch.

That said, Dunsmore clearly was not completely satisfied with the arrangement in this version, for he made another, more finished drawing soon thereafter.

The second sketch in this set, and the last of the seven to be completed, is a pastel labeled *Pres. Washington & Party Inspecting 1st Silver Coinage of the U.S. Mint*. The arrangement of the dignitaries is quite similar to that in the pencil sketch, but a good deal of Mint equipment has been added to lend context to the scene. Among the dignitaries, Tobias Lear has been moved from a spot behind the Hamiltons, to the far left of the dignitary group, taking the place of the servant with the tray of refreshments, who simply disappears from this (and also from the final) version. Prominent on the left side of the pastel is an additional coining press, and also visible is the end of a belt-driven rolling machine, with the belt extending upwards to a pulley-and-driver system running along the ceiling (this would allow the rolling machine to be driven by horses walking in circles in a horse mill). A window now appears just behind the belt. In the middle, a chair now is shifted into the foreground, although no one is seated in it, and in the background, a Rittenhouse grandfather's clock stands against the wall. Just to the right of the clock there now appears a hearth complete with roaring fire. On the right side, we find a new, low cabinet, with a set of large scales resting upon it. The Mint Windsor chair is placed against the cabinet, with Voigt appearing to have risen from the chair to approach Mrs. Washington. All of this architectural detail suggests that this sketch benefited from the artist having seen the interior of the Middle Building.

Dunsmore added another new element to this pastel, a Windsor chair prominently placed in the middle of the tableau. The chair bears a striking resemblance to a drawing located in the Dunsmore papers at the New-York Historical Society. This drawing reveals important details about the final work. First, as it is dated June 26, 1914, one can tentatively place *Sketch for Mint Picture* before this date and the subsequent *Pres. Washington & Party Inspecting 1st Silver Coinage of the U.S. Mint* after it. Dunsmore further identifies the chair type as a "David Rittenhouse chair," from the John Wister House Museum in Germantown, Pennsylvania. Whether the chair personally belonged to Rittenhouse, or was perhaps constructed by a member of the Rittenhouse family, is not clear. The greater significance is that Dunsmore desired to insert yet another historical allusion in the painting, rather than drawing in random objects. In the final version of the painting, the artist further creates interplay between the Rittenhouse chair, Martha Washington, and Rittenhouse himself engaging the First Lady in the inspection of the first coins. To summarize, while the three chairs in the final version are all of the Windsor style, two are attributed by the artist to Rittenhouse, while the third, placed against the desk, was taken from an example on display at the Philadelphia Mint.

The transition from this pastel sketch to the final painting of *Washington Inspecting the First Money Coined by the United States* reveals a few additional details. On the left side, the additional coining press has acquired a working operator, a rather incongruous touch, in that the noise of an operating press would have completely disrupted the dignitaries' visit. There is also a new door just behind this press's operator, and to his right, straight out of the previous sketches depicting the engraver, a hat and cloak hang on the wall. More of the rolling machine is visible in the painting, and the window now has mullions. A few changes have also taken place among the dignitaries. A Persian rug has been placed beneath their feet (another incongruous touch in what essentially was a factory), an additional "Rittenhouse" chair appears, and Martha Washington is now seated in it. Finally, to make the dignitary group more compact, Tobias Lear has been moved once more, this time from the far left of the group to the background, flanked by Mrs. Hamilton in front of him and to the left, and by Washington on the right. On the right side of the painting, a drawing of Miss Liberty as she appears on the half disme has been affixed to the wall, just behind David Rittenhouse. The Windsor chair by the bench with the scales has been rotated so as to become more visible, and a set of shelves now appears just over the scales.

In the absence of further correspondence between Frank Stewart and the Osborne Company, of course, there can be no definitive determination about the evolution of the sketches. After extensive study of the suite of seven, however, the authors have become convinced that the order was as we have explained it above. First, Dunsmore experimented with three views depicting dignitaries arriving outside of the Middle Building. Stewart probably found this set wanting, both on historical details, and because it did not adequately celebrate the occasion of the first coinage. Dunsmore then tried his hand at two versions of an engraver, possibly Robert Scot, at work, but although this introduced the concept of coinage and brought in minting equipment, Stewart probably still vetoed it on the grounds that it de-emphasized the number of dignitaries, obscured their faces, and still did not adequately spotlight the first coinage. Finally, with the third set, Dunsmore produced two sketches that provided what Frank Stewart wanted: a focus on the occasion of the first coinage, front stage and center for the dignitaries come to mark the event, and a "realistic" view, set inside of the Mint's Middle Building, surrounded by lots of authentic coining apparatus.

The result of all this painstaking preparation, and trips—quite literally—back to the drawing board, *Washington Inspecting the First Money Coined by the United States*, was an instant hit in numismatic circles, despite its blatant historical inaccuracies (starting with the fact that there is no evidence that the gathering it portrayed ever actually occurred), and it has nonetheless stood the test of time.

Stewart first saw the work sometime in early 1915, per a letter from John Ward Dunsmore dated February 25th of that year:

Dunsmore *Sketch for Mint Picture.* Collection of the New-York Historical Society, accession no. INV.14700.

Pres. Washington & Party Inspecting 1st Silver Coinage of the U.S. Mint, John Ward Dunsmore.

Sketch of "Rittenhouse Chair," John Ward Dunsmore. Collection of the New-York Historical Society, accession number INV.14696.

Dear Mr. Stewart,

I am sending you today, under separate cover a photograph of the painting which I did for you last summer *Striking of the 1st National Silver Coins–1792*. I trust this will keep the subject in your mind until the picture itself reaches you. [The Osborne Company no doubt retained the painting during the subsequent production of color lithographs.] I am very truly yours

John Ward Dunsmore
96 Fifth Ave. New York

Stewart mounted Dunsmore's letter of transmittal with a black-and-white photograph and a list of the names and placement of the characters in the painting. Retained in the Stewart Collection at Rowan University, a note in Stewart's hand at the bottom of the display proudly indicates "Picture inspired by Frank H. Stewart."

As with all research projects, useful information is inevitably forthcoming following publication, and *Inspecting* is no exception. On May 10, 1915, Stewart wrote the following to Jeannette Eckfeldt, wife of the Mint assayer:

> I wish I had known of the tongs and shovel of the first U.S. Mint [held in the Eckfeldt family collection] in time to have them put in the painting "Inspection of the first coins of the first U.S. Mint." It is a beautiful picture by Dunsmore and I hope you will be able to take a look at it.[110]

Today, the painting is just as iconic as it was when it was created in 1914, the first year of the Great World War. It might be argued, in fact, that it has become too much of an icon, to the point that some people who should know better have begun to regard it as a factual depiction of an actual event. The "U.S. Coin History" section of US-Coin-Values-Advisor.com, for example, has this to say about the minting of 1792 half dismes: "The coins were struck in the basement of John Harper, a citizen of Philadelphia. On hand to witness the event were the Washingtons, Rittenhouse, Jefferson, Hamilton, and other dignitaries."[111] Despite the occasional misapprehension, *Inspecting* continues to inspire current collectors. The May 15, 2007, edition of *Numismatic News*, for example, carried this headline: "Painting to Highlight Show." As the text accompanying the headline made clear, a lithographic reproduction of *Inspecting* was a main draw for the Garden State Numismatic Association's 32nd Anniversary Convention, May 17 through 19, 2007.[112] The allure of *Inspecting* shines on for numismatists as brightly as ever.

The seven Dunsmore sketches, as tentative and sometimes even as primitive as they may appear, allowed the artist to develop his ideas, and allowed the patron to reject ideas he did not like. These sketches provided both the opportunity to grope their way toward the final, and highly successful work of art that we know—and celebrate—to this day.

The finished version of *Inspecting*, owned by the City of Philadelphia and on permanent loan to Independence National Historical Park.

THE FIRST PRESS OF THE FIRST MINT

The "first Mint press," like the first Mint itself, became an ignored relic with an uncertain fate. While Stewart rued the failed attempts to preserve the Declaration House and the first Mint, he could at least take comfort in the fact that a proper excavation was executed at 37 through 39 North Seventh Street, and that an attractive volume was issued to commemorate his years of digging through earthly soil and dusty archives. The "first Mint press," on the other hand, received no such special treatment, and the question of its mere survival remains today mired in a number of technical issues.

The story begins, oddly enough, with the closure of the first Mint in the 1830s and the subsequent transition to the new facility at Chestnut and Juniper. Technology, ever accelerating, was the watchword of the day, and was poured out in full measure in architect William Strickland's Grecian temple. Franklin Peale, assistant assayer (later chief coiner), had been dispatched to Europe in 1833 to investigate the latest coining advances in the mother countries, and upon returning in 1835 introduced a number of innovations into the Mint. The Contamin reducing lathe allowed engravers to work in large clay or wax models instead of directly on die steel. Improvements in assaying procedures allowed for more accurate measurements of bullion purity. Peale's most important contribution, however, was the introduction of the steam-powered coinage press, which greatly increased the coining capacity of the Mint. Mint Director Robert M. Patterson, whose father had first introduced steam power into other Mint operations in 1816,[113] described the promising situation to the treasury secretary Levi Woodbury in a letter dated September 26, 1835:

> We have just completed under the superintendence of Mr. Peale, a model of a coining press, formed from plans he saw in successful operation in France and in Germany, and possessing many manifest advantages over the Screw press now employed in the Mint. Among these one of the most important is that [it] admits the immediate and easy application of steam power. At present our larger presses require the operation of three men each, while I am sure that one man could attend two of the new presses.[114]

The young American republic now had a respectable coinage factory with modern machinery. Washington's birthday, 1836, was chosen as the day to mark the inauguration of the first steam press. Christian Gobrecht was dispatched to engrave dies for a medal commemorating the event, and the first steam press medals were naturally struck using the first steam press itself. Mint officials understood the import of the affair, and although the goal of Washington's birthday was not met, Mint Director Robert M. Patterson was able to report progress on March 23, 1836, to the secretary of the treasury, Levi

The second U.S. Mint, at Juniper and Chestnut streets, in 1901.

Woodbury. "They [the first steam coinage medals] are the first ever struck by this power in America," Patterson wrote. "We must consider this day, therefore, as marking an epoch in our coinage."[115] Gobrecht's die was used to execute the Mint medals marking the occasion—a few were struck with the date of Washington's birthday, February 22nd (Julian MT-20), others with the actual striking date, March 23rd, re-engraved over the February date (Julian MT-21).

Less than a year later, on January 23, 1837, Patterson followed up with a letter to President Jackson proclaiming the success of the new technology:

> the performance of the press, in which the power of the lever is substituted for that of the screw, has answered all our expectations. Since that time [March 1836], all the copper coins have been struck by this

press, and it has been lately used with success for coining half dollars. The workmen are now engaged in making other steam presses; and as these are completed, the coining by human labor will be abandoned, and the work that can be executed in . . . the Mint will be greatly increased.[116]

The first steam press ably served the Mint and was eventually sold as scrap metal in 1875[117] to George Bache Soley (1836–1908), who had begun working at the Mint in 1859 as an apprentice machinist.[118] Beginning around 1876, Soley used the press to strike any number of tokens and medals, some based on reductions of government dies, for example Baker-299, a reduction of the Duvivier Washington head. Especially popular was the Lord's Prayer medalet, one version featuring an obverse bust of Washington with the inscription GOD AND OUR COUNTRY, while the reverse presented a recitation of the Lord's Prayer in tiny font. Soley sold the pieces at fairs and expositions, aiming directly at decent, God-fearing Americans who came from small towns to see the latest wonders in the big city. The Philadelphia Centennial Exhibition in 1876 was a natural starting point for Soley, but at the same time represented an ending, for it was the last of the great 19th-century expositions to be based on steam power.[119]

The U.S. Mint sold Soley pieces as well, but in 1894, the Secret Service shut down the operation, being troubled by the fact that Soley had access to Mint dies.[120] At the same time, Secret Service agent William J. McManus also forbade the Mint from selling copies of *History of the Philadelphia Mint*, on the grounds that it contained depictions of U.S. coins. The volume referred to is no doubt George Evans's *Illustrated History of the United States Mint*, which is known to have been sold at the Mint in this era.[121] Gene Hynds, the Soley researcher, has pointed out that Soley and Evans had offices near each other, and suggested that the Soley pieces were distributed as free premiums to purchasers of Evans's book. Indeed, commenting on the Soley Lord's Prayer medalet, Evans includes the following note in an 1892 edition of his book:

> This fac-simile presents the smallest space in which the Lord's Prayer was ever known to be struck on metal. It was made on the first "Steam Coining Press," used by the U.S. Mint in 1836. This press is now in the possession of G.B. Soley, Philadelphia. These medalets are not for sale at the Mint, but are presented to purchasers of the Mint book.[122]

Evidently, the Mint sale of Soley tokens began after this writing (1892) and ceased upon the Secret Service action in late 1894. In any event, Soley was undeterred by the Secret Service, exhibiting at the St. Louis World's Fair in 1904 and other venues.[123] A likely Soley emission, which appeared at the Pan American Exposition in Buffalo, New York, in 1901, bears the inscription MADE BY FIRST COINAGE PRESS USED IN U.S. MINT. This proba-

First Steam Press Coinage medal (reverse), struck in 1836 to commemorate the transition from the screw press to the steam press. Julian MT-20, "February 22nd" variety.

First Steam Press Coinage medal. Julian MT-21, "March 23rd" variety.

Julian MT-21, reverse overdate detail.

bly refers to the first steam press, not to the first screw press of the early days of the mint.

In 1927 his widow donated the press to the Franklin Institute in Philadelphia, and in 2000 the press was placed at the American Numismatic Association in Colorado Springs, Colorado, where it currently resides. To commemorate the occasion, the ANA employed the press to strike gold, silver, and copper specimens of a medal evoking the design of Gobrecht's first steam coinage medal.

While the first steam press is well memorialized, in large part due to the efforts of Mr. Soley, the history of the "first Mint press" is less definitive. The first mention in print comes from the *Philadelphia Evening Bulletin*, probably in 1861:

> The coins of 1792 were struck on a press which was set up in an old coach-house in Sixth-Street above Chestnut, directly opposite Jayne-Street. This last described press was made by Adam Eckfeldt, for many years the chief coiner of the National Mint.[124]

The author's source for this information is unknown, but Sylvester Crosby, in quoting the above passage in 1897, added that he had received a letter from the Philadelphia collector Joseph J. Mickley in 1874, who in turn was said to have personally spoken with Adam Eckfeldt, "who was present and witnessed the coinage of some of

these pieces."[125] While all the individuals involved were certainly reputable, there can be no denying that the situation had already devolved to second- and third-degree hearsay. Mickley's relationship with the Eckfeldt family, however, is confirmed by a Mickley business card still in the possession of the Eckfeldt family.

Eric P. Newman and R.W. Julian offer, in opposition to the statement attributed to Eckfeldt by Mickley, an article from the June 1831 issue of *Atkinson's Casket*, a Philadelphia publication which states in part:

> From a source entitled to the highest credit, we have obtained the following particulars, which seem to be appropriate here.
>
> "The Mint of the United States was instituted by an act of Congress, of April 2d, 1792, and a few specimens of silver coins, viz: of half dismes, and executed about the close of that year, which were the first silver coins issued under authority of the United States. The emission of copper commenced in 1793, and that of gold coins in 1795."[126]

Who was the "source entitled to the highest credit?" Had the writer inquired at the Mint, as seems likely, it is not hard to imagine that Eckfeldt, a long-serving and high-ranking employee, was summoned to describe the early history of that institution. But if it was Eckfeldt, why

Probable Soley token from the Pan American Exposition, 1901.

Gold medal commemorating the installation of the first steam coinage press at the ANA.

Joseph J. Mickley business card, from the Eckfeldt family collection.

does he refer to the "close of the year," when in fact the half dismes were struck in July? A lapse of chronological recall after 40 years is certainly understandable, but in any case, misinformation had already crept into the narrative.

The Eckfeldt family held oral traditions regarding the first press. A reporter, whose source was almost certainly Jacob B. Eckfeldt, grandson of Adam, wrote in 1915:

> And one step further up this golden generational tree takes the record back to the original Jacob Eckfeldt, great-grandfather of the present number [Jacob B.] who, while not an assayer, has to his credit an equally distinguished record. For it was this old Jacob Eckfeldt who was known in Washington's time and before as a skilled machinist with ideas in his head beyond the mere welding together of bits of iron and copper. He it was who made the first coining press, the medium through which the young nation converted its all too scanty-supply of gold, silver, and copper into "coin of the realm." This press is still extant; in fact, it was on exhibition recently at the electric exhibition in New York, where it served as one end of an object lesson in the progress made in the money-making craft in the past hundred and fifty years or thereabouts.[127]

The Eckfeldt family archive contains a placard, possibly displayed along with the press in the *ca.* 1915 New York exhibition, which states, "First Press Used to Coin United / States Money in Philadelphia / Made By / Adam Eckfeldt and father, Jacob Eckfeldt / In / 1798 [sic, 1792 is the correct date]." Whether Jacob B. Eckfeldt was the source of this information cannot be said with certainty— but he is quite likely the individual who placed this placard in the family collection. Eckfeldt was clearly proud of the family history, and rightfully so, but was this contraption indeed the "first press?"

The earliest visual evidence of the "first Mint press" is its appearance in Dunsmore's *Washington Inspecting the First Money Coined by the United States.* Unveiled in Philadelphia on January 1, 1916,[128] the Dunsmore painting seems to have led to another depiction of the press that was very similar to Dunsmore's model. The reverse of the 1928 Assay Commission medal bears the inscription "FIRST COINING PRESS U.S. MINT 1793," while depicting two workmen at the screw press. Interestingly, the Assay Commission medal for the very next year bears the image of *Ye Olde Mint*, suggesting that someone in the Mint deliberately picked the Stewart-commissioned artworks as a basis for the successive Assay Commission medals. In any case, the medallic image of the screw press

First Press placard, from the Eckfeldt family collection.

Jacob B. Eckfeldt, 1882, from the Eckfeldt family collection.

Reverse of the 1928 Assay Commission medal, AC-72.

Reverse of the 1929 Assay Commission medal, AC-73.

is clearly derived from Dunsmore's *Washington Inspecting*, the only apparent difference being the weight placed at the end of the flywheel. Obviously, the medal was based on the painting, or both were based on another common source. As the "first Mint press" resides today at the fourth U.S. Mint in Philadelphia, one can compare it with the Dunsmore and the 1928 Assay Commission medal and reasonably infer that Dunsmore was in fact painting the "first Mint press" as identified by the U.S. Mint since at least 1914, the date placed by Dunsmore in the lower left-hand corner of *Washington Inspecting*. An unattributed description of the painting found in the John Ward Dunsmore papers at the New-York Historical Society, probably written by Dunsmore himself, or perhaps Frank H. Stewart, puts closure to the matter by simply stating that "this press was painted from the original one still preserved at the Mint."[129]

Following the Dunsmore presentation and subsequent rendering on the Assay Commission medal, the next mention of the first press appears in 1965, when Eugene S. Ferguson, editor of *Early Engineering Reminiscences (1815–40) of George Escol Sellers*, comments on a photograph of the "first Mint press" which matches Dunsmore's depiction. Ferguson noted, "Early coining press used in the U.S. Mint. This machine was restored from disassembled parts, leaving the arrangement of levers in some doubt. The fly weight is too small to fit the author's description."

The attribution of this particular piece of machinery as the "first Mint press" presents a number of other problems. Quite obvious is the assay medal inscription which attributes a date of 1793 to "first press," whereas it is well established that the first striking of U.S. coinage actually occurred in July 1792.[130] Beyond this somewhat pedantic point, there are more serious considerations, and the authors are indebted to Craig Sholley for the following analysis.

The size of the Dunsmore press is inconsistent with presses purchased by the Mint in 1794 and 1795. Stewart notes a press purchased on March 25, 1794, of John Rutter, for $69.06.[131] The weight is "13 cwt. 25," or 13-1/4 hundredweight, this being 112 pounds per the British measurement, or 1,484 pounds total. Three additional presses were purchased on February 2, 1795, from Samuel Howell Jr., two "small presses" weighing "14 cwt." or 1,568 pounds each, and a "large press" weighing in at "1 ton 11 cwt.," or 3,472 pounds.[132] On May 7, 1795, another Howell press is mentioned, weighing 1,836 pounds.[133] Note that even the "small" presses are on the order of 1,500 pounds. Sholley estimates that the Dunsmore press weighs about 600 pounds. Other contemporary presses are larger than that drawn by Dunsmore, such as that shown by Samuel Thompson in his 1783 *An Essay on Coining*.[134] The size of Thompson's screw press is consistent with that shown in another contemporary source, Denis Diderot's *L'Encyclopédie* (published serially from 1751 to 1772). Indeed, Dunsmore's "first Mint press" is

actually similar in size to the planchet-cutting press depicted by Thompson.

The weight and size of the press dictate the force that can be applied by the screw to the dies. "This press would not have had sufficient force to reliably strike even the 1792 half dismes or 1793 half cents," Sholley commented. "I observed Mint personnel use this press to strike lead or white metal medallions at the Baltimore ANA Convention in 1985. The operator had to exert great force to strike even this soft metal and became exhausted from the effort after three or four strikes. Owing to the lack of force and mechanical ejection, the operator could only achieve one strike every 30 seconds or so. The press also nearly toppled several times due to the poor support."[135]

Beyond the physical dimensions of the "first Mint press," there is an important design consideration; the presence of the L-shaped handle attached to the "first Mint press" flywheel. This attachment is more typical of cutting presses, used to cut planchets from strip, as seen in Thompson's depiction.[136] Dunsmore himself seems a bit confused on this point, painting the "L" device hanging on the wall adjacent to the press, rather than attached to the press itself. The engraver of the 1928 Assay Commission medal (Julian/Keusch AC-92), Adam Pietz, who surely knew the difference between a cutting and a coining press, also omitted the "L" handle from his depiction of the first press. Dunsmore, not a noted authority on minting technology, was more likely deliberately ambiguous, not attaching the handle to the press, but leaving it near the "scene of the crime," just in case.

The U.S. Mint has continued to present a machine designated as the "first Mint press" at a number of venues, including the ANA Convention in Washington, D.C, in 1971. The August issue of *The Numismatist* for that year reported as follows:

> Mrs. Mary T. Brooks, director of the Mint, is planning a special mint exhibit at the ANA's 80th anniversary convention, to be held Aug. 10–14 at the Washington Hilton Hotel, in the nation's capital. This will be the first time the mint has had a major exhibit at an ANA convention. Mrs. Brooks has disclosed, through convention general chairman Herbert W. Price, Jr., that a highlight of the display will be the old hand-operated press used for the first strikes of United States silver coins for regular circulation. This press has been preserved through the years, and will be brought to Washington from the United States Mint in Philadelphia, where it is normally on display. It had been hoped that special medallic mementoes might be struck on the press, but some of the wooden segments have splintered, and steady use was deemed too risky. Instead, a souvenir piece will be reproduced by the Philadelphia Mint, and made available to convention visitors at a nominal cost.

Screw press from Samuel Thompson's "An Essay on Coining," 1783.

Planchet-cutting press from Samuel Thompson's "An Essay on Coining," 1783.

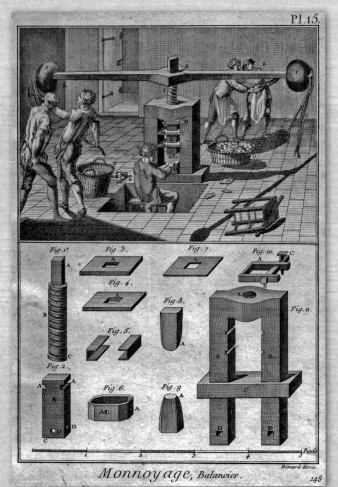

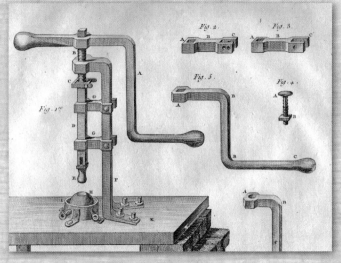

Cutting press contemporary to the first U.S. Mint, from Diderot's *Encyclopédie* (1751–1772). Note the design of the main lever.

Screw press contemporary to the first U.S. Mint, from Diderot's *Encyclopédie* (1751–1772).

The "souvenir piece" was the First Coinage medal, United States Mint medal No. 705. This medal depicts the Duvivier bust of Washington on the obverse along with a rendering of Dunsmore's *Washington Inspecting*, engraved by Frank Gasparro, on the reverse. The obverse bears the inscription GEORGE WASHINGTON PRESIDENT OF THE UNITED STATES 1789" while the reverse is inscribed "UNITED STATES MINT / PHILADELPHIA / 1792–1971."

Despite reservations concerning reliability of the machinery, the U.S. Mint issued a press release on August 9, 1971, indicating the intention to resurrect the first press the following day:

> The United States Mint exhibit will be officially opened by Director of the Mint, Mary T. Brooks, at 10:00 a.m. Tuesday, August 10 in the Washington-Hilton's Exhibition Hall. Soon thereafter the first United States coining press will be returned to service after standing idle for 160 years, striking small Washington medals in lead. Due to the age of the press, it was thought inadvisable to strike medals in harder medal.[137]

The *New York Times* reported on August 29th of that year: "After standing idle for 160 years, the press was returned to service to strike small Washington medals in lead. Because of the press's age it was deemed inadvisable to make medals of a harder metal for the public demonstrations." Dunsmore himself presided over the strikings, at least symbolically, as the Times also reported, "Mr. Dunsmore's painting was photographically enlarged to provide a backdrop for the exhibition, in which this country's first official coinage press was the feature." The authors are unaware of any extant specimens of these strikes.

At a Kennedy Space Center exhibit in 1976, the Mint was better prepared. While the "first Mint press" was on display, visitors could also strike their own commemorative medal on a "special automated coining press," for the price of one dollar. This piece featured on the obverse the fourth U.S. Mint, engraved by Michael G. Iacocca, a member of the Mint's engraving staff. The reverse again featured Gasparro's medallic recreation of the Dunsmore scene, reused from the 1971 medal.[138]

The "first Mint press" was used again in 1985 at the Baltimore ANA Convention as described above, and finally used at least once at a later date, as evidenced by the existence of a white metal example of the Mint Bicentennial medal (United States Mint medals nos. 721, 722) currently residing in a Midwest collection. This medal, dated 1992, depicts the Frank Gasparro representation of Dunsmore's *Washington Inspecting* from the 1971 First Coinage medal discussed above, while the reverse reproduces a number of United States federal and commemorative coinage designs. The Midwest collection example exhibits a very poor strike, attesting to the inability of this particular piece of machinery to competently strike coinage. The "first Mint press" today resides in the exhibit area of the fourth U.S. Mint on Fifth Street in Philadelphia.

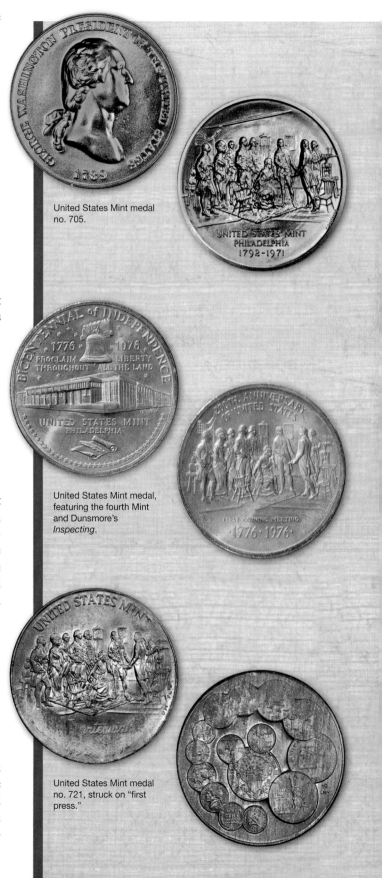

United States Mint medal no. 705.

United States Mint medal, featuring the fourth Mint and Dunsmore's *Inspecting*.

United States Mint medal no. 721, struck on "first press."

THE STEWART CALENDAR ART SET AS A WHOLE

With the publication of the 1916 *Washington Inspecting* calendar, the calendar art of the Frank Stewart Electric Company reached its logical conclusion. Stewart started the series in 1910 with an agricultural theme, continued in 1911 using reproductions of patriotic paintings, and in 1913 by selecting *In the Gloaming*. In 1914 the series became more personal for Stewart, as *Peak on Peak Against the Turquoise Blue* represented, to Stewart at least, memories of a pleasant journey from New Jersey to California. The landscape of the Yosemite remained true to the calendar art genre, portraying a popular nature scene and appealing to the increasing public appetite for pleasure travel. Stewart's second calendar for 1914, *Cradle of Liberty*, brought the series to Philadelphia, and more particularly to Independence and Congress Halls, with both of which Stewart had a close association. Clearly the calendar art series was becoming more personal to Stewart, and the trend continued in 1915.

With *Ye Olde Mint*, the 1915 subject, Stewart completely strayed from the calendar art mainstream. Gone were the lovely Indian maidens, the bucolic nature settings, the landscapes in full array of valleys, earth, and water. Instead, Stewart chose a historic building, and at that one rather unknown to the public—the first U.S. Mint. Independence Hall was a mildly acceptable calendar art subject; Mount Vernon was even better. But the Mint? Clearly, Stewart was completely in charge of the operation; no calendar art maker in his right mind would go after such a subject. The idea obviously came directly from Stewart, and no doubt was completely funded out of his own pocket. This was not a joint venture with the Osborne Company but rather Stewart using his ample checkbook to portray his prize on Seventh Street as artistically as could be accomplished.

In 1916, *Washington Inspecting* took the series as far as it could go. Lamasure, the calendar artist, was out, and John Ward Dunsmore, no mere illustrator, but a widely respected artist, was commissioned to take the Lamasure image further. Instead of an external view of the Mint, Dunsmore takes us to the heart of the first Mint complex—the first floor of the Middle Building—and bathes the creation of the nation's first coinage in the imagery of the founding fathers, surely the highest praise that could be heaped upon Stewart's inner sanctum. It was part ego on Stewart's part—after all, he *was* the Master of the First Mint, but at the same time one must recognize Stewart's rabid dedication to historical preservation. In *Washington Inspecting*, we find all the elements of Stewart's personality—part promoter, part amateur historian, part patron of the arts, and not the least bit afraid to mix all of these in a work of enduring mythology.

Indian medallion from the façade of the Frank H. Stewart Electric Company Old Mint building.

Stewart gave some consideration to a 1917 calendar, as indicated by a 1916 letter from A.H. Nash, a Philadelphia representative of the American Art Company:

> I have been corresponding with my people out at Winnebago, Neb, also the Indian Department for information about the first Indian Honor Medals casted [sic] in the old mint. I have received two letters stating that they are trying to give me as correct information as possible and also the dates and that I will hear more about the history of these in the near future.
>
> I wrote a letter to the President of our Company giving him in detail the unique way you have been advertising with calendars using the historical old mint as an interesting subject to attract attention.
>
> I received a letter from the President saying that they would be willing to go the limit with you in getting the best historical artist to paint a picture on the plans that you and I talked about when we met.
>
> You will hear from me from time to time as I receive new information and will possibly call on you in the near future.[139]

Stewart had great interest in Indian history, especially that of his native southern New Jersey. Indeed, Stewart placed an emblem of an Indian on the façade of the Stewart Electric Company building.[140] To tie together the ideas of Indian Peace Medals and the Old Mint was surely an enticing prospect. Sweetening the pot was the fact that the great Sauk leader, Chief Black Hawk, had visited the Mint while in Philadelphia in 1833, as described in his autobiography:

> We visited the place where they make money, (the mint) and saw the men engaged in it. They presented each of us with a number of pieces of the coin as they fell from the mint, which are very handsome.[141]

One can only speculate at the artistic interpretation that Stewart might have commissioned, and without doubt more than a few such conceptions might today be less than politically correct. Unfortunately for Stewart, Black Hawk's visit was almost certainly to the second, and not the first U.S. Mint. While the account is not definitive on this point, it seems natural that anyone showing off the Mint in 1833 would have chosen the far more spectacular second location on Chestnut Street, which opened for business in January of that year.[142]

Another connection between the American Indian and the first Mint lies in an early proposal of Robert Morris, who suggested that the nation's coinage include a "crown" of gold, value $10, which would depict an Indian trampling a crown—symbolizing Britain—beneath his feet.[143] Nothing seems to have come of this idea, or for that matter Stewart's Indian calendar conception. Beyond this proposed 1917 calendar emission, a cryptic handwritten note in the Stewart Collection alludes to a 1926 calendar, tersely asking "What do you think of these items for the blank places on our 1926 calendar?"[144] But like the 1917, no such examples are currently known. A correspondent of Stewart's remarked in 1923, "I suppose it is rather rank and bold in me to say that I very much miss the Stewart Calendar, the bare place in my room reminiscent of the fine large Stewart Calendars that have been with me lo! these several years."[145] Stewart's holiday giveaway in late 1917 consisted of a single print rather than a full calendar. With a fishing theme, *The Biggest One Got Away* was ordered by Stewart to the extent of a thousand copies, perhaps giving some idea of the original distribution of the Dunsmore and Lamasure reproductions.[146] Thus, John Ward Dunsmore's *Washington Inspecting* remains today the apex and finale of the Frank H. Stewart Electric Company calendar series.

DUNSMORE'S DISTRIBUTION

Washington Inspecting was distributed in several forms—large- and small-format calendars, and in stand-alone prints, also large and small. The large print, sized 16-1/4 by 25 inches, bears the Osborne Company stock no. 1216 in the lower left-hand corner. The only confirmed copy of this print resides with the Ocean County (New Jersey) Coin Club, which has periodically displayed the lithograph at area coin shows.[147] The print was donated to the club in 1994 by long-time ANA Librarian William S. Dewey, who reported having acquired the print sometime in the 1930s in New York City. Literature accompanying the print suggests that it was employed as a promotional item by "THE BANK FOR SAVINGS," said to have been created in 1819, and quite likely referring to the New York institution of the same name. As Osborne owned reproduction rights to the image, they were free to reissue or license the work to other clients in various for-

mats.[148] The Dewey copy evidences cropping at the bottom of the image, most notably cutting off the artist's signature at the lower left-hand corner. Whether this was done at the time of production or later is unclear.

A possible second copy of this print resides in the W. David Perkins collection and was previously owned by Charles Ruby. This example has a visible size of 13 by 19 inches, but has been substantially cropped by an oval mat. The coloring of the Ruby-Perkins print, reproduced on the cover of George Frederick Kolbe's 73rd sale, is considerably different from other copies, washed out and lacking the contrast usually seen.[149] Kolbe later issued a standalone print of this image in a limited edition of 125 copies. While the color is less than vibrant, it offers the advantage of clearly distinguishing between this and other examples.

The small format print exhibits Osborne Company stock no. 1226 in the lower left corner. An example is at the American Numismatic Society in New York City, currently hanging in the office of curator Robert Hoge, while at least two others reside in the Stewart Collection at Rowan University, sized 7-1/2 by 10 inches. The Historical Society of Pennsylvania retains two copies of the print no. 1226, and the Free Library of Philadelphia also has a copy. Stewart donated any number of copies of the print at the time of issue, and, while not explicitly stated, these were probably of the smaller size in order to facilitate distribution. The distribution list included a number of numismatic glitterati. Dr. C. Winfield Perkins, a great-grandchild of Adam Eckfeldt, wrote to Stewart in February 1916:

> While visiting My [sic] Aunt Miss Eckfeldt the other day she showed me a very interesting print entitled "The inspection of the first coins of the First U.S. Mint" the painting by Dunsmore. . . . As I have inherited numerous things from that side of the house I would be pleased to have one of those prints to frame for my office. So please send me one with the bill.[150]

Perkins seems to have taken the Dunsmore depiction quite literally, for later it appears that he related the following information to a Philadelphia reporter:

> Adam Eckfeldt . . . was the first coiner of the United States and made the first coins in 1792 in the first United States mint in Philadelphia. That was a signal event in American history. The coins were made in the presence of David Rittenhouse, director of the mint; George Washington and Mrs. Washington, Alexander Hamilton and Mrs. Hamilton, Thomas Jefferson and other prominent guests.[151]

Farran Zerbe, former president of the American Numismatic Association, acknowledged receiving prints,[152] as did the New York coin dealer Thomas Elder:

Thomas Elder (top) and Farran Zerbe, recipients of Stewart prints, as photographed at the 1908 ANA convention.

Allow me to thank you for the prints of the U.S. Mint [a likely reference to a print of *Ye Olde Mint*], and the Striking of the First Coins, which I was pleased to receive some while ago, but which I have not acknowledged. I am very enthusiastic over these, especially the last one, which is very beautiful indeed.[153]

B. Max Mehl, the Texas coin king, had the bright idea to turn the print into a calendar, apparently unaware that Stewart had already done so. He wrote Stewart in May 1916:

Your picture of the "First Coining of United States Money at the First Mint" has been admired so much that I thought it would be a very appropriate thing for me to do to have a neat calendar made of it. Would you please advise me whether you know of any novelty house or printing house who would undertake to make them for me. Also, of course, whether or not you would permit the picture to be reproduced for that purpose with full credit being given to you or to your firm.[154]

Word of Stewart's pictures made the rounds, and even Mint employees were asking for copies, as shown by a query received from J.M. Hetrich on the letterhead of the Denver Mint Melter and Refiner's Department, where he served as a clerk:

I should be glad to receive from you, if you have them to spare, the two pictures, "Ye Olde Mint," and "Inspection of Coins," copies of which I have seen and greatly admire. Thanking you in advance for an early communication on the subject, or for the pictures themselves.[155]

Hetrich later related to Stewart:

Your favor of the [October 1923] 16th inst. at hand, together with the two beautiful pictures which you so kindly furnished me. I have had them suitably framed and hung at home. They are much admired. They have great historical value to the patriotic citizen. They are the best thing in mint "literature." I thank you for the gift.[156]

Shortly thereafter came another plea from the Denver Mint, this time from E.P. Schell, a workman in both the melter and refiner's department and the ingot melting room:

I am enclosing you a check for $1.00 to cover[?] part the cost postage [sic]. I am very anxious to obtain a pair or set of the pictures you are issuing of the early Mint. I have been in the U.S. Mint service forty one years and feel quite an interest in the matter. I will certainly appreciate it if I can get them.[157]

Schell's note has a pencil notation indicating that the prints were sent, and the check returned. Oscar Hinrichs, a clerk in the Denver Mint's chief clerk's office, requested of Stewart "three copies to be framed and hung in different offices of this building" and acknowledged receipt of same several days later.[158] News of the pictures reached the Mint in San Francisco as well, as John W. Pack, assayer's assistant in the weighing room, made inquiries about the "those colored pictures of the old Mint."[159] J.C. Bates, cashier of the San Francisco Mint, acknowledged receiving two prints in 1921.[160]

Apart from the prints, Stewart's target for Dunsmore's work was the 1916 Frank H. Stewart Electric Company calendar, and like the prints, these were issued in large and small formats. The large-format calendar bears the Osborne Company stock no. 1206. The overall calendar measures 23-3/4 by 30 inches, while the *Washington Inspecting* image itself is 15-7/8 by 21-3/8 inches. *Washington Inspecting* has been vertically cropped on the right side, no doubt in order to center it on the calendar, resulting in the removal of a portion of Washington's silver service. Two copies are known, one in the Stewart Collection at Rowan University, and a second in the collection of Pennsylvania coin dealer Frank Greenberg. Greenberg's copy was acquired from Jospeh L. Massetti, who was reported to have acquired a number of these calendars from Stewart's estate, some missing the *Washington Inspecting* print.[161] Harry Forman, in 2007, confirmed that he had purchased and resold a number of Stewart calendars from Massetti, about "seven or eight."[162] Certain Stewart-related ephemera currently remains with Massetti's grandsons, Steve and Robert Whitney.

The small-format calendar, carrying the Osborne Company stock no. 1226, is known in the Stephen A. Crain collection and was acquired in July 2000.[163] The calendar measures 16 by 15 inches, while the *Washington Inspecting* image itself is 10 by 7 inches. Another example (possibly the same as the preceding) appeared in Craig Whitford's sale of Mint memorabilia in October 1995. The Stewart Collection at Rowan University also has one. As small-format prints and small-format calendar bear the same Osborne stock number, these were likely printed at the same time with some prints being used for calendars while remainders were distributed as standalone lithographs.

Over 20 letters of acknowledgement for these calendars are preserved in the Stewart papers, and probably many more were distributed and not acknowledged in writing.[164] Like the lithographs, the precise size of this calendar was not recorded in correspondence, but was probably the small format. Some of the letters acknowledge receipt of multiple copies. The majority of the correspondents are manufacturers such as the Central Iron & Steel Company of Harrisburg, Pennsylvania, or the Trexler Lumber Company of Allentown, Pennsylvania. Stewart probably sold industrial lighting to both concerns. Acknowledgements are dated from December 1915 through February 1916, with the U.S. Mint thanking Stewart on December 27th for two copies. Clifford Hewitt, foreman of machinists, signed the letter for the Philadelphia Mint.[165] In general, calendars seem to have been sent to active customers, while the prints were reserved for more casual contacts.

Stewart possessed lithographs of both *Ye Olde Mint* and *Washington Inspecting* as late as 1923, when Jeannette Eckfeldt, wife of Mint assayer Jacob B. Eckfeldt, entreated Stewart with "enthusiasm over 'those pictures.'" Stewart responded by sending along a few copies of *Ye Old Mint* and *Washington Inspecting*. "They were made to be given away and I know that you and your people appreciate them," Stewart wrote.[166] The following year, a letter of acknowledgement for two copies of each was sent to Stewart by Robert J. Grant, the director of the Mint in Philadelphia, who indicated that one of the sets would be forwarded to the former Mint Director Raymond T. Baker. "I will take great pleasure in framing to decorate my room," Grant said of the remaining set.[167] Similarly, the nearby Historical Society of Pennsylvania retains two sets of the two prints.[168]

Frank Reilly's *Director of the First U.S. Mint, Inspecting Initial Coinage, Philadelphia, 1792.*

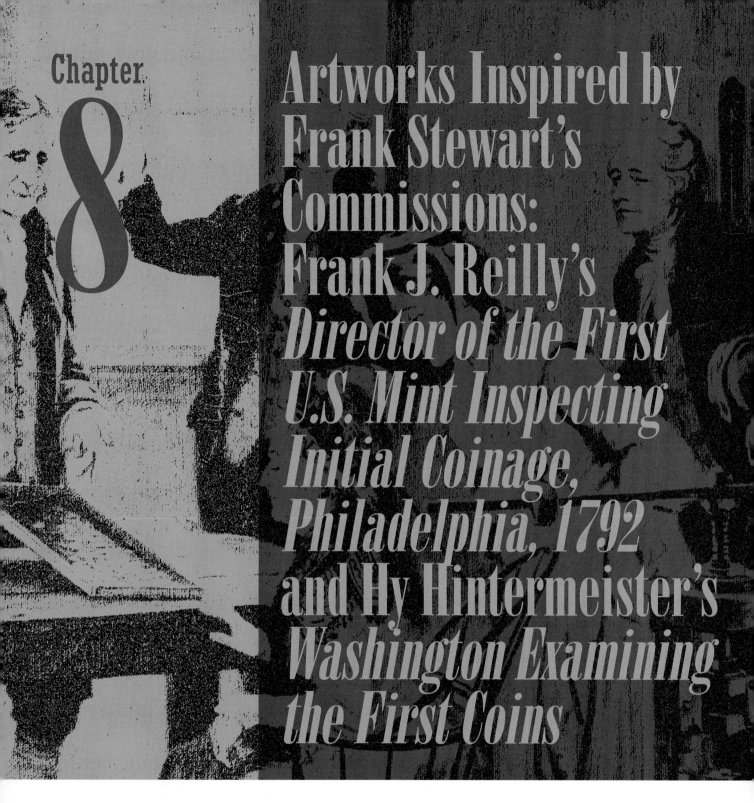

Artworks Inspired by Frank Stewart's Commissions: Frank J. Reilly's *Director of the First U.S. Mint Inspecting Initial Coinage, Philadelphia, 1792* and Hy Hintermeister's *Washington Examining the First Coins*

Imitation, the hoary cliché assures us, is the sincerest form of flattery, and if that be so, John Ward Dunsmore's *Washington Inspecting the First Money Coined by the United States* is a much-flattered painting. Not one, but two of America's leading illustrators, Frank Joseph Reilly and "Hy" (Henry) Hintermeister, were moved to paint similar scenes that clearly drew their inspiration from Dunsmore's tableau. And, in the ultimate act of flattery, *Washington Inspecting the First Money Coined by the United States* was actually forged by an unknown dauber and sold at public auction clearly identified as a fraud. All of the paintings—honest productions and forgery alike—are directly traceable to Dunsmore in their settings, subject matter, and telling details. The two canvases created by the imitators, however, vary sufficiently in their treatment of the familiar scene set in the Mint's Middle Building as to merit examination on their own account.

Interestingly, while *Washington Inspecting* proved a magnet to imitators, Edwin Lamasure's *Ye Olde Mint* did not. It may be that subsequent artists bought Stewart's claim that *Ye Olde Mint* provided the absolutely authentic view of the buildings and the yard of the first Mint, and considered that topic to be closed. *Washington Inspecting*, on the other hand, was clearly an interpretative piece, and if Dunsmore could present his version of the momentous event, then so could other artists. Further, Dunsmore had chosen to include George Washington in his realization, surely a character more worthy of artistic ambition than a set of humble buildings. While Dunsmore set a high standard, we shall see that his successors embraced admiration more than originality.

There does exist, however, one piece of fine-arts flattery on the subject of *Ye Olde Mint*. In the early 1990s, Michigan coin dealer Craig Whitford launched a one-man crusade to promote the upcoming 1992 bicentennial celebration of the U.S. Mint. In the actual event, despite Whitford's considerable exertions, the 200th birthday of the first U.S. Mint passed with relatively little fanfare. No commemorative coin was authorized, and the celebration was limited to a dinner held in Philadelphia on April 2, 1992, the anniversary of the passage of the Mint Act, attended by treasury department and Philadelphia officials, with the keynote speaker being Q. David Bowers. During the run-up to 1992, Whitford had repeatedly attempted to secure a photograph of the *Ye Olde Mint* watercolor from its place of display, the fourth Philadelphia Mint. Frustrated by bureaucratic unresponsiveness, Whitford finally commissioned a Lansing, Michigan, artist named Natalie Hause to produce a new interpretation of *Ye Olde Mint*. Hause did so quite effectively, painting in oil on canvas. Like Reilly and Hintermeister, she omitted some details, and added others, so that the final production truly is an interpretation, and not merely a copy. Just how well Ms. Hause did can be gleaned from the little-known fact that the illustration of *Ye Olde Mint* on the cover of David Lange's 2005 Whitman Publishing, LLC, book, *History of the United States Mint and its Coinage*, is the Hause version, not Lamasure's original. Whitman later used the Hause image on the program cover for the 2009 Philadelphia Coin and Collectibles Expo.

Before there was Natalie Hause, however, there were Frank Joseph Reilly and Henry Hintermeister. Both of these painters were trained in their craft during the autumnal days of the "Golden Age of Illustration," when the coincidence of increasing literacy and decreasing printing costs created a boom in the number of illustrated

Natalie Hause rendering of Lamasure's *Ye Olde Mint*.

publications. The needs of the daily newspapers could be served by "special artists" like Frank H. Taylor, who rapidly sketched the action on the spot. For magazines, and especially books, however, less frequent deadlines allowed for the employment of illustrators, artists who could convincingly render people, places or things. The skilled illustrator could supply recognizable portraits of the founding fathers for an American history book, or appropriately handsome versions of Elizabeth Bennett and Fitzwilliam Darcy for a new edition of *Pride and Prejudice*. The best illustrators became indelibly associated with the publications that carried their work. The very image of Alice in Wonderland, for example, was forever fixed in readers' minds by the illustrator John Tenniel.

The heyday of the illustrator, which had begun in the United States after the Civil War, was ebbing by the end of the 19th century, and the 20th century ushered in a long, slow retreat from the heights of halcyon. Technological advances made it more economical to reproduce photographs in publications, but the real blow came from changing tastes in art. First impressionists, then cubists, then abstractionists of varying stripes took the art world by storm. Year by year the realism represented by the illustrators lost ground to what has been called "the shock of the new." A 1926 review of John Ward Dunsmore's work concluded, "[historical] genre as a type fell into disrepute along about the last decade of the nineteenth century. Even today many artists have a horror of the story-telling picture."[1] The illustrators, however, were not completely marginalized. While nonrepresentational art reigned supreme in the bigger cities, within the walls of the academy, and among society's wealthier members, realism stubbornly held sway in smaller towns, among people without advanced degrees, and across the vast mass of Americans who were below the 90th percentile of income.

Illustrators accordingly survived—and some even thrived—in popular culture. The covers of the great 20th-century mass circulation magazines—*Saturday Evening Post, Colliers, Liberty*—usually featured a whimsical illustration front and center. Large corporations whose ads paid the bills for these magazines—railroads, automakers, distillers, and tobacco companies—frequently employed illustrators to put human faces on their products. And, of course, illustrators were needed to personify literary characters and historical figures that predated the 1840s. The best-known example of the 20th-century illustrator, of course, is Norman Rockwell, whose hundreds of *Saturday Evening Post* covers have become part of America's cultural patrimony, but dozens more toiled at the easel, notable in their day, but now remembered mainly by art historians. Their ranks included Howard Pyle, Dean Cornwell, Harvey Dunn, Phillip Gordon, Harrison Fisher, R. Atkinson Fox; and of course, Edwin Lamasure, Frank Reilly, and the Hintermeisters, father John Henry and son Henry, whose combined work was often signed "Hy" Hintermeister. In the years following World War II, the needs of commerce led Frank Reilly and Henry Hintermeister to create homages to Dunsmore's *Washington Inspecting*. Frank Reilly went first, and in the process provided a firm rebuke to the old saw that "those who can't do, teach."

FRANK JOSEPH REILLY: "REVOLUTIONARY TEACHER"

Frank Joseph Reilly was born on August 21, 1906, in New York City, near Broadway, where his father was a theatrical manager.[2] In 1929, he enrolled at the Art Students League in New York City, the foremost school of art in the United States (Augustus St. Gaudens, for example, served on its faculty). At the League, Reilly studied drawing for three years under the celebrated anatomist George Bridgeman, and painting for a year and a half under one of the League's founders, Frank Vincent DuMond. Reilly's choice of school held another numismatic connection—for the Art Students League building, at 215 West 57th, was the site of the American Numismatic Association convention in 1922. In 1933, Bridgeman died, and Reilly, at the age of 27, replaced him as instructor. Even as he launched his teaching career, Reilly served as an apprentice to one of America's leading muralists, Dean Cornwell.[3] There followed a highly successful career as an illustrator, but it was as a teacher that Frank Reilly truly made his lasting mark on the world of art, until his premature death on January 15, 1967.[4]

To say that Frank Reilly was a teacher of art is an understatement akin to saying that Socrates was a man with a philosophical method. Reilly's zeal for instruction was unmistakable; as one observer noted, "None can deny his almost evangelical consecration to teaching art."[5] His talent for transmitting lessons was no less formidable; as his old mentor, Dean Cornwell, remarked: "I've often said Frank could teach a wooden Indian to draw and paint, provided, of course, the wooden Indian wanted to paint."[6] And students voted with their feet, crowding the lecture halls at the Art Students League, as well as at the Grand Central School of Art, the National Academy of Design, the Pratt and the Moore Institutes, and at the Woodstock branch of the Art Students League.[7] During the more than three decades that Frank Reilly taught at the League, his courses were the most popular on offer, with the waiting list routinely longer than the number of available slots.[8] At the height of his instructional fame, a student could expect to cool his heels for more than two years before a space came open in one of the master's classes.[9] In 1961, Reilly left the Art Students League, opening the Frank Reilly School of Art at 111 West 57th Street,[10] just a few doors east of the longstanding Stack's Rare Coin firm. The venue had changed, but the result was the same: Students lined up to take courses from the "the number one art teacher in America."[11] So successful was the Reilly school that he made plans for a West Coast branch, plans that were cut short only by his sudden illness and death in 1967.[12]

A Reilly course left an indelible impression upon the students—as many as 60 per session—who crowded his classrooms. One such scholar recorded his vivid memories:

> As the steady stream of students entering the large studio continued, the crowded room would begin to feel claustrophobic. Some opted to wait in the hallway just outside the door, hoping to have a private moment with their revered teacher before class would actually begin. Then, seemingly larger than life, Frank Reilly would enter the room. As always, he would be dressed in a suit, white shirt and tie, projecting more the image of a Wall Street banker, than a noted instructor at the historic Art Students League of New York. . . . His classes at the "League" were always the most popular and highly attended. The waiting list to enter a Reilly course exceeded the number of students in attendance. In some instances, these conditions would make it difficult to see the model posing at the head of the class. With so many students, Reilly would focus his greatest effort on the advancement of his senior pupils, knowing that through sheer observation and osmosis his information would reach all of his students.[13]

Doug Higgins, one of Reilly's star pupils, recalls that Reilly was able to handle courses with such huge enrollments only by being methodical in his scheduling:

> The teaching program of Frank Reilly consisted of communicating an accumulation of knowledge and skills beginning with the elementary and then building to the advanced. He primarily taught the art of drawing and then painting the nude figure. . . . The classes were from seven to ten o'clock each weeknight and included a 10-minute break every hour. The time was kept by the monitor who called the poses and kept order. After a pose was called, students were not allowed to enter the room and disturb the class. The poses were 5, 15 and 30 minutes in length, beginning with the 5s.[14]

No amount of good organization, however, could allow Reilly to provide complete attention to each of his thousands of students. Candido Rodriguez, an artist who eventually became one of Reilly's classroom monitors, recalled the first time the master criticized his work. It was at the Art Students League in the fall of 1954 when Rodriguez was only 17 years old:

> Reilly would critique the drawing classes once a week on Tuesday. These classes (morning, afternoon, evening) were huge and Reilly never had enough time to see every student. It took a few months before he got to me. By this time I had a pile of drawings done in class and at home. Reilly quickly scanned through them, turned to me and said, "Son, if I told you everything that is wrong with these drawings you will need a physcharist [sic]." With that he took my pencil, broke it to an appropriate length, showed me how to sharpen and hold it. He then demonstrated his famous 6-line figure. All this took about five minutes, he moved on and he didn't get back to me for another few months.[15]

Despite the fact that Reilly might take months to give a young student personal attention, and in spite of his blunt assessments when he finally did offer one-on-one instruction, his students uniformly admired him. For example, Tom Palmer, a pupil at the Frank Reilly School of Art during the 1960s, reminisced that "Frank Reilly looked like a NYC policeman, [a] no-nonsense guy who expected you to follow the rules, but as I found out later, a warm-hearted mentor who patiently helped you out when you needed it."[16] Reilly's students demonstrated the value of the education received at the hands of the master by leaving their own marks upon the world of art. Two of the leading Western Americana artists, James Bama and Tom Ryan, were Reilly students; as was Robert Schulz, who created the cover artwork for dozens of paperback editions of Agatha Christie mysteries and Zane Grey novels. Robert A. Maguire was another prolific paperback books illustrator, and Joseph Bowler was one of the foremost romantic illustrators for women's magazines. Some of the iconic works of popular art have emerged from the easels of Reilly alums, such as the famous poster for the movie "Jaws," a Roger Kastel creation depicting a swimming woman about to be devoured by an enormous great white shark shooting up from the depths.

The master's most celebrated student by far was certainly the most surprising. Reilly, after all, was the leading exponent of drawing and painting the human figure: a holdout realist in a post-realist art world. Peter Max (who once did the artwork for an American Numismatic Association auction catalog cover) was the artist most identified with the 1960s and 1970s psychedelic style in art. Max said, "I studied figure drawing for seven years [1957–1964], life drawing from nude models, learning body and fabric, light and shadow."[17] Max's tribute to his besuited "square" mentor was more than a little surprising:

> Many thanks to you, Frank, for a teaching program that is so hip. . . . He was fantastic. In my whole life I never came across anyone like that who had so much to give. Once I had the basics to fall back on, I was completely able to go way out into my fantasies formed by living ten years in China. I had the tight instruction of Reilly, but I was always able to put into it what I needed.[18]

Among the legion of Reilly students, one has left an enduring mark upon the numismatic arts. Charles L. Vickers studied under the master at both the Art Students

League and the Frank Reilly School of Art. After stints at the Franklin Mint and as the proprietor of his own studio, Vickers joined the U.S. Mint's Sculptor-Engraver staff in December of 2003. His sculpting credits encompass eight coins, including the reverses of the Minnesota, Nebraska, and Washington state quarters, plus the obverse of the John Adams Presidential and the reverse of the Thomas Jefferson First Spouse gold commemorative coins. Vickers is probably best known in numismatic circles, however, for designing and sculpting the 2001 George W. Bush Official Inaugural Medal.[19] Reilly's influence on numismatics, therefore, stretches far beyond the single coin-themed canvas he painted to encompass the coins in our pockets.

Frank Reilly's career as an art educator was succinctly summarized in the definitive encyclopedia, *The Illustrator in America*: "Frank Joseph Reilly . . . (1906–1967), was a great teacher."[20] That greatness did not perish with him in 1967. Even during his lifetime, the master had an eye on eternity, for he established the Frank J. Reilly Fund to support in perpetuity one of his pet educational projects, the "Artists at Work" film series.[21] Reilly filmed interviews with artists such as Dean Cornwell, James Montgomery Flagg, Harvey Dunn, Robert Brackman, and John Sloan, and the Reilly Fund supported the educational use of these films for classroom instruction.[22]

Reilly's own efforts to preserve his teaching methods, however, paled next to those made by his students. A number of them established the Reilly Heritage Foundation immediately after his death in order to keep the Reilly School operating. Despite their best efforts, the school was closed in 1968, when its lease terminated. Undaunted, however, a number of Reilly's alums began teaching at the Art Students League using Reilly's methods, including Robert Schulz, Michael Ariano, Lou Donato, and George Passanito.[23] In time, a number of them banded together to create a cooperative studio called the Reilly League of Artists, headquartered in White Plains, New York, where Reilly's instructional methods live on. Cesare Borgia, a student of the master for seven years, is the League's principal instructor.[24]

Even if artists are unable to get personal instruction from Reilly alumni at the Art Students League or at the Reilly League of Artists, publications by Frank Reilly's loyal students give them access to the master's methods. The most comprehensive was written by Jack Faragasso, who directed the Frank Reilly School of Art after Reilly's passing. Entitled *Mastering Drawing the Human Figure*, and "dedicated to the memory of Frank J. Reilly, who taught so many," its 256 copiously illustrated pages provide a thorough manual of the Reilly method.[25] For those who desire a briefer introduction, there is Doug Higgins's *The Frank Reilly School of Art*.[26] A more technical manual, which explains Reilly's six lines, nine values of gray, and his chroma scales, was written by another of his students,

Apollo Dorian.[27] It is clear that Reilly's influence on the world of art, both directly through his students, and indirectly through the next generations trained by his alumni, is truly immense. His teaching legacy lives on: 42 years after his death, the Society of Illustrators named him the Distinguished Educator for 2009. On the representational end of the spectrum, at least, Reilly's influence is second to no other in the American art world. No wonder that Kurt Steine titled his Reilly biography *Revolutionary Teacher*.

FRANK JOSEPH REILLY: CORPORATE COMMISSIONS

Frank Reilly was, quite obviously, a teacher of art without peer. In his case, however, those who can teach also can *do*. He left behind a series of canvases notable for their meticulous craftsmanship and careful research to assure period authenticity. For every painting, Reilly created a series of sketch studies to accurately capture the action. He consulted his own collection of artistic images, his extensive personal library, and supplemented these with institutional resources. Whether his subject was natural, industrial, or historical, Reilly was obsessed with getting it right.

As an illustrator, Reilly tended to work for patrons, and as one of the foremost practitioners of illustration, his commissions tended to come from the first rank of corporate sponsors. As Kent Steine has noted:

> Throughout the years Reilly accumulated an impressive list of clients who sought him out for the quality of his work and his impeccable professionalism. He painted covers for most of the leading magazines of the time in addition to story illustration. As an advertising illustrator his work was highly regarded. As a testament to this, publications like *The Saturday Evening Post*, *Colliers*, *Cosmopolitan*, and *Good Housekeeping*, along with publishers such as Bantam and Pocket Books (all clients of Reilly's), would send their art directors to Reilly's classes to present actual assignments to his students. In return, these various publishers, design studios and advertising agencies had "first look" at the best of Reilly's protégés.[28]

Frank Reilly obviously was no stranger to the covers of magazines, but he was also very much at home among the inside advertising pages that paid the publishers' bills. The Pennsylvania Railroad, one of the wealthiest corporations of its day, called upon Reilly during the 1940s to illustrate certain of their advertisements. Even today, the master's presentations of streamlined diesel locomotives evoke a modernistic feel and project the speed and power of America's railroads at their zenith. Another of Reilly's major corporate patrons was the Continental Distilling Corporation (or rather, its parent company, Publicker Industries, of Philadelphia), the creator of such major brands of ardent spirits as Inver House Scotch and Rittenhouse Rye Whiskey. It was one of the Continental commissions that inspired Reilly to paint *Director of the First U.S. Mint Inspecting Initial Coinage, Philadelphia, 1792.*

Publicker Industries owed its existence to an early and innovative form of recycling. Around the turn of the 20th century, a Connecticut barrel maker named Harry Publicker was reclaiming old barrel staves for new barrels. He realized that old whiskey barrels were saturated with spirits that had soaked into them during the aging process. He discovered that by steaming them, he could extract a gallon or more of whiskey from the staves of a single old barrel. It was not unlike Elias Boudinot in the First Mint, extracting precious metal from furnace ashes. Harry steamed merrily away, and after 1912, when he built a distillery on the banks of the Delaware River between Bigler Street and Packer Avenue in Philadelphia, he transitioned from the barrel business to the beverage and industrial alcohol trade. With the advent of Prohibition in 1920, the beverage side of the business withered, but the industrial side flourished. Publicker lost no time after the repeal of Prohibition in getting back into the beverage alcohol game, for in August of 1933, Publicker Industries established a subsidiary, Continental Distilling Corporation. Later in that year, Continental filed a trademark application for its first brand, Charter Oak.[29]

For more than 50 years, Continental Distilling mixed and sold more than 110 different marques of hard liquor. Their brands were often named for historical figures or places; the biggest seller was Old Hickory Bourbon, followed by Inver House Scotch, but Philadelphia Blended Whisky, Rittenhouse Rye Whiskey, and Keystone State Rye Whiskey were also prominent on their product list.[30] Continental prospered during the post-war years, contributing mightily to Publicker Industries' solid growth. In 1946, Publicker became a publicly traded company, and by the Eisenhower era it was one of America's largest corporations. Its factories covered 35 acres along the Delaware River, and in 1955, *Fortune* magazine's inaugural list of the nation's 500 largest companies pegged Publicker at number 452. In subsequent years, it marched up the list to number 451 (1956) and 439 (1957). More than 5,000 employees owed their livelihoods to Publicker's chemical empire.[31]

Sadly, Continental Distilling and its mother company provide yet another example of late 20th-century American industrial decline. Publicker was out-competed in its core business areas, and beginning in 1981, began to run afoul of regulatory agencies monitoring the disposal of hazardous waste on their site along the Delaware. In 1985, they divested what was left of Continental Distilling, and in 1986, down to 300 employees, they sold their Philadelphia operations to the Overland Company, which declared bankruptcy itself only a few months later and abandoned the site. Within a few years, the old Publicker works became the Environmental Protection Agency's 500th (and largest with more than 2,000,000 gallons of toxic sludge) Superfund cleanup site.

In 1998, the remnants of Publicker tried a radical shift in business plan. Out went the booze—*Sic transit Gloria mundane*—and in came computer chip-embedded "smart card" technology. The only vestige of Publicker's former glory was found in the new company's name: PubliCard.[32] After buying five smart card-related businesses between 1998 and 2000, PubliCard became a casualty of the millennial high-tech business crash, selling or closing all but one of the subsidiaries by the end of 2002. They limped along until 2007, when PubliCard filed for Chapter 11 bankruptcy protection.[33] Out went the "new economy"—*Sic transit Gloria geeky*—and in came the apparent demise of Publicker Industries. Yet, faint echoes of that old luster remained. Inver House lives on as a brand of Thai Beverages, and Rittenhouse Rye was sold to Heaven Hill Distilleries of Bardstown, Kentucky, under whose auspices it was named "North American Whiskey of the Year" in 2006.[34]

Just as Rittenhouse Rye came back, so too did PubliCard. On January 30, 2008, the United States Bankruptcy Court for the Southern District of New York approved PubliCard's reorganization plan to emerge from bankruptcy as Chazak Value Corporation. The new company will remain in the smart card business, but also focus on acquiring privately held businesses that have succession issues, or which seek to restructure themselves.[35]

FRANK JOSEPH REILLY: THE COMMISSION

In 1947, Frank Reilly received a commission from Continental Distilling Corporation that would become his most enduring artistic legacy: a suite of 15 canvases specifically painted for one of Continental's top-selling brands, Philadelphia Blended Whisky. These paintings were described by the editors of *American Artist* magazine as "a notable series depicting significant historical events in early Philadelphia. These have appeared in national periodicals and have been sought by scholars and historical societies all over America."[36] Among the views in this series were *The Committee Examining the Recast Liberty Bell*; *B. Franklin, First Postmaster General, Hands Mail Over to a Post Rider, Philadelphia, 1775*; *Final Drafting of the Declaration of Independence, Philadelphia, June 1776*; and *Director of the First U.S. Mint, Inspecting Initial Coinage, Philadelphia, 1792*. In the finished ads, the paintings appeared in an elegant full-page oval format, over the tag line: "Philadelphia Blended Whisky: the Heritage Whisky."

The original oil painting of *Director Inspecting* is rectangular, and measures 25-1/2 by 39-1/2 inches. Even a cursory comparison of Reilly's work to that of Dunsmore's *Inspecting the First Coinage* will show just how much he owed to Dunsmore's 1914 composition. There is a clear echo in the titles, from *Washington Inspecting* to *Director Inspecting*. One immediately sees that the three elements that anchor the background of *Washington Inspecting*: the Rittenhouse grandfather clock, the sketch of Miss Liberty facing left, and the shelving unit to the extreme right, all presented in the same places as in the background of *Director Inspecting*. A wooden chair sits on a Persian rug in the middle of both scenes; a rolling mill and a coin press anchor the left and right sides of each canvas, although Reilly did configure his versions somewhat differently. A host of finer details, such as coloration and shadow placement, also confirm Reilly's ongoing debt to Dunsmore.

It would be a mistake, however, to conclude that Reilly's canvas was merely a knockoff of Dunsmore's opus. The biggest departure lies in Reilly's rejection of Dunsmore's "cast of thousands" approach to painting the scene. Whereas Dunsmore painted ten figures into the picture, six of whom were visiting dignitaries, Reilly halved the number of people and seems to have painted out the celebrities altogether (the gentleman to Rittenhouse's right could be President Washington, but if so, no one seems to be paying much attention to him). This brings us to the second major difference: the focus of the picture. Dunsmore has made Martha Washington, in her regal purple dress, the centerpiece of *Inspecting*, with nary a coin in sight; Reilly has made the coin, held by Director

David Rittenhouse, the focal point. It must be conceded, however, that in order to make the coin visible, the master has pumped up the diminutive half disme to the dimensions of a silver dollar.

In effect, Reilly chose to depict a scene prior to that offered by Dunsmore, focusing on the moment the first coinage was created, as opposed to the moment it was ceremonially presented to higher authorities. This change in time allowed him to limit the *dramatis personae* to Rittenhouse and his colleagues at the Mint, and changes the focus from a set-piece ceremony to a spontaneous celebration.

David Rittenhouse stands in the precise center of the canvas, gazing with satisfaction at a large coin held properly between his left thumb and index finger. To Rittenhouse's right is a gentleman who could be Washington or Alexander Hamilton, but who is probably just a Mint worker, holding a purse that is designed to be filled with the new coinage. There is a man at work on either end of the coin press, one operating the press, the other plucking newly struck coins from the press and placing them into a copper bucket. This betrays the fact that Reilly did not have a strong grasp of the minting process as of 1792. He did a reasonable job of painting the rolling machine in the left foreground, and clearly modeled the machine in

FINAL DRAFTING OF THE DECLARATION OF INDEPENDENCE, PHILADELPHIA, JUNE 1776*

Frank Reilly's recreation of the drafting of the Declaration of Independence.

the right background after the "first Mint press" in the U.S. Mint, as had Dunsmore before him.[37] Reilly, however, added a perpendicular piece to the coinage press, creating a T-shaped contraption apparently meant to be a combination of a planchet cutter and a coin press. This ungainly mule is apparently engaged in both operations at the same time, for both scissel and struck coins appear to be issuing simultaneously from the press, with the worker to Rittenhouse's left plucking coins from the scrap and tossing them into a bucket.

Director Inspecting had its time in the sun during the 1947 Philadelphia Blended Whisky advertising campaign, after which the canvas, along with the other 14 in the series, went into the Publicker Industries' archives. It emerged again, along with six others, to illustrate a book by Gerald W. Johnson, entitled *Pattern for Liberty: The Story of Old Philadelphia*.[38] Johnson (1890–1980) was a friend and colleague of H.L. Mencken at the Baltimore *Sun* and a popular historian. *Pattern for Liberty* was scholarly enough to be reviewed by *The William and Mary Quarterly*, although with faint praise as "an enjoyable essay."[39] *Director Inspecting* faces page 132 of the book, even though the first Mint or its products do not rate a single mention in the book's text.

Director Inspecting's next foray into print came courtesy of author Thomas W. Becker. Apparently, Becker had a

knack for finding forgotten paintings, for when he wrote *The Coinmakers: The Development of Coinage from the Earliest Times* in 1967, he included a full-color reproduction of *Director Inspecting*.[40] Reilly's painting was included once more in the book's second edition, in 1970. In both editions, *Director Inspecting* was credited to "Publicker Distilleries, Philadelphia."

There *Director Inspecting* remained, until Publicker Industries' successor company, PublicCard, nosedived in late 2000. In the ensuing years, there was a fire sale of old company assets, and most of the remaining canvases from the 1947 Philadelphia Blended Whisky campaign ended up in the hands of Jordan Berman, the proprietor of The Illustrated Gallery in Philadelphia. In 2005, after happening upon a copy of *Pattern for Liberty* in a Cape Cod antiquarian book store, Joel J. Orosz bought the painting from Berman.

HENRY "HY" HINTERMEISTER: THE ELUSIVE CHILD OF TWO FATHERS

Unlike Frank Reilly, whose lengthened shadow still covers the world of illustrators, Henry Hintermeister left no students to revere his memory. What should be the simple act of recalling Hintermeister's career is immensely complicated by the fact that there was the father, Swiss-born

Frank Reilly's *Director of the First U.S. Mint, Inspecting Initial Coinage, Philadelphia, 1792.*

John Henry (1869–1945) and the son, Henry Adamaugust (1897–1970), and the "Holy Ghost," Hy Hintermeister, who was an amalgam of the two (approximately 1920–1945). For when young Henry graduated from the Pratt Institute, his father offered him not merely a partnership, but in fact a merged identity in the family firm.[41] John Henry Hintermeister painted under his own name before Henry's advent, signing his canvases "J. Hy Hintermeister." Most of the paintings that emerged from the Hintermeister Studio from 1920 to 1945 were, at least to some extent, the joint effort of both artists, with John Henry working by day, and Henry A. working by night, and most bore the shared *nom de peinture* of "Hy Hintermeister."[42]

Because of this distinctive alliance, the adjective "prolific" has been attached to Hy Hintermeister in the world of illustration just as naturally as it has been attached to Q. David Bowers in the world of numismatic literature. Hintermeister expert Hugh Hetzer has traced over 1,170 images created by these two illustrators, about 40 of which feature George Washington.[43] Early on in their partnership, in 1925 to be precise, the Osborne Company, last seen in this narrative as the patron of Edwin Lamasure, commissioned John Henry to create a series of annual calendars that featured the high points of American history from 1775 to 1787. The series proved to be extremely popular with Osborne's clientele, and it remained in production until well after Hintermeister *pere's* death in 1945, keeping "Hy" very busy in the process.[44] More prosaically, the Hintermeister Studio also churned out endless variations upon the genre scene: boys fishing, children frolicking with dogs, tender moments between friends. In fact, the paintings for which "Hy Hintermeister" is best remembered are the "Gramps" and "Grandma" series from the 1930s through the 1950s, all of which depict grandparents romping adventurously (not to say recklessly) with their grandchildren on wobbly stilts, high-flying swings, or careening soap box derby racers.[45]

The Hintermeister pair, like Edwin Lamasure, sold works to both Osborne and the Thomas D. Murphy Company. The Murphy relationship began in 1937 and seems to have lasted for more than 30 years. Among these calendars include a number dedicated to safety, a theme of course borrowed from popular culture but nonetheless an upstanding promotional vehicle for any number of advertisers. Titles like *Safely Guarded* and *Stop and Look* appear in this series.[46]

The Hintermeister partnership was broken only by the death of John Henry, who passed away at his home at 4622 14th Avenue in Brooklyn on February 10, 1945.[47] Son Henry carried on, still—confoundingly—signing many canvases he did after his father's death as painted by "Hy Hintermeister." Henry remained active, with his studio near his home in Tuckahoe, New York, until his death, on June 18, 1970, at his winter home in Pinellas, Florida.[48]

WASHINGTON INSPECTS THE FIRST MINTING OF AMERICAN COINS

The roots of this painting extend back to the 1925 commission received by John Henry Hintermeister to paint a series of historical calendar illustrations. In practice, this became a series of paintings featuring the exploits of General George Washington. It could be argued with some justification that in many ways, American history during that span truly *was* the history of Washington, and the enduring popularity of the General made the series such a success that John Henry decided to keep giving the public what it wanted. According to Hugh Hetzer, "Sixteen of the Washington portraits were completed by John Henry, starting even before the Osborne commission, in 1923, and continuing through 1942. After that, Henry added 20 or so more, up to the mid-1960s." Hetzer further states, "I know that the HyH [Hy Hintermeister] picture in question was done in 1952 or 3. It was copyrighted in 1953. Thus it was done by Henry A."[49]

Hetzer's judgment is confirmed by the records of the United States Copyright Office, which reveal application number GU21919, registered by Henry Hintermeister, 9 Warren Avenue, Tuckahoe, New York [for] Oil Painting, "The First United States Coins," application received 8/6/1953."[50] We know, as we will shortly see, that this painting was an Osborne commission, so presumably it was yet another in the long-running series first authorized nearly 30 years previously.

The actual canvas, like Reilly's work, reveals the definitive inspiration of Dunsmore's *Washington Inspecting*. Most of the Dunsmore cast of characters is retained, although the focal point of the painting is moved to the left of the canvas. There, standing behind a small table, we see David Rittenhouse tilting a tray of newly struck half dismes for the better inspection of Martha Washington, who is seated at the other side of the table from the Mint director. To Rittenhouse's left, and directly behind Martha, George Washington admires (impeccably held between the thumb and index finger as in the Reilly painting) a sparkling half disme. Also like Reilly, Hintermeister felt compelled to inflate the dimensions of the diminutive half disme to a much more visible size. Completing the scene on the left side of the canvas, Chief Coiner Henry Voigt stands directly behind Rittenhouse, peering appreciatively at the personages admiring his handiwork.

Shifting to the right side of the canvas, Elizabeth Hamilton leans over Martha Washington's right shoulder to examine the half dismes, while her husband, Alexander, peers at the coins from just behind his wife. Standing directly behind Hamilton is a gentleman who could be Washington's personal secretary, Tobias Lear, or perhaps Mint contractor Adam Eckfeldt. Standing in front of Hamilton, with his arms crossed, is Thomas Jefferson. Only Lear or Eckfeldt and an anonymous Mint worker from Dunsmore's composition are missing in the Hintermeister tableau. The final element is in the foreground, a table that holds the Hintermeister version of the press used to strike the coins.

It appears that Hintermeister studied both Dunsmore's *Washington Inspecting* and Reilly's *Director Inspecting* before painting *The First United States Coins.* The obligations to Dunsmore are many and obvious, beginning with the "cast of thousands," or at least 80 percent of that cast. The tray of coins, Martha Washington as the center of attention, a Mint employee at the coining press, the drawing of Miss Liberty affixed to the wall, and the use of coining machinery as props are all reminiscent of Dunsmore. The one element clearly borrowed from Reilly was that of a central figure examining a coin in an upright and collector-approved holding stance. In Reilly's painting, it was Rittenhouse facing right, while in Hintermeister's, it was Washington facing left, but as a compositional element, it is too striking to be a mere coincidence.

Aesthetically, the nearly 40 years that separate the work of Dunsmore, Reilly, and Hintermeister does not witness an improvement; in fact, quite the opposite is true. Duns-more's *Washington Inspecting* is, whatever its shortcomings as a historical document, a fully realized work of art. Dunsmore's mania for all things Revolutionary shines through in the details of the clothing, the hair styles, and the period furnishings. The portraits are strong and recognizable, the proportions are accurate, and the colors are both true to life and vivid. Reilly's work does not quite come up to the same standard. Although the master's famed "Six Lines" allowed him to confidently paint the human form, his draperies are not as strongly rendered. The weakest point is the coloration; Reilly was the first to admit that this was not his specialty, which expresses itself most obviously in the unusual hues of the clothing. Clearly, Reilly was a more accomplished teacher than a practitioner. Henry Hintermeister, however, does not quite make the Reilly grade, for his figures lack strong definition, and the softer focus, in everything from the facial features to the pastel color scheme, renders the whole scene with a decidedly non-18th century quality. Dunsmore quite simply set a very high standard that his talented imitators could not quite match.

Henry Hintermeister's *The First United States Coins.*

THE FIRST UNITED STATES COINS: FATE OF THE CANVAS AND ITS PRINTS

The fate of the canvas for *The First United States Coins* can be summarized in a single word: unknown. Hintermeister experts Rick and Charlotte Martin point out that it is entirely possible that once the canvas had fulfilled its purpose as a template for making prints, it may simply have been discarded.[51] This has been the melancholy fate of many illustrators' paintings, including a number of those produced by the Hintermeisters. Alternatively, it may be hidden in a private collection.

Prints were made from the painting, and presumably used on Osborne calendars for 1953 and perhaps for 1954. Again, despite a diligent search, the authors have not been able to find any calendars displaying this artwork. Thanks to Pete Smith, however, we know that a print of *The First United States Coins* was exhibited by the Northwest Coin Club of Minnesota's Twin Cities during National Coin Week, April 21–27, 1958. The exhibits, set up in the window of the Northwestern National Bank,

featured a type coin collection that won the Blue Ribbon Sweepstakes at the 1957 Minnesota State Fair. Beside this set, there was a framed Hintermeister print on an easel. An accompanying label gave the title as *Washington Inspects the First Minting of American Coins*, and informs the viewer that it was "REPRODUCED FROM THE ORIGINAL PAINTING BY HENRY HINTERMEISTER" and "published by the Osborne Company, Cincinnati, Ohio, USA."[52] The authors have searched, again without success, for the archives of the Osborne Company, where the original painting may still reside.

The Hintermeister image was also marketed directly to those in the numismatic community. D. Wayne Johnson, better known as Dick Johnson, the first editor of *Coin World*, reminisced in early 2007 in the *E-Sylum*, the electronic newsletter of the Numismatic Bibliomania Society:

> The painting distributed by Dayton coin dealer Jim Kelly was an entirely different version, but based on the same theme if not the original painting [that is, the Dunsmore painting of *Washington Inspecting*]. I

Northwest Coin Club exhibit, 1958.

have one hanging above my desk now that I purchased from Jim Kelly perhaps 50 years ago. . . . It bears the signature lower left of Hy (Henry) Hintermeister (born 1897) a New York City artist.[53]

Johnson later clarified his description of the image in his possession as a painting reproduced from the original via a mechanical process. An examination of the most likely marketing vehicle, *Kelly's Coins and Chatter*, a house organ that was published between 1948 and 1961, reveals no offerings. Kelly evidently had an interest in the subject, for in the March 1949 issue he published Stewart's oft-reproduced image of the first Mint façade with touring car to the right. Still, *The First United States Coins* seems determined to maintain its status as the most mysterious and elusive of the artworks inspired by Frank H. Stewart.

The imitators of Dunsmore's *Washington Inspecting* were established artists who delivered solid work, but neither Reilly nor Hintermeister made a deep or lasting impression upon the Stewart legacy of Mint-related art. The fact that Reilly's work was last published in a numismatic book in 1970 and that the Hintermeister painting seems never to have been published at all in a numismatic venue speaks volumes about their ultimate impact. Both Reilly and Hintermeister may have set out to flatter Dunsmore by using his artwork as their starting point, but both have slipped into the shadow of the New York illus-

trator, only to be rediscovered here at long last. No wonder that no artist has attempted such flattery again for more than 50 years after Hintermeister last did so.

FLATTERY AND FORGERY

While the Reilly and Hintermeister "reinterpretations" are fraught with shortcomings, they are at least legitimate and original paintings. One cannot say as much of a painted copy of *Washington Inspecting* that appeared on the market in 1989, being featured in the Collector's Auctions, Ltd., sale no. 33 in September of that year.[54] Dick Johnson, the cataloger, related that the consignor identified the artist as a "New Jersian [sic] of great talent but little morals whose previous work was copying Rembrandts and other masterpieces." These forgeries, it was said, landed the painter in jail. The consignor further indicated that the painting had been purchased in a Philadelphia art gallery. Johnson recalled that the reproduction was signed by "John Ward Dunsmore," and that the forger had painted "craze" (tiny cracks) into the work in order to simulate age.[55] The painting is described as 24 by 35-7/8 inches, oil on canvas. Johnson separately suggested that the consignor was Harry Forman;[56] however, when queried in 2007, Forman had no recollection of the event.[57] Kurt Krueger purchased the copy out of the Johnson sale and retains it in his collection. This copy was exhibited at the 1991 ANA convention in Chicago.

Forged copy of *Washington Inspecting*.

Upon first glance, the forged copy of *Washington Inspecting* looks very much like the Dunsmore original; when comparing the images side-by-side, there is no question but that the artist who painted the forgery meant it to be a precise copy of the original. A closer comparison, however, uncovers a number of distinguishing differences between the two canvases.

The Dunsmore original is characterized by use of brilliant color, especially in Martha Washington's lilac dress and Jefferson's red vest. These features on the forgery are much drabber, and the entire painting is suffused with a brownish tone. Dunsmore rendered the portraits of his subjects with some delicacy, while the forgery artist was much coarser, as can readily be seen in the faces of the Washingtons and of Hamilton. The original is characterized by sharp background details, particularly in the equipment, such as the coin press, the tools hanging on the wall above it, and the Rittenhouse clock, while in the forgery these background pieces are rather muddy.

In fact, the differences are distinctive enough to make the forgery more a backhanded homage than dangerous deception. It is clearly a copy, right down to the forged signature of the artist in the lower left-hand corner of the canvas, but not one so skillfully presented as to deceive a careful observer.

This forged copy may have passed through the hands of one George A. Almoney, a Secret Service agent (1889–1939). James Almoney, the son of George, tells the story:

> My dad had a passion for antiques, particularly items of a historic nature. At some point he uncovered an oil painting by John Ward Dunsmore which he donated to the Service depicting the initial minting of U.S. coins at the Philadelphia mint. It hung in the Chief's office several years, but is now kept somewhere else. The picture was reproduced in 1940 for inclusion in "Know Your Money," a booklet used to help merchants and citizens detect counterfeit money. My copy is signed by then-Chief Frank J. Wilson, "Good Luck to Jimmy Almoney." The handwritten cover letter from Chief Wilson [December 21, 1940] to my mother read: "I want you and Jimmy to know I am thinking of you at this Christmas season. I am sending Jimmy a Know Your Money booklet just issued by the Secret Service Division. I am sure George would be pleased to know that in this book we copied the picture which you sent me of the production of the first United States money at the Philadelphia Mint. Happy New Year to you and Jimmy and may God bless both of you."[58]

It is certain that Almoney did not possess the original *Washington Inspecting* by Dunsmore, for this was comfortably ensconced in Congress Hall and ultimately provided for in Frank H. Stewart's will. Whether Almoney held an oil painting, as family tradition indicates, or a lithograph, is open to debate. The halftone illustration used in *Know Your Money* is not definitive, although it seems that the tops of some lettering can be detected in the lower left corner, which would suggest the Osborne Company lithograph. Further, Wilson's use of the phrase "first United States money," is somewhat evocative of the precise phrase Osborne placed in the lower left corner of the lithograph—"Washington Inspecting the First Money Coined by the United States." Still, Kurt Krueger's forged example had to originate somewhere, and it is possible that Almoney should be included in the ownership chain of this interesting copy.

Frank J. Reilly in his studio. Peter A. Juley & Son photo.

BUREAU OF CITY PROPERTY
113 CITY HALL
PHILADELPHIA

December 13,1909.

Dear Sir;

Might I ask,if you will present the City of
Philadelphia,with a pamphlet on the first U.S.Mint in
"Sugar Alley"this city .For the library at INDEPENDENCE
HALL. I am Sir.

Very truly yours,

Curator Independence Hall.

Frank H.Stewart Esq.,

Philadelphia.

9

The Fate of the Stewart Collection: Congress Hall, the National Park Service, and Rowan University

Frank H. Stewart was a man of many avocations: a hunter, a fisherman, a clubman, and an amateur historian. In none of his hobbies, however, did he cut so wide a swath as in his avid collecting of Americana. Stewart's interests were almost as broad as the field itself: he gathered paintings, manuscripts, books, relics, and even bric-a-brac. Some of these items, such as the only surviving record of the 1765 Stamp Act Congress, were of scholarly significance. Taken as a whole, however, the feat for which Stewart is justly remembered is the aggregation of artifacts known as the "Old Mint Collection," consisting of coins and medals struck at the First United States Mint, relics (such as pieces of hardware and timber salvaged from the Mint buildings), and the paintings relating to the Mint by Edward Lamasure and John Ward Dunsmore. Stewart, a man who had more than a passing acquaintance with many a historical society, had some very definite ideas about where he wanted these collections to go, both before and after his death. Nor was he shy about how he wanted his collections preserved and exhibited. As we shall see, however, Stewart's wishes were not always followed to the letter; indeed, sometimes they were flouted.

In Chapter Five we have already recounted Frank H. Stewart's first significant donation of artifacts, that of the Old Mint Collection to Congress Hall. To review briefly, Congress Hall is the "west wing" of Independence Hall, located on the corner of Chestnut and Sixth Streets, only one and a half blocks south and one block east of the first Mint's North Seventh Street site. Proximity, though a powerful allure, was not as compelling as the history associated with this structure. It was called Congress Hall because it was in this chamber that Congress met when Philadelphia served as the capital city of the United States from 1790 to 1800, and it was the setting for many memorable events, including George Washington's second inaugural, John Adams's inaugural, and the ratification of the Bill of Rights. Probably most compelling to Stewart, however, was the fact that it was in Congress Hall that the first Mint was born, with the passage of enabling legislation on April 2, 1792.

Congress Hall served many roles after the federal government decamped for Washington, D.C., in 1800, and by the early 20th century it was so run down that the city of Philadelphia contemplated demolishing it. The American Institute of

Architects stepped forward, however, and helped to raise the funds needed for restoration. The work was completed in 1913, when Congress Hall was ceremoniously reopened by President Woodrow Wilson, and the refurbished structure became the city of Philadelphia's historical museum.

Wilfred Jordan, who served as Congress Hall's curator, was a friend of Frank H. Stewart, and laid the cornerstone at the dedication of Stewart's "Old Mint" building construction site on January 27, 1912.[1] Stewart held his Old Mint Collection for a couple of years after the last of the first Mint's buildings came down in 1911, but one can imagine Jordan's arguing that the best home for them was in the very building where the Mint was birthed, and now remodeled to the latest in early 20th-century standards.

Jordan opened his campaign on December 13, 1909, when he wrote to Stewart requesting a copy of his recently published booklet, *Ye Olde Mint*, for the Independence Hall library.[2] Stewart fulfilled this request promptly, for the very next day, Jordan sent a thank-you note, including with it a strategic suggestion: "If you have in your posses-sion any coins or other curios bearing on this historic building which you might feel disposed to deposit in the Museum here, I can assure you that they would be greatly appreciated."[3]

Stewart nibbled at the bait dangled by the patient curator, but he did not bite all at once. On July 22, 1910, for example, Jordan issued a receipt to Stewart for the gift of a hand-forged bolt from the first Mint. In this note, Jordan allied himself with Stewart's desire to preserve the remaining structures (the First and Middle Buildings) at the old Mint: "In reference to our conversation yesterday, I will say, that, sometime in the very near future, I would like to see you and present a plan whereby this most interesting edifice can be preserved, for future generations of the American people."[4] If such a plan was devised, it cannot be located today.

Stewart and Jordan remained in touch, for on November 5, 1913, Jordan wrote to Stewart to summarize a recent conversation between the two in which Stewart had proposed gifting to the City of Philadelphia his collection of colonial and U.S. coins, including material

Independence Hall jigsaw puzzle, adapted from Edwin Lamasure's *Cradle of Liberty*. Congress Hall is to the left.

excavated from the first Mint. Jordan, not surprisingly, was over the moon. "It goes without saying that I, personally, highly appreciate your liberality in making this offer, and I can assure you it will be graciously accepted by the City," Jordan wrote.[5] That Stewart also agreed to furnish the display cases only sweetened the pot. Stewart was receptive to Jordan's enthusiasm, but made it clear to the curator just how he wanted the Old Mint Collection exhibited. In a letter of November 7, 1913, he offered the artifacts to Congress Hall "subject to the understanding and acceptance that the old collection be known and labeled as the 'Old Mint Collection,' to be kept intact at Congress Hall of Independence Hall and open to the public view. In other words, it is not my object to give this rare, historical collection away to find it, at some future time, packed away in boxes or closets."[6] Such conditions are the bane of a curator's existence, for they limit flexibility for future exhibitions and tie the hands of future curators. Jordan nonetheless accepted Stewart's conditions, whether sincerely, or with fingers crossed, it is now impossible to say.

On October 22, 1914, accordingly, Stewart made a gift of his Old Mint Collection to Congress Hall. Accession no. 525 lists 197 items in the lot, beginning with 133 federal coins created at the first Mint, all of which Stewart had purchased from coin dealers such as Henry Chapman; 13 items consisting of 29 planchets and pieces of "rolled copper" that had been excavated from the Mint site; 20 items consisting of 48 colonial and state coins, also collected by Stewart; and 29 items consisting of 86 relics from the first Mint, such as 49 clay testing cups, a metal boot scraper, and a section of roofing timber from the Midle Building.[7] Clearly, Stewart was pleased with the way this initial gift was handled, for on February 16, 1915, he wrote to Jordan: "Enclosed is a half cent of 1831 to be added to the Old Mint collection. This makes one of each date of 1/2 cents for every year 1793 to 1832 that they were coined and together with the complete collection of cents for the same years makes copper coinage complete."[8] In the same letter, Stewart also enclosed an 1821 admission token from Charles Willson Peale's Philadelphia Museum, a Mint-struck piece that he felt belonged at Congress Hall because the Peale Museum had been located for several years within Independence Hall. This "era of good feelings" seems to have extended a few more years, for on February 15, 1918, Stewart augmented the Old Mint Collection by adding two paintings, Edwin Lamasure's *Ye Olde Mint* and John Ward Dunsmore's *Washington Inspecting the First Money Coined by the United States.* These did not come as an outright gift, but rather as a loan, for the accession record shows that both paintings were "subject to recall on demand."[9] Apparently, Stewart was too attached to make them an irrevocable gift to Congress Hall.

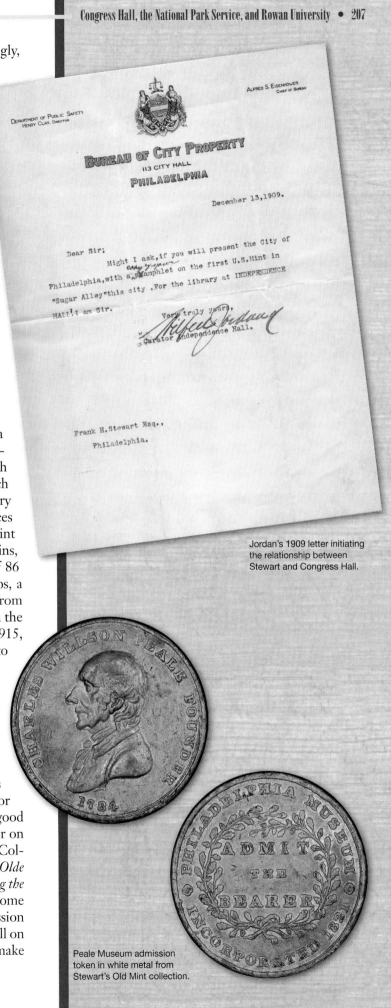

Jordan's 1909 letter initiating the relationship between Stewart and Congress Hall.

Peale Museum admission token in white metal from Stewart's Old Mint collection.

Wilfred Jordan reciprocated via a special gift in 1915:

> It gives me great pleasure to present to you one of the six mallets used in striking the Liberty Bell on the 10th day of February, 1915, the sound emanating from which was carried over the wire of the Bell Telephone Company from Independence Hall to the office of the Mayor at San Francisco, thus inaugurating a continental telephone service. The sound of the Liberty Bell was distinctly heard in San Francisco, in response to which the officials there had a bugler from one of the National Guard Regiments of California blow taps.
>
> You will notice that I speak of six mallets. The one I have presented to you is to my mind really the most interesting of the six as well as the most valuable as a relic, for it was used first on the evening of February 10th at 8:03 P.M. when Independence Hall was first directly connected with San Francisco to test the line. You therefore not only have the instrument that was used officially in striking the Liberty Bell for the first time since 1835 when it tolled the funeral solemnities of Chief Justice John Marshall, but this mallet was the medium of first producing the sound carried over the long distance telephone wires from Philadelphia to San Francisco some hours before the official event took place.[10]

Jordan initially stuck to the bargain he had made to exhibit the Old Mint Collection intact and indefinitely. A second-floor room was set aside for the collection at least by early 1915, for Jordan wrote to Stewart on March 4, 1915, about placing a print of *Ye Olde Mint* "in the Old Mint Room at Congress Hall."[11] As the years went by, however, the curator began to chip away at the agreement, albeit with Stewart's case-by-case permission. By 1920, he returned a number of duplicates and bulky objects, because "the new case arrangement [in] the room which has been devoted to coins, there is not sufficient room to further exhibit these objects here."[12] This return was most emphatically *not* made because the Old Mint Collection was unpopular with Congress Hall's patrons. On the contrary, at least some of the artifacts had proved too popular for their own good. Jordan, for example, asked Stewart's permission to cut off a section of roof timber so that the remainder could be protected within an exhibit case, for "We found that in exhibiting it as heretofore, on a pair of wooden trusses, that the visitors from time to time have chipped pieces from it to carry away as souvenirs."[13]

Jordan's good relationship with Stewart survived what can only be described as a potential disaster over a botched exchange arrangement. It began when Stewart, on May 15, 1915, made a gift of 209 tokens and medals, mostly English Conder tokens, to Congress Hall.[14] These tokens were somewhat far afield from the Philadelphia-area collecting mission of Congress Hall, so Jordan was interested in trading them to fill the gaps in the federal coinage series of the Old Mint Collection. To do so, he turned to Frederick D. Langenheim, one of Philadelphia's most respected numismatic scholars. Langenheim had been the curator of Numismatics at the Numismatic and Antiquarian Society of Philadelphia since 1890.[15] From 1919 to 1932, he would serve as the honorary curator of numismatics at the Philadelphia Museum of Art.[16] In 1920, he also became the honorary curator, department of numismatics, at the Pennsylvania Museum and School of Industrial Art.[17] Clearly, if there was a gentleman and a scholar in the coin world of Philadelphia, it was F.D. Langenheim.

After some preliminary correspondence, on November 19, 1918, Jordan wrote to Langenheim: "I am sending you by messenger, put up in separate packages, 359 coins and tokens and 18 pieces of currency which I would appreciate your examining for us at your convenience, and would ask that you take out all those pieces which might be acceptable to you for trading purposes to fill in gaps in our coin collection. I would also like to have some suggestions from you as to how we might dispose of the remaining specimens, either by sale or by exchange. Any of the pieces that you think we should keep in our collection, if you will set aside, I would also appreciate it."[18] Jordan also attached a list of coins missing from the Congress Hall collection, which consisted of a half cent of 1796; one cent of 1793; half dimes of 1797, 1801, 1802, 1805, and 1829; dimes of 1797, 1802, 1803, 1814, 1820, 1821, 1822, 1823, 1824, 1827, 1828, 1830, 1831, and 1832; quarter dollars of 1804, 1805, 1807, 1815, 1819, 1820, 1822, 1823, 1824, 1825, 1827, 1828, 1831, and 1832; half dollars of 1796, 1797, 1801, 1802, 1803, and 1820; and of course, a dollar of 1804. Further, the only coins in all of the gold series on hand were half eagles of 1804 and 1806. The 359 coins and tokens that Jordan sent to Langenheim comprised virtually all of Stewart's gift of May 15, 1915, plus additional pieces from the Old Mint Collection. This was done with Stewart's consent, for in a follow-up letter of January 3, 1919, Jordan writes to Langenheim: "I am sending you by messenger thirty-five U.S. half dollars, duplicates of our coin collection, presented by Mr. Frank H. Stewart which he signifies we may also use in exchange, thus enabling us to develop more fully our little coin cabinet here, as fully explained to you in previous letters."[19]

Then the trouble began. Jordan wrote a letter of reminder to Langenheim on April 15, 1919, apparently receiving no response. The next letter in the file is dated May 12, 1920, in which the curator tells Langenheim that "Mr. Frank H. Stewart called upon me the other day, and during our conversation asked about the tokens and other coins which he presented to the City some time ago with the rest of his Old Mint Collection and which we did not deem desirable for our exhibit here he having granted permission you will recall for us to dispose of them in a trade."[20] No answer was received to this rather diplomatic missive, nor to another letter Jordan sent on August 11.

Finally, the next day, the embarrassed curator wrote to Stewart, enclosing a copy of his May 12 letter, saying "As I told you on your last visit here, which I think was in May, Mr. Langenheim has sent us nothing in exchange for the specimens given him and a year has almost elapsed."[21] Jordan's math was a bit fuzzy, for the tokens and medals had been sent to Langenheim a year and nine months previously.

The file then jumps to a letter from Jordan to Frank Stewart on February 7, 1922, in which the curator states: "Relative to our conversation today concerning the tokens which you presented to the City with your Old Mint Collection recorded in accession Nos. 708 and 850, I would ask you permission to trade these in for coins in use in America during Colonial times, together with coins which we need to make the United States Coin Collection more complete, particularly early gold pieces."[22] Stewart's reply was written on Frank H. Stewart Electric Company stationery, which was emblazoned across the top with his "Old Mint Electrical Supplies" logo, a return address of "Old Mint Building, 37 and 39 North Seventh Street," and a reproduction of Lamasure's "Ye Olde Mint," labeled "First U.S. Mint." In it Stewart says: "You have my permission to exchange the tokens for such coins as you may desire for the Independence Hall Collection."[23] Attached to this correspondence is a copy of accession no. 850, indicating that every item in it was exchanged.

What the record does not reflect, however, was how the exchange was effected. Did the distinguished Mr. Langenheim shake off his dilatory ways and redeem himself by making shrewd exchanges? Or did Jordan recover the tokens and medals from Langenheim and use another agent in order to make the exchanges? The record is silent.

In 1923, an acquaintance of Dunsmore, A. Bertram Gilliland, complained to Stewart that the Dunsmore painting and the Old Mint exhibit had been moved to a storeroom, apparently open to the public only by special request. Stewart replied that he would "investigate the matter at once." Whether Stewart's investigation produced an outcome to his satisfaction is unrecorded.[24]

After the Gilliland excitement, the Old Mint Collection entered a long period of quiescence. Neither Stewart nor Jordan appears to have sought to add to it very much during the next quarter century. The records reveal an occasional request from the publisher of a text book, asking permission to reproduce *Ye Olde Mint* or *Washington Inspecting*, but very little else. Indeed, the next incident of real interest comes from a letter dated January 6, 1949, from the Woodbury Trust Company:

> RE: Estate of Frank H. Stewart Mr. Stewart departed this life on October 14, 1948, and we have been appointed as one of the executors of his estate. We have in our files an old receipt, No. 42, dated October 30, 1915, for two paintings loaned the City of Philadelphia for exhibition purposes at Indepen-

dence Hall as follows: 1. "The First United States Mint Building" 2. "Inspecting the First Coins." Under paragraph fifth of Mr. Stewart's will, he bequeaths as follows: "I give and bequeath to the City of Philadelphia the two pictures belonging to me pertaining to the First United States Mint, which are now on exhibition in Congress Hall, Philadelphia." We would appreciate your execution, of the proper receipt by the proper city officials for this bequest under the will of Mr. Stewart.[25]

This letter was acknowledged by Mr. N.H. Rambo Jr., Chief of the Bureau of City Property, on March 17, 1949, with the note that "These paintings are now hanging in Congress Hall, having been loaned to the City of Philadelphia on October 30, 1915."[26] Apparently, the two paintings had been exhibited in Congress Hall for more than two years before the loan was made official on February 15, 1918. Thus it was that Edwin Lamasure's *Ye Olde Mint* and John Ward Dunsmore's *Washington Inspecting the First Money Coined by the United States*, finally, after more than three decades, became the property of the City of Philadelphia and its museum at Congress Hall.

THE NATIONAL PARK SERVICE

These paintings, and the Old Mint Collection, were destined to be administered by the City of Philadelphia for only a brief time after 1949. In fact, the winds of change were blowing even before Stewart made his bequest of the paintings. On June 28, 1948, Congress had authorized the creation of National Park status for Independence Hall.[27] It was, however, a classic "unfunded mandate," for no appropriation was attached to the legislation. Local Philadelphia leaders banded together to raise the necessary funds, and on January 1, 1951, the entire complex, including Congress Hall, was consolidated under the National Park Service as Independence National Historical Park. The leaders of the new park celebrated by climbing the Independence Hall bell tower on New Year's Eve to ring in 1951.[28]

For the next nearly 20 years, the change in custodian had little practical consequence for the Old Mint Collection, with one major exception. As we shall see, by 1967, when Charles Hoskins, the director of the Money Museum at the National Bank of Detroit, and his assistant Thomas W. Becker, visited the Independence National Historical Park, they discovered—so much for Stewart's expressed

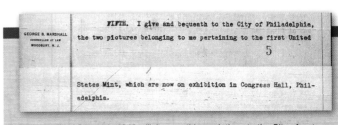

Fifth article of Stewart's 1946 will, bequeathing paintings to the City of Philadelphia. Curiously, the paintings are unnamed.

desire to have it perpetually on exhibition—the Old Mint Collection, packed away in storage in the basement of the First Bank of the United States Building (one of the structures that comprises the Independence National Historical Park).[29] The Old Mint Collection had been relegated to storage because the National Park Service had decided to focus its interpretation of Independence Hall upon the latter part of the 18th century, when it played its most momentous role in American, and indeed, world history.

Fortunately, another Philadelphia institution—or more properly, institution-in-process—was interested in the Old Mint Collection: the still under-construction fourth Mint of the United States. On July 7, 1967, M.O. Anderson, superintendent of Independence National Historical Park, at the suggestion of Arthur Sipe, then vice president of the American Numismatic Association, wrote Mint Director Eva Adams, offering to lend, on a long-term basis,

> relics of the first Philadelphia Mint, salvaged at the time of its dedication [sic, "destruction" was meant] about 1912. These are under our jurisdiction as part of the Independence Hall Collection, which we hold on permanent loan from the City of Philadelphia.[30]

Leaving aside the interesting proposition that artifacts would go to the Mint on a long-term-loan basis when they were already on a permanent-loan basis from the City of Philadelphia, Anderson's offer was a clear winner for both parties. As Anderson went on to state in the same letter, the artifacts were not germane to Independence Hall's exhibition plans, and as for the Mint, it was almost entirely devoid of any artifacts illustrating its early history. Attached to Anderson's letter was a list of 46 objects from the Old Mint Collection. Prominent among them were the paintings *Ye Olde Mint* and *Washington Inspecting*.[31] It is important to note that this was but a fraction of the Old Mint Collection, which contained many more coins and artifacts than were offered here. Director Adams accepted Anderson's offer on behalf of the Mint on August 2, 1967, but problems with construction delayed the actual transfer of the collection until the grand opening of the fourth Philadelphia Mint in 1969.[32]

Interestingly, the list of objects actually conveyed in 1969 differs slightly from Anderson's original 1967 proposal. While Lamasure's *Ye Olde Mint* went to the new Mint for exhibition in 1969 (indeed, a free interpretation of it was used as the cover art for the booklet produced for the grand opening),[33] *Washington Inspecting* was nowhere to be found on the loaned object list.[34] Over the next few months the Park Service would send more artifacts to round out the pieces already on exhibit. For example, on July 3, 1969, the Mint received the deed of sale to the first Mint property (when it was sold to Michael Kates in 1836), and an iron boot scraper.[35] This loan agreement between the Independence National Historical Park and

the Mint was to be reviewed, and if desired, renewed, on an annual basis. Distressingly, some of the items came up missing during subsequent yearly requests for extension of the loan. Twenty-two photographs that Frank H. Stewart had taken of the old Mint's buildings circa 1909 were among those artifacts that were lost (although they were apparently rediscovered in the Mint's Washington, D.C., headquarters in 2006).[36] It got worse, however, for a comprehensive accounting in 1982 revealed that only five of the 14 clay acid testing cups loaned in 1969 still remained, and, worst of all, one of the two silver center cent planchets had also gone astray.[37] This latter story has a happy ending, for the authors verified during a visit in the summer of 2009 that both of the silver center cent planchets were safely in the Mint's possession.

It was providential that Lamasure's *Ye Olde Mint* never went missing. Nor did Dunsmore's *Washington Inspecting* get lost, although it traveled a different path than *Ye Olde Mint* from 1969 until 1994. If one goes back to the original list of "Relics of the First United States Mint in the Independence Hall Collection," which accompanied M.O. Anderson's July 7, 1967, letter to Eva Adams, we find the listing of the Dunsmore painting crossed off, with the hand-written notation "loaned to U.S. Treasury."[38] Since the Bureau of the Mint was one of the divisions of the Treasury, it might seem that the intent was to send the painting to the Mint. The facts, however, tell a very different story. On February 5, 1957, *Washington Inspecting* was loaned to the Alexander Hamilton Bicentennial Commission for an exhibit on Hamilton's life to be held at the Treasury Department in Washington, D.C.[39] When the Hamilton exhibit came to an end on April 30, 1958, the Treasury Department's director of administrative services wrote to Independence National Historical Park's M.O. Anderson: "It would be appreciated if the loan of this painting were extended until June 30, 1959, during which time it would be on display in the regular Treasury exhibit room."[40] This request was approved, as were subsequent extensions through 1969, and the painting itself continued to hang in the Treasury's exhibit room.

On April 13, 1970, however, the assistant to the director of the Treasury's office of administrative services wrote to Independence Hall with two pieces of significant news. "We are now in the process of developing a new exhibit which will eliminate the desirability of this painting. The Bureau of the Mint is interested in acquiring the painting for display in the new Mint Building in Philadelphia, and I have agreed to ask whether you will loan them the painting."[41] Independence Hall quickly agreed to lend *Washington Inspecting* to the Mint, but it was fated to be nearly a quarter century before that would actually happen. Another letter from the assistant to the director explains why: "We have, meanwhile, had a request from the Director of the Mint, Mrs. Mary Brooks, that the portrait be loaned for hanging in her office, which is located in the main Treasury Building."[42] Chester L. Brooks (not related to Mary), superintendent of the Independence National Historical Park, responded by writing that the public exhibition of *Washington Inspecting*, both during the Hamilton Bicentennial and in the Treasury Department exhibit room thereafter, served a public educational function. He closed by saying, "Since this is our first responsibility, I must ask that you convey our apologies to Mrs. Brooks, and request the painting to be transferred to the Philadelphia Mint as originally agreed, or returned to this Park."[43]

In providing this answer, fully justifiable under the mission of his institution, Chester Brooks had made, in Mary Brooks, a formidable adversary. Mrs. Brooks was from Idaho, but had largely grown up in Washington, D.C., where both her husband and her father had served as U.S. Senators. In addition to her own sharply honed political instincts, she also had pals in high places: one particular friend was the first lady, Mrs. Pat Nixon. On June 22, less than a month after Chester Brooks had denied her request to hang *Washington Inspecting* in her office, she wrote this note to John Milley, supervisory curator at Independence National Historical Park:

> This will confirm Roy Cahoon's recent telephone conversation with you concerning my desire to temporarily hang the beautiful Dunsmore painting, "Inspecting the First Coins," in my office. As Mr. Cahoon explained, I have refurnished the Director's office with restored antique pieces from the first San Francisco Mint Superintendent's Office and would like to display the painting with this collection when I have a showing in the near future for the Press. It would then be transferred to the Philadelphia Mint as originally agreed.[44]

Mrs. Brooks here reveals herself as a deft bureaucratic infighter, for she was able to get her way without leaving an inordinate amount of blood on the floor. The painting would be placed in an appropriate educational context, there would be a press event that could serve in place of public exhibition, and eventually Independence Hall would get its way when the painting was transferred to the Mint. Independence Hall would soon discover that, like a camel, once Mary Brooks got her nose under the tent, it would prove very difficult to keep her out. The next letter in the file comes from Charles R. Hoskins, by now a public information officer at the Mint:

> I have been told that it is the Director's intention to transfer the painting to the Philadelphia Mint. However, the Director wishes to retain it in her office for a few more months, because the American Numismatic Association is meeting in Washington in mid-August, 1971. She intends to open her office to all the Conventioneers to give them an opportunity to see the painting, the furniture and the other interesting Mint artifacts which are to be assembled for that occasion.[45]

The advent of a new superintendent at Independence National Historical Park inspired Brooks to concoct a new set of rationales for keeping *Washington Inspecting* hanging in her office, during the year 1972. After lauding Dunsmore's work as "the most famous painting relating to this [sic] of the Mint" Brooks gets down to business:

> It now hangs in my office, where it has been seen by Mrs. Richard Nixon, Secretary and Mrs. Connally and many other dignitaries, as well as thousands of school children. Because I have launched a youth education program to encourage learning more about our nation's coins and medals, I am particularly desirous of having the painting on view in my office. By appointment, it is open for tours and the many children and others who have visited always express delight in the painting.[46]

Mrs. Brooks' extension request for 1973 cites the fact that the Treasury Building has been declared a National Historic Landmark site, and thus "my office now has more visitors than ever."[47] And so Mrs. Brooks continued to get her way, with *Washington Inspecting* gracing her office until Hobart Cawood's note of January 3, 1974, which stated:

> We would be pleased to extend our loan to your office of Dunsmore's painting "Inspecting the First Coins" for another year. I wish to advise you, however, that we shall recall the painting at the termination of this loan period, for use in our own exhibits in the First Bank of the U.S.[48]

The next item in the file is a receipt showing that on January 9, 1975, Mrs. Brooks finally relinquished the painting to Independence Hall.[49] Ironically, the long-time Mint director had prevented *Washington Inspecting* from getting to the Mint for public display.

For more than 15 years thereafter, *Washington Inspecting* hung at Independence Hall's exhibit space at the First Bank of the United States, and later in the portrait gallery of the Second Bank of the United States. In 1992, however, the U.S. Mint planned a brief, one-week exhibition to celebrate its bicentennial, and received permission from Independence Hall to borrow *Washington Inspecting* to be its centerpiece.[50] This loan exposed the fact that Dunsmore's painting was in need of professional restoration. Two years later, *Washington Inspecting* was entrusted to a professional conservator, Carole Abercauph, who stretched the canvas, and cleaned, inpainted, and varnished the painting to restore it to its former glory.[51] At this time as well, the frame was re-gilt by Howard Stephen Serlick, a Philadelphia gilder.[52]

The sprucing up came just in the nick of time, for an August 2, 1994, press release by the Mint announced that Martha Aikens, superintendent of the Independence National Historical Park, would present the painting, on a long-term-loan basis, to Phillip N. Diehl, director of the Mint.[53] Thus was *Washington Inspecting* reunited with *Ye Olde Mint*, after a hiatus of 25 years. It rejoined other artifacts from Stewart's Old Mint Collection on the mezzanine-level museum at the fourth U.S. Mint. To these objects, the Mint added a few artifacts of its own, such as the so-called "first screw press" and Windsor chairs, both of which Dunsmore had painted into his picture.

Frank H. Stewart's Old Mint Collection lives on today, albeit not in the single unified, perpetual exhibition that he had in mind. Both paintings, and a host of other relics, are on permanent exhibit at the fourth Philadelphia Mint, while the balance of the collection, including most of the coins and medals, are in storage at the Independence National Historical Park. The fourth Mint's mezzanine-level museum is possible only because of Frank H. Stewart's foresight in preserving artifacts of the first Mint, and commissioning works of art to commemorate it.

ROWAN UNIVERSITY

Stewart's Old Mint Collection landed very close to home, for both the fourth U.S. Mint and Independence National Historical Park are within a two-block radius of numbers 37 and 39 North Seventh Street. There is a conspicuous exception to this tight orbit, however, and that is the large collection of Stewart's Americana, including many Mint-related items, held at Rowan University in Glassboro, in the heart of southern New Jersey, more than 25 miles south of the old Mint. Glassboro captured the world's attention in 1967, when it hosted a summit conference between President Lyndon B. Johnson and the Soviet Union's premier, Alexi Kosygin. How Glassboro's Rowan University captured Stewart's attention makes for an interesting story, especially since it involves a case of the "big one that got away" for another historical institution.

From 1914 to 1938, Frank H. Stewart made his home in the city of Woodbury, New Jersey, less than five miles from the Delaware River, due south of Philadelphia. Woodbury is located in Gloucester County, and it happened that Gloucester County was possessed of a historical society, albeit one that was moribund and broke. This did not deter him, for "Frank H. Stewart was welcomed into the Society in early 1916 and elected trustee later that same year."[54] Calling upon his business acumen, Stewart devised a detailed plan to get the Society into the black. At a "slimly attended" annual meeting in January of 1918, the "Stewart plan of financing the Society was approved. At this meeting, President John G. Whitall was elected president emeritus and Frank H. Stewart became our second president."[55]

The Gloucester County Historical Society proved wise in its choice of leader, for Stewart energized the Society during his 19 years at the helm, raising money to pay off the debt, buying a permanent meeting place, and launching an active publications program, many of which were written by Stewart himself.[56] His proudest achievement, however, was his successful petitioning for a room and a vault to be included in the new County Building. The fireproof vault would hold the Society's archives, and the adjoining room, staffed by a curator, could be used by researchers. The success of this plan propelled the Gloucester County Historical Society into the first rank of local historical societies in the nation.[57]

The Gloucester County Historical Society, therefore, was the leading candidate for the childless Stewart to bequeath his large aggregation of Americana, and this was clearly his original intention, for his will of July 17, 1941, left his collections of books, manuscripts, watches, coins, medals, buttons, hunting and fishing tackle, and Indian relics to the Society, along with the income from an endowment of $20,000 to help support them.[58] Then, abruptly, on December 8, 1941, the day after Pearl Harbor was bombed, Stewart dropped a bombshell of his own upon Gloucester County, adding a codicil to his will that revoked the paragraph leaving his collections to the Historical Society.[59] Stewart never left a written explanation for this decision. A variety of speculations have been advanced to explain Stewart's change of heart, ranging from the County's abandonment of plans to build a library named after him, to unfounded rumors about his relationship with his sister-in-law, but the most persuasive reason involves the vault in the County Building. According to this story, Stewart happened to encounter a member of the County Freeholders Committee removing Gloucester County Historical Society archives from the vault, and replacing them with County records. Stewart angrily concluded that historical materials were not valued in Gloucester County, and revoked his intended gift.[60]

With the codicil of January 8, 1941, the disposition of Stewart's Americana Collection reverted to the hands of the trustees of the Stewart estate. On April 1, 1946, however, he wrote a new and final will that left his entire collection of Americana to the New Jersey State Teachers College at Glassboro (the Teachers College became Rowan College in 1992, and Rowan University in 1997). This gift specifically included, in the ninth paragraph of his will, "My pen and ink sketches, photos and relics of the First United States Mint, together with all paintings not otherwise herein disposed of."[61] The entire collection consisted of:

> Approximately 2,500 volumes on New Jersey History, 200 volumes about Indians, 800 volumes related to United States History, 125 volumes about New Jersey genealogy, 75 volumes about the United States Mint, 200 rare books, 3,672 Southern New Jersey manuscripts, documents and deeds, 126 Colonial newspapers, and 50 maps and atlases.[62]

It should be noted that the Gloucester County Historical Society did not completely lose out on artifacts from the first Mint. As previously discussed, Stewart gave one of the door sills from the first Mint buildings to his friend, Dr. John C. Curry, at the time of demolition in 1911. Dr. Curry brought the door sill to his home in Woodbury, where it resided for several years. Dr. Curry's son eventually donated it to the Historical Society, which has placed it in the entryway to its library.[63] The Society also received the oak bench made of roofing timber from the Middle Building of the first Mint.

The New Jersey State Teachers College took possession of the Stewart collection a few months after Frank Stewart's death, to be precise, in August of 1949. A space in College Hall was dubbed the "Stewart Room," and became the locus of cataloging activity.[64] With the advent of the first Savitz Library in 1956, the collections were moved to a more commodious version of the Stewart Room.[65] When the second Savitz Library was opened in June of 1963, the Stewart collection was transferred there.[66] The Stewart Collection currently resides in the Campbell Library at Rowan.

The portion of the Stewart collection referring to the Mint is essentially the research file or archives Stewart gathered during the course of writing *Ye Olde Mint* (1909), *Our New Home and Old Times* (1913), and *History of the First United States Mint* (1924). He was an indefatigable researcher, and the collection reflects his thorough harvesting of available evidence. It contains original correspondence, documents copied from archival sources, printed ephemera, photographs, pen and ink sketches, deeds, clippings, and handwritten notes. These reveal that nearly all of Stewart's writing about the Mint was based on primary sources. In fact, any criticism of Stewart's writing must focus not on its base of evidence, but rather on its lack of analysis: his writings often read as if they are a long series of quotations tied together by only desultory commentary.

Stewart was an omnivorous collector of historical source material, gathering everything from John Smith's Indian-issued "safe conduct pass" to Betsy Ross's marriage certificate. It should be noted that many other collectors would have stepped forward to preserve memorabilia such as these. In the case of the first Mint, however, there was literally no one else during the early 20th century interested in preserving its artifacts and documentation. Had Stewart not done so with both energy and zeal, most of this material would have been irretrievably lost to history. Not only did he collect well, but in choosing Congress Hall and the New Jersey State Teachers College at Glassboro, he also chose long-term custodians well, for his collections have been faithfully preserved and made accessible to scholars during the more than six decades since his death. Given his lifelong proclivity to collect and preserve the materials of history, it would seem that the original spelling of his surname, "Steward," was a most appropriate appellation for this avid amateur historian.

YE OLDE MINT: THE FATE OF A PAINTING

During the years since it was commissioned, Lamasure's *Ye Olde Mint* has endured an odyssey of varying esteem, often appreciated and sometimes ignored, usually lovingly cared for, but sometimes cavalierly treated. For the first few years after it was painted, Frank H. Stewart apparently kept it on exhibition in his Old Mint Building, along with what he called his "Old Mint Collection": pictures, artifacts, documents and bric-a-brac, all with a direct connection to the vanished structures on North Seventh Street. Within a few years, as we have seen, Stewart sought a long-term home for what he clearly believed to be a collection of national historical significance. As Stewart recalled:

> At one time I was rather inclined to think that I was making a mistake in giving the various things to the City instead of the Philadelphia Mint, but yielded to wishes of curator Wilfred Jordan of Independence Hall, who planned to gather relics for Congress Hall, which pertained to acts of Congress when Philadelphia was the nation's capitol.[67]

The Congress Hall Accession Record, dated February 25, 1918, establishes that in the case of *Ye Olde Mint*, Stewart's presentation was in fact not a gift, but rather a loan "subject to recall on demand." Subsequent entries in the accession record indicate that the painting was "willed to the city after the death of Mr. Stewart October 14, 1948."[68]

From the time that it was lent in 1918 until it became a permanent gift in 1948, *Ye Olde Mint* seems to have been on exhibit in Congress Hall. In 1951, however, the U.S. National Park Service, Department of the Interior, inherited on permanent loan, the City of Philadelphia's collection at Congress Hall, and *Ye Olde Mint*, along with the rest of the Old Mint Collection, suffered something of a fall from grace. The Independence National Historical Park was charged with a far broader collecting scope than that of the City of Philadelphia, and Stewart's Old Mint artifacts were not near the top of their priority list. The Old Mint Collection was taken off exhibition, relegated to storage, and our next glimpse of it does not come until 1967, when two numismatists who are forgotten today, but who were prominent in their own day, had a "close encounter" with it in storage.

The duo were Charles R. Hoskins, then the curator at the National Bank of Detroit Money Museum, later public information officer at the U.S. Mint, and ultimately, the first director of the American Numismatic Association Certification Service, and Thomas W. Becker, then Hoskins's assistant director at the Money Museum, and later author of *The Coin Makers*.[69] Searching for illustrative material for *The Coin Makers*, Becker approached Eva Adams, then director of the United States Mint, requesting to take photographs at the Mint which depicted modern coinage technology. Adams complied with Becker's request, and also added a "surprise": she had recently located the Lamasure painting in the storage of Independence Hall National Park.[70] A decade later, Becker recounted the results of their voyage of discovery: "I was elated to find the Lamasure stacked away in the basement of the First National Bank Building in downtown Philadelphia."[71] This is not as perplexing as it sounds, for the Independence National Historical Park was also responsible for the First Bank of the United States building on Third Street, just south of Chestnut Street, only two blocks east of Independence Hall,[72] and in 1967, the basement of this building provided storage for the Independence National Historical Park artifact collection.[73]

Hoskins and Becker spent four hours in the basement of the First Bank of the United States Building, carefully documenting, in writing and in photographs, both the paintings and the artifacts from the Old Mint Collection, such as a silver center cent planchet, also in storage there. The duo lavished special attention on Lamasure's famous work, for they "took a long series of color slides of the painting, moving in closer and closer to capture various details."[74] Becker made the following notes on *Ye Olde Mint:*

> The Lamasure painting is pastel [watercolor] measuring 34-7/8" across the top and 24" up and down both sides. The painting is on thin cardboard, one solid sheet, and the entire piece of material is now in a very bad state of repair. . . . The measurements are of the painting unframed.[75]

According to Becker, the color slides "were later turned over to the Bureau of the Mint except for my own set which has always remained in my possession."[76] Upon inquiry from the authors, Becker was able to locate only two of the images, one of the watercolor itself, and another, taken by Charles Hoskins, depicting Becker the photographer at work. The remainder, sadly, were lost in a robbery of Becker's residence.[77] Lest Becker's article convey the impression that *Ye Olde Mint* was continuously stored in the basement of the First Bank of the United

States building from 1950 to 1967, it should be noted that the National Park Service was happy to lend it for exhibition at other institutions. From January 8 through February 24, 1965, for example, several items from the Old Mint Collection, including the Lamasure, were loaned to the Brooklyn Public Library's "U.S. Mint" exhibition. On the loan form, Independence National Historical Park valued the painting at $100, almost certainly less than Frank Stewart had paid for it a half century before.[78]

Fewer than three years after it returned from Brooklyn, the picture of the old Mint building was offered to the builders of the new. M.O. Anderson, the superintendent of Independence National Historical Park, wrote on July 7, 1967, to Eva Adams, the director of the U.S. Mint, as follows:

> I am writing at the suggestion of Mr. Arthur Sipe, Vice President of the American Numismatic Association, to call to your attention certain specimens in our collection which would be, I think, ideal for display in the new Philadelphia Mint. The pieces in question are relics of the first Philadelphia Mint, salvaged at the time of its demolition about 1912. . . . If you are interested in having any or all of the specimens for exhibit in the new Mint, we would be glad to arrange for a long-term loan. They are not germane to our exhibition plans and we are anxious to have them placed where they can be used most appropriately.[79]

Frank H. Stewart would have been distressed to learn that his prized Old Mint Collection was no longer "germane" to the exhibition plans of the Independence National Historical Park. Indeed, Anderson's list included all of the objects in Stewart's Old Mint Collection, including Lamasure's painting. Eva Adams replied to Anderson's letter in due course:

> I need not tell you with what delight your letter of July 7th was received. We are, indeed, most interested in exhibiting the relics of the first Philadelphia

Thomas Becker photographing *Ye Olde Mint,*
1969, as captured by Charles Hoskins.

Thomas Becker's photograph of *Ye Olde Mint,* 1969.

Mint mentioned therein. Your generous offer of the specimens, on a long-term loan basis, is accepted with thanks. Frank Gasparro, our engraver at the Philadelphia Mint, is working with the exhibit material and I am asking him to call you and make the arrangements necessary to effect the delivery of such objects.[80]

It is not known if this exchange of letters later inspired Adams to recommend that Hoskins and Becker visit and photograph the Old Mint Collection. In any event, Gasparro followed up quickly, for a note jotted on a carbon copy of Anderson's July 7 letter to Adams reads: "Mr. Gasparro came August 11th, and said that they would like to borrow all items, but will not collect them until after removal to the new Mint building in 1968. "[81]

The fourth Philadelphia Mint building, however, was not ready for occupancy until the summer of 1969. On April 2 of that year, Eva Adams wrote to the new superintendent of Independence National Historical Park, Chester L. Brooks, to inform him that the Mint was ready to accept the loan, and asking him to convey the artifacts to the Mint's recently engaged consultant, none other than Charles R. Hoskins.[82] On May 9, Brooks responded, saying that most of the requested artifacts had already been delivered to Hoskins, while a few were being cleaned at the National Park Service Laboratory in Springfield, Virginia. An attached list of the artifacts already delivered shows that *Ye Olde Mint* was not among those being cleaned. The list documents that 55 accessions, consisting of 79 separate objects, were loaned to the Mint for exhibit purposes for one year, renewable annually upon request.[83] Hoskins wrote on May 13, 1969, confirming that "The Lamasure painting and about 40 or 50 artifacts from the first U.S. Mint" had been safely received at the new Mint building at Arch and Fifth Streets.[84]

The fourth U.S. Mint was officially dedicated during ceremonies on August 14, 1969. *Ye Olde Mint*, or at least a bowdlerized version of it, was front and center on the commemorative booklet produced for the occasion. The uncredited artist chose a perspective similar to that depicted by Lamasure, but reduced the number of structures to only one, the Front Building, and replaced Lamasure's sun-dappled day with a snowy and cloudy afternoon in deep winter. The tableaux is entitled *Ye Olde Mint in 1792*, and the moment is pegged at yuletide, judging from the couple in a two-horse open sleigh who are transporting their Christmas tree, and the carolers serenading the closed double doors of the Mint. A man with a dog on a leash completes the human cast, and on first glance he appears to be hailing an unseen hansom cab, but on closer examination is found to be waving to the woman in the sleigh. For all of its flights of fancy, however, this illustration also pays homage to the 1854 Richards photo, in the form of the fragment of picket fence to the west of the building, with the tree standing in front of it.[85] It is also noteworthy that the Mint had adopted Stewart's coined phrase of "Ye Olde Mint" to describe its first home.

The Lamasure painting entered the Mint in 1969, on a long-term loan, and indeed, every year since then, the Independence National Historical Park has extended the loan to the Mint. *Ye Olde Mint* has been on show most of that time in the mezzanine exhibit area of the fourth Mint, right next to Dunsmore's *Washington Inspecting*. When the authors visited the Philadelphia Mint during the summer of 2007, they found blank spots in the exhibition area where both *Ye Olde Mint* and *Washington Inspecting* customarily hang. No label explained the reason for their absence, and no Mint employee could be found to provide a reason. The authors learned that both paintings had been recalled by Independence National Historical Park for cultural research and conservation. On January 26, 2009, photos of both paintings were taken by Jeremy Katz, and in honor of the earlier Hoskins photo of Becker, Leonard Augsburger captured Jeremy Katz the photographer at work. By the autumn of 2009, both *Ye Olde Mint* and *Washington Inspecting* were once more hanging in their customary places.

Opening ceremony program for the fourth Mint in Philadelphia, 1969.

Jeremy Katz in 2009, in the basement of the Second Bank of the United States in Philadelphia, as captured by Leonard Augsburger.

136

Decorative eagle, from the façade of the Old Mint Building.

Chapter 10

The Last Days of Frank H. Stewart

Frank H. Stewart never claimed to be a scholar, yet his resume is crammed with books, booklets, and pamphlets he produced on subjects with the gravitas of numismatics, biography, and history. It cannot be said that he was a polished author—his training was apparently confined to Prickett's Business School's course on commercial writing—nor can he be called a thoroughgoing scholar. Yet Stewart was most assuredly an amateur enthusiast on topics numismatic (especially regarding the first U.S. Mint); biographical (focusing on the heroes of the Revolutionary War); and historical (particularly the chronicles of his home state of New Jersey). Two of his earliest booklet projects featured the first Mint: his inaugural effort, *Ye Olde Mint*, in 1909 and *Our New Home and Old Times* in 1913.

Stewart's *raison d'être*, even if he did not know it yet, was that of an archivist and recorder of history. His career arguably began in 1890, at the age of 17, in the form of his first diary, in which he carefully noted for posterity the observations of a young man making his way from the country to the city and carving a piece of the American pie for himself. Subsequent diaries, now missing, carried the story further.[1] By 1907, at the age of 34 and having achieved substantial success in the electrical supply industry, Stewart was amply prepared to return to his life's avocation, and what better place to start than with his own commercial concern, which by coincidence or fate, just happened to be dripping with history?

STEWART'S SMALL BEGINNINGS: *YE OLDE MINT* AND *OUR NEW HOME AND OLD TIMES*

The full title of Stewart's maiden publication was *Ye Olde Mint: Being a brief description of the first U.S. Mint, established by Congress in the year 1792, Seventh Street and Sugar Alley (now Filbert Street) Philadelphia*. The booklet is octavo in size, 6 by 8-3/4 inches, with tan card covers and a stapled binding. Its cover depicts a flowering plant rendered in the art nouveau style, rather reminiscent of a Tiffany lamp, with the title presented atop the plant as *Ye Olde Mint*. At the base of the plant are the words "Compliments of Frank H. Stewart Electric Co. 35 North Seventh St. Philadelphia," which suggests that the company had not occupied the old Mint buildings for business purposes. The booklet contains 24 pages and six unnumbered black-and-white photographs, reproduced in half tone, of the Mint buildings and the artifacts removed from them. The copyright owner is listed as the Frank H. Stewart Electric Company.

Stewart began his booklet with a foreword:

> The great majority of the rare United States coins were made in buildings still standing at 37 and 39 North Seventh Street in Philadelphia, or, to be more exact, in the coinage building in the rear of these numbers. Until recently these buildings were unmarked, and the people of the neighborhood in a great many instances were unaware of the fact that for a period of forty (40) years all of the United States coins were made so near at hand. Those who daily walked past the buildings had nothing to direct their attention to them, and it is safe to say that not 500 persons in Philadelphia could point out what at one time was one of the most important buildings in the United States, as well as the first erected under authority of Congress for Federal purposes.[2]

Stewart obviously believed that Philadelphians had forgotten, in the space of nearly three generations, the important place that the old Mint had once held in American commercial life. The passage also demonstrates that his research convinced him that the Middle Building was the coinage factory, and that the three Mint buildings were the first constructed by the federal government. As we have seen, he was wrong on both counts.

Stewart then revealed, at the end of the foreword, his purpose in writing *Ye Olde Mint*:

> The author purchased the buildings and feels that it is his duty to do what he can to describe them before they are demolished, and also at the same time to publish such data in his possession as may prove interesting or valuable to the limited few who collect rare coins or are in any way interested in what was an exceedingly important department of our early national life.[3]

Visions of wrecking crews were already dancing in Stewart's head by 1909, but so were notions of preservation through publication. The booklet *Ye Olde Mint* was Stewart's first attempt to do just that. After the four-page foreword, the balance of the booklet is presented as a single essay, unencumbered by chapters or subheadings. Stewart begins with a couple of pages on the connections between George Washington and the first Mint, then spends three pages describing the three buildings and copper coins and planchets discovered when the Rear Building came down. A painstaking four and a half pages are devoted to tracing the people who had owned the original three lots of the first Mint, beginning with William Penn himself, and concluding with Frederick Hailer, the last private owner (although Stewart also spells his name as "Wailer").[4] The rest of the booklet is devoted to

an idiosyncratic history of the Mint and its operations, jumping back and forth in time and place, but mainly focusing on its first decade, 1792 through 1802. The booklet closes with a transcription of a letter from George Washington to Thomas Jefferson, June 9, 1792, regarding the purchase of the first Mint lots.

A professional historian Stewart was not, but his enthusiasm for research is everywhere apparent. His reconstruction of the Mint property's ownership chain was meticulous, if not always accurate in every detail. Besides transcribing "Hailer" as "Wailer," he managed to render the surname of Jean-Pierre Droz, a Swiss medalist, as "Drotz." Nor were his historical judgments always sound. For example, Stewart states, "From a national viewpoint the old Mint buildings are the most historical in the United States, because they were the first to be erected by the authority of the Federal Government for public use."[5] As we have seen, the Mint structures were not the first to be erected by the United States government, and even if they had enjoyed that distinction, it does not necessarily follow that they would be the "most historical."

More accurate, and thus more valuable, than the text are the six full-page photographs that accompany it. The frontispiece is the classic view of the Front Building, with "1792 Ye Olde Mint" painted on the façade, and an open touring car parked in front. The second photo depicts the façade of the Middle Building, "undoubtedly the first brick building erected by act of Congress for public use," according to its caption.[6] The third illustration zeros in on the "vault within a vault" found in the basement of the Middle Building, while the fourth shows a general view of half of that basement. The fifth illustration offers a scrap of scissel (a piece of waste copper strip from which a half cent planchet had been punched), along with eight planchets, all found either when the Rear Building was razed, or during excavations for the four-story warehouse that replaced it. Two of these planchets were for the legendary silver center cent (or silver "centre" cent, as Stewart has it).[7] The final photo depicts six coins found in the excavation made for the basement of the four-story warehouse. Four are large cents, including those dated 1826, 1832, and 1834; two are half cents, one dated 1825; while the other, the date of which is effaced, is a Draped Bust type, minted from 1800 to 1808. Stewart, in 1922, indicated that the photographic negatives were retained by the Newell Studio in Philadelphia.[8]

Ye Olde Mint did indeed offer a brief description of the first U.S. Mint, but more significantly, it provided the most thoroughly-researched look at the first Mint published up to that time. Stewart did all he could to disseminate his booklet widely, for it was distributed "Compliments of Frank H. Stewart Electric Company" to all who displayed interest.[9] He laid into all copies a small circular advertising his business, most of which were discarded by the new owners. The copy in the collection of the Historical Society of Pennsylvania retains

Front cover of Frank H. Stewart's
Ye Olde Mint, 1909.

Excavation coins, photographic
plate from Frank H. Stewart
Collection, Rowan University.

this rare item, which notes the availability of the latest Stewart Electric Company catalog, by this time a 700-page hardcover behemoth offering thousands of items.

Stewart's distribution of *Ye Olde Mint* began towards the end of 1909, for in early December of that year he began receiving letters of acknowledgement from historical societies, libraries, and industrial concerns.[10] Stewart also distributed the booklet to the numismatic community, where it was immediately well received. Farran Zerbe, the president of the American Numismatic Association, wrote to Stewart on December 10, 1909, saying, "I have already heard many approving remarks regarding the enterprise shown by you in your late publication."[11] Zerbe requested additional copies. Next in line was the keeper of the Mint Cabinet. On January 6, 1910, curator T.L. Comparette wrote to acknowledge a recent tour of the first Mint property, and included a list of the numismatic elite who might also appreciate copies.[12] Many celebrated collectors of the era, Brand, Woodin, Clapp, Granberg, and others, found their way onto Comparette's list, and all presumably received copies of *Ye Olde Mint*.

Stewart's pamphlet was a success in promoting the Stewart Electric Company, but in one crucial respect Stewart's *Ye Olde Mint* was a disappointment, for it failed to inspire any of its readers to take action to preserve the remaining pair of old Mint structures. And while it might be unfair to lay blame upon the coin collectors of the time, one must acknowledge at least complicity—for the numismatic community was well informed, but failed to act. Thus, less than two years after the booklet's publication, the demolition began on North Seventh Street, and soon after, Stewart's new "Old Mint Building" would rise on the spot. Interestingly, this is an outcome that Stewart accurately forecasted:

> The first United States mint buildings are indeed historical in more ways than one, and while a number of suggestions have been made for their preservation it is highly probable they will eventually be located by the means of a bronze tablet on the front of the steel and concrete structure in contemplation for the use of the Frank H. Stewart Electric Company, who now occupy the buildings adjoining them on the south and east. The retention of the buildings on the present site is prohibited on account of the great value of the land and its location in the heart of the business section, and their removal by private enterprise to another site unlikely because of the great expense that such removal would entail.[13]

After these forebodings were fulfilled, in 1913, Stewart made his next excursion into the realm of writing, when he authored and published *Our New Home and Old Times*. In 1911, after making one last fruitless attempt to save them, Stewart demolished the old Mint edifices, and replaced them with a six-story structure of steel, concrete, and brick. He attached this new building to the four-story

warehouse already standing on number 631 Filbert Street (the lot directly to the east and south of numbers 37 and 39 North Seventh), thus recreating the original configuration of the first Mint (116 feet deep by 37 feet wide), on these three L-shaped lots.[14]

Just prior to the publication of the booklet, he prepared a six-page circular entitled *Our New Home* that provided a brief overview of the new building and the ongoing enterprise. At the time of this writing the exterior construction of the new building was complete, but the interior was not quite ready for business. The circular was probably printed in large quantities and delivered along with sales material, or freely distributed to more casual contacts. The full treatment, *Our New Home and Old Times*, was a greatly expanded version that included a substantial photographic record of the newly christened "Old Mint Building."

Our New Home and Old Times is octavo in size, six by nine inches, with tan card covers and a stapled binding. A few copies were bound in green-grey cloth; one remains in the collection of the Gloucester County (New Jersey) Historical Society while another appeared in Craig Whitford's sale of Mint memorabilia in October 1995. The cover bears some similarity to that of *Ye Olde Mint*, for its central vignette is also an art nouveau motif, although instead of a flowering plant, it appears to be a leaf (or possibly a butterfly) mounted on a stanchion. Both the title and the motif are enclosed by triple-ruled lines, with boxes at all four corners. The back cover contains the logo that Stewart adopted to brand his highest-quality line of electrical products, consisting of the words "OLD MINT" within a double-ruled line in the shape of a sideways coffin, with "STEWART'S" above and "GOLD STANDARD" below. The booklet contains 48 pages and 22 black-and-white photographs reproduced in half tone, depicting the interiors of Stewart's new building, along with some items of numismatic import.

Unlike *Ye Olde Mint*, the subject matter of which was exclusively numismatic, *Our New Home* is mainly about the Old Mint Building and the electric supply business, with an occasional dollop of numismatic information tossed in. Stewart took great pride in the structure he had erected on the old Mint's site: "Our new building, known as the 'Old Mint Building,' is probably the first new building to be called an old building in the history of architecture."[15] He waxes eloquent about the amenities of the Old Mint Building—its elevators, tramways, and fire tower—and expresses his satisfaction that if all of its steel bins were laid end to end, they would stretch for more than half a mile in a straight line.[16] Some 19 of the 22 photographs in the booklet focus on the Old Mint Building's interiors (13); exterior (four); and its cornerstone-laying ceremony (two).

In typical Stewart fashion, the topics meander. A nearly three-page essay on electric wiring is succeeded by sections on the Stewart Electric Company's catalog, its building by authority of congress, during the first administration of our first president the immortal George Washington. Certain rare coins made in the old buildings we tore down have recently sold at auction at prices ranging from one hundred to thirty-six hundred dollars each. Individual examples of each of the gold, silver and copper coins made in the first U. S. Mint in perfect condition would bring more at auction than it cost to erect our new building, and that is no small sum. We have a modest collection sufficiently large enough to enthuse those interested in old and rare coins, some of which were found on the site of the old mint building.

We invite you to investigate our new building, stock and equipments. Any one of our officers or employees will take great pleasure in showing you the many new ideas which will be used in our electrical supply house for the first time. Our business was established in February, 1894, and we are making a collection of electrical antiquities which were in use at the time we started in business over eighteen years ago, to show you, if you are interested in the great strides made in electrical appliances.

FRANK H. STEWART ELECTRIC CO.

STEWART'S
OLD MINT
GOLD STANDARD

OUR NEW HOME

OLD MINT BUILDING
37 & 39 N. 7th St., Philadelphia

OLD MINT BUILDING

THE illustration on this folder is a photographic reproduction of our new home in which shelving and other necessary equipment is now being placed. The building is L shaped and occupies three city lots, Nos. 37 and 39 North Seventh street and 631 Filbert street, and is next door to our old location 35 North Seventh street.

It has a freight elevator on Filbert street, a fire tower on an alley in the rear of the building, and a passenger elevator on Seventh street, also a dumb elevator and a chute, three stairways and tramways for handling heavy materials.

It is built of steel, concrete and brick, and is a fire-proof building of the best type. Over one thousand steel bins are being placed in the third and fourth floors alone. These bins are three feet wide, and thirty-two inches deep, and eighteen inches high, and adjustable. These if placed end to end would reach over half a mile in a straight line. The fifth and sixth floors will be used for goods in original cases, the first floor as a store and shipping room, and the basement which is eleven feet in depth will be used for iron conduits and heavy materials such as porcelain, glass, etc. The entire second floor will be used for office purposes.

The architectural appearance of the front of the building easily places it among Philadelphia's most artistic and pleasing modern buildings. It is of glazed tile and tapestry brick. Mr. E. F. Bertolett was its architect, and to him is due great credit as a conscientious and careful supervisor. It was erected by E. F. Dotts & Co., who also are entitled to great credit in carefully following the well thought out plans of Mr. Bertolett.

Strength, utility and beauty, without extravagance have been combined in the erection of this building and installation of its equipment. The electrical materials were made by manufacturers who are noted for the superior quality of their products and taken by the electrical contractor right from our own stock.

The steam heat is furnished by two large heaters which can be used together or separately. The plans were made to take care of a sprinkler system which will be put in later after our stock placing arrangements are completed.

The historical feature of the site is perpetuated by bronze tablets and the name of the building.

In the demolition of the old buildings many interesting finds were made and these will be fully described in a history of the property now about to be published.

The weight capacity of the building is sufficient to load a freight train a mile long thirty thousand pounds to the car.

The building was erected by the president of our Company for the sole use of our business and is a physical illustration of the business principles and policies formed and followed in the development of our business. Unswerving fidelity to those characteristics which have enabled us to occupy what is said by many who have a knowledge of the facts to be the best building in America, devoted exclusively to an electrical supply business will be maintained.

For a great many years we have been more or less hampered by not having sufficient room to satisfactorily handle our congested stocks located in the old buildings and neighboring warehouses, and our customers and friends now have a right to expect even better stocks and service than we have been able to offer and give them in the past.

We were the first, and consequently now the oldest to do an exclusively electrical supply business in the City of Philadelphia, and it is a curious coincidence that we should occupy the site of the first U. S. Mint, as well as the first property purchased for the erection of first public

Our New Home circular, written just before the Old Mint Building opened for business.

Stewart's *Our New Home and Old Times,* a 1913 pamphlet.

The numismatic content of *Our New Home*, though relatively slight, still has some items of note. It begins with the frontispiece, which features the bronze tablet that Stewart had been contemplating when he wrote *Ye Olde Mint* in 1909. Affixed to the front façade of the Old Mint Building, the tablet read: "ON THIS SITE WAS ERECTED THE FIRST U.S. MINT A.D. 1792 THE FIRST PUBLIC BUILDING AUTHORIZED BY CONGRESS. COINAGE CONTINUED HERE 40 YEARS. BUILDING RAZED A.D. 1911."[19]

There are photographs of two chairs and one bench that were constructed of timbers salvaged from the old Mint, with the note that the bench was a Christmas gift to Frank H. Stewart in 1911, the year that the last of the old Mint edifices were demolished.[20] He reports that all three were made of oak joists from the Middle Building, which were so hard that the cabinet maker had to be paid extra for working with them, and that all were part of his office furnishings. The bench today resides in the collection of the Gloucester County Historical Society; the whereabouts of the chairs are unknown. These were not the only wooden relics, for about two dozen gavels and the same number of paperweights, made of the same oak joists, were crafted by James Barton of Camden, New Jersey, and distributed at the cornerstone-laying ceremony to participants and special guests.[21] There is also a picture of the hand-made lockset that came off the Front Building, although it is not described in the text.[22]

The deed of sale of the first Mint from the United States to Michael Kates is pictured in a full-page format, along with an explanation that it was found in an old safe by descendent Louis Kates; Stewart's memorable judgment was that "It is a piece of parchment and the penmanship is above reproach."[23] He also used this section to make a declaration of future literary intentions:

In the past two years data has [sic] been collected by us pertaining to the original mint property, which when added to the finds made when the buildings were demolished, will make a book of considerable historical interest. Those fortunate enough to possess a copy of Ye Olde Mint booklet have some idea of what may be expected in the final write-up of information in our possession, a great deal of which has never been published. If you want a copy, send in your request now.[24]

As it happened, Stewart was hardly the first would-be author who was overly optimistic about his publication date, for *History of the First United States Mint* did not appear until 1924. This does demonstrate, however, that he was planning to write the book very soon after the old Mint structures came down.

pictorial calendars, and its museum of old electrical devices (current whereabouts unknown). Stewart himself signed a four-page disquisition on his reminiscences of the electrical supply business. The Master of the Mint closed his booklet with no less than six pages of "Odds and Ends" wherein it is possible to learn, should one be so inclined, that "J.W. Parker had a lot of fun with a windowful of feathers blown around by a sturdy C&C Electric Fan."[17] This section also contained Stewart's bold, if inaccurate prediction that "Solar heat and water power will supply all the electrical energy 100 years hence. There is no use of worrying about coal."[18]

Not strictly numismatic, but somewhat numismatically inspired, were the medallions and sculptural elements on the façade of the Old Mint Building. There were six medallions, three set in the space between the third and fourth floors, and three set in the space between the fourth and fifth floors. The two pictured in *Our New Home* evoke coins without actually copying them, with one similar, but not identical, to an Indian Head cent

obverse, and another, with a wreath surrounded by 13 stars, bringing to mind (at least in terms of the wreath) the Indian Head cent Laurel Wreath reverse of 1859.[25]

In the space between the first and second floors were small alcoves that held a carved eagle, perched on a shield, which in turn rested on bundled foliage. Stewart clearly modeled these eagles on Peter, the famed mascot of the Mint, for the photo's caption states that "the Mint eagle

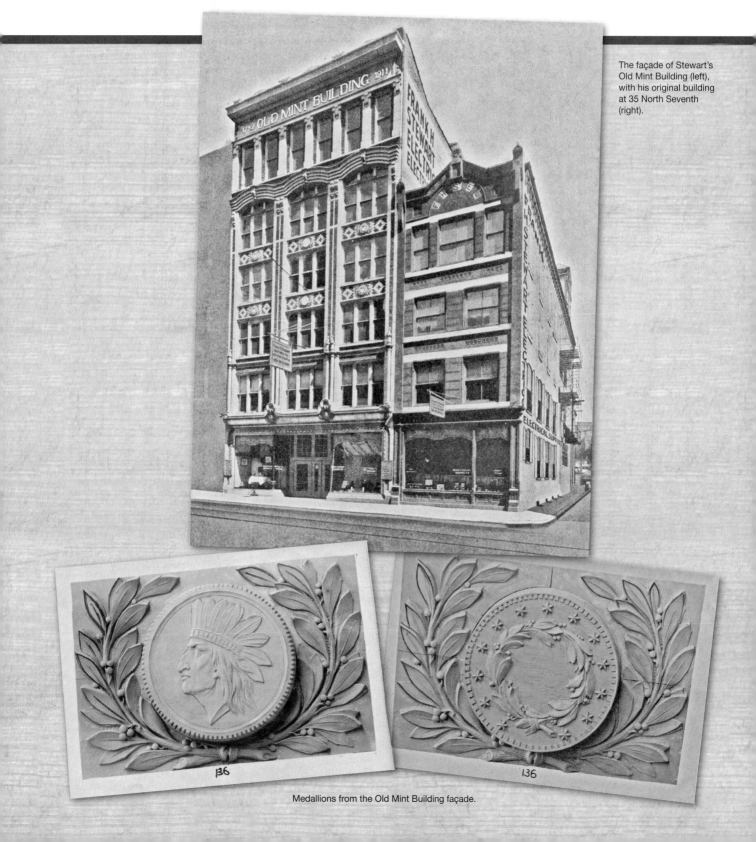

The façade of Stewart's Old Mint Building (left), with his original building at 35 North Seventh (right).

Medallions from the Old Mint Building façade.

Decorative eagle, from the façade of the Old Mint Building.

Eagle guarding the visitor's entrance to the current U.S. Mint, 2009.

was a noted bird."[26] Like the Old Mint Building, today's fourth U.S. Mint is similarly guarded by eagles at the entrance.

Our New Home seems to have been primarily distributed within the electrical trade, as part advertising and part history. Although several snippets are of interest to coin collectors, the majority of the content promotes the history, capability, and of course the new facility of the Stewart Electric Company. For this reason the pamphlet is little known today among numismatists. Stewart began receiving letters of acknowledgement for *Our New Home* in May 1913.[27]

Ye Olde Mint and *Our New Home* occupy a distinctive niche in numismatic literature, that of the "rehearsal" publication. Both were written as Frank H. Stewart was still in the business of learning about the old Mint: its people, its processes, its history. They are therefore inherently incomplete and occasionally inaccurate, but by the same token, they are fresh and bursting with the excitement of new discoveries. Much of what they contain is incorporated in his 1924 *History of the First United States Mint*, but a few important textual details and pictures of the Old Mint Building can be found only in these two booklets. Stewart himself certainly thought highly of his inaugural efforts, for he placed a copy of *Ye Olde Mint* in the cornerstone of the Old Mint Building, and had *Our New Home* been published then, no doubt it would have been included, as well.[28] In his address on that occasion, Stewart said, "This building represents my life's work. It is built of enduring steel and concrete. It is the best that I can do."[29] Surely he felt very much the same way about *Ye Olde Mint*, *Our New Home*, and later, *History of the First United States Mint*. They also represent his enduring life's work—the best that he could do—and for that, we should all be grateful.

THE HISTORY OF STEWART'S *HISTORY OF THE FIRST UNITED STATES MINT*

Following Stewart's "rehearsal" publications, the author continued to collect data into the 1920s, and ultimately faced the conundrum of every archival researcher: when to publish? If one seeks to be as thorough as possible, there will always be new sources to investigate and the work will never reach closure. Conversely, the need to share one's work with the public is compelling, and so a balance must be reached, deadlines must be accepted, and books produced. Leonardo da Vinci's observation that "Art is never finished, only abandoned" likely resonated with Stewart. There too, is the frustration of an unfinished project, which one senses in Stewart's own words regarding *History of the First United States Mint*:

I should like to make it more comprehensive in its scope but think it is better to print it as it is than run a probable risk of its never being put in type. . . . Month by month and year by year fragment by fragment data was [sic] found but the greatest work of all has been to compile it in its present form. It has all been rewritten and rearranged at least three times and probably should be gone over again but it is far better to print it as it is than to run the risk of its never being printed at all. The very nature of the whole thing is so variable[?] that it is impossible to connect it together except by an undue use of paper and ink. Nearly all the halftones were made over ten years ago.[30]

Stewart had been at it since 1907, and further reflected on the journey that was *History*:

When I purchased the property formerly occupied by the first Mint of the United States in Nineteen Hundred and Seven I tried to find something about its history and the effort resulted in a hunt that has lasted over seventeen years. . . . At the outstart my interest was in the old Mint buildings only but gradually this thought was overwhelmed by a desire to learn something about its people and its operations. . . . During all the years that have passed I have searched as my time permitted in every every [sic] possible way for information about the proposition. I have bought manuscript papers at auction, made two trips to Washington to search Robert Morris's diary, read old newspapers, searched old account books and the Mint records, interviewed the descendants of those first connected with the Mint and if anything has escaped me it has been simply because I had no clue.[31]

As time passed, information became harder to come by, as demonstrated by a 1921 letter from Stewart to Henry William De Saussure, a descendant of the shortly tenured second director of the Mint:

If possible I should like to have a copy of any data that you may have concerning your ancestor in connection with the Mint. . . . I understand you have a letter from Washington to him and that the same probably refers to the Mint. . . . We have no doubt your ancestor was a very distinguished gentleman, and would like to have something authentic that will do him full credit in my contemplated history of the First United States Mint.[32]

De Saussure apparently responded, but for all of Stewart's work in tracking down the descendant and initiating a correspondence, the result was a mere

sentence in the final work.[33] Stewart got a bit luckier with a batch of old Mint reports, "70 pieces, being reports from 1796 to 1828" that appeared in a single auction lot of the American Art Association in 1921. Whether Stewart was the successful bidder is unrecorded, although as many of these survive in the Stewart papers it seems that he was.[34]

Compounding Stewart's delay is that he seems to have been more attracted to catching fish than catching coins at this stage of his life. Indeed, of the surviving photographs of Stewart, he is typically found smiling only when accompanied by fish. In 1922, he rued the demise of the *American Angler*:

Stewart with catch, probably taken in Florida or California.

It is with a great deal of regret that I learn the AMER-ICAN ANGLER has ceased to exist. It was a mighty fine magazine and appealed to me more than any other because it was devoted to the one thing in which I am most interested, namely, fishing. I feel that fisherman have lost their most valuable friend in the magazine world and my regret is that such is the case.[35]

In 1921, Stewart considered serial publication of his work in *The Numismatist*. His original query is now missing, but on May 24th, editor Frank G. Duffield responded:

In reply to your letter of the 21st inst., I would say that I believe your proposed articles on the first U.S. Mint for publication in The Numismatist would be of general interest, and we will be glad to publish them from month to month. I am supposing that while they are largely historical, there is more or less numismatics in them. I would suggest that when the first use appears it be accompanied with an introduction by yourself, explaining that they will be continued from month to month, as well as stating their scope.[36]

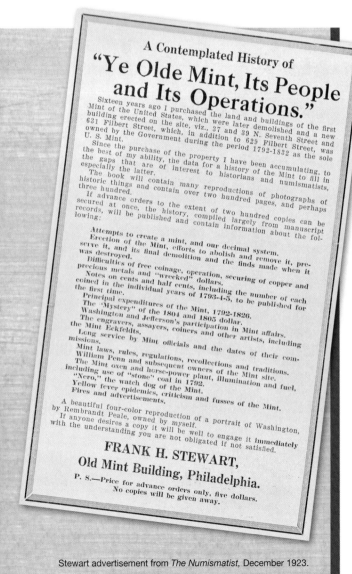

Stewart advertisement from *The Numismatist*, December 1923.

For whatever reason, Stewart abandoned the idea, and in an attempt to gauge public interest in a full-length volume, took a full-page advertisement in the December 1923 issue of *The Numismatist*, announcing "a contemplated history of 'Ye Olde Mint, Its People and Its Operations.'"[37] Stewart later changed the title in favor of the more formal *History of the First United States Mint: Its People and Its Operations*. In doing so, Stewart eschewed the sentimentality of "Ye Olde Mint," preferring the cloak of historical veracity over the romantic marketing he had draped upon the façade of the first Mint. Stewart's prospectus promised a book "compiled largely from manuscript records," and the choice of the word "compiled" suggests that even Stewart saw himself as a collector of historical facts more than a historian, perhaps recognizing his own shortcomings in contextualizing the mass of raw data that he had carefully accumulated over the years. Stewart solicited advance orders at five dollars, the equivalent of about 60 today. "No copies will be given away," he added.

Stewart's marketing campaign was not as successful as he anticipated, and a somewhat dejected tone marked his letter of December 10, 1923, to Frank G. Duffield. Stewart once again raised the idea of serial publication:

Judging from the fact that I only received one reply to my advertisement in the Numismatist and the further fact that you gave it an editorial, for which I thank you, I feel that it would be a waste of money to get out the contemplated history.

Some time when you are in Philadelphia I should like to show you the copy for the book, and also to ask at this time whether you think it would be worth while to run it as a serial in your magazine and make some arrangement with the printer whereby I could have, say, One Hundred [sic] copies printed and bound in a book. I already have practically all of the necessary half tone engravings for illustration purpose.

I feel that there would be a certain demand from reference libraries, and even though the coin collectors and dealers would have no interest in it, I should like to see the most prominent of the libraries have a copy of the book.[38]

Duffield apparently did not respond to Stewart's idea immediately, for only eight days later Stewart followed up:

Up to date I have received orders for seven of the Old Mint Histories which would hardly warrant the idea that it will be very much in demand by collectors. It has occurred to me that possibly it might be divided into chapters and run 30 to 40 pages at a time in the Numismatist and that arrangement could be made with the printer so that eventually the entire number of pamphlets could be bound together to the extent of a hundred or more copies so as to be placed in reference libraries. You may think this matter over at your leisure and let me know the result of your opinion.[39]

On the very same day, Stewart seemed to close the matter entirely, writing to G.M. Emery of Washington, D.C., that "I have decided that the demand for the history of the Old Mint would not be sufficient for me to go ahead with the publication of the book as contemplated."[40] Stewart returned pre-orders, as he wrote to Waldo C. Moore on December 12, 1923, that "I have received but few replies to the advertisement." Stewart sent back Moore's check for five dollars.[41] His letter to William Festus Morgan of New York on the same day was even more despondent:

> The lack of additional orders for copies of the history of The Old Mint has been such as to make me think it would be useless to waste a lot of money on its printing. It would probably cost me $20.00 for each copy sold on top of a few thousand dollars which has already been spent on it. It would be well, therefore, for you not to expect your order to be filled.[42]

Duffield seems not to have been receptive to the idea of serial publication; certainly at least the record is silent on the matter. The publication of the mammoth article on Lincolniana in the February 1924 issue of *The Numismatist* may have deterred the editor from accepting a second work of similarly gargantuan scope. Conversely, Duffield may have simply considered Stewart unreliable after the 1921 exchange.

Stewart made inquires with his own printer, R.R. Donnelley & Sons Company, of Chicago, who printed thousands of Stewart's mammoth electrical catalogs. Surely a concern with which Stewart did much business might be interested. Alas, even Donnelley begged off, indicating that they were merely contract printers and not publishers.[43] Stewart also tried The MacMillan Company in New York, which presumably passed on the project.[44]

The next mention of *History* comes in the May 1924 issue of *The Numismatist*, in which Frank H. Stewart replied to the query of Henry Russell Drowne, published in the April issue, relating to the former practice of denominating the dollar into 90 parts, rather than 100.[45] Stewart indicated that Drowne's query "may probably be satisfactorily answered by the following extracts from my manuscript 'History of the First U.S. Mint, Its People and Its Operations.'" Thus, by this time Stewart had settled upon the final title, and seems to have purposed to get the book published once and for all.

Stewart's preliminary copies of *History* are today preserved in the Stewart Collection at Rowan University. The earliest copy is contained within four similar binders, approximately 12 by 9-1/2 inches, all with removable pages.[46] The leaves contain a combination of longhand and typed script, with handwritten edits throughout. From here Stewart advanced to bound copies. The first of these is 11-3/8 by 8-5/8 inches and bound in olive cloth.[47] The individual leaves exhibit the "Old Mint" logo watermark used on stationery of the Frank H. Stewart Electric

Frank G. Duffield, 1908, from an ANA convention photograph.

Company, yet bear the imprint of the Gloucester County Historical Society—a veritable mélange of Stewart's professional and personal life. On the leaves, rectos only, are pasted various typewritten sections, with notes in Stewart's hand interspersed here and there. The table of contents is similar to the final version, with some reordering, and the preface found in the ultimate work is not present here. No illustrations are included. A second bound copy, typewritten with light edits in hand, is sized 11-3/8 by 8-7/8 inches, rectos only, in red cloth with leather fore corners. This volume is part of the "Writings of Frank H. Stewart" series, no. 6 in a group of identically bound volumes probably made at Stewart's direction. Like the previous bound copy, no illustrations are present.

Sometime in 1924, Stewart initiated the typesetting with Sinnockson, Chew & Sons, of Camden, New Jersey. A letter from Chew to Stewart dated July 21st indicates that the author and publisher were in the process of placing images within the text.[48] Of course, as all researchers know, the surest way to generate disruptive information is to initiate the irrevocable act of printing. Stewart was no exception, and only encouraged the process by continuing to perform research. His persistence was rewarded in October 1924 with perhaps his most important documentary finding, in Washington, D.C., at the Department of State archives. He uncovered correspondence from Jefferson to Washington, a letter of transmittal for two Voigt silver center cents which, when taken in conjunction with the Voigt account book entry on the same subject, constructs a solid timeline surrounding the manufacture of these pieces. That Stewart had uncovered two silver center cent planchets in the 1907 demolition of the Rear Building only sweetened the pot. But by now it was too late to rework the new information into the main text, so Stewart elected to document Jefferson's letter in an appendix.[49]

After the appendix was prepared on October 28th, the first typeset copy of *History* was delivered to Stewart in December 1924, and is inscribed by Stewart:

This interleaved book was bound in advance of the delivery of the regularly bound copies of the book. It was delivered to me the latter part of December 1924 by Wm. H. Chew on the steam train from Camden to Salem where he lives. Frank H. Stewart Woodbury NJ 1/20/1925.[50]

Stewart's residence was within walking distance of the Woodbury train station, conveniently located on the route from Camden to Salem. Chew, the printer, seems to have visited Stewart's Cooper Street manse personally, bearing the fruit of Stewart's 17 years of labor. The copy is bound in gray cloth, and is slightly oversized, 9-5/8 by 6-5/8 inches, as compared to the 9-by-6-inch regular edition. Stewart made minimal handwritten notations on the interleaved pages. A second interleaved copy, bound identically to the regular edition and bearing notes in Stewart's hand, also exists in the Stewart Collection.[51] Given Stewart's inscription on the first interleaved copy, it is clear that despite the 1924 publication date on the imprint, *History* was not publicly available until early 1925. Further, although Stewart made notes on the interleaved pages, none of these were absorbed in the final edition, for which the typesetting remained identical. One senses that Stewart simply wanted to be done with the project. Still, Stewart used these interleaved copies to save information of interest. For example, in the second interleaved copy, he notes, "Lafayette visited the Mint in Oct. 1825 when he was in Philadelphia. Oct. 1, 1946."

History seems to have been exclusively distributed by William J. Campbell, a "bookseller and publisher" located at 223 South Sydenham Street in downtown Philadelphia. Stewart had an existing relationship with Campbell, who bought and sold books on his account.[52] An undated four-page sales circular, echoing much of the copy from the December 1923 *Numismatist* advertisement, indicates that *History* was "for sale only by William J. Campbell."[53] The volume was priced at five dollars, "less than the actual expense of collecting and printing the material," and the edition was limited to 500 copies. The table of contents given in the circular matches perfectly the table of contents as stated in the book itself. By June 1925, Campbell was apparently advertising the work and had received offers to publish reviews in exchange for free copies.[54]

Campbell's circular apparently misled some into believing that Campbell was the publisher in addition to the distributor, for in 1926, author Jesse P. Watson, in *The Bureau of the Mint: Its History, Activities and Organization*, cited a second edition of Stewart's *History*, said to have been published by Campbell in 1925.[55] This supposed second edition is today unknown, while the imprint of the first edition clearly indicates "Privately Printed 1924." The Campbell circular, carefully read, is suggestive of the idea that Campbell was in fact the publisher; perhaps a case of "implication by omission," an attempt to impart additional legitimacy to a book that was effectively self-published, while not deliberately asserting a mistruth. Marketing it was called, and Stewart was good at it.

This subterfuge proved quite successful. For example, Michael A. Powills, librarian of the Chicago Coin Club and a pioneering numismatic bookseller, wrote to Campbell on June 29, 1931, requesting a copy of *History of the First United States Mint*, adding that he believed "Mr Frank H. Steward" to be deceased. Respoindng on July 3, on behalf of the Campbell firm, John J. Campbell informed Powills that he had referred the inquiry to Mr. Stewart, "who is still very much alive."[56]

The frontispiece of *History* is a color plate of a George Washington portrait by Rembrandt Peale, which was in Stewart's collection. Stan Henkels, the Philadelphia auctioneer, related to Stewart some of the history of the rendering:

> The former owner's father wanted an oil portrait of Washington, and he went to Rembrandt Peale to get one. Rembrandt Peale informed him that he had

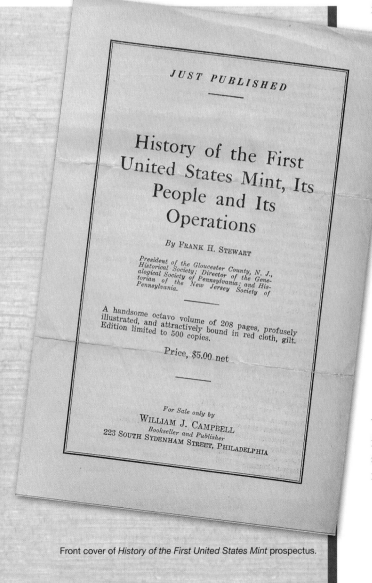

Front cover of *History of the First United States Mint* prospectus.

none finished, but he could paint him one in a couple of weeks. The gentleman wanted it right away, and Peale then told him that he had one of his studies of his famous port-hole portrait of Washington, which he could touch up and complete in a short time if that would suit him. The bargain was made.[57]

Some difference of opinion regarding the authenticity of Stewart's Peale arose. Henkels and Charles Henry Hart, director of the Pennsylvania Academy of the Fine Arts, had previously made an unsuccessful offer of $800 on the painting, thus attesting to their endorsement of the Rembrandt Peale origin.[58] Wilfred Jordon, curator at Congress Hall, thought it was a copy.[59] Jonce I. McGurk, New York art dealer, disagreed, writing to Stewart that:

> Yours is by Rembrandt Peale and is what is known as the Port hole portrait of which Baker says there are 75 [reference is made to William Spohn Baker's *The Engraved Portraits of Washington*]. The portrait is an ideal of what Rembrandt Peale thought Washington looked like when he was a boy. The first port hole portrait was painted in 1820 after many attempts for 20 years and was sold Congress.[60]

McGurk added that he was interested in purchasing the portrait. Thus, it seems that the art dealers desired Stewart's Peale while a single curator questioned the authenticity. The painting today remains in the Stewart Collection at Rowan University.

A rare variant of *History* is known, with a second portrait plate, depicting Frank Stewart. Charles Davis first brought this to the attention of the numismatic community in 1992:

> Meanwhile, at the recent Garden State Numismatic Association show in New Jersey, we were shown a copy of Frank Stewart's 1924 *History of the First United States Mint*. While appearing to be the usual red cloth edition, this copy contained a presentation inscription from the author noting that it was one of a few copies bound with an extra plate. The plate turned out to be a sepia toned portrait of the author bound in between the second and third signatures. We would be most interested to know if any of our readers have seen a similar copy.[61]

A similar copy[62] indeed exists in the Stewart Collection at Rowan University, and is marked in pencil, "rare," while another copy, inscribed by Stewart, is found in the Gloucester County (New Jersey) Historical Society. A note in Stewart's hand, located in the Stewart papers, indicates "25 copies to have an insert of my photograph."[63] Stewart's left profile pose in the portrait plate is typical, for:

> At the time when Frank took daily trips into Philadelphia on business, he always traveled by ferry. One day, the ferry gate accidentally fell on Frank and damaged his right eye. In all photographs taken after that time [sic; Stewart's right eye shows in at least one photograph], Frank Stewart was careful to position himself so that his right eye did not show.[64]

Stewart's accident occurred about 1903, for in that year he signed a release of The Philadelphia and Camden Ferry Company, in consideration of the sum of $800, "in consequence of being struck by sliding door while in the act of passing out of waiting room of The Philadelphia and Camden Ferry Company, at the foot of Market Street, Philadelphia."[65] Later, his passport described the condition as paralysis of the eyelid.

A tradition exists that many of the first printing of Stewart's *History* were destroyed. The first mention of this is in the September 1960 issue of *The Numismatist*.[66] "Although five hundred copies of this book were printed in 1924," the writer notes, "unverified reports say that three hundred were destroyed." The writer seems to have had contact with William H. Chew, of Sinnickson, Chew & Sons, the printers of Stewart's book; so it is possible that Chew, age 92 at the time, was the author's source. Besides having personally delivered the first copy of *History* to Stewart, Chew printed other Stewart works, such as *Notes on Old Gloucester County, New Jersey* (1917). Chew had an ongoing relationship with Stewart, and would have been in a position to know the history of *History*. The 1960 *Numismatist* article may have been the source used by Elvira Clain-Stefanelli, who in 1965 wrote that the work was "Rare since most of first edition destroyed in fire."[67] Note that the idea of "fire" had now been introduced. In 1968, Warren A. Lapp clarified further: "Only 500 copies were printed, and almost half of these were destroyed in a fire before the book was distributed."[68] Charles Davis, writing on Stewart's *History* in *American Numismatic Literature* (1992) noted that "The work has long been considered scarce as the single first printing was largely destroyed in a fire. . . . As we once owned a copy comprised of soiled (sooty?) untrimmed leaves in a library buckram, one might surmise that Stewart salvaged a number of copies and sold or donated them to institutions."[69]

An inquiry to the Gloucester County Historical Society, where the books may have been stored, indicated that no fires or floods were known to have occurred at that site.[70] Stewart also used other storage locations, for the inventory of his will notes 300 copies of his biography of Nicholas Collin located at a "storehouse" in Woodbury, New Jersey, along with other personal property.[71] Another possible location for a fire, of course, would have been the storerooms of the William J. Campbell booksellers in Philadelphia, the distributors of *History*.

No copies of *History of the First United States Mint* are mentioned in Stewart's probate papers, although Stewart seems to have had a supply of the books into the 1940s. One extant copy of the book is inscribed by Stewart and dated 1942, while another contains the inscription "presented by the author" with the date 1943.[72] If in fact

Stewart did have a supply of books in the 1940s, he was not especially liberal with them, for the New Jersey numismatic researcher Damon Douglas wrote to Stewart in March 1943, as follows:

> I heard again of your "History of the First U.S. Mint" which I had never had the pleasure of reading. The only copy I could locate was the one in the Newark Museum where I spent two very pleasant hours hastily reading it and making notes. It is a grand piece of work and deserves a place of honor on every American coin collectors [sic] book shelf. I would like very much to purchase a copy for myself and I am wondering if you can tell me where I might be able to get one.[73]

The flattering tone was not sufficient to procure a copy from Stewart, for two months later Douglas wrote again to Stewart:

> About a month ago I was lucky enough to pick up a copy of your fine "History of the First U.S. Mint" at

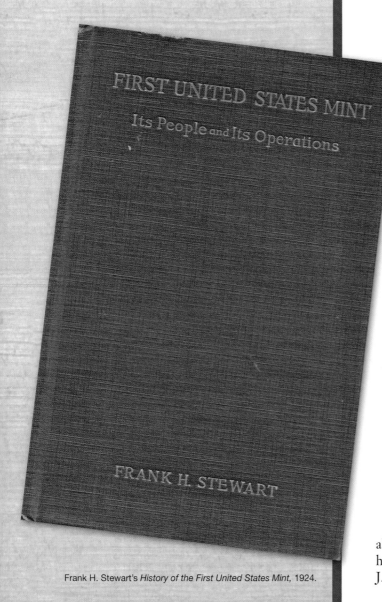

Frank H. Stewart's *History of the First United States Mint*, 1924.

an auction sale, (the first time I have ever seen it show up at a sale, and from your letter [Stewart's reply to the initial Douglas letter is not preserved] I can understand that the floating supply must be about nil). I've enjoyed reading it again and will always value it most highly.[74]

Other correspondents had more luck. Richard G. Helman of Kansas City, in 1944, purchased a copy from Stewart for $15, noting that "I appreciate your offer to get me a copy."[75] William H. Arthur of New Jersey also wrote to Stewart in 1944, "Received your letter of January 10th and was greatly pleased to hear that you might be able to obtain a copy of the book for me."[76] The situation is not entirely clear, but suggests that Stewart had a source of copies, perhaps not readily accessible. A likely possibility is that Stewart retained copies in storage. A 1951 letter from F.J. Schaefer of Haverford, Pennsylvania, to Dorothy Hammond, librarian at the Glassboro State Teachers College (today Rowan University) further clarified:

> Thank you for sending another copy of "First United States Mint" for which I enclose my check for $4.12. Also the Stewart calendar of the First mint building. Received the list of Colonial notes which I return with notation which refers to certain pages in the Standard Catalogue which is also enclosed. You will note that none of the notes you have are scarce.[77]

F.J. Schaefer had purchased the remainder of Stewart's coin collection from the estate. Schaefer's letter suggests that Glassboro was deaccessioning duplicates of the book from the Stewart collection, in addition to at least one Stewart calendar and certain colonial currency. Hammond was probably not aware that Stewart had been selling the same book for $15, as this price is deeply buried in his personal correspondence, and Hammond was more occupied with cataloging the New Jersey history content of the Stewart papers.

While Schaefer endeavored to procure desiderata from the Stewart Collection, a Glassboro resident claimed to possess something even better – the very first copy of the book. The assertion was made by John. J. Carey Sr. in 1962:

> It [Stewart's book] is a Collector's item and has never been sold. When Mr. Stewart published this book only 100 copies were issued and he gave them to his friends, and I was given the first copy. . . . The original source for the Stewart book was furnished by me when I was ordered to pack up all the old documents we had stored in the Phila. Mint and which I sent to the Smithsonian Institute in Washington, D.C.[78]

Carey's assertions, while most interesting, are questionable. Stewart clearly sold copies of his book, both through himself and through the Philadelphia bookseller William J. Campbell, whose circular advertised an "edition limited to 500 copies," disagreeing with Carey's figure of 100. As for Carey providing the source material for *History*, Stewart had been at the task of investigating the first Mint ever since the publication of *Ye Olde Mint* in 1909, while Carey more likely refers to the removal of the Mint Cabinet to the Smithsonian Institution in 1923.[79]

A better candidate for the first copy of *History* resides in the Hagley Library in Wilmington, Delaware. It is inscribed by Stewart as follows:

> This book has the distinction of being the first one to come from the bindery in the Rittenhouse building [at] N.W. cor. 7th + Arch Sts. Phila. on Jan. 17, 1925. David Rittenhouse lived there. I went after the book and took it to Trenton where I spoke before the Trenton Historical Society at their annual meeting.

This copy does not have the added portrait plate of Stewart, as found on the copies in the Stewart Collection at Rowan University and at the Gloucester County Historical Society. Nevertheless, with Stewart's signed inscription, this example has the best claim to being, literally, the "first" history of the U.S. Mint.

History remained in demand, for in 1965 Aaron Feldman (of "Buy the book before the coin" fame) offered a copy at $45, a substantial price at the time for a numismatic book.[80] A copy in Craig Whitford's October 6, 1995, sale of Mint Memorabilia, lot 413, fetched $125. Today, *History* remains quite desirable, with original copies selling for $200 and more in numismatic literature auctions. A 1974 reprint, by Quarterman Publications, has eased the demand somewhat, but even this volume is listed by online booksellers at $100 and up. The reprint is a faithful reproduction, although the plates, only halftones to begin with in the original edition, are somewhat degraded. The authors are aware of no sales of the original edition with the added portrait plate. Stewart's claim of 25 copies with the portrait plate is not accompanied by an invoice from the printer, and seems doubtful. The authors estimate the value of this version at $1,000.

Stewart was legitimately, if not hyperbolically, proud of *History*, and reflected later:

> Strange as it may seem the first building the United States Government erected under an appropriation of Congress had never received much attention at the hands of historians of Philadelphia. I consider the book a standard on the subject. It is in most of the leading libraries of the United States and added a great deal to the glory of the Frank H. Stewart Electric Company, who used the name "Old Mint" as its trade mark. Washington, Jefferson, Hamilton, Rittenhouse, Benjamin Rush, and other famous Americans participated in the establishment of the first mint and its operations.[81]

FRANK H. STEWART ON MARK NEWBY AND THE ST. PATRICK COINAGE

Frank H. Stewart's last numismatic work was hardly his best, but was undoubtedly his bravest. In 1947, battling heart disease, and with but a year to live, Stewart tackled one of American numismatics' abiding enigmas, Mark Newby's St. Patrick coinage. Stewart's attraction to the Newby coppers paralleled that of Joseph C. Mitchelson, who took a similar interest in his own local coinage of Connecticut. Mitchelson, as previously discussed, unsuccessfully negotiated with Stewart to obtain one of the silver center cent planchets discovered during the first Mint excavation. Mitchelson delivered a paper to the New York Numismatic Club in 1910, in which he explained his fascination with the Higley coppers of Connecticut:

> as I have lived within a short distance of the place where these pieces were made, off and on, for my whole life, the [copper] mines being within sight of my home, I have consented to give the members here all the information that has come my way. Being

The 1974 Quarterman Publications reprint of *History of the First United States Mint*.

interested in the subject probably more than anyone else on account of these coins having been made in my own town, I have made inquiries from all the old residents in that section of the country in the hope of being able to add something to the very little that is known regarding them. I have really devoted a lot of my time to the subject ever since I was a boy.

Mitchelson went on to relate further background on the subject of the Higleys.[82] Then, like Stewart, Mitchelson donated his collection to an institution, in this case the Connecticut State Library.[83]

Stewart no doubt felt a similar sentimental attachment to the Newby coppers of West Jersey, and, in spite of his age, his illness, and especially despite the well-nigh impenetrable mysteries surrounding his subject, Stewart did a credible job. True, he made some errors in his 1921 article in *The Numismatist*, "Mark Newby: The First Banker in New Jersey and his Patrick Halfpence," but that put him in the select company of Dr. Edward Maris and Sylvester Sage Crosby, among others.[84] In fact it is not too much to say that the St. Patrick coinage has baffled historians and fabulists alike since they were first struck more than three centuries ago. This coinage remains a puzzlement; so much so that, in 2006, the American Numismatic Society convened a Coinage of the Americas Conference exclusively to delve into its stubborn set of secrets.

There is general agreement that the St. Patrick coins first came to America through the hands of Mark Newby, a Quaker born in England around 1638, who emigrated from Ireland to New Jersey on November 18, 1681.[85] Once in "West Jersey" (today's southern portion of the state, bordering the Delaware River), Newby became involved in the finances and politics of his home township of Newton. He was elected to the Second Session of the General Free Assembly of West Jersey, which met in early May of 1682. During that session an act passed that tied him forever to the St. Patrick coinage:

> And for the more Convenient paymt. of small summes, bee it Enacted, by Authority aforesaid, that Marke Newbie's halfe pence called Patrick's halfe pence shall, from and after the said Eighteenth Instant, passe for halfe pence Current pay of this Province, provided hee the said Marke give sufficient security to the speaker of this house for the use of the Generall Assembly from tyme to tyme being.[86]

This act provided New Jersey with its first circulating coins, gave Britain's American provinces their first official copper coinage, and made Mark Newby, who was required to post 300 acres of land as security, one of the province's first bankers.[87]

Newby's story was similar to that of Joseph Steward, Frank H. Stewart's immigrant ancestor, seven generations back in the paternal line of Stewart's family tree.

Steward came from England to America in 1682 with a group of persecuted Quakers. Aged 14 at the time, Steward's previous involvement in the Quaker community is unknown, but clearly he was an active member following his arrival, and he married within the church. Like Newby he settled in West Jersey, acquiring property which remained in the family as late as 1907.[88] The Newby coinage thus resonated with Stewart not just because of geographical proximity, but because of cultural and religious reasons as well.

The aforementioned facts are known about the St. Patrick coinage. Just about everything else surrounding it is prone to dispute. To start with, the coinage comes in two planchet sizes, neither of which bears a denomination on its face. By tradition, the smaller coin is called a farthing, and the larger is denominated a halfpenny, although the "farthings" are many times heavier than other 17th-century Irish farthings. The basic obverse of both farthing and halfpenny depicts a kneeling king playing a harp, with the Latin motto FLOREAT REX (may the king prosper), divided by a crown. The reverse of both farthing and halfpenny depicts St. Patrick, although on the farthing he holds a metropolitan cross with the motto QVIESCAT PLEBS (may the people be at ease), while on the halfpenny the saint holds a crozier in his left hand and a trefoil in his right, surrounded by people, with the arms of the city of Dublin in a shield to his left, with the motto ECCE GREX (behold the flock). A distinctive anti-counterfeiting device was a brass splasher, usually applied over the crown on the obverse, thus making the St. Patrick coinage the first bimetallic coins to circulate in the British provinces. Both halfpennies and farthings boasted reeded edges to deter would-be clippers. The halfpence are many times scarcer than the farthings, but both come in a bewildering assortment of die varieties (nine for the halfpence, and about 250 for the farthings), many of the varieties known by only one or two survivors.[89] Why there should be such a profusion of varieties has never been satisfactorily explained.

Another important point in dispute is when the coins were struck. Numismatic writers William Nicholson, the bishop of Derry, in *The Irish Historical Library* (1724); Stephen Martin Leake, in *Nummis Britannici Historia: or, An Historical Account of English Money, from the Conquest to the Uniting of the Two Kingdoms by James I, and of Great Britain to the Present Time* (1726); James Simon, in *An Essay Towards an Historical Account of Irish Coins and of the Currency of Foreign Monies in Ireland* (1749); and Henry Noel Humphreys, in *The Coin Collector's Manual, Volume 1, or Guide to the Numismatic Student in the Formation of a Cabinet of Coins* (1853) all asserted a striking date of 1641 or 1642, thus associating the St. Patrick coinage with King Charles the First of England. Sylvester Sage Crosby, in *The Early Coins of America* (1875); Edward Maris, in *A Historic Sketch of the Coins of New Jersey, With a Plate* (1881); and Aquilla Smith, in "On the Copper Coins

1737 Higley threepence, a pet coin of J.C. Mitchelson.

J.C. Mitchelson, from the October 1911 issue of *The Numismatist.*

St. Patrick farthing.

St. Patrick farthing in silver.

St. Patrick halfpenny.

Commonly Called St. Patrick's" from *The Proceedings of the Kilkenny and South-Eastern Archaeological Society* (1855) cited sources including John Evelyn, in *Numismata: A Discourse of Medals Antient and Modern* (1697); and Walter Harris, in *The History and Antiquities of the City of Dublin* (1766) to claim that the coinage was struck during the 1670s and circulated on the Isle of Man, thus associating them with King Charles the Second.

Along with the question of when, there is the riddle of where. Given the Irish devices on the coins, most authorities have assumed that they were minted in Dublin, by the British Colonial authorities, or in Kilkenny, by the Catholic Confederation that existed from 1642 to 1648. Alternatively, Crosby quotes Dr. Robert Cane as concluding that the St. Patrick coinage was struck on the continent of Europe and brought to Ireland for the use of the Catholic Confederation.[90] More recently, Brian J. Danforth presented extensive research to buttress his findings that the person responsible for striking the coins was Pierre (Peter) Blondeau at the London Tower Mint, and that the coins were circulated from 1667 through 1669 by the Lord Lieutenant of Ireland, James Butler, Lord Ormond, as a non-regal issue, primarily in order to pay the army during a turbulent period in Irish history.[91] Danforth's conclusions have not been universally accepted; William Nipper, for example, notes that Sir Edward Ford, a knight and inventor, in 1664 made a proposal to the Fishery Company to coin farthings from Swedish copper. His plan was ultimately rejected, but as a consolation prize of sorts, he was granted permission to make farthings for Ireland. Ford went to the Emerald Isle, but died there before he could put his plan into operation. It is unclear if anyone in Ireland was able to pick up Ford's fallen banner and strike halfpence there.[92]

The uncertainty swirling around the St. Patrick coinage extends even to the identity of the king on the obverse of both the farthing and the halfpenny. Most of the numismatists who have studied these pieces see in the kneeling king playing the harp a clear reference to the Old Testament King David, who has been depicted in this pose in numerous images that date back more than a thousand years. Edward Maris, however, perceived a double identity: "In the figure representing King David kneeling, I recognize the undoubted features of Charles the First."[93] Walter Breen heartily concurred in his *Encyclopedia*, and added that this conclusively proved that the St. Patrick coinage was struck during the reign of that monarch.[94]

Any writer willing to step into this numismatic puzzle wins points for moxie, but Frank H. Stewart had a dual inducement for doing so. Not only had his ownership of the first Mint buildings provided him with an interest in early American numismatics, but his penchant for history, especially that of his home state of New Jersey, made Mark Newby and his St. Patrick coinage an irresistible subject. The first money in New Jersey handled by the province's first banker: here was a magnetic attraction.

Stewart approached it (along with other topics) in a pamphlet published by the Gloucester County Historical Society when he presided over that institution, "Notes on Old Gloucester County." The editor of *The Numismatist*, Frank G. Duffield, read Stewart's "Notes," and issued an invitation to write an article on Newby and his coinage. Stewart complied, and "Mark Newby and his Patrick halfpence" appeared in *The Numismatist* for February, 1921.

In this piece, Stewart stuck mainly to Mark Newby's biography, with only small excursions into the subject of the St. Patrick coinage. Stewart got the details pretty much right, and his most glaring error—the statement that Newby was a resident of London and lived in Ireland only a short time before emigrating to New Jersey—was due to the paucity of information available in 1921. It was not until David Gladfelter's research was published in 1974 that it became clear that Newby had lived in Dublin from 1663 to 1681.[95] Stewart ventured into less certain territory when he talked about the St. Patrick coinage, for as the title suggests, he covered only the halfpenny, utterly ignoring the farthing. His confusion deepened when he quoted from Francis Bazley Lee's 1902 *History of New Jersey as a Colony and as a State* that there are two common varieties of the coin, then went on to describe the farthing and the halfpenny as if they were merely two varieties of the same coin.[96]

For more than a quarter century after the publication of the article in *The Numismatist*, Stewart wrote no more of Newby and the St. Patrick coinage, but his interest in the man and the money never flagged. Finally, in 1947, Stewart, by now the president emeritus of the Gloucester County Historical Society, published a second article on the subject, "Mark Newby: The First Banker in New Jersey and His Patrick Halfpence." This article appeared in a pamphlet, published by the Society, that served as an anthology of Stewart's writings on miscellaneous topics of New Jersey history. The other articles, eight in all, range from "Letters of George Washington" to "Early Settlers in Newton Township," and include two pieces that focus on artifacts from the Stewart collection destined to find a home at Rowan University: Betsy Ross's marriage license and the "Safe Conduct Pass" issued by Virginia Indians to Captain John Smith in 1607.

Stewart's foreword to his Newby article begins with a confession of "a couple of errors" in his 1921 article in *The Numismatist*.[97] He took care to correct his earlier misunderstanding regarding "varieties" of the coins when he noted, "they were of two sizes, the smaller of which is now termed a farthing."[98] And Stewart knew whereof he spoke about the halfpenny and the farthing, for he disclosed: "The writer has two of the large and six of the small size in his possession, and there is another one he gave to the city of Philadelphia, with the rarities of the First United States Mint, 1792–1832."[99] Actually, Stewart's collection totaled 14 St. Patrick specimens, for "Since the preceding pages were set in type, an auction sale of six of Newby's coins by the Numismatic Gallery occurred at the Buffalo, N.Y. convention of the American Numismatic Association August 23–27, 1947. The writer was fortunate in securing all six of the specimens by mail bids."[100] Indeed, Abe Kosoff and Abner Kreisberg, doing business as the Numismatic Gallery, offered six examples of St. Patrick coinage from the Prann collection in their *ANA 1947 Convention Auction Sale*, as lots 921 "halfpenny"; 922 "halfpenny"; 923 "farthing"; 924 "farthing"; 925 "farthing"; and 926 "farthing in silver." Stewart's successful bids were: 921—$13; 922—$17.50; 923—$12; 924—$8.50; 925—$5; and 926—$26.[101] The Master of the Mint thus swept the field on these six coins with bids that totaled $82.

Stewart's first-hand acquaintance with the coins allowed him to describe them minutely, if somewhat colorfully. For example, after discussing the assorted birds, snakes and turtles found on various specimens, Stewart saved time and printer's ink by saying that the reverse of one of his farthings "shows the usual 'varments'."[102] He was unaware, however, of the use of the brass splasher as an anti-counterfeiting device, for in describing another of his farthings, he wrote that "some previous owner has tested the king's head with a drop of acid which has left a brassy appearance."[103] In general, Stewart's descriptions are closely observed, allowing the specialist to identify the varieties he held in his collection. The half-tone illustrations published in his pamphlet, however, are not of his coins, but rather appeared "by the friendly cooperation of Wayte Raymond, Inc., Mineola, New York."[104]

This pamphlet amply displays Stewart's strengths as a historian, especially the publication of original research. The inventory of Mark Newby's personal property, the bond of Newby's wife Hannah, in connection with his estate, items about Mark Newby's land holdings, and information regarding the genealogy of the Newby family, all served to illuminate the context of his life. As is usual with Stewart, however, these primary documents are presented verbatim, with little in the way of authorial insights.

Stewart did make one exceptional foray into analysis, and frankly the pamphlet would have been stronger without it. Noting that the inventory of Newby's estate contained one small iron furnace, one pair of small scales and weights, three sieves, along with quantities of silver plate, pewter and brass, Stewart concluded: "I know from the research for my history of 'The First United States Mint, its People and Its Operations,' scattered over a period of 17 years, that all of these items would be essential for a mint such as Mark Newby might have had on his plantation in Old Gloucester County."[105] Stewart was sufficiently intrigued to entitle a subheading of his pamphlet "Did Newby Strike Coins at Newton?" which question he never quite answered in the affirmative, although he did say that "the inventory of the estate printed herewith

tends to suggest he hoped to strike some here in New Jersey."[106] Unfortunately, Frank H. Stewart stands alone on this question, for no other scholar believes that Newby struck any of his St. Patrick coinage in New Jersey.

Stewart closed his little pamphlet—and his numismatic literature career—with graceful admissions that his was not the last word on the subject. After a brief digression on the topic of United States 1804 silver dollars, Stewart wrote "Newby's Patrick halfpence . . . are a greater mystery than the 'gem of our coinage.'"[107] And, in a sentence that could serve as a coda for any scholar who has grappled with this demanding topic, he concluded "The writer has been trying to catch up with Newby since 1918 and still has some distance to travel."[108]

Mark Newby and the St. Patrick coinage provide the perfect platform for Frank H. Stewart, mixing seamlessly as it does his two great writing passions: New Jersey history and numismatics. As an enthusiastic amateur, Stewart delved deeply into Mark Newby's biography and unearthed what he could about the St. Patrick farthings and halfpence. What he found, he shared openly with all, and what baffled him, he also freely admitted. In light of

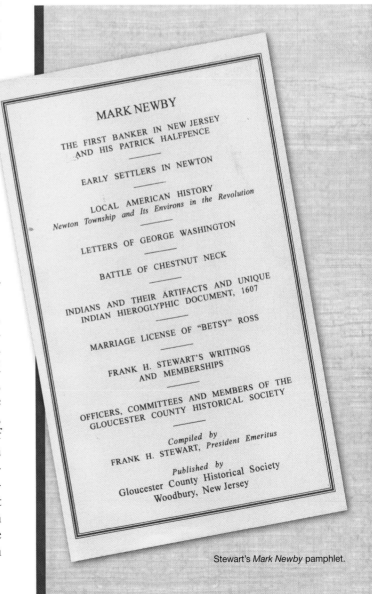

Stewart's *Mark Newby* pamphlet.

such passion and generosity, it seems churlish to quibble too much with his errors, particularly given the inherent difficulty of the topic he chose. Frank H. Stewart's farewell article was thus not a triumph, but it was a microcosm of the man and his honest efforts to expand the boundaries of knowledge in his chosen fields. That should be enough for all who, like Stewart, still have "some distance to travel" in pursuit of numismatic truth.

STEWART ELECTRIC TURNS OUT THE LIGHTS

Frank H. Stewart, the electric entrepreneur, retired in June 1928, a month after his 55th birthday.[109] Stewart sold his business to the General Electric Supply Company, the wholesale distribution arm of General Electric. General Electric was buying up not just Stewart Electric, but a host of independent electrical distributors.[110] The days of the "little man" gave way to national concerns as electrical giants like Westinghouse and GE joined Henry Ford and others in the age of large-scale industrialization. Stewart was also squeezed by the retailers, as he later recalled:

> The chain retail stores with their low priced products were another difficulty that butted into the electrical retail field and made every man, woman, and youth an embryo electrician, to the distraction of the manufacturer, wholesaler, and electrical contractor.[111]

The sale price to GE is unrecorded, but Stewart had valued the company at $461,000 in 1923.[112] With no children, Stewart sold out to the new economy, and settled into his Main Line-style mansion in downtown Woodbury, New Jersey. An area resident recalled Stewart ambling about the town following his retirement:

> During the early 1930's a tall [Stewart stood five feet, ten inches[113]] elderly gentleman could be seen daily walking along the Main street. He resembled, with his steel gray mustache, General Pershing. The gold headed cane that he swung as he strode along added to his air of distinction. He would stop in a cigar store on the highway and pay for his dozen El Producto cigars with brand new paper money that he extracted from his billfold. This was in the depression years when most people were rolling their own cigarettes.[114]

General Electric had little use for Stewart's "Old Mint" brand. A single company letterhead, featuring the "Old Mint" logo, survives in the Stewart papers, with the heading "GENERAL ELECTRIC SUPPLY CORPORATION / SUCCESSOR TO / FRANK H. STEWART ELECTRIC CO."[115] But while Stewart left the "Old Mint" behind, he did not leave the Frank H. Stewart Electric Company behind. Stewart had sold his business, but not his name, which still operated as a holding com-

pany for Stewart's considerable personal assets. He established a new office in downtown Philadelphia, moving to the Land Title Building.[116] Designed by Daniel H. Burnham and constructed in 1897, with an annex in 1902, the Land Title Building still graces the southwest corner of Broad and Chestnut Streets, just a block south of Penn Square. Ironically enough, this landmark office tower stands only a stone's throw from the Widener Building, constructed on the site of the second United States Mint at Chestnut and Juniper. Although the second Mint was long gone by the time Stewart arrived in the neighborhood, he must have noted that, move as he might, he always seemed to land in the shadow of a U.S. Mint.

Beginning in 1929, Philadelphia directories listed General Electric Supply in Stewart's former premises on North Seventh Street, while the Stewart Electric Company was now listed on 102 South Broad. The Stewart Electric company retained the Land Title building address until 1950, following Stewart's death, at which time the company was officially dissolved by the Commonwealth of Pennsylvania at the request of the Stewart estate.[117]

Stewart died of congestive heart failure on October 14, 1948, at Cooper Hospital in Camden, New Jersey.[118] He was buried in Harleigh Cemetery, also in Camden, next to his wife Rose Kirby Stewart, who preceded him in death in 1937.[119] Stewart requested in his will "a modest and respectable granite marker . . . at the graves of myself and my beloved wife, Rose Kirby Stewart, and suitably inscribed thereon my name, with the date of my birth and my death, and below that the name of my said wife, with the date of her birth and of her death."[120] Stewart, ever the historian, clearly desired to ensure that the facts and figures were recorded for the next generation. While Stewart's birth and death dates were duly engraved in granite, his executors failed to do the same for his wife, whose epitaph reads simply "ROSE KIRBY / BELOVED WIFE OF / FRANK H. STEWART." Stewart had had more eccentric ideas about his own epitaph, and proposed the following in a 1929 will:

> FRANK H. STEWART
>
> Born May 7th, 1873
>
> Died (date of death)
>
> MERCHANT AND HISTORIAN
>
> WHO, LIKE A WORN OUT COIN
>
> HAS BEEN RETURNED TO THE MINT
>
> TO BE REMADE BY THE CHIEF COINER OF THE UNIVERSE

"Those who know me will understand the reasons for this little sentiment on my part," he added in the will.[121] For whatever reason, this epitaph, with its clear echoes of Benjamin Franklin's "printer's epitaph," was deleted in a later version of the will.

Stewart's final will was a detailed 15-page document with 58 numbered provisions.[122] His two paintings of the First Mint received fifth billing on the list, and were explicitly bequeathed to the City of Philadelphia. Stewart's caretaker in his final days, his sister-in-law Ida Jane Kirby Landis, received $5,000 per year for the duration of her life, while his brother's widow, Helen Pancoast Stewart, was granted the income from a trust fund of $50,000. With no children, Stewart left bequests to a multitude of collateral relations, cousins and children of cousins, and most of these individuals received the somewhat odd sum of $495.00. Stewart's cat "Scooter" scored

Current and vintage views of the Stewart home at 510 Cooper Street in Woodbury, New Jersey, today owned by Rowan University and serving as the president's residence.

Frank H. Stewart, 1947, overlooking the Red Bank, New Jersey, Revolutionary War battle site.

The grave markers of Frank H. Stewart and his wife Rose at Harleigh Cemetery in Camden, New Jersey.

Frank and Rose Stewart, from the Frank H. Stewart passport, 1921.

the $495.00 as well, which was placed under the supervision of Ida Jane Kirby Landis "as compensation to her for providing for my pet black cat." Stewart further made institutional gifts to hospitals, churches, and historical and genealogical societies. These received varying amounts between one and several thousand dollars. Following the lengthy enumeration of gifts, Stewart left the residue of his estate to the public trust, to be used "for the purpose of public parks or recreation grounds." This remainder, administered by the First National Bank and Trust Company of Gloucester County, generated $45,000 annually as of 1972.[123] As recently as 2004 the Stewart Trust granted property to the borough of Glassboro, New Jersey.[124]

Stewart's estate was well diversified, including American and foreign stocks and bonds. He seems to have favored energy stocks, concentrating on oil, gas, electric, and public utilities. He spread his portfolio widely, investing a few hundred here and a few thousand there, yet the accumulated sum at the time of his death totaled nearly half a million dollars. He was a big believer in real estate, and held approximately 75 New Jersey mortgages, typically valued at a few thousand dollars apiece. Among his assets was the Old Mint Building, which gathered, for example, $6,000 rent in 1944.[125] All told the estate was appraised at $800,000, the equivalent of about $7,000,000 today.[126] The value in current dollars is perhaps understated, for Stewart's collection of manuscripts and historical documents was accounted for at a mere $5,000, while the iconic paintings of the First Mint, *Ye Olde Mint* and *Washington Inspecting the First Money Coined by the United States*, perhaps six-figure items today, were appraised at $250 and $500, respectively.

Despite Stewart's comparative wealth and affinity for numismatics, his coin collection at the time of his passing was modest. David Bullowa, the Philadelphia coin dealer, appraised the collection and was paid $25 for his services on June 21, 1949. Bullowa was apparently not interested in handling the accumulation, which was sold to F.J. Schaefer, a second-tier coin dealer of the era, on July 13, 1949, for $1,485.00.[127] An inventory of the collection was not found in the Stewart estate papers, but likely included Stewart's Newby coppers as discussed in his 1947 pamphlet on the same topic. A Stack's fixed price list from 1945 to 1946 found among the Stewart papers contains check marks next to a Newby farthing (priced at $3.50) and a New Jersey cent (uncirculated, priced at $10).[128] The collection may have also included a 1795 large cent, cataloged as "Doughty 70 [Sheldon-78]," "Unc. Slight scratch through hair on obverse," and sold by the Guttag Brothers for $12.50 to Stewart in 1923, long after Stewart was donating coins to Congress Hall.[129]

Stewart Electric Company or not, commerce on North Seventh Street continued unabated. While the General Electric Company assumed the premises at 35–39 North Seventh Street, this was apparently under lease to Stew-

art, who continued to own the real estate. General Electric Supply is listed at the address through the 1930 city directory. Sometime in the early 1930s the Franklin Institute used the property, for in November 1933, Stewart circulated a post card advertising the building for rent:

> For Rent—Well-Known Building
>
> The modern fire-proof type, steel, concrete and brick building, suitable for wholesale, retail, manufacturing or warehousing at 37 & 39 North Seventh Street, and 631 Filbert Street, known as the Old Mint Building, on the site of the First United States Mint, is for rent.
>
> This building was formerly occupied by the Frank H. Stewart Electric Co. and at present by the Franklin Institute, who will move February 1st [1934] or before, if desirable. The lot size on Seventh Street is 36 ft. 10 in. by 116 feet, with an ell on Filbert, 20x17 ft. In the rear is an alley across which is 629 Filbert, 3 stories high, also for rent cheap.
>
> The Old Mint Building is six stories high with an extra deep basement. It has oil burners and Otis elevators and is adaptable to almost any kind of business and has stood the test of use by outstanding concerns. The property, because of historical associations, is one of the best known buildings in Philadelphia.
>
> A low rent, low insurance, excellent location, and adaptability make it a rare proposition and bargain.
> FRANK H. STEWART
> 1014 Land Title Building, Philadelphia[130]

Stewart continued to lease the buildings, and apparently some use was made of the "low insurance" provision of his advertising circular, for in November 1941 a fire occurred in the 37–39 North Seventh Street building. Stewart thought enough of the event to paste a news clipping in a scrapbook:

> The building is occupied by the Arrow Decorating and Fixture, Co., which manufactures the background decorations for store window displays. . . . The fire started among some papers, paints, fibre materials and finished products, including figures of Santa Claus stored in the basement. . . . The flames were eventually brought under control . . . after the fireman had flooded the basement with five feet of water. . . . Hoses were strung out in crisscross fashion throughout the fire area. This blocked eastbound traffic on Arch st., and northbound traffic on 7th st., delaying hundreds of persons headed for work.[131]

A building permit issued for repairs indicated that the property was being used as a "decorating & fixture store," and that the damage was estimated at $19,000. That damage was extensive is further demonstrated by the description of the necessary repairs: "Repair fire damage; carpentry work, electrical work, heating, plastering, masonry work, plumbing, painting, roofing, etc."[132] Stewart's fire insurance was cancelled shortly thereafter.[133] The conflagration was not enough to induce Stewart to sell his beloved Old Mint Building, but in 1945, Stewart did sell 35 North Seventh Street, adjoining but not part of the original Mint, to William A. Goldberg.[134] Goldberg himself dealt with fire at 35 North Seventh Street the following year, this time to the tune of $6,000.[135]

Stewart refused to let go of the First Mint property in life, but his estate administrators possessed no such sentimentality. The property at 37–39 North Seventh Street, along with 629–631 Filbert Street, were sold by the Stewart estate to one Mary Dierkes in 1949, who promptly resold all four lots to William A. Goldberg in July of the same year.[136] Goldberg in turn sold the Old Mint lots to the Gold Seal Electric Supply Company in 1950, which had already set up shop at 35 North Seventh.[137]

Gold Seal did not last long at the location, for by 1964 the Philadelphia Redevelopment Authority had acquired much of the property in the immediate vicinity and applied for permits to raze the Seventh Street and Filbert Street lots. The building permits were terse, condemning Stewart's Old Mint Building to "complete demolition."[138] While the First Mint survived well into its second cen-

tury, Stewart's building endured barely 50 years. John L. Cotter, in his masterful *The Buried Past: An Archaeological History of Philadelphia*, states:

> In preparation for the construction of the federal buildings [to be erected at the site], the entire block between Market, Arch, Sixth, and Seventh streets was cleared of buildings in 1968, and in February 1969 a construction crew began excavating to a depth of 15 to 20 feet. The excavation revealed some deep pits that extended below the excavation floor, and as the work progressed, the site drew a number of artifact collectors.[139]

Cotter, along with a team of University of Pennsylvania students, had opportunity to dig the site in June 1969. The team was nowhere near as lucky as Frank Stewart. The site was subject to "uncontrolled artifact collection," a euphemism for scavenging, and Cotter unearthed little of numismatic interest. Several pieces of fire-tolerant earthenware, thought to have been used to fire-test metal, were recovered from a pit located near the northeast corner of the Middle Building. Cotter theorized that this was the same well in which Stewart had located bone cups, also used for fire-testing, in 1911. Cotter's team found multiple bone

The Old Mint Building in 1938.

A view of the Old Mint Building, 1960.

fragments in the same pit.[140] Thus, no numismatic delicacies were uncovered in the "last dig," or if there were, their secrets have been well protected. For the most part only ordinary ceramics and glass were reported, objects deemed worthless long ago by the inhabitants of the site, and not of much interest either to the modern day numismatist.

Area residents thought the building actually *was* the first Mint, which may have encouraged a few to have a try at it themselves. A newspaper reported:

> Most of the neighbors insist it was "the first U.S. Mint." The waitress in Uncle John's Better Bar & Restaurant, 29 N. 7th St., said it was. So did the proprietor of a nearby plumbing house. Even Tony Gluhoski, of the Cleveland Wrecking Co., said it was the old Mint. "We've been looking, but we haven't found any money stuck between the floor boards," he said.[141]

The last picture of the "Old Mint," which replaced the first Mint, was found in a March 1965 Philadelphia newspaper. It was taken just as the process of demolition had begun, evoking the last photo of the Front Building, which Stewart had snapped 54 years previously.

From the excavation rose the William J. Green Federal Building, bounded by Sixth and Seventh Streets to the east and west, and by Arch Street and the former Filbert Street (eradicated as part of the 1960s demolition) to the north and south. What were once approximately 30 Philadelphia city lots were now unified to host an immense Federal structure, perhaps an ironic commentary on the bureaucratic growth in the modern era. At nearly 2,000,000 square feet, the multi-story Green building dwarfs the 5,000-square-feet footprint allocated to the First Mint of the United States in 1792. A plaque on the western side of the property commemorates the First Mint site.

The seeming impenetrability of the William J. Green monolith has not deterred modern-day relic hunters, whose focus on sites in the vicinity of the first Mint property has proven fruitful. In 2006, detectorist Matt Mille uncovered a 1798 dollar copper trial while working a vacant lot in downtown Philadelphia. Although the numismatic press reported the location as "a construction site adjacent to the location of the first U.S. Mint,"[142] Mille later clarified that "the site did not abut the original Mint site but was close to it."[143] The exact location was

The Gold Seal Electric Supply Company at 35 North Seventh, 1944.

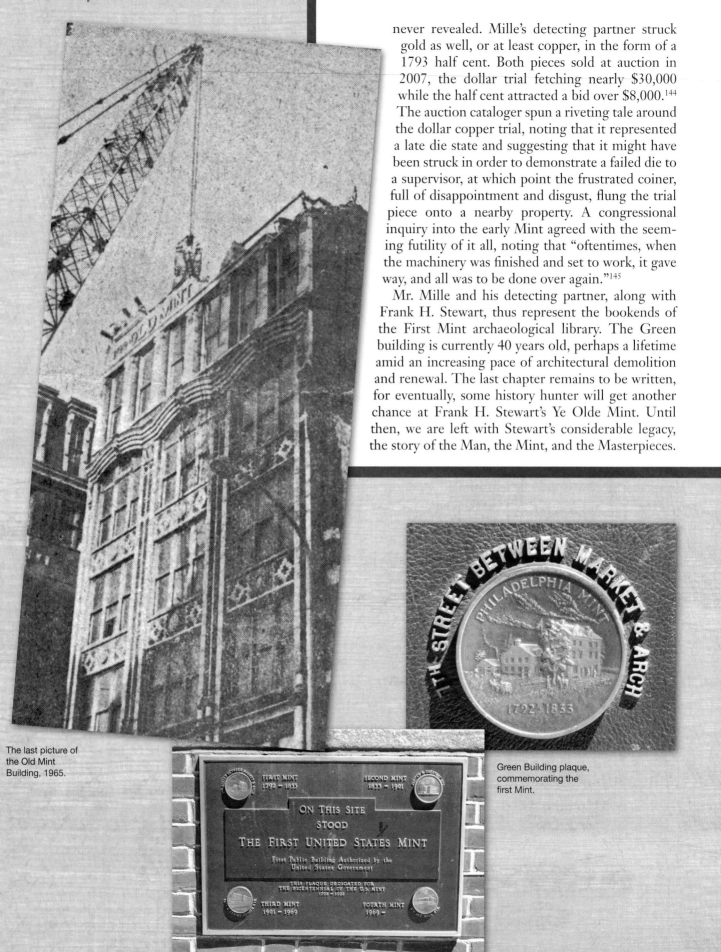

never revealed. Mille's detecting partner struck gold as well, or at least copper, in the form of a 1793 half cent. Both pieces sold at auction in 2007, the dollar trial fetching nearly $30,000 while the half cent attracted a bid over $8,000.[144] The auction cataloger spun a riveting tale around the dollar copper trial, noting that it represented a late die state and suggesting that it might have been struck in order to demonstrate a failed die to a supervisor, at which point the frustrated coiner, full of disappointment and disgust, flung the trial piece onto a nearby property. A congressional inquiry into the early Mint agreed with the seeming futility of it all, noting that "oftentimes, when the machinery was finished and set to work, it gave way, and all was to be done over again."[145]

Mr. Mille and his detecting partner, along with Frank H. Stewart, thus represent the bookends of the First Mint archaeological library. The Green building is currently 40 years old, perhaps a lifetime amid an increasing pace of architectural demolition and renewal. The last chapter remains to be written, for eventually, some history hunter will get another chance at Frank H. Stewart's Ye Olde Mint. Until then, we are left with Stewart's considerable legacy, the story of the Man, the Mint, and the Masterpieces.

The last picture of the Old Mint Building, 1965.

Green Building plaque, commemorating the first Mint.

Facing north on the east side of Seventh Street; the Green Building is to the right. The plaque commemorating the first Mint is barey visible on the brick wall facing North Seventh Street.

The southwest corner of the Green Building, penetrating the sky.

1798 dollar trial in copper, unearthed in 2006, close to the first Mint site.

The 1798 dollar, just after being discovered.

1793 half cent, found near the First Mint site.

Afterword

The Mint as it Was, the Mint as Stewart Fixed it in Memory

The German historian Leopold von Ranke (1795–1886), considered one of the founders of the modern source-based discipline, often charged his students to write history *wie es eigentlich gewesen ist*, or "as it actually was." Ranke sought not to judge the past, nor to instruct the future; he simply wanted to do justice to what had actually happened. In the case of the first U.S. Mint, with its paucity of pertinent records and its antiquity (it was no longer part of living memory in Philadelphia even before the 20th century dawned), any attempt to write its history *wie es eigentlich gewesen ist* faces huge obstacles. These challenges are exacerbated by the good-faith efforts of Frank H. Stewart to preserve the first Mint's buildings, and later its memory, through his writings and the paintings he commissioned. But it is not too late to apply Ranke's principle to the first Mint, nor to Stewart's labors on its behalf. Stripped away of traditional tales and fanciful embellishments, there is still ample nobility in both Mint and man, to adhere to Ranke's dictum.

To begin to capture the Mint as it was, it is important to recall that before Frank Stewart, there was real confusion in Philadelphia about its very location. Like the Graff House before it, an alternative site was proposed. Stewart extracted the following from a book written about the history of Chestnut Street: "There is a tradition extant that the first building used in Philada. for accommodating of the Mint was located on Mint Court, which runs from Raspberry Lane between Cherry & Race, and above 8th. We are assured that there is no substantial ground for this belief."[1] There was indeed no basis for the supposition that the first Mint had been located on Mint Court. An ancient memory may have given rise to this fallacy, however, for it is true that the 1792 half dismes were struck, before the Mint was ready, in the cellar of John Harper's saw making establishment at Sixth and Cherry Streets. Even 19th-century numismatists of Philadelphia could be confused on the point. Ebenezer Locke Mason Jr., in 1885, placed the old Mint at Seventh and Jayne, a block south of its true location.[2] An early 20th-century collector, writing in *The Numismatist*, mistakenly put it at Sixth and High Street (now Market)—close, but not quite.[3]

The point to be drawn from these yarns is quite simple: The first U.S. Mint was always a modest, workaday affair. Its footprint was so small, most Philadelphians, unless directly connected with the establishment, were unaware of its existence. It did not help that the coining operations were not apparent to Seventh Street pedestrians, who daily strolled past a façade which masked the inner workings of the enterprise. One author concludes that, "The Mint was so small and evidently so uninteresting to the Philadelphians that map makers of 1800 who indicated public buildings on their plans of the city did not think it worth their while to show the location of the only currency factory in the country."[4] The Mint itself, too small for its mission and increasingly technologically backward for its times, had no choice but to labor as hard as it could simply to meet the demands for its products. There was not a moment during these grinding workdays to pause in order to document the work they were doing, or to describe the buildings in which they were providing such hard labor. The workdays blended one into another, and structures went up, burned down, were rebuilt and remodeled, all without a chronicler to note their stories. No wonder, then, that no one is sure of exactly when the old Mint was abandoned—in 1832, 1833, or even later—and no wonder that some even thought that there was a Mint on Mint Court. It all demonstrates that recapturing the first Mint *wie es eigentlich gewesen ist* is a daunting task, indeed.

This task is made no lighter by the first Mint's latter-day successor. The U.S. Mint, the fourth one, sits in Philadelphia just two and a half blocks from the site of the first one, but psychicly, it may as well be a million miles away. The current Mint does have an Office of the Historian, but one quickly finds that the history of the Mint has been fractured by time and circumstance. The Mint cabinet, the story of the Mint in coinage, was transferred to the Smithsonian in 1923, while many of the documentary records have been transferred in bits and pieces to various outposts of the National Archives and Records Administration. As a result, a comprehensive view of the first Mint is not to be found in the fourth.

The absence of a coherent narrative is a breeding ground for misinformation, so it is not surprising that the Mint's Internet site, as recently as 2009, stated that "The first Mint was erected at 7th and Arch Streets," a location that is half a block north of the actual site.[5] Nor is this the only such error, for the History of the Mint page states that "in [sic] July 18, 1792, he [David Rittenhouse] purchased two lots for $4,266.67."[6] The actual number of lots was three. Moreover, the Mint has ceded its own mythology, for Stewart's imprint is found very forcefully on the same page, as evidenced in the following statements:

> The original facility was a 3-story building, the tallest building in Philadelphia in 1792, and became known as "Ye Ole[sic] Mint". . . . Legend states that President George and Mrs. Martha Washington donated their personal silver for the production of the half-disme. The presentation of what may have

occurred was demonstrated in the John Ward Dunsmore painting "Inspecting the First Coins."[7]

In effect, Ye "Ole" Mint has become an orphan, unclaimed alike by its own city, its own public, and even by its own direct descendant institution. A large vacuum sits where there ought to be information, and sometimes rumors, speculation and outright errors are attracted to that vortex. Over the years, however, mostly what has been drawn to that vacuum is Frank H. Stewart. It is Stewart, rather than the Mint itself, who fixed the collective visual memory of the Mint in our minds. First, of course, he rolled out Edwin Lamasure's *Ye Olde Mint*, a beautifully composed, colorfully painted depiction of three brick buildings in an open, almost bucolic setting. Second, he commissioned John Ward Dunsmore's *Washington Inspecting the First Money Coined by the United States*, an artfully composed roll call of notables supposedly examining the new 1792 half dismes. Third, there is the classic photograph of the Front Building alone, but this time in an urban setting with a touring car parked in front of it, and the letters spelling out "Ye Olde Mint" painted right onto the façade of the building.

The implication is clear: the Lamasure painting must depict the Mint as it looked in 1818; the Dunsmore painting demonstrated how important the Mint had been from the beginning; and the photograph shows how the neighborhood had closed in on this gallant old survivor of the nation's dawning days. And that is exactly how it has been etched into the minds of numismatists ever since: the three separate "little buildings that could" in the Lamasure painting; Washington, Jefferson and Hamilton visiting the Mint; and the brave little house in the big city. All three images, compelling though they may be, are fundamentally misleading. There never was a time, as we have seen, when there were only three Mint buildings on North Seventh Street, nor was there ever a time when the president and key members of his cabinet visited the Mint; nor was there ever a time when the Mint buildings were not crowded by neighborhood structures on all sides. *Ye Olde Mint* depicts a scene that never really existed, not in 1818, not in 1792, not ever. *Washinton Inspecting the First Money Coined by the United States* similarly commemorates an event that never actually occurred. Even the later photograph is also misleading in its way. Yes, commercial structures crowded both sides of the old Front Building at numbers 37 and 39 North Seventh Street. But the edifice at number 35 was leased by Frank H. Stewart, and the old Mint building itself was rented to tradesmen during the last seven decades of its life. It was not becoming overwhelmed by the commercial hurly-burly of the turn-of-the-20th-century North Seventh Street in Philadelphia; it was in fact an active participant in that bustle.

Be all that as it may, however, it is understandable that Stewart has, more than any other person, created the image of the first Mint in our minds. It is equally undeniable that the Stewart image is preferable to that produced

Postcards of *Ye Olde Mint* (Natalie Hause version) and *Washington Inspecting*, produced by the Numismatic Card Company in 1985 and 1986.

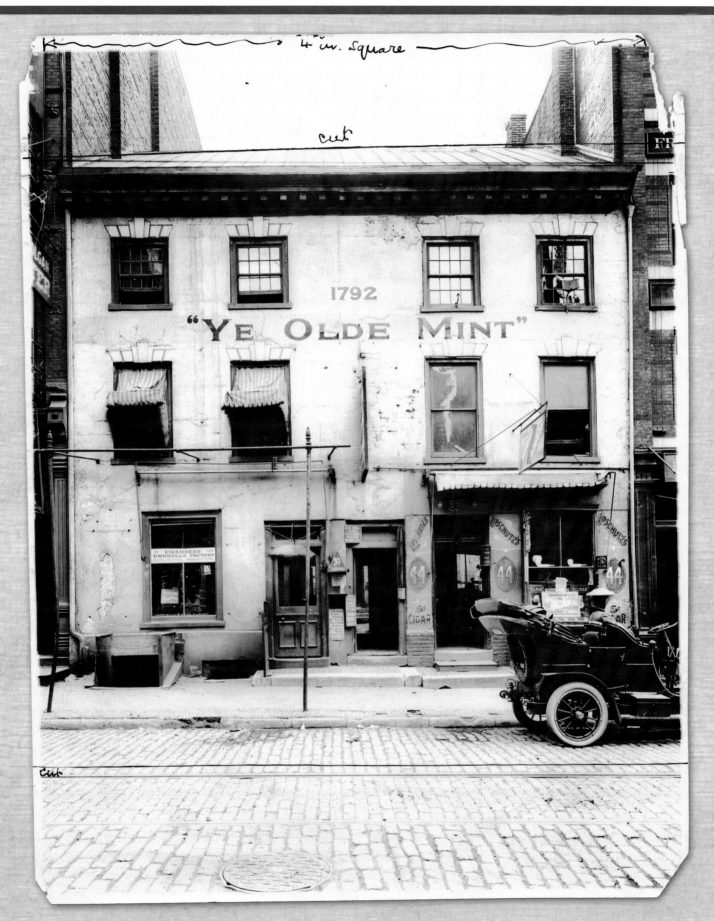

The well-known photograph of the first U.S.
Mint, by R. Newell & Sons, Philadelphia.

by all other comers, which is to say, no image at all. Yet, the Stewart image is not a good match with the history of the first Mint *wie es eigentlich gewesen ist*. In fact, in subsequent decisions, Stewart actually, if unintentionally, added more layers of obfuscation to the image of the Mint.

In 1907, when Stewart first purchased the L-shaped property comprising numbers 37 and 39 North Seventh and number 631 Filbert Street, he was in immediate need of space to augment his rented quarters at number 35 North Seventh. His eye fell on the dilapidated Rear Building and its attached stable, and their history hardly seemed to matter: "He immediately tore down the small building located in the rear of the property and erected a building which was connected with the property at 35 North Seventh Street (N.E. corner 7th & Filbert)."[8] This was hardly the act of a committed historic preservationist, although to be fair to Stewart, he did take some photographs of the Rear Building before unleashing the wrecking crew, and he also salvaged some historically important planchets from the rubble. Still, as he came to learn more of the history of the Mint campus, he regretted not having done a more thorough excavation.[9]

Then, four years later, the Frank H. Stewart Electric Company was once more running out of space, and this time it was the Front and Middle Buildings sitting in Stewart's cross-hairs. So far as it can be determined today, Stewart had done nothing to preserve these buildings except to have a single conversation with Congress Hall curator Wilfred Jordan on the subject.[10] In any case, by his own admission, he waited until the 11th hour to attempt to preserve the Middle building. It was not until July 7, 1911, that he sent a letter to the mayor of Philadelphia, John E. Reyburn, and when the answer came back, on August 2, that no appropriation was possible because the City Council was adjourned for the summer, Stewart lost no time in letting the contract for demolition, and the Middle Building was razed before the end of that month.[11] As with the rear buildings, Stewart later wished he had done differently, writing in 1915 that "I now regret that I did not feel able to offer to reconstruct the building at my expense."[12]

By connecting the four-story structure he erected in 1907 with the six-story Old Mint Building constructed in 1911, Stewart succeeded in exactly replicating the L-shaped footprint of the first Mint. He consciously evoked the vanished Front Building in his Old Mint Building, right down to the double doors fronting North Seventh Street. Although the result was much grander than the first Mint buildings, in the minds of some, it remained fraudulent. On March 25, 1965, the *New York Times* had this to say:

> Philadelphia, March 24 (AP)—They're tearing down Philadelphia's "grand old fake," a six-story building that it has long been contended, without proof, is America's first Mint, built in 1792. The words "Old Mint Building" and the alleged construction date are carved into the stone façade, just under the roof line.

Also carved into the stone are six Indian Head Pennies. The pennies prove the building's claim to a place in United States history is a fake. Indian Heads were not minted until 1864.[13]

The writer for the *Times* was not exactly well posted on numismatics, for Indian Head cents were first produced for circulation in 1859, not 1864. Further, the Indian heads carved into the façade of the Old Mint Building likely reflected Stewart's fascination with Indian history and not necessarily with Indian cents, none of which appear in the Stewart Collection accession records of Congress Hall. Nor do they exactly match the Indian cent, for starters depicting a male and not a female. More important, though, was the reporter's "debunking" of claims that Stewart never actually made, namely that the Stewart Electric Company Old Mint Building was America's first Mint. To some folks, at least, Stewart had fixed the first Mint in memory in another way, in a structure built more than a century later. It seems that in attempting to pay homage to the first Mint, Stewart was guilty, in some minds at least, of creating a fraudulent imitation.

Whether the image of the first Mint fixed in one's mind comes from Lamasure's painting or Dunsmore's, from the "touring car" photo of "Ye Olde Mint," or even from the "grand old fake" as reported by the *New York Times*, the resulting picture is simply inaccurate. To form an image of the Mint as it actually was at the height of its activity, just prior to its closing in or about 1833, one needs to let go of the iconography Stewart bequeathed to us, and become immersed in the first Mint *wie es eigentlich gewesen ist*.

The Mint as it actually was in 1833 would have made any visitor feel like Gulliver on a trip to Lilliput, or to give the simile a more American flavor, like Washington standing, pillar dollar in hand, on the bank of the Rappahannock. So tiny was the footprint of the Mint that any moderately gifted athlete would have experienced no trouble in flinging a silver dollar from one side completely over the other side of the yard.

The Mint as it actually was in 1833 was in an urbanized setting, not placed apart from its neighbors, but rather living cheek-by-jowl with them. Residential buildings crowded literally up to the edges of the "Sugar Alley Mint" buildings on the north, south and east sides, with only the west side, fronting North Seventh Street, providing any open space. So close were the neighbors that one of their burn barrels, as we have seen, set the Mint ablaze in 1816. In short, the first Mint was as much a neighborhood fixture as a government institution.

The Mint as it actually was in 1833 was not a single edifice or even three separate structures, but rather clusters of adjoining or interconnected buildings. The Front, Middle, and Rear Buildings, as well as the stable, were connected by a series of covered walkways and a tunnel, which transformed the four into a single functional structure. The four shops were attached to each other and accessible one to another by communicating doors.[14] Only the rented Cromley Furnace Building stood alone in the Mint yard, unconnected to any other edifice. These integrated structures allowed the Mint to squeeze every last ounce of efficiency from their doll's-house facilities.

The Mint as it actually was in 1833 would have left a visitor seeking a glimpse of junketing dignitaries seriously disappointed. In 1833, as in the previous 41 years of its existence, the Mint's employees toiled in utter obscurity, unvexed by the attentions of governmental luminaries; indeed, unvexed by luminaries of any sort. With the exception of a (possible) single visit from George Washington, no president, no secretary of state, no secretary of the treasury, no first lady came to witness the Mint's processes or to examine its products. The Mint was located neither in the nation's commercial capital of New York City, nor in its political capital of Washington, D.C., but rather in Philadelphia, where anonymity settled over it like a comfortable old cloak. Even Philadelphia's own chroniclers focused on the second Mint to the exclusion of the first, naturally preferring the graceful Grecian temple of Numisma to a hodgepodge of broken-down brick and frame structures. As a result of this preference, as well as the advent of photography soon after it was built, the surviving imagery of the second Mint far outnumbers that of the first.

The Mint as it actually was in 1833 was not only small and obscure, but also very much a family affair. The Patterson, Moore, Eckfeldt, and DuBois families, interconnected by marriage and by birth, accounted for about 15 percent of the 36-person workforce, with an almost complete monopoly of the executive positions. Nepotists these officers may have been, but they were busy nepotists, for each employee of the Mint was responsible for producing the coinage needs for nearly a million people. Attempting to meet these daunting demands made for long days and little time for reflection. The 18th-century coiners would today be amazed at the effort spent reconstructing their coinage progressions, as scholars labor to unwind decisions influenced by expediency or chance as circumstances dictated.

The Mint as it was in 1833 was not so much the romantic "Ye Olde Mint" celebrated in paintings and photographs, but rather a workplace so technologically backward as to foist an embarrassment upon the young American nation. The 19th century was preeminently the age of steam in factories, ships, and other power plants. Yet in 1833, the Mint possessed just one small steam engine, and that was dedicated to the rolling process. Every American coin struck through the beginning of the year 1833 owed its existence to the exertions of, as George Escol Sellers put it, the "bare-armed vigorous men" who swung the arms of the hand-powered coinage presses.[15] In one sense, "Ye Olde Mint" was just that: an institution many years behind its times, especially when compared to European mints, both public and private.

The Mint as Stewart fixed it in our memories consisted of three separate buildings, set in an ample yard, an institution important enough to be visited by three of the most luminous of the nation's founding fathers, and quaint enough to literally carry the wording of "Ye Olde Mint." The Mint as it actually existed was a tiny, hemmed-in cluster of integrated structures, devoid of the attention of dignitaries, rife with nepotism and starved of the latest technology.

The Mint as Stewart fixed it in our memories, was a place of romance, a tidy domain of neat brick buildings set in a pastoral meadow seemingly at some distance from the hustle and bustle of Philadelphia's urban life. The Mint as it actually existed was a Dickensian jumble of rough brick and frame structures, connected by improvised walkways and a tunnel, smack in the middle of the urban life of Philadelphia. It was more an eyesore than a showplace, which led Director Samuel Moore to admit that its buildings presented a "repulsive aspect."[16]

The Mint, as Stewart fixed it in our memories, was a place of productivity, where workers stood at their posts efficiently striking the coin of the realm. The Mint as it actually existed was a place of backbreaking labor, requiring of its employees 11-hour days and six-day workweeks.

Frank H. Stewart, "Master of the Mint," *ca.* 1945, featuring a rare perspective allowing the viewer to see his injured right eye.

As one visitor to the Mint in 1828 noted: "I and Mr. Fisk went to see the United States Mint. There they were, striking off half dollars in one room, and cents in another. . . . It took three men to do this; all of them had hold of the machine at a time, and it appeared to be pretty hard labor."[17] The Mint was more an old-fashioned sweatshop than a smoothly operating workshop, calling on its employees to compensate for its lack of modern technology with the sweat of their brows.

The first Mint, as Stewart fixed it in our memories, was set in a moment in time when it was forever 1792, as depicted by Dunsmore, or 1818, as painted by Lamasure. The first Mint as it actually existed consisted of a constantly evolving yard, in which, over the space of four decades, structures were built, burnt, rebuilt, rented, and remodeled as needed. It was more a movie than a photograph, in a constant state of evolution, and toward the end of its run, of devolution.

The distinctions between the first Mint as Stewart fixed it in our memories and the first Mint as it really existed are many, and essential to recognize. In so doing, however, it is equally important to keep the contributions of Frank H. Stewart in their proper perspective. If the paintings he commissioned pertaining to the first Mint are not entirely accurate, or are over-romanticized, it is also the case that no one else—before or since—has commissioned a painting to commemorate this institution. If the tableaux presented by the paintings are too neat and tidy, it is also the case that the Mint's rougher edges were not fully revealed until decades after Stewart's research and writing were completed. If he presents us with but a partial picture of the first Mint at its most comely, it is also the case that his writings discussed the Mint's other structures and times of trouble.

What should be remembered, ultimately, is not the relatively few details that Frank H. Stewart got wrong, but the great multitude of concepts that he got right. A businessman, without the benefit of higher education, Frank H. Stewart's amateur history of the Mint is nonetheless meticulously researched, source-based, and mostly accurate. Without his work to save the artifacts and commemorate the history of the first Mint, virtually all record of this institution would be lost to us. More than 80 years on, the vast majority of Stewart's findings and conclusions have stood the test of time. When laying the cornerstone of his Old Mint Building, Stewart said, "Every one of us here assembled owes a tribute to the past and the legacy to the future."[18] There can be no disputing that, in his research and writing about "Ye Olde Mint," Stewart paid his tribute to the past and left a splendid legacy to the future. Frank H. Stewart, in his earnest efforts to tell the story of the first Mint *wie es eigentlich gewesen ist*, has achieved an immutable place in the pantheon of numismatic worthies; truly earning the title of "Master of the Mint."

Frank H. Stewart's Old Mint Building.

The Stewartiana Catalog

Collectors eventually become collectible themselves, and Frank H. Stewart is no exception. Numismatists today pursue items in a number of categories associated with Stewart and the first Mint:

AO-1xx: *Washington Inspecting* and Associated Items

AO-2xx: *Ye Olde Mint* and Associated Items

AO-3xx: Numismatic Publications of Frank H. Stewart

AO-4xx: Frank H. Stewart Electric Company Ephemera

For the two paintings, *Washington Inspecting* and *Ye Olde Mint*, a host of derivative items have been created in multiple media. Many of these were produced by Craig Whitford's Numismatic Card Company in the 1980s. For each painting, the following classifications are used.

AO-x00: Original Art and Artistic Adaptations

AO-x20: Calendars and Lithographs

AO-x40: Post Cards, Postal Covers, and Souvenir Cards

AO-x60: Medallic Realizations

AO-x80: Miscellaneous

AO-1xx: *WASHINGTON INSPECTING* AND ASSOCIATED ITEMS

Original Art and Artistic Adaptations

AO-101. The original painting by John Ward Dunsmore. Oil on canvas. Dimensions 29-1/4 inches high by 43-1/2 inches wide. Painted in 1914. Owned by the City of Philadelphia and on permanent loan to Independence National Historical Park. Currently loaned, on a year-to-year basis, by Independence Hall to the Fourth United States Mint, where it is on display in the mezzanine museum.

AO-102. Engraving by Wilbert(?) Mathieu, 1944, with figures removed.[1] From an unattributed news clipping in the Stewart Collection (as shown here). Location of original art unknown.

AO-103. Forged copy appearing in Collector's Auctions, Ltd., sale no. 33, September 23, 1989, lot 1364. Dimensions 24 by 35-7/8 inches, oil on canvas (as shown). Kurt Krueger collection.

AO-104. Six- by ten-foot mural, "photographically enlarged" for the U.S. Mint exhibition at the 1971 ANA convention in Washington, D.C.[2] Possibly displayed on the exterior of the fourth U.S. Mint, *ca.* 1980, facing west.[3] Current location unknown.

Calendars and Lithographs

AO-121. Frank H. Stewart Electric Company calendar, 1916. Osborne Company, stock no. 1226. Small format calendar, 16 by 15 inches, image size 10 by 7 inches. One known example in the Stephen A. Crain collection, another in the Stewart Collection at Rowan University.

AO-122. Frank H. Stewart Electric Company calendar, 1916. Osborne Company, stock no. 1206. Large format calendar, 30 by 23-3/4 inches, image size 21-3/8 by 15-7/8 inches. Known examples reside in the Frank Greenberg collection and in the Stewart Collection at Rowan University.

AO-123. Small lithograph. Osborne Company, stock no. 1226. 10 by 7-1/2 inches. Likely representing remainders from AO-121 production. The American Numismatic Society has a copy.

AO-124. Large lithograph. Osborne Company, stock no. 1216. 25 by 16-1/4 inches. Possibly not associated with the Frank H. Stewart Electric Company. One example known, Ocean County (New Jersey) Coin club.

AO-125. Ruby-Perkins lithograph. Image size 19 by 13 inches, ovally cropped, coloration lacking contrast. Reproduced by George Kolbe in a limited edition of 125 copies, *ca.* 1998. W. David Perkins collection. Adapted for the cover of Kolbe's 73rd sale, June 1998 (as shown).

AO-126. DuPont safety calendar, March 1941. Image size approximately 15 by 9 inches. One example known, Hagley Library, Wilmington, Delaware.

Post Cards, Postal Covers, and Souvenir Cards

AO-141. Color post card, Numismatic Card Company, 1985. Dimensions 5-7/8 by 4-1/8 inches. Photographic reproduction of the Dunsmore painting. Reverse text:

"INSPECTING THE FIRST
UNITED COINAGE"

By John W. Dunsmore
Martha Washington sits before a tray of silver half dismes held by first Chief Coiner, Henry Voight [sic], looking on around her are President Washington, Thomas Jefferson, Treasury Secretary Alexander Hamilton and Mrs. Hamilton. Newly appointed Director of the Mint, David Rittenhouse, offers a coin from the tray for the First Lady's inspection. It is known that President Washington had a great interest in the Mint and provided some of his family silver for the production of our Nation's first silver coinage.

A0-142. Souvenir card, Numismatic Card Company, 1987. Dimensions 10 by 8 inches. Featuring an ovally cropped, black-and-white reproduction of the Dunsmore painting, image size 5-1/4 by 2-1/2 inches. Text above image, SOUVENIR CARD / TWO-HUNDREDTH ANNIVERSARY / of the / UNITED STATES MINT / Philadelphia, Pennsylvania.

AO-143. Post card, Eastern National Park & Monument Association, USM-1, 6 by 4-1/4 inches. Featuring a rectangularly cropped four-color reproduction of the Dunsmore painting. Text on mailing side (shown) describes the striking of the 1792 half dismes. Undated, but reported by Pete Smith as being for sale in the fourth Mint museum store in 2000.

Medallic Realizations

AO-161a. 1965 Assay Commission medal, AC-109. The reverse bears Frank Gasparro's rendering of *Washington Inspecting*. Auction appearances include Stack's Keusch, November 2008:5347 ($805).

AO-161b. 1971 Assay Commission medal, AC-115. Same reverse as preceding except for date. Auction appearances include Stack's Keusch, November 2008:5353 ($4312.50).

AO-161c. 1975 Assay Commission medal, AC-119. Same reverse as preceding except for date. Auction appearances include Stack's Keusch, November 2008:5357 ($1092.50).

AO-162. United States Mint Medal No. 705, 1971.[4] First Coinage Medal. Bronze, 1-15/16 inches in diameter. Obverse bust of Washington, based on Duvivier's *Washington Before Boston*. Peripheral legend GEORGE WASHINGTON PRESIDENT OF THE UNITED STATES 1789. Reverse rendition of Dunsmore's *Washington Inspecting* by Frank Gasparro. Issue price one dollar. This medal made its debut at the 1971 ANA in Washington, D.C., at the U.S. Mint exhibit.[5] Available directly from the Mint as of August 2007 at a price of $3.50.

AO-163. United States Mint medal, 1976. Bronze, 1-1/2 inches in diameter. Obverse view of the fourth U.S. Mint, with Liberty Bell above. Reverse depiction of Dunsmore's *Washington Inspecting*, as on preceding, with slight differences. Distributed at the U.S. Mint exhibit at the Kennedy Space Center Bicentennial Exposition, 1976. At least 15,000 were struck. Issue price one dollar.[6] This medal was repackaged with the 40 percent silver bicentennial coinage and presented as an ANA Convention souvenir set, purchase price ten dollars, at the 1976 New York ANA Convention.[7] FIRST COINING MEETING / • 1776 • 1976 • in obverse exergue. An example appeared in Whitford, October 1995:53.

AO-164a. United States Mint medal no. 721, 1992. Bronze, 3 inches in diameter. Obverse features Frank Gasparro rendering of *Washington Inspecting*, while the reverse displays an array of historical U.S. coinage designs. BICENTENNIAL / 1792–1992 in obverse exergue.

AO-164b. United States Mint medal no. 722, 1992. Similar to preceding, except diameter 1-1/2 inches. A trial in white metal, struck on the Mint's "first press," is depicted.

Washington Inspecting Original Art and Artistic Adaptations

AO-101.

AO-102.

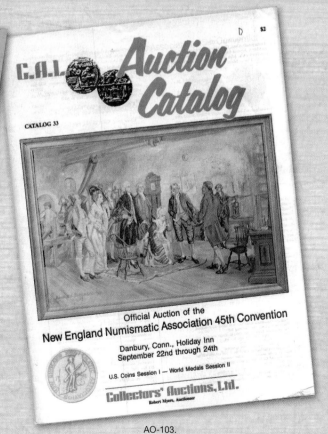

AO-103.

Washington Inspecting Calendars and Lithographs

AO-122.

AO-123.

Washington Inspecting Calendars and Lithographs

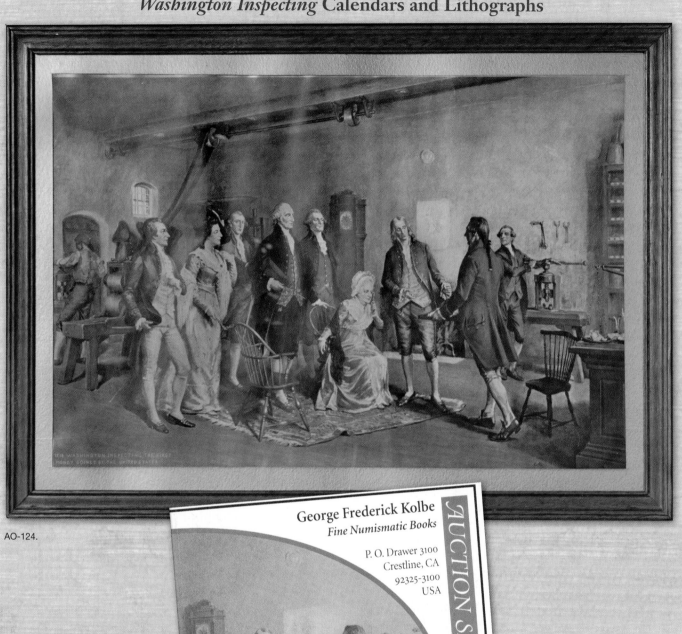

AO-124.

AO-125.

Washington Inspecting Post Cards, Postal Covers, and Souvenir Cards

AO-141.

"INSPECTING THE FIRST UNITED STATES COINAGE"
by John W. Dunsmore

Martha Washington sits before a tray of silver half dismes held by first Chief Coiner, Henry Voight. Looking on around her are President Washington, Thomas Jefferson, Treasury Secretary Alexander Hamilton and Mrs. Hamilton. Newly appointed Director of the Mint, David Rittenhouse, offers a coin from the tray for the First Lady's inspection. It is known that President Washington had a great interest in the Mint and provided some of his family silver for the production of our Nation's first silver coinage.

SOUVENIR CARD

TWO-HUNDREDTH ANNIVERSARY
of the
UNITED STATES MINT
Philadelphia, Pennsylvania

1792      1992

"Inspection of the First U.S. Coins"

The first United States Mint was established by the Act of April 2, 1792, and coinage operations commenced the following October. The first United States coins consisted of silver half dismes. This scene, painted in 1914 by artist John W. Dunsmore, depicts what might have taken place at this ceremony.

First Lady, Martha Washington sits before a tray of silver half dismes held by first Chief Coiner, Henry Voight. Standing around her, looking on are President Washington; Secretary of State, Thomas Jefferson; Treasury Secretary, Alexander Hamilton and Mrs. Hamilton. Newly appointed Director of the Mint, David Rittenhouse, offers a coin from the tray for the First Lady's inspection. Standing at the coining press is Adam Eckfeldt, later also a Chief Coiner.

Tradition states that President Washington, who had taken a great interest in the Mint, provided some of his family silver for the production of our Nation's first silver coinage.

Souvenir Card Series
1987

AO-142.

THE INSPECTION OF THE FIRST U.S. COINS
by John W. Dunsmore

The first coin struck by the United States government was the half disme, produced during July 1792. According to tradition, President George Washington supplied some of his own silver for these first experimental coins. The portrait on the half disme, emblematic of Liberty, may have been modeled by Martha Washington. Robert Birch, an engraver and Adam Eckfeldt, later to become chief coiner, engraved the dies for the disme and half disme.

USM-1
© Eastern National Park & Mon. Assoc.

AO-165. Philadelphia Bicentennial Medal, 1993. Included as part of the five-coin "Philadelphia Set," along with a 1993 American silver eagle, plus gold half, quarter and tenth eagles of the same year. Similar to preceding, except now in silver and with modified exergue. The Mint packaging indicates:

> The Philadelphia Bicentennial Medal is a silver medal in proof condition produced at the Philadelphia Mint specifically for The Philadelphia Set. A modification of the Mint's United States Mint Bicentennial Medal 1792–1992, the Philadelphia Bicentennial Medal is struck to recognize the 200th anniversary of the striking of the first regular issue U.S. Coins produced for general circulation by the Philadelphia Mint —the large one cent coins struck in March 1793.

BICENTENNIAL / PHILADELPHIA in obverse exergue. An example of the Philadelphia Set appeared in Heritage Long Beach, September 2005, lot 6535 ($747.50).

Miscellaneous

AO-181. United States Mint Bicentennial Celebration program, April 2, 1992. Noted speakers include Q. David Bowers, U.S. Mint superintendent John Martino, Philadelphia mayor Edward G. Rendell, and others. Outer cover features a black-and-white reproduction of the Dunsmore painting.

AO-2XX: *YE OLDE MINT* AND ASSOCIATED ITEMS

Original Art and Artistic Adaptations

AO-201. The original watercolor by Edwin Lamasure, painted *ca.* 1913. Dimensions 23-1/2 inches high by 33-1/2 inches long. Currently owned by the City of Philadelphia and on permanent loan to Independence National Historical Park. On display at the U.S. Mint in Philadelphia as of 2009. Currently loaned by Independence Hall, on a year-to-year basis, to the fourth U.S. Mint, where it is on display in the mezzanine museum.

AO-202. Sepia-toned lithograph of original watercolor, with various modifications by Frank H. Taylor, *ca.* 1920, but prior to 1926, for it appears in *The Independence Square Neighborhood* (Philadelphia: Penn Mutual Life Insurance Company, 1926). The original art resides in the Gloucester County (New Jersey) Historical Society. Examples of the lithographs (as pictured here) are discussed below (AO-227).

AO-203. Engraving of Lamasure's *Ye Olde Mint* used on Frank H. Stewart Electric Company stationary (as shown here), 1918 or before. Location of original art unknown.

AO-204. "First Real Old Mint," 1919, detail from Frank H. Stewart sketch appearing in the Ocean City Fishing Club 1919 Year Book (as pictured here). Original art possibly in Stewart Collection at Rowan University, but presently unlocated.

AO-205. Adaptation of *Ye Olde Mint*, with Benjamin Franklin and kite, used on the front cover of *Stewart's Current Flashes*, a house organ of the Frank H. Stewart Electric Company, October 1920 (as pictured here). Original art possibly in Stewart Collection at Rowan University, but presently unlocated.

AO-206. Adaptation of *Ye Olde Mint*, Henry B. McIntire, published in *The Philadelphia Inquirer*, July 12, 1936, as part of a "Philadelphia Then and Now" series, which featured old and recent views of various Philadelphia sites. In this example, an adaptation of *Ye Olde Mint* is depicted, adjacent to a photograph of Stewart's Old Mint Building. Location of original art unknown.

AO-207. Pencil copy of *Ye Olde Mint*, J. Warren Sheppard, date unknown. Stewart Collection at Rowan University. Original art only; no known reproductions.

AO-208. Adaptation of *Ye Olde Mint*, artist unknown, 1969. Used for program of the opening ceremonies of the fourth United States Mint, 1969. An adaptation of *Ye Olde Mint* graces the program cover. The location of the original art is unknown. A copy of the program (AO-282), as pictured here, resides in the Independence Hall National Park library in Philadelphia.

AO-209. Adaptation of *Ye Olde Mint*, Nancy and Mal Dunn, 1969. Used on the fourth United States Mint PNC (Philatelic Numismatic Cover), 1969, as pictured here (AO-244). The location of the original art is unknown.

AO-210. *Ye Olde Mint* rendering by Pam Lubinski, *ca.* 1985, commissioned by Craig Whitford. Location of original art (pen and ink?) unknown. Reproductions, as pictured here, are discussed below (AO-242, AO-245).

AO-211. Painted copy by Natalie Hause, 1985, entitled *Our First Mint*. Oil on canvas, size 24 by 36 inches, first appearing in Craig Whitford's sale of Mint memorabilia, October 112.5995:244. This copy was executed under the commission of Whitford and later used for post cards, as pictured here (AO-243). The painting resides in an Illinois collection.

Calendars and Lithographs

AO-221. Frank H. Stewart Electric Company calendar, 1915, featuring a lithographic reproduction of Lamasure's *Ye Olde Mint*. Overall 16-3/4 by 15 inches, *Ye Olde Mint* image size 7 by 12 inches, cropped from original watercolor. Two examples known, one from Craig Whitford's October 1995 sale, lot 242, and a second in the Stewart Collection at Rowan University. Osborne Calendar Company stock no. 1914 in lower right corner.

Washington Inspecting Medallic Realizations

AO-161a.

AO-161b.

AO-161c.

AO-162.

AO-163.

AO-164a.

AO-164b.

AO-165.

Washington Inspecting Miscellaneous

**UNITED STATES MINT
BICENTENNIAL CELEBRATION**
1792 -- 1992
April 2, 1992
PROGRAM

5:00 p.m.	**Public Lecture** *Federal Reserve Bank*	**Q. David Bowers** *Noted Researcher, Historian & Author of Mint History*
		David A. Kimball *Historian (Retired) Independence National Historical Park*
5:30 p.m. -- 7:30 p.m.	**Cocktail Reception** *U.S. Mint Lobby*	
6:00 p.m.	**Presentations**	
	Opening Remarks	**John Martino,** **U.S. Mint Superintendent**
	Mayoral Proclamation	**Honorable Edward G. Rendell** Mayor of Philadelphia
	City Council Citation	**Honorable W. Thacher Longstreth** Philadelphia City Councilman
	Pennsylvania Senatorial Citation	**Honorable Allyson Y. Schwartz** Pennsylvania State Senator
	Welcome	**A.E. Wolf** Chairman of the Board National Constitution Center
		Hugh B. Hanson President Historic Rittenhouse Town
6:30 p.m.	**Closing**	**John Martino**

Celebration hosted and sponsored by:

National Constitution Center

VR

Historic Rittenhouse Town

AO-181

We are grateful to acknowledge the following supporters:

American Speedy Printing, Jenkintown, PA
Dock Street Brewing Company
Eastern National Park & Monument Association
Federal Coin Fund
Finance Company of America
Meridian Bank
Philadelphia Convention & Visitors Bureau
Philadelphia Savings Fund Society
The Royal Pickwickians
Second Pennsylvania Regiment Fifes & Drums
Simpson Paper Company
Tiffany's Bakery
Williamhouse-Regency

* *List may be incomplete at time of printing*

On the Cover... "Inspecting the First Coins", by John Ward Dunsmore.
Photograph courtesy of Independence National Historical Pa

Ye Olde Mint Original Art and Artistic Adaptations

AO-201.

AO-202.

AO-203.

Ye Olde Mint Original Art and Artistic Adaptations

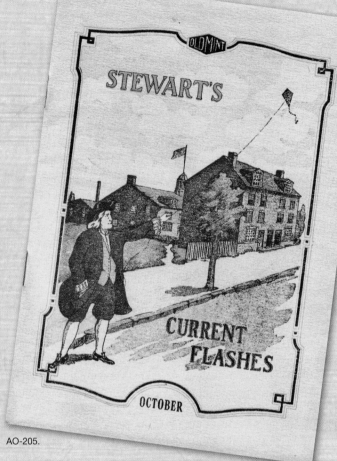

AO-205.

AO-204.

AO-206.

Ye Olde Mint Original Art and Artistic Adaptations

AO-207.

1st Mint-1792

AO-209.

UNITED STATES MINT

INDEPENDENCE MALL
PHILADELPHIA

YE OLD MINT 1792

AO-208.

Ye Olde Mint Original Art and Artistic Adaptations

AO-210.

AO-211.

AO-222. Frank Stewart Electric Company calendar, 1915. Same as preceding except large format calendar, overall 24 by 25 inches, *Ye Olde Mint* image size 14-3/4 by 20-3/4 inches, uncropped. The Stewart Collection at Rowan University has multiple examples. Osborne stock no. 1904 at lower right corner.

AO-223. Postcard sized lithograph, 5 by 6-1/4 inches and cropped. At least 14 examples exist in the Stewart Collection (box B) at Rowan University, Osborne stock no. 1924. Possibly an early sample during postcard production, as the final postcard used the same stock number but a smaller (more cropped) format (AO-241).

AO-224. Small color lithograph of *Ye Olde Mint*, 7 by 12 inches, same image used for AO-221, likely representing remainders from the calendar production, *ca.* 1914. The Stewart Collection at Rowan University has multiple copies. The Gloucester County (New Jersey) Historical Society has one copy, accession no. 1978.26 in that collection. Osborne stock no. 1914.

AO-225. Large color lithograph of *Ye Olde Mint*, as used on the large format calendar above (AO-222). Osborne stock no. 1904. The only known example is in the Historical Society of Pennsylvania, with two pencil notations on the reverse: "Mint large size" and "Frank H. Stewart March 16, 1915."

AO-226. Black-and-white reproduction of *Ye Olde Mint* on card stock, image size 13-1/2 by 7-7/8 inches. Ex. George Kolbe Mail Bid Sale October 4, 1986, lot 281 (realized $30.00). Osborne stock no. 1914 in lower right corner.

AO-227. Lithographic reproduction of Frank H. Taylor's adaptation of *Ye Olde Mint* (AO-202). The Stewart Collection at Rowan University retains multiple copies. In addition, a copy appeared in Whitford, October 1995, lot 246. Another copy, possibly same as preceding, was handled by John Kraljevich Americana & Numismatics in 2009.

Post Cards, Postal Covers, and Souvenir Cards

AO-241a. Color postcard, 5-1/2 by 3-1/2 inches. "1924 [Osborne stock number] 'YE OLDE MINT' ©[19]14 E. LAMASURE" at lower right corner, *ca.* 1914. Postage indicated as one cent. The image has been horizontally and vertically cropped from the original Lamasure watercolor. An example in the Historical Society of Pennsylvania is postmarked 1915 (exact month not legible). The reverse text reads:

> FIRST UNITED STATES MINT.
>
> The birthplace of our National Coinage. First public building erected by Act of Congress, under personal

supervision of Washington, 1792. Located 37 and 39 N. Seventh St. and 631 Filbert St., Philadelphia.

> The new building now on the site of the old Mint buildings is the home of Frank H. Stewart Electric Company who own the beautiful, original, historical picture "Ye Olde Mint," the only one ever made of the three buildings, and from which this print was copied.

An example appeared on ebay.com, item #360081186922, 8/27/2008, selling for $104.01. Other copies have sold at widely varying prices. Multiple examples exist in the Stewart Collection at Rowan University. Note, the Osborne stock number (#1924) has caused some cataloguers to attribute the year of production to 1924, not 1914 (as per the copyright date).

AO-241b. Color postcard as above, but postage now indicated as one and a half cents. Two examples reside in the collection of the Historical Society of Pennsylvania. Date of issue 1924 or later. The reverse text has been expanded:

> FIRST UNITED STATES MINT
>
> The birthplace of our National Coinage and the first public buildings erected by the U.S. Government in 1792, under the direction of President Washington.
>
> Oxen, horses and manual labor furnished all of the power of the Mint prior to 1816, during which time it was protected by a lone watchman and a watchdog. Anthracite coal was used in the forges as early as 1793.
>
> Relics of the Mint, and the original picture of it by Lamasure, are on exhibition in Congress Hall, 6th and Chestnut Streets, where the Mint Act was passed April 2, 1792, when Philadelphia was the Capital of the United States.
>
> The new six-story fireproof building on the site of the three old Mint buildings, located at 37 and 39 N. 7th Street and 631 Filbert Street, is occupied by the Frank H. Stewart Electric Co., whose founder and president has compiled a history of the First U. S. Mint (1924), which may be consulted in Libraries and Historical Societies.

AO-242a. Black-and-white postcard, 3-1/2 by 5-1/2 inches. Rendering of *Ye Olde Mint* by Pam Lubinski (AO-210, here unsigned), cropped circularly and surrounded by text, "1792 • LIBERTY • 1992 PHILADELPHIA, PENNSYLVANIA." Numismatic Card Company, 1985. Reverse text:

> UNITED STATES MINT BICENTENNIAL
> Philadelphia, Pennsylvania
> 1792–1992
> The Numismatic Card Company's official Logo commemorating the Bicentennial of our First United States Mint at Philadelphia.

Ye Olde Mint Calendars and Lithographs

AO-210.

AO-222.

Ye Olde Mint Original Art and Artistic Adaptations

AO-223.

Ye Olde Mint Post Cards, Postal Covers, and Souvenir Cards

AO-241a.

PLACE
STAMP HERE.

Domestic:
ONE CENT.

Foreign:
TWO CENTS

...ly to be written here

FIRST UNITED STATES MINT.
The birthplace of our National Coinage. First public building erected by Act of Congress, under personal supervision
of Washington, 1792. Located 37 and 39 N. Seventh St. and
631 Filbert St., Philadelphia.
The new building now on the site of the old Mint buildings
is the home of Frank H. Stewart Electric Company who own
the beautiful, original, historical picture "Ye Olde Mint," the
only one ever made of the three buildings, and from which
this print was copied.

AO-242b. Black-and-white postcard, 3-1/2 by 5-1/2 inches. Rendering of *Ye Olde Mint* by Pam Lubinski (AO-210), uncropped without text. Numismatic Card Company, 1985. Reverse text:

OUR FIRST MINT
PHILADELPHIA, PENNSYLVANIA
At 10:00 A.M. on July 31, 1792, David Rittenhouse laid the foundation stone of the first United States Mint, located on Seventh Street, the first Mint drew not much more attention than any other business. But it must have been quite a sight to peer through the Mint windows and watch as coins were being produced.

AO-242c. Black-and-white postcard, 3-1/2 by 5-7/16 inches. Numismatic Card Company logo on front. Pam Lubinski rendering (AO-210) of *Ye Olde Mint* on reverse, below which an elongated Roosevelt dime (AO-267c) is mounted. Numismatic Card Company, 1987. Reverse text:

"YE OLDE MINT"
The establishment of our Nation's first Mint came with the Mint Act of April 2, 1792. Following this action, President Washington appointed scientist, eminent astronomer and philosopher David Rittenhouse to the position of Mint Director.

Property for the Mint was purchased by Rittenhouse on July 18, 1792 for the sum of $4266.67. Construction began on July 19, 1792 with the destruction of an old distillery which was on the property.

Our first Mint consisted of three buildings. The first building which was erected, the coinage building (middle), was completed on September 7, 1792. The front building, facing Seventh Street, served as the administrative building. The third and last building housed the melting and refining equipment.

Following 40 years of service, 1792–1832, operations were moved to the newly constructed Mint, the second in Philadelphia.

AO-243. Color postcard, 5-7/8 by 4-1/8 inches. Reproduction of AO-211, the Natalie Hause adaptation of *Ye Olde Mint*, Numismatic Card Company, 1986. Reverse text (notice similarities to text of AO-241a):

FIRST UNITED STATES MINT
Philadelphia, Pennsylvania
The Act of April 2, 1792 provided for the establishment of the first United States Mint. These buildings were the birthplace of our National Coinage. The first U.S. Mint also had the distinction of being the first public building erected by an Act of Congress, under the personal supervision of President Washington.

This modern reproduction of the famous picture 'Ye Olde Mint,' originally painted by Edwin Lamasure in 1914, was recreated by the brush of Artist Natalie Hause, from which this print was made.

AO-244. Fourth United States Mint PNC (Philatelic Numismatic Cover), 1969. Rendering of *Ye Olde Mint* at lower left, with 13-starred American flag. United States Mint bronze medal (stock no. 701) inset into envelope, commemorating the opening of the fourth United States Mint. The medal itself remains available directly from the United States Mint at a nominal price. An insert with the PNC indicates:

E-14, Philadelphia Mint Opening Day Commemorative. 33mm bronze medal depict main entrance of new $37 million mint, world's largest and most productive, on Independence Mall. It's [sic] rotary presses, 99 dies to the roller, will revolutionize world money-making techniques. They can produce 10,000 coins per minute. Sculptor of the medal is Frank Gasparro, Chief Sculptor-Engraver of the Mint. Envelope face is decorated with full color sketch (by Nancy and Mal Dunn) of nation's first mint in Philadelphia, then U.S. capitol, with 13 star flag that flew during that era. Postmarked 8-14-69, Mint opening day and release date of medal, in Philadelphia, with two 6 cent White House flag stamps. Reverse of mint-struck medal portrays American eagle with outspread wings, holding in his beak the scales of Justice and clutched in his talons an olive branch and key denoting an office of state, Treasury Department symbols that antedate the Constitution. On the eagle is superimposed a U.S. relief map with stars marking the 7 mint sites, past and present, which are identified on the envelope.

AO-245a. Souvenir card, 8-1/2 by 11 inches, card stock. Pam Lubinski rendering of *Ye Olde Mint* (AO-210) centered, above which reads, SOUVENIR CARD / TWO-HUNDREDTH ANNIVERSARY / of the / UNITED STATES MINT / Philadelphia, Pennsylvania. Numismatic Card Company, 1985.

AO-245b. Same as preceding except without text, 9 by 12 inches, *ca.* 1985.

Medallic Realizations

AO-261a. 1929 Assay Commission medal, AC-73. The reverse of this and AO-261b through AO-261d feature a rendering, by Adam Pietz, of Lamasure's *Ye Olde Mint*. Auction appearances include Bowers & Ruddy Willing, June 1976:53 ($40); Bowers & Merena Leidman, April 1986:4237 ($187); Bowers & Merena Dreyfuss, April 1986:5078 ($132); Bowers & Merena Fredd, November 1995:1122 ($192.50); Bowers & Merena Harlan, December 2003:3536 ($299); Heritage Long Beach, September 2006:6612 ($373.75); Stack's Keusch, November 2008:5325 ($1,150).

Ye Olde Mint Post Cards, Postal Covers, and Souvenir Cards

AO-242b.

UNITED STATES MINT BICENTENNIAL
Philadelphia, Pennsylvania
1792-1992

The Numismatic Card Company's Official Logo commemorating the Bicentennial of our First United States Mint at Philadelphia.

AO-242a.

OUR FIRST MINT
PHILADELPHIA, PENNSYLVANIA

At 10:00 A.M. on July 31, 1792, David Rittenhouse laid the foundation stone of the first United States Mint. Located on Seventh Street, the first Mint drew not much more attention than any other business. But it must have been quite a sight to peer through the Mint windows and watch as coins were being produced.

Ye Olde Mint Post Cards, Postal Covers, and Souvenir Cards

"Ye Olde Mint"

The establishment of our Nation's first Mint came with the Mint Act of April 2, 1792. Following this action, President Washington appointed scientist, eminent astronomer and philosopher David Rittenhouse to the position of Mint Director.

Property for our first Mint was purchased by Rittenhouse on July 18, 1792 for the sum of $4266.67. Construction began on July 19, 1792 with the destruction of an old distillery which was on the property.

Our first Mint consisted of three buildings. The first building which was erected, the coinage building (middle), was completed on September 7, 1792. The front building, facing Seventh Street, served as the administrative building. The third and last building housed the melting and refining department.

Following 40 years of service, 1792–1832, operations were moved to the newly constructed Mint, the second in Philadelphia.

AO-242c.

AO-243.

FIRST UNITED STATES MINT
Philadelphia, Pennsylvania

The Act of April 2, 1792 provided for the establishment of the first United States Mint. These buildings were the birthplace of our National Coinage. The first U.S. Mint also had the distinction of being the first public building erected by an Act of Congress, under the personal supervision of President Washington.

This modern reproduction of the famous picture "Ye Olde Mint", originally painted by Edwin Lamasure in 1914, was recreated by the brush of Artist Natalie Hause, from which this print was made.

Ye Olde Mint Post Cards, Postal Covers, and Souvenir Cards

MINTING OF
U.S. COINS
Philadelphia, Pa.
—1793—
Denver, Colo.
—1906—
San Francisco, Calif.
—1854—
Charlotte, N. C.
—1838-1861
Dahlonega, Ga.
—1838-1861
Carson City, Nev.
—1870-1893
New Orleans, La.
—1838-1909

AO-244.

SOUVENIR CARD

TWO-HUNDREDTH ANNIVERSARY
of the
UNITED STATES MINT
Philadelphia, Pennsylvania

1792   1992

"Ye Olde Mint"

The Act of April 2, 1792 provided for the establishment of the first United States Mint. This Federal law also made provisions for a Mint Director, Assayer, Chief Coiner, Engraver and Treasurer. On April 14, 1792, President Washington appointed David Rittenhouse as the first Director of the Mint. Construction began on July 19, 1792 and at 10:00 A.M. on July 31st, David Rittenhouse laid the foundation stone. The foundations and walls were completed and the frame work of the roof was raised August 25th. The building was completed September 7th. Frank H. Stewart, who authored the "History of the First United States Mint: Its People and Its Operations" in 1924, states, "It is easy to imagine that immediately upon the completion of the Mint building that the patriot, Rittenhouse, ordered the Stars and Stripes hoisted above it so that the first Mint of the United States must have had the unique distinction of being the first of all Government owned buildings dedicated for public use and purpose, to display the National colors."

Souvenir Card Series
1985

AO-245a.

AO-261b. 1930 Assay Commission medal, AC-74. Appearances include Bowers & Merena Dreyfuss, April 1986:5079 ($176); Bowers & Merena Salisbury, September 1994:2288 ($302.50); Bowers & Merena Harlan, December 2003:3537 ($207); Heritage Long Beach, September 2006:6613 ($345); Stack's Keusch, November 2008:5326 ($1,035).

AO-261c. 1932 Assay Commission medal, AC-76a. Appearances include Bowers & Merena Dreyfuss, April 1986:5081 ($187); Bowers and Merena Salisbury, September 1994:2290 ($220); Bowers & Merena Harlan, December 2003:3539 ($287.50); Heritage Long Beach, September 2006:6615 ($299); and Stack's Keusch, November 2008:5328 ($1,610).

AO-261d. 1940 Assay Commission medal, AC-85. Appearances include Bowers & Merena Dreyfuss, April 1986:5088 ($440); Presidential Coin and Antique, June 1991:306 ($522.50); Bowers and Merena Salisbury, September 1994:2296 ($440); Bowers & Merena Salisbury, November 1995:1133 ($467.50); Bowers and Merena Harlan, December 2003:3546 ($345); and Stack's Keusch, November 2008:5337 ($,1265).

AO-262a. 1952 Assay Commission medal. The reverse of this and AO-262b feature Frank Gasparro's adaptation of *Ye Olde Mint*. Appearances include Bowers & Merena Dreyfuss, April 1986:5089 ($1100); Bowers & Merena Rich, March 2002:3589 ($2,990).

AO-262b. 1977 Assay Commission medal. Frontal view of Front Building. The only Assay Commission medal struck in large quantity, this medal remains widely available. Appearances include Ebay no. 170249405154, closing August 17, 2008, which sold at $20.85, and another, no. 310078925853, closing September 4, 2008 at $20.50.

AO-263. 1964 Metal Arts Company medal, designed by Toivo Johnson, engraved by Robert Stephan Schabel. Part of a series honoring U.S. Mint engravers. Diameter 3 inches. *Ye Olde Mint* on reverse.

AO-264. 1967 Main Line Coin Club 20th Anniversary Medal. Obverse legend: ★ 1792 ★ FIRST UNITED STATES MINT PHILADELPHIA, reverse MAIN LINE / COIN CLUB / 20th Anniversary / 1947–1967. Whitford's October 1995 sale catalog noted examples in silver and bronze.

AO-265. First Mint commemorative medallion, 1992. Obverse legend about upper periphery: PHILADEL-PHIA MINT, with 1792–1833 in exergue. Frank H. Taylor's version of *Ye Olde Mint* is featured. Part of a commemorative plaque located at the Green Building (First U.S. Mint site) in present-day Philadelphia.

AO-266. 1992 Numismatic Association of Southern California medal. Upper obverse legend: 37th ANNUAL NASC CONVENTION / GOLDEN STATE COIN SHOW / JAN. 31 – FEB. 2, 1992 / PASADENA, CALIF. Lamasure's *Ye Olde Mint* is featured on the obverse, and in exergue FIRST U.S. MINT, PHILADELPHIA / BICENTENNIAL / 1792–1992. Whitford's October 1995 sale catalog noted examples in silver, bronze and aluminum.

AO-267. 1993 Chris Victor-McCawley Personal Medal. Copper. Obverse similar to AO-236 with the exception of the obverse legend: C.V.M. P.O. BOX 2967 / EDMOND, OK. 73083 / 405-341-2213, and in exergue FIRST U.S. MINT / PHILADELPHIA, PA. / 1793–1993. The reverse features three 1793 large cent types with the centered inscription EARLY AMERICAN COPPERS. As of 2007 examples were still available directly from McCawley at a nominal cost. Also issued in bronze and silver.

AO-268a. United States Mint Bicentennial Elongated, 1992, rolled on U.S. cent. *Ye Olde Mint* centered with 1792 / 1992 to left and right, upper legend U.S. MINT BICENTENNIAL, lower legend PHILADELPHIA. Craig Whitford October 1995:24. Same die used to elongate nickels and quarters.

AO-268b. United States Mint Bicentennial Elongated, 1992, rolled on U.S. cent. *Ye Olde Mint* centered top to bottom, upper legend U.S. / MINT / 200 Years / Apr. 2, 1792, lower legend PHILADELPHIA / Craig A. Whitford / Numismatist / ANA LM 3705 / 1992.

AO-268c. United States Mint Bicentennial Elongated, 1992, rolled on U.S. Roosevelt silver dime. *Ye Olde Mint* centered with 1792 / 1992 to left and right, upper legend U.S. MINT BICENTENNIAL, lower legend PHILA-DELPHIA. Craig Whitford, October 1995:24. Two hundred examples apparently rolled, as a postcard in the author's collection (AO-242c), upon which an example is mounted, indicates "Silver 155/200." Same die used to elongate nickels and quarters.

AO-268d. United States Mint Bicentennial Elongated, 1992, rolled on 1987 one-tenth ounce gold American eagle. Unique, ex. Craig Whitford, October 1995:25. *Ye Olde Mint* centered with 1792 / 1992 to left and right, upper legend U.S. MINT BICENTENNIAL, lower legend PHILADELPHIA.

AO-269. Gallery Mint Museum medal, 1994, marking the 202nd anniversary of the U.S. Mint. "Act of April 2 / 1792" beneath *Ye Olde Mint* figure, MCMXCIV in exergue. Reverse recreation of the 1792 disme.

AO-270. American Numismatic Association 2000 Convention (Philadelphia) medal and Convention badge. The reverse depicts all four of the Philadelphia Mints, with the first Mint clearly derived from the Lamasure image. Issued in various formats and featured in *The Numismatist*, February, 2010 (convention badge illustrated here).

Miscellaneous

AO-281. *Ye Olde Mint*, bearing Osborne stock number 1924, laminated onto metal plate with faux woodgrain border, 5 by 7 inches. Peer-Glaze Company of Philadelphia label on reverse. Examples exist in the Stewart Collection at Rowan University.

AO-282. Program for the opening ceremonies of the fourth U.S. Mint, 1969 (see illustration under AO-208).

AO-283. Commemorative Ornament, diameter 2-5/8 inches. *Ye Olde Mint*, encircled by the text BICENTENNIAL OF THE UNITED STATES MINT. Treasury Historical Association, 1992, still available as of 2008 from the Treasury Historical Association.

AO-3xx: NUMISMATIC PUBLICATIONS OF FRANK H. STEWART

AO-301. *Ye Olde Mint*, Philadelphia: Frank H. Stewart Electric Company, 1909. Per Charles Davis, reprinted in *Mehl's Numismatic Monthly* (January–February 1910).

AO-302. *Our New Home and Old Times* (Philadelphia: Frank H. Stewart Electric Company, 1913).

AO-303. Letter to the editor, *The Numismatist*, vol. 27, no. 1 (January 1914): 19. Stewart discusses his search for old prints of the first U.S. Mint.

AO-304. "The First United States Mint," *Mehl's Numismatic Monthly*, vol. 6, nos. 7–8, whole nos. 67–68 (July–August 1915).

AO-305. "The First U.S. Mint and Its First Coins," *The Numismatist*, vol. 29, no. 2, (February 1916). This reprints the text from the brochures accompanying the 1915 and 1916 Frank H. Stewart Electric Company calendars.

AO-306. Letter to the editor. *The Numismatist*, vol. 29, no. 8 (August 1916): 366. Stewart comments on an (apparent) 1796 half cent donated to Congress Hall.

AO-307. "Mark Newby, of West New Jersey, and his Half Pence," *Year Book* [of] *The New Jersey Society of Pennsylvania*, The New Jersey Society of Pennsylvania, 1920.

AO-308. "Mark Newby and His Patrick Halfpence," *The Numismatist*, vol. 34, no. 2 (February, 1921).

AO-309. "Extracts From the Diary of Robert Morris," *The Numismatist*, vol. 36, no. 3 (March, 1923).

AO-310. Letter to the editor, *The Numismatist*, vol. 37, no. 5 (May 1924): 365. Response to Henry Russell Drowne, discussing odd denominations of the U.S. dollar.

AO-311a. *History of the First United States Mint* (Philadelphia: Frank H. Stewart Electric Company), 1924.

AO-311b. Identical to above, with a portrait plate of Frank H. Stewart inserted between pp. 6–7. One copy known in the Stewart Collection at Rowan University (notated on flyleaf "special photo page 7 rare"), and a second in the Gloucester County (New Jersey) Historical Society.

AO-311c. *History of the First United States Mint*, Quarterman Publications reprint, 1974.

AO-312. "George Washington and the First U.S. Mint," *The Numismatist*, vol. 38, no. 4 (April 1925).

AO-313. Letter to the editor, *The Numismatist*, vol. 39, no. 12 (December 1926): 662. Discusses a Joseph Wright medal of George Washington, and the consideration of the Continental Congress for the formation of a Mint.

AO-314a. *Mark Newby: The First Banker in New Jersey and His Patrick Halfpence*, privately published, 1947.

AO-314b. *Mark Newby: The First Banker in New Jersey and His Patrick Halfpence*, Gloucester County Historical Society reprint, 2001.

AO-4xx: FRANK H. STEWART ELECTRIC COMPANY FIRST MINT EPHEMERA

AO-401. Postcard, black and white, photograph of 35–39 North Seventh Street facing southeast. Undated, *ca.* 1908. Text above buildings reads "The first United States Mint. / Now belonging to the Frank H. Stewart Electric Co., 35 N. 7th St., Phila." Reverse attribution is "1247. Rosin & Co., Phila. & N. Y." Example shown is from David Sklow collection. An example in the Historical Society of Pennsylvania collection is postmarked August 2, 1908.

AO-402. Similar to AO-401, except now colorized and with expanded text: "The first United States Mint. First buildings erected by Federal Government, 1792. Now belonging to the Frank H. Stewart Electric Co., 35 N. 7th St., Phila." Reverse attribution is "No. 1501 Rosin & Co., Phila. & New York." Example shown is from Dan Hamelberg collection, a second appeared in the John J. Ford Reference Library Part II, lot 1260 (Stack's/Kolbe, June 2005). The New Jersey collector J. de Lagerberg had at least one example as of 1920.[8]

AO-403. Postcard, black and white, photograph of 35–39 North Seventh facing northeast. Undated, *ca.* 1908. The reverse contains no attribution information. Possibly a prototype for AO-401, the attribution to Frank H. Stewart is tentative. Example shown is from David Sklow collection.

AO-404. Similar to AO-403, now showing only 37–39 North Seventh, with identical reverse. Example shown is from John Dikun collection.

Ye Olde Mint **Medallic Realizations**

AO-261a.

AO-261b.

AO-261c.

AO-261d.

AO-262b.

AO-263.

AO-264.

AO-265.

Ye Olde Mint Medallic Realizations

AO-266.

AO-267.

AO-268a.

AO-268b.

AO-269.

AO-268c.

Ye Olde Mint Miscellaneous

AO-270.

AO-283.

Frank H. Stewart Electric Company First Mint Ephemera

AO-401.

AO-403.

AO-402.

AO-404.

Frank H. Stewart Purchases From Chapman Sales

Samuel Hudson Chapman and Henry Chapman, brothers, formed a numismatic partnership in Philadelphia in 1878. The "young Turks" were not the least bit shy in challenging the existing numismatic establishment, and the pair revolutionized auction cataloging forever with the emission of the Bushnell sale catalog in 1882, a lavish production replete with flowing descriptions and photographic plates. The Chapman's charged $5 for plated copies of the sale, "a preposterous price for a coin sale catalogue" thought one among the dealer fraternity.[1] Critics derided the scholarship therein, but were competitively forced to adapt similar presentations. By the time Stewart began collecting in the early 1900s, the brothers had become part of the establishment themselves, with a long string of auction sales to their credit. A number of the Chapman bid books record purchases by Frank H. Stewart.

Confusing the issue, however, is that a second Frank H. Stewart was simultaneously active on the numismatic scene. The sequence is this. In the 1901 Wilcox sale, one Frank H. Stewart is identified in the Chapman bid book as having purchased a 1794 dollar at $100. In December, 1903, the following ad appeared in *The Numismatist*:

> TO EXCHANGE.—1794 silver dollar, cost $110.00, for a 1799 copper cent of equal value. F.H. Stewart, 32 Fountain St. Grand Rapids, Mich.[2]

Unstated in the Wilcox catalog, but noted in other Chapman catalogs of the period, for example the May 1901 sale, is that the Chapmans charged a 10% commission for executing bids, thus explaining Stewart's reported cost of $110.00. The same 1794 dollar shows up again in the Chapman's July 1904 Barker sale, now selling for $75.00. It thus appears that this coin originally sold to Frank H. Stewart of Grand Rapids, Michigan, who unsuccessfully attempted to trade it, and a few months later consigned it back to the Chapmans at a loss.

The Numismatist, later in July 1909 identifies a Frank H. Stewart as president of the West Michigan Numismatic Society,[3] almost certainly the same individual who purchased and sold the 1794 dollar detailed above. Further investigation reveals that an F.H. Stewart of Grand Rapids, Michigan, joined the ANA in 1900 and placed wanted ads in *The Numismatist* in that year.[4] It is also known that the F.H. Stewart of Grand Rapids offered a hoard of 1856 flying eagle cents to the

Chicago collector Virgil Brand in 1904.[5] Thus, references to "Frank H. Stewart" in the Chapman bid books must be used cautiously.

In addition to the purchases detailed here, Stewart is listed as a registered bidder in the S.H. and H. Chapman sale of May 8, 1906, (per the Chapman bid book in the ANS collection) and the Henry Chapman sales of February 20, 1908, September 30, 1908, and December 12, 1909, (per Chapman bid books in the Dan Hamelberg collection). A note in the Henry Chapman bid book of February 20, 1908, indicates that Stewart personally attended the sale, more likely suggesting the Frank H. Stewart of Philadelphia, who worked only a few blocks away from the Chapman offices. The lot descriptions below are taken verbatim from the Chapman catalogs.

Finally, Stewart appears as a registered bidder in three Lyman Low sales: October 1901, December 1906, and January 1907.[6] No actual purchases are recorded. The October 1901 sale in particular points to Stewart of Philadelphia, for his name is given in the bidder list as "F.H. Steward," but later in a cross-referenced list as "Stewart." The ambiguity in the spelling of the last name likely indicates Stewart of Philadelphia, who used the "Steward" spelling in his early years.

S.H. & H Chapman: Meigs, Breton, and Paul Collections, May 3–4, 1901.

Lot 113 [Gold Coins] U.S. 1880 1/4 Dollar. Duplicate of last [Indian head]. Proof. [$2.00]

Lot 143 [Medals] Lincoln. Fine head r. Emancipation Proclaimed. Bronze. Perfect. Size 29. [$1.00]

Lot 191 [United States Fractional Currency] 3d issue. 50c. Justice. Autograph signatures of Colby and Spinner. Rev. Carmine back. A 265. Slight nick on lower corner. [$2.00]

Lot 202 [Specimen Currency – CSA] 15c. Grant and Sherman. Autograph sigs. of Jeffries and Spinner. Red back. Separate. Wide margin. Slightly yellowed. Very rare. [$6.50]

Lot 203 [Specimen Currency – CSA] 15c. Grant and Sherman. Duplicate of last. [$6.50]

Lot 275 [United States Coins] 1873 Standard Proof set. $1, $1/2, $1/4, $1/10, $1/20, 3c., Silver. Nickel, 3c., 5c. Copper, 2c., 1c. In fine morocco case. Set. [$7.00]

Lot 278 [United States Coins] 1802 Cent. Extremely fine. Strong, even impression. Dark steel-brown color. [$2.20]

Lot 420 [U.S. Fractional Currency] 4th issue. 50c. Lincoln. Fine. [$1.00]

Lot 497 [American Colonial and State Coins] 1787 Fugio Cent. As last, but reading STATES UNITED. Uncirculated. Bright red. [$0.75]

Lot 817 [Foreign Copper Coins] England. Geo. III. Bust in sunken field. 1, 2 pence, 1797. Unc. Splendid pair. 2 pcs. [$2.70]

1794 dollar from the S.H. & H. Chapman
Barker sale, July 1904, lot 610.

Lot 1015 [Bronze Medals]. Victoria. Bust l, by *Wyon*. R. Queen enthroned surrounded by beautiful emblematical figures. On 50th Anniversary of Reign, 1887. 40. [$2.00]

Lot 1155 [Complete Set of Minor Proof Coins]. 1873. Complete minor proof set. 1c., 2c., 3c., 5c. Set. Rare and rapidly advancing, the last 2c. sold at auction brought $4.25. [$4.75]

Lot 1173 [United States Dollars] 1795. Bust. Fine. Very scarce. [$3.00]

Lot 1232 [United States Cents] 1802. Extremely Fine. Light nicks on obv. Steel color. [$2.05]

Lot 1242 [United States Cents] 1806. Very fine. Surface lightly eroded. Pale olive color. Rare so fine. [$3.00]

Lot 1251 [United States Cents] 1813. Fine. Small nicks. Dark olive color. [$1.75]

S.H. & H. Chapman: Hopkins, Harrison, et al Collections, July 22, 1901.

Lot 454. [Minor Proof Sets] 2c. 1864, 5, 9, 70, 72. Uncirculated. Red. 5 pieces. [$0.20 each]

Lot 568. [Proof Sets] 1858 Complete proof set. $1, $1/2, $1/4, $1-10, $1-20, 3c., 1c. nickel. Extremely rare. It is said only 70 of the dollars were coined. 7 pieces sold as 1 set. [$45.00]

S.H. & H. Chapman: C.S. Wilcox Collection, November 6–7, 1901.

Lot 150 [United States Three Dollars] 1875 proof $3 (underbidder). Of the greatest rarity—but 20 coined! The only specimen offered at auction in ten years! Originally from the Parmelee collection through S.H. & H. Chapman to Seagrave to S.H. & H. Chapman again, and sold in set to Wilcox. [Realized $210.00]

Lot 301 [United States Dollars] 1794 dollar. Excessively rare, far more so than collectors are aware, and our experience verifies this assertion when we say that in our 26 years in the business we have never been offered a 1794 dollar. [Realized $100.00]

Lot 608 [United States Half Dimes] 1792 half dime (underbidder). The first coin struck after the establishment of the U.S. Mint and *Geo. Washington* supplied some of his silverware to provide the material. He also mentioned them in his fourth annual address. [Realized $17.00]

S.H. & H. Chapman: Geo. Eavenson, et al Collections, April 16–17, 1903.

Lot 1221 [Canadian Coins and Tokens] Louis XV. Bust. R. Indian Standing. 1751 (L 255). Louis XV. Bust. R. Galley. 1755 (L 284) Originals. Fair. 510, 515. 2 pcs. [Realized $2.00]

Lot 1271 [Canadian Coins and Tokens] Ship. R. HALF PENNY TOKEN. Poor, corroded. Rare. 1005. [Realized $0.20]

Lot 1304 [Medals] Victoria. Diamond Jubilee. Bust l. 1837–1897. R. 8 shields. CANADA CONGRATULATES HER QUEEN. Silver. Proof. In case, 22. [Realized $0.65]

Lot 1308 [Medals] King Edw[ard] and Queen Alexandra. Busts. R. Tree with shields of Provinces. CANADA'S COMMEMORATION. Bronze. Proof. Size 22. In case. [Realized $0.60]

S.H. & H. Chapman: Louis S. Risse Collection, June 17–19, 1903.

Lot 151 [England] 1887 Victoria. Jubilee, 1887. Set, 5, 4, 2 1/2, 1, 1/2, 1/4 shillings. The 6 pence has reverse with SIX PENCE. Uncirculated; a few slightly chafed. 8 pcs. [95 cents]

Lot 389 [Foreign Silver Coins, Genoa] 1666 Virgin and child on cloud. R. Cross. Crown. V.g. [$1.30]

Lot 521 [Foreign Copper Coins, England] Geo. III. Cart wheel two pence 1797. Uncirculated. Light olive, traces of red. [$2.00]

Lot 671 [Washington Coins] 1791 Cent. Same as last in every respect [Bust of Washington in costume. WASHINGTON PRESIDENT 1791. R. Large eagle, ONE CENT above.] [$2.60]

Lot 931 [Half Dollars] 1802 Good. Rare. [$2.00]

Lot 932 [Half Dollars] 1803 Very good. [$1.00]

Lot 939 [Half Dollars] 1821 Uncirculated. Sharp imp. Scarce. [$1.00]

Lot 1156 [Cents] 1831 Die cracked around stars. Small letters. Very fine. Light olive. [$0.55]

Lot 1202 [Cents] 1857 Large and small dates. Very fine. 2 pcs. [$0.35]

Lot 1792 [Numismatic Books] Scott's Silver and Gold Coin Catalogue. Cuts throughout. Slight tear in cover, but clean and perfect. Rare. 8vo. Paper. N.Y., 1893. [$3.00]

Lot 1798 [Numismatic Books] Snowden, J.R. Ancient and Modern Coins in the Cabinet Collection at the Mint of the United States. 27 plates embossed in metallic colors. 407 pp. 8vo., cloth. Phila., 1860. [$3.00]

S.H. & H. Chapman: Ralph R. Barker, Esq. Collection, July 7–8, 1904.

Lot 610 [United States Silver Dollars] 1794 Fine for this coin. Well and evenly struck. A few almost invisible scratches in field before head. Slight edge dent. Cost $100 at our Wilcox sale, Nov. 6–7, 1901. Very rare, far more so than collectors are aware of; and our experience in 28 years in the business verifies this assertion when we state that we have never been offered a 1794 dollar outside of a regular collection. See plate. [$75.00]

Lot 1182 [United States Pattern Pieces] 1863 2c. Bust of Washington r. GOD AND OUR COUNTRY *1863*. R. Similar regular issue. Copper. Proof slightly smeared. [$1.50]

S.H. & H. Chapman: J.F. McCabe, Esq. Collection, June 7, 1905.

Lot 574 [Half Cents] 1795 Let ed. Holed, 1797 corroded, 1800, '3, '4, '5, '6, '7, '9, '10, '25, '6, '8, '9, '32, '3, '4, '5, '50, '1, '3, '4, '5, '6, '7. 10 poor, rest good to very fine. 51 pcs. [$0.125 each].

HALF DIMES.

608 1792 Bust of Liberty l., 1792 beneath, around LIB.(erty) PAR.(ent) OF SCIENCE & INDUSTRY. R. Eagle flying left, UNI. STATES OF AMERICA HALF DISME*. Extremely fine. Shows some file marks in planchet on cheek. Very rare. The first coin struck after the establishment of the U. S. Mint and *Geo. Washington* supplied some of his silverware to provide the material. He also mentions them in his fourth annual address.

1792 half disme lot description, from the S.H. & H. Chapman *Wilcox* sale, November 1901, lot 608.

Appendix C

Early Fire Insurance Surveys of the First Mint Campus

The authors acknowledge Pete Smith for the following transcriptions.

THE 1837 INSURANCE SURVEY

SURVEY, made February 16th 1837 and reported to the

Franklin Fire Insurance Company of Philadelphia

For Michael Kates

Two, Three story Brick buildings, rough cast in front, situate nos. 27 and 29 North Seventh Street, east side, between High and Mulberry Streets in the City of Philadelphia, Also two, 2 story brick buildings in the rear of the above and all formerly occupied as the United States Mint; One Thousand dollars insured on No. 1, One thousand dollars insured on No. 2, Eight hundred dollars insured on No. 3, and Two hundred dollars insured on No. 4. Insured without exception.

No. 1, is 19 feet 6 in. front by 34 feet deep; the first story has an entry and stairway off a door frame front with square transom and 4 lights of glass, panel door and a plain door frame back, the other part is occupied as a silver platers shop and had a forge in it, a door frame the same front with 9 light sash door, lifting shutter and a swelled front bulk window, 25 lights 10 by 16 glass, panel shutters, cornice and bed mould, and a 36 light Venetian window 8 x 10 glass back, outside panel shutters, heart floor, washboard, and story 8 feet 8 inches high in the clear; The stairs from the first to the second story are doglegged, close string, sap steps and white pine risers, 3 feet going, square ballisters and painted rail; The stairs from the second to the third story are winders, square steps and winders, as described.

No. 2 is 17 feet 4 inches front by 31 feet deep, a door frame and sash door front the same as No 1, and a bulk window 25 lights 10 by 17 glass front and 10 bent lights of glass, panel shutters, cornice and bedmould, plain door frame back and a 24 light 9 by 11 window, panel shutters, heart floor and story 9 feet high in the clear, this story is now occupied as a painters shop.

The second and third stories of both houses has the wall taken down in the centre between the houses about 18 feet from the front wall, the joist over the opening in each story being supported by a girder with turned columns under it in each story; a small room back in each house, the north room having 2-18 light windows 8 by 10 glass, with panel shutters, fireplace in it with mantel, panel breastwork, single worked panel doors, surface and washboard, the south room has a 15 light 8 by 10 window back and a doorway leading on to a platform to Building No. 3; 4-24 light 8 1/2 x 11 window front, 2 in each house, wood mantel each end and side closets and paneled breastwork, surface and washboard, plain ovolo mouldings and washboard, heart pine floor and story 9 feet high in the clear, and all occupied as school rooms.

The Third Story is as the second story and finished in the same manner, 4-16 light 8 1/2 x 11 windows front and 16 light and a 12 light back in No. 2, and a 12 light ditto in No. 1. Heart floor story 8 feet 4 in high and occupied as a Lyceum and chemical experiment rooms, each story warmed by coal stoves.

The Garrett of both houses is in one room. The two being lathed and plastered yellow pine floor, double pitch roof 12 feet pitch, cedar shingled, wood eaves and cornice front and back, modillions to front eave. Wood spouts back to No. 2, and tin spouts in No. 1, Copper gutter and 1 conductor front, a 12 light semicircular top dormer window front and plain ridge top ditto back 8 by 10 glass, cheeks shingled, common scantling window framed with stone heads front, stud partitions in both houses, and first, second and third stories lathed and plastered, the cellar of each house has been vaulted and a passage under the yard back into No. 3 which is a 2 story Brick Building 30 feet front by 35 feet deep, first story occupied as the Apprentices Library, the second story and garrett occupied as a manufactory for coloured paper having a steam engine used for the said purpose.

The first story has a plain door frame, panel door, and marble sill and a 6 light 8 by 10 window front, 4-24 light 8 x 10 windows on the north side, heart pine floors, washboard, plain window casings and mouldings, story 11 feet high in the clear, and all lathed and plastered, 3 turned columns under a girder supporting the second floor, room warmed by a coal stove.

The second story has 3-16 light 8 x 10 windows front and a door opening on to a platform to No. 1, 4 windows the same on the north side, 2 ditto and a doorway back opening into the stairway. Heart floor, a room partitioned off by a planed board partition, story 8 ft. 6 in. high in the clear and not plastered;

steam engine Boiler is placed in a large fire place on the south side and appears to be safe; a step ladder to loft overhead which is occupied as a drying loft, white pine floor, double pitch roof 12 feet pitch, cedar shingles, copper gutters and conductors, a 16 light ridge top dormer window in front and back, moulded brick eaves, a large semicircular window and sash in north and south gable ends, battlement walls, each side, scantling window framed, panel shutters to first and second stories.

No. 4 is a two story brick building 18 feet wide by 27 feet long occupied as a machinist shop and having a forge in each story, The first story has a door back with a 9 light sash over it and 2-18 light 8 by 10 windows, 1 window the same and 2-18 light windows front panel shutters to all, earth floor, and the south end wall taken partly down and opening into a frame building (two stories high and not insured) story 10 feet high in the clear.

The second story is 8 feet high in the clear, yellow pine floor 3-12 light 8 by 10 windows back, 1-16 light north end and 2-12 light in the west side, and a doorway into stairway, 2 doors south and opening into frame building, room lathed and plastered, double pitch roof 8 feet pitch, cedar shingles, plain brick eaves, battlement walls common scantling window framed.

D H Flickwir Surveyor

The 1772 Shubert House Survey

Survey

Michael Shubert Dwelling House situate on the East side of Seventh Street between High & Mulberry Streets.

17 feet 9 inches front by 31 feet deep—3 story high, 14 & 9 inch walls Two Rooms & an entry on the first floor Front finished with Breast surface & skirting Back room furnished with Breast tabernacle frame wainscoted pedestal high & Double cornice round Entry wainscoted pedestal high & single cornice Second Story Finished with Breast surface & skirting in both Rooms Third Story Plain Board newel stairs Plastered partitions Garrett plastered Painted Inside & outside Modillion Eves Front away out on the Roof—Quite New.

Sam Wetherille

10 m/o. 5th. 1772

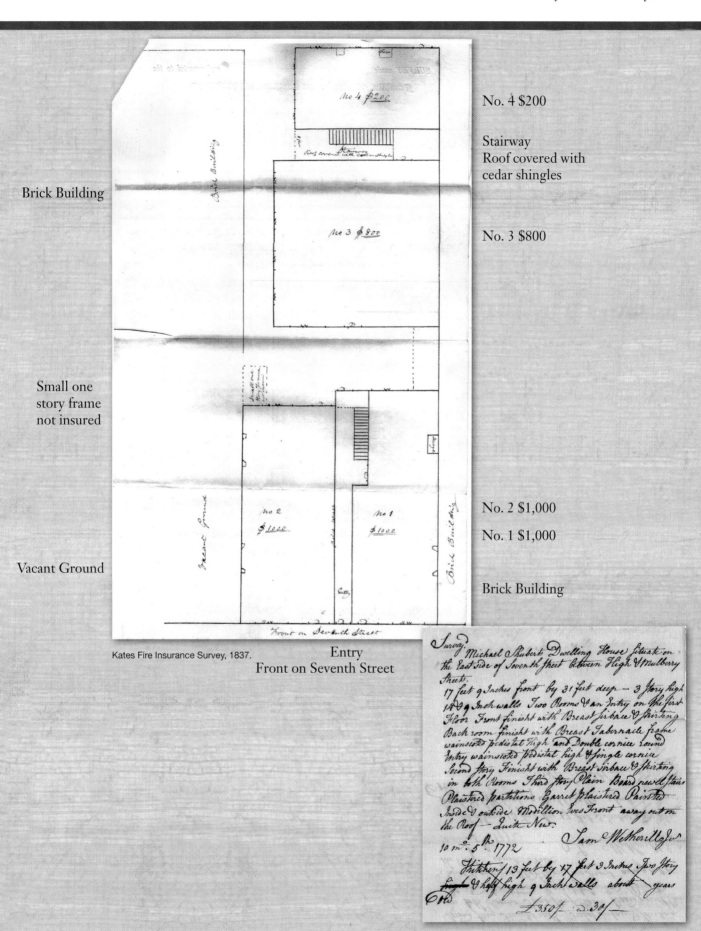

No. 4 $200

Stairway
Roof covered with
cedar shingles

No. 3 $800

Brick Building

Small one
story frame
not insured

No. 2 $1,000

No. 1 $1,000

Vacant Ground

Brick Building

Kates Fire Insurance Survey, 1837.

Entry
Front on Seventh Street

Shubert Fire Insurance Survey, 1772.

Appendix D

Seventh Street Lot Numbering

L ike many other American cities, Philadelphia cast off old ways in the 19th century and adopted a standardized system of numbering its streets and buildings. City blocks were changed to run in hundreds, odd house numbers were confined to the south and east sides of streets, and so on. Remarkably, no single source summarizes the changes effected by Philadelphia's Ordinance of 1856, which mandated the more orderly streeting system.[1] Thus, conversion tables must be built from a variety of sources. Unfortunately, the 1849/1850 R.P. Smith map of Philadelphia, which contains lot numbers for portions of central Philadelphia, does not extend to the section of Seventh Street which contains the first Mint lots. Using city directories to untangle the jumble of street numbers is complicated by the fact that no reverse directories exist for this period; fortunately, an electronically searchable version of the 1861 directory is available.[2] By searching for Seventh Street entries in 1861 and comparing with a city directory prepared prior to the Ordinance of 1856, a table of old and new style street numbers can be created:

Entry	1856 Directory	1861 Directory
Alfred Genay, painter	3 N. 7th Street	9 N. 7th Street
John Heumann, bootmaker	5 N. 7th Street	11 N. 7th Street
Alexander S. Ferguson, sexton	7 N. 7th Street	21 N. 7th Street
John G. Craig, painter	21 N. 7th Street	31 N. 7th Street
Herman M. Dorschimer, baker	25 N. 7th Street	35 N. 7th Street
James T. Brodie, metallic roofer	29 N. 7th Street	39 N. 7th Street
John Briggs, ticket agent	47 N. 7th Street	53 N. 7th Street
Silas Frost, brassfounder	49 N. 7th Street	55 N. 7th Street

While this table is not comprehensive, it can be seen that house numbers changed for all of the listed Seventh Street entries. The first U.S. Mint, numbered at 27–29 N. 7th Street at the time of its creation, was changed to nos. 37–39 by the Ordinance of 1856. Further corroboration is provided by the October 23, 1792, issue of *Dunlap's American Daily Advertiser*, which places the mint at 29 N. 7th. Throughout the text, we have consistently used modern lot numbers.

work, and every other branch of the carving, gilding, and looking-glafs bufinefs at the very loweft rates.   3aw3w   October 3.

THE HIGHEST PRICE
Will be Given for
OLD COPPER,
At the Mint,
North Seventh ftreet, No. 29.   Sept. 1. eotf
OFFICE
For the Sale of Real Eftates, &c.

Dunlap's American Daily Advertiser, October 23, 1792.

Appendix E

The Frank H. Stewart Photographs of the First Mint Demolition

During the Mint demolition, Stewart created his own photographic record of the proceedings. These snapshots are today preserved in the Stewart Collection at Rowan University in Glassboro, New Jersey. Stewart wrote captions on the reverse of most of these images, which are presented here verbatim. Stewart offered several comments on his photography:

> Of course, you know about the 2-A Brownie camera which is to me the most important part of my equipment. I have carried one every time I have been away from home for the past fifteen years and find it has been worthwhile.[1]

In the *Ocean City Fishing Club 1919 Year Book*, which Stewart compiled, he included an illustration of himself working at his desk, with the Kodak Brownie resting on the desktop. In *History of the First United States Mint*, Stewart added that he took snapshots of the site during the demolition.[2] A pre-publication draft of the work clarified further:

> I myself kept a small camera always at hand and took about fifty snapshots of what seemed interesting to me. Unfortunately, the light was poor for snapshots, because of the surrounding buildings, and a great many of them cannot be reproduced without retouching the negatives.[3]

Thus, the quality of the photographs varies, but in any case, this is Stewart's most personal account of the final days of the first Mint of the United States, as told in his own pictures.

2nd floor of coinage building after floor boards were removed, looking northeast from building 631 Filbert

Carrying out the girder that supported the roof of Coinage building.

Looking down on top of burglar proof [vault] of 1792

Coinage building looking northwest after second floor boards taken off

Looking down on second floor of coinage building towards southwest

Dust airing from coinage building just after big slab of bricks were pushed forward

Shows flooring of second floor and stairway hole

Shows top of building after the roof and rafters were removed also shows how the building on 37 extending [sic] back about 2 ft. of 39 N. 7th

Showing coinage building after top floor and roof knocked down. This building was leveled to ground in about 24 hrs excepting back wall

Coinage building

Shows floor on 2nd story 39 N. 7th

Old Mint. Front view taken Saturday August 11th, 1911 [sic—Saturday was the 12th, not the 11th]

Taking out the queer thing made of two planks bolted together with a sort of spring joist fastened at the bottom edge. This supported the roof of the coinage building and took the place of the original which was burned off. The end was left in wall after being sawed off and I saved it to make souvenirs. It shows strong evidence of fire.

Showing two chimneys on wall of 41 N. 7th

Showing difference in depth of two buildings 37 and 39 N. 7th

After the front buildings had been torn down

Back hallway door of 37 and 39 N. 7th

Looking down the alley between the Coinage building and 41 N. 7th from 3rd story window of concrete building 631 Filbert

Big piece of front wall of coinage building being tumbled

Coinage building

Tin roof of 35 and 37 N. 7th from top of Coinage building

Looking from top of Coinage building towards 7th St. Sun happened to be just right to light up old hallway in center, and room on first floor of 37 [North Seventh] occupied by Chambers the Umbrella man. Doorways shown are the hallway door and the rear door in 37 [North Seventh]. The place where the old stairway leading to second floor was is shown to the left of the hall door.

Demolition of coinage building

Demolishing north wall of Coinage building

7th St. crowd watching excavations at old mint

Tumbling piece of wall of Coinage building

Watching excavations at old mint Watching excavations at old mint

Digging for relics

Throwing down back wall of Coinage building

Basement of 37 N. 7th showing windows in north wall of basement

Arch in basement wall Coinage building shadow is in well [orientation not clear]

Well hole back of men

Back end of front buildings looking north taken from old outside stairway

Reporter of Philadelphia Record holding set of iron bars taken from rear of basement window of 39. Bars badly corroded

F.H.S. and Kieran Colgan watching excavation [Colgan was a printer on the east side of Seventh Street]

Well in block hole. Showing arch in north wall of coinage building built in wall. Below this arch was a solid brick pier about 4 ft. sq. Evidently built to keep the basement from caving in under the wall into the well or else to keep anyone from digging through the side of well into the mint basement. The pier was below floor level of basement which was paved.

The arch at top was built in line of wall dividing the two basements. The other thing may have been a vault or fireplace but I could not figure what it was. It [was] projecting into the basement of 37 [North Seventh]

Ruin of burglar proof [vault] of 1792 after demolishment [orientation not clear]

Snapshot of stairway (brick) in basement of 39 N. 7th

Peoples Press [?] leader horses

Picture of front buildings taken about 1 P.M. Friday Aug 4th [1911] just before I left for Ocean City to visit Fisher. When I saw the buildings again on Tuesday Aug 8th the roof was off and buildings were down to the 3rd floor boards

Time exposure of brick arch stairway in basement of 39 N. 7th

Burglar proof [vault] of 1792 after demolishment [orientation not clear]

Working excavations at old mint

Crowd on side walk watching excavations of Old Mint buildings

People from off street at noon time—digging for relics

Snapshot of arched brick stairway—about a dozen steps of brick. No wood in stairway. Probably[?] taken[?] place of the part demolished in the past.

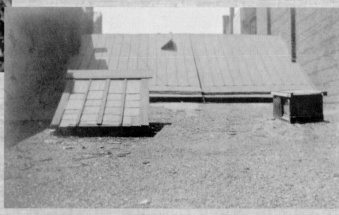

Roof of coinage building and 37 & 39 N. 7th from 3rd story window 631 Filbert

This shows the rear wall of the filled in basement also shows where the workmen caved in an unfilled well. This is the well I was told about by an old man as being in existence when he was a boy. Both the basement and well were in the yard and paved over.

Notes

PREFACE

1. Frank H. Stewart MSS, unnumbered box, Rowan University, draft for *Historic Seventh Street*.

INTRODUCTION

1. Frank H. Stewart, *History of the First United States Mint: Its People and Its Operations* (Philadelphia: printed for the author, 1924), 148.

2. Frank H. Stewart, *Mark Newby: The First Banker in New Jersey and His Patrick Halfpence* (Woodbury, N.J.: Gloucester County Historical Society, 1947), 39.

3. See for example, Mark Twain's *Huckleberry Finn*, or, more numismatically, Elizabeth Johnston's *A Visit to the Cabinet of the United States Mint, at Philadelphia* (Philadelphia: J.B. Lippincott & Co., 1876), 19. See also *Mason's Coin Collectors' Herald*, vol. 3, no. 1 (June 1881): 35. Frank H. Stewart himself was guilty of the practice, as in *History of the First Mint*, 160.

4. *The President's House in Philadelphia: Part I*, http://www.ushistory.org/presidentshouse/plans/pnhb/phI.htm (accessed July 24, 2007).

5. Stewart, *History of the First United States Mint*, 5.

6. *American Journal of Numismatics*, vol. 1, no. 4, 27. Later, *The Numismatist* published a photograph of the desk upon which the Declaration was penned (*The Numismatist*, vol. 38, no. 2, February 1925, 79).

7. Thomas Donaldson, *The House in Which Thomas Jefferson Wrote the Declaration of Independence* (Philadelphia: printed for the author, 1898), 58, 69.

8. Grant Miles Simon, *Part of Old Philadelphia: A Map Showing the Historic Districts and Sites From the Founding Until the Early 19th Century* (Philadelphia: The American Philosophical Society, 1966).

9. Ibid.

10. "The Declaration House" (Graff House), http://www.ushistory.org/declaration/graff.htm (accessed September 24, 2007).

11. Donaldson, *The House*, 71.

12. Ibid., 61, 72.

13. Charles B. Hosmer Jr., *Presence of the Past: A History of the Preservation Movement in America Before Williamsburg* (New York: G.P. Putnam's Sons, 1965), 84.

14. Donaldson, *The House*, 55–56.

15. Ibid., 55–56, 60.

16. See Joel J. Orosz, "Dr. James Mease: A Forgotten Pioneer of Numismatic Literature." *The Asylum*, XIX: 4, 128–134.

17. Donaldson, *The House*, 67–69.

18. Joel J. Orosz and Carl R. Herkowitz, "George Washington and America's 'Small Beginning' in Coinage: The Fabled 1792 Half Dismes," *American Journal of Numismatics*, Second Series, 15 (2003): 120–121.

19. Ibid., 111–114.

20. Donaldson, *The House*, 70.

21. Ibid., 71–73.

22. Hosmer, *Presence of the Past*, 84.

23. Donaldson, *The House*, 74.

24. Ibid., 75.

25. Ibid., 77.

26. Ibid.

27. Ibid., 78–81.

28. Ibid., 80.

29. http://www.gutekunst-archiv.de/Gutekunst_Art.htm (accessed October 20, 2007).

30. George Frederick Kolbe, *Numismatic Literature Sale 104* (Crestline, Calif.: George Frederick Kolbe, November 1, 2007), 96.

31. Donaldson, *The House*, 82.

32. Hosmer, Presence of the Past, 85.

33. Donaldson, *The House*, facing 93.

34. John L. Cotter, Daniel G. Roberts, Michael Parrington, *The Buried Past: An Archeological History of Philadelphia* (Philadelphia: University of Pennsylvania Press, 1993), 129.

35. Ibid., 130.

36. Continental currency recovered from the Declaration House, possibly cached by Jefferson, is today in possession of Independence Hall National Historical Park.

37. Ibid.

CHAPTER 1

1. Felicie F. Squyres, "The Stewart Room: Its History, Contents and Usage" (term paper for L.S. 600, seminar in current issues and library seminar, graduate division of Glassboro State College, Rowan University, 1973), 7.

2. Ibid., 8.

3. Stewart, *History of the First United States Mint*, 134.

4. Judith Austin Brown, "Frank H. Stewart: A Biography" (term paper for L.S. 600, seminar in current issues and library seminar, graduate division of Glassboro State College, Rowan University, 1972), 11.

5. Stewart, *History of the First United States Mint*, 137.

6. Squyres, "The Stewart Room," 10.

7. Stewart, *History of the First United States Mint*, 162.

8. Craig A. Whitford, *The Numismatic Card Company Archive Collection of U.S. Mint Memorabilia*, mail bid sale, October 6, 1995, lots 242 and 243.

9. Frank H. Stewart, "George Washington and the First U.S. Mint," *The Numismatist*, XXXVIII:4 (April 1925), 215.

10. Stewart, *History of the First United States Mint*, 149.

11. Ibid, 149–55.

12. Ibid., 159.

13. Editors of *Coin World*, *Coin World Almanac*, 5th ed. (New York: Pharos Books, 1987), 161.

14. United States Mint website, http://www.usmint.gov/historianscorner (accessed September 23, 2007).

15. Stewart, *History of the First United States Mint*, 64.

16. http://www.easternscaffolding.com/byrne-green.htm (accessed September 23, 2007).

17. Don Taxay, *The U.S. Mint and Coinage: An Illustrated History from 1776 to the Present* (New York: ARCO Press, 1966), 79–82.

18. Robert I. Alotta, *Street Names of Philadelphia* (Philadelphia: Temple University Press, 1975), 14–15, 98.

19. Kenneth Roberts and Anna Roberts, translator and eds., *Moreau de St. Méry's American Journey [1793–1798]* (Garden City, N.Y.: Doubleday & Co., Inc., 1947).

20. John Hebron Moore, "A View of Philadelphia in 1829: Selections from the Journal of B.L.C. Wailes of Natchez," *Pennsylvania Magazine of History and Biography*, LXXVIII (July 1954): 356.

21. Caspar Souder, *History of Chestnut Street from the Founding of the City to 1859* (Philadelphia: King & Baird, printers, 1860), 146, originally appearing in *Thomas Westcott's Sunday Dispatch* (October 9, 1858), as part of a series.

22. Stewart, *History of the First United States Mint*, 139, 145–146.

23. Squyres, "The Stewart Room," 9.

24. Frank H. Stewart, *Our New Home and Old Times* (Philadelphia: Frank H. Stewart Electric Company, 1913), 3.

25. Stewart, "George Washington and the First U.S. Mint," 215.

26. Stewart, *History of the First United States Mint*, 166.

27. Michael Ewing, "About Edwin Lamasure Jr.," http://www.savvycollector.com/DamageCorner/tabid/96/ArtistID/467/Default.aspx (accessed September 24, 2007).

28. Stewart, *History of the First United States Mint*, 167.

29. Robert P. Hilt II, *Die Varieties of Early United States Coins: Volume 1, Silver and Gold Coins, 1794 to 1798, Dies 1794 Through 1797* (Omaha: RTS Publishing Company, 1980), vii.

30. Stewart, *Our New Home and Old Times*, 16.

31. John L. Cotter, et al., *The Buried Past: An Archaeological History of Philadelphia* (Philadelphia: University of Pennsylvania Press, 1993), 34–36.

32. Florence Seville Berryman, "Dunsmore's Epic of the American Revolution," *Daughters of the American Revolution Magazine*, LX, no. 11 (November 1926): 648.

33. Florence Seville Berryman, "Dunsmore's Epic of the American Revolution: Part II," *Daughters of the American Revolution Magazine*, LXI, no. 1 (January–December 1927): 26.

34. Frank H. Stewart, "Inspection of the First Coins of the First United States Mint," printed brochure/overleaf attached to a 1916 Frank H. Stewart Electric Company calendar, owned by Steve Crain.

35. Orosz and Herkowitz, "George Washington and America's 'Small Beginning' in Coinage," 126–127. See also "The 1792 Pattern Disme" discussion in chapter 5.

36. Stewart, "Inspection of the First Coins of the First United States Mint."

37. Carl Binger, *Revolutionary Doctor: Benjamin Rush (1746–1813)* (New York: W.W. Norton & Company, Inc., 1966), 113–114. Further on medallic realizations of Leutze's painting, see Hank Spangenberger, "Washington's Christmas Gift—Victory at Trenton in 1776," *Numismatic Scrapbook Magazine* (December 1968): 1857–1862.

38. Orosz and Herkowitz, "George Washington and America's 'Small Beginning' in Coinage," 128–32.

39. Stewart, *History of the First United States Mint*, 191.

CHAPTER 2

1. Frank H. Stewart, "Recollections and Traditions of the Electrical Business," Frank H. Stewart MSS, box 7, Rowan University, 1926, 1. Stewart did not attend the Philadelphia Centennial but later visited the 1904 World's Fair in St. Louis. An admission pass is located in Frank H. Stewart MSS, box N, Rowan University.

2. *Mason's Coin Collectors' Magazine*, vol. 1, no. 2 (July 1884): 18.

3. *American Journal of Numismatics*, vol. 11, no. 3 (January 1877): 72.

4. R.W. McLachlan, "Fifty Years a Collector," *The Numismatist*, vol. 24, no. 10 (October 1911): 361. See also the Gospel of Mark 12:38–44. Further discussion of the widow's mite in the Mint Cabinet is found in *The Numismatist*, vol. 13, no. 4 (April 1900): 128. See also George G. Evans, *Illustrated History of the United States Mint* (Philadelphia: George G. Evans, 1892), 68–69.

5. Arlie R. Slabaugh, *American Centennial Tokens and Medals* (Tecumseh, Mich.: Paul A. Cunningham, 1981), 11.

6. *Numisma*, vol. 2, no. 3 (May 1878): 7.

7. Nicholas B. Wainwright, *History of the Philadelphia Electric Company 1881–1961* (Philadelphia: Philadelphia Electric Company, 1961), 13.

8. Ibid., 19.

9. Stewart, "Recollections and Traditions of the Electrical Business," Frank H. Stewart MSS, box 7, Rowan University, 1926, 5.

10. Ibid., 23.

11. Stewart, "Recollections and Traditions of the Electrical Business," Frank H. Stewart MSS, box 7, Rowan University, 1926, 2.

12. *Testimony Taken by the Committee Appointed to Investigate the Bureau of Engraving and Printing*, 55th Congress, 3rd sess., doc. 109, Part 2, 12. Congressional Serial Set no. 3734. The authors acknowledge Q. David Bowers for pointing out this resource.

13. Stewart, "Recollections and Traditions of the Electrical Engineer," Frank H. Stewart MSS, box 9, Rowan University.

14. Ibid., 204.

15. HK-188, HK-189. See Heritage Auctions, February 2007, sale 430, lot 52.

16. HK-246, HK-249, HK-251, HK-252.

17. *Coin World* (November 24, 2008): 44. The artistic juxtaposition of classic and modern motifs was in vogue at the time. See *Coin World* (June 8, 2009): 32.

18. Brown, "Frank H. Stewart: A Biography," 2.

19. Frank H. Stewart, *Notes on Old Gloucester County New Jersey Volume III* (Baltimore: Genealogical Publishing, 1977), 240.

20. E.S. Steward, *The Stewart Family of New Jersey* (Philadelphia: Press of Allen, Lane & Scott, 1907), 50–51. Also see the 1880 United States Federal Census, Pilesgrove, Salem County, New Jersey, roll T9_797.

21. Frank H. Stewart, *Reminiscences of Sharptown, N.J.* (privately published, 1931–1932), 13.

22. Stewart, *Notes on Old Gloucester County New Jersey Volume III*, 21.

23. Frank H. Stewart to Howard D. Fisher, February 16, 1924, Frank H. Stewart MSS, box 6, Rowan University.

24. Ibid.

25. Stewart, *Reminiscences of Sharptown, N.J.*, 15.

26. Brown, "Frank H. Stewart: A Biography," 7.

27. Ibid., 8.

28. Stewart, *Notes on Old Gloucester County New Jersey Volume III*, 243.

29. Frank H. Stewart to Howard D. Fisher, February 16, 1924, Frank H. Stewart MSS, box 6, Rowan University.

30. Stewart, *Notes on Old Gloucester County New Jersey Volume III*, 21.

31. Frank H. Stewart, 1890 diary, Frank H. Stewart MSS, box 6, Rowan University.

32. Stewart, *Notes on Old Gloucester County New Jersey Volume III*, 22.

33. Stewart, *Reminiscences of Sharptown, N.J.*, 11. While Stewart claimed to have "manufactured" the Huling name on the spot, a daguerreotype in Frank H. Stewart MSS, box H, Rowan University, is identified as "step daughter of Aunt Hannah Hulings." Thus, the Huling(s) name seems to have had some family connection.

34. Prickett College of Commerce Graduating Exercises program, May 31, 1892, Frank Stewart MSS, box 6, Rowan University. Stewart graduated twice from Prickett, in 1891 and again in 1892.

35. Ibid.

36. Burnett was the maiden name of Stewart's mother. Squyres, "The Stewart Room: Its History, Contents and Usage," 1.

37. Stewart, *Notes on Old Gloucester County New Jersey Volume III*, 243.

38. Frank H. Stewart, autobiographical papers, Frank H. Stewart MSS, box 6, Rowan University.

39. Stewart, *Reminiscences of Sharptown, New Jersey*, 13–14.

40. Frank H. Stewart to Howard D. Fisher, February 16, 1924, Frank H. Stewart MSS, box 6, Rowan University.

41. Frank H. Taylor MSS, box 2, Historical Society of Pennsylvania.

42. Stewart, *Notes on Old Gloucester County New Jersey Volume III*, 22.

43. Ibid., 23.

44. Brown, "Frank H. Stewart: A Biography," 13.

45. Stewart, *Notes on Old Gloucester County New Jersey Volume III*, 23.

46. Stewart, *Mark Newby: The First Banker in New Jersey and His Patrick Halfpence*, 41.

47. Frank H. Stewart diary, October 26, 1893, Frank H. Stew-

art MSS, box 6, Rowan University.

48. Brown, "Frank H. Stewart: A Biography," 15.

49. Stewart, *Notes on Old Gloucester County New Jersey Volume III*, 23.

50. Brown, "Frank H. Stewart: A Biography," 15. Brown cites Stewart's 1919 diary (now missing) in stating that Stewart initially did business at 20 North Seventh. Elsewhere Stewart noted that "the business . . . has been located on Seventh Street since its inception, with the exception of the first few months of 1894." (Frank H. Stewart MSS, box 6, Rowan University). Stewart's company literature from 20 North Seventh is undated, while a Stewart letterhead addressed 1208 Green Street is dated March 1, 1894. Stewart's "Electrical Industry" (Frank H. Stewart MSS, unnumbered box, Rowan University) indicates that the sequence was 1208 Green Street, then 41 North 7th, then 20 North 7th, then 35 North 7th.

51. Ibid., 16.

52. Stewart, *Our New Home and Old Times*, 7.

53. Brown, "Frank H. Stewart: A Biography," 15. Brown indicated 1308 Green, but this appears to be a typographical error as a Frank Stewart letterhead exists for 1208 Green. Autobiographical notes in Stewart's own hand (Frank H. Stewart MSS, box 6, Rowan University) agree with the 1208 Green address.

54. Lease agreement between Frank H. Stewart, P. Logan Bockius and J.W. Parker, Frank H. Stewart MSS, box 9, Rowan University.

55. Frank H. Stewart, "How to start a business on a small capital," Frank H. Stewart MSS, box 7, Rowan University, undated.

56. Ibid.

57. City of Philadelphia Deed Abstract, lot 154, May 13, 1919. The price was $32,000 per the purchase agreement found in Frank H. Stewart MSS, box D, Rowan University.

58. *Polk's-Boyd's Philadelphia Directory* (Philadelphia: R.L. Polk and Co., 1925).

59. Stewart, "How to start a business on a small capital," Frank H. Stewart MSS, box 7, Rowan University, undated.

60. Frank H. Stewart MSS, card file box, Rowan University.

61. Brown, "Frank H. Stewart: A Biography," 22. The marriage certificate survives in Frank H. Stewart MSS, Rowan University.

62. Frank H. Stewart to Eli Steward, May 27, 1896, Frank H. Stewart MSS, box 6, Rowan University, 1.

63. Stewart, "How to start a business on a small capital," Frank H. Stewart MSS, box 7, Rowan University, undated.

64. Frank H. Stewart to Howard Fisher, February 16, 1924, Frank H. Stewart MSS, box 6, Rowan University, 8.

65. "Articles of Agreement" between Stewart and Bockius, March 16, 1895, Frank H. Stewart MSS, box 6, Rowan University, 1.

66. Frank H. Stewart to Howard Fisher, February 16, 1924, Frank H. Stewart MSS box 6, Rowan University, 8; also Frank H. Stewart, "Electrical Industry," Frank H. Stewart MSS, unnumbered box, Rowan University.

67. Clement Lippincott to Frank H. Stewart, January 30, 1899, Frank H. Stewart MSS, box 6, Rowan University.

68. Frank H. Stewart to Eli Steward, May 27, 1896, Frank H. Stewart MSS, box 6, Rowan University.

69. "Reception and Dinner to Mr. Frank H. Stewart by the Employees of the Frank H. Stewart Electric Co.," May 6, 1910, Frank H. Stewart MSS, box 9, Rowan University.

70. Sales 1894–1906, Frank H. Stewart MSS, box 9, Rowan University.

71. Sales and Profits 1899–1902, Frank H. Stewart MSS, box 9, Rowan University.

72. Frank H. Stewart Electric Company Articles of Incorporation, filed June 15, 1904, Pennsylvania charter book, no. 76, p. 286. Later, the government challenged Stewart's incorporation accounting; it seems that Stewart exchanged intellectual property rather than cash for some or all of his shares. See *Frank H. Stewart Electric Co. v. The United States*, 65 Ct. Cl. 21; 1928 U.S. Ct. Cl. LEXIS 527; 5 U.S. Tax Cas. (CCH) P1547; 6 A.F.T.R. (P-H) 7384 (accessed via lexis. com). Ultimately, Stewart lost a $6,000 tax judgment.

73. *List of Charters of Corporations Enrolled in the Office of the Secretary of the Commonwealth During the Two Years Beginning June 1, 1903, and Ending May 31, 1905* (Harrisburg, Penn.: Harrisburg Publishing Co., 1905), 59. Accessed via books .google.com.

74. United States Patent 992821, May 1911.

75. United States Patents 627215, 656431, 846158. http://www .google.com/patents accessed June 1, 2009.

76. *Polk's-Boyd's Philadelphia Directory* (Philadelphia: R. L. Polk and Co., 1925), 110.

77. *Stewart's Current Flashes*, vol. 2, no. 6 (November 1921), 10. Rowan University Stewart collection, box 5, folder 14.

78. *Ivanhoe Metal Reflectors and Fittings for Industrial Illumination* (July 1920), Frank H. Stewart Electric Co., distributors.

79. Burnett Stewart to Frank H. Stewart, February 13, 1911, Frank H. Stewart MSS, box 9, Rowan University.

80. Squyres, "The Stewart Room: Its History, Contents and Usage," 17. Stewart's retirement date is also alluded to in his *Reminiscences of Sharptown, N.J.*, 19.

81. Frank H. Stewart, autobiographical papers (*ca.* 1916), Frank H. Stewart MSS, box 6, Rowan University.

82. Squyres, "The Stewart Room: Its History, Contents and Usage," 9.

83. Frank H. Stewart, *Indians of Southern New Jersey* (Woodbury, N.J.: Gloucester County Historical Society, 1932), 3–4.

84. Ibid.

85. Ibid., 3.

86. Frank H. Stewart to Howard D. Fisher, February 16, 1924, Frank H. Stewart MSS, box 6, Rowan University.

87. Stewart, *Our New Home and Old Times*, 4.

88. City of Philadelphia Deed, April 20, 1907, WSV no. 831, 227–230. John L. Kates died on January 27, 1898.

89. In 1890, an attempt to pay the ground rent in actual Spanish dollars might have led to litigation. Per John Kraljevich (*Coin World*, March 30, 2009, 32), "Nuisance lawsuits persisted well into the late 19th century revolving around the Spanish milled dollar. Since many decades-old contracts were still stipulated in 'milled dollars,' the clever or unscrupulous would attempt to pay off landlords and partners in old Spanish coins—then worth just 72 cents on the dollar. Hundreds of such cases found their way into courts across America." Regarding the extinguishment of the ground rent, Stewart noted, "John L. Kates paid off the ground rent which was in existence for nearly one hundred years. It was last owned by a church whose members were colored. They obtained a good price for the ground rent when sold," per Frank H. Stewart MSS, box K, Rowan University.

90. Autobiographical Papers, Frank H. Stewart MSS, box 6, Rowan University.

91. Stewart, *History of the First United States Mint*, 162.

92. "Application For Erection of New Buildings," City of Philadelphia Permit no. 6191, August 28, 1907. Also see Frank E. Hacker to Frank H. Stewart, December 5, 1938, Frank H. Stewart MSS, box S2, Rowan University.

93. Stewart, "How to start a business on a small capital," Frank H. Stewart MSS, box 7, Rowan University, undated.

94. Stewart, "Recollections and Traditions of the Electrical Business," Frank H. Stewart MSS, box 7, Rowan University, 1926, 3.

95. *The Evening Bulletin* (Philadelphia), April 24, 1907, and *Philadelphia North American*, September 8, 1907.

96. Historical Society of Pennsylvania, Society Print collection, Streets, Seventh Street, box 60, folder 2. The clipping exhibits a handwritten date (November 20, 1907) but is unattributed as to the source.

97. An example of this postcard in the Historical Society of Pennsylvania collection is postmarked August 2, 1908.

98. S. Hudson Chapman to Frank H. Stewart, December 6, 1909. Frank H. Stewart MSS, box 5, Rowan University.

99. *The Numismatist*, vol. 23, no. 1 (January 1910): 2.

100. *For the Man Who Buys Electrical Supplies* (Philadelphia: Frank H. Stewart Electric Company, 1910), 8. Frank H. Stewart MSS, box 6, Rowan University.

101. Ibid., 11.

102. *The Numismatist*, vol. 34, no. 4 (April 1921): 149. Yet another numismatic banquet is noted in George Kolbe's sale no. 110, June 2009, lot 280.

103. "Frank H. Stewart Electric Co. Employee's Outing 1924," Frank H. Stewart MSS, box D, Rowan University.

104. "Extracts From an Address Delivered by Frank H. Stewart Before the Association of Electrical Contractors and Dealers of New Jersey" (Philadelphia: Frank H. Stewart Electric Company, 1920), 9–10.

CHAPTER 3

1. Raymond H. Williamson, "The Coinage of the First U.S. Mint: 'Lifting the Curtain,'" *The Numismatist*, 64, no. 4 (April 1951): 387.

2. Russell F. Weigley, ed., *Philadelphia: A 300-Year History* (New York: W.W. Norton, 1982), 4–5.

3. Thomas Hamilton, *Men and Manners in America*, two volumes (Edinburgh: William Blackwell, 1833); reprinted two volumes in one (New York: Augustus M. Kelley, 1968), 337–8.

4. Richard Saul Wurman and John Andrew Gallery, *Man-made Philadelphia: A Guide to its Physical and Cultural Environment* (Cambridge, Mass.: The MIT Press, 1972), 79.

5. Stewart, *History of the First United States Mint*, 35–36.

6. Theodore J. Crackel, ed., "George Washington to the Senate of the United States, April 13, 1792," *The Papers of George Washington Digital Edition* (Charlottesville: University of Virginia Press, Rotunda, 2007), http://rotunda.upress .virginia.edu/pgwde/print -Pre10d158 (accessed November 26, 2009).

7. Thomas Jefferson to George Washington, June 9, 1792, *Thomas Jefferson Papers*, ser. 1, General Correspondence, 1651–1827, Library of Congress.

8. David Rittenhouse to Thomas Jefferson, June 16, 1792, Barbara B. Oberg and J. Jefferson Looney, eds., *The Papers of Thomas Jefferson Digital Edition* (Charlottesville: University of Virginia Press, Rotunda), 2008, http://rotunda.upress.virginia .edu:8080/founders/default .xqy?keys=TSJN-print-01-24 -02-0082 (accessed November 25, 2009).

9. David Rittenhouse to George Washington, July 9, 1792, *Thomas Jefferson Papers*, ser. 1, General Correspondence, 1651–1827, Library of Congress.

10. James Hardie, A.M., *The Philadelphia Directory and Register* (Philadelphia: Printed for the author by T. Dobson, 1793), 121.

11. Ibid., 149. The directory gives 29 North Seventh, which is 39 North Seventh per the new numbering assigned in 1856.

12. "The First Assayer of the United States Mint," *American Journal of Numismatics*, vol. 16, no. 4 (April 1882): 80. In email to the authors, January 17, 2010, R.W. Julian noted that "As far as I know Coxe did not arrive at the Mint until 1793 and thus could not have influenced the Mint site."

13. Elias Boudinot, "Chairman of the Committee Appointed to Examine and Report on the State of the Mint, Report Communicated to the House of Representatives, February 9, 1795," *American State Papers: Finances*, vol. 1 (Washington, D.C.: Gales and Seaton, 1832), 353.

14. Stewart, *History of the First United States Mint*, 27.

15. 41 North Seventh was subdivided in 1788 by Elizabeth Sterner(?), with the western portion granted to Jacob Grumlick (son-in-law) and his wife Elizabeth (daughter of Sterner), and the eastern portion to Henry Grim (Philadelphia Deed Book ser. D, vol. 47, 259).

16. The eastern portion of 43 North Seventh is discussed in Philadelphia Deed Book series D, vol. 71, 57, and series EF, vol. 26, 569. Daniel Trump is found in the 1795 Philadelphia city directory at 43 North Seventh (modern numbering), presumably the western portion, although this is not explicitly indicated in the directory.

17. Stewart, *History of the First United States Mint*, 25.

18. Ibid.

19. Henry William De Saussure, "Mint," Communicated to the U.S. Senate, December 14, 1795. *American State Papers: Finances*, vol. 1 (Washington, D.C.: Gales and Seaton, 1832), 757.

20. Don Taxay, *The U.S. Mint and Coinage* (New York: ARCO Publishing, 1966), 127–130.

21. Elias Boudinot to Thomas Jefferson, April 17, 1802, as cited in J.J. Boudinot, *The Life, Public Services, Addresses and Letters of Elias Boudinot, LL. D.* (Boston and New York: Houghton, Mifflin and Company, 1896), volume 2, 161–162.

22. Stewart, *History of the First United States Mint*, 29.

23. Stewart, *Ye Olde Mint* (Philadelphia: Frank H. Stewart Electric Company, 1909), 8. Stewart's claim was likely based on Evans's *Illustrated History of the United States Mint* (Philadelphia: George G. Evans, Publisher, 1892), 14. The authors are grateful to Pete Smith for this citation.

24. James Rankin Young, *The United States Mint at Philadelphia* (Philadelphia: Captain A.J. Andrews, 1903), 7.

25. http://www.Portlandheadlight .com (accessed September 18, 2007).

26. http://www.nps.gov (accessed September 18, 2007).

27. Edgar H. Adams to Frank H. Stewart, November 29, 1908, Frank H. Stewart MSS, box 5, Rowan University.

28. Thomas Jefferson to George Washington, June 8, 1792, op cit.

29. Newsclipping from Jeannette L. Eckfeldt scrapbook, *The Philadelphia Evening Bulletin*, March 9, 1925.

30. Stewart, *History of the First United States Mint*, 36.

31. Clement Biddle, *Philadelphia Directory*, Philadelphia, 1791. The actual directory listing is 29 North Seventh, which is the same as the modern 39 North Seventh.

32. Survey, Michael Shubert dwelling house, Cancelled Philadelphia Fire Insurance Surveys no. 1639 (Michael Shubert), Philadelphia Contributionship Archives.

33. Frederick Hailer and Wife Christiana [to] the United States of America, Philadelphia Deed Book ser. D, vol. 35, 399, July 18, 1792, transcription from Frank H. Stewart MSS, box 12, folder 1, Rowan University. Another possible source for Stewart was James Ross Snowden, *A Description of Ancient and Modern Coins in the Cabinet Collection of the United States*, (Philadelphia: J.B. Lippincott & Co., 1860), 98. Snowden does not credit his source, but apparently it was the same deed.

34. William Barton, *Memoirs of the Life of David Rittenhouse, L.L.D., F.R.S., Late President of the American Philosophical Society, Interspersed With Various Notices of Many Distinguished Men, With an Appendix Containing Sundry Philosophical and Other Papers, Most of Which Have Not Hitherto Been Published* (Philadelphia: Edward Parker, 1813), 386.

35. William Lambert to Thomas Jefferson, April 17, 1792, Barbara B. Oberg and J. Jefferson Looney, eds., *The Papers of Thomas Jefferson Digital Edition* (Charlottesville: University of Virginia Press, Rotunda,

2008), http://rotunda.upress
.virginia.edu:8080/founders/
default.xqy?keys=TSJN-print
-01-27-02-0787 (accessed
November 29, 2009).

36. John Beckley to Thomas Jefferson, March 18, 1801, Barbara B. Oberg and J. Jefferson
Looney, eds., *The Papers of Thomas Jefferson Digital Edition* (Charlottesville: University of Virginia Press, Rotunda, 2008), http://rotunda.upress
.virginia.edu:8080/founders/
default.xqy?keys=TSJN-print
-01-33-02-0291 (accessed November 26, 2009).

37. *Travels Through North America During the Years 1825 and 1826 by His Highness Bernhard, Duke of Saxe-Weimar Eisenach. 2 vols.* Philadelphia: Carey, Lea and Carey, 1828, vol. 2, 179; *Philadelphia Press*, August 1, 1857. The authors would like to acknowledge R.W. Julian for these citations.

38. Stewart, *Ye Olde Mint*, 13.

39. David Rittenhouse to Thomas Jefferson, March 25, 1793, Barbara B. Oberg and J. Jefferson Looney, eds., *The Papers of Thomas Jefferson Digital Edition* (Charlottesville: University of Virginia Press, Rotunda, 2008), http://
rotunda.upress.virginia
.edu:8080/founders/default
.xqy?keys=TSJN-print-01-25
-02-0416 (accessed November 26, 2009).

40. Stewart, *History of the First United States Mint*, 69. See also *Dunlap's American Advertiser*, October 23, 1792, 4.

41. Taxay, *The U.S. Mint and Coinage*, 80.

42. Stewart, *History of the First United States Mint*, 158.

43. Elias Boudinot to Albert Gallatin, March 22, 1802, in Walter Lowrie and Matthew St. Clair Clarke, eds., *American State Papers: Finances*, vol. 1 (Washington, D.C.: Gales and Seaton, 1832; reprinted Buffalo: William S. Hein & Co., Inc., 1998), 745.

44. Pete Smith to Joel Orosz, e-mail communication, January 25, 2010.

45. Taxay, *The U.S. Mint and Coinage*, 80.

46. David Rittenhouse to George Washington, July 9, 1792, op. cit.

47. David Rittenhouse, "Mint," Communicated to the U.S. Senate by the President of the United States, November 20, 1794, *American State Papers, Finances:* vol. 1 (Washington, D.C.: Gales & Seaton, 1832), 317.

48. Elias Boudinot, "Report on the State of the Mint," February 9, 1795, op. cit.

49. Elias Boudinot, "A Statement of the Application of Moneys Advanced from the Treasury of the United States, for the Support of the Mint Establishment, from the Institution Thereof, to the 31st of December, 1797" (Appendix B of Boudinot's 1798 *Report of the Director of the Mint*), *American State Papers, Finances*, vol. 1 (Washington: Gales & Seaton, 1832), 606.

50. "Committee Instructed to Enquire into the Expediency of Prolonging the Continuance of the Mint at Philadelphia," Report to House of Representatives, February 4, 1823, *American State Papers: Finances*, vol. 4 (Washington: Gales & Seaton, 1858), 225.

51. Stewart, *History of the First United States Mint*, 24.

52. Stewart, *Ye Olde Mint*, 7.

53. Taxay, *The U.S. Mint and Coinage*, 80.

54. Stewart, *History of the First United States Mint*, 169.

55. State of Delaware, *Standards for Measurement*, Title 6, Commercial Trade, Subtitle III, Weight, Measures and Standards, chapter 53. Standards for mason work. http://
delcode.delaware.gov/title6/
c053/index.shtml (accessed May 9, 2008).

56. Stewart, *History of the First United States Mint*, 157, 161–163, with a photograph of one of the vaults on p. 163.

57. Ibid., 170.

58. Stewart, *History of the First United States Mint*, 162; Taxay, *The U.S. Mint and Coinage*, 80.

59. Stewart, *History of the First United States Mint*, 164.

60. Andrew W. Pollock III, *United States Patterns and Related Issues* (Wolfeboro, N.H.: Bowers and Merena Galleries, 1997), 10.

61. Ibid.

62. R.W. Julian, "The Mint in 1792," *The Numismatic Scrapbook Magazine*, XXVIII, 4 (April 1, 1962): 1241–1243.

63. Stewart, *History of the First United States Mint*, 156.

64. Taxay, *The U.S. Mint and Coinage*, 73.

65. *Views in Philadelphia, and Its Vicinity, Engraved from Original Drawings*, (Philadelphia: C.G. Childs, engraver, 1827–1830), pages unnumbered.

66. Joseph Jackson, *Market Street Philadelphia: The Most Historic Highway in America—Its Merchants and Its Story*, (Philadelphia: published by the author, 1918), 116.

67. David Rittenhouse to George Washington, November 27, 1792, quoted in Julian, "The Mint in 1792," 1243, 1245.

68. Stewart, *History of the First United States Mint*, 77.

69. Mark Borckardt, ed., *Walter Breen's Encyclopedia of Early United States Cents, 1793–1814* (Wolfeboro, NH: Bowers and Merena Galleries, 2000), 34.

70. James Ross Snowden, *A Description of the Medals of Washington; of National and Miscellaneous Medals; and of Other Objects of Interest in the Museum of the Mint* (Philadelphia: J.B. Lippincott & Co., 1861), 16.

71. Stewart, *History of the First United States Mint*, 165.

72. David Rittenhouse to Tobias Lear, December 27, 1792, Theodore J. Crackel, ed., *The Papers of George Washington Digital Edition* (Charlottesville: University of Virginia Press, Rotunda, 2008), http://
rotunda.upress.virginia
.edu:8080/founders/default
.xqy?keys=GEWN-print-05
-11-02-0345 (accessed November 26, 2009).

73. Stephen Decatur Jr., *Private Affairs of George Washington: From the Records and Accounts of Tobias Lear, Esquire, his Secretary* (Boston: printed by the Riverside Press for Houghton Mifflin, 1933), 323.

74. Ibid.

75. Unidentified printed history of the Apprentice's Library of Philadelphia, one leaf of which is laid into a copy of Frank H. Stewart's *Our New Home and Old Times;* inscribed by Stewart to "Wm. M. Mervine," and housed at the Hagley Library in Wilmington, Delaware. Quoted portion comes from page 35 of this history. Mervine (1874–1914) was the author of genealogical works.

76. Stewart, *History of the First United States Mint*, 157.

77. Taxay, *The U.S. Mint and Coinage*, 80.

78. Ibid.

79. Warren A. Lapp, M.D., "A Description of the First U.S. Mint," *Penny-Wise*, vol. 2, no. 5 (September 15, 1968), 157.

80. Denis Diderot and Jean le Rond d'Alembert, eds., *L'Encyclopédie, ou Dictionnaire des Sciences, des Arts et des Métiers*, Paris: André François le Breton, 1751–1777; Monnoyage Plate no. 7, depicting a horse mill by Abot de Bazinghem, 1764.

81. Pete Smith to Joel J. Orosz, email message, November 18, 2009.

82. Stewart, *History of the First United States Mint*, 157.

83. Lapp, "A Description of the First U.S. Mint," 156.

84. Ibid., 156–157.

85. Stewart, *History of the First United States Mint*, 135, 137.

86. Karl Moulton to Leonard Augsburger and Joel J. Orosz, e-mail communication, February 22, 2008.

87. Lapp, "A Description of the First U.S. Mint," 156.

88. Boudinot, "A Statement of the Application of Moneys Advanced from the Treasury of the United States, for the Support of the Mint Establishment, from the Institution Thereof, to the 31st of December, 1797," 606.

89. Taxay, *The U.S. Mint and Coinage*, 81.

90. Ibid., 82.

91. Ibid.

92. Henry Garrett, testimony in *Lex v. Kates*, December Term, 1888, Frank H. Stewart MSS, box 12, Rowan University, 14.

93. Ibid., 30.

94. Charles E. Peterson, ed., *The Carpenters' Company of the City and County of Philadelphia 1786 Rule Book* (no place of publication: Bell Publishing Company, 1971), "End Frame" caption facing plate I.

95. Taxay, *The U.S. Mint and Coinage*, 80.

96. Ibid.

97. Stewart, *History of the First United States Mint*, 25–26, 28. See also Joseph Wood, "Brief of Defts [sic] Title," *Wood v. Kates*, 1847, Frank H. Stewart MSS, box 12, Rowan University.

98. Taxay, *The U.S Mint and Coinage*, 80.

99. *Philadelphia Deed Book:* ser. EF, vol. 26, 569–571; ser. GS, vol. 5, 34–39.

100. Adam Eckfeldt, testimony in *Wood v. Kates*, 1847, Frank H. Stewart MSS, box 12, Rowan University.

101. Ibid.

102. *Philadelphia Deed Book:* ser. IH, vol. 3, 205; ser. TG, vol. 376, 503; and Philadelphia Deed Abstracts, lot 149.

103. Robert C. Smith, ed., "A Portuguese Naturalist in Philadelphia, 1799," *The Pennsylvania Magazine of History and Biography*, LXXVM (January 1954), 49.

104. Eugene S. Ferguson, ed., *Early Engineering Reminiscences (1815–1840) of George Escol Sellers* (Washington, D.C.: The Smithsonian Institution, 1965), xv.

105. Ibid., 62.

106. Ibid., 63–64.

107. *American Journal of Numismatics*, vol. 3, no. 7, 52.

108. Raymond H. Williamson, "A Visit to the U.S. Mint in 1812," *The Numismatist*, no. 1 (January 1951): 7–8.

109. George Adams Boyd, *Elias Boudinot* (New York: Greenwood Press, 1952), 249.

110. William E. DuBois, *A Record of the Families of Robert Patterson (the Elder), Emigrant from Ireland to America, 1774; Thomas Ewing, from Ireland, 1718; and Louis DuBois, from France, 1660; Connected by the Marriage of Uriah DuBois with Martha Patterson, 1798. Part First, Containing the Patterson Lineage* (Philadelphia: John C. Clark, 1847), 39.

111. Stewart, *History of the First United States Mint*, 27–28.

112. Ibid., 28; Taxay, *The U.S. Mint and Coinage*, 82.

113. Eckfeldt testimony, op. cit.

114. Ferguson, *Early Engineering Reminiscences (1815–1840) of George Escol Sellers*, 66.

115. "Fire at the Philadelphia Mint 100 Years Ago," *The Numismatist*, XLV, no. 5 (May 1932): 307.

116. 'Penn,' "The First United States Mint," *The Numismatist*, XXIII, no. 1 (January 1910): 3.

117. Stewart, *History of the First United States Mint*, 133–34.

118. *Philadelphia Democratic Press*, January 11, 1816, 2. The authors are grateful to Wayne Homren for providing this citation.

119. Patterson Dubois, "Sparks from the Mint Fire," *American Journal of Numismatics*, vol. 21, no. 1 (July 1886): 11.

120. Ibid.

121. Stewart, *History of the First United States Mint*, 157; Lapp, "A Description of the First U.S. Mint," 157–58.

122. Dubois, "Sparks from the Mint Fire," 12.

123. Stewart, *History of the First United States Mint*, 133–34.

124. Ibid., 162.

125. http://www.usflag.org/index.html (accessed September 9, 2008).

126. Robert Patterson, *Annual Report of the Director of the Mint for 1819* (Washington, D.C., 1820), 2.

127. Taxay, *The U.S. Mint and Coinage*, 98, 80.

128. Moore, "A View of Philadelphia in 1829," 356.

129. Taxay, *The U.S. Mint and Coinage*, 144–145.

130. Stewart, *History of the First United States Mint*, 136.

131. Ibid., 27, 136–137.

132. Ibid., 83.

133. Ferguson, *Early Engineering Reminiscences (1815–1840) of George Escol Sellers*, 67.

134. Stewart, *History of the First United States Mint*, 123, 138.

135. Jacob Eckfeldt to Frank H. Stewart, February 3, 1916, Frank H. Stewart MSS, box 12, Rowan University.

136. Stewart, *History of the First United States Mint*, 139–141.

137. Ibid., 139.

138. Ibid.

139. George Tucker Bispham, Esq., in evidence for the plaintiff, *Lex v. Kates*, December Term, 1888, Frank H. Stewart MSS, box 12, Rowan University, 6–7.

140. Ferguson, *Early Engineering Reminiscences (1815–1840) of George Escol Sellers*, 67–68.

141. Bill in Equity, *Lex v. Kates*, December term, 1888, Frank H. Stewart MSS, box 12, Rowan University, 1–3.

142. Stewart, *History of the First United States Mint*, 144.

143. Unidentified printed history of the Apprentice's Library of Philadelphia, op. cit., Hagley Library.

144. Ibid.

145. Ibid., 36. Also laid into the Mervine copy of *Our New Home and Old Times* is a lithographic copy of Edwin Lamasure's *Ye Olde Mint* with a printed caption: "Apprentice Library Co. occupied first floor Jan. 1836–May 1841."

146. Stewart, *History of the First United States Mint*, 147.

147. Survey, Made February 16, 1837, and Reported to the Franklin Fire Insurance Company of Philadelphia, 1.

148. Ibid., 2.

149. Ibid.

150. Frank H. Stewart, typescript for *History of the First United States Mint*, dated August 16, 1911, Frank H. Stewart MSS, box K, Rowan University.

151. Record Group 104, Inventory Entry 40, Account Book of Coinage Expenses, 1795–1835, National Archives, Mid-Atlantic branch, Philadelphia. The authors are indebted to R.W. Julian for bringing this to our attention.

152. Hexamer and Locher, *Maps of the City of Philadelphia, 1858–1860*, vol. 1, plate 12, map collection, Free Library of Philadelphia.

153. Karl Moulton, *Henry Voigt and Others Involved With America's Early Coinage,*, 145.

154. "B." [Benjamin Betts], "The First United States Mint," *American Journal of Numismatics*, vol. 3, no. 7 (November, 1868), 52–53. The identification of Betts is possible, but not definite.

155. Young, *The United States Mint at Philadelphia*, 3,5.

156. Stewart, *History of the First United States Mint*, 134.

157. Stewart, *Our New Home and Old Times*, i.

CHAPTER 4

1. *The North American*, Philadelphia, September 8, 1907.

2. Ibid.

3. Frank H. Stewart, *Ye Olde Mint*, 3.

4. *The Numismatist*, vol. 23, no. 1 (January 1910): 2.

5. "From Charcoal to Gas in the Minting of Gold," *Gas Logic*, vol. 7, no. 4 (April 1910): 3.

6. *The North American*, Philadelphia, September 8, 1907.

7. Frank H. Stewart, "Indians of Southern New Jersey," (Woodbury, N.J.: Gloucester County Historical Society, 1932), 5.

8. Thomas L. Elder to Frank H. Stewart, undated, but probably late 1908, Frank H. Stewart MSS, box 5, Rowan University.

9. Farran Zerbe to Frank H. Stewart, November 20, 1908, Frank H. Stewart MSS, box 5, Rowan University. Zerbe first met Adams at Henry Chapman's Stickney sale in August 1907 per *The Numismatist*, vol. 20, no. 8 (August 1907): 231, and as Zerbe indicates in this letter that he introduced Adams to Stewart, it is quite possible that Stewart personally attended the Stickney sale.

10. Howland Wood to Frank H. Stewart, November 30, 1909. Frank H. Stewart MSS, box 5, Rowan University.

11. T. L. Comparette to Frank H. Stewart, January 6, 1910, Frank H. Stewart MSS, box 5, Rowan University.

12. J. C. Mitchelson to Frank H. Stewart, November 16, 1908, Frank H. Stewart MSS, box 5, Rowan University.

13. Professional Coin Grading Service U.S. Coins Forum, February 18, 2008, http://forums.collectors.com/messageview.cfm?catid=26&thread id =639735 (accessed March 11, 2009).

14. Stewart, *History of the First United States Mint*, 160. The chronology in *History of the First United Mint* is not precise on this point, though it suggests that the die was found in August or September 1911.

15. Ibid., 105.

16. Walter Breen, *Walter Breen's Encyclopedia of United States Half Cents 1793–1857* (South Gate, Calif.: American Institute of Numismatic Research, 1983), 316.

17. "Coin Dies Abandoned in the Old U.S. Mint," *The Numismatist*, vol. 23, no. 9 (December 1910): 258–259. For more on Charles Warner, see *The Numismatist*, vol. 18, no. 12 (December 1905): 363–365, also Bowers & Merena, Bass I, May 1999:2136.

18. O.C. Bosbyshell to James Pollock, October 21, 1878, as quoted in Arlie R. Slabaugh, "Mickley and the Mint Dies," *Numismatic Scrapbook Magazine*, vol. 31, no. 4, whole no. 350 (April 1965): 973.

19. Ibid. Further confirmation of the destruction is provided in a letter from Preston to Pollock, October 25, 1878, National Archives Record Group 104, entry 235, vol. 17, 139. The authors acknowledge Roger W. Burdette for this citation.

20. *American Journal of Numismatics*, vol. 13, no. 3 (January 1879): 76.

21. *American Journal of Numismatics*, vol. 17, no. 1 (July 1882): 23.

22. *Proceedings of The Numismatic and Antiquarian Society of Philadelphia for the Years 1907, 1907, 1909* (Philadelphia: published by the Society, 1910), 43.

23. R.W. Julian, "All About the Half Cent," *The Numismatist*, vol. 121, no. 12 (December 2008): 65. Breen suggests that the 1811 restrike first appeared in Edward Cogan's December 1859 sale, and notes that John Haseltine attributed their creation to Mickley in his January 1883 sale catalog. See Walter Breen, *Walter Breen's Encyclopedia of United States Half Cents 1793–1857* (South Gate, Calif.: American Institute of Numismatic Research, 1983), 315.

24. Mark Borckardt and William Metropolis, "Restriking the Issue: The Large Cent Restrikes of 1804, 1810 and 1823," appearing in "America's Large Cent," *Coinage of the Americas Conference Proceedings no. 12,* (New York: The American Numismatic Society, 1998), 161. The authors acknowledge Mark Borckardt's thorough discussion of first Mint dies in this article.

25. Charles Steigerwalt, "So-Called Mint Restrike Cents," *The Numismatist*, vol. 20, no. 4 (April 1907): 99. Goldberg's Naftzger sale (February 2009) presents a good selection of 1823 restrike cents, including an example in silver.

26. *American Journal of Numismatics*, vol. 13, no. 4 (April 1879): 92.

27. R.W. Julian, *Medals of the United States Mint: The First Century 1792–1892* (El Cajon, Calif.: The Token and Medal Society, 1977), 31. The medal in question is Julian IP-1. The price is indicated by a letter from Preston to Snowden, October 30, 1878, National Archives Record Group 104, entry 235, vol. 17, 173. The authors acknowledge Roger W. Burdette for this citation.

28. Russell Rulau and George Fuld, *Medallic Portraits of Washington*, 2nd ed., (Lola, Wis.: Krause Publications, 1999), 100.

29. Walter Breen, "Blundered Dies," *The Whitman Numismatic Journal*, vol. 3, no. 5 (May 1966): 325–326.

30. David J. Davis, et al, *Early United States Dimes 1796–1837* (Ypsilanti, Mich.: John Reich Collectors Society, 1984), 86.

31. Rulau and Fuld, *Medallic Portraits of Washington*, 2nd ed., 49. Also see George Fuld, "A Group of Restruck Patterns," *The Numismatist*, vol. 111, no. 5 (May 1998): 515, 518. In e-mail to the author (Augsburger, January 11, 2009), Fuld identified the two seized dies as Judd-461 and Judd-466 Washington head obverses.

32. W. Elliot Woodward, *Catalogue of the Numismatic Collection Formed by Joseph J. Mickley, Esq.* (Roxbury: L.B. Weston, printer, Guild Row, 1867). Lot 2134 was a Birch pattern cent, lot 2136 the Dickeson restrike.

33. *Empire Topics*, no. 5 (February–March, 1959), 14, 15. An example recently appeared in Stack's Americana Sale, January 2009:8567. See also *The Numismatist*, vol. 25, no. 5 (May 1912): 186, for a contemporary opinion of the piece. Curiously, even fakes of the Dickeson piece, a fantasy to begin with, are known—W. Elliot Woodward's October 1884 sale, lot 894, catalogs an electrotype.

34. Heritage, September 1997, lot 7697.

35. Steve M. Tompkins, *Early United States Quarters 1796–1838* (Sequim, Wash.: Steve M. Tompkins & Destni, Inc., 2008), 328–329.

36. Ibid.

37. J. Hewitt Judd, M.D, *United States Pattern Coins* (Atlanta, Ga.: Whitman Publishing, LLC, 2009).

38. Craig Sholley, "The Early U.S. Coining Dies in the ANS Collection," appearing in "America's Large Cent," *Coinage of the Americas Conference Proceedings no. 12* (New York: The American Numismatic Society, 1998), 85. For more on the 1820 half eagle die, see Robert Hoge, "An Early Half Eagle Obverse Die," *The Numismatist*, vol. 107, no. 10 (October 1994): 1489.

39. Nancy Kelly and Richard Oliver, "A Mystery to Die For," *Coin World* (December 12, 2005): 46, 66.

40. John M. Kleeberg, "A Pair of Morgan Dollar Dies in the Collection of the American Numismatic Society," appearing in "America's Silver Dollars," *Coinage of the Americas Conference Proceedings no. 9* (New York: The American Numismatic Society, 1993), 123.

41. Larry Briggs, *The Comprehensive Encyclopedia of United States Liberty Seated Quarters* (Lima, Ohio: Larry Briggs Rare Coins, 1991), 171.

42. Goldberg's Pre-Long Beach Auction, no. 57, lot 2202.

43. Mary Brooks, January 26, 1972, correspondence courtesy of Greg Allen Coins. The recipient's name has been occluded.

44. Mary Brooks, February 9, 1973, correspondence courtesy of Greg Allen Coins. The recipient's name has been occluded.

45. Eric von Klinger, "Discarded Dies by Hundreds," *Coin World* (November 10, 2003): 96, 98. Also see Barbara Gregory, "Kenneth E. Hopple," *The Numismatist*, vol. 122, no. 5 (May 2009): 99.

46. http://www.coinworld.com/news/031802/news-2.asp (accessed December 31, 2008). See also Steve Bieda, "An Olympic-Sized Challenge: Collecting Canceled Dies," *The Numismatist*, vol. 123, no. 1 (January 2010): 44–48.

47. http://catalog.usmint.gov/webapp/wcs/stores/servlet/ProductDisplay?catalogId=10001&storeId=10001&productId=14649 (accessed December 31, 2008).

48. Frank H. Stewart MSS, box 11, Rowan University.

49. Stewart, *History of the First United States Mint*, 160.

50. Ibid., 158.

51. Ibid., 159.

52. Frank H. Stewart MSS, box 11, Rowan University.

53. Stewart, *History of the First United States Mint*, 134.

54. Wilfred Jordan to Frank H. Stewart, February 20, 1918, Independence Hall Accession Records, no. 525.

55. Frank H. Stewart to Wilfred Jordan, February 21, 1918, Independence Hall Accession Records, no. 525.

56. Stewart, *Our New Home and Old Times*, 20.

57. Frank H. Stewart MSS, box K, Rowan University.

58. Stewart, *History of the First United States Mint*, 136.

59. Frank H. Stewart to Wilfred Jordan, November 7, 1913, Independence Hall Accession Records, no. 525. The chair does not appear in the cataloged and numbered lists of this accession. However, it does appear in a single unnumbered, handwritten list, which is probably a preliminary, working copy of the Stewart accession.

60. Author's interview with Harry Forman, July 31, 2007, also voicemail communication from Catherine Bullowa in response to author's query of March 2, 2009.

61. Stewart, *Our New Home and Old Times*, 20.

62. Frank H. Stewart MSS, box 1, Rowan University.

63. George W. Price (Recording Secretary, The Salem County Historical Society) memorandum, March 10, 1914, Frank H. Stewart MSS, box 12, Rowan University.

64. Frank H. Stewart personal note, May 16, 1924, Frank H. Stewart MSS, box 12, folder 4C, Rowan University.

65. Accession no. 1975.54.

66. Verified by author in person on July 31, 2007.

67. *Proceedings of the Numismatic and Antiquarian Society of Philadelphia, for the Years 1910, 1911, and 1912, vol. 26* (Philadelphia: Published by the Society, 1913), 80–81.

68. Craig Whitford Numismatic Auctions, *The Numismatic Card Company Archive Collection of U.S. Mint Memorabilia*, October 6, 1995.

69. Verified by author in person on July 31, 2007.

70. George B. Cucore, "Mint Nostalgia Preserved Through Historical Timber," *Coin World* (December 7, 1962).

71. *The Numismatist*, vol. 73, no. 11 (November 1960): 1637.

72. Cucore, "Mint Nostalgia Preserved," op. cit.

73. Warren A. Lapp, M.D., "Surviving Mementoes of the First U.S. Mint," *Penny-Wise* vol. 3, no. 4 (July 1969): 116.

74. Cucore, "Mint Nostalgia Preserved," op. cit.

75. *The Numismatist*, vol. 80, no. 8 (August 1967): 1018.

76. ANA curator Douglas Mudd to Leonard Augsburger, September 19, 2007

77. *The Numismatist*, vol. 73, no. 11 (November 1960): 1637. The gavel and sounding board were pictured in *Coin World* (September 9, 1960): 3.

78. Ibid.

79. *Numismatic Scrapbook Magazine* (December 1968): 1918. Kaptik's obituary is found in *The Numismatist*, vol. 91, no. 5 (May 1978): 953.

80. E-mail from Eric Newman to the authors, November 19, 2009.

81. Cora Frieman to Frank H. Stewart, December 2, 1909, Frank H. Stewart MSS, box 5, Rowan University.

82. Cora Frieman to Frank H. Stewart, February 23, 1910, Frank H. Stewart MSS, box 5, Rowan University.

83. Cora Frieman to Frank H. Stewart, May 7, 1910, Frank H. Stewart MSS, box 5, Rowan University.

84. Frank H. Stewart, "Ye Olde Mint," *The Philadelphia Rotarian* (February 1, 1915): 4.

85. Ben R. Browne, "Recollections of the First U.S. Mint Building," handwritten single page, dated March 1942, laid into the Wm. M. Mervine copy of Frank H. Stewart's *Our New Home and Old Times*, housed at the Hagley Library in Wilmington, Delaware.

86. Posting by "MrHalfDime," PCGS U.S. Coins forum, http://forums.collectors.com/messageview.cfm?catid=26&threadid=755196&STARTPAGE=1 (accessed January 3, 2010).

87. Frank H. Stewart to James C. Griscom, June 14, 1923, Frank H. Stewart MSS, box D, Rowan University.

88. Stewart, *History of the First United States Mint*, 165. Curry and Stewart were both members of the New Jersey Society of Philadelphia, per the 1918 yearbook of that organization.

89. *Bulletin of the Gloucester County Historical Society*, vol. 7, no. 5 (September 1960): 1. Also see

The Numismatist, vol. 73, no, 9 (September, 1960): 1319.

90. Jeannette R. Eckfeldt to Frank H. Stewart, May 18, 1925, Frank H. Stewart MSS, box 5, Rowan University.

91. Jeannette R. Eckfeldt to Frank H. Stewart, April 29, 1925, Frank H. Stewart MSS, box 5, Rowan University. Eckfeldt served 64 years before retiring in 1929 and passed away at the age of 92 in 1938, per an unattributed news clipping dated September 8, 1938 in Frank H. Stewart MSS, scrapbook 1.

92. *Mehl's Numismatic Monthly*, vol. 6, nos. 7–8, whole nos. 67–68 (July–August, 1915): 107. Stewart attributes the chairs to the second Mint, but see following.

93. *The E-Sylum*, vol. 10, no. 10, March 11, 2007, http://www.coinbooks.org/club_nbs_esylum_v10n10.html (accessed March 14, 2009). Here, an Eckfeldt descendant relates that the chair in the family matches that used by Dunsmore in the *Inspecting* painting. Further corroboration is found in a letter from J.J. Eckfeldt to Jeannette Eckfeldt, January 12, 1916, in which the writer refers to a chair in the Dunsmore painting "like Emmy [presumably a relative] has," Frank H. Stewart MSS, box R, Rowan University. J.J. Eckfeldt was probably John Jacob Eckfeldt, son of Jeannette Eckfeldt. A grandson of Jacob B. Eckfeldt had no knowledge of the tongs and shovel (interview with Joel Orosz, March 1, 2010).

94. Chas. M. Jones to Frank H. Stewart, January 30, 1918, Frank H. Stewart MSS, box 12, Rowan University. Stewart and DuBois were acquainted, as indicated by Patterson DuBois to Frank H. Stewart, February 22, 1916, Frank H. Stewart MSS, box R, Rowan University.

95. Stewart, *History of the First United States Mint*, 161.

96. Independence Hall accession records, no. 525.

97. Christopher Morley, *Travels in Philadelphia* (Philadelphia: David McKay Company, 1920), 169–170.

98. *Philadelphia North American*, August 15, 1911, from Frank H. Stewart MSS, box 11, Rowan University.

99. Independence Hall accession records, no. 509.

100. Independence Hall accession records, no. 525.

101. Stewart, *History of the First United States Mint*, 164, 160.

102. *American Journal of Numismatics*, vol. 2, no. 10, whole no. 22 (February 1868): 89–90.

103. Rusty Goe, *The Mint on Carson Street* (Reno, Nev.: Southgate Coins and Collectibles, 2003), 26–27.

104. Ibid., 487.

105. *The Numismatist*, vol. 16, no. 5 (May 1903): 148.

106. *The Register of Philadelphia*, July 11, 1829, 28. Also see *Coin World* (April 20, 2008): 20 and *Niles' Register* (July 18, 1829).

107. Nancy Oliver and Richard Kelly, "What was Stolen from Former Mint Cornerstone?" *Coin World* (April 27, 2009): 1, 5.

108. Ibid.

109. *American Journal of Numismatics*, vol. 11, no. 2 (October 1876): 39.

110. *New York Times*, September 10, 1874, 5. The Museum of American Finance is now at this site; see *Chicago Tribune*, March 11, 2008, 4.

111. *Numismatic Scrapbook Magazine*, vol. 31, no. 9, whole no. 355 (September 1965): 2461.

112. *Numismatic Scrapbook Magazine*, vol. 23, no. 7, whole no. 257 (July 1957): 1439.

113. American Numismatic Rarities, *Drew St. John Sale*, June 2005, lot 396. The lot realized $32,200.

114. *Coin World*, April 12, 2004; also see the *E-Sylum*, vol. 7, no. 14 (April 4, 2004) and vol. 7, no. 16 (April 18, 2004).

115. *The Numismatist*, vol. 22, no. 12, (December 1909): 355.

116. *Philadelphia Record*, July 30, 1911. Clipping from Frank H. Stewart MSS, box 11, Rowan University.

117. J. Louis Kates to Frank H. Stewart, April 19, 1915, Frank H. Stewart MSS, box 12, Rowan University.

118. *Philadelphia Inquirer*, February 7, 1898.

119. Stewart, *Ye Olde Mint*, 6.

120. Stewart, *History of the First United States Mint*, 24. See also James Ross Snowden, *A Description of Ancient and Modern Coins in the Cabinet Collection at the Mint of the United States* (Philadelphia: J.B. Lippincott & Co., 1860), 99.

121. Unattributed news clipping, Frank H. Stewart MSS, box 11, Rowan University.

122. J. Louis Kates to Frank H. Stewart, April 19, 1915, Frank H. Stewart MSS, box 12, Rowan University.

123. Unattributed news clipping, Frank H. Stewart MSS, box 11, Rowan University.

124. Frank H. Stewart to Historical Society of Pennsylvania, August 30, 1911, Frank H. Stewart MSS, box 12, Rowan University.

125. Frank H. Stewart, "George Washington and the First U.S. Mint," *The Numismatist*, vol. 38, no. 4 (April 1925): 215.

126. Stewart, *History of the First United States Mint*, 189.

127. Ibid., 195.

128. *Numismatic Scrapbook Magazine*, vol. 31, no. 5, whole no. 351 (May 1965): 1290.

129. Stewart, *History of the First United States Mint*, 197.

130. Stewart, *Reminiscences of Sharptown, N.J.*, 11.

131. *The Numismatist*, vol. 38, no. 4 (April 1925): 231.

132. *The Pitman Grove Review*, December 3, 1908, Frank H. Stewart MSS, unnumbered scrapbook, Rowan University.

133. *American State Papers: Finances*, vol. 1, 356.

134. Hon. William Harper, *Memoir of the Life, Character, and Public Services of the Late Hon. Henry Wm. De Saussure, Prepared and Read on the 15th February, 1841, at the Circular Church, Charleston, by Appointment of the South Carolina Bar Association* (Charleston, S.C.: printed by W. Riley, 1841), 21–22.

135. Stewart, *History of the First United States Mint*, 155. The friend is unnamed here, but was possibly one Joseph Pate, as mentioned in Stewart's *Reminiscences of Sharptown, N.J.*, 6–7.

136. *Philadelphia Record*, April 27, 1907, 6. News clipping from Frank H. Stewart MSS, box 11, Rowan University.

137. Stewart, *History of the First United States Mint*, 155.

138. *American State Papers: Finances*, vol. 1, 688.

139. *Boston Weekly Messenger*, July 19, 1832. The authors are grateful to R.W. Julian for this citation.

140. *American State Papers: Finances*, vol. 3, 57.

141. *Historical Magazine* (May 1858), as cited in Q. David Bowers, *American Numismatics Before the Civil War* (Wolfeboro, N.H.: Bowers and Merena Galleries, 1998), 54.

142. *The Numismatist*, vol. 16, no. 5 (May 1903): 151.

143. "A Clever Swindle," *The Numismatist*, vol. 21, no. 5 (May 1908): 155.

144. *The Numismatist*, vol. 37, no. 4 (April 1924), 307.

145. "The Natural Dissemination of Gold," *American Journal of Numismatics*, vol. 20, no. 2 (October 1885): 35.

146. Bowers and Merena, *American Numismatic Association Auction*, July 2003, lot 3472.

147. Semi-Quantitave X-Ray Analysis report, August 18, 2003, from Ledoux & Company, Teaneck N.J., to National Guaranty Corp., Sarasota, Fla.

148. *American Journal of Numismatics*, vol. 20, no. 1, whole no. 109 (July 1885): 22.

149. *The Numismatist*, vol. 16, no. 7 (July 1903): 186.

150. *Philadelphia Record* photograph morgue at the Historical Society of Pennsylvania, vol. 7, 2982, January 24, 1937.

151. Stewart, *History of the First United States Mint*, 155.

152. Stewart, "Ye Olde Mint," *The Philadelphia Rotarian* (February 1, 1915): 4.

153. Joseph F. Meredith, sketch of the Rear Building, *ca.* 1913. Frank H. Stewart MSS, box 12, Rowan University.

154. Stewart, *History of the First United States Mint*, 155.

155. Will of Frank H. Stewart, Gloucester County Surrogate's office, W-3087-48, book 6, folio 336, filed March 31, 1949, 51.

CHAPTER 5

1. Stewart customer letter, July 26, 1905, Frank H. Stewart MSS, box F, Rowan University.

2. Frank H. Stewart MSS, card file box, Rowan University.

3. *The North American*, Philadelphia, September 8, 1907.

4. *The Numismatist*, vol. 21, nos. 10–11 (October–November 1908): 305.

5. Stewart revealed his ANA membership number, no. 1099, in his monograph *Mark Newby The First Banker in New Jersey and His Patrick Halfpence* (Woodbury, N.J.: Gloucester County Historical Society, 1947), 15. Stewart joined the ANA in December 1908, per *The Numismatist* of that month, and remained a member until his death in 1948 (email from Douglas Mudd, ANA curator, to Augsburger, October 7, 2008). Confusing the issue is the existence of a 1909 ANA membership card, no. 446, in the Stewart papers at Rowan University. This appears to be in error, as no. 446 was assigned to one S.M. Thompson (see *The Numismatist*, vol. 15, no. 10 (October 1902): 315, and *The Numismatist*, vol. 23, no. 3 (March 1910): 88. A 1920 ANA membership card for Stewart, with the correct number, exists in the Stewart papers. Stewart is mentioned as being an ANA member in the April 1925 issue of *The Numismatist*, vol. 38, no. 4: 231, and a subscriber to the George Heath Memorial Fund in October of the same year (vol. 38, no. 10: 516).

6. *The Numismatist*, vol. 23, no. 1 (January 1910): 1 and vol. 23, no. 2 (February 1910): 41.

7. Sydney P. Noe to Frank H. Stewart, August 2, 1918. Frank H. Stewart MSS, box I, Rowan University. Per email from ANS archivist Jospeh Ciccone to author (Augsburger), October 1, 2009, Frank H. Stewart does not appear in the ANS historical membership card file. Howland Wood, ANS Acting Secretary, made a second overture in 1923, found in Frank H. Stewart MSS, box I, Rowan University.

8. Frank H. Stewart, *Mark Newby: The First Banker in New Jersey and His Patrick Halfpence*, 5.

9. "Frank H. Stewart, Historian, Dead," unattributed news clipping from the Stewart vertical file at the Gloucester County (N.J.) Historical Society, dated October 15, 1948. The obituary is signed by L.B.M., probably L.B. Moffett of the Peirce School in Philadelphia, from which Stewart hired many graduates. A "Louis B. Moffet" [sic] was elsewhere linked with Stewart; see *Bulletin of the Gloucester County Historical Society*, vol. 16, no. 6 (December 1978): 21. Moffett and Stewart were further both members of the New Jersey Society of Pennsylvania, per the yearbook of that organization in 1920.

10. Stewart, *History of the First United States Mint*, 152, quotes Sellers. Stewart queried the *American Machinist* regarding Sellers's contributions to that periodical, and on December 29, 1920, received a response detailing Sellers's *Early Engineering Reminiscences* which appeared from 1884 to 1895 (Frank H. Stewart MSS, box 12, Rowan University). George Evans is referred to on p. 75, which also mentions the Voigt account books, while the *American State Papers* are noted on pp. 61, 74. Crosby is mentioned in Stewart's *Mark Newby: The First Banker in New Jersey and His Patrick Halfpence*, p. 3. Wayte Raymond's *Coin Collector's Journal* is mentioned on p. 5 of the same pamphlet, and on p. 15 is found a description of Stewart's working relationship with Ted R. Hammer, ANA librarian and curator. *The Numismatist*, *American Journal of Numismatics*, and Scott's *Coin Collector's Journal* citations are found in Stewart's hand on a loose sheet, Frank H. Stew-

art MSS, box 12, Rowan University.

11. *American Journal of Numismatics*, vol. 3, no. 12 (April 1869): facing p. 93.

12. James Neiswinter, "Joseph N.T. Levick," *Coinage of the America's Conference Proceedings no. 12*, (New York: American Numismatic Society, 1998), 15.

13. Independence Hall accession record no. 525.

14. *The Coin Collector's Journal*, vol. 12 (1887): 66, citing *Dunlap's American Daily Advertiser*, Philadelphia, February 9, 1791.

15. Independence Hall accession record no. 525.

16. *American Journal of Numismatics*, vol. 1, no. 2, whole number 2 (June 1866): 12. Reference was likely made to the "Dr. Edwards" struck copies, which today are collectable in their own right—the Rouse example in Goldberg's September 2008 sale brought $11,500. See also George F. Kolbe's sale no. 111 (January 2010), lot 11, describing a contemporary broadside condemning the practice.

17. Charles Warner, *Catalogue of the Large and Valuable Collection of Coins and Medals*, June 5–7, 1867, lots 364, 365.

18. "Government Seizures," *American Journal of Numismatics*, vol. 20, no. 4 (April 1886): 94.

19. Roger S. Cohen Jr., *American Half Cents*, (published by the author, 1971), 20. Also see W. Elliot Woodward, *Nineteenth Sale*, November 11–16, 1878, 4.

20. Independence National Historical Park Outgoing Loan Extension no. L.1997.7. The catalog numbers for the specimen in question are no. 9278 (Independence Hall) and no. 37019 (U.S. Mint).

21. Independence Hall accession record no. 525.

22. Auctions by Bowers and Merena, Inc., *The Herman Halpern Collection*, March 24–25, 1995, lot 2307.

23. Walter Breen, *Walter Breen's Encyclopedia of Early United States Cents 1793–1814* (Wolfeboro, N.H.: Bowers

and Merena Galleries, 2000), 365. Additional commentary is found in *Penny-Wise*, vol. 29, no. 3, consecutive issue no. 168 (May 15, 1995). Also see Walter Breen, *Walter Breen's Encyclopedia of United States Half Cents 1793–1857*, (South Gate, Calif.: American Institute of Numismatic Research, 1983), 163.

24. "The 1861 D Gold Dollar and 1796 Half Cent," *The Numismatist*, vol. 29, no. 8 (August 1916): 366.

25. Attributions courtesy of Steve Tompkins, communicated to author (Augsburger), August 19, 2008.

26. S.H. & H. Chapman, *The Collection of Coins of the United States Formed by Major William Boerum Wetmore, U.S.A. of New York City*, June 27–28, 1906, lot 380.

27. *Mehl's Numismatic Monthly*, vol. 6, no. 5, whole no. 65 (May 1915): 78.

28. Neil Carothers, *Fractional Money*, (New York: John Wiley & Sons, Inc., 1930), 76–77.

29. Frank H. Stewart MSS, box 5, folder 6, Rowan University. In 1920, Pugh alerted Stewart to the presence of the Voigt account book in the Mint library—this is detailed in a loose note dated December 31, 1920, in Frank H. Stewart MSS, box 12, Rowan University.

30. Stewart, *History of the First United States Mint*, 108–111.

31. Q. David Bowers, *Silver Dollars and Trade Dollars of the United States*, (Wolfeboro, N.H.: Bowers and Merena Galleries, Inc., 1993), 468–477. The Chapmans appear in the pedigree notes for the Stickney, Watters, Dexter, Cohen, and Adams specimens.

32. Ibid., 473.

33. Stewart, *History of the First United States Mint*, 117.

34. Frank H. Stewart, *Ye Olde Mint*, 5. In *Our New Home and Old Times*, 7, Stewart mentions the sale of an unspecified coin at $3,600, probably referring to the Stickney 1804 dollar, auctioned by Henry Chapman in June 1907. In *History of the First United States Mint*, 110, he discusses the Stickney 1804

in greater detail. See also *American Journal of Numismatics*, vol. 2, no. 4 (August 1867): 41–42.

35. Ibid.

36. "From Charcoal to Gas in the Minting of Gold," *Gas Logic*, vol. 7, no. 4 (April 1910): 3.

37. *American Journal of Numismatics*, vol. 10, no. 4 (April 1876): 77–78.

38. John L. Cotter, Daniel G. Roberts, and Michael Parrington, *The Buried Past: An Archaeological History of Philadelphia*, (Philadelphia: University of Pennsylvania Press, 1993), 118, 146–147.

39. Ibid., 116.

40. Independence Hall Catalog Records for accession no. 850, specimen 20, 138.

41. Email to author (Augsburger), May 29, 2009.

42. *Coin Collectors Journal*, vol. 2 (March 1877): 45.

43. Congress Hall accession record no. 850, Independence Hall National Park catalog number 9323.

44. Orosz and Herkowitz, "George Washington and America's 'Small Beginning' in Coinage," 118.

45. James A Bear Jr. and Lucia C. Stanton, eds., *Jefferson's Memorandum Book—Accounts, with Legal Records and Miscellany, 1767–1826*, in *The Papers of Thomas Jefferson*, 2nd ser., vol. 2 (Princeton University Press, 1997), 1874.

46. Orosz and Herkowitz, "George Washington and America's 'Small Beginning' in Coinage," 127.

47. Bear and Stanton, *Jefferson's Memorandum Book*, 1874.

48. Orosz and Herkowitz, "George Washington and America's 'Small Beginning' in Coinage," 144.

49. John C. Fitzpatrick, *The Writings of George Washington from Original Manuscripts, 1745–1799* (Washington, D.C.: United States George Washington Bicentennial Commission, 1939), vol. 32, March 10, 1792–June 30, 1793, 210.

50. Henry Chapman, *Catalogue of a Varied Collection of Ancient and Modern Coins*, (Philadelphia: October 14, 1919), 21.

51. Stewart, *History of the First United States Mint*, 120–121.

52. Ibid., 121.

53. Frank H. Stewart to Albert P. Gerhard, December 13, 1920, Frank H. Stewart MSS, box D, Rowan University.

54. Thomas Elder, *Collection of Edward H. Eckfeldt, Jr.* (New York: Elder Coin and Curio Company, 1924), 99.

55. Orosz and Herkowitz, "George Washington and America's 'Small Beginning' in Coinage," 127–134.

56. *Mason's Coin Collectors' Magazine*, vol. 1, no. 9 (February 1885): 96. Edward Cogan, Philadelphia coin dealer, presented the same idea earlier, in 1864; see George Kolbe's 111th sale, January 9, 2010, lot 46. Also see Stack's 65th Anniversary Sale, October, 2000, lot 478, for a modern presentation of the 1792 silver disme.

57. William H. Sheldon, with the collaboration of Dorothy I. Pascal and Walter Breen, *Penny Whimsy* (New York: Harper & Row, 1958), 7.

58. Heritage Auction Galleries, *Baltimore ANA*, July 2008, lot 1406.

59. Ibid.

60. Stewart, *History of the First United States Mint*, 164.

61. Ibid., 76. In email to authors, January 17, 2010, R.W. Julian wrote of the account book for later 1792, "I have been unable to find it. Stewart certainly had access to it."

62. Ibid., 202.

63. P. Scott Rubin, "Auction Appearances and Pedigrees of the 1792 Silver Center Cent," appearing in "America's Copper Coinage 1783–1857," *Coinage of the Americas Conference Proceedings no. 1*, (New York: American Numismatic Society, 1985).

64. *Philadelphia Ledger*, November 8, 1908, clipping from Frank H. Stewart MSS, box 11, Rowan University.

65. Handwritten prospectus for *History of the First United States Mint Its People and Its Operations*, Frank H. Stewart MSS, box 5, Rowan University.

66. Stewart, *Mark Newby: The First Banker in New Jersey and His Patrick Halfpence*, 10.

67. J.C. Mitchelson to Frank H. Stewart, December 7, 1908, Frank H. Stewart MSS box 5, Rowan University.

68. *The Numismatist*, vol. 13, 112, 162. Mitchelson was assigned ANA member ID no. 190.

69. Stewart, *Mark Newby: The First Banker in New Jersey and His Patrick Halfpence*, 10.

70. Frank H. Stewart, "George Washington and the First U.S. Mint," *The Numismatist*, vol. 38, no. 4 (April 1925): 213.

71. Frank H. Stewart MSS, box K, Rowan University.

72. Roger W. Burdette, *Renaissance of American Coinage 1909–1915*, (Great Falls, Va.: Seneca Mill Press, 2007), 324.

73. An inventory exists at http://uspatterns.com/constatlib.html, accessed June 8, 2009.

74. J.C. Mitchelson to Frank H. Stewart, January 10, 1910, Frank H. Stewart MSS, box 5, Rowan University.

75. "Relics of the First U.S. Mint," Independence Hall National Park accession record no. 525.

76. Paul Gilkes, "ANACS authenticates 14th Silver Center 1¢," *Coin World*, vol. 50, issue 2543 (January 5, 2009): 1.

77. "Our New Home," undated circular of the Frank H. Stewart Electric Company, *ca.* 1913. Frank H. Stewart MSS, box 1, Rowan University.

78. Stewart, *History of the First United States Mint*, 118.

79. Ibid., 119.

80. Ibid., 119.

81. Frank H. Stewart MSS, box 11, Rowan University.

82. Stewart, *History of the First United States Mint*, 160.

83. Stewart, *History of the First United States Mint*, 158.

84. Ibid., 119.

85. Ibid., 119.

86. Ibid., 118. The coin is further listed in John M. Kleeberg, *Numismatic Finds of the Americas* (New York: The American Numismatic Society, 2009), 481.

87. Attribution per email from John McCloskey to Leonard Augsburger, May 22, 2009.

88. Stewart, *History of the First United States Mint*, 160.

89. Ibid., 36.

90. Stewart, *History of the First United States Mint*, 116, discusses J.C. Mitchelson. See also Anderson Auction Company, March 4, 1915. Like Stewart, Mitchelson gifted his collection to an institution—the Connecticut State Library, where it is preserved today. See *American Journal of Numismatics*, vol. 45, no. 4 (October, 1911): 208–209.

91. Stewart, *History of the First United States Mint*, 117.

92. David Tripp, *Illegal Tender*, (New York: Free Press, 2004), 51–52. Also see *The Numismatist* (August, 1971): 1163–1164, regarding transfer of the Tiffany pieces from the third to the fourth Philadelphia mint.

93. T.L. Comparette, *Catalogue of Coins, Token, and Medals in the Numismatic Collection of the Mint of the United States at Philadelphia, PA*, (Washington, D.C.: Government Printing Office), 1914.

94. *American Journal of Numismatics*, vol. 45, no. 2 (April 1911): 45. Also http://en.wikipedia.org/wiki/William_B._Van_Ingen, accessed October 22, 2008.

95. Frank H. Taylor, *The Philadelphia Electrical Handbook* (New York: American Institute of Electrical Engineers, 1904), 26.

96. Edward M. Riley, "The Independence Hall Group," *Transaction of the American Philosophical Society*, vol. 43, part 1, 1953.

97. *Pennsylvania Magazine of History and Biography*, vol. 22, 1898, 252.

98. Stewart, *Mark Newby: The First Banker in New Jersey and His Patrick Halfpence*, 39.

99. *Public Ledger*, September 21, 1913.

100. Independence Hall accession records, no. 493, July 22, 1910. This first accession consisted of a single item, a "hand hammered iron door bolt, removed from the First U.S. Mint, Philadelphia," accession no. 893, April 16, 1919, the last from Stewart, consisted of a set of 26 presidential medals.

101. Frank H. Stewart to Wilfred Jordan, November 7, 1913, Independence Hall accession records, no. 525.

102. Brown, "Frank H. Stewart: A Biography," 31.

103. Dean P. Johnson, "Treasure Hunt: At the Frank H. Stewart Room in Rowan's Library," *Rowan Magazine*, vol. 3, no. 3 (Summer 1998): 3.

104. Stewart, *Reminiscences of Sharptown, N.J.*, 23.

105. Frank H. Stewart MSS, card file box, Rowan University.

106. Frank H. Stewart, Letter to the Editor of the Philadelphia Public Ledger, May 27, 1929, Frank H. Stewart MSS, unnumbered box. "ADDRESSES / LETTERS / F.H.S" vol. Also see Frank H. Stewart to Geo. Wharton Pepper, April 10, 1923, Frank H. Stewart MSS, box L, Rowan University, in which Stewart protests the proposed move of the Mint collection to Washington, D.C.

107. Stewart, *Reminiscences of Sharptown, N.J.*, 11, 19.

Chapter 6

1. *American Journal of Numismatics*, vol. 3, no. 7, whole no. 31 (November 1868).

2. Library Company of Philadelphia, catalog no. (5)2526.F.6a.

3. John Dye, *Dye's Coin Encyclopedia: A Complete Illustrated History of the Coins of the World* (Philadelphia: Bradley & Company, 1883), 1065.

4. *Mason's Monthly Illustrated Coin Collector's Magazine*, vol. 1, no. 1, (June 1884): 9. The image was reused by Mason in February 1885.

5. George Evans, *Illustrated History of the United States Mint* (Philadelphia: George G. Evans, 1892), 13. An advertisement for the Electro-Tint Engraving Company, appearing on p. 183, indicates "The engravings in this book are specimens of our work." The same engraving appears again in *Numismatic Scrapbook Magazine*, vol. 24, no. 5, whole no. 267 (May 1958): 929.

6. *The Numismatist*, vol. 27, no. 1 (January 1914): 19.

7. From an unattributed news clipping in the Jane Campbell scrapbooks at the Historical Society of Pennsylvania, vol. 28, 210. This news clipping includes an image virtually identical to Newell and is captioned "FIRST MINT OF THE UNITED STATES IN 1898." The Newell/Stack family image was reproduced in Frank Spadone's *The Flying Eaglet*, vol. 3, no. 5 (September 1957), an example of which appeared among a group lot, in David Sklow's sale of October 2009, lot 818, realizing $150.00.

8. *Youth's Companion*, vol. 75, no. 28 (July 11, 1901). A copy appeared in David Sklow's sale no. 5, October 4, 2008, lot 244, realizing $240.00.

9. James Rankin Young, *The United States Mint at Philadelphia* (Philadelphia: Captain A.J. Andrews, 1903), 5.

10. W. Burnett Stewart to Frank H. Stewart, March 13, 1911, Frank H. Stewart MSS, box 9, Rowan University. Burnett writes, "Do you contemplate renting the cigar store at 37 as there has been three or four parties asking about it, at present we have nothing in it."

11. The image here is a news clipping dated April 27, 1907, from Frank H. Stewart MSS, box 11, Rowan University. The same image appears in the Jane Campbell scrapbooks at the Historical Society of Pennsylvania, vol. 28, 201, and is there attributed to the *Evening Bulletin*, June 12, 1906.

12. Library of Congress catalog LC-USZ262-99223, http://hdl.loc.gov/loc.pnp/cph.3b45269, accessed May 22, 2009. The authors acknowledge David Sklow for locating this image.

13. News clipping attributed to the *North American*, April 24, 1907, Frank H. Stewart MSS, box 11, Rowan University.

14. Stewart used the photograph in *History of the First United States Mint*, 14. Photographic prints have appeared in Whitford, October 6, 1995, lot 247

and Sklow sale no. 5, October 4, 2008, lot 250 (realizing $2,337). The image appeared in *The Bowers Review*, no. 2 (March–April 1961), also *The Numismatist* (January 1910).

15. An ad for the "Lipschutz '44' Cigar Co., Philadelphia, Pa.," with no further address given, appears in the *Atlantic County Record* (March–April 1911), http://www.atlanticlibrary.org/Newspapers/AtlCoRecord/ACR03041911.pdf, accessed December 26, 2009.

16. "Independence National Historical Park, Specimen Record, Independence Hall Collection," accession no. 525, specimen 22, 004.

17. Stewart, *History of the First United States Mint*, 166.

18. Ibid., 124.

19. Stewart Room, Rowan University, catalog entry St.C. 332.46 E92 1886.

20. *The Numismatist*, vol. 27, no. 1 (January 1914): 19. Stewart's letter is dated December 4, 1913.

21. Frank H. Stewart, "The First United States Mint," *Mehl's Numismatic Monthly*, vol. 6, nos. 7–8, whole nos. 67–68 (July–August, 1915): 107.

22. Frank H. Stewart, compiler, *Ocean City Fishing Club 1919 Year Book*, 36.

23. Stewart, *History of the First United States Mint*, 166.

24. Nancy Gustke, *The Special Artist in American Culture* (New York: Peter Lang Publishing, 1995), 18.

25. Gustke, *The Special Artist in American Culture*, 16, 27.

26. Ibid., 63.

27. Ibid., 20.

28. Stewart, *Reminiscences of Sharptown, N.J.*, 11.

29. Frank H. Taylor to Frank H. Stewart, July 18, 1916. Frank H. Stewart MSS, box 5, Rowan University.

30. Frank H. Taylor to Frank H. Stewart, undated. Frank H. Stewart MSS, box 12, Rowan University.

31. Frank H. Taylor to Frank H. Stewart, undated. Frank H. Stewart MSS, box 11, Rowan University.

32. This photo is currently (June 2009) exhibited in the display case of the Stewart Room, Rowan University.

33. Gustke, *The Special Artist in American Culture*, 203.

34. Ibid., 14.

35. Brown, "Frank H. Stewart: A Biography," 1.

36. Ibid., 29.

37. Johnson, "Treasure Hunt: At the Frank H. Stewart Room in Rowan's Library," 3.

38. Gustke, *The Special Artist in American Culture*, 104, citing *The Crossman: Alexandria Bay, N.Y.* (Philadelphia: Alfred M. Slocum Co., 1901).

39. Gustke, *The Special Artist in American Culture*, 131.

40. Ibid., 100.

41. Frank H. Taylor, "The Story of a Copper Coin," Frank Taylor MSS, Historical Society of Pennsylvania.

42. Michael L. Plant et al, *History of the Bureau of Engraving and Printing 1862–1962* (Washington, D.C.: Treasury Department, 1962), 2.

43. Carothers, *Fractional Money*, 156.

44. *The Coin Collector's Journal*, vol. 6 (October 1881): 159.

45. A history of the Heath counterfeit detectors by Eric Newman is found in *The American Numismatic Association Centennial Anthology* (Wolfeboro, N.H.: Bower & Merena Galleries, 1991), 241–271.

46. Plant, *History of the Bureau of Engraving and Printing 1862–1962*, 9. The authors were not able to independently verify this story using the *New York Times* archive.

47. Carothers, *Fractional Money*, 156.

48. Plant, *History of the Bureau of Engraving and Printing 1862–1962*, 24, 27.

49. Ibid., 40.

50. Ibid., 34.

51. Ferguson, *Early Engineering Reminiscences (1815–1840) of George Escol Sellers*, 74–77.

52. Plant, *History of the Bureau of Engraving and Printing 1862–1962*, 35.

53. "Report of Committee to Investigate the Bureau of Engraving and Printing," 55th Cong., 3rd sess., doc. 109, part 2, 12.

54. Plant, *History of the Bureau of Engraving and Printing 1862–1962*, 108. See also *The Numismatist*, vol. 25, no. 11 (November 1912): 435.

55. Ibid., 90.

56. Ibid., 101–102.

57. Stewart, *History of the First United States Mint*, 123.

58. Ibid., 122.

59. Robert Patterson, *A Report of the Director of the Mint, of the Operation of that Establishment during the Year 1816* (Washington: printed by William A. Davis, 1817).

60. Joseph E. Ralph to George B. Cortelyou, June 28, 1908, National Archives, record group 318, entry 5, vol. 239, 119.

61. Stewart, *History of the First United States Mint*, 125.

62. Elizabeth Johnston, *A Visit to the Cabinet of the United States Mint, at Philadelphia* (Philadelphia: J.B. Lippincott & Co., 1876), 19. See also *American Journal of Numismatics*, vol. 27, no. 4, whole no. 140 (April 1893): 85, and *The Numismatist*, vol. 16, no. 7 (July 1903): 212.

63. Evans, *Illustrated History of the United States Mint*, 43.

64. Roger W. Burdette, *Renaissance of American Coinage 1909–1915* (Great Falls, Va.: Seneca Mill Press, 2007), 222–224.

65. Ibid., 28–29.

66. William M. Meredith to Leslie Mortimer Shaw, February 10, 1902, National Archives, record group 318, entry 5, vol. 128, 396.

67. Ibid., 396–397.

68. See for example National Archives, record group 318, entry 10, vol. 8, which lists employees and associated recommendations.

69. http://bioguide.congress.gov/scripts/biodisplay.pl?index=K000062, accessed July 4, 2008.

70. National Archives, record group 318, entry 10, vol. 22 gives the most complete list of Lamasure recommendations, which appear piecemeal throughout other BEP archives.

71. "Report of Committee to Investigate the Bureau of Engraving and Printing," 55th Cong., 3rd sess., doc. 109, part 2, 10. For more on Chapman, see Albert Nelson Marquis, *Who's Who in America A Biographical Dictionary of Notable Living Men and Women in the United States 1906–1907* (Chicago: A.N. Marquis & Company, 1906), 314.

72. National Archives, record group 318, entry 9, vol. 4, 178.

73. Ibid., 178, and also vol. 6 of the same series, 187.

74. "Report of Committee to Investigate the Bureau of Engraving and Printing," 55th Cong., 3rd sess., doc. 109, 18.

75. National Archives, record group 318, entry 9, vol. 6, 187, also 1870 U.S. Census, Philadelphia, 91st district, 28th ward, 18.

76. Joseph E. Ralph to Franklin MacVeagh, March 23, 1910, National Archives, record group 318, entry 5, vol. 279, 52.

77. National Archives, record group 318, entry 9, vol. 7, 185.

78. National Archives, record group 318, entry 5, vol. 190, 234.

79. National Archives, record group 318, entry 11, vol. 21, 237.

80. "Report of Committee to Investigate the Bureau of Engraving and Printing," 55th Cong., 3rd sess., doc. 109, 3, 8. The total BEP payroll was $107, 259.34, of which the Division of Engraving consumed $79,455.

81. Joseph E. Ralph to Frank Lamasure, et al, October 30, 1909, National Archives, record group 318, entry 5, vol. 270, 91.

82. Plant, *History of the Bureau of Engraving and Printing 1862–1962*, 92.

83. National Archives, record group 318, entry 12, box 52, Engraver's file, September 18, 1919.

84. *Annual Report of the Secretary of the Treasury on the State of the Finances for the Fiscal Year Ended June 30, 1919*, (Wash-

ington: Government Printing Office, 1920), 170. Accessed via books.google.com.

85. National Archives, record group 318, entry 12, box 100, Engraver's file, April 23, 1923.

86. National Archives, record group 318, entry 11, vol. 21, 237.

87. *Coronet*, vol. 17, no. 10, whole no. 100 (February 1945): 87–88.

88. National Archives, record group 318, entry 10, vol. 21, also vol. 24, 631.

89. National Archives, record group 318, entry 10, vol. 24, 631.

90. National Archives, record group 318, entry 10, vol. 21.

91. Plant, *History of the Bureau of Engraving and Printing 1862–1962*, 8. Today, Casilear is remembered for his contributions to Laban Heath's *Infallible Counterfeit Detector* series.

92. "Report of Committee to Investigate the Bureau of Engraving and Printing," 55th Cong., 3rd sess., doc. 109, part 2, 301.

93. *Washington Post*, July 6, 1916, 14 (Edwin Lamasure obituary).

94. Ibid.

95. Brochure accompanying Mount Vernon at Sunset 1912 calendar (Red Oak, Iowa: Thomas D. Murphy Company, ©1909), author's collection.

96. *Washington Post*, September 25, 1894, 6, and October 24, 1894, 12.

97. 1910 United States Census, Washington, D.C., precinct 8, district 167, 8A, indicates that Lamasure and his wife, Bertha, had been married for 13 years as of the census date (April 21, 1910), thus placing the marriage in 1896 or 1897.

98. *Washington Post*, December 1, 1894, 3.

99. *Mount Vernon at Sunset*, (Red Oak, Iowa: Thomas D. Murphy Company, ©1909), author's collection.

100. *Washington Post*, August 11, 1906, 7.

101. *Washington Post*, August 11, 1901, 18.

102. *Washington Post*, March 2, 1894, 8.

103. http://en.wikipedia.org/wiki/Louis_Prang, accessed September 22, 2008.

104. *The Fresno Morning Republican*, October 10, 1912, 11, also *Catalog of Copyright Entries Part 4, New Series, Vol. 5, nos. 1–4, January 1910* (Washington: Government Printing Office, 1910), 70.

105. Bettie McKenzie, *The People's Art 1889–1989: One Hundred Years of Calendars from the Thos. D. Murphy Company of Red Oak, Iowa* (Red Oak, Iowa: The Montgomery County Historical Society, 1991).

106. Kathi Wagner, Director, Red Oak (Iowa) Public Library to Leonard Augsburger, November 26, 2008.

107. "Death of Edwin Lamasure," *Washington Post*, July 6, 1916, 14.

108. *Across Panama Building the Canal Reproduced From Original Water Colors by Edwin Lamasure*, 1915 calendar for the J.F. & W.H. Warren Company, Worcester, Mass., author's (Augsburger) collection.

109. Rick and Charlotte Martin, *Vintage Illustration: Discovering America's Calendar Artists 1900-1960*, (Portland, Ore.: Collector's Press, 1997), 11.

110. Frank H. Stewart MSS, Calendars box, Rowan University.

111. *For the Man Who Buys Electrical Supplies* (Philadelphia: Frank H. Stewart Electric Company, 1910), 11. Frank H. Stewart MSS, box 6, Rowan University.

112. Frank H. Stewart MSS, "Frank Stewart Prints" box, Rowan University. Further on Washington, music, and numismatics, the celebrated Philadelphia collector Joseph J. Mickley is said to have repaired a Washington violin in 1856. See William E. Du Bois, "Recent Additions to the Mint Cabinet," *American Journal of Numismatics*, vol. 11, no. 4 (April 1877): 86.

113. Stewart, *Our New Home and Old Times*, 15.

114. *Catalog of Copyright Entries Part 4: Reproductions of a Work of Art; Drawings of Plastic Works of a Scientific or Technical Character; Photographs; Prints and Pictorial Illustrations; Works of Art, New Series, Vol. 5, nos. 1–4, January 1910* (Washington: Government Printing Office, 1910), 460, accessed via books.google.com.

115. Kathi Wagner, Director, Red Oak Public Library to Leonard Augsburger, November 26, 2008.

116. Unattributed clipping, Frank H. Stewart MSS, box 6, Rowan University. The price was $75.00, per an invoice from Murphy to Stewart, January 4, 1912, Frank H. Stewart MSS, box M, Rowan University. The Murphy stock number was 757.

117. Brown, "Frank H. Stewart: A Biography," 17.

118. Stewart, *Mark Newby: The First Banker in New Jersey and His Patrick Halfpence*, 42. Stewart's phrase, "Golden Gate to Golden Horn," matches an 1892 travel book title, authored by one Charles H. Matters, perhaps a volume which resided in Stewart's library.

119. Ibid., 29.

120. Stewart, *Reminiscences of Sharptown, N.J.*, 7.

121. "YE OLDE MINT," single sheet, printed on both sides, attached to the back of the Frank H. Stewart Electric Company calendar for 1915 (Philadelphia: Frank H. Stewart Electric Company, 1915), collection of Pete Smith. The circulars accompanying the 1915 and 1916 Stewart Electric calendars were reprinted in the February 1916 issue of *The Numismatist*.

122. Stewart, *Our New Home and Old Times*, 15.

123. "Assignment of Copyrights," Copyright Office of the United States of America, vol. 50, 174. The copyright date of 1912 allowed time for production in 1913, in order to issue a 1914 calendar by the end of the year.

124. Stewart, *Our New Home and Old Times*, 16.

125. Ibid.

126. Stewart, *History of the First U.S. Mint*, 195.

127. *Cradle of Liberty* was displayed at Congress Hall, along with *Ye Olde Mint*, for at least some period of time. George E. Nitzsche, *University of Pennsylvania Its History, Traditions, Buildings and Memorials, Seventh Edition* (Philadelphia: International Printing Company, 1918), 322.

128. Stewart, *Mark Newby: The First Banker in New Jersey and His Patrick Halfpence*, 32.

129. Thomas W. Becker, "Home of Our First Mint," *COINage* (May 1977): 102.

130. Ibid.

131. Ibid.

132. Stewart, *History of the First United States Mint*, 168.

133. Frank H. Stewart MSS, box K, Rowan University.

134. Browne, "Reflections of the First Mint Building," op. cit., 1.

135. Ibid, 125–126.

136. "YE OLDE MINT," single sheet, printed on both sides, attached to the back of the Frank H. Stewart Electric Company calendar for 1915 (Philadelphia: Frank H. Stewart Electric Company, 1915), collection of Pete Smith.

137. Ferguson, *Early Engineering Reminiscences (1815–1840) of George Escol Sellers*, 63.

138. Mrs. Jacob Weber to Frank H. Stewart, May 6, 1915, Frank H. Stewart MSS, box N, Rowan University.

139. Frank H. Stewart MSS, box K, Rowan University.

140. "Flag of the United States: Wikipedia, The Free Encyclopedia," http://en.wikipedia.org/wiki/Flag_of_the_United_Statesno. historical_progression_A_dumps, accessed December 10, 2009.

141. See documentation in chapter two.

142. Stewart, *History of the First United States Mint*, 166.

143. Ibid., 147.

144. John McDowell to Frank H. Stewart, March 26, 1913,

Frank H. Stewart MSS, box 12, Rowan University, cf. Stewart, *History of the First United States Mint*, 166.

145. Stewart, *History of the First United States Mint*, 166.

146. Ibid.

147. Ibid.

148. Ibid., 151.

149. Ibid., 134.

150. Ibid., 146–147.

151. Ibid., 168.

152. Ibid., 124, 166.

153. Ibid., 151.

154. Ibid., 14.

155. *Philadelphia Ledger*, April 28, 1907, clipping from Frank H. Stewart MSS, box 11, Rowan University.

156. Stewart, *History of the First United States Mint*, 169.

157. Frank H. Stewart MSS, box 12, Rowan University.

158. Ibid.

159. Ibid.

160. Ibid.

161. Frank H. Stewart, "Ye Olde Mint Checklist," Frank H. Stewart MSS, box 12, Rowan University.

162. Ibid.

163. The authors were not able to locate the original application in the Washington, D.C., copyright office. However, a renewal application from the Osborne Company, no. K49455, is dated December 26, 1941. Renewal application was typically executed exactly 28 years after initial publication, coinciding with the expiration of the original copyright.

164. *Electrical World* (April 3, 1915): 865.

165. Frank H. Stewart MSS, clippings box 2, miscellaneous 3, Rowan University.

166. Pete Smith, e-mail communication to Leonard Augsburger, May 2, 2006.

167. Stewart, "YE OLDE MINT," single sheet, printed on both sides, attached to the back of the Frank H. Stewart Electric Company calendar for 1915.

168. Ibid.

169. Ibid.

170. Stewart, *History of the First United States Mint*, 166.

171. Ibid.

172. Ferguson, *Early Engineering Reminiscences (1815–1840) of George Escol Sellers*, 63. Stewart does not mention the molasses lady in either *History of the First Mint* or *Ye Olde Mint*. However, the brochure accompanying the 1915 Stewart Electric Company *Ye Olde Mint* calendar, almost certainly written by Stewart himself, makes mention both of the "molasses-candy woman" and "the famous watchdog of the First Mint."

173. Stewart, *History of the First United States Mint*, 125.

174. Ibid., 166.

175. Frank H. Stewart to Horace T. Carpenter, February 1, 1932, Independence Hall accession records, SN 13.102, Acc. 147, INDE 15789.

176. http://en.wikipedia.org/wiki/Conestoga_wagon, accessed August 23, 2008.

177. The Independence Square Neighborhood (Philadelphia: The Penn Mutual Life Insurance Company, 1926), 48.

178. "Frank H. Taylor's 413 numbered 'Old Philadelphia' prints," http://www.bryn-mawr.edu/iconog/fht/pfht/pfht.html, accessed September 29, 2009.

179. "Electrical Industry," Frank H. Taylor MSS, unnumbered box, Rowan University.

180. Arthur Frazier, *Joseph Saxton and His Contributions to the Medal Ruling and Photographic Arts (Smithsonian Studies in History and Technology, no. 32)* (Washington, D.C.: Smithsonian Institute Press, 1975). The Taylor image is depicted in George Wilson, *Yesterday's Philadelphia* (Miami, Fla.: E.A. Seemann Publishing, Inc., 1975), 32. Besides the first American photograph, Saxton made important advances in medal ruling, see also *A Manual of Gold and Silver Coins of All Nations*, (Philadelphia: Assay Office of the Mint, 1842), 186–189.

CHAPTER 7

1. DeWitt M. Lockman Interviews, New-York Historical Society MSS, January 28, 1927, 1.

2. "Sketch of facts pertaining to life of John Ward Dunsmore," John Ward Dunsmore MSS, New-York Historical Society.

3. DeWitt M. Lockman Interviews, New-York Historical Society MSS, January 28, 1927, 3.

4. Ibid., 9.

5. *1870 United States Census*, Washington township, Decatur County, Ind., 6.

6. Florence Seville Berryman, "Dunsmore's Epic of the American Revolution," *Daughters of the American Revolution Magazine*, vol. LX, no. 11, whole no. 401 (November 1926): 646, 648.

7. DeWitt M. Lockman Interviews, New-York Historical Society MSS, January 28, 1927, 10.

8. Ibid., 11, and February 12, 1927, 33.

9. Ibid., 8.

10. *1870 United States Census*, Washington Township, Decatur County, Ind., 32.

11. DeWitt M. Lockman Interviews, New-York Historical Society MSS, January 28, 1927, 11. Lockman refers here to "Thomas S. Nolan," but this is a typo, cf. Lockman, February 2, 1927, 4.

12. *1870 United States Census*, Washington township, Decatur County, Ind., 41.

13. DeWitt M. Lockman Interviews, New-York Historical Society MSS, January 28, 1927, 8.

14. Mary Noble Welleck Garretson, "Thomas Noble and His Paintings," *New-York Historical Society Quarterly Bulletin*, vol. 24, no. 4 (October 1940): 118.

15. Ibid. This painting currently resides in the New-York Historical Society, inventory no. 1939.250.

16. Ibid., 114.

17. DeWitt M. Lockman Interviews, New-York Historical Society MSS, February 2, 1927, 2.

18. Ibid., 3.

19. Ibid.

20. Lockman, February 2, 1927, gives "2 M. le Prince," but Dunsmore states the address as "22 M. le Prince" in personal correspondence, John Ward Dunsmore MSS, New-York Historical Society. By 1878 Dunsmore is listed at 53 rue Notre-Dame-des-Champs (Lois Marie Fink, *List of American Exhibitors and Their Works, American Art at the Nineteenth Century Paris Salons* (Washington: National Museum of Art, 1990). Both addresses are in the Latin Quarter near the Luxembourg Garden.

21. Greensburg, Ind., *Standard*, November 1, 1875, clipping from John Ward Dunsmore MSS, New-York Historical Society.

22. Ibid., December 22, 1875.

23. *The National Cyclopedia of American Biography* (New York: James T. White & Company, 1909), 366.

24. Florence Seville Berryman, "Dunsmore's Epic of the American Revolution," *Daughters of the American Revolution Magazine*, vol. LX, no. 11, whole no. 401 (November 1926): 648.

25. DeWitt M. Lockman Interviews, New-York Historical Society MSS, February 2, 1927, 9.

26. Ibid., January 28, 1927, 5.

27. Lockman, February 2, 1927, 4, refers to Couture as "Coutois," a typographical error. The identification is made from Lockman placing "Coutois" in Villiers-le-Bel, where Couture resided.

28. New-York Historical Society, inventory no. 14708.

29. DeWitt M. Lockman Interviews, New-York Historical Society MSS, February 2, 1927, 4–5.

30. *Cincinnati Commercial*, November 1877, clipping from John Ward Dunsmore MSS, New-York Historical Society.

31. DeWitt M. Lockman Interviews, New-York Historical Society MSS, February 12, 1927, 31.

32. John Ward Dunsmore to Joseph Dunsmore, May 30, 1876, John Ward Dunsmore

MSS, New-York Historical Society.

33. Ibid.

34. DeWitt M. Lockman Interviews, New-York Historical Society MSS, February 2, 1927, 12.

35. Ibid., February 8, 1927, 1.

36. Ibid, February 2, 1927, 8, and "Early Paintings by John Ward Dunsmore," John Ward Dunsmore MSS, New-York Historical Society.

37. *Boston Daily Globe*, February 25, 1883, clipping from John Ward Dunsmore MSS, New-York Historical Society. This sketch currently resides at the New-York Historical Society, accession no. 1937.1792, there with penciled notations *fait le jour après sa morte* ("made the day after his death") and *á Villier le bel* ("at *Villier-le-bel*").

38. *Kokomo Tribune*, October 4, 1879, clipping from John Ward Dunsmore MSS, New-York Historical Society.

39. "Sketch of facts pertaining to the life of John Ward Dunsmore," John Ward Dunsmore MSS, New-York Historical Society.

40. DeWitt M. Lockman Interviews, New-York Historical Society MSS, February 2, 1927, 10. Probably the artist Frank D. Millett is referred to, who went on to design a number of United States Mint medals.

41. *The National Cyclopedia of American Biography* (New York: James T. White & Company, 1909), 366.

42. DeWitt M. Lockman Interviews, New-York Historical Society MSS, February 12, 1927, 17, also http://en.wikipedia.org/wiki/Duke_of _Marlborough, accessed August 27, 2008.

43. World War I draft registration for Malcolm Dunsmore, Morris County, New Jersey; roll: 1712357; draft board: 2. The connection between father and son is confirmed by the description of Malcolm's injured hand, Lockman, February 12, 1927, 18.

44. *Boston Herald*, September 18, 1881, clipping from John Ward Dunsmore MSS, New-York Historical Society.

45. *Boston Daily Globe*, February 25, 1883, clipping from John Ward Dunsmore MSS, New-York Historical Society.

46. "Early Paintings of John Ward Dunsmore," John Ward Dunsmore MSS, New-York Historical Society. The authors have not located this medal. For medals of the Ohio Mechanics Institute, see Presidential Coin and Antique Auction Seventy-Seven, June 2007, lots 135–136, and 138.

47. Ibid.

48. DeWitt M. Lockman Interviews, New-York Historical Society MSS, February 12, 1927, 19.

49. John Ward Dunsmore MSS, New-York Historical Society. The catalog is dated Saturday, December 1st, with no year. A perpetual calendar suggests that 1883 is the most likely candidate. The *Macbeth* work is plated.

50. *The National Cyclopedia of American Biography* (New York: James T. White & Company, 1909), 366.

51. "Early Paintings of John Ward Dunsmore," John Ward Dunsmore MSS, New-York Historical Society.

52. Richard J. Koke et al., *American Landscape and Genre Paintings in the New-York Historical Society* (Boston: New-York Historical Society in association with G. K. Hall and Company, 1982), vol. 1, 285.

53. *The National Cyclopedia of American Biography* (New York: James T. White & Company, 1909), 366.

54. "Sketch of facts pertaining to the life of John Ward Dunsmore," John Ward Dunsmore MSS, New-York Historical Society.

55. DeWitt M. Lockman Interviews, New-York Historical Society MSS, February 8, 1927, 5.

56. "No Gum, No Art," *The Daily Huronite*, April 10, 1890, 3.

57. *New York Times*, May 4, 1890, 13.

58. *Detroit Tribune*, November 8, 1890, clipping from John Ward Dunsmore MSS, New-York Historical Society.

59. DeWitt M. Lockman Interviews, New-York Historical Society MSS, February 8, 1927, 6, also *United States Census*, 1900, Hamilton County, Ohio, district 23, 9, which respectively places Noble and Dunsmore at 2308 and 2312 Kemper Lane.

60. Mary Noble Welleck Garretson, "Thomas Noble and His Paintings," *New-York Historical Society Quarterly Bulletin*, vol. 24, no. 4, October 1940, 119.

61. Ibid., 123. This work resides today in the New-York Historical Society, inventory no. 1940.274.

62. *Cincinnati Enquirer*, August 8, 1897, 32.

63. DeWitt M. Lockman interviews, New-York Historical Society MSS, February 12, 1927, 7.

64. Ibid., 8.

65. Garretson, "Thomas Noble and His Paintings," 123.

66. DeWitt M. Lockman Interviews, New-York Historical Society MSS, February 12, 1927, 10.

67. Ibid.

68. Ibid., 12.

69. Ibid., 11.

70. *New York Times*, June 17, 1908.

71. DeWitt M. Lockman interviews, New-York Historical Society MSS, February 12, 1927, 1–2.

72. Ibid., 2.

73. Reginald P. Bolton, *Relics of the Revolution: The Story of the Discovery of the Buried Remains of Military Life in Forts and Camps on Manhattan Island* (New York: privately published, 1916), 5.

74. Ibid., 10.

75. Ibid., 11.

76. DeWitt M. Lockman Interviews, New-York Historical Society MSS, February 12, 1927, 10.

77. "Unearthing Relics in Wild Spots of New York City," *New York Times*, December 28, 1919, SM5.

78. Letter of recommendation from Reginald P. Bolton, September 28, 1921, and letter of acceptance from John Ward Dunsmore October 19, 1921,

John Ward Dunsmore MSS, New-York Historical Society.

79. John Ward Dunsmore correspondence, William L. Calver MSS, New-York Historical Society. Dunsmore spoke to the N-YHS on April 3, 1928, using stereopticon images, probably of his own paintings.

80. *New York Times*, March 23, 1915, 6.

81. DeWitt M. Lockman Interviews, New-York Historical Society MSS, February 12, 1927, 20.

82. Margaret Dunsmore to Oscar Barck, September 8, 1944, John Ward Dunsmore correspondence, William L. Calver MSS, New-York Historical Society.

83. DeWitt M. Lockman Interviews, New-York Historical Society MSS, February 12, 1927, 12-13.

84. Mary Noble Welleck Garretson, "Thomas Noble and His Paintings," 122.

85. John Ward Dunsmore to Richard J. Jones, November 21, 1925. John Ward Dunsmore MSS, Wagnalls Memorial Library, Lithopolis, Ohio.

86. *Early American Paintings: Catalog of an Exhibition Held in the Museum of the Brooklyn Institute of Arts and Sciences* (New York: Museum of the Brooklyn Institute of Arts and Sciences, 1917), 95.

87. DeWitt M. Lockman Interviews, New-York Historical Society MSS, February 12, 1927, 10.

88. Ibid., 14.

89. Ibid., 15–16.

90. Ibid., 21.

91. United States Copyright Office claimant files, John Ward Dunsmore, March 25, 1922.

92. DeWitt M. Lockman Interviews, New-York Historical Society MSS, February 12, 1927, 16.

93. United States Copyright Office claimant files, John Ward Dunsmore, December 7, 1933.

94. John Ward Dunsmore MSS, correspondence file, New-York Historical Society. George A. Zabriskie was a distant relative (fifth cousin, once removed)

of one Andrew Christian Zabriskie, President of the American Numismatist Society. Andrew at one time sought a merger between the ANS and New-York Historical Society. See George Olin Zabriskie, *The Zabriskie Family; a Three Hundred and One Year History of the Descendants of Albrecht Zaborowskij (ca. 1638–1711) of Bergen County, New Jersey*, published by the author, 1963. Also see *The E-Sylum*, vol. 12, no. 18 (May 3, 2009), http://www.coinbooks .org/ club_nbs_esylum_v12n18. html, accessed June 21, 2009.

95. *New York Herald Tribune*, October 3, 1945, 18.

96. Margaret Dunsmore to Oscar Barck, December 14, 1942, John Ward Dunsmore correspondence file, William L. Calver MSS, New-York Historical Society.

97. Ibid., September 8, 1944.

98. Lilly Ney to Oscar Barck, October 5, 1945, John Ward Dunsmore correspondence file, William L. Calver MSS, New-York Historical Society.

99. *New York Times*, April 11, 1934, 18.

100. Lilly Ney to Oscar Barck, December 13, 1945, John Ward Dunsmore correspondence file, William L. Calver MSS, New-York Historical Society.

101. United States Copyright Office, reg. no. G51229, December 24, 1915.

102. "Assignment of Copyrights," Copyright Office of the United States of America, vol. 61, 374, December 27, 1915.

103. That Stewart furnished nameplates in 1918 is clear. Wilfred Jordan to Frank H. Stewart, February 14, 1918, ACC 147, Independence Hall Library. Stewart's donation is described as "engraved brass plates, washed in gold."

104. Stewart, *History of the First United States Mint*, 120.

105. *Washington Inspecting the First Money Coined by the United States*, John Ward Dunsmore MSS, "Lists of Paintings" file, New-York Historical Society.

106. Ibid.

107. "Adam and Jacob Eckfeldt U.S. Mint Retirement Medals Information Sought," *The E-Sylum*, vol. 10, no. 10 (March 11, 2007). In addition to this chair, Stewart (*History of the First United States Mint*, 82–83) reported that the Eckfeldt family, as of 1924, also possessed the fire tongs and shovel of the first Mint, as well as 1797 correspondence related to a large screw press under construction. Finally, Adam Eckfeldt's 1839 retirement medal (Julian MT-18), in gold, was still in the family at the time of Stewart's writing.

108. Charles M. Jones to Frank H. Stewart, January 30, 1918, Frank H. Stewart MSS, box 12, Rowan University.

109. Frank H. Stewart to the Osborne Company, May 11, 1914. Frank H. Stewart MSS, box 12, folder 4A, Rowan University.

110. Frank H. Stewart to Mrs. J.B. Eckfeldt, May 10, 1915, Eckfeldt family archive.

111. "U.S. Coin History: The First U.S. Mint Survives Political Factionalism," http://www.us-coin-values -advisor.com/the-first-us -mint.html, accessed June 10, 2006.

112. "Painting to Highlight Show," *Numismatic News* (May 15, 2007): 33.

113. Robert Patterson, *A Report of the Director of the Mint, of the Operation of that Establishment during the Year 1816*, (Washington, D.C.: Printed by William A. Davis), 1817.

114. Cathy L. Clark, "Steam Power: A Pressing Issue," *The Numismatist* (March 2000): 287–291.

115. R.W. Julian, *Medals of the United States Mint: The First Century 1792–1892* (El Cajon, Calif.: The Token and Medal Society, Inc., 1977), 193.

116. Kenneth M. Failor, *Medals of the United States Mint* (Washington, D.C.: U.S. Government Printing Office, 1972), 250.

117. Email from Gene Hynds to author (Augsburger), October 7, 2007.

118. Pete Smith, "Soley Struck Tiny Medals," *The Numismatist* (July 2000): 772–773.

119. David E. Nye, *Electrifying America: Social Meanings of a New Technology, 1880–1940* (Cambridge, Mass.: The MIT Press, 1990), 37.

120. *New York Times*, December 21, 1894; also see *The E-Sylum*, vol. 11, no. 44 (November 2, 2008).

121. George Frederick Kolbe, *Auction Sale 104*, November 2007, lot 796.

122. George G. Evans, *Illustrated History of the United States Mint* (Philadelphia, Pa.: George S. Evans, Publisher, 1892), 12th plate following p. 88.

123. Clark, "Steam Power: A Pressing Issue," 287–291.

124. Orosz and Herkowitz, "George Washington and America's 'Small Beginning' in Coinage," 126–127.

125. Ibid.

126. *Atkinson's Casket, or Gems of Literature, Wit and Sentiment* (June 1831): 270. The authors acknowledge Eric P. Newman and R.W. Julian for this citation.

127. "50 Years in the Mint," *The Ambler Gazette*, undated news clipping in the Eckfeldt family archive, *ca.* April, 15, 1915, the 50th anniversary of Jacob B. Eckfeldt's employment in the Mint.

128. "Inspection of the First Coins of the First United States Mint," brochure accompanying the 1916 Frank H. Stewart Electric Company calendar, Frank H. Stewart MSS, Rowan University. Much of the text of the brochure was reprinted in *The Numismatist*, vol. 29, no. 2 (February 1916): 63.

129. *Washington Inspecting the First Money Coined by the United States*, John Ward Dunsmore MSS, New-York Historical Society.

130. Orosz and Herkowitz, "George Washington and America's 'Small Beginning' in Coinage."

131. Stewart, *History of the First United States Mint*, 175.

132. Ibid., 178.

133. Ibid., 179.

134. Francis D. Campbell, "Library News," *American Numismatic Society Magazine*, vol. 5, no. 3 (Winter 2006): 54–55.

135. Email to author (Augsburger), March 18, 2007.

136. Ibid., 98–100.

137. http://www.usmint.gov/ historianscorner/index.cfm ?action=DocDL&doc =pr434.doc, accessed October 18, 2008.

138. *New York Times*, July 11, 1976.

139. A.H. Nash to Frank H. Stewart, February 14, 1916, Frank H. Stewart MSS, box 12, Rowan University.

140. Stewart, *Our New Home and Old Times*, 41.

141. J.B. Patterson, ed., *Autobiography of Ma-Ka-Tai-Me-She-Kia-Kiak, or Black Hawk* (Oquawka, Ill.: J.B. Patterson, 1882), 85, accessed via books.google.com.

142. Taxay, *The U.S. Mint and Coinage*, 149.

143. *Mason's Coin Collectors' Magazine*, vol. 1, no. 1 (June 1884): 10.

144. Frank H. Stewart MSS, box 5, folder 12, Rowan University.

145. John Rulon Downer to Frank H. Stewart, December 13, 1923, Frank H. Stewart MSS, box D, Rowan University.

146. Edward Stern & Company, Engravers and Printers, to Frank H. Stewart, October 30, 1917, and November 1917, Frank H. Stewart MSS, box S2, Rowan University. *The Biggest One Got Away* is not explicitly named in the Stern correspondence but is inferred by an adjacent letter in the file acknowledging receipt of a copy, William Stevenson to Frank H. Stewart, December 21, 1917.

147. Correspondence from Jim Majoros to Leonard Augsburger, February 11, 2007, also email to the author (Augsburger) July 9, 2009. *The Numismatist*, vol. 108, no. 9 (September 1995): 1158, describes an exhibition of the lithograph in 1995.

148. For example, the DuPont Company in 1941 issued a safety-themed calendar bearing the *Washington Inspecting* image, a copy of which exists in the John Ward Dunsmore vertical file at the Smithsonian Archives of American Art.

149. George Frederick Kolbe, *Auction Sale no. 73*, June 13, 1998, lot 251, also email from W. David Perkins to authors, July 11, 2009.

150. Dr. C. Winfield Perkins to Frank H. Stewart, February 20, 1916. Frank H. Stewart MSS, box 12, folder 24, Rowan University. Perkins (1878-1954) was the son of Charles Perkins and Sarah Eckfeldt (daughter of Adam C. Eckfeldt), per email from Pete Smith, July 12, 2009.

151. "Eckfeldt Farewell Medal Has New Home," *The Numismatist*, vol. 39, no. 4 (April 1926): 191. Also see *The Evening Public Ledger* (Philadelphia), April 15, 1926.

152. Farran Zerbe to Frank H. Stewart, March 27, 1916, Frank H. Stewart MSS, box R, Rowan University.

153. Thomas Elder to Frank H. Stewart, January 27, 1916. Frank H. Stewart MSS, box 5, folder 15, Rowan University. Also see Thomas Elder to Frank H. Stewart, December 31, 1915, Frank H. Stewart MSS, box R, Rowan University.

154. B. Max Mehl to Frank H. Stewart, May 20, 1916. Frank H. Stewart MSS, box 11, Rowan University. Also see B. Max Mehl to Frank H. Stewart, December 28, 1915, Frank H. Stewart MSS, box R, Rowan University.

155. J.M. Hetrich to Frank H. Stewart, October 12, 1916. Frank H. Stewart MSS, box 5, Rowan University. Hetrich is enumerated in the 1912 Mint employee list, see National Archives record group 104, entry 362, box 1. The authors acknowledge Roger W. Burdette for this citation.

156. J.M. Hetrich to Frank H. Stewart, October 28, 1916. Frank H. Stewart MSS, box D, Rowan University.

157. E.P. Schell to Frank H. Stewart, January 3, 1917. Frank H. Stewart MSS, box 5, Rowan University. Schell is named in the 1912 Mint employee list, op cit.

158. Oscar Hinrichs to Frank H. Stewart, January 10, 1916, and January 18, 1916, Frank H. Stewart MSS, box R, Rowan University. Hinrichs is found in the 1912 Mint employee list, op. cit.

159. John W. Pack to Jacob B. Eckfeldt, April 20, 1921, and Frank H. Stewart to Jeannette Eckfeldt, April 27, 1921, Frank H. Stewart MSS, box D, Rowan University. Pack later acknowledged receipt of two pictures, per correspondence from John W. Pack to Frank H. Stewart, June 14, 1921, Frank H. Stewart MSS, box L, Rowan University. Pack is named in the 1912 Mint employee list, op cit.

160. J.C. Bates to Frank H. Stewart, May 16, 1921, Frank H. Stewart MSS, unnumbered box, Rowan University. Bates's title is given in the 1912 Mint employee list, op cit.

161. Authors' interview with Frank Greenberg, December 28, 2006.

162. Authors' interview with Harry Forman, July 31, 2007.

163. Stephen A. Crain to Leonard Augsburger, March 25, 2006, and email to author (Augsburger), July 8, 2009.

164. Frank H. Stewart MSS, box 5, Rowan University.

165. Frank H. Stewart MSS, box 5B, folder 11, Rowan University.

166. Jeannette Eckfeldt to Frank H. Stewart, undated, and Stewart to Eckfeldt, December 18, 1923, both in Frank H. Stewart MSS, unnumbered box, Rowan University.

167. Robert J. Grant to Frank H. Stewart, April 3, 1924, Frank H. Stewart MSS, Rowan University. Stewart's letter of transmittal to Grant, April 1, 1924, is found in Frank H. Stewart MSS box D, Rowan University.

168. "Question of the Week" for August 9, 2009, http://www.hsp.org/default.aspx ?id=1404, accessed August 29, 2009. Historical Society of Pennsylvania Collection V89, Small Prints box 27.

CHAPTER 8

1. Florence Seville Berryman, "Dunsmore's Epic of the American Revolution," *Daughters of the American Revolution Magazine*, vol. 40, no. 11, whole no. 401 (November 1926): 645–646.

2. Bonnie J. Silverstein, "Frank J. Reilly, The Man and His Method," *American Artist*, 43 (March 1979): 47.

3. Ibid.

4. "Frank Reilly, 60, Art Teacher Dies," *New York Times*, January 16, 1967, 41.

5. Ernest W. Watson and Arthur L. Guptill, "Frank J. Reilly: Painter, Illustrator, Teacher," *American Artist*, 22, (June 1948): 42.

6. Silverstein, "Frank J. Reilly," 42.

7. Ibid., 42–47.

8. Kent Steine, "Frank Reilly (1906–1967): Revolutionary Teacher," http://www.american artarchives.com/reilly.htm, accessed November 13, 2005.

9. Michael Aviano, Askart, http://www.askart.com/askart/a/michael_aviano/michael_aviano.aspx, accessed November 13, 2005.

10. "Frank Reilly, 60, Art Teacher Dies," 41.

11. Stein, "Frank Reilly (1906–1967)," 15.

12. Ibid.

13. Ibid.

14. Doug Higgins, "The Frank Reilly School of Art," 12, http://www.dhfai.net/Artiststatement2.html, accessed August 18, 2008.

15. Candido Rodriguez, "Frank Reilly: Highly Intelligent, Complex and Really Interesting," 3, http://www.todaysinspiration.blogpost.com/2008/05/frank-reilly-highly-intelligent-complex.html, accessed August 21, 2008.

16. Tom Palmer, "Frank Reilly: A no-nonsense guy . . . A warm-hearted mentor," 3, http://www.todaysinspiration .blogpost.com/2008/5/Frank-reilly-no-nonsense-guy-warm.html, accessed August 18, 2008.

17. Richard VanBusack, "Art to the Max," http://www.metroactive.com/papers/metro/10.22.98/peter-max.9842.html, accessed November 13, 2005.

18. Silverstein, "Frank Reilly, The Man," 70.

19. http://www.usmint.gov/about_The_Mint/sculptor_engravers-index.cfm?/=yes&action=aspx, accessed August 21, 2008.

20. Walt Reed, *The Illustrator in America: 1860–2000 (3rd edition)* (New York: Publisher, The Society of Illustrators by HarperCollins International, 2001), 290.

21. Watson and Guptill, "Frank J. Reilly: Painter," 41.

22. Silverstein, "Frank Reilly, The Man," 47.

23. Ibid., 49.

24. http://www.reillyleague.com/aboutus.htm, accessed August 18, 2008.

25. Jack Faragasso, *Mastering Drawing the Human Figure: From Life, Memory, Imagination; with Special Section on Drapery*, no place or publisher, 1998.

26. Doug Higgins, *The Frank Reilly School of Art*, no place, publisher, or date of publication.

27. Apollo Dorian, *Frank J. Reilly—Illustrator's Bible: A Manual for Realist/Representational Painters*. No place of publication, Apollo Dorian Publishing, no date.

28. Steine, *Frank Reilly, Revolutionary Teacher*, 5–6.

29. John Lipman, "American Whiskey: Continental Distilling Corporation, Publicker Industries Incorporated," http://www.ellenjay.com/pub_publicker.htm, accessed August 18, 2008.

30. Dave Ziegler, "Publisher/Continental Distilling/Brands," http://www.straightbourbon.com/forms/showthreadsphp?t=7573, accessed August 23, 2008.

31. "Publicker Industries: An American Distiller of the Past

Century," http://www.encyclo central.com/13042-Publicker _Industries_An_American _Distiller_of_The_Past _Century.html, accessed November 17, 2008.

32. http://www.lileks.com/match/ gallery/131.html, accessed November 13, 2005.

33. http://www.finance.aol.com/ company/publicard-inc/card/ nue/company-description, accessed October 16, 2008.

34. http://www.heaven/hill.com/ tr-recent-stitml?article =NTM4NnN1cGVyNTM4 m3N1y3J1d, accessed August 23, 2008.

35. http://www.prnewswire.com/ cgi-bin/stories.pl?ACCT=109 &STORY=/www/story/01-31 -2008/ 0004746986&EDATE- 66k, accessed August 23, 2008.

36. Watson and Guptill, "Frank J. Reilly: Painter," 42.

37. Ferguson, *Early Engineering Reminiscences (1815–1840) of George Escol Sellers*, 64.

38. Gerald W. Johnson, *A Pattern for Liberty: The Story of Old Philadelphia* (New York: McGraw Hill, 1952).

39. Wallace Evan Davies, "A Pattern for Liberty: The Story of Old Philadelphia," *The William and Mary Quarterly, 3rd Series, 10, 2* (April 1953): 281.

40. Thomas W. Becker, *The Coinmakers: The Development of Coinage from the Earliest Times*, (Garden City, N.Y.: Doubleday, 1967).

41. Richard and Charlotte Martin, *Vintage Illustrations: Discovering America's Calendar Artists, 1900–1950* (Portland, Ore.: Collector's Press, 1997), 116.

42. Hugh Hetzer, "The Hintermeister's," no place, publisher, or date of publication, 1, 3.

43. Ibid., 1.

44. Richard and Charlotte Martin, *Vintage Illustrations*, 116.

45. Ibid., 116–118.

46. Kathi Wagner, director, Red Oak (Iowa) Public Library to Leonard Augsburger, November 26, 2008.

47. "John Henry Hintermeister, A Portrait Painter," *New York Times*, February 12, 1945.

48. "Henry Hintermeister, 73, Painter of Historic Subjects," *New York Times*, June 19, 1970.

49. Hugh Hetzer, e-mail communication with Leonard Augsburger, August 22, 2007.

50. Henry Hintermeister, *Application for Registration of a Claim to Copyright in a Work of Art*, no. GU21919, August 6, 1953, United States Copyright Office.

51. Richard Martin, telephone conversation with Joel J. Orosz, February 5, 2007.

52. Pete Smith, e-mail communication with Leonard Augsburger, October 22, 2008.

53. D. Wayne "Dick" Johnson, post to the *E-Sylum* (January 8, 2007).

54. Collector's Auctions, Ltd., sale no. 33, September 23, 1989, lot 1364.

55. D. Wayne "Dick" Johnson, post to the *E-Sylum* (January 14, 2007).

56. D. Wayne "Dick" Johnson, email to Joel J. Orosz, June 17, 2005.

57. Author's interview with Harry Forman, July 31, 07. See also Leonard Augsburger and Joel J. Orosz, "An Evening with Harry Forman," *The Asylum*, vol. 25, no. 3, consecutive issue no. 97 (Summer 2007).

58. Correspondence from James Almoney to author (Augsburger), February 2006. George A. Almoney had other numismatic connections, as one of the agents assigned by the Secret Service to investigate the Baltimore gold hoard (1934). The treasury department also prepared a film version of "Know Your Money," which was presented at the American Numismatic Association Executive Board meeting in August, 1945 (see *The Numismatist*, vol. 58, no. 10 (October 1945): 1093.

CHAPTER 9

1. Stewart, *Our New Home and Old Times*, 28.

2. Wilfred Jordan to Frank H. Stewart, December 13, 1909, Frank H. Stewart MSS, box 5, Rowan University.

3. Wilfred Jordan to Frank H. Stewart, December 14, 1909, Frank H. Stewart MSS, box 5, Rowan University.

4. Wilfred Jordan to Frank H. Stewart, July 22, 1910, Frank H. Stewart MSS, box 12, Rowan University.

5. Wilfred Jordan to Frank H. Stewart, November 5, 1913, Frank H. Stewart MSS, box 12, folder 3, Rowan University.

6. Frank H. Stewart to Wilfred Jordan, November 7, 1913, acc. 525, Independence Hall Library.

7. Acc. 525, Independence Hall Library, 1912–1950.

8. Frank H. Stewart to Wilfred Jordan, February 26, 1915, acc. 708, item 31, Independence Hall Library.

9. Receipt 747, Independence Hall Library, 1912–1944.

10. Wilfred Jordan to Frank H. Stewart, June 24, 1915, Frank H. Stewart MSS, box N, Rowan University.

11. Wilfred Jordan to Frank H. Stewart, March 4, 1915, acc. 525, Independence Hall Library.

12. Wilfred Jordan to Frank H. Stewart, October 8, 1920, acc. 525, Independence Hall Library.

13. Wilfred Jordan to Frank H. Stewart, February 20, 1918, acc. 525, Independence Hall Library.

14. Acc. 850, Independence Hall Library, 1912–1950.

15. *Report of the Proceedings of the Numismatic and Antiquarian Society of Philadelphia for the Years 1890–1891* (Philadelphia: published by the Society, 1892), 7.

16. http://www.philamuseum.org/ pma_archives/ead.php?c=DEP &s=s188, accessed February 1, 2009.

17. http://www.archive.org/ stream/annualreportofpe40 philaoft/annualreportofpe40 philaoft_djvu.txt, accessed February 1, 2009.

18. Wilfred Jordan to S.[sic] D. Langenheim, November 19, 1918, acc. 850, Independence Hall Library.

19. Wilfred Jordan to S.[sic] D. Langenheim, January 3, 1919, acc. 850, Independence Hall Library.

20. Wilfred Jordan to F.D. Langenheim, May 12, 1920, acc. 850, Independence Hall Library.

21. Wilfred Jordan to Frank H. Stewart, August 12, 1920, acc. 850, Independence Hall Library.

22. Wilfred Jordan to Frank H. Stewart, February 7, 1922, acc. 850, Independence Hall Library.

23. Frank H. Stewart to Wilfred Jordan, February 8, 1922, acc. 850, Independence Hall Library.

24. A. Bertram Gilliland to Frank H. Stewart, February 5, 1923, and Frank H. Stewart to A. Bertram Gilliland, February 8, 1923, Frank H. Stewart MSS, box D, Rowan University.

25. Henry E. Frederick, assistant trust officer, Woodbury Trust, to Warren A. McCullough, curator, Independence Hall, January 6, 1949, SN13.102, Acc. 147, Frank H. Stewart, INDE 15789, Independence Hall Library.

26. N.H. Rambo Jr. to Henry E. Frederick, March 17, 1949, SN13.102, Acc. 147, Frank H. Stewart, INDE 15789, Independence Hall Library.

27. "Independence Hall," *Wikipedia*, http://en.wikipedia.org/ wiki/Independence_National _Historical_Park, accessed February 2, 2009.

28. Constance M. Greiff, *Independence: The Story Behind the Creation of Independence National Historical Park*, chap. 42, http://www.ushistory.org/ihu/ dreams/dreams.42.htm, accessed February 2, 2009.

29. Thomas W. Becker, "Home of Our First Mint," *Coinage* (May 1977): 10. However, the current chief curator of Independence National Historical Park, Karie Diethorn, suggests the location may have been the Second Bank, stating "People often confuse the two buildings, and Second Bank has always been the main museum collections storage area," (email to author December 29, 2009).

30. M.O. Anderson to Eva Adams, July 7, 1967, Independence Hall Library Museum records.

31. "Relics of the First U.S. Mint in the Independence Hall Col-

lection," accompanying M.O. Anderson to Eva Adams, July 7, 1967, Independence Hall Library Museum Records.

32. Eva Adams to M.O. Anderson, August 2, 1967, Independence Hall Library Museum records.

33. *United States Mint, Independence Mall, Philadelphia, Ye Olde Mint in 1792, the Department of the Treasury*, Independence Hall Library Museum records.

34. Loan form, Independence National Historical Park, May 9, 1969, to U.S. Mint, accompanying Chester L. Brooks to Eva Adams, May 9, 1969, Independence Hall Library Museum records.

35. Loan receipt, July 3, 1969, signed by Charles R. Hoskins, Independence Hall Library Museum records.

36. Augustine A. Albino, administrative officer, U.S. Mint, to Robert L. Giannini, museum curator, July 29, 1982, Independence Hall Library Museum records. Some of the rediscovered photos were published in Debbie Bradley, "'P' Mint Grows With U.S." *Numismatic News*, vol. 59, no. 30 (July 27, 2010): 1, 42–44.

37. John C. Milley, chief of museum operations, to Angela Zungolo, U.S. Mint, August 11, 1982, Independence Hall Library Museum records.

38. M.O. Anderson to Eva Adams, July 7, 1967, op. cit.

39. Worth Bailey, museum consultant, loan receipt, February 5, 1957, acc. 147, Independence Hall Library.

40. Paul McDonald to M.O. Anderson, May 20, 1958, acc. 147, Independence Hall Library.

41. Catherine V. Coleman to Frederick Hanson, April 13, 1970, acc. 147, Independence Hall Library.

42. Catherine V. Coleman to Chester L. Brooks, May 19, 1970, acc. 147, Independence Hall Library.

43. Chester L. Brooks to Catherine V. Coleman, May 28, 1970, acc. 147, Independence Hall Library.

44. Mary Brooks to John Milley, June 22, 1970, acc. 147, Independence Hall Library.

45. Charles R. Hoskins to John Milley, February 8, 1971, acc. 147, Independence Hall Library.

46. Mary Brooks to Hobart Cawood, January 25, 1972, acc. 147, Independence Hall Library.

47. Mary Brooks to Hobart Cawood, December 20, 1972, acc. 147, Independence Hall Library.

48. Hobart Cawood to Mary Brooks, January 3, 1974, acc. 147, Independence Hall Library.

49. Receipt for *Washington Inspecting* dated January 9, 1975, acc. 147, signed by Hobart Cawood, Independence Hall Library.

50. Martha B. Aikens to John T. Martino, March 31, 1992, acc. 147, Independence Hall Library.

51. Carole Abercauph, invoice to Independence Hall, April 12, 1994, acc. 147, Independence Hall Library.

52. Howard Stephen Serlick to Karie Diethorn, March 20, 1994, acc. 147, Independence Hall Library.

53. Ann Marie DiSerafino, news release "Park Service Loans U.S. Mint Historic Painting," August 2, 1994, acc. 147, Independence Hall Library. Also see *Coin World* (August 22, 1994): 7.

54. Frances W. Shute, "The Stewart Years," *Bulletin of the Gloucester County Historical Society*, vol. 16, no. 6 (December 1978): 21.

55. Ibid.

56. Squyres, "The Stewart Room," 13.

57. Ibid., 14.

58. Ibid., 26.

59. Ibid.

60. Brown, "Frank H. Stewart," 50.

61. Squyres, "The Stewart Room," 29.

62. Ibid., 50.

63. Ibid., 11.

64. Ibid., 35.

65. Ibid., 36.

66. Brown, "Frank H. Stewart," 52.

67. Stewart, *History of the First United States Mint*, 117.

68. "Independence National Historical Park, Specimen Record, Independence Hall Collection," item 1, specimen 7047, acc. 747, cat. INHP 11938.

69. *New York Times*, August 29, 1971, identifies Becker as the assistant director of the National Bank of Detroit Money Museum.

70. Author's interview with Thomas W. Becker, November 7, 2008.

71. Becker, "Home of Our First Mint," 10.

72. Grant Miles Simon, "Part of Old Philadelphia: A Map Showing Historic Buildings and Sites," (Philadelphia: American Philosophical Society, 3rd rev.), 1966.

73. Discussion with Karie Diethorn, chief curator of Independence National Historical Park, August 1, 2007.

74. Becker, "Home of Our First Mint," 10.

75. Ibid., 102.

76. Ibid.

77. Author's interview with Thomas W. Becker, November 7, 2008.

78. Leonore Braun to David H. Wallace, February 8, 1965, Independence Hall Library Museum records.

79. M.O. Anderson to Eva Adams, July 7, 1967, Independence Hall Library Museum records.

80. Eva Adams to M.O. Anderson, August 2, 1967, Independence Hall Library Museum records.

81. M.O. Anderson to Eva Adams, July 7, 1967, op. cit.

82. Eva Adams to Chester L. Brooks, April 12, 1969, Independence Hall Library Museum records. Hoskins was hired by the U.S. Mint on August 13, 1970, as a consultant to Brooks, per a U.S. Mint press release dated August 22, 1970, www.usmint.gov/historianscorner/index.cfm?action=DocDL&doc=pr419.pdf, accessed on October 24, 2008. Prior to this he consulted for the Mint while still in the capacity of director of the Money Museum of the National Bank of Detroit. See

also *The Numismatist*, vol. 121, no. 11 (November 2008): 103.

83. Chester L. Brooks to Eva Adams, May 9, 1969, Independence Hall Library Museum records.

84. Charles R. Hoskins to Fred Hansen, May 13, 1969, Independence Hall Library Museum records.

85. *United States Mint, Independence Mall, Philadelphia, Ye Olde Mint in 1792, the Department of the Treasury*, Independence Hall Library Museum records.

CHAPTER 10

1. Squyres, "The Stewart Room: Its History, Contents and Usage," 21, notes a diary of 1906.

2. Stewart, *Ye Olde Mint*, 3–4.

3. Ibid., 4.

4. Ibid., 12.

5. Ibid., 8.

6. Ibid., facing page 5.

7. Ibid., facing page 20.

8. Frank H. Stewart to The Cromwell Publishing Company, August 3, 1922, Frank H. Stewart MSS, box D, Rowan University.

9. Stewart, *Ye Olde Mint*, front cover.

10. Frank H. Stewart MSS, box 5, Rowan University.

11. Farran Zerbe to Frank H. Stewart, December 10, 1909, Frank H. Stewart MSS, box 5, Rowan University.

12. T.L. Comparette to Frank H. Stewart, January 6, 1910, Frank H. Stewart MSS, box 5, Rowan University.

13. Stewart, *Ye Olde Mint*, 8.

14. Stewart, *Our New Home and Old Times*, 3.

15. Ibid.

16. Ibid.

17. Ibid., 48.

18. Ibid., 45.

19. Ibid., frontispiece.

20. Ibid., 5.

21. Ibid., 20.

22. Ibid., 6.

23. Ibid., 12–13.

24. Ibid., 15.

25. Ibid., 41.

26. Ibid., 42.

27. Frank H. Stewart MSS, box 7, Rowan University.

28. Stewart, *Our New Home and Old Times*, 36.

29. Ibid.

30. Frank H. Stewart MSS. box 5, Rowan University.

31. Ibid.

32. Frank H. Stewart to Henry William De Saussure, December 6, 1921, Frank H. Stewart MSS, box D, Rowan University.

33. Isabelle DeSaussure to Frank H. Stewart, December 1, 1921, indicated that her cousin Henry William DeSaussure possessed a letter from Washington acknowledging De Saussure's resignation. Stewart makes a brief mention of the exchange between Washington and De Saussure in *History of the First United States Mint*, 89.

34. American Art Association to Frank H. Stewart, January 29, 1921, referring to their sale of February 1, 1921, lot 658. Frank H. Stewart MSS, box I, Rowan University.

35. Frank H. Stewart to J.A. Cruikshank, January 14, 1922, Frank H. Stewart MSS box I, Rowan University.

36. F.G. Duffield to Frank H. Stewart, May 4, 1921, Frank H. Stewart MSS, box G, Rowan University.

37. *The Numismatist*, vol. 36, no. 12 (December 1923): 607. The cost of the ad was $10, per a letter from Stewart to Frank G. Duffield, editor of *The Numismatist*, November 7, 1923, Frank H. Stewart MSS, box D, Rowan University.

38. Frank H. Stewart to Frank G. Duffield, December 10, 1923, Frank H. Stewart MSS, box D, Rowan University.

39. Frank H. Stewart to Frank G. Duffield, December 18, 1923, Frank H. Stewart MSS, box D, Rowan University. Three of the orders were received from the Guttag Bros. in New York, per a letter from the Guttag Bros. to Frank H. Stewart, December 4, 1923, Frank H. Stewart MSS, box D, Rowan University.

40. Frank H. Stewart to Mr. G.M. Emery, December 18, 1923, Frank H. Stewart MSS, box D, Rowan University.

41. Frank H. Stewart to Waldo C. Moore, December 1923, Frank H. Stewart MSS, box S2, Rowan University.

42. Frank H. Stewart to Wm. Festus Morgan, October 12, 1923, Frank H. Stewart MSS, box S2, Rowan University.

43. C.F. Beezley Jr. to Frank H. Stewart, December 4, 1923, Frank H. Stewart MSS, unnumbered box, Rowan University.

44. Frank H. Stewart to The Mac-Millan Company (Ruth N. Bryant), April 1, 1924, Frank H. Stewart MSS, box S2, Rowan University.

45. *The Numismatist*, vol. 37, no. 5 (May 1924): 365.

46. Frank H. Stewart MSS, box G, Rowan University. In addition, three typescript copies, in various stages of completion, are filed in the Stewart collection under the call number 332.46.

47. St. C. 332.46 S849h [no copy number present], Stewart Collection, Rowan University.

48. William H. Chew to Frank H. Stewart, July 21, 1924, Frank H. Stewart MSS, box O, Rowan University.

49. Stewart, *History of the First United States Mint*, 202; also see *The Numismatist*, vol. 38, no. 4 (April 1925): 213.

50. St. C. 332.46 S849h copy 2, Stewart Collection, Rowan University.

51. Ibid., copy 5.

52. Frank H. Stewart MSS, unnumbered box, Rowan University.

53. "Just Published / History of the First United States Mint, Its People and Its Operations," undated, Frank H. Stewart MSS, Rowan University.

54. Frank H. Stewart MSS, box 5, folder 13, Rowan University. Two German publications, *Literarische Wochenschrift* and *Weltwirtschaftliches Archiv*, sent postcards to Campbell in Philadelphia.

55. Jesse P. Watson, *The Bureau of the Mint: Its History, Activities and Organization* (Baltimore: Johns Hopkins Press, 1926), 78, accessed via books.google.com. The Campbell circular and the Watson bibliographic reference (to the supposed 1925 edition) both indicate a page count of 208 pages, while all known copies have 209. Watson further misspells Stewart's name as "F.E. Stewart." Watson was clearly aware of the 1924 edition, for this is correctly cited as "privately printed." While the evidence is not definitive, it seems possible that Watson was referring to the Campbell circular when preparing his bibliography, and (incorrectly) inferred the existence of a 1925 edition published by Campbell.

56. Michael A. Powills to William J. Campbell, publisher, June 29, 1931, and John J. Campbell to Michael A. Powills, July 3, 1931, both letters in the library of Joel J. Orosz. The authors thank George Frederick Kilbe for locating these letters.

57. Stan V. Henkels to Frank H. Stewart, January 6, 1921, Frank H. Stewart MSS, box D, Rowan University.

58. Ibid.

59. Wilfred Jordan to Frank H. Stewart, January 4, 1921, Frank H. Stewart MSS, unnumbered box, Rowan University.

60. Jonce I. McGurk to Frank H. Stewart, January 10 (?), 1921, Frank H. Stewart MSS, box L, Rowan University.

61. *The Asylum*, vol. 10, no. 3 (Summer 1992): 18.

62. St. C. 332.46 S849h copy 3, Stewart Collection, Rowan University.

63. Frank H. Stewart MSS, box O, Rowan University.

64. Brown, "Frank H. Stewart: A Biography," 43.

65. Release of The Philadelphia and Camden Ferry Company, November 27, 1903, Frank H. Stewart MSS, box 6, Rowan University.

66. "A Stone is Moved," *The Numismatist*, vol. 73, no. 9 (September 1960): 1319.

67. Elvira Clain-Stefanelli, *Select Numismatic Bibliography* (New York: Stack's, 1965), 262.

68. Warren A. Lapp, M.D., "A Foreword," *Penny-Wise*, vol. 2, no. 5, consecutive issue no. 8 (September 15, 1968): 154.

69. Charles Davis, *American Numismatic Literature* (Lincoln, Mass.: Quarterman Publications, 1992), 174.

70. Email to author (Augsburger), April 14, 2008.

71. Will of Frank H. Stewart, Gloucester County Surrogate's Office, W-3087-48, book 6, folio 336, filed March 31, 1949, 44.

72. Authors' collections.

73. Damon Douglas to Frank H. Stewart, March 6, 1943, Frank H. Stewart MSS, 1942–1943 Correspondence Box, Rowan University.

74. Ibid., May 4, 1943.

75. Richard G. Helman to Frank H. Stewart, March 2, 1944, Frank H. Stewart MSS, box I, Rowan University.

76. William H. Arthur to Frank H. Stewart, January 16, 1944, Frank H. Stewart MSS, box I, Rowan University.

77. F.J. Schaefer to Dorothy Hammond, August 13, 1951, Frank H. Stewart MSS, box R, Rowan University.

78. John J. Carey Sr. to Eric P. Newman, July 30, 1962, and August 20, 1962.

79. Vladimir Clain-Stefanelli, *History of the National Numismatic Collections* (Washington, D.C.: U.S. Government Printing Office, 1968), appendix VIII.

80. *Numismatic Scrapbook Magazine*, vol. 31, no. 5, whole no. 351 (May 1965): 1511.

81. "Electrical Industry," Frank H. Stewart MSS, unnumbered box, Rowan University. Undated but 1942 or later.

82. "The Higley Coppers," *The Numismatist*, vol. 40, no. 12 (December 1927): 740–743, citing *Mehl's Numismatic Monthly* (June 1910). Also see *The Numismatist*, vol. 23, no. 4 (April 1910): 121; and vol. 23, no. 5 (June 1910): 152.

83. Q. David Bowers, *Whitman Encyclopedia of Colonial and Early American Coins* (Atlanta, Ga.: Whitman Publishing, 2009), 233.

84. *The Numismatist*, vol. 34, no. 2 (February 1921): 44. The editor of *The Numismatist*, F.G. Duffield, encouraged Stewart to write this article, per correspondence from Duffield to Frank H. Stewart, August 9, 1920, Frank H. Stewart MSS, box L, Rowan University.

85. Roger S. Siboni and Vicken Yegparian, "Mark Newby and His St. Patrick Halfpence," in Oliver D. Hoover, ed., *Newby's St. Patrick Coinage, Coinage of the Americas Conference Proceedings, no. 16*, (New York: The American Numismatic Society, 2009), 290, 298.

86. Ibid., 298.

87. William Nipper, "Old and New Takes on the St. Patrick Coinage," in Hoover, ed., *Newby's St. Patrick Coinage*, 69.

88. E.S. Steward, *The Steward Family of New Jersey* (Philadelphia: Press of Allen, Lane & Scott, 1907), 11.

89. Nipper, "Old and New Takes on the St. Patrick Coinage," 71. Nipper's estimate of the number of half pence varieties (30) is incorrect. *The C4 Newsletter* (Winter 2009): 20.

90. Sylvester Sage Crosby, *The Early Coins of America* (Boston: published by the author, 1875), 136.

91. Brian J. Danforth, "St. Patrick Coinage Revisited," *The Colonial Newsletter*, 45 (April 2005): 2786.

92. Nipper, "Old and New Takes on the St. Patrick Coinage," 94–97.

93. Edward Maris, *A Historic Sketch of the Coins of New Jersey, with a Plate* (Philadelphia: printed for the author, 1881), 4.

94. Walter Breen, *Walter Breen's Complete Encyclopedia of U.S. and Colonial Coins* (New York: Doubleday, 1988), 34.

95. David Gladfelter, "Mark Newby: Quaker Pioneer," *Token and Medal Society Journal*, 14, no. 5 (1974): 171.

96. Frank H. Stewart, "Mark Newby and His Patrick Halfpence," *The Numismatist*, XXXIV, no. 2 (February 1921): 45.

97. Stewart, *Mark Newby: The First Banker in New Jersey and His Patrick Halfpence*, 3.

98. Ibid.

99. Ibid.

100. Ibid., 8.

101. Abe Kosoff and Abner Kreisberg, *ANA 1947 Convention Auction Sale*, Numismatic Gallery, New York, 1947, lots 921–926.

102. Stewart, *Mark Newby: The First Banker in New Jersey and His Patrick Halfpence*, 7.

103. Ibid., 9.

104. Ibid., 5.

105. Ibid., 11.

106. Ibid.

107. Ibid., 15.

108. Ibid.

109. Stewart, *Reminiscences of Sharptown, N.J.*, 19.

110. William E. Rothschild, *The Secret to GE's Success* (New York: The McGraw-Hill Companies, Inc., 2007), 62. General Electric retained General Electric Supply Company until 2006 when it was divested to Rexel, a French concern. GE Supply was rebranded as Gexpro in 2007.

111. "Electrical Industry," Frank H. Stewart MSS, unnumbered box, Rowan University, 39. Undated, but 1942 or later.

112. Federal Trade Commission to Frank H. Stewart, December 8, 1923, Frank H. Stewart MSS, box D, Rowan University.

113. Brown, "Frank H. Stewart: A Biography," 27.

114. http://members.nova.org/~dayalan/Days_of_Yore/Woodburys_top_citizen.html, accessed August 15, 2009.

115. Frank H. Stewart MSS, 1942–1943 Correspondence, Rowan University.

116. Stewart reported having "an office in the Land Title building in Philadelphia," in *Stewart Clan Magazine*, vol. 9, no. 4 (October 1930–1931): 200, accessed via books.google.com.

117. "Articles of Dissolution," February 1, 1950, Commonwealth of Pennsylvania, Department of State.

118. Brown, "Frank H. Stewart: A Biography," 47.

119. Ibid., 25.

120. "Will of Frank H. Stewart," Gloucester County Surrogate's Office, wills book 6, folio 336, November 10, 1948, 2nd clause.

121. Frank H. Stewart MSS, Wills File, February 26, 1929, Rowan University. Stewart's epitaph is clearly modeled after that of a young Benjamin Franklin.

122. Ibid.

123. Brown, "Frank H. Stewart: A Biography," 48.

124. Borough of Glassboro Council meeting minutes, March 9, 2004, http://www.glassboroonline.com/PDF/minutes_03_09_04.pdf, accessed August 31, 2009.

125. "Cash Recapitulation 1944 Frank H. Stewart Electric Co.," Frank H. Stewart MSS, box D, Rowan University.

126. "Inventory of Frank H. Stewart, Deceased," Gloucester County Surrogate's Court, inventories book no. 24, 220, August 12, 1949.

127. "First and Final Account of Woodbury Trust Company, George H. Carnall, and Henry B. Frederick, Executors u/w [under will] Frank H. Stewart, deceased," 27, 180. Gloucester County Surrogate's Office, docket no. 12498.

128. Frank H. Stewart MSS, box D, Rowan University.

129. Guttag Bros. to Frank H. Stewart, October 16, 1923, and October 30, 1923, and Frank H. Stewart to Guttag Bros., October 25, 1923, and October 29, 1923, Frank H. Stewart MSS, box D, Rowan University.

130. Postcard, November 15, 1933, cancelled and returned to sender. Frank H. Stewart MSS, Rowan University.

131. "Fire at 37–39 N. 7th is Hard to Find," news clipping dated November 12, 1941, source unattributed. Frank H. Stewart MSS, scrapbook no. 7, Rowan University.

132. "[City of Philadelphia] Application for Permit for Additions, Alterations, Repairs, One-Story Structures, Frame Buildings, Bay Windows, Heaters, Boilers and Engine Foundations, Demolitions, etc.," no. 6927, December 22, 1941.

133. Mutual Assurance Company Policy no. 9500, Historical Society of Pennsylvania.

134. City of Philadelphia Deed Abstract, 35 North Seventh Street, lot 154, December 27, 1945.

135. "[City of Philadelphia] Application for Permit for Additions, Alterations, Repairs, One-Story Structures, Frame Buildings, Bay Windows, Heaters, Boilers and Engine Foundations, Demolitions, etc.," no. 4081, December 16, 1946.

136. City of Philadelphia Deed Abstract, 37–39 North Seventh Street and 631 Filbert, lots 159–160, May 3, 1949, and July 15, 1949, and City of Philadelphia Deed Abstract, 629 Filbert, lot 157, April 29, 1949, and July 15, 1949.

137. City of Philadelphia Deed Abstract, 37–39 North Seventh Street and 631 Filbert, lots 159–160, August 28, 1950.

138. "[City of Philadelphia] 'A' Application for Permit for Additions, Alterations, Repairs, One-story Structures, Foundations, Hot Air Systems, Air Conditioning, Signs, Demolitions, Statement of Occupancy, etc.," no. 9838, October 8, 1964, and no. 9835, October 8, 1964.

139. John L. Cotter, Daniel G. Roberts, Michael Parrington, *The Buried Past: An Archeological History of Philadelphia* (Philadelphia: University of Pennsylvania Press, 1993), 194.

140. Ibid., 215.

141. *Philadelphia Bulletin*, March 23, 1965. Newsclipping from Eckfeldt family archive.

142. Paul Gilkes, "Metal detectorist finds 1798 dollar copper trial," *Coin World* (July 30, 2007): 1.

143. Email communication from Matt Mille to the author (Augsburger), August 12, 2007.

144. Stack's, *The J.A. Sherman and Roraima Shield Collections*, August 2007, lot 3025 and lot 225.

145. Elias Boudinot, "Mint," Communicated to the House of Representatives, February 9, 1795. *American State Papers: Finances*, vol. 1, 353.

AFTERWORD

1. Caspar Souder, *History of Chestnut Street from the Founding of the City to 1859*, extract in Frank Stewart MSS, Seventh Street Folder, Rowan University. The original appeared in *Thomas Westcott's Sunday Dispatch*, October 9, 1858, as part of a series.

2. *Mason's Coin Collectors' Magazine*, vol. 1, no. 9 (February 1885): 95. Jayne Street is today known as Ranstead.

3. *The Numismatist*, vol. 27, no. 2 (February 1914): 71.

4. Jackson, *Market Street Philadelphia*, 116.

5. http://www.usmint.gov/about _the_mint/mint_facilities/index .cfm?action=PA_facilities, accessed May 7, 2009.

6. http://www.usmint.gov/ historianscorner/index.cfm ?action=Roles, accessed May 7, 2009. Rittenhouse actually purchased three lots for this sum,

the two mentioned in addition to 631 Filbert. See Stewart, *History of the First United States Mint*, 25.

7. Ibid.

8. Frank H. Stewart, "Frank H. Stewart Electrical Company History," *ca.* 1920, Frank H. Stewart MSS, box 6, Rowan University.

9. Stewart, *History of the First United States Mint*, 155.

10. Wilfred Jordan to Frank H. Stewart, July 22, 1910, op. cit.

11. Stewart, *History of the First United States Mint*, 157–158.

12. *The Philadelphia Rotarian*, February 1, 1915, from Frank H. Stewart MSS, box 5, Rowan University.

13. *New York Times*, March 25, 1965, 61.

14. Hexamer and Locher, *Maps of the City of Philadelphia, 1858–1860*, vol. 1, plate 12, Map Collection, Free Library of Philadelphia.

15. George Escol Sellers, op. cit.

16. Samuel Moore, op. cit.

17. George Stark, ed., *The Granite Monthly* (November 1881), cited from Bowers & Merena Galleries *The Coin Collector*, no. 131 (June 17, 2001): 10.

18. Stewart, *Our New Home and Old Times*, 31.

APPENDIX A

1. Unattributed news clipping dated May 18, 1944, from Frank H. Stewart MSS, scrapbook 3, Rowan University.

2. *The Numismatist*, vol. 84, no. 12 (December 1971): 1811.

3. Per a post by Bill Jones, April 12, 2004, on the PCGS U.S. Coins forum, http://forums .collectors.com/messageview .cfm?catid=26&threadid =279190&STARTPAGE=1, accessed August 30, 2007.

4. Failor, "Medals of the United States Mint," 281.

5. *The Numismatist*, vol. 84, no. 12 (December 1971): 1811, also *New York Times*, August 29, 1971.

6. *New York Times*, July 11, 1976.

7. Ibid., August 22, 1976.

8. J. de Lagerberg to Frank H. Stewart, December 14, 1920, and December 17, 1920, Frank H. Stewart MSS, box N, Rowan University.

APPENDIX B

1. *Numisma*, vol. 6, no. 3 (May 1882).

2. *The Numismatist*, vol. 16, no. 1 (December 1903): 378.

3. *The Numismatist*, vol. 22, no. 7 (July 1909): 202.

4. *The Numismatist*, vol. 13, 247, 249, 303, 311, 338. Stewart was assigned ANA member ID no. 214,

5. Q. David Bowers, *Virgil Brand: The Man and His Era* (Wolfeboro, N.H.: Bowers and Merena Galleries, 1983), 105. Also see Q. David Bowers, *Adventures With Rare Coins* (Los Angeles, Calif.: Bowers and Ruddy Galleries, 1980), 76.

6. The Lyman Low bid books appeared in George F. Kolbe's sale no. 111, January 2010, lots 103, 105–112.

APPENDIX D

1. Jefferson M. Hoak, *Architectural Research in Philadelphia* (Philadelphia: The Athenæum of Philadelphia, 2001), 12.

2. http://www.philageohistory .org/citydir, accessed February 4, 2009.

APPENDIX E

1. Frank H. Stewart to George M. Andrews, November 8, 1922, Frank H. Stewart MSS, box I, Rowan University.

2. Stewart, *History of the First United States Mint*, 158, 161.

3. Frank H. Stewart MSS, box K, Rowan University.

Selected Bibliography

(FOCUSING ON SIGNIFICANT NUMISMATIC REFERENCES)

American Journal of Numismatics:

 vol. 1, no. 2, June 1866, 12.

 vol. 1, no. 4, August 1866, 27.

 vol. 2, no. 4, August 1867, 41–42.

 vol. 2, no. 10, February 1868, 89–90.

 vol. 3, no. 7, November 1868, 52–43.

 vol. 3, no. 12, April 1869, facing 93.

 vol. 10, no. 4, April 1876, 77–78.

 vol. 11, no. 2, October 1876, 3.

 vol. 11, no. 3, January 1877, 72.

 vol. 11, no. 4, April 1877, 86.

 vol. 13, no. 3, January 1879, 92.

 vol. 17, no. 1, July 1882, 23.

 vol. 20, no. 1, July 1885, 22.

 vol. 27, no. 4, April 1893, 85.

 vol. 45, no. 2, April 1911, 45.

 vol. 45, no. 4, October 1911, 208–209.

American Numismatic Society. Numerous archival collections.

American State Papers. Washington, D.C.: Gales and Seaton, 1832. *Finance*, vol. 1, 688; vol. 3, 57.

Barton, William. *Memoirs of the Life of David Rittenhouse, L.L.D., F.R.S., Late President of the American Philosophical Society. Interspersed with Various Notices of Many Distinguished Men, With an Appendix, Containing Sundry Philosophical and Other Papers, Most of Which Have Not Hitherto Been Published.* Philadelphia: Edward Parker, 1813.

Becker, Thomas W. "Home of our First Mint," *COINage*, May 1977, 9–10, 102.

——. *The Coinmakers: The Development of Coinage from the Earliest Times.* Garden City, N.Y.: Doubleday, 1970.

Boka, Al. "The History of Sugar Alley," *Penny-Wise*, November 2009, 320–326.

Borckardt, Mark, ed. *Walter Breen's Encyclopedia of Early United States Cents, 1793–1814.* Wolfeboro: Bowers and Merena Galleries, 2000.

Bowers, Q. David. *Silver Dollars and Trade Dollars of the United States: A Complete Encyclopedia.* Wolfeboro: Bowers and Merena Galleries, 1993.

——. *Whitman Encyclopedia of Colonial and Early American Coins.* Atlanta: Whitman Publishing, 2009.

Breen, Walter. *Walter Breen's Encyclopedia of United States Half Cents, 1793–1857.* South Gate, Calif.: American Institute of Numismatic Research, 1983.

——. *Walter Breen's Complete Encyclopedia of U.S. and Colonial Coins.* New York: Doubleday, 1988.

Brown, Judith Austin. "Frank H. Stewart: A Biography." A Project Submitted in Partial Fulfillment of the Requirements for L.S. 600, Seminar in Current Issues and Library Seminar, in the Graduate Division of Glassboro State College, 1972 (Located in the Stewart Collection, Rowan University).

Burdette, Roger W. *Renaissance of American Coinage, 1909–1915.* Great Falls, Va.: Seneca Mills Press, 2007.

Carothers, Neil. *Fractional Money.* New York: John Wiley & Sons, Inc., 1930.

Cooper, Denis R. *The Art and Craft of Coinmaking: A History of Minting Technology.* London: Spink & Son, 1988.

Crackel, Theodore J. *The Papers of George Washington, Digital Edition.* Charlottesville: University of Virginia Press, Rotunda, 2008. http://rotunda.upress.virginia.edu

Donaldson, Thomas. *The House in Which Thomas Jefferson Wrote the Declaration of Independence.* Philadelphia: Avil Printing Company, 1898.

Evans, George. *Illustrated History of the United States Mint.* Philadelphia: George S. Evans, 1892.

Failor, Kenneth M. *Medals of the United States Mint.* Washington, D.C.: U.S. Government Printing Office, 1972.

Ferguson, Eugene S., ed. *Early Engineering Reminiscences (1815–1840) of George Escol Sellers.* Washington, D.C.: Smithsonian Institution, 1965.

Hardie, James, A.M. *The Philadelphia Directory and Register.* Philadelphia: Printed for the author by T. Dobson, 1793.

Historical Society of Pennsylvania. Numerous manuscript collections.

Independence National Historical Park. Numerous manuscript collections.

Johnston, Elizabeth. *A Visit to the Cabinet of the United States Mint, at Philadelphia.* Philadelphia: J.B. Lippincott & Co., 1876.

Julian, R.W. *Medals of the United States Mint: The First Century.* El Cajon, Calif.: The Token and Medal Society, 1977.

——. "The Mint in 1792." *The Numismatic Scrapbook Magazine*, vol. 28, no. 4, April 1, 1962, 1241–1243.

Lange, David W. *History of the First United States Mint and Its Coinage.* Atlanta: Whitman Publishing, 2005.

Lapp, Warren A., M.D. "A Description of the First U.S. Mint." *Penny-Wise*, vol. 2, no. 5, September 15, 1968, 157.

——. "Surviving Mementoes of the First U.S. Mint." *Penny-Wise*, vol. 3, no. 4, July 1969, 116.

Mason's Coin Collector's Magazine

 vol. 1, no. 1, June 1884, 10.

 vol. 1, no. 2, July 1884, 18.

 vol. 1, no. 9, February 1885, 95, 96.

Mason's Monthly Illustrated Coin Collector's Magazine, vol. 1, no. 1, June 1884, 9.

Mehl's Numismatic Monthly

 vol. 6, no. 5, May 1915, 78.

 vol. 6, nos. 7–8, July–August 1915, 107.

Moulton, Karl. *Henry Voigt and Others Involved with America's Early Coinage.* Sunnyvale, Calif.: The Cardinal Education Foundation, 2007.

National Archives, Record Group 318.

Newman, Eric P. Numerous e-mail communications.

Nipper, William. "Old and New Takes on the St. Patrick Coinage." In Oliver Hoover, ed., *Mark Newby's St. Patrick Coinage*, American Numismatic Society Coinage of the Americas Conference, November 11, 2006, 67–101.

The Numismatic Scrapbook Magazine:

   vol. 23, no. 7, July 1957, 1439.

   vol. 30, no. 4, April 1964, 909.

   vol. 31, no. 5, May 1965, 1290, 1511.

   vol. 31, no. 9, September 1965, 2461.

The Numismatist:

   vol. 13, various nos., 1900, 112, 162, 247, 249, 303, 311, 338.

   vol. 16, no. 1, January 1903, 378.

   vol. 16, no. 5, May 1903, 148, 151, 186.

   vol. 16, no. 7, July 1903, 186.

   vol. 18, no. 12, December 1905, 363–365.

   vol. 21, no. 5, May 1908, 155.

   vol. 21, nos. 10–11, October–November 1908, 305.

   vol. 22, no. 7, July 1909, 202.

   vol. 22, no. 12, December 1909, 355.

   vol. 23, no. 1, January 1910, 1–2.

   vol. 23, no. 2, February 1910, 41.

   vol. 23, no. 9, September 1910, 258–259.

   vol. 27, no. 1, January 1914, 19.

   vol. 27, no. 2, February 1914, 71.

   vol. 34, no. 2, February 1921, 44.

   vol.34, no. 4, April 1921, 149.

   vol. 36, no. 12, December 1923, 607.

   vol. 37, no. 4, April 1924, 307.

   vol. 37, no. 5, May 1924, 365.

   vol. 38, no. 4, April 1925, 231.

   vol. 45, no. 5, May 1932, 307.

   vol. 72, no. 5, May 1959, 542.

   vol. 73, no. 9, September 1960, 1319.

   vol. 73, no. 11, November 1960, 1637.

   vol. 80, no. 8, August 1967, 1018.

   vol. 84, no. 12, December 1971, 1811.

   vol. 121, no. 11, November 2008, 103.

Oberg, Barbara B. and J. Jefferson Looney, eds. *The Papers of Thomas Jefferson, Digital Edition.* Charlottesville: University of Virginia Press, Rotunda, 2008. http://rotunda.upress.virginia.edu

Orosz, Joel J. and Carl R. Herkowitz. "George Washington and America's 'Small Beginning' in Coinage: The Fabled 1792 Half Dismes." *American Journal of Numismatics, New Series*, vol. 15 (2003), 111–156.

"Penn." "The First United States Mint." *The Numismatist*, vol. 23, no. 1, January 1910, 1–5.

——. "The First United States Mint." *The Numismatist*, vol. 23, no. 2, February 1910, 39–42.

Pennsylvania Magazine of History and Biography, vol. 22, 1898, 252.

Philadelphia, City of. Archives. Numerous record groups.

Pollock, Andrew III. *United States Patterns and Related Issues.* Wolfeboro: Bowers and Merena Galleries, 1994.

Rowan University. Frank H. Stewart Collection.

Sklow, David. U.S. Mint Postcard Collection.

Smith, Pete. Numerous e-mail communications.

——. "Soley Struck Tiny Medals." *The Numismatist*, vol. 113, no.7, July 2000, 772–773.

Snowden, James Ross. *A Description of Ancient and Modern Coins, in the Cabinet Collection at the Mint of the United States.* Philadelphia: J.B. Lippincott & Co., 1860.

Souder, Caspar. *History of Chestnut Street from the Founding of the City to 1859.* Philadelphia: King and Baird Printers, 1860.

Squyres, Felicie F. "The Stewart Room, Its history, Contents and Usage." Term Paper for L.S. 600, Seminar in Current Issues and Library Seminar, in the Graduate Division of Glassboro State College, 1972. (Located in the Stewart Collection of Rowan University.)

Stewart, Frank H. "Autobiographical Papers." MSS box 6, Stewart Collection, Rowan University.

——. "Diary." MSS box 6, Stewart Collection, Rowan University.

——. "George Washington and the First U.S. Mint." *The Numismatist*, vol. 38, no. 4, April 1925, 213–215.

——. *History of the First United States Mint: Its People and Operations.* Philadelphia: Author, 1924.

——. "Inspection of the First Coins of the United States Mint." Printed brochure attached to the back of Frank H. Stewart Electric Company calendars.

——. "Mark Newby and His Patrick Halfpence." *The Numismatist*, vol. 34, no. 2, February 1921, 2.

——. "Mark Newby: The First Banker in New Jersey and His Patrick Halfpence." Woodbury, N.J.: The Gloucester County Historical Society, 1947.

——. "Notes on Old Gloucester County New Jersey Volume III." Baltimore: Genealogical Publishing, 1977, 23, 240.

——. *Our New Home and Old Times.* Philadelphia: Frank H. Stewart Electric Company, 1913.

——. "Reminiscences of Sharptown, N.J." Author, 1931–1932.

——. "The First United States Mint." *Mehl's Numismatic Monthly*, vol. 6, nos. 7–8, July–August 1915.

——. *Ye Olde Mint.* Philadelphia: Author, 1909.

Taxay, Don. *The U.S. Mint and Coinage.* New York: ARCO Publishing, 1966.

United States Mint. http://www.usmint.gov/historianscorner/index.cfm?action=DocDL&doc=pr434.doc

Whitford, Craig A. *The Numismatic Card Company Archive Collection of U.S. Mint Memorabilia.* Mail bid sale, October 6, 1995. Lansing, Mich.: Craig Whitford Numismatic Auctions.

Williamson, Raymond H. "A Visit to the U.S. Mint in 1812." *The Numismatist*, vol. 64, no. 1, January 1951, 4–10.

——. "The Coinage of the First U.S. Mint: Lifting the Curtain." *The Numismatist*, vol. 64, no. 4, April 1951, 386–387.

Index

Page numbers in italic indicate images of the subject.

20 North Seventh, 19
35 North Seventh Street, 36, 46, 49, 57–58
37 and 39 North Seventh Street, xii, 1–2, 25, 26–27, 33, 35–36, *36*, 40–41, 43, 44, 46, 58, 60, 63–64, 66–68, 85, 107, 122–123, 126, 239–240. *See also* Front Building and Old Mint Building
41 and 43 North Seventh Street, 36–37, 49
629 Sugar Alley, 37, 42, 46–47, 63
631 Sugar Alley, 35–36, 40, 46
700 Market Street, xvii. *See also* Graff House
702 Market Street, xiii
710 Market Street, xv
1792 YE OLDE MINT, 25

Adams, Edgar H., 38, *39*, 72, 109
Adams, Eva, 72, 210
Adams, John 76, 90, 115
Administration Building, 2, 4, 38. *See also* Front Building
agriculture, 18
Agriculture Hall, 87
Almoney, George A., 203
American Artist, 196
American Journal of Numismatics, 13, 66, 74, 87, 91, 96, 99
American Numismatic Association, 72, 83, 95
American Numismatic Rarities, 87
American Numismatic Society, 75, 77–78
American State Papers, 96
Anderson, M.O., 210
Apprentices Library of Philadelphia, 63
Art School in Cincinnati, 160
Art Students League, 193–195

Baird, Spencer Fullerton, xv
Bank of the United States, 87
Barton, James, 81
Barton, William, 40, *41*
Bashlow, Robert, 76
Becker, Thomas, 198, 209, 213
Berman, Jordan, 198
Betts, Benjamin, 65–67
Biggest One Got Away, The, 131
Birth of Our Nation's Flag, The, 10, *10*
Bit of Philadelphia at Seventh and Filbert Streets, A, 154
Bockius, P. Logan, 22
Bosbyshell, O.C., 74
Boudinot, Elias, *35*, 35–37, 39, 41–42, 49, 51, *54*
Bowers, Q. David, 77
Breen, Walter, 73, 76
Bressett, Ken, 102
Briggs, Larry, 78
Brooks, Mary, 72, 78, 211
Browner, Ben R., 85
Bullowa, Catherine, 81
Bullowa, David, 239

Bureau of Engraving and Printing, 14, 15, 135
Bureau of the Mint: Its History, Activities and Organization, 228
Buried Past, The: An Archaeological History of Philadelphia, 240

calendars, 28
Carson City dies, 79
Carson City Mint, 79
Centennial Exhibit, 13
Centennial medals, 14
cents, 90–92
Chambers Umbrella Factory, 126
Chapman, Samuel and Henry, xvi, 95, 102, 105
Childs, George K., 73
City of Philadelphia xvii, 1, 3–5, 8, 14, 32–33, *33*, 50, 115, 210, 240
Civil War, 134
Cleveland Wrecking Company, 89
Cloud, Joseph, *54*
Coin Collector's Journal, 96
Coin World, 78–79, 82
Coinage Building, 2–3, 38, 80. *See also* Middle Building
Coinage law of January 18, 1837, 27
Coinmakers, The: The Development of Coinage from the Earliest Times, 198
College Hall, 213
Comparette, Thomas L., 110
Conestoga wagon, 153
Congress Hall, 96, 115–117, *116*, 239
   reconstruction, 115, 143
Continental Distilling Corporation. *See* Publicker Industries of Philadelphia
Cope, Caleb, 133
Cope, Porter F., 133
copper alloy, 90
cornerstones, 86, 87, 86
Cornwell, Dean, 193
Cotter, John L., 240
counterfeiting, 72, 138
Coxe, Albion, 35
Cradle of Liberty, 142
Cromley, Thomas, 49, 56
Crosby, Sylvester Sage, 96, 108
Cucore, George, 82
Curry, John C. D.D.S., 85
customs, 76

Daggett, John, 78
Dallett, Gillies, xv
Davis, David, 76
Davis, Robert Coulton, 75
De Saussure, Henry William, 37, *54*, 90
Decatur, Stephen, 45
Declaration House, xi–xiii, xvi, *xviii*, 1
Declaration of Independence, xi. *See also* Declaration House
Delaware County Coin Club, 83
Delaware Valley Coin Club, 85

Description of the Medals of Washington, A, 45
Detroit School of Art, 164
Dickeson, Montroville, 71, 73, 76, 77
Did Newby Strike Coins at Newton, 235
Dierkes, Mary, 240
dimes, 100–101, *101*
Director of the First U.S. Mint Inspecting Initial Coinage, Philadelphia, 1792, 195–198, *198*
   and *First United States Coins*, 200
   and *Washington Inspecting*, 196–197, 200
   See also Reilly, Frank Joseph
dismes, 108
dollar coins, 102–104, *103–104*
   1804 silver dollar, 102–103, *103*
Donaldson, Thomas xv–xvii, 1, 3
DuBois, Patterson, 85
DuBois, William E., 51, *55*, 85
Duffield, Frank G., 226
Dunsmore, John Ward, *9*, 9–10, 38, 159–189, 192
   as professor, 164
   last days of, 169–170
   military service, 168
   sketches of, 170–177
   See also Washington Inspecting the First Money Coined by the United States
Dunsmore, Joseph Pollack, 159
Dunsmore, Margaret Anette Ward, 159
Dye's Coin Encyclopedia, 120

Early Coins of America, The, 108
Early United States Dimes, 1796-1837, 76
Eckfeldt family, 52, 249
Eckfeldt, Adam, 49–50, *51*, *53*, 56, 59, 62–63, 81, 85, 105
Eckfeldt, Edward H. Jr., 106
Eckfeldt, Jacob B., 81, 85
Eckfeldt, Jacob Reese, *54*
Eckfeldt, John Jacob, *53*
Edison, Thomas, 14
Elder, Thomas, 27, 71, 106
electricity, 14
Electro-Tint Engraving Company, 120
Ellis, Joseph D., 88

Fantastic 1804 Dollar, The, 102
Farmer, Richard, 33
First Bank of the United States, xviii, 198
first Mint, 19, *33*, 33–69, *36*, *43*, *47*, *48*, *57*, *58*, *59*, *63*, *65*, *68*, 71, *120*, 241, 248–250
   art and iconography, 7–11, 239, 245–250
   building layouts, *66*, *67*, *68*
   coinage production, 100–102, 109, 245, 249–250
   construction, 41–46, 56, 58–60, 65
   debate about location, 244–245

demolition, 2–4, 6, 10, 41, 44, 108, 128, 248
dies, 72–80
fire, 46, 56–58, 60–61, 147
gold, 90
later excavation, 240–241
myths and misconceptions, 4, 31–32, 37–39, 46, 241, 245–248
preservation, 2–4, 7, 244, 248
press, 179–185
purchase of mint property, 34–35, 43, 46, 49
relics, 80, 85–86
sale, 62–63
security, 36–37, 47, 49, 56
Stewart room, 81
Stewart's excavations, 93, 96, 103, 108–112, 248
timber, 80–86
First Photograph Made in America, 157
First United States Coins, The, 199–203, *200*, *201*
   and *Director Inspecting*, 200
   and *Washington Inspecting*, 199–200
Ford, Sir Edward, 234
Forman, Harry, 81, 202
Fort Jones Museum, 77
fourth Mint, xviii, 4, 63, 80–81, 245
Frank H. Stewart Electric Company, 1–3, *3*, 5–8, 7, 13, 56, 67–69, 85, *107*, 128, 248
   brands, 25–29, 107, 115–116
   calendars, 140, 151, 186–189
   history, 19, 22–25, 236
Frank Reilly School of Art, 193–195
Early United States Dimes, 1796-1837, 76
Franklin Fire Insurance Company of Philadelphia, 38, 63–64, 147
Franklin Institute, 131, 239
Franklin, Benjamin, 34, 37
Free Library of Philadelphia, 120
Frieman, Cora, 84
Front Building, *30*, 46, *47*, 64–67, 71, 245–248, *247*
   and fire, 58–59
   construction, 41–45
   use, 49
Frossard, Edouard, 14, 99
furnace buildings, 46, 56, 64–65

Garden State Numismatic Association, 178
Garrett, Henry S., 48–49
Genealogical Society of Pennsylvania, 24
General Electric Company, 19, 236, 239
General Services Administration, 72, 78
George I, King of England, 91
Gerhard, George S., 105–106
Gloucester County (New Jersey) Historical Society, 24, 81, 85, 116
gold coins, 111, *111*
Gold room, 92–93

Gold Seal Electric Supply Company, 240, *241*
Goldberg, William A., 240
golden penny, 91
Graff House, xii–xiii, 1, 3, 60
   demolition of, xv–xvi
   replica, xvii
Graff, Jacob Jr., xi, xvi, xiv
Gratz, Hyman, xiii–xiv
Gratz, Jacob, xiv
Great Central Sanitary Fair in Philadelphia, 131
Griffith, Robert E., 37, 49
Grim, Henry, 37, 46, 49
Grumlick, Jacob and Christiana, 37
Guide Book of United States Coins, 75
Gutekunst, Frederick F., xv
Guttag Brothers, 239

Hailer, Frederick, 33, 39–41, 43
half cents, 99, 99–100
half dimes, 100, *101*
half dismes, 35, 100, 105–108, *106*, 197, 199
half dollars, 102, *102*
Hallahan, J.P., 82
Hallahan, John D., 82
Hamilton, Alexander, 10, 99
Hamilton, William, 37
Harper, John, 35, 105, 108
Harris, John, 83
Haseltine, John W., 76
Hause, Natalie, 192
Hetzer, Hugh, 199
Hexamer Insurance Company, 38
Higley coppers, 231
Hilt, Robert P., 8
Hiltzheimer, Jacob, xii–xiii, xv
Hintermeister, Henry "Hy", 191, 198–203
   confusion over identity, 198–199
   John Henry Hintermeister, 198–199
   See also The First United States Coins
Historic Sketch of the Coins of New Jersey with a Plate, xvi
Historical Society of Pennsylvania, 87–89
History of the First United States Mint, 38, 40, 44–46, 49, 64, 88, 92, 96, 109–110, *130*
History of the First United States Mint at Philadelphia, 130
History of the First United States Mint: Its People and Its Operations, 226
History of the United States Mint and its Coinage, 192
History of the United States Mint, 25, 72, 80
Hodgins, William, 72
Holme, Thomas, 32–33
Hoskins, Charles, 198, 209, 213
Huling, adoption of name, 17
Humphreys, Whitehead, 37

Illustrated Gallery, The, 198
illustration, 192–195
Illustrations of Philadelphia, 120

In the Gloaming, 140
Independence Hall, 17, 76, 80, 96, 116, *117*, 206
Independence National Historic Park, 111, 213
Indian Queen Inn, xiii, *xviii*
Isle of Man, 234

Jackson, Joseph, 44
Jefferson, Thomas, xi, xi–xiv, 10, 34, 39–41, 44, 108
    and half dismes, 105–107
    writing the Declaration of Independence, xi–xiv, 60
Jenks, John Story, 75
Johnson, D. Wayne, 201–202
Jordan, John W., 88
Jordan, Wilfred, 116, 248
Julian, R.W., 44, 72, 76

Kaptic, Alexander, 84
Kates family, 1–2, 6, 25, 32, 49, 58, 63–69, 74, 87, 125
Kelly's Coins and Chatter, 202
Kelly's Oyster House, xiii
Krueger, Kurt, 202–203

Laboratory and School of Analytical Chemistry, 63
Lamasure, Edwin Jr., 5, 7, 7–8, 119, 136–149, 139, 151–152, 186, 205. *See also* Ye Olde Mint
Lamasure, Edwin Sr., 14, 134
Lamasure, Frank, 137
Lammer, Francis J., 89
Landis, Ida Jane Kirby, 236, 239
Lange, David, 192
Langenheim, Frederick D., 208
Lapp, Warren A., 46, 56, 83
large cents, 96–99, *98–100*, 109
Lear, Tobias, 45
Leutze, Emanuel, 10
Levick/Crosby Plate, 96, 97
Levy-type Company, 120
Lex v. Kates, 48
Library Company of Philadelphia, 120
Library of Congress, 125
Lipschutz "44" Cigar Company, 126
Lovett, Robert Jr., 76

Madison, James, 56, 58
Maris, Dr. Edward, xv
Mason, E.B., 13
Mason, Ebenezer Locke Jr., 74, 108, 244
Mastering Drawing the Human Figure, 195
McAllister, John A. Jr., xiii, xiv, 105–106
McClellan, Elizabeth, 115
McDowell, John, 84
McNear, Charles, 72
Medals of the United States Mint, 76
Medonca, Hipolito Jose da Costa Pereira Furtado de, 49–50
Mease, Dr. James, xiii, xiii–xiv
Mehl, Max B., 77, 95
Mehl's Numismatic Monthly, 95
Meredith sketch, 148
Mickley collection, 77
Mickley, James, 73
Mickley, Joseph J., 74–75, 76
Middle Atlantic Numismatic Association, 83
Middle Building, 62, 64–65, 71, 80, 248
    construction, 58–59
    debate over construction, 42–45
Mill House, 41, 43–45
    debate over location, 46, 57
    fire, 46, 56–58, 60–61
Mille, Matt, 241–242

Mint Act, The, 34, 115, 192
Mint animals
    Black Diamond, 136
    Nero, 135
    Peter, 135
    Prince, 135
Mint cabinet, 13, 17, 72, 110, 116, 245. *See also* U.S. Mint Coin Collection
    Adam Eckfeldt's, 27
Mint Yard, 60
Mitchelson, J.C., 109, 110
    letter to Stewart, 72
Money Museum at the National Bank of Detroit, 209
Moore, Dr. Samuel, 38, 46, 51, *55*, 62, 249
Moulton, Karl, 46

National Archives and Records Administration, 72, 245
National Mall, xv
National Museum, xv
National Park Service, 209
Nealis, T.F., 87
Nevada State Museum, 79
    display of cornerstone coins, 86
New England Rare Coin Galleries, 78
New Jersey Society of Pennsylvania, 24
New York Produce Exchange, 87
New York Sun, 72
Newby, Mark, 89
    St. Patrick coinage, 231–235
Newell photograph, 125–126, 145
Newell studio, 218
Newman, Eric, 84, 102
New-York Historical Society, Field Exploration Committee, 167
North American, 96
Notes on Old Gloucester County, New Jersey, 131
Numismatic and Antiquarian Society of Philadelphia, 82
Numismatic Scrapbook Magazine, 89
numismatics, 7–8, 50, 69, 96, 102, 105, 107
Numismatist, The, 51, 95–96, 244
    on first Mint dies, 73
    on first Mint timber, 82
    on Mint restrikes, 75
    on the rumor of the golden penny, 91

O'Brien, Thomas, 87
Ocean City, N.J., Fishing Club, 24
Old Mint brand, 25–29
Old Mint Building, 6, 239–240, *240, 242*, 248, *250*
Old Mint collection, 207–208
Old Mint Gold Standard, 27–28
Oliphant, Mary Emma, 15
Olympics, 80
Orosz, Joel J., 198
Osborne Company, 7–8, 152–153, 199
Our New Home and Old Times, 220–224

Painting Data, 149
Panic of 1893, 18
Patterson family, 51–52, 249
Patterson, Robert, 50–51, *55*, 56–58, 135
Patterson, Robert Maskell, 51, *55*
Peak on Peak Against the Turquoise Blue, 140
Peale Museum, xviii, 76, 207
Peale, Charles Willson, 50, 76
Peale, Franklin, 63, 76
Peale, Rembrandt, 228–229

Peale, Titian, 63
Penn National Bank, xv, 1
Penn, William, 32–33, 131
Pennsylvania Land Company, 33
Pennsylvania Museum and School of Industrial Art, 208
Pennsylvania Society of the Colonial Dames of America, 115
Perkins, Jacob, 50
Philadelphia Coin Club, 83, 84
Philadelphia Electric, 14, 19
Philadelphia *Inquirer*
    Kates family search for cornerstone, 87
Philadelphia *Item*, 18
Philadelphia Methodist Hospital, 87
Philadelphia Mint, 13, 14
Philadelphia Sketch Club, 132
Philadelphia Street Scene 1809, 61
Pierce, O.D., 18
Pitman (New Jersey) Grammar School, 89
Poulson, Charles, 120
Pratali, Wayne, 78
President's House, 60
Prickett's College of Commerce, 16–18
Provident Life and Trust Building, 88
Publicker Industries of Philadelphia, 195–196, 198
Pugh, Ellis, 102

quarters, 101, *102*

railroads, 18
Ralph, Joseph E., 137
Ranke, Leopold von, 244
Rear Building, 64–65, 71, 108, 248
    fire, 58–59
    construction, 41, 43–45
    remodeling, 58
    use, 44, 48–49
Red Book, 75
Redevelopment Authority of Philadelphia, 89
Reilly, Frank Joseph, 191, 193–198
    and Continental Distilling Corporation, 196, 198
    as teacher, 193–195
    corporate commissions, 195–196
    influence, 195
    See also Director of the First U.S. Mint Inspecting Initial Coinage, Philadelphia, 1792
Reminiscences of Sharptown, 132
restrikes, 75
Revolutionary War, 161
Reyburn, John E., 248
Richards, Frederick De Bourg, 65–67, 119
Rittenhouse, David, 8–11, 39–42, 45, 197, 199
    and half dismes, 105–107
    cornerstone laid by, 87–88
    extraction of gold, 90
    founding director of U.S. Mint, *11*, 33–37, *34–35, 53, 105*
    scientist, 34
Rittenhouse, Elizabeth, 106
Robert Newell & Son, 131
Rockwell, Norman, 193
Rowan University, 102, 116, 212–213
    Stewart collection, 128, 131
Rubin, P. Scott, 109
Rush, Benjamin, 10–11, *11*

Salem a Century Ago, 138

Salem County (New Jersey) Historical Society, 81
San Francisco Mint, 78, 92
Schaefer, F.J., 239
Second Bank of the United States, xviii
Second Mint, 6, 6, 61–62, *62*, 71, 99
Secret Service, 72, 78
Sellers, Coleman, 50
Sellers, George Escol, 50–51, 56, 63, 74, 96, 145, 249, *50*
Sellers, Nathan, 50
Sellers, William, 74
Seventh Street neighborhood, 1, 36, 71, 95, 239
Sharptown, New Jersey, 15–16
Sheldon, William H., 108
Shubert, Michael, 33, 39–41
silver center cent, 108–110, *109*
Sipe, Arthur, 84
Smelting Building, 2, 38. *See also* Rear Building
Smith, Pete, 38, 60, 201
Smithsonian Institution, xv, 50, 76, 245
Snowden, James Ross, 45, *45*
Soley, George, 63
Southwestern View of Washington Square, A, 154
special artist, 131
St. Mery, Moreau de, 5
St. Patrick halfpence, 234
stable, 40, 41, 45–46, 61, 64–65, 248
Stack Family Library, 120
Stack's Rare Coins, 193
steam power, 61, 156
Steigerwalt, Charles, 75
Steine, Kent, 195
Steward, Frank, 17
Stewart, Abigail Rose Kirby, 20–21
Stewart, Eli, 15, 22
Stewart, Frank H., xi, *xii*, 2–4, *16*, 18, 86, *96, 238, 249*
    and artists, 7–10, 106
    and Congress Hall, 115–117, 239
    collections, 24, 98–103, 106–117, *111–114*, 205–215, 239, 248
    early life of, 2, 15–16, 95
    estate of, 209, 239–240
    interests, 1–2, 7, 14, 18, 24, 31, 95–96
    interpreting Mint site, 37–40, 42–45, 49, 56, 58, 64–65, 245–248
    last days of, 217–250
    legacy, 249–250
    Mint preservation and destruction, 11, 244, 248
    misconceptions, 2–3
    purchase of Mint site, 6, 49, 67–69, 95, 248
    See also Frank H. Stewart Electric Company
Stewart, Helen Pancoast, 236
Stewart, William Burnett, 15, 17, 22–23

Taxay, Don, 41, 43–44, 56
Taylor, Frank H., 4, 7–8, 119, 130–131, 193
Third Mint, *115*, 115–116
Thomas D. Murphy Company, 199
Tom Thumb Hamburger Stand, xvi
Treasury, 76
Trumbull, John, 9
Trump, Daniel, 37

U.S. Centennial of American Independence, 13

U.S. Mint bicentennial, 192
U.S. Mint coin collection, 115. *See also* Mint Cabinet
U.S. National Park Service, xvi
United States Centennial medal, 13
United States Coinage of 1793, 108
United States Mint at Philadelphia, 38, 67, 123
United States Pattern, Trial and Experimental Pieces, 109

Van Ingen, William B., 115
Voigt, Henry, 35, 96, 108

Warner, Charles K., 73, 99
Washington Crossing the Delaware, 10
Washington Inspecting the First Money Coined by the United States, 2, 9, 9–11, 105–108, 170–189, 191, 239, 245, *246*
    and *Director Inspecting*, 196–198, 200
    and *First United States Coins*, 199–200
    imitators and forgeries, 202–203
    See also Dunsmore, John Ward
Washington Society of Bank Notes Engravers, 137
Washington, George, 8–11, *34*, 35, 39, 44–45, 60, 108, 115
    and gold coinage, 90
    and half dismes, 105–107
    believed to have set cornerstone, 87
    in art, 192, 199
    regarding currency, 100
Washington, Martha, 105–106, 199–200
Watch House, 46, *47*, 64–65
Weaver, John, 82
Weinberg, Fred, 80
Weisgerber, Charles, 10
Whitford, Craig, 82–83, 192
William J. Green Jr. Federal Building, 4, 241–242, *243*
William Sellers & Co., 74
Williamson, Raymond H., 51
Wilson, Woodrow, 115
Wood, Howland, 72
Woodin, William H., 109
Woodward, W. Elliot, 77
Workshops, 46–51, 56, 64–65
World War I, 137
World's Fair, 13–14

Ye Olde Mint, 2–4, 7–11, *8*, 37–38, *37*, 46, 58–60, *59*, 119, 143–158, 192, 239, 245, *246*
    booklet, 206
    calendar, 151
    evolution of, 146
    fate of, 213–215
    Natalie Hause rendering, *192*
    publication, 218
    See also Lamasure, Edwin Jr.
YE OLDE MINT signage, 124
Yorke, Samuel, 49, 56, 59
Yosemite, 140
Young, James Rankin, 38, 67
Youth's Companion, 122

Zerbe, Farran, 72